BURPEE
COMPLETE GARDENER

BURPEE
COMPLETE GARDENER

A COMPREHENSIVE, UP-TO-DATE, FULLY ILLUSTRATED REFERENCE FOR GARDENERS AT ALL LEVELS

ALLAN ARMITAGE
MAUREEN HEFFERNAN
CHELA KLEIBER
HOLLY H. SHIMIZU

EDITED BY BARBARA W. ELLIS

MACMILLAN • USA

MACMILLAN
A Simon & Schuster Macmillan Company
1633 Broadway
New York, NY 10019-6785

Library of Congress Cataloging-in-Publication Data

Burpee complete gardener / Maureen Heffernan ... [et al.].
    p.   cm.
    Includes index.
    ISBN 0-02-860378-8 (hc)
    1. Gardening. I. Heffernan, Maureen. II. W. Atlee
        Burpee Company.
    SB453.B89 1995
    635—dc20   95-13141
                                       CIP

Manufactured in the United States of America
10 9 8 7 6 5 4 3 2 1

EDITOR, BARBARA W. ELLIS
DESIGN BY STAN GREEN, GREEN GRAPHICS

PHOTOGRAPHY CREDITS

Pamela Harper: Table of Contents, pages 4–7, 9, 11–12, 13 (top), 15–37, 40–44, 48, 53 (top), 55 (left), 56 (top), 57, 58 (top), 60, 61 (top), 63 (top), 64, 70–73, 75-76, 78 (top), 79 (top), 86 (right), 87–88, 89 (left), 90 (top), 92, 93 (bottom), 98–102, 104–107, 108 (top), 109–110, 111 (left), 112–115, 116 (left), 117 (bottom), 118, 119 (bottom), 121–122, 123 (top), 124, 125 (left), 126–133, 135, 136 (bottom), 138 (bottom), 140–142, 143 (bottom), 144–149, 150 (bottom), 151, 152 (top), 155–157, 159, 160 (bottom), 162, 164–169, 171–172, 174, 175 (bottom), 176–178, 179 (top), 182 (top), 183, 187 (bottom), 189 (bottom), 192, 194–217, 220, 248, 254, 264–267, 270, 272–273, 277–281, 283 (right), 284–289, 290–293, 295, 296 (left), 297–300, 301 (top), 302, 303 (right), 306–317.

W. Atlee Burpee Co.: pages 10, 46–47, 50–52, 53 (bottom), 55 right, 58 (bottom), 61 (bottom), 65, 66 (top), 67–69, 74, 77, 78 (bottom), 81–82, 84–85, 89 (right), 90 (bottom), 93 (top), 94–96, 103, 108 (bottom), 111 (right), 116 (right), 117 (top), 119 (bottom), 120, 123 (bottom), 134, 137, 138 (top), 139, 143 (top), 152 (bottom), 153–154, 161, 170, 173, 175 (top), 180–181, 182 (bottom), 184–186, 187 (top), 189 (top), 190–191, 225–246, 249–253, 255–260, 271 (left), 282, 283 (left), 294, 301 (bottom), 303 (left), 304 (right).

Stan Green: pages 2–3, 8, 38–39, 54, 56 (bottom), 59, 63 (bottom), 80, 86 (left), 125 (right), 150 (top), 160 (top), 218–219, 222, 262–263, 271 (right), 274 (left), 275–276, 318–319.

Barbara W. Ellis: pages 13 (bottom), 49, 62, 66 (bottom), 79 (bottom), 83, 136 (top), 158, 179 (bottom), 274 (right), 296 (right), 304 (left).

ILLUSTRATION CREDITS

Elayne Sears: All illustrations by Elayne Sears, except where noted below.

W. Atlee Burpee Co.: 325, 327, 329, 331, 335 (bottom), 342, 343 (right), 345, 368, 340–346.

SPECIAL THANKS

This book is the product of many hands and many talents—writers, photographers, illustrators, designers, editors, and copyeditors have all played a part in its production. But we owe special thanks to the gardeners who grew the plants and created the scenes shown in the photographs in this book. We express our gratitude to them all, and especially to the following: Trevor and Janet Ashbee, Elsa and Mike Bakalar, Arlene Bartlett, Shirley Beach, Elda and Ray Behm, Dan Borroff, Sydney and Martin Eddison, Jerry Flintoff, Barbara Flynn, Lee Goosens, Mary Henderson, Mrs. Julian (Polly) Hill, Mrs. Calvin Hosmer, Gladys and Alain Huyghe, Daniel John, Louise Kappus, Liz Knowles, Mrs. Gavin Letts, Mary Ley, Sheila Magullion, Kathryn Mcholm, Phoebe Noble, Lee Nydegger, John and the late Jane Platt, Loleta Powell, Rob Proctor, Joanna Reed, Mr. and Mrs. J. P. Smith, Bill and Bunny Soltis, Sir John Thouron, Mr. and Mrs. A. Van Vlack, Louise Weekes, Norma and Gerald Wilson, Wayne Winterrowd and Joe Eck.

C O N T

E N T S

INTRODUCTION

Next to language, the richest expression of diversity in America is found in our home gardens. Gardeners across this vast country have developed a fascinating array of unique regional gardening styles. These styles—developed in response to the local climate, ethnic traditions, and a myriad of other factors—range from urban aesthetic statements to deceptively simple gestures that communicate the values of country living. But make no mistake: In this land of "do it yourself," each and every garden, regardless of its style, reflects its owner's personality and individuality.

Nowadays, we approach gardening with the same vigor and determination we bring to fixing up our houses. No other nation can claim to have as many hardware stores, and our passion for weekend home-improvement projects has inspired both serious and comic television programs. The Burpee Complete Gardener was written with that same do-it-yourself spirit in mind. It is designed to help and inspire gardeners at every level—to make your newfound passion a long-term commitment, stimulate a neglected "green thumb," or help you express your own individuality through your garden.

Why was Burpee chosen to put together this ambitious gardening project? In a word, experience. The Burpee Company was established 120 years ago by a group of dedicated gardeners and plant breeders who recognized that European flowers and vegetables were not suited to the unique climates and soils of North America. Many nineteenth-century farmers and gardeners lost their crops because they were growing these inappropriate European varieties. Company founder W. Atlee Burpee started a long-term project to select strong plants from among the struggling survivors. His goal was to develop improved "American" varieties of our favorite flowers and vegetables. Beginning with 'Golden Bantam', the first yellow sweet corn, and 'Fordhook', the first bush lima bean, Burpee bred and introduced an entire generation of new home garden crops. I am especially pleased that we can share some of the rich history of the Burpee Company in this book. At the beginning of every chapter you will find either a cover from one of the early Burpee catalogs (like the one on this page) or a catalog page that sold those early flowers and vegetables.

Today, as I travel to many regions of our nation I am pleased to see field after field, and garden after garden, of Burpee's marigolds, melons, eggplants, and zinnias. We still breed, grow, and harvest over half of the seed we sell, as in Mr. Burpee's time. Our customers continue to call and write to us about their experiences and ideas. And we still travel the world in search of new colors, forms, and flavors to delight the eye and excite the palate. Now we add to our many challenges a new one: to make a more "joyful noise" about gardening, so that all sorts of people are inspired to become capable and knowledgeable gardeners. Such is the aim of the Burpee Complete Gardener.

Happy gardening!

GEORGE BALL, JR.
President, W. Atlee Burpee & Co.

1

GARDENING FROM THE GROUND UP

GARDENING IS BOTH AN ART AND A SCIENCE. Designing a pleasing garden layout, and creating gorgeous plant groupings within that layout, allow nearly endless scope for exploring your creativity. As with art, making a beautiful garden can be a transcendent experience—one that restores and renews your heart, mind, and soul. Creating a great garden is a real challenge, but it can bring you, and everyone who visits your garden, a great deal of pleasure and joy.

Before mastering the *art* of gardening, however, you need to understand the *science* that makes it work. In the following chapters, you'll find out how knowing about your soil and climate can help you create a beautiful, thriving garden. You'll also find all kinds of tips and techniques that will help you design your garden—from mapping your site to planning its layout and working with color and texture. When you combine this knowledge with your own outdoor experience and common sense, you'll be well on your way to creating your own garden masterpiece.

WHOLE-YARD APPEAL. *The flowing design of this garden encompasses the entire yard. A ribbon of white sweet alyssum helps unite beds filled with marigolds, dahlias, and petunias, along with a variety of shrubs and perennials.*

CHAPTER ONE

GETTING STARTED

THE FIRST RULE OF SUCCESSFUL GARDENING IS TO WORK WITH, NOT AGAINST, THE NATURAL SETTING. While it's possible to grow plants that aren't well adapted to your climate and conditions, it takes a lot more fussing, and the results may not be worth the trouble. For instance, shade-loving plants, such as impatiens and hostas, will suffer in a hot, sunny garden no matter how much you pamper them. And heat-loving vegetables, such as okra, will grow poorly and may not even produce a crop in the short, cool summers of far-north gardens. But when you match the right plant with the right place, you've set the stage for healthy, vigorous growth, prolific flowering, and generous harvests.

So how do you know which plants are right for your yard? The key is knowing what growing conditions—what kind of climate, how much light, and what kind of soil—your yard has to

5

SUN-BAKED COLOR. *Brilliant blooms abound in this full-sun garden, planted with perennials that thrive in well-drained soil, including lilies, sedum, roses, lavender, and coreopsis.*

offer. Once you know these factors, you can read the plant portraits in later chapters to learn about the needs of the plants you'd like to grow. When you find a match between the plants' needs and what you can provide, you're in business!

In this chapter, you'll learn how to identify your existing garden conditions. As you go through the chapter, make notes about the different things you discover about the features of your yard. These notes will be invaluable when you move on to actually create a garden plan and choose the plants you want to grow. They'll also be helpful for future reference if you decide to rework parts of your layout to reflect your changing tastes and needs.

UNDERSTANDING YOUR CLIMATE

"Climate" is a catch-all term that combines many different factors, including high and low temperatures, frost dates, rainfall, and wind. All of these factors will affect the way your plants grow.

TEMPERATURE

Although you can change some growing conditions, such as the quality of your soil, there's not much you can do to change the yearly high and low temperatures your garden experiences. That makes it espe-

A LUSH SHADE GARDEN. *A shady site doesn't have to be dark and colorless. This spring garden is filled with a host of shade-loving plants, including ferns, primroses, hostas, epimediums, fringed bleeding heart (Dicentra eximia), and wild sweet William (Phlox divaricata).*

cially important to choose plants that can tolerate those temperatures.

Although heat does have an effect on plant growth, its influence hasn't been investigated as much as that of cold temperatures. Your area's coldest winter temperatures will dictate which perennials, trees, and shrubs will survive from year to year in your area. The United States Department of Agriculture (USDA) has determined that there are distinct temperature zones (called hardiness zones) for the United States, including Alaska and Hawaii. They have produced a zone map that is absolutely indispensable for all gardeners who want to know which perennials, trees, and shrubs are likely to thrive in their area. (These zones don't apply to annuals, such as marigolds, since these plants naturally die before winter anyway.)

The USDA Plant Hardiness Zone Map divides the country into 11 different temperature regions, based on the average annual low temperatures. It assigns a zone number to each region, which corresponds to a range of low temperatures. (For example, if you live in Philadelphia, you live in Zone 6. That means that your average annual minimum temperatures range between 0° and −10°F.)

In the plant portraits later in this book, as well as in catalog descriptions, you'll find hardiness zone

SUMMER PASTELS. *Pastel-flowered yarrows (Achillea spp.), ornamental grasses, and blue viper's bugloss (Echium vulgare) make a lovely summer combination that thrives in full sun and well-drained soil.*

EASY ANNUALS. *Zinnias, cosmos, and cleome are all easy-to-grow annuals that can be started from seed sown right where the plants are to grow. Sow cosmos and cleome after danger of heavy frost has passed; sow zinnias after all danger of frost has passed.*

ranges for perennials, trees, shrubs, and other plants that can live for more than two years. If "Zones 6 to 9" is listed for a plant, for instance, it means that you should have luck growing that plant if you live in Zone 6, 7, 8, or 9. Zones 10 and 11 may be too hot, while Zones 1 through 5 are probably too cold.

These guidelines aren't foolproof, since you may occasionally have a record-cold winter. If the temperature drops well below the average low temperature, plants that are normally considered hardy in your zone may be killed off. To be on the safe side, especially with trees and shrubs, you may want to look for plants that are hardy to one zone colder than the one you live in. (For instance, if you live in Zone 6, a plant listed for Zones 5 to 9 would be more dependable than one listed for Zones 6 to 9.)

To find out which hardiness zone you live in, turn to the official USDA Plant Hardiness Zone Map on page 407 and locate where you live on the map. Jot down your area's specific zone number with your garden notes, and keep it in mind anytime you buy perennials, trees, shrubs, and other permanent plants from catalogs or garden centers.

FROST DATES

If you're raising annual flowers and vegetables, hardiness zones won't tell you if the plants you want to grow will thrive in your temperatures. For these plants, you need to know the average dates of the first and last frost in your area. These fixed dates determine the beginning and end of your regular growing season.

The average last spring frost date is particularly important if you grow your own transplants from seed. It will give you a guideline for knowing when it's time to start seed indoors, as well as when it's safe to sow seed outdoors or set out transplants. The average date of the first fall frost will tell you when to dig up or protect tender plants that could get damaged or killed by freezing. The number of days between these two dates is the average length of your growing season. This is important to know for vegetables, since it will tell you if a particular crop can produce a harvest in the growing season your garden offers. (You'll learn more about the importance of the growing season in Chapter 7, Vegetables.)

The last and first frost dates are fixed averages for a given area, based on many years of tracking weather patterns. To find the average dates for your particular area, call your local Cooperative Extension Service office, which is listed in the county or city government listings of your telephone directory. Or ask at your local garden center or nursery. Keep in mind that these are averages, so the actual date of the last spring or first fall frost will change a bit from year to year. Some years, a freak snowstorm may hit when it should be the last frost-free day; an early frost may hit in September in an area where it normally doesn't until mid-October. So while it's handy to use these dates for planning, just be aware that they will be slightly different each year, and be prepared to adjust your plans accordingly.

RAINFALL

The amount of water a garden receives is not necessarily restricted to natural rainfall patterns. For instance, if you live in a dry climate, you can still grow moisture-loving plants if you are willing to spend the time and money needed to provide extra water. However, this is working *against* your natural environment and not *with* it.

As water becomes more of a precious resource, it is increasingly important to plan your garden with

LUSH MOISTURE-LOVERS. *Hostas, rhododendrons, variegated Solomon's seal* (Polygonatum odoratum *var.* thunbergii *'Variegatum'), and ferns create a garden full of texture and interest. All thrive in rich, moist soil.*

water-saving techniques in mind. To do that, you need to be familiar with the average rainfall patterns in your area. If you've lived in one area for years, you probably already know roughly how often it rains, and whether dry spells are common. If you're new to an area, ask neighboring gardeners or the local Cooperative Extension Service office about the amount of rainfall you can expect through the year.

To find plants that are adapted to your area's natural moisture, check the plant portraits later in this book. If you live in a region where rainfall is scarce or undependable, look for plants that like dry soil. In high-rainfall areas, plants that prefer evenly moist to wet soil are a better choice. You can also find out about plants that do well in your area by visiting parks and cemeteries, where plantings are usually left to grow without a lot of fuss. If plants are thriving there with no watering, chances are good that the same kinds will do well in your yard, too.

WIND

The amount of wind a site gets is another important climatic factor to consider before planning your garden. Strong summer winds can topple tall flowers and vegetables, while dry winter winds may damage soft-leaved evergreen trees and shrubs.

Since wind speed and direction can vary greatly, there aren't any rules or guidelines to go by—you'll just have to observe the site for yourself. Note any spots where existing plants tend to fall over easily, or where evergreens tend to get brown tips after winter. As you walk through your yard, also note

LEAFY PROTECTION. *A tall hedge protects the perennials and annuals in this garden from prevailing winds. An edging of impatiens, ageratums, and zonal geraniums provides a ribbon of summer-long color. The dark green leaves of the hedge behind help set off the colors of the flowers.*

which areas of your yard seem to be subjected to the strongest breezes.

Knowing where strong winds may be a problem will prevent you from placing plants that are susceptible to wind damage in exposed locations. If your entire garden area is exposed to strong winds, you may need to install fencing or plant a natural windbreak of cold-hardy evergreen trees and shrubs.

LEARNING ABOUT LIGHT

Before you can plan a garden or choose plants for it, it's critical to know how many hours of sunlight the site receives each day. While you can get very specific about light conditions, most references break light levels down into three simple groups: full sun, partial shade, and full shade. (Some books and catalogs use the term "partial sun," which is really only another way of saying "partial shade.")

As the earth moves around the sun, the amount of light either increases or decreases during each season. The three basic light classifications are usu-

ally meant to describe the amount of sun during the prime growing months, which for most parts of the country are April through August.

FULL SUN

"Full sun" generally means that a site receives, or a plant needs, *at least* 6 hours of sun each day between 10 A.M. and 6 P.M. In cooler northern gardens, plants needing full sun do best with 8 or more hours of sun, since the light is not as intense there as in the warmer southern zones. Full sun is best for most vegetables, herbs, fruit trees, and roses, as well as many kinds of flowers.

PARTIAL SHADE

Partial-shade plants don't need either full, direct sun or full shade. They prefer dappled shade, where the light is filtered through the leaves of deciduous trees, such as maples or dogwoods, during the summer months. A partially shaded site gets either dappled light all day or some direct sunlight for less than 6 hours each day.

MANAGING MICROCLIMATES

Within your yard, there are variations in growing conditions that can make one site very different from another. For instance, a garden under a large maple tree may always be dry, even though summer rain is plentiful, while a spot under a downspout may be consistently soggy. A flower bed along the house may stay warmer in winter than a bed farther out in the yard, offering a special spot for plants that would not ordinarily survive the cold.

The parts of a yard that vary from normal climatic conditions are called microclimates. By identifying the microclimates that exist in your yard, you can select just the right plants for each spot. The more closely you can match a plant's needs with the right microclimate, the happier your plant will be and the more successful you will be as a gardener.

To find the microclimates in your yard, carefully observe your garden's natural conditions throughout the seasons. The next time there is a frost, for example, note which areas seem to be hit, and which areas do not. Low-lying areas will naturally collect cooler air and are considered frost pockets. Avoid siting plants that are susceptible to early or late frosts—such as vegetable crops and fruit trees—in these areas.

In spring and summer, you may notice that bulbs and other perennials planted on the south side of your house bloom earlier than the same flowers on the west or east side. And flowers on the north side bloom latest of all. Garden sites with a southern exposure receive more sun, and the soil there heats up faster in the spring. Therefore, these are the best sites for vegetable gardens and for plants that like warm conditions.

Plants that need cooler conditions, on the other hand, appreciate east-facing sites, where they receive cool morning light but are shielded from the hot afternoon sun. Shade cast by trees, large shrubs, or trellises

COLORFUL HEAT-LOVERS. *Reflected heat can pose a problem for plants growing next to roads or concrete walkways. Soil compaction can be a problem on such sites as well. Fortunately, many annuals, such as these marigolds, thrive in heat and less-than-ideal soil.*

can also provide ideal conditions for cool-loving plants.

Each year you garden, you'll notice more and more differences between the planting sites you've established in your yard. Jotting down notes on these microclimates will allow you to fine-tune your planting plans and move plants around in the right season to take advantage of these special conditions.

Keep in mind that sites that are partially shaded by deciduous trees in summer may be in full sun in winter and spring. That makes these sites perfect for crocuses, daffodils, and other spring bulbs that need full sun in early spring. As the trees leaf out and start casting shade, the bulbs will die back to the ground, and delicate partial-shade plants will start to grow. While there aren't many edible plants that thrive in partial shade, these light conditions are ideal for a wide range of flowers and shrubs.

FULL SHADE

A fully shaded site receives no direct light. Full shade is common on the north side of a house, and in spots sheltered by evergreen trees and shrubs. While full shade limits your plant choices fairly dra-

EPIMEDIUM GRANDIFLORUM. *This spring-blooming perennial has handsome foliage and thrives in shade. Grow it as a groundcover or in a woodland garden.*

HELLEBORUS NIGER. *The creamy flowers of shade-loving Christmas rose are a welcome sight in winter or early spring. The leaves are attractive all season.*

HOSTAS 'BLUE UMBRELLAS' AND 'TRUE BLUE'. *Shade-loving hostas come in an astounding array of foliage colors. For best effect, plant a variety of these plants.*

matically, you may still be able to create beautiful plantings with shade-lovers such as hostas, rhododendrons, ferns, and mosses.

UNDERSTANDING YOUR SOIL

Like the plants it supports, soil is alive and changing. It is made up of many parts, including small particles of weathered rock, as well as organic matter, air, and water. The amount of organic matter, air, and water can change, depending on how you manage your garden. Working compost into the soil, for instance, will raise the level of organic matter. Watering will increase soil moisture, while loosening the soil by digging or tilling can add air. The mineral part of soil, however, is relatively unchangeable. Finding out what kinds of particles make up your soil will tell you a lot about how to handle it.

IS IT CLAY, SAND, OR LOAM?

Soil mineral particles are divided into three basic groups—sand, silt, and clay—depending on their size. Soils from different areas, even from different parts of your yard, can vary noticeably in the proportions of sand, silt, and clay they contain. Sandy soil is, not surprisingly, high in sand; clayey soil is high in clay. A soil with balanced amounts of sand, silt, and clay is called a loam. Each kind of soil has different traits.

Clay Soil: The bane of many gardeners, clay soil is mostly composed of tiny particles less than $\frac{1}{12,500}$ of an inch across. Their tiny size means that the particles are easily compacted. Compaction of clay particles leads to two common clay soil problems: waterlogging (after heavy rain or irrigation) or crusting (after a dry spell). When clay soil is wet, it clings to your shovel and looks like a dense, heavy, cloddy paste. When clay soil is dry, the surface looks like cracked, hard pottery pieces.

Many garden plants don't thrive in heavy clay soil, because the roots receive either too much or too little water, and there is little or no oxygen for roots to grow properly. Clay soils are also slow to warm up in the spring, discouraging seed germination and promoting seed rot.

If your soil is on the clayey side, don't despair—

it is still possible to create a gorgeous garden. In fact, there are some advantages to clay. For one thing, clay soil holds more moisture and nutrients than sandy or loamy soil, so it is better suited to plants that appreciate extra moisture. And clay soil doesn't require frequent fertilizing.

You can moderate many of the problems of clay by digging generous amounts of organic amendments, such as compost, peat moss, or leaf mold, into the soil. Garden gypsum (hydrated calcium sulfate) can also be added to clay soil to loosen up the compacted particles, although it may increase the acidity of the soil.

Sandy Soil: Sandy soil contains tiny mineral pieces that are significantly bulkier than clay particles. Unlike clay soil, sandy soil has a light, loose feel, and water drains through it quickly. In fact, sandy soil may drain so quickly that the water is gone before the roots can reach it. As the water drains through, it also picks up nutrients and carries them downward, out of the reach of plant roots.

Sand is terrific for plants that like very dry and well-drained soil. But for most plants, sandy soil needs frequent watering and fertilizing to supply what they require to grow.

There is one similarity between sandy and clay soil: Both benefit from additions of organic matter. In sandy soil, organic matter fills the open spaces between the large particles, giving water and nutrients something to hang on to so they aren't washed away so quickly. Digging in a layer of compost, chopped leaves, or other organic matter before planting, and adding more each year, will turn a dry, sandy soil into a great growing site for a wide variety of garden plants. Adding organic matter to a clay soil helps water drain through it and makes it easier to work.

Loamy Soil: Loamy soil contains a good balance of large sand particles, tiny clay particles, and medium-sized silt particles. If your garden site has naturally loamy soil, consider yourself very lucky; it provides excellent growing conditions for most garden plants. The sand particles contribute a loose feel and good drainage, while the silt and clay particles hold the nutrients and water that roots need.

WHAT IS THE PH?

Along with their mineral content, soils are also classified by their pH—their level of acidity or alkalin-

A DRY-SOIL PAIR. *Sedum 'Autumn Joy' and hardy prickly pear cactus (Opuntia humifusa) thrive in sun and very well-drained soil. The prickly pear bears showy yellow flowers in spring.*

DRY-SOIL GROUNDCOVERS. *Hens and chicks (Sempervivum spp.) are an ideal groundcover for hot, dry sites. They come in many forms, and planting a variety creates an interesting patchwork of color and texture. Here, two types are shown growing with blue fescue (Festuca cinerea).*

WHAT KIND OF SOIL DO YOU HAVE?

To determine if your soil is sandy, clayey, or loamy, pick up a handful of lightly moist earth from your garden and rub it between the palms of your hands. Look at the result, then match it with what you've already observed about your soil:

• Does the soil in your hand form a sticky ball that doesn't fall apart when you tap it? After a rain, does water seem to take a long time to drain away? If so, you have clay soil.

• Does the soil run through your hand without forming any kind of clump or ball? When you water your garden, does the water quickly soak right in, with little runoff? If so, your soil type is sandy.

• Does the soil in your hand form a ball that crumbles easily when you tap it? Does your soil naturally seem to be evenly moist but never waterlogged? If so, you probably have loamy soil.

ity. The pH scale ranges from 1.0 to 14.0, with 7.0 being neutral. If a soil's pH is higher than 7.0, it is alkaline; if the pH is below 7.0, it is acidic. Most garden soils in the United States fall somewhere between 4.5 and 8.0.

It's important to know what pH you're dealing with, because it can have a great effect on which nutrients are available to your plants. When the pH is too high or too low, your plants may get too much of some nutrients and too little of others. At a high (alkaline) pH, for instance, calcium and iron get chemically "locked" into the soil, so they are not available to plant roots. This is why pines, azaleas, and rhododendrons growing in alkaline soil often have yellow leaves—they are not getting enough iron, because the soil is not naturally acidic enough to supply it.

Soil pH also affects the balance and health of soil microorganisms. Earthworms, for example, do not tolerate very acidic soil. A pH between 6.0 and 7.0 is best for most beneficial soil microorganisms. This same range is ideal for most plants; a slightly acidic 6.5 is optimal. (Acid-loving plants, such as rhododendrons, azaleas, camellias, dogwoods, and blueberries, prefer a lower pH, from 4.5 to 6.0.)

Many different factors can affect soil pH, including the amount of rainfall your area receives and the kinds of minerals that are common in the soil. Acid soils are more common in the eastern half of the United States, which tends to get lots of rain. Dry, western gardens are more likely to have alkaline soil. Alkaline soil is also common along building foundations, where the lime from the concrete leaches out into the surrounding soil. Since acidity and alkalinity can vary widely, even on one property, it's worth finding out the pH of your garden beds. Then you can look for plants that are naturally adapted to that pH, or else decide how to adjust the pH to match the plants you want to grow.

Testing Soil pH: Checking soil pH is fairly easy. Do-it-yourself soil-testing kits are available from garden supply catalogs and most garden centers. A very quick and easy way to measure pH is to use one of the metal probe-type pH meters: You insert the probe into the soil, wait 60 seconds, and then check the gauge to find out the pH level. There are also soil-testing kits that use a chemical solution to test soil pH and nutrient content.

The most accurate and reliable way to learn about your soil is to buy a test kit from your local Cooperative Extension Service office. This kit contains instructions for collecting a soil sample and sending it to a state lab for analysis. Along with pH, the analysis may include information on your soil's sand, silt, and clay content, as well as its nutrient levels. In most cases, the lab will make specific recommendations regarding how much lime or sulfur you need to add to the soil to raise or lower the pH.

When testing your garden soil, be sure to take readings or soil samples from different sites, since pH and nutrient values can vary even within a small area.

Adjusting Soil pH: If your pH tests show that your soil is between 6.0 and 7.0, you really don't need to bother adjusting the pH (unless, of course, you're growing acid-loving plants such as rhododendrons or camellias).

If your pH is too low, you'll need to add lime to your soil. Garden lime (calcium carbonate) is readily available at garden centers, hardware stores, and discount home-and-garden centers. Applying about 5 to 10 pounds of garden lime for every 100 square feet of garden area will raise the soil pH by one full number (from 5.0 to 6.0, for instance). Add the right amount for your needs, based on the results of your soil analysis, and work it into the top few inches of soil. You can apply lime any time of the year, but it's best to add it several months before planting time. (Just leave several weeks between applying fertilizers and adding lime; the two don't mix well.)

Too much lime is as bad as too little, so don't be tempted to add more than you need. Take another soil test next year to see if the soil needs more lime, and if so, how much. Once the pH is in the right range, continue to check it every few years, and add more lime as needed.

If alkaline soil is your problem, you need ground sulfur, calcium sulfate, iron sulfate, aluminum sulfate, or garden gypsum. Like lime, these materials are readily available from garden centers. Apply them according to the package directions, depending on how much you need to lower the pH. Pine needles, pine bark, peat moss, and manure can also lower soil pH, although they work much more gradually. Once you get the pH to the right level, mulching plants with pine needles or pine bark can help keep the soil balanced.

HOW'S THE FERTILITY?

A fertile soil is rich in the major nutrients that plants need to develop and grow. Plants absorb all of these nutrients through their root systems.

The primary nutrients are nitrogen, phosphorus, and potassium. Nitrogen is the essential element that plants break down to make their own food through photosynthesis. When nitrogen is lacking, plants will grow slowly, producing weak stems and yellowish leaves. An infusion of nitrogen into the soil has an immediate effect, stimulating plant growth and greening up the foliage. Too much nitrogen, however, promotes soft, succulent growth that is prone to damage and disease. It also encourages leafy growth at the expense of blooms, so flowering plants may produce few, if any, flowers in high-nitrogen soil.

Phosphorus is critical for good root, seed, flower, and fruit development, since it promotes cell division. If your soil is deficient in phosphorus, you will see a reddish to purple color develop on the leaves and stems of plants. It is a good practice to sprinkle some phosphorus—in the form of colloidal phosphate or rock phosphate—into freshly dug garden beds so the roots will have easy access to this important nutrient.

Potassium, or potash, promotes photosynthesis and root development, and builds strong cell walls.

LATE-SUMMER PERENNIALS. *This sun-loving combination will thrive in any moist but well-drained soil. Purple coneflowers, black-eyed Susans, and lavender Russian sage* (Perovskia atriplicifolia) *will also tolerate dry soil. Scarlet rose mallow* (Hibiscus coccineus), *behind them, grows best if the soil remains moist.*

It also helps plants retain moisture and keeps them from drying out in the summer and winter. A lack of potassium in the soil will show up in poor root development, susceptibility to wilting and wilt diseases, and a bronzy color on the foliage. Potassium is highly soluble, so it leaches out of the soil fairly quickly. If your soil is naturally low in potassium, it's a good idea to add a boost of high-potassium fertilizer (such as potassium sulfate or potassium nitrate) at the beginning of each growing season.

How do you know if your soil has the right balance of nutrients? If the plants that are already in your yard seem vigorous and healthy, that's a good clue that the right nutrients are there. To get a better idea, though, you can test the soil yourself with a kit, or get it tested by a lab, as explained in "Testing Soil pH" on page 14.

Improving Soil Fertility: You can supply nutrients to plants in either organic or chemical fertilizer forms. As long as the nutrients are available, the

IRIS ENSATA. *Spring-blooming Japanese irises are ideal for wet-soil sites along a pond, or wherever water tends to stand in spring. They will also grow in rich, well-drained soil.*

WET-SOIL COMPANIONS. *Japanese primroses* (Primula japonica), *ferns, forget-me-nots, and umbrella plants* (Peltiphyllum peltatum) *all thrive in wet soil.*

HOSTAS AND FERNS. *For a wet site in shade, purple-flowered ajuga, sweet woodruff* (Galium odoratum), *ferns, and hostas make happy companions.*

plant doesn't care if they come from chemical or organic sources. What really matters is how fertile your soil is to begin with, and how fast you need to get the nutrients to your plants.

If your soil is naturally rich in organic matter, chemical fertilizers are usually not necessary for good plant growth. Compost, manures, and other forms of organic matter contain lower amounts of the three primary nutrients than do their chemical counterparts, but they release a slow, balanced supply that's great for steady plant growth. Yearly additions of compost or well-rotted manure should keep the soil in good condition. (For more information on choosing fertilizers, see Chapter 11, Planting and Caring for Your Garden.)

WHAT'S THE DRAINAGE LIKE?

Poor drainage is the cause of many untimely plant deaths. When the soil is filled with water, roots can't get the air they need to function, and they suffocate. The symptoms of waterlogged soil are similar to those of too-dry soil: wilting and eventual death.

Garden sites that have poor drainage are often at the bottom of a slope. Flat or low-lying areas can also be prone to waterlogging. Clay soils, as well as shallow soils over hard, rocky subsoil, are often wet, too.

Testing Drainage: Fortunately, it is relatively easy to diagnose poor drainage problems in soil. If you can still see standing water in areas of your yard several hours after a heavy rain, your soil is probably not well drained, and chances are, it is not good for most garden plants. To get a more accurate picture, try this simple test:

1. Take a 46-ounce aluminum can (like the kind Hawaiian Punch comes in) and remove its top and bottom.
2. Dig a 4-inch-deep hole in an area of your yard where you want to measure soil drainage.
3. Set the can securely in the hole, and back-fill the soil firmly around the outside of the can.
4. Fill the can with water up to the top, and check how far the water level drops in hour.

If you have well-drained soil, the water level should drop about 2 inches in an hour. This drainage rate is ideal for most garden plants.

If the water level drops more than 4 to 5 inches in an hour, your soil drains too quickly; add more organic matter.

If the water level drops less than 1 inch in an hour, your soil is poorly drained and needs serious help to make it suitable for most plants.

Improving Drainage: There are several ways to speed up soil drainage. If the soil is compacted or high in clay, organic matter is probably the answer. Dig or till in generous amounts of compost, chopped leaves, or other organic matter regularly. Do so before planting every year, if you're growing vegetables or annual flowers. For more permanent plantings, such as perennials and shrubs, till in organic matter at least a year ahead and again before planting.

Loosening the soil with digging and organic matter can also help to improve drainage in low-lying areas. If it doesn't help in your case, you may need to regrade the area so water won't have low spots to collect in. For small spots, you can regrade the area yourself, by adding soil and organic matter to the low areas and using a rake to smooth out the surface. For large-scale regrading, it's best to get the advice of a landscape contractor.

If your site is flat, and tilling and adding organic matter doesn't help, you will probably need to install a drainage system. Unless the drainage problem is very extensive and unusually severe, you may be able to install a system yourself without having to hire a professional contractor.

To make a drainage system, dig a trench about 1 foot wide directly in the problem area. Begin digging the trench about 1 foot deep, then gradually increase the depth until one end is at least a few inches lower than the other end. Make the trench long enough to carry the water to a spot where it can drain without causing problems. Don't end the trench at the street or your property line, for instance, or by a path or entryway; choose an out-of-the-way spot within your property. If there is no suitable area to end the trench and direct the water, dig a drainage pit hole about 3 feet by 2 feet wide and $1\frac{1}{2}$ to 2 feet deep at the lower end of the trench, and fill it with gravel.

Now, lay plastic drainage pipe in the trench. Choose pipe that is 3 to 4 inches in diameter, with a line of small holes along one side. Fit pieces of pipe for longer areas, or cut them to fit smaller areas. Make sure the holes are facing upward when you are setting the pipe in the trench. Next, lay a piece of landscape fabric over the pipe to prevent the holes

A RAISED BED GARDEN. *Raised beds—whether built of wood or concrete, like the garden shown here— are an ideal solution to poor soil. Purple coneflowers, phlox, cleome, Russian sage* (Perovskia atriplicifolia), *lamb's ears* (Stachys byzantina), *and ornamental grass* (Pennisetum alopecuroides) *fill this late-summer garden*

from becoming clogged with soil particles and organic debris. (Landscape fabric is porous; don't substitute black plastic, which isn't.) Fill the trench with about 6 inches of gravel, and top the gravel layer with soil. As you replace the soil, try to slope it a bit to direct the water toward the pipe and away from your garden beds.

If you followed all the steps properly, the pipes should be effective for many years before they become clogged up. When this happens, replace them with new pipes and regrade as necessary.

Yet another way to cope with poor soil—no matter what the cause—is to create raised beds. Raised beds are garden areas where you build up the soil so that the surface is above the normal soil level. If drainage problems aren't too severe, you can rake the soil into broad mounds a few inches high. To make beds higher than about 6 inches, build frames from landscape timbers, cinder blocks, or rocks to hold up the soil. (Avoid pressure-treated timbers or creosoted railroad ties, which can release harmful substances into the soil.) Loosen the top layer of existing soil within the frame by digging in a 2- or 3-inch layer of organic matter. Fill the frame the rest of the way with a mixture of good topsoil and organic matter. When the mixture settles in a few weeks, it should be 1 to 2 inches below the top of the frame.

SUMMER SPLENDOR. *Free-form beds filled with phlox, delphiniums, bellflowers, daisies, and other perennials celebrate summer. Lawn paths between the beds make it easy to enjoy—and care for—the flowers close-up.*

CHAPTER TWO

DESIGNING YOUR GARDEN

IF YOU'RE NEW TO GARDENING, THE IDEA OF DE-SIGNING YOUR OWN LANDSCAPE CAN SEEM RATHER INTIMIDATING. Even more advanced gardeners may shy away from writing down their ideas, preferring to dig rather than draw. And there's no doubt about it—you *can* create a nice garden without ever putting pencil to paper.

But before you skip to the next chapter, consider the following advantages of creating a customized plan for your plantings:

• Garden planning can be lots of fun. It doesn't necessarily mean sitting at a desk, drowning in papers and protractors: It's looking at books, magazines, and catalogs for ideas; visiting other gardens for inspiration; and daydreaming about what *you* always wanted to have in your garden. The actual paper planning can be as formal or informal as you like.

19

• Planning can save you money. Deciding now what you want for your garden can prevent you from making costly mistakes—like planting a big shade tree right where you eventually would like to put a new garage or deck. Planning ahead also means you'll be able to keep an eye out for bargains, so you can phase in your design as you find the right plants and materials at the right price.

• Garden planning can save you time, too. Advance planning lets you look at your property as a whole, rather than in bits and pieces, so you can design your yard for easy maintenance from the start. You can also identify problem spots—like tough sites where nothing seems to grow well, or awkward, hard-to-mow areas—and include solutions in your plan.

• Good planning leads to results that are attractive *and* practical. No one knows better than you how you currently use your yard and how you'd like to use it in the future. You can choose where you want paths to be, where the vegetable garden would be most convenient, and where your favorite flowers will go without having to work around previous mistakes.

In this chapter, you'll learn all the basics of creating a great garden plan, from making a site map to deciding what kind of and how many plants to buy. Along the way, you'll find lots of exciting and inspiring ideas to help you plan a landscape that's perfectly suited to your own wants and needs.

START WITH A SITE MAP

The best way to begin your dream garden is with a site map—a plan of what already exists on your property. You don't need to be an experienced architect or draftsman to create a usable map; as long as you can read it, it doesn't matter how rough it is. What's important is the actual *process* of making the map. By spending a little time really looking at your yard, measuring and observing the existing features, you can create a layout that takes full advantage of what your site has to offer.

Exactly how much of the site you'll map will depend on your plans. If you just want to spruce up the front yard, for instance, it's not necessary to spend time mapping the backyard, too. But if you have the time, it's a good idea to map your whole site at once. That way, you'll already have the map done if you decide to develop a new area. Mapping

the entire site may also give you some new ideas for planning your landscape as a whole.

Follow these steps to create your site map:

1. Carefully measure the boundaries of your garden site with a 50- or 100-foot carpenter's measur-

A COLORFUL GARDEN ROOM. *Stone walls and beds of flowers enclose an enticing outdoor sitting area. Perennials providing early-summer color include peonies, foxgloves, coral bells, hardy geraniums, pinks* (Dianthus spp.), *clustered bellflowers* (Campanula glomerata), *meadow rue* (Thalictrum aquilegifolium), *and violet sage* (Salvia X superba).

ing tape. If your garden is irregularly shaped, break it up into smaller squares or rectangles; measure the individual areas, then add up their measurements.

2. As best you can, draw the site to scale on a piece of graph paper. A scale of 1 inch on paper to

FOUNDATION FLOWERS. *Instead of all-too-common foundation shrubs, this home is decorated with flowers, which not only add instant appeal to the landscape but can also be enjoyed from indoors. Easy-care perennials in this garden include phlox, heliopsis, Shasta daisies, tiger lilies, and Gloriosa daisies. Clumps of red dahlias provide additional color.*

1 foot on the ground should give you enough room on the map to write in some details. If you can't fit your whole yard on one sheet, either tape several sheets together or use a smaller scale (such as 1 inch on paper to 2 feet on the ground).

3. For future reference, draw an arrow on the

SWEEPS OF COLOR. *Mass plantings of easy-care perennials and ornamental grasses create a garden that's bold and appealing as well as low-maintenance. Black-eyed Susans (Rudbeckia fulgida), Russian sage (Perovskia atriplicifolia), lamb's ears (Stachys byzantina), and silver grass (Miscanthus spp.) provide months of color and interest.*

sketch to indicate which way is North.

4. Sketch in any existing features—for example, the house and other structures, trees, shrubs, flower beds, vegetable gardens, driveways, sidewalks, and patios or decks.

5. Indicate on the sketch the location of overhead power and telephone lines, as well as underground electric cables, water pipes, sewer lines, and septic tanks. Before you dig into your yard by hand or with machinery, you want to be sure that you won't hurt yourself or your utility lines. If you don't know exactly where these lines are located, call your local utility services.

6. Go back to the notes you made as you learned about your site in Chapter 1. On your map, mark where particular spots have special features, such as summer shade, poor drainage, or exposure to strong winds.

7. Make several photocopies of your site map. Keep the original and one copy in your garden notebook. Use the extra copies when you're sketching out different ideas for your layout. When you've found a layout you like, transfer it to the clean copy you set aside.

PLAN TO RELAX. *Don't forget to plan an area for just sitting and enjoying the outdoors. This secluded seating area is heavily planted to provide privacy, and is decorated with daylilies, purple coneflowers, geraniums, a yucca plant, and other perennials.*

IDENTIFY YOUR NEEDS

Once you know what you have, it's time to think about what you need. Sit down with a pencil and your garden notebook, and start writing down the practical things that you know you need to consider in your plan—for instance, a path between the house and the mailbox, an area for kids and pets to play, or a place for a clothesline. This list should include features that you feel you absolutely must have in your yard, such as a vegetable garden for fresh produce, a flower bed to brighten a dull corner, or a tree to shade a porch or patio.

MAKE A WISH LIST

Now comes the fun part: thinking about what you'd really like to put in your garden. You probably already have some ideas, inspired by things you've seen in books, magazines, catalogs, and other gardens. A wish list gives you a place to put down those ideas so you can remember them when it's time to actually lay out the plan.

Next to your needs list, start writing down all the fun ideas that come to mind. Always wanted an herb garden? Add it to the list. Would you love to have fruit trees, or a cutting garden so you can have armloads of fresh flowers for arrangements? Jot down those ideas, too.

When the ideas start slowing down, think about

A BUTTERFLY GARDEN. *You can invite butterflies into your garden with plantings of butterfly-attracting flowers. This garden features annuals, including cosmos, cleome, calliopsis (Coreopsis tinctoria), heliotrope (Heliotropium sp.), cornflowers (Centaurea cyanus), and Mexican sunflowers (Tithonia sp.).*

VEGETABLES AND FLOWERS. *This simple Colonial-style garden provides room for a traditional vegetable garden along with beds of flowers, such as larkspur and yarrow, for cutting. Simple raised beds ensure excellent soil drainage.*

the following points, and write down any thoughts they inspire:

• Why are you making the plan in the first place? Do you just want to add some color and interest to your front- and backyard? Or do you want to reduce maintenance so you can spend less time working on your yard and more time enjoying it?

• Are there any existing features you want to highlight, downplay, or hide completely? Perhaps you'd like to screen off the area where you keep your trash, or highlight a particularly beautiful view.

• Would you like your garden to have a formal look, with very simple, elegant lines, or do you prefer a more casual, natural look? The features you include in your landscape may differ, depending on your preferences. If you're not sure what you like best, see "What's Your Style?" on page 25.

• What special things would you like to add to your landscape? How about plants to attract birds, butterflies, and other wildlife? Or a water garden or fountain to add the calming sounds of water? Or

maybe a fragrant or white-and-silver garden to highlight a pool or patio? The possibilities are endless! For even more ideas, see "Choosing a Theme" on page 29.

• If you're not the only one who uses your landscape, ask the other family members what they think—they may also have great ideas for the wish list. (They may have things to add to your needs list, too.)

CREATE A PRACTICAL PLAN

Actually making your garden plan is a lot like putting together a jigsaw puzzle: You take the frame that your site has to offer and figure out how to fit in all the pieces to make a pleasing picture. Like most things in life, the final design will be a compromise between dreams and reality. The trick is to cram in as many of your dreams as possible!

WHAT'S YOUR STYLE?

There are two general kinds of garden design: formal and informal. The style you choose for your property could be either one of these or a blend of the two. The key is to match your garden style with the natural look of your property and with the look you like best.

In a formal design, plants are arranged in geometrically shaped beds laid out symmetrically. Other features of this style include straight edges, clipped hedges, topiaries, and finely mown lawns, as well as flagstone paths and brick walls. Formal gardens can be especially grand on large properties, but the simple, restrained style can also be elegant and practical for very small areas.

Informal gardens have a more casual, free-flowing look. The idea is not to make the site look neglected, but rather to let the plantings and materials look a little more natural. A good example of an informal planting is the classic English cottage garden, with its abundance of blooms all jostling for attention. An increasingly popular informal American garden style is "wildscaping," which includes habitat plantings, butterfly gardens, wildflower gardens, and native plant gardens. Among other features of informal landscapes are curving lines and casual-looking materials such as wood-chip paths and post-and-rail fences.

If you're not sure which style you like best, look through books and magazines, walk through your neighborhood, and visit botanical gardens to find examples. Let your home give you clues, too. A formal-looking brick or frame house generally looks best with a more formal landscape, while a more informal home can lend itself to a casual garden layout. If your house is one style but you like another, try using some features of both. You might, for instance, choose formal-looking flagstone paths but arrange the plantings within the beds in a more informal style.

FORMAL BALANCE. *Clipped yews on either side of the brick steps are an easy clue that this garden has a formal design. The straight brick walk and circular brick terrace are also formal elements. The perennial beds on either side of the walkway have a formal feel, even though they aren't strictly mirror-image plantings.*

INFORMAL MOVEMENT. *The rustic fence and natural-looking plantings of perennials shown here are characteristic of an informal design. The meadowlike clumps of bee balm, daylilies, and yuccas in this garden also create a feeling of movement and excitement—both hallmarks of informal gardens.*

MAKING A ROUGH PLAN

Start by taking a copy of your site map and sketching in the features from your needs list. Also, mark any changes you definitely plan to make, such as removing overgrown shrubs or redirecting awkward paths.

Now look at your wish list and see which of those ideas would work. If you have lots of room, you may be able to fit in everything you want. If space is limited, try to imagine an area that could serve a double purpose. Say, for instance, you want a flower bed *and* a garden of herbs for cooking, but you don't have room for both. You could combine both kinds of plants in one garden to make an area that's practical as well as pretty.

WATER IN THE GARDEN. *A pond or water garden adds magic to any landscape. Garden visitors such as birds, wildlife, and humans alike will find it irresistible. This garden, which sits on the edge of a wild area, is surrounded by black-eyed Susans, gayfeathers (Liatris sp.), Joe-Pye weed (Eupatorium sp.), and ornamental grasses.*

PRETTY INSIDE AND OUT. *When planning any garden, take time to consider what it will look like from inside your home. This garden is as appealing from indoors as it is out.*

While this isn't the time to decide exactly which plants will go where, keep the growing conditions in mind when you choose garden sites. Most vegetables need as much sun as they can get, so you may want to pick the vegetable garden site first and fit the more adaptable flower gardens around it. A low-lying spot is a natural choice for a water garden or a bed of moisture-loving perennials.

If you want to include a play area for children or a place for outdoor entertaining, a flat site is best. If the flat areas of your yard are limited, save them for these uses, and plant your gardens on the slopes. For details, see "Straighten Slopes with Terraces" on page 27.

Don't forget to consider how the different features will look from inside the house. Check the view from the windows you look out most frequently, and see what you can add for special excitement, such as shrubs and flowers for winter interest, or a mixed planting and a water garden to attract birds.

Also, mark where you want any new pathways to go, and where you want the flower beds and vegetable garden to be.

Once you've done as much as you can, it's time to take a long, hard look at the results. If there's anything left on your needs list that didn't fit in, decide if it really must be in there. If it does, look again to find a spot for it, even if it means taking out one of your dream ideas. No matter how much you want a perennial border, for instance, it won't help you if what you need is a place to park that second car.

You'll also need to consider how much time and money you can spend on the garden. Despite wishful thinking, there is no such thing as a no-maintenance garden. Be realistic about how much time you can spend on mowing, pruning, staking, weeding, and watering. When you don't have the time to care for it, even the best design will soon look neglected and shabby. If you are a beginning gardener, or a busy person without a lot of extra time, you're better off keeping the design simple, at least for a few years. As your skills, wants, and needs change, you can always go back and add features later on.

FINE-TUNING YOUR MASTER PLAN

It's time to put the finishing touches on your landscape plan. The key to a professional-looking layout is to use the same principles the pros use: repetition and balance.

Repetition: Repeating different design elements is an important part of creating a sense of unity. These elements include both the "hardscape" features and the plants themselves.

"Hardscape" refers to the constructed features of a landscape, such as paths and walkways, decks and patios, and walls and fences. By using the same, or very similar, kinds of materials for these features, you can visually link the different elements together. The specific material you choose depends a lot on the style of your house, as well as your preference for a formal or informal garden style. For example, if your home is brick, using brick for garden walls, paths, and patios will give a unified, formal look to your landscape. Gravel paths and picket fences can look charming with small Colonial-style houses.

Repeating plants can also unify your garden design. This does not mean that you have to grow the same plants in all your beds and borders to create mirror-image plantings. It's okay to jumble things

STRAIGHTEN SLOPES WITH TERRACES

Sloping sites can be tricky to plant and even trickier to maintain. With a little work, though, slopes can actually be ideal garden spots for vegetables, flowers, and groundcovers that thrive in particularly well-drained soil. The trick is to turn the slope into a series of broad steps, called terraces. You can do this by installing a series of low retaining walls across the slope and filling in behind them with soil to create flat planting areas.

Wood, stone, concrete, railroad ties, and bricks are all popular materials for building retaining walls. Don't use creosote-treated railroad ties or pressure-treated lumber, since these materials may release harmful chemicals into the soil. The terraces should be the same length and width as the sloped area, and at least 8 to 12 inches high.

If you want to install a few low terraces on a gentle slope, you can probably do the work yourself. If the slope is steep, however, you're probably better off hiring a landscape contractor or builder who knows how to build safe, durable walls.

GARDEN ON A TERRACE. *A low stone wall transforms this sloping site into a level area that is ideal for gardening. Basket-of-gold (*Aurinia saxatilis*), candytuft (*Iberis sempervirens*), and irises thrive in the well-drained conditions above the wall.*

up a bit, but try to repeat some elements, such as a particular color or texture. You could do this by using one particular plant, such as lamb's ears (*Stachys byzantina*), as an edging for all the beds. Or you could choose a few favorite colors and grow different plants with those colors throughout the yard.

Balance: Achieving balance is critical in good

REPETITION. *Pink-flowered yarrow, spun through this border like cotton candy, creates a unified garden picture that is pleasing to the eye; orange daylilies and orange-and-yellow Gloriosa daisies serve as accents. Foliage colors help unify the design, too: Silver-leaved artemisia echoes the color of the building.*

BALANCE. *The clumps of perennials that line this walk-way are balanced because they have similar visual weight. A pair of pink spiraeas in the foreground gives way to mismatched clumps of yarrow, sundrops (Oenothera spp.), lady's-mantle (Alchemilla mollis), and shocking-red Maltese cross (Lychnis chalcedonica). A pair of red-leaved roses (Rosa glauca) at the end of the walk completes the composition.*

garden design. When you look at the garden, it should not appear greatly weighted to one side or one area. While one area may have a captivating specimen tree or an eye-catching island flower border, it shouldn't overwhelm the entire garden. A small tree in the middle of a big lawn can look as unbalanced as a big tree in a small lawn.

Symmetrical plantings—such as flower beds on both sides of a path—are one way to balance your layout. Unless you're striving for a formal look, however, perfect symmetry can get boring. To avoid this, try to use similar-size masses of different plants. One large tree on the right side of a yard, for instance, could be balanced with three smaller trees on the left side.

LAY OUT BEDS AND BORDERS

Now that you know where you want everything to go in your garden, you can start thinking about the details, such as the size and shape of the planting areas. There is no right or wrong shape or size—it depends on the amount of room you have and on the look you're striving for. Formal beds are usually rectangular, with crisp, straight edges. Vegetable gardens are also usually square or rectangular, since the crops are normally planted in rows or blocks. Informal, ornamental planting areas have more flowing outlines.

A great way to try out different shapes before digging is to outline the bed with a hose or rope. Move the hose or rope around until you find a shape you like. If you are designing a bed that you'll look at mainly from indoors, go into the house and look out the window. If necessary, adjust the shape of the bed to create the most pleasing view. When you're satisfied with the results, sketch the shape and size of the bed onto your master plan.

PICK PLANTS FOR YOUR PLANS

Once you've determined the exact shape and size of the bed or border, you're ready to design the planting scheme for that space. The best way to do this is to make an enlarged drawing of the garden bed. Take the exact measurements of the bed and draw it to scale on graph paper, as you did for the master plan. Next to the outline, jot down everything you know about the site, including the amount of sun and shade it gets, the soil type, the drainage characteristics, and the soil fertility. (You'll find this information in the garden notes you collected in Chapter 1.)

Armed with all this information, you can start selecting the plants. Make a list of plants that appeal to you, then go through the list to make sure they will grow well in the conditions available on your site. Then check to make sure you've included some plants for all seasons to ensure that the landscape will be interesting year-round. Finally, decide how to group the plants to create the most pleasing combinations.

THE PATH TO SUCCESS

As you plan your landscape, don't forget that well-designed paths and walkways are an invaluable addition to any property. Their most obvious purpose is to give you a fast and safe way to reach different parts of your yard, but they can also serve many other functions. For instance, a path through a planted area lets you maintain the plants in the beds without stepping on and compacting the soil. Paths and walkways can also visually link different parts of the garden, drawing your eye from one spot to another.

If the walkway is curved, it lends an informal, easygoing mood to the garden. Curved walkways also add charm and a bit of mystery to the garden, by beckoning visitors to see what's behind the next curve of the path. A straight walkway can make an area look longer and give it a formal feel.

If the walkway will get heavy use, it should be at least 4 to 5 feet wide so that two people can walk side by side. Less frequently used paths should be about 2 feet wide.

Many different materials are available for making paths and walkways. Choose the one that best fits your style, needs, and budget. The following are some of the most commonly used materials:

Wood chips or shredded bark: Easy and eco-nomical to use, these materials add a natural, informal feeling to the garden. Use them alone, or edge them with bricks, wood, or other materials for a more finished look.

Wood blocks: Wood blocks lend a natural and rustic look to a garden. However, they can be slippery when wet.

Concrete pavers: These durable materials come in different sizes and patterns, and are available from most garden centers.

Flagstone: Flagstone is one of the most beautiful and durable materials you can use for walkways. It is hard to install, because the individual stones are extremely heavy to lift and lay out, but it's worth the cost and effort.

Brick: This very durable and handsome material looks good in most gardens, especially more formal ones. There are dozens of ways to lay out brick to achieve various patterns and styles. Use paving bricks, which are better suited for garden use than ordinary bricks.

Gravel: Gravel is both economical and easy to lay out, but it does need to be replenished a bit each year. Edge it with wood or bricks, and rake it every so often so it doesn't scatter with wear and weather. Gravel pathways go well in herb, rock, Japanese, and wildflower gardens.

AN INTRIGUING PATHWAY. *Charm and mystery abound along this simple pathway. Note the transition between one area and the next as the path passes under the arbor. Rustic stone gives way to concrete pavers to mark the steps, then brick sets the tone for the sitting area beyond.*

CHOOSING A THEME

With thousands of plants to choose from, how do you know where to start? Knowing what kinds of plants you're looking for will make the search much easier. Check your wish list to see if you had an idea for a garden theme—for example, an evening garden or a fragrant garden. If you didn't have a specific idea then, now's a good time to choose one.

Theme gardens are a wonderful way to develop and indulge your passion for a particular type of garden or group of plants. You could carry one theme through all of your gardens, or use different themes

to make charming "rooms" within the landscape. For instance, you might choose to plant a fragrant garden to welcome visitors to your front door, a soothing Japanese garden in a quiet side yard, and a colorful children's garden in part of the backyard. Or perhaps you are especially fond of one particular kind of plant, such as daylilies, roses, or herbs. Any of these themes make a good starting point for your plant choices.

Listed below are other inspiring ideas for fun and exciting theme gardens. Once you've selected a theme, turn to the later chapters in this book to learn more about annuals and biennials, perennials, bulbs, roses, vegetables, herbs, groundcovers, and vines. Each chapter includes plant portraits, with details on the needs and characteristics of the best garden plants. Read through the portraits and look at the photographs to find plants you'd like to try. Check the entries to make sure the plants you like can survive in your climate and under the growing conditions your site has to offer. Jot down the names of all the suitable plants you find until you have a plant list for each garden bed. Then move on to "Planning for Four-Season Interest" on page 33 to help fine-tune your plant choices.

Handy Kitchen Garden: Traditional kitchen gardens are making a comeback. If you enjoy having garden-fresh vegetables and just-picked herbs for cooking, this kind of garden could be for you. For gourmet salads, try a special salad garden with different kinds of lettuce, edible flowers, spinach, arugula, and other greens. If you enjoy Mediterranean cooking, how about a planting of tomatoes, eggplants, onions, garlic, basil, and other herbs? Or maybe Mexican cooking is more your style; try a garden filled with tomatoes, onions, cilantro, tomatillos, and an assortment of hot peppers. For a garden that's both beautiful and bountiful, combine colorful vegetables such as red and yellow tomatoes, purple eggplants, and red, yellow, and green peppers.

A Pretty and Practical Cutting Garden: Bring the outdoors in with fresh flower arrangements scattered throughout your home. Creating a special gar-

TUCKED-IN BEDS. *Flower beds filled with foxglove, bellflowers, and lady's-mantle (Alchemilla mollis) add delicate beauty to a small nook off a brick patio edged with lavender cotton (Santolina chamaecyparissus). A stone bench provides an appealing perch from which to enjoy the view.*

BOLD COLOR AND SHAPE. *Phlox, bee balm, cleome, and a host of other perennials create a spectacular effect in this informal planting. Large clumps of flowers ensure that this border is bold and striking, even from a distance.*

den just for cut flowers will spare your more visible flower beds from your scissors. Look for annuals and perennials with long, sturdy stems and long-lasting flowers; fragrance is a plus, too. Baby's breath (*Gypsophila* spp.), China asters (*Callistephus chinensis*), annual statice (*Limonium sinuatum*), Shasta daisies (*Chrysanthemum* X *superbum*), snapdragons, poppies, lilies (*Lilium* spp.), and zinnias are just a few of the many wonderful flowers that are ideal for cutting gardens.

An Easy Everlasting Garden: Enjoy beautiful blooms all year long by growing your own everlasting flowers. Durable, easy-to-dry flowers and seedpods look great in the garden and in arrangements,

wreaths, potpourri, and other crafts. Try a variety of annuals and perennials, including yarrows (*Achillea* spp.), statice (*Limonium* spp.), strawflowers (*Helichrysum bracteatum*), globe amaranth (*Gomphrena globosa*), and bells-of-Ireland (*Moluccella laevis*).

A Wonderful Wildlife Garden: Add grace and beauty to your summer garden with plants that provide food and shelter for wildlife. To attract butterflies and hummingbirds, for example, try growing colorful flowers such as red salvia (*Salvia coccinea*), cosmos, snapdragons, and marigolds.

A Color-Theme Garden: If you have a favorite color, that's a great place to start for choosing a garden theme. Try a soothing purple-and-blue garden, or a planting of sunny yellows and golds. For an exceptionally elegant look, consider a silver, gray, and white garden with lamb's ears (*Stachys byzantina*), 'Silver Lace' dusty miller (*Chrysanthemum ptarmiciflorum* 'Silver Lace'), 'White Porcelain' mealy-cup sage (*Salvia farinacea* 'White Porcelain'), and 'Snowflake' candytuft (*Iberis sempervirens* 'Snowflake').

An Easy-Care Garden: When low maintenance is your main concern, look for tough, adaptable plants that can thrive with minimal fussing. A few good candidates include cleome (*Cleome hasslerana*), cornflower (*Centaurea cyanus*), cosmos (*Cosmos* spp.), 'Purple Dome' aster (*Aster novae-angliae* 'Purple Dome'), 'Moonbeam' coreopsis (*Coreopsis verticillata* 'Moonbeam'), marigolds, zinnias, and daylilies (*Hemerocallis* spp.).

A Colorful Children's Garden: Giving children their own garden space to plant and maintain is the best way to pass on your love of plants and gardening. Make a tepee-shaped structure with tall garden stakes (be sure to leave room for a door!), and plant fast-growing beans and mini-pumpkins around the base to make a child-size hideaway. Around the outside, plant brightly colored flowers, cherry tomatoes, and fast-growing radishes. A tepee garden makes a great theme garden within a larger vegetable garden area.

PLANNING FOR
FOUR-SEASON INTEREST

To get the most enjoyment from your ornamental gardens, make sure you include plants that will be attractive in each season.

Spring: Seeing the first bulbs come up in spring is a joyful reminder that winter is over. Include tulips, daffodils, hyacinths, crocuses, and other early-blooming beauties in beds, borders, among groundcovers, and under deciduous trees. Plant them among hostas, daylilies, and other plants that can hide the yellowing bulb foliage as it dies back in late spring.

Summer: Summer is an easy time to plan for color. Combine long-blooming annuals with summer-flowering perennials for summer-long beauty.

Fall: Deciduous trees and shrubs are often the stars of the fall garden, with their stunning cool-weather foliage colors. Add extra excitement to the season with fall-flowering asters, chrysanthe-

A COTTAGE GARDEN. *Sunflowers, cosmos, purple coneflowers, Artemisia 'Silver King', and a variety of other flowers complement the white picket fence in a cottagey mix.*

VEGETABLES, FLOWERS, AND HERBS. *Here, a kitchen garden mixes flowers for cutting with herbs and vegetables for the table.*

A COLOR THEME. *Blue delphiniums and hardy geraniums, pink dianthus, and silver-leaved lamb's ears and artemisia create a serene mood with subtle color.*

SUMMER-LONG COLOR. *Perennials mixed with annuals, including marigolds and zinnias, provide a swath of color below this low retaining wall from early summer to frost.*

A COOL COMBO. *The lavender-blue blooms of grassy-leaved Siberian iris (Iris sibirica 'Sea Shadows') combine effectively with pink-flowered broom (Cytissus 'Hollandia') and Dianthus 'Bath's Pink'.*

mums, sedums, and Japanese anemones (*Anemone* X *hybrida*).

Winter: You will probably want to add evergreen plants to provide some color in the wintertime.

A GARDEN FOR THE SENSES

Color is one of the first things you notice about any flower garden, and there's unlimited scope for creating stunning color combinations. But you can do more than just look at your garden—you can smell it and listen to it as well.

Fabulous Fragrance: Flower and foliage fragrances are among the most delightful and memorable features of a garden. When selecting garden plants, always include at least a few that will send you into olfactory ecstasy. Some fragrant favorites of gardeners include flowering tobacco (*Nicotiana sylvestris*), moonflower (*Calonyction aculeatum*, also known as *Ipomoea alba*), honeysuckles (*Lonicera* spp.), sweet peas (*Lathyrus odoratus*), lavender, roses, tuberose (*Polianthes tuberosa*), and hyacinths. Herbs such as sage, thyme, rosemary, and mint are ideal for adding scented foliage.

Plant fragrant plants where you can enjoy them often—near doorways, decks and patios, benches, pools, and hot tubs. Place containers of aromatic plants on porches, balconies, and decks.

Soothing Sound: Many gardeners wouldn't think of selecting plants for sound, but it's definitely worth considering. Ornamental grasses such as Japanese silver grass (*Miscanthus sinensis*) and fountain grass (*Pennisetum* spp.) make a wonderful rustling sound when the wind rushes through them. You can also add sound by attracting songbirds to your garden with shelter and food plants—berry bushes, sunflowers, and ornamental grasses are all good choices.

Also, be sure to include plants with interesting winter structure, such as ornamental grasses, and perennials with long-lasting seed heads, such as 'Autumn Joy' sedum and gloriosa daisies (*Rudbeckia* spp.).

CREATING GREAT PLANT COMBINATIONS

Planting a flower garden and watching the gorgeous tapestry of color and foliage unfold over the season is one of a gardener's greatest pleasures. What makes each garden unique is the gardener's selection and placement of specific combinations of plants. There are endless possibilities for breathtakingly beautiful, playful, and unusual plant combinations.

As seed and nursery companies come out with

BOLD CONTRAST. *Magenta phlox, yellow yarrow, violet larkspur, and red penstemon provide a lively color contrast in this informal planting.*

FOLIAGE TEXTURE. *Both the texture and color of the foliage in this planting provide interest. The bold, corrugated leaves of hostas contrast with the more delicate textures provided by a variety of golden-leaved and variegated plants.*

BALANCED HEIGHT AND SCALE. *A mass planting of lady's-mantle (*Alchemilla mollis*) creates a frothy skirt for a shrub rose. The larger planting of lady's-mantle visually balances the taller rose.*

ever more glorious plants each year, it's easy to get lost in blissful daydreaming about all kinds of possible plant combinations. Start by looking at your plant list to see which plants might look best together, based on their color, texture, height, and scale.

Color: Color is probably the most memorable and beautiful characteristic of flower gardens. Just as you choose the style and design of your garden, you can also select a mood for your garden, by using certain colors. If you like the softness and soothing quality of an overcast day, you probably are drawn to cooler colors like blue, gray, dark green, and soft pink. On hot summer days, cool color combinations offer visual relief from the heat. If you prefer the brilliancy of a bright sunny day, you may want to combine hot colors like red, yellow, bright pink, magenta, orange, and scarlet. Hot color combinations are bold and exciting, but they can also be jarring if the colors clash too much, so choose carefully.

Color can also help make a garden look bigger or smaller than it really is. For example, cool colors can make flower gardens look larger or farther away. Hot colors tend to jump right out at you, so they're great if you want to make outlying beds look closer.

Unless you're trying to create a color-theme garden, it's fun to experiment with different flower and foliage colors in the same planting. You can create eye-catching effects by contrasting hot and cool colors, such as red roses with the soft blue flowers and grayish green leaves of Russian sage (*Perovskia atriplicifolia*). For a more subtle look, combine plants that share similar colors, such as yellow lilies with yellow-and-green-leaved hostas.

Texture: When deciding which plants to grow together, keep in mind that textures can add almost as much interest as color. Try bold, spiky plants, such as yuccas (*Yucca* spp.) and grasses, with plants that have small or rounded leaves, like creeping thyme or nasturtiums. Lacy, finely cut leaves look wonderful against bold, flat foliage: Try pairing ferns with hostas in a shady site, or curled-leaf parsley with fuzzy lamb's ears in a sunny spot.

The trick to using texture effectively is to avoid going overboard. Too many different textures can make a garden look jumbled.

Height and Scale: Always know how tall and wide each plant will get before giving it a place in your garden. Take the plant's size into account when deciding where to put it and which companions to group it with. Tall plants generally look best at the back of the border, with medium-sized plants in the middle and short plants along the front.

It's okay to mix the heights up a little to get a less rigid look. The best way to do this is to site a few spiky-flowered plants, such as foxgloves (*Digitalis purpurea*) and mulleins (*Verbascum* spp.), near the front; it's easy to see around these spikes to view the plants behind them. Tall plants with airy foliage or flowers, such as Russian sage (*Perovskia atriplicifolia*) and blue lace flower (*Trachymene coerulea*), are also ideal for this purpose.

CLASSIC PERENNIAL COLOR. *Gardens are almost always works-in-progress. Plants that self-seed or that need dividing are just two factors that affect a design as the years go by. Let experimentation figure in your plans as well: Make room for flowers you've never tried or colors you've never combined. This garden features phlox, daylilies, bee balm, bellflowers (*Campanula *spp.), balloon flowers (*Platycodon *sp.), ligularia, and globe thistle (*Echinops ritro).*

TURN YOUR DREAM INTO REALITY

You have your maps and your plant lists. Now it's time to move to the next step: installing the garden. Don't think you have to do it all at one time. Now that you have a plan, it's easy to phase in the garden over several years, as time and finances permit.

Ideally, you should begin with the big projects. Start by removing any unwanted trees and shrubs. This is also the time to do any major regrading of the soil and to put in drainage pipes or trenches. Next, plant larger trees, privacy hedges, and wind screens so they'll get established as soon as possible. Then construct any raised beds, garden walls, or other masonry structures. It's also helpful to lay out your paths before you plant.

Of course, it's not much fun to wait several years before starting on your actual garden plantings. To spruce up your yard in the meantime, experiment with container plantings and annual flower beds. If you have time, you may even want to start a small, temporary perennial garden. When you're ready to start the permanent plantings, you can dig up the perennials, divide them, and use them to fill your new gardens. It's also easy to start the vegetable garden in the first year or two, since you'll know where you want it to go, and it will provide a well-deserved reward for all your hard work.

While you can do much of the work yourself, there are some jobs that are best left to qualified professionals. For your personal safety and to protect your property, hire pros to cut down large trees and remove the stumps, do major regrading and terracing, correct severe soil drainage problems, and build large masonry structures.

Once the big jobs are done, you can move on to laying out the garden beds. If possible, dig the beds at least a few weeks before you plan to plant, so the soil will have a chance to settle. Refer back to your master plan to make sure you're putting the bed in the right place. Outline each bed with a hose, a rope, or stakes and string so you'll know where to dig. (For details on soil preparation and planting, see Chapter 11, Planting and Caring for Your Garden.)

PART II

PLANT PORTRAITS

DECIDING WHAT TO GROW IS ONE OF THE MOST ENJOYABLE ASPECTS OF GARDENING. What gardener hasn't spent an enjoyable few hours pouring over the pages of a catalog, or wandering the aisles of the local garden center? There are always new plants to try, whether they are old favorites your grandmother once grew or plants you've never heard of before. But deciding what to grow can be intimidating, too. It can also be frustrating if your new purchases don't perform well in your garden.

In the chapters that follow, you will find all the information you need to grow a host of annuals, perennials, bulbs, roses, vegetables, herbs, groundcovers, and vines. You will find photographs and descriptions of hundreds of terrific plants, along with tips for growing them from seed, ideas for using them in the garden, problems to watch out for, and much more. For a successful, thriving garden that is easy to care for, use this information to fill your garden with plants that will grow vigorously in the sun, soil, and climate conditions your yard has to offer.

ANNUAL COLOR. *China asters (Callistephus chinensis) and flowering tobacco (Nicotiana alata)
make happy companions in a bed with zonal geraniums that are just coming into bloom.*

CHAPTER THREE

ANNUALS AND BIENNIALS

DEPENDABLE AND EASY TO GROW, ANNUALS AND BIENNIALS ARE THE BACKBONE OF MANY AMERICAN FLOWER GARDENS. Marigolds, petunias, geraniums, and other favorites offer colorful flowers and season-long bloom that can brighten up any yard and add a welcoming touch to entryways. In this chapter, you'll learn about the many exciting advantages of growing these beautiful and versatile plants. Plus, you'll find a gallery of plant portraits to help you choose the best annuals and biennials for your yard.

WHAT ARE ANNUALS AND BIENNIALS?

Technically, an annual is any plant that completes its life cycle in one year: It germinates, grows leaves, blooms, pro-

ANNUALS FOR CONTAINERS. *Many annuals are ideal for pots, tubs, window boxes and other types of containers. Pots of red-flowered geraniums add summer-long color and interest to this sun-splashed terrace.*

duces seed, and dies all in one growing season. Marigolds, cosmos, and sweet peas are all examples of true annuals. Biennials, such as foxgloves, complete the same cycle, but over two years. They produce only leaves the first year, waiting until the second year to flower, set seed, and die.

While these definitions can be helpful, plants don't always fit neatly into categories. As some gardeners say, plants don't read books, so they may not behave the way books say they should! Petunias, impatiens, and geraniums, for example, are staples of the annual garden, but botanically speaking, they are actually perennials. (In most areas, they are killed by frost at the end of the season.) And some biennials, including forget-me-nots, will grow, bloom, and set seed in just one year if you start them indoors in late winter. Many biennials also produce lots of seedlings, so they may bloom in your garden for many years, as perennials do.

So, while it's helpful to know how an annual or biennial is *supposed* to act, it's more important to

consider how the plant will actually grow in your garden. In the plant portraits in this chapter, in seed catalog descriptions, and on seed packets, you'll see that the plants commonly grown as annuals are classified as "tender," "half-hardy," or "hardy," depending on their tolerance for cold temperatures.

Tender annuals, such as petunias and begonias, have no tolerance for frost. They must be sown indoors in spring and transplanted outside after all danger of frost has passed, or sown directly in the garden when the soil is warm. Snapdragons, dusty miller, and other half-hardy annuals can be sown outdoors a few weeks before the last frost, but after the last heavy frost. If they self-sow (drop seeds that grow into new plants), their seed can often survive the winter and may germinate the following year. Hardy annuals, including sweet peas and larkspur, can tolerate a light frost. Sow them outdoors as soon as you can work the soil in spring. If they self-sow, their seed can survive the winter and germinate the following year.

EASY-CARE COLOR. *In this simple but cheerful planting, a sheet of golden and orange marigolds along a rustic fence provides a colorful salutation to passersby from early summer to frost.*

WHY GROW ANNUALS AND BIENNIALS?

Annuals and biennials have many distinct advantages over perennials, not the least of which is that they tend to be easier to maintain in the garden. Unlike perennials, they do not become overcrowded, so they don't need to be dug up and divided. Also, because their life cycles are relatively short, annuals and biennials often have fewer pest and disease problems than longer-lived plants. There is little need to worry about winter protection for biennials, and annuals require no protection at all. You can allow an annual bed to sit all winter long without a winter mulch, because there are no plants that can be pushed out of the soil by the repeated freezing and thawing. (In fact, this cycle of freezing and thawing is good for the soil, because it breaks it up, making it more friable and easier to work in the spring.)

Another advantage of planting annuals and biennials is that you can easily change your garden design every year or two. You have the freedom to experiment with different plant heights, flower types, and individual colors and color combinations. Annuals and biennials allow you to try something new in containers, mixed borders, mass plantings, and edgings. In fact, every garden should have some areas set aside for annuals, because every gardener should try something new every year.

The versatility of annuals is especially helpful for beginning gardeners. Perennial gardens usually take about three years to mature, so you have to wait a long time to see if your design and plant choices worked out. And if you don't like the results, it can take a lot of work to rearrange the plants. On the other hand, if you make a mistake in your choice of an annual in a border, you will know fairly quickly, and you can always try something else next year. As you watch your annuals, you'll develop a sense for the colors and heights that you like, which will give

ANNUALS AND PERENNIALS. *Plant annuals right in perennial gardens to add color all season long. In this garden, zonal geraniums* (Pelargonium *spp.*) *and petunias in drain-tile planters create a sculpturelike effect. They're mixed with cranesbills* (Geranium pratense) *and irises.*

you confidence as you plan all kinds of flower gardens in the future.

As you develop an eye for garden design, you'll appreciate the versatility of annuals even more. By including different annuals every year, you can change the look of your garden without having to replace expensive perennials. And since annuals tend to come into their own in midsummer, just when many perennials are entering a midsummer slump, they can keep the color going until the perennials come back for their fall finale. Annuals are also invaluable filler plants for new perennial borders, when young perennial plants are just starting to grow.

In fact, annuals' fast-growing habit makes them

ideal for any new garden. If you move into a new home that has not been landscaped, or if you live in an apartment and only have a balcony to serve as a garden, annuals can give you an instant, long-blooming garden in just one season. They can serve as quick hedges to hide an unsightly view, or fill in until slower-growing, more permanent woody hedges grow large enough to serve as a screen. Annual vines can cover an arbor or pergola by midsummer the same year they are planted, providing shade and privacy while clematis or other more permanent vines are getting established.

In any garden, annuals and biennials are great values. They are often available as seed, which is the most inexpensive way to grow plants. If you purchase bedding plants in large numbers, it can add up fairly quickly, but it is still much cheaper than buying large quantities of perennials. Some annuals and biennials—including cleome, impatiens, and foxgloves—will even self-sow, so you may get plants without having to buy them or start them indoors! If they come up where you don't want them, just weed them out before they bloom, and they won't return. Keep in mind that self-sown seedlings from hybrids may not look like the original plants. It can be fun to see what you get, but allowing them to grow should be done in the spirit of experimentation rather than as part of your design.

Perhaps the best thing about annuals is that they are the garden plants we all started with, or should start with. They are the best plants for children, since they can initiate a love of gardening at an early age that will last a lifetime. And for those of us who started late, annuals are still the way to begin, giving us the confidence to go on and try something new. It is possibly the memory of our first successful gardening attempts that makes us unable to give annuals up when we go on to bigger challenges. But we would not keep planting annuals for sentimental reasons alone. Any sentimentality about annuals is always rewarded with those familiar, reliable bursts of color that say "It's summer!" so eloquently.

PLANT PORTRAITS

The following plant portraits are by no means an exhaustive list of the many fine annuals and biennials that American gardeners can grow and enjoy. The plants covered here were selected for their superior garden performance, reliability, popularity, or special qualities, such as their suitability as fresh-cut or dried flowers. They are also easy to find, either as seed from mail-order catalogs or as bedding plants at local garden centers.

The plants are listed by their botanical names in bold type. These names are recognized all over the world. Since they can be real tongue twisters, you'll find pronunciations under each entry name. You'll also find the common name (or names) of the plants, which often vary from region to region. Next, the entry tells you if the plant is usually grown as a tender annual, a half-hardy annual, a hardy annual, or a biennial. Each entry also provides a

GROWING TIPS AT A GLANCE

Each of the following plant portraits includes simple symbols to highlight special features you need to know about each annual and biennial. If you're not sure what any of the symbols mean, refer back to this key.

- ○ Full sun (more than 6 hours of sun a day; ideally all day)
- ◑ Partial sun (some direct sun, but less than 6 hours a day)
- ● Shade (no direct sun)
- ✳ Drought-tolerant
- ❀ Prefers cool temperatures
- ✂ Good as a cut flower
- ❀ Good as a dried flower or seedpod
- ❦ Fragrant
- ▼ Grows well in containers

description of the plant, including its height, color, and bloom time. Growing guidelines and suggested garden uses complete the portraits to ensure flower gardening success!

Ageratum houstonianum
ad-jer-AY-tum hew-stow-nee-AY-num.
Ageratum, floss flower. Tender annual.

Characteristics. Height: 6 to 30 inches. Colors: Blue, purple, pink, and white.

With their tight clusters of powder-puff blooms, ageratums add a soft, almost fluffy texture to beds and borders. The flower buds are darker in color than the fully opened flowers, and because they don't open all at once, the clusters often have an interesting two-toned look. The plants are mound-shaped, forming undulating ribbons of color when they are in full bloom. Ageratums come in a wide range of blue shades, from light powder blue through deep oceanic blue to lavender as well as white and pink. Many cultivars are named after bodies of water, including 'Blue Danube Hybrid', 'Blue Lagoon', 'Pacific', and 'Adriatic'. Some names, such

Ageratum houstonianum

as 'Blue Mink', suggest the luxuriant texture of the flowers.

Because of their reliable garden performance, ageratums are favorite annuals for use in flower beds or wherever a broad sweep of color is desired all summer long.

How to Grow. Sow seed indoors about 6 weeks before the last frost. The seeds need light to germinate, so just scatter them over the planting medium and press them lightly into the surface. Keep the medium moist by covering the trays or pots with clear glass or plastic until seedlings appear. Transplant hardened-off seedlings to the garden when all danger of frost has passed. Bedding plants are readily available at garden centers.

Ageratums grow best in a warm, rich, well-drained soil in full sun, or plant in light shade where summers are long and hot. They tolerate heat and drought but should be watered during prolonged dry periods for continuous bloom. Deadheading keeps the plants looking tidy and encourages more blooms to form.

Uses. The compact dwarf ageratum cultivars, including 'Blue Danube Hybrid', are at their best in mass plantings. They make excellent edging plants and blend well with other low-growing annuals in window boxes and other containers. The taller cultivars, such as 'Blue Horizon Hybrid', are ideal for annual or mixed borders. The flowers are excellent for cutting for fresh or dried bouquets.

ALYSSUM, SWEET. See *Lobularia maritima*

Amaranthus spp.
am-er-AN-thus. Love-lies-bleeding, summer poinsettia. Half-hardy annual.

Characteristics. Height: 3 to 5 feet. Colors: Brown, green, red, and yellow.

The amaranthus family is large and includes many wildflowers, weeds, and edible grains. Love-lies-bleeding (*Amaranthus caudatus*) and summer poinsettia (*A. tricolor*) are two popular species for annual gardens.

Love-lies-bleeding grows up to 5 feet tall and produces long, deep red, tassel-like flower clusters, which remain on the plants until autumn. Yellow and green cultivars are also available but are less common. The plants and flowers have a luxuriant, old-fashioned, even overgrown look. Love-lies-bleeding adds a coarse texture to the garden, so you may want to site it where you'll see it from a little distance, such as near the back of a border. A dramatic plant, it can make a striking focal point in the right place.

Amaranthus tricolor

Summer poinsettia is grown for the rich color combinations of its foliage. 'Joseph's Coat' has green-and-red leaves tipped with yellow. 'Illumination' has bright red upper leaves and yellow, green, and chocolate brown on its lower leaves.

How to Grow. Both love-lies-bleeding and summer poinsettia are easy to grow from seed. Sow the seed indoors about 8 weeks before the last frost. Transplant hardened-off seedlings to the garden after all danger of frost has passed and when night temperatures remain above 50°F. Bedding plants are not readily available.

Native to India, the plants thrive in warm summer weather. They tolerate hot, dry conditions in full sun. Foliage colors tend to be brighter where the soil isn't very rich.

Uses. The flowers of love-lies-bleeding are fascinating in dried flower arrangements. Both species make interesting focal points in the garden. They also look attractive planted along a fence or wall as a hedge.

Antirrhinum majus

Antirrhinum majus

an-ter-EYE-num MAY-jus. Snapdragon.
Half-hardy annual.

Characteristics: Height: 6 to 36 inches. Colors: Pink, red, salmon, yellow, orange, white, and bicolors.

Snapdragons are long-time garden favorites for their elegant, lightly fragrant flower spikes in a wide variety of compatible colors. Besides soft pastels, deep reds, and burgundies, snapdragons come in an exquisite range of bicolors. Bicolor combinations include orange with yellow, salmon with apricot, cherry red with rose, and many lighter and darker shades of the same color. The florets on the flower spikes resemble tiny dragons' heads, which snap open and shut when you squeeze the "jaws." Part of the charm of snapdragons, no doubt, comes from our childhood memories of snapping snapdragon flowers—an irresistible urge some of us have not outgrown.

Snapdragons are tender perennials that are normally grown as tender or half-hardy annuals. They can remain outside all winter in frost-free areas. They also do well in greenhouses.

How to Grow. Because snapdragons bloom best in cool weather, you should start the seed indoors 8 to 12 weeks before the last frost. The seed needs light to germinate, so scatter it over the surface of the planting medium. Cover trays or pots with glass or plastic to keep the medium moist while the seeds are sprouting; remove the cover when seedlings appear. When the seedlings are 3 to 4 inches tall, pinch the tops off to encourage better branching. Snapdragons tolerate light frost, so you can transplant hardened-off seedlings to the garden after the last heavy frost. Bedding plants are readily available at garden centers.

Snapdragons bloom best in well-drained, moist soil, in cool late-spring or early-summer temperatures. They can tolerate light shade but bloom much better in full sun. Snapdragons tend to stop producing flowers when hot weather arrives, but they will usually rebloom when the weather cools off in late summer if you cut back the spent flower stalks. The flowers that follow the initial bloom tend to be smaller than the first flowers, but there are often more of them. Taller cultivars need staking. Snapdragons are susceptible to rust fungus, which appears as orange or brown spots on the underside of the foliage. If the disease is a problem in your garden, try growing resistant cultivars.

Uses. Snapdragons are available in a broad range of heights, so they can be used in many ways in the garden. The very small cultivars, such as 'Floral Carpet Hybrid', work well as an annual groundcover, as an edging, or in pots or window boxes. The spiky form of taller cultivars adds an attractive accent to annual and mixed borders. (Deadheading is particularly important in these spots, to keep the plants flowering.) Tall snapdragon cultivars also make remarkably long-lived cut flowers.

ASTER, CHINA. See *Callistephus chinensis*
BABY'S BREATH. See *Gypsophila elegans*
BACHELOR'S BUTTON. See *Centaurea cyanus*

Begonia X semperflorens
beh-GO-nee-uh sem-per-FLOR-enz.
Wax begonia. Tender annual.
○ ◑ ● ✳ ▼

Characteristics: Height: 6 to 12 inches. Colors: Pink, red, and white.

Wax begonias are among the most versatile and reliable annuals available. They grow well in sun or shade, are rarely bothered by pests or diseases, and require very little maintenance in the garden. Wax begonias tend to have a uniform growth habit and bloom freely from early summer to frost, making them popular subjects for mass plantings or formal designs where color and form must be constant all season.

Wax begonia flowers are generally 1 to 2 inches across, although cultivars are available with flowers up to 3 inches wide. The plants bloom so freely that the flowers create masses of color in the garden. The light or dark green, bronze, or red foliage provides an attractive contrast to the flowers. The common name "wax begonia" refers to the waxy texture of the leaves.

How to Grow. Since wax begonias take several months to bloom from seed, you'll need to sow the seed indoors 12 weeks before the last frost. The seeds are so small, some Burpee customers have complained that they didn't get any seeds in the packet—only dust! Because the tiny seeds are diffi-

cult to handle, you might want to mix them with a little sand to help you sow them more evenly. Begonias require light to germinate, so just scatter them as evenly as you can over the surface of the planting medium. Cover the pots or trays with glass or clear plastic to keep the seed from drying out; remove the cover when seedlings appear. Adding bottom heat will speed germination.

When the seedlings are large enough to handle, thin them to 6 inches apart in the flat, or move them to individual pots. Transplant hardened-off seedlings to the garden when all danger of frost has passed. The stems and foliage of wax begonias are brittle and break easily, so handle the plants carefully. Bedding plants of begonias are always available at garden centers.

Wax begonias grow easily in most soils but prefer rich, well-drained soil. They tolerate full sun to fairly dense shade. These dependable plants need little maintenance and are rarely bothered by pests or diseases once they are established in the garden.

Uses. Wax begonias are the perfect bedding plant for sun or shade. They make colorful edgings and fill window boxes and other containers with masses of color. They also make good houseplants, since they stay compact in pots and do not require bright light to bloom well.

BELLS-OF-IRELAND. See *Moluccella laevis*
BLANKET FLOWER. See *Gaillardia pulchella*
BLUE LACE FLOWER. See *Trachymene coerulea*

Begonia X semperflorens

Brachycome iberidifolia

Brachycome iberidifolia

BRAK-ee-kohm eye-ber-id-ih-FOE-lee-uh.
Swan River daisy. Tender annual.

Characteristics: Height: 10 to 18 inches. Colors: Pink, blue, violet, and white.

Swan River daisy produces masses of small, lightly scented, daisylike flowers on mounded plants with delicate, feathery foliage. When they bloom, the bright little daisies are so prolific that they almost cover the foliage. The bloom period is unfortunately short—from 3 to 6 weeks—but the spectacular display outweighs this drawback. The short bloom season makes Swan River daisy a good subject for containers, particularly hanging baskets, which can be removed easily. (Make successive sowings into several hanging baskets so you'll have a new basket ready when the previous one is starting to look tired.) The common name refers to the region of Australia where the plant grows wild.

How to Grow. Where summers are short, it is best to start seeds indoors 6 weeks before the last spring frost. Set hardened-off seedlings in the garden after the last heavy frost. You can also sow seed directly in the garden after all danger of frost has passed. Make successive sowings every 3 weeks for continuous bloom all summer. Plants in hanging baskets are sometimes available at better garden centers.

The plants prefer full sun, cool temperatures, and well-drained, rich, sandy soil. They benefit from extra fertilization throughout the summer. Deadheading will prolong the flower display.

Uses. Swan River daisy is ideal for hanging baskets and other containers, and is an excellent choice for rock gardens. It is also good for edging and beds, as long as you can replace it with fresh plants for continuous bloom. The mildly fragrant flowers make enchanting small bouquets.

Brassica oleracea

BRASS-ik-uh oh-ler-AY-see-uh. Flowering
cabbage, flowering kale. Hardy annual.

Characteristics. Height: 12 inches. Colors: Foliage in pink, red, green, and white.

Flowering cabbage and flowering kale are ornamental versions of the familiar vegetables. They are among the few bedding annuals that are planted primarily for their fall display. However, they are not grown for their flowers, but rather for the splendid coloration cold weather brings out in their foliage. When night temperatures remain cold, the green foliage of the low-growing, cabbagelike plants turns a striking combination of either green and creamy white, or green and pink or red. Flowering cabbage and kale are often used in public gardens and commercial plantings to replace tender annuals killed by the first frost in fall. The plants hold their color and can last for weeks after the first frost.

Gardeners often ask if flowering cabbage and kale are edible. They *are* edible, but they taste extremely bitter. While they would look attractive

Brassica oleracea

in a salad, there are far better-tasting colorful lettuce cultivars available.

How to Grow. Start seeds indoors from early to mid-summer for fall transplanting to the garden. Set home-grown or purchased transplants in the garden from mid- to late summer. If you are waiting to use them to replace summer flowers after the first frost in fall, make sure you harden the plants off before transferring them outside. You can also grow them from seed sown directly in a holding bed in the garden in early to mid-summer; let the plants grow in the holding bed until you are ready to move them to their fall locations. Bedding plants are readily available for fall planting.

Like their tastier counterparts, flowering cabbage and kale prefer rich, well-drained soil. Unlike their vegetable relatives, however, they cannot tolerate light shade. The plants will be tall and leggy, with rather pale colors, unless they are grown in full sun. Because flowering cabbage and kale belong to the same botanical family as regular cabbage and kale, broccoli, and brussels sprouts, they tend to share the same diseases. For that reason, choose a new spot for your flowering cabbage and kale each year, and don't grow them where any of their relatives grew the year before.

Uses. These colorful plants are invaluable for their fall display in beds, window boxes, and tubs. Grow them as accents or as edgings. Use flowering cabbage and kale to replace frost-killed tender annuals.

Browallia speciosa
broh-WALL-ee-uh spee-see-OH-suh.
Browallia. Tender annual.

Characteristics. Height: 10 to 18 inches. Colors: Blue, lavender, and white.

Browallia is prized for its rare blue color, ease of cultivation, and neat, well-branched habit. The masses of blue, lavender, or white star-shaped flowers bloom continuously on strong, low-growing plants all summer until the first fall frost. Browallia tolerates as much shade as impatiens does, so it's ideal for adding an unusual blue accent to shady gardens. Before the first frost in fall, take cuttings or bring the plants inside during the winter.

How to Grow. Browallia takes a long time to bloom from seed, so start it indoors about 8 weeks before the last spring frost. Seeds need light to germinate, so just scatter them over the surface of the medium. Keep them moist by covering the pots or trays with glass or clear plastic until seedlings appear. When the seedlings are 4 to 5 inches tall, pinch the tops to encourage bushiness. Transplant hardened-off seedlings to the garden when the danger of frost has passed. Bedding plants of browallia are usually available at garden centers.

Browallia prefers fertile, well-drained soil and a sunny or partially shady location. It can tolerate sun if you keep it watered, but in areas with very warm

Browallia speciosa

summers, it prefers partial shade. In too much shade, it will grow leggy and will not bloom well. Native to the rain forests of Central America, browallia can tolerate high humidity, but it does not perform well under hot, dry conditions. Mist it every day if you are growing it in hanging baskets or other containers. If you are growing browallia inside as a houseplant, be sure to mist it daily, or place the pot on a bed of pebbles to maintain higher humidity.

Uses. Browallia is a fine annual for beds and borders, as well as hanging baskets, window boxes, and other containers. The blue shades contrast beautifully with white, silver, and pink flowers and foliage. You can also grow browallia as a houseplant in winter in a sunny window.

BUSY LIZZIE. See *Impatiens* spp.

Calendula officinalis
kuh-LEN-dew-luh off-ish-in-AL-iss.
Pot marigold. Hardy annual.
○ ☀ ✂ ❄

Characteristics. Height: 10 to 24 inches. Colors: Yellow, gold, orange, and cream.

In Shakespeare's time, pot marigolds were more likely to be found in kitchen and herb gardens than in ornamental flower borders. Their edible flowers and foliage have long been used to flavor soups and stews, and the flowers used to be grown for medicinal purposes, including the removal of warts.

Calendula officinalis

Nowadays, these charming annuals are popular for adding cool-season color in the flower garden. The bright yellow, gold, orange, and cream flowers resemble chrysanthemums, both in looks and in fragrance. Single and double forms are available. Dwarf cultivars are ideal for flower beds; tall cultivars are good for cutting. Children love growing pot marigolds because the seeds are easy to handle and grow quickly. The bright blooms make pretty and fragrant bouquets.

In public gardens, pot marigolds are often planted with pansies in early spring, replaced in summer with warm-season annuals, then brought back for the cool weather of fall. At home, however, you don't need to take as much trouble with them. Pot marigolds will tolerate some hot summer weather if you keep the roots cool with a light mulch and water the plants regularly. They are not at their best in the heat of summer, but they should revive when cool weather returns.

How to Grow. After the last hard frost in spring, direct-sow the seeds where you want the plants to grow in the garden. Pot marigold seeds resemble comma-shaped worms, and more than one Burpee customer has sent back seed packets with a note indicating that the seeds were devoured by the worms in the packet! When the seedlings are 3 to 4 inches tall, thin them to 12 to 15 inches apart. In areas with mild winter weather, you can sow seed in the garden in fall for early-spring bloom. Plants are sometimes available at garden centers.

Pot marigolds thrive in well-drained soil and full sun. Deadheading encourages continuous blooming. The spent flower heads look somewhat like the flower buds. However, if you look closely, you'll notice that the spent heads have green, wormlike seeds that are beginning to form in the center.

Uses. Easy-to-grow pot marigolds are ideal plants for children and other beginners. Compact cultivars add cool-season color to beds, edgings, and containers. The rich gold and yellow shades combine beautifully with blues and purples. The taller cultivars make terrific cut flowers. These old-fashioned favorites also deserve a place in herb gardens, as well as Shakespearean and Colonial American period gardens.

CALIFORNIA POPPY. See *Eschscholzia californica*

Callistephus chinensis

kal-ih-STEF-us chin-EN-sis. China aster.
Hardy annual.

○ ❄ ⁍❀ ▼

Characteristics. Height: 6 to 36 inches. Colors: Pink, red, blue, purple, yellow, and white.

China asters are versatile, showy annuals suitable for cutting gardens, borders, and pots. Like their relatives, the chrysanthemums, they come in a variety of flower types and a broad range of gorgeous colors. There are single daisylike flowers, doubles with ribbonlike petals, and fluffy, fully double pompons. Extra-dwarf cultivars, including 'Pot 'n Patio Mixed', are especially well suited for growing in containers. Taller cultivars have been developed for borders and cutting.

How to Grow. For an early start, you can sow the seed indoors in peat pots 6 weeks before the last frost in spring. (Transplant hardened-off seedlings outside after all danger of frost, taking care not to damage the roots.) In most cases, though, you'll get the best results by sowing seed directly in the garden where the plants will grow, since they do not transplant well. China asters are not normally available as bedding plants.

China asters prefer well-drained, fertile soil and full sun. They thrive in cooler temperatures and appreciate extra watering in hot summer weather. Pinch off the spent flowers to encourage constant blooming. Taller cultivars need staking.

Unfortunately, China asters are susceptible to several serious diseases, including Fusarium wilt and root rot. To avoid problems with these diseases, plant China asters in a different place each year. These plants are also subject to aster yellows, a disease that affects Canterbury bells, marigolds, and other annuals. Infected plants turn yellowish, and the flowers and foliage become distorted. There is no cure; destroy infected plants. Aster yellows is spread by leafhoppers, so controlling these pests can help prevent the spread of the disease.

Uses. The taller cultivars of China asters are excellent for cutting. Dwarf cultivars make colorful edgings and container plants. All kinds work well in mixed and annual borders. They are easy to grow in a greenhouse in winter for cut flowers.

Callistephus chinensis

Campanula medium

kam-PAN-yew-luh MEE-dee-um.
Canterbury bells. Biennial.

○ ◐ ❄ ⁍❀

Characteristics. Height: 2 to 3 feet. Colors: Blue, lavender, pink, and white.

This old-fashioned favorite makes an unforgettable display in the spring border, especially in mass plantings. Canterbury bells is a hardy biennial, blooming the second year after sowing. The first year, the plants form low-growing rosettes that tend to be evergreen. The following spring, the rosettes produce tall spikes of bell-shaped florets in pretty pastel shades of blue, lavender, pink, and white. Single and double cultivars are available. 'Cup-and-Saucer Mixed' has florets that resemble tiny, exquisite cups and saucers.

How to Grow. For spring bloom the following year, sow seeds in summer directly in the garden in a protected area. In the fall, move the plants to their

Campanula medium

blooming location. You can also sow seed indoors in trays in the summer and transplant the seedlings to the garden in the fall. If you want to try for first-year bloom, sow Canterbury bells indoors 10 to 12 weeks before the last frost in spring. Sprinkle some of the growing medium over the surface until the seed is just barely covered. Transplant hardened-off seedlings to the garden in early spring. Plants are sometimes available at garden centers.

Canterbury bells prefer well-drained, fertile soil and full sun. They will tolerate light shade but will not bloom as well. All cultivars require staking, and the plants will grow best where summers are cool. The plants are susceptible to aster yellows, which causes yellowed and distorted foliage (see the previous entry for more details); remove and destroy infected plants.

Uses. Canterbury bells make terrific spring-blooming bedding plants. They also make handsome additions to flower beds and borders or cottage-style gardens. You can also grow them as container plants in cool greenhouses in winter. Their showy blooms make attractive, long-lasting cut flowers.

CANTERBURY BELLS. See *Campanula medium*
CAPE DAISY. See *Venidium fastuosum*
CARNATION. See *Dianthus* spp.

Catharanthus roseus
kath-uh-RAN-thus ROH-zee-us.
Vinca, periwinkle. Tender annual.

Characteristics. Height: 4 to 15 inches. Colors: Pink, purple, and white.

Vinca is a very satisfying annual to grow. It is rarely bothered by pests and diseases, it tolerates drought without wilting, and it does not need deadheading or staking. Plus, it continues blooming all summer through heat, humidity, and drought, right up to the first frost in fall. Five-petaled flowers bloom profusely on well-branched plants with glossy, dark green foliage. Newer cultivars have larger flowers (up to 2 inches across) that come in a wider range of colors, including deep rose and orchid. Many flowers have a center "eye" of a contrasting color.

How to Grow. Start seed indoors 10 to 12 weeks before the last spring frost. The seed needs light to germinate well, so just scatter it over the surface of the planting medium. Cover the flats or pots with glass or clear plastic until the seedlings emerge. Transplant hardened-off seedlings to the garden when the danger of frost has passed. Bedding plants are always available at garden centers.

Vinca tolerates a wide range of soil conditions, but prefers well-drained, sandy soil. Plants grow best in full sun or partial shade. They need little care once they are established in the garden.

Catharanthus roseus

Uses. Vinca is a reliable plant for beds and borders in full sun or partial shade. Because of its uniform growth and compact size, it makes an ideal edging or annual groundcover. Vinca is also great for window boxes and other containers. The pastel pink shades contrast beautifully with deep blues and purples.

Celosia spp.
sell-OH-see-uh. Celosia, cockscomb.
Half-hardy annual.

Characteristics. Height: 6 to 30 inches. Colors: Pink, red, orange, apricot, and cream.

Celosia is unmatched for its intense color and unusual flower shapes. Two species are popular in the garden: cockscomb or crested celosia (*Celosia cristata*) and plumed celosia (*C. plumosa*). Cockscomb has broad, rounded, brain-shaped flower heads with an incredibly soft, velvety texture. 'Red Velvet' produces one huge, bright crimson flower head— up to 10 inches across—on each plant. Plumed celosia produces more graceful, feathery flower heads that look like flames or paintbrushes. 'Apricot Brandy', an intense apricot-orange, is one of the most unusual colors in annuals. It is breathtaking when paired

Celosia cristata with ornamental grasses

with the deep purple of heliotrope or annual lobelia. Both types of celosia have attractive, stiff, pointed leaves; some are light or dark green, while others have a yellowish orange tinge.

How to Grow. Sow seed indoors 5 to 6 weeks before the last frost in spring, or directly outside after all danger of a heavy frost has passed. The seeds need light for germination, so just scatter them over the surface. Indoors, cover the trays or pots with glass or clear plastic to maintain moisture until the seeds sprout; outdoors, mist the seedbed daily to keep it moist. Transplant hardened-off seedlings to the garden when the danger of frost has passed. Celosia is a popular annual and is usually available as bedding plants at garden centers.

Celosia is easy to grow in moist, well-drained, fertile soil. Plants prefer full sun. Tall cultivars may need staking.

Uses. Both cockscomb and plumed celosia make excellent, eye-catching bedding plants in annual and mixed borders. Lower-growing cultivars work well in containers and as edging plants. Both types of celosia make terrific, long-lasting cut or dried flowers.

Centaurea cyanus
sen-TAR-ee-uh sy-ANN-us. Bachelor's buttons, cornflower. Hardy annual.

Characteristics. Height: 12 to 30 inches. Colors: Blue, lavender, pink, rose, and white.

Bachelor's buttons add an informal, old-fashioned look to the garden. They are easy to grow, require little maintenance, and make lovely cut flowers, fresh or dried. Although they are prized for the intensity of their "cornflower blue" flowers, other colors are also available, including pastel pinks and mauves and maroon. Bachelor's buttons come in varying heights, from dwarf, 12-inch-tall edging cultivars to graceful, 30-inch-tall cutting cultivars. Plants normally bloom freely all summer, but tend to be at their best in cooler temperatures.

How to Grow. Bachelor's buttons do not transplant well, so you'll get the best results by sowing them directly where they are to bloom. Wait to sow the seed until after danger of a heavy frost. Because bachelor's buttons are so easy to direct-sow, and

Centaurea cyanus

Chrysanthemum ptarmiciflorum 'Silver Lace'

because they are difficult to transplant, they are not generally available as bedding plants.

Bachelor's buttons are easy to grow in full sun, in any well-drained soil. Taller cultivars require staking. Pinch or shear off spent flowers for continuous bloom. Plants are drought-tolerant and rarely bothered by pests or diseases.

Uses. Bachelor's buttons are excellent for cutting and drying. They are perfect for a cottage garden, wildflower meadow, or border. Dwarf cultivars are good for edging and containers.

CHINA ASTER. See *Callistephus chinensis*
CHINESE FORGET-ME-NOT. See *Cynoglossum amabile*

Chrysanthemum ptarmiciflorum

kris-ANN-the-mum tar-mih-sih-FLOR-um.
Dusty miller. Half-hardy annual.
○ ▼

Characteristics. Height: 6 to 10 inches. Colors: Silver foliage, yellow flowers.

The name "dusty miller" actually refers to several different silver-leaved plants—most commonly *Chrysanthemum ptarmiciflorum* and *Cineraria maritima*. *C. maritima* 'Silverdust' has finely cut, velvety silver foliage. *Chrysanthemum ptarmiciflorum* 'Silver Lace' has a finer, more delicate texture and a stiffer

habit. Both have a compact habit, making them ideal companion plants for other low-growing annuals. Dusty miller will bloom, but most gardeners prefer to cut off the small flowers.

How to Grow. Start seed indoors, as dusty miller tends to grow slowly. Sow 'Silver Lace' 12 weeks before the last expected spring frost and 'Silverdust' about 2 weeks later. Transplant hardened-off seedlings to the garden when the danger of frost has passed. Dusty miller is readily available at most garden centers.

Dusty miller prefers well-drained, sandy soil but is easy to grow in any soil. It requires full sun and will become lanky in the shade. The plants need little maintenance once they are established.

Uses. Dusty miller is invaluable for its velvety, silvery foliage, which looks very attractive when contrasted with pinks, blues, purples, and even whites. It makes an excellent edging, border, rock garden, or container plant. Use the cut foliage for contrast in fresh flower arrangements.

Clarkia amoena

KLARK-ee-uh uh-MEE-nuh.
Godetia. Hardy annual.
○ ❄ ❧ ▼

Characteristics. Height: 1 to 2 feet. Colors: Rose, pink, salmon, lavender, and bicolors.

These exquisite wildflowers are native to the

Clarkia amoena

mountains of the American West. The flowers are cup-shaped and softly colored, with four shiny, satiny petals. While the species has single flowers, cultivated forms with both single and double blooms are available. Cultivated forms often have ruffled petals as well. Single forms may feature a contrasting blotch of color in the middle of the petals, or a white central blotch surrounded by pink or red. The mounded plants bloom best in the cool weather of early summer.

How to Grow. Godetia does not transplant well, so you'll have the best results if you direct-sow. Prepare a seedbed and sow the seed where you want the plants to grow, after the danger of heavy frost has passed. In frost-free areas, sow seed in fall for early-spring bloom. The seeds need light to germinate, so just barely cover them with soil. Be sure to keep the seedbed moist until the seedlings appear. Since the plants do not transplant well, bedding plants are not readily available at garden centers.

Godetia is easy to grow in full sun and any well-drained soil, especially poor soil. It requires little maintenance in the garden and is rarely bothered by pests and diseases. Godetia prefers cool temperatures and blooms best in early summer, before the hot weather arrives.

Uses. Godetia makes a beautiful, long-lasting cut flower. This native American wildflower naturalizes well in a wildflower meadow. It also looks wonderful in borders, cottage gardens, rock gardens, and containers.

Cleome hasslerana

klee-OH-mee has-ler-ANN-uh.
Spider flower. Hardy annual.

Characteristics. Height: 3 to 6 feet. Colors: Pink, purple, rose, and white.

These towering background annuals make a dramatic statement in any garden. From early summer to frost, the bushy, well-branched plants are topped with airy heads of spidery flowers in soft pastel colors. The blooms are followed by long, narrow seedpods, each full of a long row of seeds. The foliage has a distinctive fresh fragrance somewhat like that of tomato foliage. Spider plants have two kinds of foliage: long, narrow lower leaves and deeply cut, handlike upper leaves. Mature plants develop short thorns along the stems, so beware when thinning plants or cutting flowers.

Cleome self-sows furiously—a drawback or a virtue, depending on how you look at it. While the seedlings are prolific enough to be weedy, they are easy to pull out, and they won't return if you don't let them bloom. And this ability to self-sow can be a bonus if you want cleome in your garden the following year, since you won't need to sow it. It also

Cleome hasslerana

gives you plenty of seedlings to share with family, friends, and neighbors. Start fresh seeds every few years to keep your cleome patch vigorous.

How to Grow. Start seed indoors 6 weeks before the last spring frost, or sow outdoors where you want the plants to grow, after the danger of heavy frost has passed. Seeds need light for germination, so leave them uncovered, but keep them moist until they sprout. When outdoor-sown seedlings are about 4 to 5 inches tall, be sure to thin them, or they'll become crowded and leggy. Bedding plants are sometimes available at garden centers.

Cleomes are easy to grow in most soils but prefer a rich, well-drained site. They tolerate drought conditions. The plants bloom best in full sun but will flower in partial shade. Give them plenty of room, since individual plants can spread 2 to 3 feet wide. They require little maintenance once established, never need staking, and are rarely bothered by pests and diseases.

Uses. Cleomes make striking, fast-growing annual hedges. Their thorns and dense foliage create an effective barrier, while the prolific pink, purple, rose, and white blooms create a pleasing mass of color that is easily visible from a distance. The tall plants are welcome additions to the back of annual or mixed borders for their long period of bloom and airy flower heads. Cleomes also make dramatic cut flowers.

COCKSCOMB. See *Celosia* spp.

Coleus blumei
KOH-lee-us blu-MAY-ee. Coleus.
Tender annual.

Characteristics. Height: 1 to 2 feet. Colors: Foliage in combinations of green, red, orange, yellow, pink, and cream.

Coleus offers extravagantly variegated foliage that brings welcome color to shady areas in the garden. The color combinations can be shocking, pleasingly bright, or softly pastel. Cultivars can have up to four contrasting colors radiating from the center of the leaves; others are mainly one color, with a contrasting edge. Leaves may be narrow or broad

Coleus blumei

and have frilled, scalloped, or sharply toothed edges.

A member of the mint family, coleus is vigorous but never invasive. Plants usually form bushy mounds, but some cultivars—including those in the 'Carefree' and 'Fiji' series—have a graceful, cascading habit that is perfect for hanging baskets.

How to Grow. Coleus grows slowly from seed, although the foliage color is apparent soon after the seedlings start growing. Sow seed indoors 10 weeks before the last spring frost. It needs light to germinate, so just scatter it over the surface of the planting medium. Keep the medium moist by covering the trays or pots with glass or clear plastic until seedlings appear. Transplant hardened-off seedlings to the garden when the danger of frost has passed. Bedding plants are readily available at garden centers in the spring.

Coleus prefers rich, well-drained soil and a shady location protected from wind. It will bloom, but the spiky flowers are generally insignificant and detract from the foliage display; remove the spikes before they bloom. You'll need to pinch the stem tips of most coleus plants to maintain their compact, bushy habit. Improved cultivars, such as those in the 'Wizard' series, have a naturally well-branched habit that doesn't require pinching.

Coleus blumei 'Wizard Sunset'

Coleus plants are extremely easy to grow from cuttings. Choose a vigorous-looking stem tip, and cut off a 3- to 4-inch piece just below a leaf joint. Pull off the bottom set of leaves and place the cutting in a glass of water, with its leaves resting on the edge of the glass and the stem in the water. Roots should appear in a week or two. Allow several roots to grow before transplanting. Check the water daily to make sure the stem is underwater, and replace it with fresh water every couple of days.

Uses. Coleus is a good choice for window boxes, pots, hanging baskets, and patio containers in partially shaded areas. It is also popular as a houseplant, because it is easy to grow in pots and tolerates the low-light conditions of many houses and apartments. Established plants are ideal for children to work with, since they are so easy to propagate from cuttings.

Consolida ambigua
kon-SOL-ih-duh am-BIG-yew-uh.
Rocket larkspur. Hardy annual.
○ ❋ ⊱❀ ❁

Characteristics. Height: 2 to 4 feet. Colors: Blue, pink, red, purple, lavender, burgundy, and white.

Rocket larkspurs are beloved for their tall, showy flower spikes, which look wonderful in the garden or indoors in fresh or dried arrangements. These versatile plants are as at home at the back of a formal mixed annual and perennial border as they are in an informal setting, such as a wildflower meadow or cottage garden. Best of all, they are so easy to grow that even novice gardeners are seldom disappointed.

Closely related to delphinium, rocket larkspur is known by several botanical names, including *Delphinium ajacis* and *D. consolida*. It is no surprise that one of the common names of this familiar favorite is annual delphinium.

How to Grow. Rocket larkspur is easy to grow from seed sown directly in the garden where the plants are to grow. In early spring, after the last heavy frost, prepare a seedbed and sow the seed. Be sure to keep the seedbed moist until the seedlings appear. For earlier bloom, start seeds indoors 6 to 8 weeks before the last frost. In frost-free areas, sow them in the fall for late-winter and early-spring bloom. Fall sowing for spring flowers sometimes

Consolida ambigua

works in areas as cool as southern portions of Zone 6 if the winter is mild. The plants will also self-sow in mild-winter areas. Rocket larkspur is not readily available as bedding plants.

These plants grow best in rich, well-drained, slightly alkaline soil, with full sun and cool night temperatures. They bloom all summer in areas where summer nights are cool and moist. In warmer regions of the country, rocket larkspurs are at their best in late spring and early fall. Most cultivars need staking.

Uses. Tall cultivars of rocket larkspur—such as 'Giant Imperial Mixed'—make excellent background plants at the back of a border. They also work well as accent plants or temporary annual hedges. Grow shorter cultivars in containers or in the middle of annual or mixed borders. All rocket larkspurs make dramatic cut flowers, fresh or dried.

CORNFLOWER. See *Centaurea cyanus*

Cosmos spp.

KOZ-mohs. Cosmos.
Half-hardy annual.
○ ✳ ✿ ⁂ ▼

Characteristics. Height: 1 to 5 feet. Colors: Crimson, rose, pink, white, yellow, and orange.

Two species of cosmos are commonly grown in the garden, but the one that most gardeners are familiar with is *Cosmos bipinnatus*. This species has feathery foliage and reddish, pink, rose, or white flowers. The popular 'Sensation' series produces plants that grow to 5 feet tall, with flowers up to 5 inches across. 'Sensation Mixed' comes in various shades of pink, burgundy, and white. The flowers of 'Seashells' have unique rolled, tubular petals. Shorter cultivars, such as 20-inch-tall 'Sonata', are attractive in patio containers.

The species *C. sulphureus* may be slightly less common, but it is equally as beautiful. As its name suggests, the flowers come in shades of yellow, orange, and orange-crimson. The foliage is less finely cut than that of *C. bipinnatus*, and the plants do not grow as tall. The All-America Selections winner 'Sunny Red' is a very intense orange-crimson color

Cosmos bipinnatus

and looks outstanding in borders; it is breathtaking next to deep purples or blues. 'Bright Lights', a mix of yellows and oranges, is popular for cutting, borders, and containers.

How to Grow. Both species are easy to grow from seed sown directly in the garden after the danger of heavy frost. You can also start them indoors 5 to 6 weeks before the last spring frost. Transplant hardened-off seedlings to the garden when the danger of frost has passed. Cosmos seedlings are readily available at garden centers.

Cosmos tolerates a wide range of soil types, particularly poor soil. In fact, too-rich soil can encourage lush foliage at the expense of flowers. Pinch off spent flowers to encourage continuous bloom. These durable plants withstand heat and drought, and are rarely bothered by pests and diseases. They need full sun to bloom well. Tall cultivars require staking to prevent their thick, hollow stems from breaking due to heavy rain or wind.

Uses. Tall cultivars of *C. bipinnatus* add a soft, airy touch to the back of an annual or mixed border. You can also use them as a fast-growing annual hedge or in a cutting garden. Since the taller cultivars are not always uniform in height, they're perfect for adding an informal look to cottage gardens. Shorter cultivars of both species are ideal near the front of the border, in containers, or as edgings. They also make beautiful cut flowers. Because cosmos is easy to grow and the seeds are large and easy to handle, it is a good choice for a children's garden.

Cynoglossum amabile

sy-noh-GLOSS-um ah-MAH-bil-ay.
Chinese forget-me-not. Hardy annual.

○ ☀ ❧ ▼

Characteristics. Height: 18 to 24 inches. Colors: Blue or white.

Chinese forget-me-not has tiny blue flowers that closely resemble those of the spring-blooming forget-me-not (*Myosotis sylvatica*). Chinese forget-me-nots, however, provide much longer bloom and tolerate warmer conditions. They add a rare deep blue that blends well with either cool pink, silver, and white shades or hot oranges, reds, and yellows. The graceful plants have an informal, loose habit and handsome, spear-shaped foliage.

How to Grow. Chinese forget-me-not grows easily from seed sown directly in the garden after danger of heavy frost. For earlier bloom, start the seed indoors 6 to 8 weeks before the last frost in spring. Seeds need light to germinate, so just scatter them over the surface of the planting medium. Keep the medium moist by covering the trays or pots with clear glass or plastic until seedlings appear. Transplant hardened-off seedlings to the garden when the danger of frost has passed. Chinese forget-me-not is not readily available as bedding plants.

This hardy annual grows well in moist soils but also tolerates drought conditions. It requires full sun for best bloom and compact growth. Deadheading

Cynoglossum amabile

keeps the plants tidy and encourages continuous bloom. Chinese forget-me-not is susceptible to tobacco mosaic virus, which causes mottled foliage and stunted growth. There is no cure for the disease; remove and destroy infected plants.

Uses. Chinese forget-me-not is attractive in containers, borders, cottage gardens, and rock gardens. The flowers are pretty in bouquets.

DAISY, CAPE. See *Venidium fastuosum*
DAISY, DAHLBERG. See *Dyssodia tenuiloba*
DAISY, SWAN RIVER. *Brachycome iberidifolia*
DAISY, TRANSVAAL. See *Gerbera jamesonii*

Dianthus spp.

dy-ANN-thus. Pinks, carnation, sweet William.
Hardy annual or biennial.

○ ☀ ❧ ❦ ▼

Characteristics. Height: 6 to 18 inches. Colors: Pink, red, purple, yellow, white, and bicolors.

The genus *Dianthus* includes many species of annual, biennial, and perennial garden flowers. All dianthus have fringed edges on the flower petals, which look as though they've been cut with pinking shears—hence the common name "pinks." (Even though many cultivars *are* pink in color, the name has no connection to the color.) Most Dianthus species also have smooth, long, narrow leaves in various shades of blue and green.

The species usually called annual dianthus (*D. chinensis*) is a popular bedding plant for borders and containers. In areas with mild winters, annual dianthus may actually grow as a perennial. The compact plants are covered with flat, round, single flowers about 1 inch across. Colors include pink, red, white, and many bicolors with picotee edges. All-America Selections winner 'Ideal Violet' is an unusual dark violet color with a rich, velvety look.

The familiar long-stemmed florist carnation (*D. caryophyllus*) is generally not suitable for gardens, but compact types are charming for bedding, containers, and small bouquets. They have the same spicy fragrance as the long-stemmed carnations, and make attractive, long-lasting cut flowers. They come in red, yellow, pink, salmon, purple, and white.

Dianthus barbatus

Sweet William (*D. barbatus*) is a biennial that blooms the second year from seed. Sweet Williams are sentimental favorites that give an old-fashioned look to the garden. They are covered with clusters of exquisite tiny, round, flat, single flowers for several weeks in spring. The small flowers resemble those of annual dianthus. Tall and dwarf cultivars are available in a wide range of colors, both solid and bicolored.

How to Grow. Start annual dianthus and carnations from seed sown indoors 8 weeks before the last hard frost in spring. Just barely cover the seed with the growing medium. Transplant hardened-off seedlings to the garden after the last heavy frost. Annual dianthus is commonly available at garden centers as bedding plants.

For sweet William, sow seed in midsummer in a protected area of the garden. Sprinkle soil over the seeds until they are barely covered, and keep the area moist. Move the seedlings to their blooming locations in late summer or early fall for spring bloom. You can also start the seed indoors in late spring or summer, then transplant the seedlings in late summer or early fall. Plants are sometimes available at garden centers.

Once you've planted sweet William, you probably won't have to worry about starting or buying plants again. Like many biennials, it readily self-sows in the garden. Dig up the seedlings in the fall and move them to wherever you want them to bloom the next year.

All pinks prefer well-drained soil and full sun. They can tolerate drought but appreciate extra watering in dry weather. They are sensitive to excess nitrogen and may develop brown leaf tips if you overfertilize them. Remove spent flowers to prolong the bloom season (but leave a few flower heads on sweet Williams if you want them to self-sow).

Uses. Annual dianthus and compact carnations are excellent in beds, borders, containers, and window boxes from summer to fall. Sweet Williams are showy in beds, borders, and edgings in spring. All pinks are great for cutting, and many cultivars have very fragrant flowers.

Digitalis purpurea
dih-jih-TAL-iss per-per-EE-uh.
Foxglove. Biennial.
○ ◑ ❄ ✄❀

Characteristics. Height: 3 to 4 feet. Colors: Pink, purple, creamy yellow, and white.

Biennial foxglove forms a basal rosette of leaves the first season from seed and blooms early the following summer. The huge flower stalks are covered with bell-shaped blooms that resemble the fingertips of gloves. The inside of each flower is irregularly marked with rather sinister-looking spots. The flowers at the bottom of the spike are the first to open. These elegant plants are popular for formal borders because they are easy to grow and provide a

Digitalis purpurea

dramatic, colorful vertical accent in shady or sunny locations. They are also marvelous for informal woodland gardens, since they self-sow reliably, providing plants for the following year without your having to scatter fresh seed.

'Excelsior' is a popular cultivar that produces florets all around the spike rather than on one side, as most foxgloves do. 'Foxy', an annual cultivar, blooms in just five months from seed.

How to Grow. Sow foxglove seed in midsummer in a protected part of the garden. Scatter the seed over the planting area and press it lightly into the soil surface. Keep the area moist until seedlings appear, then move them to their permanent location in early fall. You can also start the seed inside in spring and move the seedlings outdoors in early fall. Plants are often available at garden centers in spring and fall. You may also be able to buy them through mail-order catalogs.

Foxgloves thrive in rich, moist, well-drained soil. They grow best in partial shade but can tolerate full sun if you water them regularly in dry weather. The plants generally do not require staking in informal settings. In formal borders, however, you may want to stake the stems to keep them upright and to prevent them from being damaged by wind.

If you cut the stalks back right after bloom, you may get a second flush of flowers in late summer or early fall. But if you allow the spent flower stalks to dry on the plant before deadheading, foxgloves will almost always self-sow. You may find seedlings in unexpected places far from the mother plants. Once you learn to recognize the seedlings, you can dig them up in early fall and move them to where you would like them, or share them with friends and neighbors.

Uses. Foxgloves are at home in woodland gardens and make attractive accents at the back of mixed borders. The flowers are terrific for cutting. Keep in mind that foxgloves are highly toxic and therefore unsuitable for gardens visited by small children.

DUSTY MILLER. See *Chrysanthemum ptarmiciflorum*

Dyssodia tenuiloba
dy-SOH-dee uh ten-yew-ih-LOH-buh.
Dahlberg daisy. Tender annual.

Characteristics. Height: 4 to 8 inches. Colors: Yellow.

This charming native American annual has yellow, single daisy flowers that shade subtly to a deeper gold toward the center. The exquisite blooms cover the low-growing mounds of feathery foliage from early summer to fall.

How to Grow. For early bloom in areas with short summers, start seed indoors 6 to 8 weeks before the last frost. Transplant hardened-off seedlings to the garden when all danger of frost has passed. In areas with a long growing season, sow seed directly in the garden after all danger of frost has passed. Plants are sometimes available at garden centers.

Dahlberg daisies grow well in poor soil, and they tolerate hot, dry conditions. They need full sun. Generally free of pests and diseases, the plants are very easy to care for once they are established in the garden.

Uses. Dahlberg daisy's long bloom season and light, airy texture make it invaluable in borders, rock gardens, and container plantings. It is also useful as an annual groundcover.

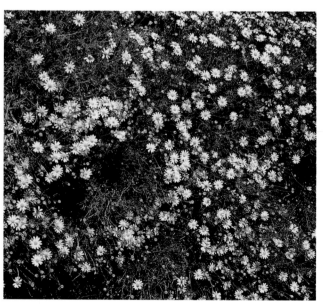

Dyssodia tenuiloba

Eschscholzia californica

Eschscholzia californica

eh-SHOL-zee-uh kal-ih-FOR-nih-kuh.
California poppy. Hardy annual.

○ ✺ ✻ ⚘ ▼

Characteristics. Height: 10 to 12 inches. Colors: Orange, pink, red, yellow, and white.

California poppy is not a true poppy (of the genus *Papaver*), but it has poppylike flowers. The plants are low-growing, with a spreading habit and ferny foliage. As its common name indicates, California poppy is native to California, where it carpets hillsides in spring. This delicate-looking flower is popular all over the United States as a cool-season annual. The wild form is orange, but cultivars come in a broad range of colors, including pink, red, yellow, and white. Some double-flowered cultivars are available.

How to Grow. California poppy does not transplant well, so plant the seed directly in the garden in early spring, after the danger of heavy frost has passed. Scatter the seed over the growing area, press it lightly into the soil, and keep the seedbed moist until seedlings appear. Thin the seedlings to about 6 inches apart when they are 3 to 4 inches tall. Bedding plants are not readily available at garden centers.

California poppy prefers sandy, well-drained, alkaline soil in full sun. It blooms best in cool tem-peratures and can die out in the hot summer heat. This low-maintenance, drought-tolerant plant is generally free of pest and disease problems. Like true poppies, California poppies often self-sow and will naturalize in favorable locations.

Uses. California poppy is pretty in beds, borders, and pots, and is an ideal plant for sunny rock gardens. In masses, it makes a showy annual ground-cover. Try it as a cut flower, too.

Eustoma grandiflorum

yew-STOH-muh gran-dih-FLOR-um.
Lisianthus. Half-hardy annual.

○ ✺ ⚘ ▼

Characteristics. Height: 18 to 36 inches. Colors: Blue, pink, and white.

Prized for its exceptionally elegant, satiny, funnel-shaped flowers, lisianthus is gaining popularity

Eustoma grandiflorum

as a cut flower and as a garden plant. This native American wildflower is sometimes called prairie gentian, since it is native to the dry prairies of the Southwest. It bears its poppylike blooms in delicate shades of deep gentian blue, silvery pink, and creamy white, all of which blend easily with other colors in the garden and in bouquets. A variety of single and double forms are available. 'The Blue Rose' is a new double-flowered cultivar that bears striking, deep purple-blue blooms with flaring petals that really look like roses! Cultivars with deep rose-pink to nearly red flowers are available as well.

Lisianthus plants can look lost in the garden if they are planted sparingly. Grown in masses, however, they are truly magnificent and sure to evoke praise from the most jaded visitor.

How to Grow. Sow seed at least 12 weeks before the last frost in spring. Press the tiny seeds into the surface of the planting medium, and cover the trays or pots with glass or clear plastic until seedlings appear. To encourage branching, pinch the seedlings several times before transplanting. After all danger of frost, carefully transplant the hardened-off seedlings to the garden. Transplants are available at well-stocked garden centers.

Lisianthus is not an easy annual to grow, since the seed tends to germinate slowly and the plants take a long time to bloom from seed. The seedlings do not transplant happily, either, so be sure to handle them carefully when transplanting. Once established in well-drained soil and full sun, however, lisianthus requires little care. It can tolerate drought and will bloom continuously until the first frost.

Uses. Lisianthus is grown primarily for its stunning, long-lasting cut flowers. The shorter cultivars are attractive in containers. All types can be used in borders or as edgings, as long as they are spaced closely together.

FLOSS FLOWER. See *Ageratum houstonianum*
FLOWERING CABBAGE OR KALE. See *Brassica oleracea*
FLOWERING TOBACCO. See *Nicotiana* spp.
FORGET-ME-NOT. See *Myosotis sylvatica*
FOUR O'CLOCK. See *Mirabilis jalapa*
FOXGLOVE. See *Digitalis purpurea*

Gaillardia pulchella

Gaillardia pulchella
gay-LARD-ee-uh pul-CHELL-uh.
Annual blanket flower. Tender annual.

Characteristics. Height: 14 to 36 inches. Colors: Red, yellow, orange, and bronze.

The native American annual and perennial blanket flowers are popular for the bright color they add to summer gardens and bouquets. Annual blanket flower has single or double, daisylike flowers in combinations of yellow, orange, bronze, and red. Most cultivars grow about 2 to 3 feet tall and look best in borders, mass plantings, or wildflower meadows. The fully double 'Red Plume' is an All-America Selections winner with unusual brick red blooms on very compact, 14-inch plants. A yellow form, 'Yellow Plume', is also available. Both are excellent for containers.

How to Grow. For earliest bloom, sow seed indoors 6 weeks before the last frost. The seed needs light to germinate, so just scatter it over the surface of the planting medium. Keep the medium moist by covering the trays or pots with glass or clear plastic until seedlings appear. Transplant hardened-off seedlings to the garden when the danger of frost has passed. You can also sow seed directly in the garden after all danger of frost. Bedding plants are sometimes available at garden centers.

Annual blanket flower prefers well-drained, sandy soil in a sunny location. It tolerates poor soil, as well as hot, dry conditions. Deadheading will extend the bloom period, which can last until the first frost in fall. The plants are rarely bothered by pests and diseases. Taller cultivars may need staking.

Uses. Annual blanket flower is prized for its bright summer colors in beds and borders. It is an excellent flower for cutting, and naturalizes well in wildflower meadow plantings. Dwarf cultivars are ideal for containers.

Gazania ringens

guh-ZANE-ee-uh RIN-genz. Gazania.
Tender annual.

Characteristics. Height: 8 to 12 inches. Colors: Yellow, orange, red, bronze, and cream.

Gazania is an eye-catching annual with single, daisylike flowers in rich desert colors. The blooms are often boldly multicolored, with striped petals and contrasting rings around the centers. The flowers grow up to 3 to 5 inches across and tend to close in cloudy weather. The foliage ranges from silver to blue-green or dark green and can be strikingly decorative. Many cultivars have names suggestive of the sun and cheerfulness, including 'Gaiety', 'Carnival', 'Sundance', 'Daybreak', and 'Sunshine'.

Gazania ringens

How to Grow. For early bloom, start seed indoors 6 weeks before the last frost and transplant hardened-off seedlings outside after the danger of frost has passed. You can also sow seed directly in the garden after all danger of frost. Bedding plants are usually available at garden centers.

Gazanias thrive under hot, dry conditions in full sun. They tolerate drought and poor soil, and require little maintenance once they are established in the garden. Gazanias are rarely troubled by pests. In humid areas, they do have a tendency to get powdery mildew, a fungal disease that causes powdery white patches on the leaves. You can usually prevent this problem by giving the plants plenty of space to ensure good air circulation.

Uses. Gazanias are grown mostly in flower beds, containers, and rock gardens. Because the flowers close in cloudy weather, they do not make good cut flowers.

GERANIUM. See *Pelargonium* spp.

Gerbera jamesonii

GER-ber-uh jame-SONE-ee-eye. Gerbera, Transvaal daisy. Tender annual.

Characteristics. Height: 15 to 24 inches. Colors: Yellow, red, orange, pink, and white.

Gerberas are popular for their large daisylike flowers, which come in a wide range of bright, clear colors. Because they have long, strong stems, they make excellent cut flowers. Although usually grown as annuals, gerberas are actually tender perennials that you can bring indoors as houseplants during the winter. In frost-free areas, gerberas are grown in the garden all year.

How to Grow. For garden plants, sow seed indoors 10 weeks before the last frost. The seed needs light to germinate, so scatter it over the surface of the planting medium. Keep the medium moist by covering the trays or pots with glass or clear plastic until seedlings appear. Transplant the seedlings to progressively larger pots as they grow, and then move hardened-off plants to the garden when all danger of frost has passed. Start the seed indoors anytime for houseplants or to grow plants

Gerbera jamesonii

for outdoor containers or window boxes. Potted plants are readily available at commercial greenhouses and garden centers.

Gerberas prefer rich, well-drained soil and full sun to light shade. They may require watering in dry weather. The plants are happy in pots (one cultivar is called 'Happipot'), window boxes, and other containers. In fact, growing these plants in containers is one of the best ways for gardeners in the North to enjoy them. For plants that look like they are growing in the garden, yet are still easy to move inside for the winter, plant pot-grown gerberas (pot and all) in beds and borders. In fall, pull up the pots to move the plants indoors for overwintering.

Gerberas bloom best when night temperatures are cool. They may stop blooming during the hottest days of summer, but will resume when the nights are cool again.

Uses. Gerberas are wonderful for cutting gardens, flower beds, patio containers, and window boxes. They also make great houseplants. Or you can grow them in a cool greenhouse in winter for cut flowers.

GLOBE AMARANTH. See *Gomphrena globosa*
GODETIA. See *Clarkia amoena*

Gomphrena globosa
gom-FREE-nuh gloh-BOH-suh.
Globe amaranth. Tender annual.

Characteristics. Height: 6 to 30 inches. Colors: Pink, rose, purple, magenta, red, orange, and cream.

Globe amaranth is an old-fashioned, cloverlike annual grown primarily for its excellent qualities as a dried flower. Its long period of bloom and neat plant habit also make it popular for beds and mixed or annual borders. Flower colors include antique-looking shades of dusty rose, pink, magenta, purple, and cream. 'Strawberry Fields' is a bright strawberry-colored cultivar used to add vibrant color to the garden, as well as to dried bouquets.

How to Grow. For earliest bloom, start seeds indoors 6 weeks before the last frost in spring. The seeds need light to germinate, so scatter them over the surface of the planting medium. Keep the medium moist by covering the trays or pots with glass or clear plastic until seedlings appear. Transplant hardened-off seedlings to the garden when the danger of frost has passed. You can also sow the seed directly in the garden after all danger of frost. Bedding plants are sometimes available at garden centers.

Globe amaranth is easy to grow in full sun and well-drained soil. It tolerates poor soil, heat, and drought, and is rarely bothered by pests and diseases.

Uses. Globe amaranth is charming in beds, bor-

Gomphrena globosa

ders, edgings, and large containers. The chaffy flower heads add an interesting texture to cottage gardens and are prized for fresh and dried flower arrangements.

Gypsophila elegans
jip-SAW-fill-uh EL-eh-ganz.
Annual baby's breath. Tender annual.

Characteristics. Height: 18 to 24 inches. Colors: White or pink.

Baby's breath is the common name for both annual and perennial species of *Gypsophila*. Annual baby's breath has tiny white or pink blooms that are widely dispersed on delicate, well-branched stems. The leaves are very fine and narrow. In the garden, baby's breath has a lighter-than-air texture, with clouds of tiny flowers blooming continuously for 5 or 6 weeks at a time. 'Covent Garden', a popular cultivar, offers masses of tiny, single white flowers on billowy, 18-inch plants.

How to Grow. For early bloom, start seeds indoors 4 or 5 weeks before the last spring frost. Seeds need light to germinate, so scatter them over the surface of the planting medium. Keep the medium moist by covering the trays or pots with glass or clear plastic until seedlings appear. Transplant hard-

ened-off seedlings to the garden when all danger of frost has passed. Annual baby's breath also grows easily from seed sown directly in the garden after danger of heavy frost. Because the bloom time is relatively short, many gardeners sow annual baby's breath every 3 weeks until summer to ensure a continuous display. Annual baby's breath does not tend to be readily available as bedding plants, possibly because of its short life span.

This annual prefers, but does not require, alkaline soil. It will grow well in most well-drained soil in a sunny location. The plants are rarely bothered by pests or diseases.

Uses. Like the perennial species, annual baby's breath is grown primarily for its tiny flowers, which are ideal for fresh arrangements and for drying. The plants add an airy look to borders and rock gardens.

Helianthus annuus
hee-lee-ANN-thus ANN-yew-us.
Sunflower. Half-hardy annual.

Characteristics. Height: 18 inches to 10 feet. Colors: Yellow, red, and brown.

Sunflowers are often listed in both the flower and vegetable sections of seed catalogs: as flowers, for their ornamental value, and as vegetables, for

Helianthus annuus 'Sunrise' and 'Sunset'

Helianthus annuus 'Mammoth'

their edible seeds. The ornamental kinds are available as single or double flowers and come in many colors, including shades of red and mahogany. The new dwarf cultivar 'Sunspot' grows only 18 inches tall and looks delightful in containers or as an edging. All sunflowers are so named because they turn toward the sun during the day. Keep this in mind when you decide where to plant these annuals, since a north-facing site may leave you with a crop of sunflowers that always turn their backs on you.

How to Grow. Sunflowers grow so quickly that they are normally sown directly in the garden after all danger of frost. Plant the seed about ½ inch deep. Thin the plants to about 2 feet apart when they are 3 to 4 inches tall. Plants are rarely available at garden centers.

Sunflowers are easy to grow in any soil, in full sun. They benefit from extra fertilization and watering in dry weather when they begin blooming. They are rarely bothered by pests or diseases.

Uses. Dwarf sunflower cultivars are fascinating in patio tubs, and the small-flowered types are good for cutting. Tall cultivars make dramatic background plantings, annual hedges, or garden accents. They attract birds to the garden, which is a disadvantage for the vegetable garden but an advantage for the flower garden. Because sunflowers are so easy and fast-growing, they are ideal plants for children's gardens.

Helichrysum bracteatum

Helichrysum bracteatum
hel-ih-KRY-sum brak-tee-AY-tum.
Strawflower. Tender annual.

Characteristics. Height: 14 to 36 inches. Colors: Red, yellow, orange, pink, purple, salmon, white, and bicolors.

The common name, strawflower, describes the papery texture of this colorful annual perfectly. The daisylike, semidouble or fully double flowers have smooth, satiny petals that shimmer in the sunlight. They come in a wide range of colors and color combinations. (One popular cultivar is called 'Bright Bikinis Mixed'.) Both dwarf and tall cultivars are available.

Strawflowers are invaluable for dried arrange-

ments. Not only do they have long stems, they also retain their color for a long time after drying. They are easy to grow and dry, too.

How to Grow. For earliest bloom, sow seed indoors 6 weeks before the last frost in spring. The seed needs light to germinate, so scatter it over the surface of the planting medium. Keep the medium moist by covering the trays or pots with glass or clear plastic until seedlings appear. Transplant hardened-off seedlings to the garden when all danger of frost has passed. You can also sow the seed directly in the garden after danger of heavy frost. Bedding plants are not generally available at garden centers.

Strawflowers prefer well-drained, sandy soil in full sun and can tolerate hot, dry conditions. They do not require staking or any special maintenance, and are rarely bothered by pests and diseases.

Uses. The quintessential dried flower, strawflower is attractive in fresh arrangements as well. All strawflowers are useful for adding color to beds and borders. The dwarf cultivars look good in containers or as edgings.

Heliotropium arborescens

Heliotropium arborescens

hee-lee-oh-TROH-pee-um ar-bor-ESS-enz.
Heliotrope. Tender annual.

Characteristics. Height: 8 to 18 inches. Colors: Purple, violet, and blue.

Heliotrope is valued for its exquisite fragrance and regal blue-purple color. You'll enjoy the vanilla-like fragrance best when the plants are sited near a resting place, such as a patio or garden bench, or by an open window. The intense deep purple, violet, or blue color combines well with silver, white, pink, yellow, and orange.

How to Grow. For early bloom, start seed indoors about 6 to 8 weeks before the last frost in spring. The seeds need light to germinate, so just scatter them over the surface of the planting medium. Keep the medium moist by covering the trays or pots with glass or clear plastic until seedlings appear. Transplant hardened-off seedlings to the garden when all danger of frost has passed. You can also sow the seed directly in the garden after the danger of frost has passed. Bedding plants are available at well-stocked garden centers.

Heliotrope prefers rich, well-drained soil in a sunny location. It is generally reliable and requires little care, other than an extra drink of water during dry spells.

Uses. Heliotrope makes a wonderful addition to beds, borders, containers, and edgings for its gorgeous color and delicious fragrance.

HONESTY. See *Lunaria annua*

Hypoestes phyllostachya

hy-poh-ESS-teez phyl-oh-STACK-yah.
Polka-dot plant. Tender annual.

Characteristics. Height: 5 to 12 inches. Colors: Green foliage with pink or white spots.

Polka-dot plant is grown for its shiny, dark green leaves splashed with pink or cream. It has long been grown as a houseplant and is now gaining popularity in the garden. The plants have a neat bushy, well-branched habit.

How to Grow. Start houseplants from seed anytime. For garden use, start seed indoors 6 weeks before the last frost in spring. Transplant hardened-off seedlings to the garden when the danger of frost has passed. You can also sow the seed directly in the garden after all danger of frost.

Polka-dot plant tolerates a wide range of conditions but grows best in rich, well-drained soil, in sun or light shade. In too much shade, the plants tend to become leggy; in too much sun, the leaf tips may turn brown if the soil gets too dry. The plants require little maintenance and are rarely bothered by pests or diseases.

Uses. Charming as a houseplant, polka-dot plant is also good for edgings, beds, and borders. It works very well in all kinds of containers, especially hanging baskets. In masses, it makes an attractive, lush annual groundcover.

IMMORTELLE. See *Xeranthemum annuum*

Impatiens spp.

im-PAY-shenz. Busy Lizzie, impatiens.
Tender annual.

Characteristics. Height: 8 to 20 inches. Colors: Pink, purple, red, orange, salmon, light blue, and white.

Busy Lizzie (*Impatiens wallerana*) is America's favorite bedding plant for shade, and for good reason. The plants are neat, well branched, and fairly uniform. The many brightly colored flowers often cover the foliage, and they bloom nonstop from

Impatiens wallerana

New Guinea impatiens

early summer to frost. The flowers come in an immense range of colors, many with splashes or "eyes" of contrasting colors. 'Super Elfin Swirl' is coral pink with a deep rose edge. 'Cherry Vanilla' is a clear white with a bright cherry splash in the center. Double-flowered forms, which look like exquisite miniature roses, are also available. Some cultivars have bronze- or chocolate-colored foliage, or variegated foliage with a creamy white edge.

The plants tend to be bushy, spreading wider than they grow tall. Older cultivars required pinching to maintain their bushiness, but newer cultivars remain compact and well branched without pinching. Taller cultivars are still available and tend to have a more old-fashioned look.

But busy Lizzies aren't the only kind of impatiens worth growing. The showy New Guinea hybrids are also gaining in popularity as newer cultivars become available. They used to be sold primarily as houseplants and were relatively expensive to produce, since they were grown from cuttings. New seed-grown cultivars have been developed that perform better in the garden, and they tolerate more sun than busy Lizzies. 'Tango', an All-America Selections winner, offers orange flowers measuring more than 2½ inches across on 2-foot plants. The 'Spectra Hybrid' series has green or variegated foliage and flowers in shades of pink, rose, red, lavender, and

white. Some plants have such attractive leaves that they could be grown for their foliage alone.

How to Grow. Both kinds of impatiens are slow to grow to blooming size, so start the seed indoors 10 to 12 weeks before the last frost in spring. The seeds need light to germinate, so scatter them over the surface of the planting medium. Keep the medium moist by covering the trays or pots with glass or clear plastic until seedlings appear. Transplant hardened-off seedlings to the garden when all danger of frost has passed.

Busy Lizzies may self-sow in the garden, but seedlings of hybrid cultivars probably won't resemble the parent plants. To get particular colors, you should start new plants from fresh seed every year. If there's a favorite color that you absolutely must have, or if you want to grow impatiens as houseplants for the winter, take cuttings of either kind from garden plants before the first fall frost. To take cuttings, cut 3 to 4 inches of healthy new growth. Remove the lower leaves and set the stems in a glass of water to root, or insert the bottom half of each stem into a pot of moist growing medium. Plants are always available at garden centers. However, mail-order seed catalogs usually offer the best selection of colors and types.

Busy Lizzies thrive in partial to full shade, while New Guinea impatiens can take more sun. Both kinds of impatiens prefer evenly moist soil. Busy Lizzies in particular will wilt dramatically in dry soil. They recover remarkably well once they are watered, but can only take so much neglect before suffering, so check them daily in hot, dry weather. Wilting occurs most often when the plants are growing in sunny locations, in containers, or under mature trees that rob the surrounding soil of precious water. For this reason, busy Lizzies do not perform as well under shallow-rooted trees, such as dogwoods and maples, as they do under deep-rooted trees, such as oaks. If the plants have rich, cool, moist soil, they will thrive, spread, and bloom continuously until frost.

Uses. Both busy Lizzies and New Guinea impatiens stay neat and attractive in patio containers, hanging baskets, and window boxes. Busy Lizzies are essential in shady borders, as edgings, and as an annual groundcover under trees. They also make good houseplants because of their tolerance for low light conditions. Add extra humidity to the dry winter air in your house by placing the pots on a bed of moist pebbles.

LARKSPUR, ROCKET. See *Consolida ambigua*

Lathyrus odoratus
LATH-ih-rus oh-door-AY-tus.
Sweet pea. Hardy annual.

Characteristics. Height: 9 inches to 5 feet. Colors: Blue, pink, purple, red, orange, and white.

At the turn of the century, sweet peas were one of the most popular garden annuals in America, and they were on the cover of many early Burpee catalogs. They were eventually surpassed in popularity by more heat-tolerant bedding plant introductions, such as marigolds and zinnias. However, sweet peas still have a pleasant, old-fashioned association for many people, and no one can grow them without friends and neighbors stopping by and exclaiming, "You're growing sweet peas! My mother (or grandmother) used to grow them!"

Sweet pea flowers are deliciously fragrant and make superb cut flowers. They come in soft, pastel colors and many rich shades of deep rose and cherry

Lathyrus odoratus

red. Early cultivars grew as vines; the vining types are still available, but dwarf forms suitable for containers have also been developed. The newer cultivars have larger flowers than their ancestors, although some have lost their fragrance in the breeding process.

How to Grow. Sweet peas, like garden peas, thrive in cool weather, so plant them early in spring (or in fall for winter bloom in frost-free areas). Direct-sow the seed ½ inch deep as soon as you can work the soil. To encourage faster germination, nick the seed coat with a nail file or soak the seed overnight before planting it. You can also start sweet peas indoors in mid- to late winter. Set the seedlings out in early spring, after hardening them off. They are not readily available as bedding plants.

Sweet peas prefer rich, moist, well-drained soil and full sun. Climbers need some kind of support to wrap their tendrils around. In a greenhouse, they climb nicely on strings or wires strung from floor to ceiling. Outside, they can climb a fence, trellis, or tall tripod. Dwarf cultivars need no support.

Uses. In the cool weather of spring, sweet peas add a wonderful old-fashioned feel to flower beds, trellises, and containers. Grow some in a cutting garden, too, for indoor enjoyment. Sweet peas make excellent cool greenhouse plants for winter cut flowers.

Lavatera trimestris

lah-vuh-TEAR-uh try-MESS-tris.
Mallow. Hardy annual.

Characteristics. Height: 2 to 4 feet. Colors: Pink or white.

Few annuals can rival mallow for sheer floral beauty. The smooth, satiny flower petals have a delicate silvery pink or snow white color that seems to radiate from within, unlike the "painted-on" look of many brightly colored flowers. Mallow flowers resemble single hollyhocks, to which they are related. They bloom with abandon from midsummer to the first frost in fall. The plants are bushy and well branched, with broad leaves shaped like those of maple trees. Taller and shorter cultivars are available, making mallow useful in many parts of the garden.

How to Grow. After all danger of frost has passed, sow seed directly in the garden where you want the plants to grow. The seeds have a hard coat and benefit from an overnight soaking in water before sowing. Scatter soil over the seed until it is just barely covered. For an earlier start, sow seeds indoors 6 weeks before the last frost. Sow them in peat pots, as mallow does not tend to transplant well. Move hardened-off seedlings to the garden when all danger of frost has passed. Plants are not generally available at garden centers.

Mallow prefers well-drained, sandy soil and full sun. It thrives in summer heat, looking its best in high summer. Taller cultivars may need staking. All cultivars benefit from deadheading. Like hollyhocks, mallow is susceptible to rust, a fungal disease that produces orange spots on the leaves. To prevent a severe rust problem, space plants at least 2 feet apart to allow for good air circulation. Remove any leaves that show signs of the disease as soon as you notice them.

Uses. Mallows look splendid in beds and borders. Taller cultivars make good background plants, garden accents, or annual hedges; shorter cultivars are excellent in containers. All are superb cut flowers.

Lavatera trimestris

Limonium sinuatum

lih-MOE-nee-um sin-yew-AY-tum.
Annual statice. Tender annual.

Characteristics. Height: 12 to 30 inches. Colors: Blue, pink, purple, red, yellow, and white.

Annual statice is popular for its crinkled, papery flower heads, which are among the easiest and most satisfying flowers you can grow for drying. The rainbow of colors ranges from pink and rose to blue, purple, yellow, and white; many have a faded, antique look. The flowers dry quickly, the colors hold up well after drying, and the winged stems are long and strong.

How to Grow. For earliest bloom, start seed indoors about 10 weeks before the last frost in spring. Sow the seed ⅛ inch deep. Transplant hardened-off seedlings to the garden when all danger of frost has passed. If your area has a long growing season, you can sow the seed directly in the garden after the danger of frost. Bedding plants are often available at garden centers.

Annual statice prefers fertile, well-drained soil and requires full sun. It tolerates hot, dry conditions well and is rarely bothered by pests and diseases.

Uses. Annual statice is a must for cutting and drying. It is also attractive in beds and borders. Dwarf cultivars add a unique touch to container plantings.

LISIANTHUS. See *Eustoma grandiflorum*

Lobelia erinus

Lobelia erinus
loh-BEE-lee-uh er-EYE-nus.
Annual lobelia. Tender annual.

Characteristics. Height: 4 to 6 inches. Colors: Blue, pink, purple, and white.

Annual lobelia is a sister of the perennial cardinal flower (*Lobelia cardinalis*). The flowers are small and single, and blue or purple shades are most common, although white- and pink-flowered cultivars are available. Many cultivars have a white "eye" at the center of each flower. These low-growing plants come in upright or trailing forms and have green, red, or bronze foliage. 'Crystal Palace' is a popular selection with astonishing cobalt blue flowers and bronze-red leaves.

How to Grow. Start seed indoors 10 to 12 weeks before the last frost in spring. The seeds need light to germinate, so scatter them over the surface of the planting medium. Keep the medium moist by covering the trays or pots with glass or clear plastic until seedlings appear. Transplant hardened-off seedlings to the garden when all danger of frost has passed. In areas with long summers, sow the seed directly in the garden after all danger of frost. Bedding plants are commonly available at garden centers.

Annual lobelia prefers rich, well-drained soil in full sun but will also bloom well in partial shade. Water the plants regularly in hot, dry weather. They bloom best in cool temperatures and may flower less when hot weather arrives. However, they usually perk up in late summer and bloom right up to the first fall frost.

Uses. Trailing forms of annual lobelia are ideal for hanging baskets and window boxes; they make an attractive annual groundcover, too. Upright types are good for flower beds, borders, edgings, or patio containers.

Lobularia maritima
lob-yew-LARE-ee-uh muh-RIT-ih-muh.
Sweet alyssum. Hardy annual.

Characteristics. Height: 3 to 6 inches. Colors: White, pink, lavender, and purple.

Sweet alyssum is a popular annual with very tiny flowers in pastel shades of lavender, pink, and rose, as well as deep purple and white. (The name of the cultivar 'Easter Basket' captures the mood of the pastel colors available.) This low-growing plant combines well with many other bedding annuals, especially as a filler plant in patio container plant-

Lobularia maritima

ings, window boxes, and hanging baskets. It has a spreading habit on the ground and a cascading habit in containers.

Sweet alyssum has a delicious, meadowy sort of fragrance, but the scent is easy to miss, since the plants are so low-growing. To enjoy your sweet alyssum to the fullest, plant it in a window box under an open window, in a planter on a deck or patio, or by a garden bench. Or try planting it along the top of a retaining wall or in a raised bed or rock garden.

How to Grow. Sow seed directly in the garden after danger of heavy frost. As a hardy annual, sweet alyssum can tolerate a light frost. Scatter the seed over the planting area as evenly as you can, and just barely cover it with a sprinkling of soil. The seed is small and easy to oversow. This is not normally a problem, however, as the plants can tolerate over-crowding. Sweet alyssum tends to self-sow if it likes the location. Bedding plants are usually available at garden centers.

Sweet alyssum can tolerate a wide range of soil conditions and is easy to maintain in the garden. It blooms best in full sun but tolerates partial shade well. It prefers cooler temperatures and tends to go to seed in hot weather. Shearing the plants back after they bloom will usually cause them to produce a new flush of growth.

Uses. Sweet alyssum is excellent for hanging baskets, window boxes, strawberry jars, and other containers where it is allowed to billow over the side. Use it as a low-growing spreader for sunny to lightly shaded beds, borders, and rock gardens. In masses, sweet alyssum makes an effective annual groundcover.

LOVE-IN-A-MIST. See *Nigella damascena*
LOVE-LIES-BLEEDING. See *Amaranthus* spp.

Lunaria annua
lew-NARE-ee-uh ANN-yew-uh.
Honesty, money plant. Biennial.
○ ◑ ✿ ✾

Characteristics. Height: 30 inches. Colors: Purple or white flowers; silvery seedpods.

Honesty is grown primarily for its papery, pearly

Lunaria annua 'Alba'

white seedpods, which add a unique look to dried bouquets. It is a biennial, producing scalloped, wedge-shaped foliage the first year, and flowers and seedpods the second year. Its pretty purple or white spring flowers make it an excellent choice for flower borders or woodland plantings. The flowers are followed by seedpods in late summer or early fall. The seedpods turn from green to brown, and eventually the outer casing starts to peel away. At that point, you can gently peel it off to reveal the shimmery white center of the pod. If you try too early, you can easily tear the center part of the pod; wait until the casing almost comes off by itself.

How to Grow. If you really want flowers and seedpods in 1 year, you can try starting the seed indoors 8 to 10 weeks before the last frost; set the seedlings out after danger of heavy frost, after hardening them off. In most cases, however, honesty grows best from seed planted directly in the garden after all danger of frost; the plants will produce flowers and seedpods the following year.

Like many biennials, honesty self-sows reliably. You can peel the outer casing from the pods right in the garden and allow the seeds to drop on the ground, then transplant the seedlings—carefully—in late summer or fall. Plants are not normally available at garden centers.

Honesty is not fussy about soil conditions and will grow and bloom well in full sun or partial shade. It does not require staking or deadheading. (If you do remove the flowers, the seedpods will not form.)

Uses. While honesty is primarily grown for its ornamental seedpods, the flowers are also decorative in beds and borders. The blooms are attractive in fresh arrangements, too.

MALLOW. See *Lavatera trimestris*
MARIGOLD. See *Tagetes* spp.

Matthiola incana

mat-thee-OH-luh in-KAH-nuh.
Stock. Hardy annual.

Characteristics. Height: 15 to 36 inches. Colors: Blue, pink, purple, yellow, red, and white.

Stock is grown primarily for its wonderful fragrance and is used primarily as cut flowers or potted plants. It is short-lived in the garden, often going to seed in hot summer temperatures, and generally needs to be replaced in bedding schemes in midsummer. The lovely flower spikes somewhat resemble hyacinth flowers in both looks and fragrance. They bloom in the soft pastel colors that are so welcome in spring. The blue-gray foliage is also attractive.

The garden cultivars developed for beds and borders grow 15 to 20 inches tall and are considered dwarf. Cultivars are also available for greenhouse growing. These grow 3 feet tall or more and take much longer to bloom. The flower spikes on greenhouse cultivars are also much more elongated than those of the bedding types; in fact, they can be up to 2 feet long. Single and double forms are available for both types.

How to Grow. Because stock blooms only in cool weather, it should be started early. In areas with

a long, cool spring season, sow seed directly in the garden after danger of heavy frost. Elsewhere, sow the seed indoors 4 to 6 weeks before the last frost. The seeds need light to germinate, so just scatter them over the surface of the planting medium. Keep the medium moist by covering the trays or pots with glass or clear plastic until seedlings appear. Transplant hardened-off seedlings to the garden when danger of heavy frost has passed. Plants are not usually available at garden centers.

Stock prefers rich, well-drained soil and full sun. Taller cultivars may need staking, although the stems are generally strong. The plants require cool temperatures to flower and will not form new blooms when temperatures rise above 65°F.

Uses. Stock is useful for beds, borders, and containers, but it is best grown for cutting and for its exquisite fragrance. Grow tall cultivars in a cool greenhouse for winter cut flowers.

Melampodium cinereum

mel-um-POH-dee-um sin-ER-ee-um.
Melam-podium. Tender annual.

Characteristics. Height: 18 inches. Colors: Yellow.

This gem of a tender annual is woefully underused in American gardens. In the past few years, it has begun to appear in public garden borders, where

Melampodium cinereum

appreciative visitors ask about the plant's identity so they can grow it at home.

Melampodium has small, yellow, 1-inch-wide daisy flowers that bloom in great abundance on sturdy, bushy plants. The flowers start in early summer and continue nonstop until frost kills the plants.

How to Grow. Start seed indoors 8 to 10 weeks before the last frost in spring. Transplant hardened-off seedlings to the garden when all danger of frost has passed. Melampodium tends to self-sow reliably. Plants are sometimes available in pots at garden centers.

Melampodium prefers rich, well-drained soil and blooms best in full sun. It tolerates a wide range of conditions, including drought and heat. The neat, compact plants never need staking and are rarely bothered by pests and diseases.

Uses. Melampodium is a reliable performer in beds, borders, edgings, and containers. The blooms make attractive long-lasting cut flowers. The plants are a welcome addition to the front of the mixed or annual border and look splendid in patio containers.

MEXICAN SUNFLOWER. See *Tithonia rotundifolia*

Mirabilis jalapa

Mirabilis jalapa

mih-RAB-ih-liss huh-LOP-uh.
Four o'clock. Half-hardy annual.

Characteristics. Height: 2 to 3 feet. Colors: Pink, purple, red, orange, yellow, white, and multicolor combinations.

Four o'clock plants grow 2 to 3 feet tall and are well branched and bushy. The botanical name *Mirabilis* refers to the miraculous diversity of flower colors produced on a single plant. Not only are individual flowers often multicolored, but different flowers on the same plant may be different colors. The funnel-shaped blooms resemble petunia flowers and only open for part of the day, theoretically starting at four o'clock (hence the common name). They often stay open all day in cloudy weather. The fact that the flowers open so late in the day bothers some people, but is not usually a problem for those who return home from work

every day just when the flowers are opening to greet them.

Every year some Burpee customers ask why their four o'clocks bloom even later than four o'clock—sometimes as late as eight or nine o'clock in the evening. No one knows for sure, but it may have something to do with the heat. We know the flowers cannot tolerate the hot, mid-afternoon sun. It's possible that they open later if the plants are located in an area that captures heat or is exposed to the late-afternoon sun.

How to Grow. Start seed indoors 4 to 6 weeks before the last frost in spring. Sow the large seeds ½ inch deep. Transplant hardened-off seedlings to the garden when all danger of frost has passed. You can also sow seed directly in the garden after the danger of frost. Bedding plants are not readily available at garden centers.

Four o'clocks are easy to grow in most soils and can withstand heat, humidity, and drought. They require full sun to bloom well but also will tolerate light shade. The plants are rarely bothered by pests or diseases.

Uses. Four o'clocks are colorful annuals for beds, borders, and containers. They make poor cut flowers because they cannot be relied on to remain open. Four o'clocks are good flowers for children to try, since they are colorful, easy to plant, and fast-growing.

Moluccella laevis

Moluccella laevis
moh-luk-SELL-uh LEE-viss.
Bells-of-Ireland. Half-hardy annual.
○ ◑ ⚘ ❀

Characteristics. Height: 2 to 3 feet. Colors: Green bracts with white flowers.

Bells-of-Ireland is a fascinating annual with an unusual green color and a unique honeycomb texture. While it is most loved by dried flower enthusiasts, it also has great value as an accent plant in beds and borders. Of course, some people might say that foliage provides enough green in the garden and that green can get boring, but the tall, pale green spikes of bells-of-Ireland are anything but common. The spikes are covered with bracts that resemble tiny suction cups, bells, or bathtubs (hence the wonderful common name "lady in the bath"), with tiny pinkish white flowers looking out. Bells-of-

Ireland are noticed and praised wherever they are planted.

How to Grow. Sow seed directly in the garden where you want the plants to grow. The seeds have a hard coat; to aid germination, soak them in water overnight before sowing. Sow the seed about ⅛ inch deep after the danger of heavy frost has passed. Bedding plants are rarely available.

Bells-of-Ireland prefers well-drained, moist soil and full sun or light shade. The plants tolerate crowding and should be spaced 9 to 12 inches apart. Stake the plants while they are still young. They are relatively free of pests and diseases.

Uses. Bells-of-Ireland is grown primarily for cutting and drying, and for the unusual color and texture it adds to beds and borders. The green bracts turn a soft straw color when dried. They add a unique texture to dried arrangements and are commonly present in large, professionally arranged dried flower displays.

MONEY PLANT. See *Lunaria annua*
MOSS ROSE. See *Portulaca grandiflora*

Myosotis sylvatica
my-oh-SOH-tiss sil-VAT-ih-kuh.
Forget-me-not. Hardy annual or biennial.
○ ◑ ❄ ⚘ ▼

Characteristics. Height: 12 inches. Colors: Blue, pink, lavender, or white.

Forget-me-nots bloom for several weeks in spring with literally unforgettable, tiny, intense blue flowers over low-growing mounds of long, narrow foliage. They are also available in shades of pink, lavender, and white, but the dainty blue flowers are what people are usually talking about when they say that a plant has "forget-me-not flowers."

Because they bloom at the same time as many spring bulbs, forget-me-nots are excellent companions for tulips, daffodils, and other early bulbs. These sturdy little plants often grow as biennials, so you can even plant them in the fall, after you plant your bulbs, for a memorable spring show.

How to Grow. Sow seed in late summer or fall for blooms the following spring. Or sow seed indoors 6 to 8 weeks before the last frost. Cover the seed

Myosotis sylvatica

with a thin layer of planting medium. Transplant hardened-off seedlings to the garden when the danger of heavy frost has passed. Plants are usually available at garden centers.

Forget-me-nots prefer cool, moist soil in partial shade or full sun. They require little care once they are established, and they are rarely troubled by pests and diseases.

Uses. Forget-me-nots are ideal for cool-season color in containers, flower beds, edgings, and even rock gardens. They are also perfect for naturalizing in woodlands. They make delightful, long-lasting cut flowers for small bouquets.

NASTURTIUM. See *Tropaeolum majus*

Nicotiana spp.

nih-koh-shee-ANN-uh.
Flowering tobacco. Tender annual.
○ ◑ ✳ ❦ ▼

Characteristics. Height: 1 to 6 feet. Colors: Pink, purple, red, green, yellow, and white.

The various kinds of flowering tobacco are relatives of commercially grown tobacco. The dramatic *Nicotiana sylvestris* produces a flower stalk up to 6 feet tall over a large rosette of enormous leaves measuring up to 2 feet long and 1 foot across. The pendulous, creamy white flowers are shaped like long, narrow trumpets and have a sweet fragrance. They bloom from mid- or late summer to the first frost in fall.

The species most commonly grown in gardens is *N. alata*. The 1- to 2-foot-tall plants are like miniature versions of *N. sylvestris*; they produce shorter, wider, more upright flowers in a wide range of colors. They also bloom earlier and for a longer time. Plants of the new 'Metro Hybrid' series grows only 12 inches tall; the flowers remain open and upright even at the hottest time of the day, when those of other flowering tobaccos close.

How to Grow. Flowering tobaccos take a long time to bloom from seed, so start them early. Plant the seed indoors 6 to 8 weeks before the last frost in spring. The seed needs light to germinate, so just scatter it as evenly as possible over the surface of the planting medium. Keep the medium moist by covering the trays or pots with glass or clear plastic until seedlings appear. Transplant hardened-off seedlings to the garden when all danger of frost has passed. Plants are usually available at garden centers.

The plants usually reseed themselves in the garden, and sometimes seedlings will appear even when flowering tobacco has been absent from the garden for years. Self-sown seedlings of hybrid cultivars won't resemble the parent plants, so you'll need to start these cultivars from fresh seed each year.

Both species of flowering tobacco prefer rich, well-drained soil. They can withstand dry conditions once they are established. They prefer full sun but will bloom well in partial shade. If blooming

Nicotiana alata 'Peace Pipe'

Nicotiana alata 'Domino Mix'

slows in midsummer, you can revive the plants by cutting them back to where fresh leaves are growing out from the basal clump—they will quickly recover and bloom continuously until the first frost. Flowering tobacco belongs to the same botanical family as tomatoes and potatoes, and is subject to many of the same pests and diseases. To minimize problems, plant it in a different area of the garden each year.

Uses. Both kinds of flowering tobacco are excellent for beds and borders. The more compact forms of *N. alata* are also well suited for containers and edgings. The blooms make good cut flowers, and many cultivars are fragrant. As an added bonus, the funnel-shaped flowers attract hummingbirds.

Nierembergia hippomanica
nee-rem-BER-gee-uh hip-oh-MAN-ih-kuh.
Nierembergia. Tender annual.

Characteristics. Height: 6 to 12 inches. Colors: Purple or white.

Nierembergia is a charming, low-growing annual that's nearly covered with dainty, cup-shaped flowers all summer until fall. The plants have a spreading habit and fine-textured, feathery foliage.

The traditional color is purple, but a new white cultivar, 'Mont Blanc', was recently named an All-America Selections winner.

How to Grow. Nierembergia takes a long time to bloom from seed, so start it indoors 10 weeks before the last frost in spring. Seeds need light to germinate, so just scatter them over the surface of the planting medium. Keep the medium moist by covering the trays or pots with glass or clear plastic until seedlings appear. Transplant hardened-off seedlings to the garden when all danger of frost has passed. Plants are sometimes available at garden centers.

Nierembergia grows best in a sheltered location that gets full sun or partial shade. The plants prefer moist, well-drained soil. They are rarely bothered by pests and diseases, and require little care in the garden other than extra watering in dry weather.

Uses. Nierembergia looks good near the front of beds and borders. The plants have a spreading habit that makes them ideal for strawberry jars, hanging baskets, and window boxes, where they can flow over the sides. As an annual groundcover, nierembergia forms an attractive, dense carpet of color. You can even grow it over winter as a houseplant.

Nierembergia hippomanica

Nigella damascena

Nigella damascena

ny-JEL-uh dah-mah-SEEN-ah.
Love-in-a-mist. Hardy annual.

Characteristics. Height: 1 to 2 feet. Colors: Blue, pink, purple, rose, and white.

Love-in-a-mist adds an old-fashioned touch to the garden. Dried flower enthusiasts grow it primarily for its unusual seedpods, which resemble miniature blowfish without some of their horns. But love-in-a-mist also has charming flowers—in rare shades of sky blue, antique pink, and white—that make a welcome addition to the mixed flower border. The foliage is feathery and delicate-looking, making the plants seem otherworldly. Site love-in-a-mist carefully in the garden; it can easily look lost among the bold colors and textures of many bedding annuals.

How to Grow. After danger of heavy frost in spring, sow the seed directly in the garden where you want plants to grow. When the seedlings are 3 to 4 inches tall, thin them to 9 to 12 inches apart. Love-in-a-mist reseeds itself reliably. Plants are sometimes available at garden centers, but they usually don't transplant well.

Love-in-a-mist prefers cool, moist soil and full sun or light shade. It grows and flowers best in cool weather. It is easy to grow and is rarely troubled by pests or diseases.

Uses. This airy annual is lovely in beds, borders, and fresh arrangements. It is excellent for containers, looks very much at home in herb gardens, and is perfect in cottage gardens. Love-in-a-mist is also prized for its fascinating puffy seedpods, which add an unusual texture to dried arrangements.

Oxypetalum caeruleum

awk-see-PET-uh-lum see-RULE-ee-um.
Oxypetalum. Half-hardy annual.

Characteristics. Height: 18 inches. Colors: Blue.

A relative of milkweed, oxypetalum bears waxy-textured, star-shaped flowers, followed by horned, milkweedlike seedpods. When the flowers bloom, they are an amazing shade of icy turquoise-blue, which changes to rich sky blue as they mature. They are long-lasting and make excellent cut flowers (if you like the fragrance, which many people do not). In the garden, they add the valuable shades of blue that are so prized in mixed borders. Oxypetalum combines beautifully with orange or pink companions.

Unfortunately, the plants themselves aren't nearly as attractive or desirable as the flowers. They grow rangy and weedy-looking, and neither staking nor pinching will make them look neat. Keep this drawback in mind when siting oxypetalum. The plants do work well in pots and can be spectacular behind shorter annuals or perennials, especially those with silver or gray foliage.

How to Grow. The plants take a long time to bloom, so start the seed indoors 10 to 12 weeks before the last frost in spring. Cover the seed with a thin layer of planting medium. When the seedlings are about 5 or 6 inches tall, pinch the tops to encourage bushiness. Transplant hardened-off seedlings to the garden when all danger of frost has passed. Plants are occasionally available at garden centers.

Oxypetalum thrives in poor, sandy soil and full sun. It does not perform well in overly rich soil. The plants tolerate dry conditions and are rarely bothered by pests and diseases.

Uses. Oxypetalum is a good plant for containers and mixed borders. Try the fresh flowers in bouquets. The seedpods are attractive in dried flower arrangements.

PANSY. See *Viola X wittrockiana*

Shirley Poppies

Papaver spp.

PAP-uh-ver. Poppy. Hardy annual.

Characteristics. Height: 15 to 36 inches. Colors: Pink, purple, red, orange, salmon, and white.

Poppies have many associations—some cheerful, some serious. They have been immortalized in the paintings of the Impressionists, and they are somber memorials of the dead of World War I. And with their gorgeous colors and crinkly petals, poppies are sure to bring joy to any garden planting.

Every year customers ask Burpee if the poppies it sells are the same as those that grew in France, on Flanders fields, at the end of World War I. The poppy they are referring to is *Papaver rhoeas*, commonly called Flanders poppy. Flanders poppies have silky, crinkled, clear red petals that form a delicate, cup-shaped bloom about 1 inch across. Although the original red Flanders poppy is still available, it has been used to produce new strains called Shirley poppies. Shirley poppies come in a wider range of colors—including pinks, whites, and bicolors—and a broader range of flower types, including doubles and semidoubles.

While Flanders and Shirley poppies are hardy annuals, Iceland poppy (*P. nudicaule*) is actually a perennial that can be treated as an annual. Its flowers look similar to those of Flanders and Shirley poppies, but the color range includes oranges and yellows.

All poppies have a basal rosette of serrated or ferny-textured leaves, thin stems, and pendulous flower buds that straighten up as they open. Annual poppies add bright summer color to the garden, generally blooming from June to the end of August.

How to Grow. Poppies have easily damaged taproots and seriously resent transplanting. Fortunately, they are easy to grow from direct-sown seed. In early spring, scatter the seed over the soil where you want the plants to grow, and keep the soil moist until seedlings appear. (In mild-winter areas, sow in fall for earlier blooms the next year.) While poppies are offered occasionally at garden centers, sowing seed is best, since they don't transplant well.

Poppies thrive in rich, sandy soil and full sun. For the most continuous bloom, remove the spent flower stems frequently. Toward the end of the season, leave some flowers to form seed; poppies often reseed when they are happy in their location.

Uses. Enjoy the beautiful blooms of these easy annuals in beds and borders. Poppies make wonderful cut flowers. Cut the flower when it is still in bud, and seal the cut end of the stem with a lighted match to prevent rapid water loss. Poppies are also excellent flowers for naturalizing in a wildflower meadow.

Pelargonium spp.

pel-ar-GOH-nee-um. Geranium.
Tender annual.

Characteristics. Height: 10 to 18 inches. Colors: Pink, magenta, red, orange, salmon, and white.

Geraniums are among the most popular flowers in American houses and gardens. These dependable plants add bold, bright colors to beds, borders, and containers from early summer to the first frost in fall. In protected locations, they can even tolerate a light frost and may be among the last annuals in bloom in the garden in autumn. You can bring them indoors to continue their display in a sunny window all winter, until it's time to put them in the garden again in the spring. Geraniums are easy to maintain, requiring only deadheading and some extra watering in dry weather.

Many types of geraniums are available for the

Pelargonium X *hortorum*

Pelargonium X *hortorum* 'Earliana Mix'
with sweet alyssum and marigolds

garden as well as the house and greenhouse. The familiar zonal geranium (*Pelargonium* X *hortorum*) has big, ball-shaped flower heads in bright shades of red, magenta, orange, pink, and white. The plants have an upright habit and rounded, scallop-edged leaves, which are plain green or have a dark ring near the edge.

Ivy-leaved geranium (*P. peltatum*) has foliage true to its common name and a cascading habit that makes it well suited for hanging baskets. The flowers are less showy than those of zonal geranium, with looser flower clusters. Martha Washington or regal geraniums (*P.* X *domesticum*) have large, crinkled leaves with a maple-leaf shape. Their gorgeous flowers bloom in astonishing bicolor combinations. They do not tolerate the hot, humid summer weather common in much of the country and are often grown in greenhouses or as houseplants.

Beautiful flowers aren't the only reason to grow geraniums; some have delightful foliage as well. Scented geraniums come in a wide array of foliage fragrances, including chocolate, peppermint, and lemon. They are usually grown in greenhouses or as houseplants, but they add a nice touch to herb and flower gardens, too.

How to Grow. Geraniums take a long time to bloom from seed, so start them indoors 10 to 12 weeks before the last frost in spring. Cover the seed with a thin layer of growing medium. Transplant hardened-off seedlings to the garden when all danger of frost has passed. Most garden centers sell pots of geraniums in spring.

Because geraniums are really tender perennials, you can keep them over the winter as houseplants. Bring the plants indoors in the fall, or take cuttings from healthy stems and root them for houseplants. You can then take more cuttings from the houseplants during the winter and root them for next year's garden.

Geraniums prefer rich, well-drained soil in full sun. They will also tolerate light shade. Deadhead them periodically to promote continuous bloom. The lower leaves have a tendency to turn yellow or dry up, especially on container-grown plants; remove the off-color leaves to keep the plants neat, and fertilize the containers to add needed nutrients.

Uses. Geraniums are popular outdoors in beds, borders, and containers of all sorts—especially window boxes. They also make excellent houseplants for a sunny spot indoors. The flower clusters add bright color to fresh bouquets. Cascading cultivars are ideal for hanging baskets.

PERIWINKLE. See *Catharanthus roseus*

Petunia X hybrida

peh-TOON-yuh HY-brih-duh.
Petunia. Tender annual.

○

Characteristics. Height: 12 to 15 inches. Colors: Blue, pink, purple, red, yellow, white, and bicolors.

Another of America's top-ten bedding plants, petunias are loved for the bright color they provide all summer until the first frost. They also have a delicious fragrance, which is often overlooked when they are planted in small numbers among plants with a stronger fragrance. If you are fortunate enough to find a bench in front of a large planting of petunias, the unforgettable scent will entice you to linger.

Petunias are sometimes classified as multiflora or grandiflora types. The multifloras produce many small flowers, while the grandifloras produce fewer, larger flowers up to 5 inches across. Double and single forms are available for both types.

How to Grow. Petunias take a long time to bloom from seed, so they need an early start. Sow the seed indoors 10 to 12 weeks before the last frost in spring. The tiny seed needs light to germinate; scatter it as evenly as possible over the surface of the planting medium. Keep the medium moist by covering the trays or pots with glass or clear plastic until seedlings appear. Transplant hardened-off seedlings

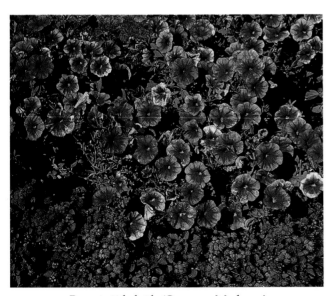

Petunia X hybrida 'Summer Madness'

to the garden when all danger of frost has passed. Most garden centers offer a broad selection of petunias as bedding plants.

Petunias grow best in full sun and rich, well-drained, sandy soil. Pinch off spent flowers for continuous blooming. Many cultivars of petunias, especially grandiflora types, tend to droop in rainy weather and take some time to recover before they continue their floral display. Petunias are also subject to botrytis, a fungal disease that causes spotting on the flowers, particularly after rainy weather. The multiflora types are more rain-tolerant and botrytis-resistant.

Around the end of July, cut your petunias back to about 4 to 6 inches, and give them a feeding of 5-10-5 or 5-10-10 fertilizer. They will come back in a few weeks and bloom all the better for this treatment, right up to the first frost.

Uses. Petunias are perfect for sunny beds and borders, and in mass plantings for a great sweep of color. They are particularly impressive cascading from hanging baskets, window boxes, and other containers. Petunias are actually tender perennials, so you can grow them on a sunny windowsill as houseplants. They are also popular for greenhouse growing in winter.

Phlox drummondii

FLOKS druh-MON-dee-eye.
Annual phlox. Hardy annual.

○

Characteristics. Height: 6 to 18 inches. Colors: Blue, pink, lavender, red, salmon, white, and many bicolors.

Annual phlox is a bright, summer-blooming annual with clusters of small, round, single or semi-double flowers in a range of colors on sturdy, mound-shaped plants. The flowers have a faint, sweet fragrance, which is most noticeable when the plants are located in raised beds or containers, or in mass plantings. You can also enjoy the fragrance by cutting the flowers for small bouquets.

How to Grow. After the last heavy frost in spring, sow the seed directly in the garden where you want the plants to grow. You can also start them indoors 6 to 8 weeks before the last frost, then trans-

Petunia 'Americana Mix'
with zinnias

plant the hardened-off seedlings to the garden when all danger of frost has passed. The seeds need darkness to germinate, so cover them with ⅛ inch of soil. Indoors, cover the flats with a sheet of newspaper until the seeds sprout. Bedding plants are not usually available at garden centers.

Annual phlox thrives in rich, well-drained soil in full sun. The plants may need extra water in dry periods but are generally tolerant of high heat. Pinch off spent flowers for continuous bloom. Otherwise, the plants require little care in the garden.

Uses. This colorful annual can be used in beds, borders, rock gardens, edgings, patio containers, and cutting gardens. It looks marvelous in masses as an annual groundcover.

PINCUSHION FLOWER. See *Scabiosa* spp.
PINKS. See *Dianthus* spp.
POLKA-DOT PLANT. See *Hypoestes phyllostachya*

POOR MAN'S ORCHID. See *Schizanthus pinnatus*
POPPY. See *Papaver* spp.
POPPY, CALIFORNIA. See *Eschscholzia californica*

Portulaca grandiflora
por-tew-LAH-kuh gran-dih-FLOR-uh.
Moss rose. Hardy annual.
○ ☀ ▼

Characteristics. Height: 5 to 6 inches. Colors: Pink, magenta, red, orange, yellow, salmon, and white.

Moss rose is a low-growing, succulent annual popular for its remarkable tolerance for heat and drought. It is ideal for rock gardens and desertlike patches in the garden where few other long-blooming, colorful annuals can thrive. The brightly colored flowers may be single, semidouble, or double, like miniature roses. They bloom on spreading plants with short, narrow, succulent foliage resembling that of rosemary. The flowers stay closed all day in cloudy weather, or open during the day and close late in the afternoon in sunny weather. This can be a drawback for those people who work outside the home and return every day to see the flowers closed. (They might want to plant *Mirabilis jalapa*, commonly called four o'clocks, instead!) New

Portulaca grandiflora

cultivars, such as the 'Sundial Hybrid' series, have been developed to bloom for longer periods.

How to Grow. For earliest bloom, start seed indoors 6 to 8 weeks before the last frost in spring. The seeds need light to germinate, so just scatter them over the surface of the planting medium. Keep the medium moist by covering the trays or pots with glass or clear plastic until seedlings appear. Transplant hardened-off seedlings to the garden when the danger of frost has passed. You may also want to try sowing the seed directly in the garden after all danger of frost. The seed is quite small, however, and it is likely to dry out when sown in the dry areas moss rose loves. Keeping the seedbed evenly moist—just until seedlings appear—may encourage better germination. Bedding plants are readily available at garden centers.

Moss rose prefers sandy, hot, dry locations in full sun. It is rarely bothered by pests or diseases and requires almost no maintenance after it has become established in the garden. The plants often reseed in favorable locations.

Uses. Moss rose is perfect for rock gardens and for beds and borders in drought-prone areas. It grows nicely between paving stones. The plants have a spreading habit, so they cascade gracefully from hanging baskets and window boxes. They also make a great annual groundcover.

POT MARIGOLD. See *Calendula officinalis*
ROCKET LARKSPUR. See *Consolida ambigua*

Salpiglossis sinuata
sal-pih-GLOSS-iss sin-yew-AY-tuh.
Salpiglossis. Tender annual.
○ ❄ ✂ ▼

Characteristics. Height: 2 to 3 feet. Colors: Blue, purple, red, yellow, brown, and white.

Salpiglossis is an unusual annual prized for its fascinating, velvety flowers. The funnel-shaped blooms resemble those of single petunias, to which this plant is related. However, salpiglossis comes in a very different range of colors, including deep red with yellow veins and magenta with black veins. One of the most striking of these colors is a rich brown with golden yellow veins, which the famous

Salpiglossis sinuata

English gardener Vita Sackville-West described as "corduroy brown."

The flowers are indeed breathtakingly beautiful, and virtually everyone who sees them wants to grow them. Unfortunately, salpiglossis is difficult to grow successfully in much of the country, since it cannot tolerate high summer temperatures. The plants thrive in areas with cool summer weather, such as the Pacific Northwest and coastal California. In the rest of the country, they perform best in a cool greenhouse in winter.

How to Grow. For earliest bloom, sow seed indoors 8 to 10 weeks before the last frost in spring. The seed needs darkness to germinate, so cover the trays or pots with newspaper until seedlings appear. Transplant hardened-off seedlings to the garden when all danger of frost has passed. In areas with cool summers, you can also sow the seed directly in the garden after all danger of frost. If you are lucky enough to have a greenhouse, you can sow seed indoors in the fall for winter flowers. This uncommon annual is rarely available as bedding or pot plants.

Salpiglossis prefers full sun and light, sandy soil that's rich in organic matter. The taller cultivars need staking.

Uses. The exotic-looking blooms of salpiglossis are very striking in cool-summer beds, borders, and containers. They also make terrific cut flowers.

Salvia splendens

Salvia spp.

SAL-vee-uh. Salvia. Half-hardy annual.

○ ◑ ✿ ❀ ▼

Characteristics. Height: 10 to 30 inches. Colors: Blue, pink, purple, red, orange, and white.

Salvias are popular and easy-to-grow additions to all kinds of sunny gardens. Several species are particularly well loved for their rich colors. The ones that are most commonly grown as annuals include scarlet sage (*Salvia splendens*) and mealy-cup sage (*S. farinacea*). *S. viridis* (also known as *S. horminum*) and *S. patens* are also grown as annuals but are less well known.

Scarlet sage has thick flower spikes covered with tubular florets. The scarlet and fiery red shades are most common, but cultivars are also available in deep purple, lavender, cream, and salmon. Most scarlet sage cultivars have deep green, wedge-shaped foliage. One of the best performing cultivars is 'Flare', which offers an extra-long season of bloom and doesn't require constant deadheading.

Mealy-cup sage is actually a tender perennial that is usually grown as an annual. (Plants often overwinter in Zones 7 to 10.) It has slender flower spikes in shades of lavender-blue and white. The bushy plants have a more graceful texture than scarlet sage, and the foliage is longer, narrower, and a lighter shade of green. The flowers are often used in dried arrangements.

Both scarlet sage and mealy-cup sage are among the most satisfying plants available, delivering a

Salvia farinacea

long season of bloom from midsummer to the first frost, and sometimes—in protected areas—even a little beyond. The sturdy, well-branched plants have a neat, upright, bushy habit and provide reliable sweeps of bright color for mass plantings.

S. viridis and *S. patens* have looser, more open flower spikes than those of scarlet sage and mealy-cup sage, and they tend to be more subtle and less free-flowering. *S. viridis* comes in shades of violet-blue, pink, and white; *S. patens* is deep blue and white. They have the same cultural requirements as scarlet sage.

How to Grow. Salvias take a long time to bloom from seed, so start them early indoors. Sow mealy-cup sage seed 10 weeks before the last frost in spring; plant scarlet sage, *S. viridis*, and *S. patens* 8 weeks before the last frost. The seed needs light to germinate, so just scatter it on the surface of the planting medium. Keep the medium moist by covering the trays or pots with glass or clear plastic until seedlings appear. Transplant hardened-off seedlings to the garden when all danger of frost has passed. Bedding plants are readily available for scarlet sage and mealy-cup sage, but not for *S. viridis* or *S. patens*.

All salvias tolerate a wide range of soil conditions, but they grow best in well-drained, rich soil. They may require some extra watering in dry weather. The plants grow well in full sun or partial shade and are rarely bothered by pests and diseases. They never need staking but do benefit from deadheading.

Uses. These versatile, colorful plants are widely grown in annual gardens, perennial gardens, mixed borders, formal massed plantings, herb gardens, wildflower gardens, cottage gardens, and containers. Compact cultivars add excitement to window boxes; tall-stemmed types are great for cutting. Mealy-cup sage also works well as a dried flower.

filling spaces in the front of the border. In containers, the free-flowering stems cascade gracefully over the sides.

How to Grow. Sow seed directly in the garden after all danger of frost has passed. Barely cover the seeds, as light helps them to germinate. Keep them evenly moist until they sprout. When the plants are 3 to 4 inches tall, thin them to about 6 inches apart. Bedding plants are sometimes available at garden centers.

Sanvitalia is easy to grow in any well-drained soil in full sun. Plants are rarely bothered by pests or diseases.

Uses. Grow sanvitalia for eye-catching color in beds, borders, or rock gardens. Its cascading habit makes it attractive in hanging baskets, strawberry jars, and window boxes.

Sanvitalia procumbens

san-vih-TAL-ee-uh proh-KUM-benz.
Sanvitalia. Tender annual.

Characteristics. Height: 6 to 8 inches. Colors: Orange or yellow.

Sometimes called creeping zinnia, sanvitalia is a charming, low-growing annual covered with bright zinnia-like, single flowers from midsummer to the first frost in fall. There are yellow and orange cultivars available, both with deep purple centers. The plants have a spreading habit, making them ideal for

Scabiosa spp.

scab-ee-OH-suh. Pincushion flower,
starflower. Hardy annual.

Characteristics. Height: 2 to 3 feet. Colors: Blue, pink, lavender, purple, red, salmon, and white.

Two annual species of scabiosa are commonly grown in American gardens. Pincushion flower (*Scabiosa atropurpurea*) is a tall, hardy annual with ball-shaped flower heads in shades of pink, blue, lavender, purple, red, and white. The flower heads are covered with silvery filaments that stick in the

Sanvitalia procumbens

Scabiosa atropurpurea

petals like pins. They bloom on graceful, 3-foot-tall plants from midsummer to frost.

Unlike pincushion flower, starflower (*S. stellata*) is grown primarily for its ball-shaped seedpods, which—as one Burpee breeder has suggested—resemble space satellites. Starflowers are prized for dried arrangements, since they have such an interesting texture and their long, stiff stems are easy to work with.

How to Grow. Sow seed directly in the garden in spring, after danger of a heavy frost has passed. Cover the seed with ⅛ inch of soil. When the seedlings are large enough to handle, thin them to 12 inches apart. For earlier bloom, you can start seed indoors 4 to 6 weeks before the last frost. Transplant hardened-off seedlings to the garden when all danger of frost has passed. Bedding plants of pincushion flower and starflower are not usually available at garden centers.

Both species prefer rich, well-drained, slightly alkaline soil in a sunny location. The plants may require staking. They are rarely bothered by pests and diseases.

Uses. Starflower adds a unique texture to dried arrangements. Pincushion flower is ideal for planting in masses at the back of the border. Its delicate blooms also make wonderful cut flowers for fresh arrangements.

Schizanthus pinnatus

skih-ZAN-thus pin-AY-tus. Schizanthus,
poor man's orchid. Tender annual.

○ ❄ ⚹❀ ▼

Characteristics. Height: 1 to 2 feet. Colors: Pink, purple, orange, salmon, yellow, and white.

This unusual cool-season annual is prized for its extraordinary, orchidlike blooms. The bushy plants have attractive, ferny foliage that makes a beautiful background for the flowers. Schizanthus would be grown more widely in American gardens if it were more tolerant of heat. It thrives in areas with cool summers, where it blooms all summer long, but it tends to burn out in hot weather. It works well as a cool greenhouse plant for winter bloom.

How to Grow. Start seed indoors 12 weeks before the last spring frost. The seeds need darkness

Schizanthus pinnatus

to germinate, so cover the trays or pots with newspaper until seedlings appear. To produce well-branched plants, pinch the young seedlings when they're a few inches tall. Transplant hardened-off seedlings to the garden when the danger of frost has passed. Bedding plants are rarely available at garden centers.

Schizanthus prefers loose, rich, moist soil and full sun. It does not like to dry out, so water it regularly in dry weather. The plants are susceptible to aster yellows, a disease that causes yellow-green, stunted growth; remove infected plants immediately to help prevent the spread of the disease. During wet periods, schizanthus is also prone to anthracnose, a fungal disease that causes leaf spots; avoid getting the foliage wet when you are watering the plants.

Uses. Schizanthus flowers are excellent for cutting and beautiful in borders and containers. This uncommon annual is a good choice for a cool greenhouse for winter cut flowers or potted plants.

SNAPDRAGON. See *Antirrhinum majus*
SPIDER FLOWER. See *Cleome hasslerana*
STARFLOWER. See *Scabiosa* spp.
STATICE. See *Limonium sinuatum*
STOCK. See *Matthiola incana*
STRAWFLOWER. See *Helichrysum bracteatum*
SUMMER POINSETTIA. See *Amaranthus* spp.
SUNFLOWER. See *Helianthus annuus*
SUNFLOWER, MEXICAN. See *Tithonia rotundifolia*

SWAN RIVER DAISY. See *Brachycome iberidifolia*
SWEET ALYSSUM. See *Lobularia maritima*
SWEET PEA. See *Lathyrus odoratus*
SWEET WILLIAM. See *Dianthus* spp.

Tagetes spp.

TAH-jeh-teez. Marigold.
Half-hardy annual.

Characteristics. Height: 8 to 36 inches. Colors: Yellow, orange, red, white, and bicolors.

Marigolds owe their popularity to their cheerful, summery blooms, which blanket sturdy, easy-care plants from midsummer to fall. They are available in a wide range of shapes and sizes, with single or double flowers that may resemble daisies, anemones, or carnations. Marigolds come in sunny shades of yellow, gold, orange, and rust-red, in both solid colors and bicolor combinations. White cultivars are also available, providing a welcome contrast to the hot colors.

Marigold flowers and foliage have a characteristic pungent scent that many people like—and many more dislike. Odorless cultivars are available for the latter group. The odor, however, can serve a purpose, as it is thought to repel insects. For this reason, vegetable gardeners have traditionally planted marigolds around their crops. Research has also indicated that the roots of French marigolds emit a substance that deters root-damaging nematodes in the soil. But perhaps the best reason to plant these annuals around vegetable or herb gardens is that they are edible, and their petals make colorful additions to salads.

In seed catalogs, you'll see marigolds divided into four groups: American or African marigolds (*Tagetes erecta*), French marigolds (*T. patula*), signet marigolds (*T. tenuifolia*), and triploid hybrids. Each group has different traits and uses in the garden.

American marigolds are medium to tall, stocky, hedge-type plants with blooms up to 4 inches across. They are available in shades of yellow, gold, orange, and white. These durable plants are most frequently used in mass plantings or large containers, as floral hedges, or for cutting. Cultivars in Burpee's award-winning 'Lady Hybrid' series are among the best American marigolds available, with sturdy stems and fully double flowers.

French marigolds are shorter than the American types and tend to bloom earlier. They have single or double flowers in shades of yellow, gold, orange, and rust, as well as intense rust-and-yellow bicolors. French marigolds are perfect for beds, borders, edgings, and containers. The 'Disco' series has exquisite single flowers in a wide range of solid colors and bicolors.

Signet marigolds have dainty single flowers on short, mounded plants with ferny foliage. They look

Tagetes erecta 'Climax Strain Orange'

Tagetes patula 'Queen Sophia'

Tagetes tenuifolia 'Lemon Gem' and 'Tangerine Gem'

so different from their more familiar American cousins that many people do not recognize them as marigolds. These plants are becoming more popular for rock gardens, containers, herb gardens, beds, borders, and edgings.

Triploid marigolds are a combination of American and French types, with the best qualities of both: vigor, compact habit, early and prolific bloom, and large flower size. They are also "mule" types, which means that they do not produce seeds; instead, they direct all their energy to producing flowers. Triploids are among the best performing marigolds available.

How to Grow. Marigolds grow easily from seed sown directly in the garden after all danger of frost. For earlier bloom, start seed indoors 6 to 8 weeks before the last frost. Just barely cover the seed with the soil or planting medium. Transplant hardened-off seedlings to the garden when all danger of frost has passed. Bedding plants are always available in a wide array of colors and types at any garden center.

Marigolds can adapt to most kinds of garden soil, but prefer a well-drained soil that is not overly rich. They must have full sun. The plants resist both heat and drought. The taller cultivars may need staking, and all types require deadheading.

Marigolds are susceptible to aster yellows, a disease that causes the plants to turn a greenish yellow color and makes the foliage texture rougher; remove infected plants immediately if you notice these

symptoms. Aster yellows and insect problems tend to be worse for the odorless cultivars and the older white cultivars.

Uses. Marigolds are great for almost all sunny garden spots, including beds, borders, edgings, containers, cutting gardens, rock gardens, cottage gardens, mass plantings—even herb and vegetable gardens! These colorful, easy-to-grow annuals are perfect confidence-builders for beginning gardeners of all ages.

Tithonia rotundifolia
tih-THOH-nee-uh roh-tun-dih-FOE-lee-uh.
Mexican sunflower. Half-hardy annual.

Characteristics. Height: 3 to 6 feet. Colors: Orange, yellow, and red.

These splendid annuals produce single, dahlia-like blooms up to 3½ inches across on towering, 6-

Tithonia rotundifolia

foot-tall plants. The flowers have velvety petals in an intense shade of scarlet-orange that's unforgettable in fresh flower arrangements. Yellow cultivars are available, but the natural orange color is so unrivaled in the garden that there seems to be no need for any other color! The sturdy, bushy plants grow 2 to 3 feet wide and have attractive, dark green, spear-shaped leaves.

'Torch' is an All-America Selections winner that grows to 6 feet tall, with deep fiery red flowers. It looks spectacular as a flowering screen or hedge, or planted by itself in front of a fence or wall or next to a door. 'Sundance' is a lower-growing, 3- to 4-foot cultivar that's easier to place in beds and borders.

How to Grow. For earliest bloom, start seed indoors 6 weeks before the last frost in spring. Cover the seed with a thin layer of planting medium. Transplant hardened-off seedlings to the garden when the danger of frost has passed. You can also sow the seed directly in the garden after all danger of frost. Bedding plants are not generally available.

Mexican sunflower, also commonly called tithonia, prefers well-drained, fertile soil in full sun. It is heat- and drought-tolerant, but it does appreciate extra water and fertilizer during its most intense growth period in midsummer. Tithonia is rarely bothered by pests and diseases. Although the plants are generally bushy and sturdy, they may need staking.

Uses. Tithonia is useful for dramatic floral hedges or accents. Grow it at the back of the border and in the cutting garden. Children love it!

Torenia fournieri
tore-REEN-ee-uh for-NEAR-eye.
Torenia. Tender annual.

Characteristics. Height: 8 to 12 inches. Colors: Blue, purple, lavender, rose, pink, and white.

Torenia is a delightful, low-growing annual that is valued in the garden for its shade tolerance. It was once available only in dark purple and blue shades, but the popular 'Clown' series has extended the color range to include rose, white, and many pleasing combinations. Torenia is also called "wishbone flower," for the little white wishbone-shaped stamens in the throat of the flower.

How to Grow. Start seed indoors 10 to 12 weeks before the last frost in spring. The seed needs light to germinate, so just scatter it over the surface of the planting medium. Keep the medium moist by covering the trays or pots with glass or clear plastic until seedlings appear. Transplant hardened-off seedlings to the garden when all danger of frost has passed. Many garden centers sell torenia as bedding plants.

Torenia prefers rich, moist, well-drained soil and light to fairly dense shade. It is rarely bothered by pests and diseases, and it requires very little maintenance once it is established in the garden.

Uses. Torenia is useful for shady beds and borders, or as an edging. In masses, it forms an attractive annual groundcover. An excellent plant for small containers and window boxes, torenia also makes a good houseplant.

Trachymene coerulea
tray-KIH-men-ee see-RULE-ee-uh.
Blue lace flower. Tender annual.

Characteristics. Height: 24 to 30 inches. Colors: Blue.

This unusual tender annual looks like a lovely blue version of Queen-Anne's-lace. The flowers are a unique shade of icy blue and add a delicate, airy texture to the border. They are most effective in the garden when planted in large numbers. The flowers have a delicate, sweet fragrance that can be lost when surrounded by more fragrant flowers. You'll appreciate the scent most when you cut the flowers and bring them inside.

The upright plants spread about 12 inches wide and have lacy, medium green foliage. They bloom best in cooler temperatures. Where summers are hot, blue lace flower may not bloom until temperatures begin to cool off in late summer.

How to Grow. Blue lace flower dislikes being transplanted. After all danger of frost has passed, sow the seed directly in the garden where you want the plants to grow. Just barely cover the seed with soil, and keep the seedbed moist until seedlings appear. When the seedlings are 4 to 5 inches tall, thin them to 9 to 12 inches apart. Bedding plants are generally not available at garden centers.

Blue lace flower prefers rich, sandy, well-drained soil in full sun. The plants may require staking. They are rarely bothered by pests and diseases.

Uses. Blue lace flower is beautiful in the middle of a border or in a cottage garden. It also makes a lovely, long-lasting cut flower. If you have a greenhouse, you can grow it in winter. While blue lace flower is not a native plant, its resemblance to Queen-Anne's-lace makes it look at home in a wildflower meadow.

TRANSVAAL DAISY. See *Gerbera jamesonii*

Tropaeolum majus
troh-pee-OH-lum MAY-jus.
Nasturtium. Hardy annual.
○ ❄ ⚮ ❦ ▼

Characteristics. Height: 1 foot (bedding types) to 6 feet (vining types). Colors: Orange, pink, yellow, red, mahogany, and white.

Nasturtiums are popular for their vibrant, sweetly fragrant blooms and interesting foliage, which resembles miniature lily pads. They are available as low-growing, bushy bedding plants up to 1 foot tall; as semidwarf, mound-shaped plants up to 20 inches tall; or as vines that climb 6 feet or more.

Tropaeolum majus

The foliage is usually light to medium green, although 'Alaska' has unusual variegated foliage and is attractive even without flowers. The edible foliage and flowers of nasturtium have a peppery flavor and add color to salads or garnishes.

How to Grow. Nasturtiums grow quickly from seed sown directly in the garden after danger of a heavy frost. Plant the large, pealike seeds ½ inch deep. Thin the seedlings to 12 inches apart when they are 3 to 4 inches tall. For earlier bloom, you can sow seed indoors 6 weeks before the last frost. Transplant hardened-off seedlings to the garden when the danger of frost has passed. Bedding plants are not normally available, possibly because nasturtiums are so easy to grow from seed.

Nasturtiums prefer poor, well-drained soil in full sun. Too-rich soil tends to encourage leafy growth at the expense of flowers. The plants grow best in cooler temperatures. They tend to bloom less in the heat of summer but revive beautifully in the first cool weather of late summer. Deadhead regularly to prolong blooming. Tie vining types to a latticelike support if you want them to climb. Nasturtiums almost always have aphids on the succulent new leaves and flowers; control the pests with insecticidal soap.

Uses. Short cultivars are useful for beds, borders, and edgings. Vining types are attractive as a temporary climbing screen or cascading out of window boxes and hanging baskets. All kinds make excellent cut flowers. Nasturtiums are good plants for children to grow because they are fast, easy, and reliable.

Venidium fastuosum
ven-ID-ee-um fast-yew-OH-sum.
Cape daisy. Tender annual.
○ ☀ ▼

Characteristics. Height: 2 feet. Colors: Orange. This handsome tender annual deserves to be grown more in American gardens. The big, brilliant orange, single daisies have dark purple rings between the base of the petals and the large black centers. They resemble large gazania flowers, both in appearance and in their tendency to close at night. They bloom all summer long on bushy plants with attractive silvery foliage.

How to Grow. For earliest bloom, start seed indoors 6 to 8 weeks before the last frost in spring. The seed needs light to germinate, so scatter it on the surface of the planting medium. Keep the medium moist by covering the trays or pots with glass or clear plastic until seedlings appear. Transplant hardened-off seedlings to the garden when the danger of frost has passed. You can also sow seed directly in the garden after all danger of frost. Bedding plants are generally not available at garden centers.

Cape daisy prefers rich, well-drained soil in full sun. The plants thrive in hot, dry conditions and are rarely bothered by pests and diseases. They are practically trouble-free once they are established in the garden.

Uses. Cape daisy is striking in beds, borders, and containers.

Verbena spp.
ver-BEE-nuh. Verbena. Half-hardy annual.
○ ⚘ 🐛 ▼

Characteristics. Height: 6 inches to 4 feet. Colors: Blue, pink, purple, red, apricot, salmon, and white.

Verbena X *hybrida* is a popular, low-growing bedding annual with bright clusters of dainty blooms that resemble primrose flowers. They come in a wide range of colors, including blue and purple shades, Valentine's Day red, all shades of pink, and white. Some cultivars bloom in solid colors; others have a gleaming white "eye" in the center of each flower. 'Peaches & Cream' is a recent All-America Selections winner that offers a subtle blend of blush and apricot shades—unique colors for verbena. The color is breathtaking when placed next to deep purple or blue flowers.

Another new annual verbena All-America Selections winner is *V.* X *speciosa* 'Imagination'. This is a spreading type that can grow 2 feet tall, with intense violet-blue flower clusters on long stems. The foliage is feathery, almost like asparagus fern. This annual looks stunning cascading out of window boxes and hanging baskets.

V. bonariensis is a lesser-known verbena that is really a tender perennial grown as an annual. It grows 2 to 4 feet tall and has very long stems topped

Verbena X *hybrida* 'Springtime Mixed'

Verbena bonariensis

with flattish clusters of violet-blue flowers. Even with its long stems, it never needs staking. *V. bonariensis* is not as easy to site in the garden as the other annual verbenas, as it can look gawky and insignificant unless planted in masses. It often reseeds, producing seedlings that can pop up in unexpected locations; leave these alone if they look right, or move them to a more pleasing location in spring. The plants may also overwinter in areas with mild winters.

How to Grow. Verbenas take a long time to bloom from seed. To get an earlier start, sow the seed indoors 10 to 12 weeks before the last spring frost. The seed needs light to germinate, so just scatter it over the surface of the planting medium. Keep the medium moist by covering the trays or pots with glass or clear plastic until seedlings appear. Transplant hardened-off seedlings to the garden when the danger of frost has passed. Bedding plants of *V. X hybrida* are readily available at garden centers; plants of the other verbena species are less commonly available.

These annuals prefer rich, well-drained, sandy soil and full sun. They do not perform well in wet or heavy soil; take care not to overwater them. Deadhead periodically to prolong the bloom season. The plants are susceptible to spider mites in very dry weather, but are rarely bothered by other pests and diseases. In general, verbenas require little maintenance once they are established in the garden.

Uses. *V. X hybrida* is popular for beds, borders, edgings, rock gardens, and window boxes and other containers. The fragrant flowers are delightful for small bouquets. *V. X speciosa* is ideal for containers, beds, and borders; it's also great as an annual groundcover. *V. bonariensis* works well as an accent in mixed borders.

VINCA. See *Catharanthus roseus*

Viola X *wittrockiana*

ed by a border of white. 'Padparadja' is a very striking, brilliant, solid orange, named after a famous orange sapphire of Sri Lanka. It has a longer bloom period than other pansies and is tolerant of summer heat.

How to Grow. For spring bloom, sow the seed indoors—covered with a thin layer of planting medium—in December or January, and transplant the hardened-off seedlings to the garden after the last heavy frost. Or sow seed in midsummer in a sheltered location in the garden, and move the seedlings in fall to their spring-blooming locations. In areas with mild winters, you can sow pansies in the fall for flowers the following spring. Pansies are commonly available as bedding plants at garden centers in early spring.

For fall-blooming pansies, sow seed in early summer in a protected garden area, and move the plants to their blooming locations in early fall. Or transplant spring-blooming plants to a sheltered location in early summer, and move them back to the garden in early fall.

Pansies prefer cool, moist soil and partial shade or full sun. They are seldom bothered by pests and diseases, and require very little maintenance once they are established in the garden. If slugs are a problem, control them with diatomaceous earth or slug bait.

Uses. Pansies are perfect for cool-season color in beds, borders, rock gardens, and edgings. They

Viola X wittrockiana

vy-OH-luh wit-rok-ee-AY-nuh.
Pansy. Hardy annual or biennial.

○ ◑ ❄ ⚶❀ ▼

Characteristics. Height: 6 to 7 inches. Colors: Blue, pink, purple, red, orange, and white.

Pansies are practically synonymous with spring. They are classic companions for early bulbs, such as tulips and daffodils, in beds or window boxes. But spring isn't the only time you can enjoy them. These cool-loving plants are also valuable for fall bloom.

Pansies are available in a wide array of colors, many with the familiar faces and whiskers we remember so well from childhood. 'Maxim Marina' is a rare sky blue with dark blue blotches surround-

are also delightful in small bouquets as well as patio containers and window boxes.

WAX BEGONIA. See *Begonia* X *semperflorens*

Xeranthemum annuum

zer-ANN-the-mum ANN-yew-um.
Immortelle. Tender annual.

○ ✄ ❀ ▼

Characteristics. Height: 2 to 3 feet. Colors: Pink, red, and white.

Like strawflower, immortelle is grown for its silky-textured, daisylike flowers, which are easy to dry for everlasting arrangements. The 1½-inch-wide flowers come in double and semidouble forms. They bloom on 2- to 3-foot plants for a relatively short period of several weeks in summer.

How to Grow. For earliest bloom, start seed indoors 6 to 8 weeks before the last frost in spring. The seed needs light to germinate, so just scatter it on the surface of the planting medium. Keep the medium moist by covering the trays or pots with glass or clear plastic until seedlings appear. Transplant hardened-off seedlings to the garden when all danger of frost has passed. Or sow seed directly in the garden after all danger of frost in spring. Bedding plants are not generally available at garden centers.

Immortelle prefers sandy, fertile soil in full sun. It may need extra watering during extended dry periods in summer. The plants are rarely bothered by pests and diseases, and require little care once they are established in the garden.

Uses. Immortelle is primarily grown for dried flowers; try just-picked blooms in fresh bouquets, too. The flowers are also attractive in beds, borders, and large containers.

Zinnia spp.

ZIN-ee-uh. Zinnia. Tender annual.

○ ✳ ✄ ▼

Characteristics. Height: 6 to 36 inches. Colors: Pink, red, orange, yellow, green, and white.

Zinnia angustifolia

As symbols of summertime, zinnias are rivaled only by marigolds. They bloom nonstop from midsummer to the first frost in fall, creating cheerful masses of color in the garden and providing cut flowers for the house all summer long.

Zinnia elegans is the zinnia grown most often in American gardens. The single, semidouble, or double flowers come in bold shades of pink, magenta, orange, yellow, and white, in both solid colors and bicolors. They range from quilled "cactus" types to ruffled and semiruffled "dahlia-type" flowers. The well-branched plants are fairly stiff and upright, and usually behave well in the garden. However, the tall cultivars can topple dramatically during summer storms, uprooting themselves and sometimes their neighbors. (Staking is the key to preventing this problem!)

Many cultivars of this garden favorite are available. 'Envy' is a fascinating green-flowered cultivar. 'Candy Cane Mixed' has pink, rose, and cherry stripes on gold flowers, which are also flecked with orange. 'Firecracker' has big double blooms with

Zinnia elegans

Zinnia 'Pinwheel Series'

twisted, yellow-tipped petals, which really do look like exploding firecrackers.

Z. *angustifolia*, also known as Z. *linearis*, is a narrow-leafed zinnia with daisylike flowers in shades of yellow, orange, and white, all with orange centers. The single flowers grow 1 to 2 inches across. The graceful plants are quite different in texture from Z. *elegans*, and have a looser, more informal look. They tend to sprawl gently on the ground, often rooting along the stems. They cascade elegantly from window boxes and patio containers, and can even be used as an annual groundcover.

Z. *angustifolia* has been gaining in popularity since Burpee's introduction of 'Star White', a welcome new color that has made this species easier to combine with other plants. (The original orange does, however, make a striking display with blues or purples.) One of the best things about Z. *angustifolia*

is that it is resistant to the two scourges of zinnias: powdery mildew and alternaria. It also tolerates more shade, heat, and drought than Z. *elegans*, and tends to self-sow. In addition, the plants do not seem to require as much deadheading as Z. *elegans*.

The 'Pinwheel' series, developed by Burpee, is a cross between these two species, combining the larger flower size of Z. *elegans* with the mildew resistance and single flower form of Z. *angustifolia*. These cultivars are available in cherry, orange, rose, salmon, and white.

How to Grow. Sow seed directly in the garden after all danger of frost. Or, for earlier bloom, start seed indoors 6 to 8 weeks before the last frost. Sow seed ¼ inch deep. Transplant hardened-off seedlings to the garden when all danger of frost has passed. Bedding plants are sometimes available at garden centers.

Zinnias are obliging, easy-care plants that tolerate a wide range of soil conditions. They do, however, grow best in fertile, well-drained soil in full sun. Constant deadheading is a must for all cultivars of Z. *elegans*. (Frequently cutting flowers for fresh arrangements serves the same purpose and is much more fun.) Taller cultivars need staking to stay upright. But if you neglect to stake your plants and they sprawl, don't despair! Zinnias have the ability to send out roots along stem that are in contact with the soil, which in turn enables them to fill empty spots in beds and borders without your help. You can even encourage this process by pinning stems to the ground with hairpins or padded wire to keep them in contact with the soil.

Zinnias are susceptible to two fungal diseases: powdery mildew, which causes powdery white patches on the leaves; and alternaria, which causes leaf spots. Space the plants generously to allow for good air circulation around the leaves, and pinch off any infected leaves as you spot them. In areas with humid summers, it is almost impossible to avoid these two diseases, but fortunately, they do not tend to attack plants until fairly late in the summer. If these diseases are a yearly problem in your garden, try growing Z. *angustifolia* or the 'Pinwheel' series. Japanese beetles can be a problem in July in areas where they thrive; unfortunately, there are no easy controls.

Uses. Zinnias are prized for beds, borders, edgings, floral hedges, containers, cutting gardens, and cottage gardens. They are perhaps at their best in mass plantings. Zinnias are excellent flowers for children to grow, since the large seeds are easy to handle and the flowers are reliably colorful. Z. *angustifolia* looks at home in wildflower meadows.

OVERFLOWING WITH COLOR. *Perennials and annuals can be combined to create a garden with nonstop color. Gloriosa and Shasta daisies, foxgloves, annual phlox* (Phlox drummondii)*, and pot marigolds* (Calendula officinalis) *provide a colorful show in this garden.*

CHAPTER FOUR

PERENNIALS

Gardeners have been growing and enjoying peonies, irises, primroses, pinks, and many other delightful perennials for hundreds of years, and with good reason. With a little care, these beautiful, dependable plants return year after year to show off their stunning flowers and fabulous foliage. Plus, it's easy to find the perfect plant for virtually any site, since perennials come in an incredible array of colors, shapes, sizes, and bloom times. In this chapter, you'll discover dozens of exciting perennials, along with inspiring ideas for including them in every part of your yard.

WHAT IS A PERENNIAL?

Before you start choosing your perennials, it's helpful to understand some of the lingo associated with them. A perennial is any plant that can live for more than two years. Technically, this includes woody-stemmed plants, such as trees, shrubs, and many vines. Sometimes the term "herbaceous perennial" is used to differentiate the soft-stemmed perennials from those that have long-lived woody stems. In most cases, though, gardeners simply call

MIX AND MATCH PERENNIALS. *Combining perennials to create effective beds and borders is challenging and fun. This garden features lush color, shape, and texture provided by garden phlox, purple coneflowers, pink yarrow, white spiked speedwell (Veronica 'Icicle'), and purple-blue mealy-cup sage (Salvia farinacea), a tender perennial often grown as an annual.*

daylilies, phlox, asters, and other plants that die back to the ground each year "perennials."

While all perennials have the ability to grow and bloom for several years, they can't all persist in every climate. Some— including petunias, impatiens, and wax begonias—can only survive from year to year where winter temperatures stay above freezing. In most areas of the country, these tender perennials are grown as annuals. (That's why you'll find these and other tender perennials covered in Chapter 3 of this book.) The perennials discussed in this chapter are called hardy perennials, since they can send up new shoots from their roots even after their tops have been killed by frost.

All hardy perennials can survive frost. However, the amount of winter cold they can tolerate varies. That's why descriptions of hardy perennials indicate a range of hardiness zones (such as "Zones 5 to 9"). These ranges correspond to the USDA Plant Hardiness Zone Map, which divides the country into 11 zones based on average winter low temperatures. The hardiness range does not account for hot temperatures in summer, summer night temperatures, rainfall, or other climatic factors that can affect how well a certain perennial will grow in a given area. But this information can at least help you narrow your plant choices to those that should thrive in your climate. If you don't know what har-

PERENNIAL GROUNDCOVERS. *Many perennials make effective, weed-smothering groundcovers. In this garden,* Geranium macrorrhizum *provides a river of colorful blooms between a clump of Siberian iris foliage and azaleas. Plant groundcovering perennials in masses, as shown here, or combine several equally vigorous plants to create a unique carpet of color.*

diness zone you live in, check the USDA Plant Hardiness Zone Map on page 407.

WHY GROW PERENNIALS?

It's hard to imagine planning a garden without perennials. And who would want to, when these versatile plants have so much to offer? For just a few dollars, you can buy perennials that will return to grace your garden year after year, without your having to hassle with buying and planting new stock every spring. While the initial cost of a perennial plant is higher than that of an annual bedding plant, you get a greater return on your money, since

you get to enjoy the perennial for many seasons. Plus, your perennials will grow larger over time, and you can divide most of them every few years. Each time you divide a perennial, you end up with two or more new plants. Suddenly, your initial investment has yielded dividends! You can start another perennial planting for free, or trade perennials with your gardening friends.

Of course, the benefits of perennials aren't just financial. These plants also offer a wealth of exciting design possibilities. While the bloom time of perennials is generally shorter than that of annuals—three to five weeks for many perennials, versus three to five months for many annuals—grouping

COLORFUL COMPANIONS. *Golden star* (Chrysogonum virginianum), *a low-growing ground-cover, makes an appealing companion in a lightly shaded spot with starry-flowered Serbian bellflower* (Campanula poscharskyana).

DON'T FORGET VINES. *For added interest and excitement, experiment with vines in perennial plantings. Here,* Clematis X jackmanii *trails happily over* Geranium endressii.

perennials with different bloom times can give you a continually changing display from spring until the first frost in autumn. Some perennials shoot up quickly at the beginning of the season, bloom in spring, and then die back to make room for slower-growing later bloomers. During the summer, a wealth of perennials fills beds and borders with spiky and bushy foliage and dramatic flowers. The show continues well into fall with colorful late-flowering perennials.

Since perennials bloom at different times, you can choose plants in several different colors to change the look of your garden through the seasons. For instance, you might plan to have pinks and yellows for spring, blues and whites for summer, and yellows and oranges for fall. You just can't get this kind of versatility with a single planting of annuals!

Another benefit of perennials is that many have attractive foliage, form, and texture, so they are beautiful even when they aren't in bloom. In fact, some have such lovely leaves that they are grown more for the foliage than for the flowers. Hostas, for example, come in an astounding array of leaf colors, textures, and patterns that can add excitement to any shady garden. Artemisias produce mounds of silvery leaves that are a perfect complement to the green foliage and colorful flowers of plants growing nearby. After blooming in early summer, blue starflower (*Amsonia tabernaemontana*) forms shrubby mounds of willowlike, green leaves that turn a fiery yellow-orange in fall. Special features like these give many perennials multiseason interest.

Alone or mixed with annuals, bulbs, herbs, roses, shrubs, and grasses, perennials are perfect for filling beds and borders. Many of these adaptable plants also look great in containers. Some are ideal for cutting or drying, too, so be sure to make some space for them in your cutting garden as well.

PLANT PORTRAITS

The perennials described in the following plant portraits were selected for their superior garden performance, popularity, versatility, ease of care, and long season of interest. Also included are a few particularly beautiful perennials that are worth the extra-special care they need to thrive. You can find all of these perennials—either seed or plants—in mail-order catalogs or at local nurseries and garden centers.

The plants are listed by their botanical names, which appear in bold type. These names are recognized all over the world, while common names often vary from region to region. The best-known common name or names are also included at the beginning of each entry.

Since botanical names can be intimidating to pronounce, pronunciations are provided under the entry names. You'll also find the common name or names of the plant, its main season of interest (generally, when it blooms), and its hardiness zones. In addition, each entry includes a description of the plant, including its height and color, along with growing guidelines and suggested garden uses. With all this information at your fingertips, you're sure to get great results from your perennial plantings!

GROWING TIPS AT A GLANCE

Each of the following plant portraits includes simple symbols to highlight special features you need to know about each perennial. If you're not sure what any of the symbols mean, refer back to this key.

- ○ Full sun (more than 6 hours of sun a day; ideally all day)
- ◑ Partial sun (some direct sun, but less than 6 hours a day)
- ● Shade (no direct sun)
- ✳ Drought-tolerant
- ❄ Prefers cool temperatures
- ✄❀ Good as a cut flower
- ❀ Good as a dried flower or seedpod
- ❦ Fragrant
- ▼ Grows well in containers

Achillea spp.
ah-KILL-ee-uh. Yarrow, sneezewort.
Summer. Zones 3 to 9.
○ ✳ ✄❀ ❀ ❦ ▼

Characteristics. Height: 2 to 5 feet. Colors: Yellow, bronze, pink, lilac, red, and white.

Yarrow has showy, flat, disklike flower clusters

Achillea millefolium

Achillea 'Coronation Gold'
with *Geranium sanguineum*

and finely divided, ferny foliage. Several species are commonly grown in gardens. Common yarrow (*Achillea millefolium*) features masses of pink, red, bronze, or white flower clusters on low-growing plants with feathery foliage. The plants have a tendency to sprawl, especially in hot summer weather, and they spread quickly. They are attractive in the front of the border and in patio containers. The All-America Selections winner 'Summer Pastels' blooms the first year from seed and comes in a wide range of antique-looking pastel colors, including rose, lavender, bronze, red, yellow, and white.

Fernleaf yarrow (*A. filipendulina*) comes in shades of yellow or gold on tall, strong plants with ferny, gray-green foliage. 'Gold Plate' grows to 5 feet tall and has deep yellow flower heads. 'Moonshine' is a hybrid with remarkably beautiful, creamy primrose-yellow flower heads; the 2-foot-tall plants have attractive, silvery gray foliage. 'Coronation Gold', one of the most popular hybrids, offers deep yellow flower heads and gray-green foliage on sturdy, 3-foot plants, which never need staking.

Sneezewort (*A. ptarmica* 'The Pearl') has a sprawling habit and masses of dainty, double white flowers reminiscent of baby's breath. The green foliage is narrow and airy, but not divided—very different from that of other yarrows.

How to Grow. Yarrow species and some cultivars will grow from seed sown in midsummer and bloom the following summer. Sow seed directly in a protected area of the garden. Move the young plants to their permanent locations in fall or early spring. 'Summer Pastels' blooms the first year from seed sown indoors 8 to 10 weeks before the last frost date. Cultivars are readily available as plants from garden centers and by mail-order.

Yarrows are vigorous growers and benefit from being divided every 2 or 3 years in spring or fall. The stems are often strong enough to be self-supporting, but taller cultivars may need staking. The plants are drought-resistant and rarely troubled by pests or diseases. Once they are established in the garden, they are trouble-free.

Uses. These long-blooming, easy-to-grow perennials are popular for both formal borders and informal cottage gardens. They also make ideal fresh cut or dried flowers. Shorter cultivars are suitable for patio containers. Taller cultivars look at home in wildflower meadows.

Alcea rosea
AL-see-uh ROH-zee-uh. Hollyhock.
Summer. Zones 4 to 8.
○

Characteristics. Height: 6 to 10 feet. Colors: Pink, red, yellow, purple, white, and black.

These stately, old-fashioned favorites have the remarkable ability to evoke memories of visiting country relatives in summer—even if you never had any! Names such as 'Old Farmyard' conjure up images of neglected stands of hollyhocks coming back year after year in front of an old barn wall, or against a farmhouse in need of new paint. While some hollyhock plants can survive for many years, they are usually described as short-lived perennials. Since hollyhocks can bloom quickly from seed, they can even be grown as annuals or biennials.

Hollyhocks are related to hibiscus and have the

Alcea rosea

same flower form, with large, overlapping petals and a long, narrow column of fused reproductive parts in the center. The flowers bloom on tall spikes on big plants with large, rounded leaves. Single-, semidouble-, and double-flowered forms are available. The more old-fashioned-looking single-flowered types were once very difficult to find, but are becoming popular again.

These perennials are susceptible to several serious pest and disease problems, including rust and mites. People who love hollyhocks grow them in spite of these problems, since no other plant can take their place in the garden or in the heart.

How to Grow. Hollyhocks are easy to grow from seed sown indoors 8 weeks before the last frost date. To aid germination, soak the seeds overnight. They need light to germinate, so just press them lightly into the surface of the planting medium. Transplant hardened-off seedlings to the garden when the danger of frost has passed. Hollyhock plants are sometimes sold at garden centers.

The plants prefer a well-drained, moist soil enriched with plenty of organic matter. They do best in full sun, and may need staking in exposed locations.

Uses. Hollyhocks provide dramatic screening when planted along a fence or wall. They are also excellent plants for the back of the border. Hollyhocks always make a statement planted as a garden accent.

Alchemilla mollis
al-kuh-MILL-uh MOL-iss. Lady's-mantle.
Early summer. Zones 4 to 7.

Characteristics. Height: 18 to 24 inches. Colors: Greenish yellow.

This striking perennial features clouds of tiny flowers that are held above lobed, light green leaves. The flowers bloom for several weeks in June and often grow so heavy that they fall back and rest on the foliage. They are a very unusual shade of chartreuse, which blends beautifully with pinks and deep purples in flower borders. The leaves have an undulating, pleated look and are covered with tiny hairs that catch and hold water droplets, giving them a fresh look after a rainfall. (Unfortunately, their tendency to hold moisture can cause plants to rot,

Alchemilla mollis
with *Thymus serpyllum*

especially in areas with hot, humid summers.) The foliage is so attractive that lady's-mantle is often used as a leafy groundcover.

How to Grow. Start with purchased plants, which are available from garden centers and through mail-order catalogs.

This charming perennial prefers cool, moist, rich soil in partial shade or full sun. It tolerates more light in cooler areas; partial shade is important in warmer regions. Divide crowded plants in spring or fall. Lady's-mantle is rarely bothered by pests or diseases.

Uses. Grow lady's-mantle as a spring-to-fall groundcover or as an edging for beds and borders. It also looks great in woodland gardens. The blooms make interesting and attractive filler flowers in cut flower arrangements.

Amsonia tabernaemontana

am-SOH-nee-uh tay-ber-nee-mon-TAN-uh.
Blue starflower. Early summer. Zones 3 to 9.

Characteristics. Height: 2 feet. Colors: Light blue.

This reliable, easy-to-grow plant isn't grown often enough in American perennial gardens. The well-behaved, 2-foot-tall, bushy mounds have handsome, willowlike leaves. The leaves are attractive in the border all season, but are especially eye-catching when they turn fiery yellow-orange in the fall. The plants bloom in June, with pretty balls of star-shaped, steel blue flowers.

Amsonia tabernaemontana

How to Grow. To raise your own plants, sow seed in midsummer directly in a protected area of the garden. Move the young plants to their permanent locations in fall or early spring. If you prefer, you can purchase plants of blue starflower, which are available at some garden centers and through mail-order catalogs.

The plants prefer a moist, well-drained soil enriched with plenty of organic matter. They perform best in full sun but can tolerate light shade; in too much shade, they grow tall and leggy. Cut the plants back by one-third after flowering, to encourage neater, more compact growth. Clumps can live for many years without division, but you can divide them in spring or fall for propagation. Blue starflower is rarely bothered by pests and diseases, and is easy to maintain through the season.

Uses. Blue starflower is a handsome plant for the middle of the border. It is one of the few herbaceous perennials that can be grown for its fall color alone. The flowers are good for cutting.

Anchusa azurea

Anchusa azurea

an-KOO-suh ay-ZER-ee-uh. Italian alkanet.
Late spring to early summer. Zones 4 to 8.

Characteristics. Height: 18 inches to 5 feet.
Colors: Deep blue or purple.

Italian alkanet is a large, rough-textured perennial with broad, hairy leaves and great quantities of unforgettable, deep blue to purple flower clusters. For several weeks in late spring to early summer, the flowers become focal points in the garden, creating a haze of regal blue that beautifully complements neighboring pinks, silvers, or whites. The older, taller cultivars require staking to prevent them from flopping on lower companions. However, better-behaved, lower-growing cultivars have been developed, including the popular 3-foot-tall 'Loddon Royalist'. 'Little John' grows only 18 inches tall.

How to Grow. To raise your own plants, sow seed of the species directly in a protected area of the garden in midsummer. Move the young plants to their permanent locations in fall or early spring. Cultivars are also available as plants from mail-order nurseries.

Italian alkanet requires well-drained soil and a sunny to lightly shaded location. Avoid overfertilizing, as it can lead to spindly plants that do not bloom well. The plants tend to be short-lived, surviving only about 3 years, but usually self-sow reliably. They generally do not live long enough to require division. Tall cultivars need staking.

Uses. Italian alkanet makes a striking accent plant for the middle or back of the border. The flowers are good for cutting.

Anemone X hybrida

ah-NEM-on-ee HY-brih-duh.
Japanese anemone. Fall. Zones 5 to 8.

Characteristics. Height: 2 to 4 feet. Colors: Pink or white.

Graceful Japanese anemones add elegance to perennial gardens, woodland plantings, and shrub borders in fall, when tired summer plantings are

Anemone X hybrida

just beginning to revive for their end-of-the-season show. The blooms resemble fully open poppy flowers, on long, waving stems that seem to be constantly in motion. They are available in single-, semidouble, and double-flowered forms, in shades ranging from deep rose to shell pink to white. 'Alba' offers pristine white, single flowers on 2-foot plants. 'Margarete' has deep rose, semidouble flowers that contrast beautifully with blue asters. 'Queen Charlotte' bears semidouble flowers in a lovely, gentle pink.

How to Grow. Japanese anemones are usually grown from purchased plants. They are available from mail-order catalogs and at some garden centers.

The plants grow best in rich, well-drained, moist soil and partial shade or full sun. They may need extra watering in dry conditions. They are relatively slow to mature and may take 2 or 3 years to bloom. Deadheading will prolong their blooming period. In northern areas, Japanese anemones need a protective winter mulch. If you want to propagate clumps, divide them or take root cuttings in spring.

Uses. Japanese anemones are wonderful in the back of the perennial border. They are perfect companions for asters and Kamchatka bugbane (*Cimicifuga simplex*). Japanese anemones also naturalize well in woodlands. The flowers are good for cutting.

Aquilegia canadensis

Aquilegia spp.
ak-will-EE-jee-uh. Columbine.
Spring. Zones 3 to 8.
○ ◑ ✿ ✿ ❦ ▼

Characteristics. Height: 2 to 3 feet. Colors: Blue, purple, pink, yellow, red, white, and bicolors.

Columbines are among the most welcome flowers of spring. The flowers always look perfect, with long, narrow sepals and cup-shaped petals, often in a contrasting color. Many cultivars have long, elegant spurs; others have shorter, inward-curving spurs; and some have no spurs at all. The green or gray-green foliage is deeply lobed and attractive enough to make a lightly textured groundcover even when the plants are not in bloom. When columbines are planted in the open, their long stems sway in the wind, making the delicate flowers look as though they are constantly in motion.

Wild columbine (*Aquilegia canadensis*) is a native American wildflower with small red-and-yellow flowers that bloom for up to 6 weeks in May and June. The plants require little assistance in the garden, taking good care of themselves and self-sowing where they are happy. They are ideal for naturalizing in woodlands or wildflower meadows, and make charming cut flowers.

Hybrid columbines (*A.* X *hybrida*) offer large flowers (up to 3½ inches across) in a wide range of solid colors and bicolors, on plants of various heights. The bright color combinations and intri-

cate flower shapes are reminiscent of a jester's hat, as the name of one series, 'Harlequin', suggests. The 'Songbird' series features extra-large flowers on compact plants that look great in containers.

How to Grow. These short-lived perennials are easy to grow from seed. The seeds germinate best when they are chilled for 3 to 4 weeks at 40°F. Sow the seed in pots or trays, chill them, then set the containers outdoors for the summer. Or sow directly in the garden in a protected area in midsummer. Move the young plants to their final locations in fall or early spring. The plants also self-sow reliably where they are happy; move the seedlings in summer or early spring to where you want plants to grow. Remember that seedlings from hybrid cultivars will probably not resemble their parents; buy new hybrid seed if you want to duplicate these plants. Columbine plants are available at garden centers and through mail-order catalogs.

Columbines prefer moist, well-drained soil in full sun or partial shade. Taller cultivars may require staking. Don't deadhead unless you want to eliminate self-sown seedlings. Mature plants resent transplanting and division; grow new plants from seed. Columbines are highly susceptible to leafminers, which cause squiggly lines to appear just below the surface of the leaf. Leafminers do not kill the plant, but they do make the foliage unsightly. Remove and destroy severely affected foliage.

Uses. Columbines are lovely for borders and excellent for naturalizing in woodlands. The blooms make good cut flowers, and the seedpods make interesting additions to dried arrangements. Compact cultivars can be grown in containers.

Aquilegia X *hybrida*

Artemisia ludoviciana 'Silver King'

Artemisia spp.

ar-teh-MEEZ-ee-uh. Artemisia.
Spring through fall. Zones 5 to 8.

Characteristics. Height: 1 to 3 feet. Colors: Silver foliage.

In the perennial garden, artemisias are grown mostly for their fragrant, finely cut silver foliage. The silver color blends well with many colors in the border, especially deep pinks, blues, and purples. Artemisia is also an important companion plant for white flowers in all-white color schemes.

Three types of artemisia are popular in American perennial gardens. 'Silver King' artemisia (*Artemisia ludoviciana* 'Silver King') grows 2 to 3 feet tall and has finely cut, silvery leaves. It can be quite invasive, especially in light, sandy soil. Some gardeners plant it in bottomless containers sunk in the ground to the rim to prevent it from creeping out of bounds. The spreading runners are easy to pull out, but this can disturb neighboring plants. The foliage of 'Silver King' is valuable in arrangements.

Silvermound artemisia (*A. schmidtiana* 'Silver Mound') is a low-growing type, reaching only 12 inches tall with an 18-inch spread. It has more finely cut foliage than 'Silver King' and is not invasive. It works well as an edging or in the front of the border, especially in areas with cool summers.

'Powis Castle' artemisia (*A. X* 'Powis Castle') is a hybrid of *A. absinthium* and *A. arborescens*. It is wonderfully well behaved in borders, staying where you put it and looking splendid all season, with aro-

matic, feathery foliage. In areas south of Zone 6, its stems tend to become woody, making it look like a gnarled, low-growing shrub. If this look doesn't appeal to you, renew the plants by cutting them back in spring and allowing new growth to come up from the ground. Farther north, plants tend to die back to the ground each winter.

How to Grow. Artemisias are usually grown from purchased plants. These three cultivars are readily available at nurseries and garden centers, and through mail-order catalogs. You can also propagate them by taking cuttings in spring.

The plants grow best in well-drained, sandy soil in full sun. They can tolerate partial shade but will grow leggy in too much shade. 'Silver King' artemisia may need staking to look neat. To encourage bushiness in all three types, pinch the plants in late spring to early summer. Use the pinched-off pieces as cuttings to propagate new plants. You can also divide 'Silver King' in spring or fall. Like many silver-leaved plants, artemisias are subject to root and foliage rot diseases, especially in areas with hot, humid summers.

Uses. These perennials are great as filler plants for borders and herb gardens. Silvermound artemisia is attractive as an edging. Artemisia foliage is excellent for cutting.

Aruncus spp.

ah-RUN-kus. Goatsbeard.
Summer. Zones 4 to 7.

Characteristics. Height: 1 to 6 feet. Colors: White.

Goatsbeard (*Aruncus dioicus*) is a large, shrubby perennial that resembles a giant astilbe. It produces airy clusters of creamy white flowers in June and July on sturdy plants that never need staking. The divided, ferny foliage is attractive all season.

Korean goatsbeard (*A. aethusifolius*) is a miniature version of *A. dioicus*. The foliage has the same ferny look as that of a dwarf astilbe. However, the flowers of Korean goatsbeard are loose and airy, not stiff and upright like those of astilbe. This perennial makes a terrific woodland groundcover or specimen plant in a shady part of a rock garden.

How to Grow. To raise your own plants, sow seed directly in a protected area of the garden in

Aruncus dioicus 'Plumosus'

Asclepias tuberosa

midsummer. Move the young plants to their permanent locations in fall or early spring. Plants of *A. dioicus* are readily available through mail-order and from some garden centers. *A. aethusifolius* is somewhat more difficult to locate but is worth the search.

Goatsbeards prefer cool, moist, well-drained soil with added organic matter. They do best in partial shade or full sun. In full sun, steady moisture is especially important. Divide for propagation in fall, or leave the plants alone to form large, showy clumps. The plants do not need staking and are rarely bothered by pests and diseases. They are very easy to care for when they are in the right location.

Uses. *A. dioicus* makes a wonderful woodland specimen plant or background plant for the back of the border. *A. aethusifolius* is good for edgings, as a woodland groundcover, or in rock gardens. The flowers of both species are good for cutting and drying.

Asclepias tuberosa
as-KLEE-pee-us tew-ber-oh-suh. Butterfly weed.
Late spring to late summer. Zones 4 to 9.
○ ✳

Characteristics. Height: 1½ to 3 feet. Colors: Orange to reddish orange.

This perennial has been referred to as the "flower with wings." Butterfly weed *does* appear to have fluttering wings for petals, since its sweet nectar attracts many butterflies. A tough native American wildflower, it has oblong leaves, flattened to slightly domed flower clusters, and a rounded, upright,

clump-forming habit. It is easy to grow in most areas of the country and doesn't become invasive.

How to Grow. Butterfly weed thrives in full sun. It is not picky about soil, though it does not like soil that is waterlogged; if the soil is too wet, the roots will rot. The plants are generally pest- and disease-free, with the exception of problems with leaf spot or rusts. Watch for early signs, and pinch off any damaged leaves. Pinch off spent flowers to extend the bloom period.

Because butterfly weed has a long taproot, it is difficult to propagate by division. Seeds germinate readily indoors if you keep the temperature of the growing medium approximately 65° to 70°F. You can also sow the seed outdoors in the fall where you want the plants to grow. Plants are readily available through mail-order and from some garden centers.

Uses. Butterfly weed is ideal for sunny sites with dry, infertile soil. It looks great in borders and in wildflower meadows.

Aster spp.
AS-ter. Aster. Late summer through fall.
Zones 4 to 8.
○ ⚘ ▼

Characteristics. Height: 2 to 7 feet. Colors: Blue, purple, red, pink, and white.

Asters are second only to chrysanthemums in importance in the fall garden. These easy-to-grow plants bloom prolifically at a time when color is especially welcome in the garden.

New England aster (*Aster novae-angliae*) is one of the species most often grown in American gardens. It includes 4-foot-tall cultivars, as well as some neat dwarf types that fit well in the middle of the border. 'Alma Potschke' is a well-behaved, 3-foot cultivar with intense-but-not-quite-hot-pink flowers. 'Purple Dome' offers striking, regal purple flowers on compact plants that grow 2 feet tall and 3 feet wide.

The hybrid Frikart's aster (*A. X frikartii*) includes a number of cultivars noted for their early bloom, which starts in June and extends through July, sometimes returning in the fall. 'Wonder of Staffa' offers lavender-blue flowers on 2-foot plants. 'Monch' is considered one of the best garden perennials; its 2½-inch, lavender-blue flowers bloom for 4 months on 3-foot-tall plants.

One of the most dramatic asters you can grow is Tartarian aster (*A. tataricus*). It produces towering 7-foot stems that (amazingly) never need staking. The stems are topped with dome-shaped clusters of lavender-blue flowers for weeks in October, and even into November in areas with late-fall frosts. The plants look stately in the back of the border or in groups in a shrub border. The cut flowers last as long as those of any aster.

How to Grow. Asters are generally grown from purchased plants, which are readily available from nurseries and garden centers, and through mail-order catalogs.

Asters can tolerate a wide range of soil conditions but prefer good drainage. They generally grow best in full sun, although some cultivars can take light shade. Pinch New England asters twice before the fourth of July to encourage bushy growth. Tall asters, with the exception of Tartarian asters, need staking. Divide the plants every 2 to 3 years in the spring to keep them vigorous; discard the woody center and replant the younger side growth. Some cultivars are susceptible to powdery mildew; give the plants plenty of room for air circulation to help prevent a serious problem. Other than needing a little pinching and staking, asters are easy to grow and require little maintenance in the garden.

Uses. Asters are invaluable for fall color in borders and for naturalizing in wildflower meadows. Try tall cultivars as landscape accents and compact cultivars in containers. All asters make attractive, long-lasting cut flowers.

Astilbe spp.
ah-STILL-bee. Astilbe.
Early summer. Zones 3 to 8.

Characteristics. Height: 1 to 3½ feet. Colors: Pink, red, peach, purple, salmon, and white.

No perennial shade garden should be without

Aster novae-angliae 'Alma Potschke'

Astilbe X arendsii

Astilbe X *arendsii* 'Cattleya'

astilbe. The feathery flower plumes are as important a feature of the June garden as columbines, bleeding hearts, and hostas. Astilbes offer attractive ferny foliage and an abundance of showy flowers. They are long-lived and easy to grow in the shade. Clip the flowers for cutting or drying, or leave them on the plants for winter interest.

Astilbe X *arendsii* is the type most often grown in American gardens. These reliable hybrids bloom in June and July, and come in a wide range of colors and plant heights. 'Peach Blossom' grows to 2 feet and bears clear blush-pink, Christmas tree-shaped flower clusters. 'Ostrich Plume' is a bright salmon cultivar; the loose, arching plumes appear on 3½-foot-tall plants. 'Fanal' offers deep red blooms and bronze-red foliage on 2-foot plants.

A. chinensis 'Pumila' is a low-growing dwarf astilbe. It has a spreading habit and makes an ideal light-textured groundcover. The stiff, lavender-pink flower spikes bloom in July or August—later than most astilbes.

A. taquetii 'Superba' offers stiff, tight, lilac-pink flower clusters in July. The 4-foot-tall plants make a terrific landscape feature in summer, and the seed-pods provide winter interest.

How to Grow. To raise your own plants, sow seed of *A.* X *arendsii* directly in a protected area of the garden in midsummer. Move the young plants to their final locations in fall or early spring. Plants of astilbe hybrids and cultivars are commonly available at garden centers and through mail-order catalogs.

Astilbes must have moist, rich soil. The plants can tolerate sun, but only if the soil is moist; they are usually grown as partial-shade plants. They never require staking and only need to be divided every 4

or 5 years if they become overcrowded. For propagation, divide plants in early spring. Astilbes are rarely bothered by pests and diseases, and require very little maintenance once they are established in the right place in the garden.

Uses. Astilbes are showy plants for the middle of a shaded, moist-soil border. They naturalize well in woodlands. *A. chinensis* 'Pumila' makes an attractive groundcover from spring through fall. Astilbe flowers are good for fresh arrangements and also are attractive dried.

BABY'S BREATH. See *Gypsophila paniculata*
BALLOON FLOWER. See *Platycodon grandiflorus*

Baptisia australis
bap-TEE-zee-uh oss-TRAL-iss. False indigo.
Early summer. Zones 3 to 8.

Characteristics. Height: 4 to 6 feet. Colors: Blue.

This perennial member of the pea family was once grown in the southeastern United States as a substitute for indigo. Now it is grown across the country for its towering spikes of deep blue, pealike flowers, which add color to the back of the perennial border in June. The shrublike plants have blue-green, compound leaves. The foliage is attractive all season and adds a fine texture to the border when the plants are not in bloom. The flowers are followed by pealike seedpods, which you can leave on the plant for winter interest or cut for dried arrangements.

How to Grow. To raise your own plants, sow the seed in pots or trays in midsummer. Place the containers in the refrigerator for 6 weeks, then move them outdoors to sprout. Or sow seed directly in a protected area of the garden in midsummer. Move the young plants to their permanent locations in fall or early spring. Plants are also available at some garden centers and through mail-order catalogs.

Like other members of the pea family, false indigo grows well in low-fertility soil. It prefers full sun but tolerates light shade. The plants are long-lived and do not like to be moved once they are estab-

Baptisia australis

Begonia grandis

lished. They do not need to be divided regularly. The flower spikes generally need to be staked. Cut plants back by one-third after blooming to keep them neat.

Uses. False indigo is attractive at the back of the border or as an accent plant. The flowers are great for cutting, and the pods can be used in dried arrangements.

BARRENWORT. See *Epimedium* spp.
BEE BALM. See *Monarda didyma*

Begonia grandis
beh-GO-nee-uh GRAN-diss. Hardy begonia.
Late summer to fall. Zones 6 to 10.

Characteristics. Height: 2 to 3 feet. Colors: Pink or white.

Hardy begonia deserves to be grown more in American shade gardens. A sister to the familiar annual wax begonia, hardy begonia has larger green leaves and pendulous clusters of small heart-shaped pink buds that open into pink flowers. The flowers bloom from August through October. The plants are not as tightly mounded as wax begonias; instead, they are upright and spreading, like some of their tropical relatives, which are grown as houseplants. 'Alba' has white flowers.

How to Grow. Start your plantings of hardy begonia with purchased plants. They are available from some nurseries, garden centers, and mail-order catalogs. A friend with an established planting is also a good source.

Hardy begonias require rich soil that stays constantly moist. They prefer partial or full shade and cannot tolerate the hot afternoon sun. The plants produce small bulbils along their stems, which fall to the ground and grow into new plants. Once a stand is established, the plants are maintenance-free; all you need to do is keep them from spreading where you don't want them to go. Dig up extra plants and start a new bed, or share them with friends.

Uses. Grow hardy begonia in the middle of the border, as an edging, in a woodland, or as an accent. It also looks attractive in front of a shrub border. A mass planting makes a fascinating spring-to-fall groundcover. Hardy begonia emerges relatively late in spring, making it a perfect filler for spaces where spring-flowering bulbs have gone dormant.

Belamcanda chinensis

Belamcanda chinensis
bel-am-KAN-duh chih-NEN-sis. Blackberry lily.
Summer. Zones 5 to 10.

Characteristics. Height: 2 to 4 feet. Colors: Bright orange with spots of red, or yellow.

The flat, swordlike, clump-forming foliage of blackberry lily looks very similar to iris foliage and grows from creeping rhizomes. The summer flowers are usually about 2 inches across and are borne on stiff, upright, forked stems. 'Hellow Yellow' is a yellow-flowered cultivar. Several weeks after the plants bloom, the seed capsules split open to expose beautiful, shiny black, berrylike seeds.

How to Grow. Blackberry lily needs rich, moist, well-drained soil and full sun to grow to its maximum height. Mulch the plants over winter to keep their roots from being pushed out of the soil by alternating freezing and thawing.

If you allow the seed to drop naturally, the plants can self-sow. You can also collect the seed in autumn and store it in your refrigerator until spring. Sow seeds indoors in early spring, and keep the planting medium warm (about 80°F is ideal). The plants will bloom the following year. To propagate by division, dig up clumps carefully in spring and gently pull them apart. Replant the rhizomes at least 1 foot apart and about 2 inches deep. Plants are

sometimes available at garden centers and from mail-order firms.

Uses. The spotted flowers of blackberry lily lend an exotic feel to the garden. The irislike foliage is attractive in naturalized plantings. The seeds add ornamental value to the plant, and stems with seed capsules are lovely for winter flower arrangements.

BELLFLOWER. See *Campanula* spp.

Bergenia cordifolia
ber-GEN-ee-uh kor-dih-FOE-lee-uh. Heartleaf bergenia. Spring. Zones 3 to 8.

Characteristics. Height: 1 foot. Colors: Pink or white.

Heartleaf bergenia is a low-growing perennial planted mostly for its large, leathery, heart-shaped leaves. The leaves are dark green, often with a reddish tint; they sometimes develop a deeper red fall color. While the foliage is considered evergreen, it often has a worn look in winter. The pink or white flower clusters appear in spring, but in areas with cold spring weather, the flower buds may be killed and may never bloom.

How to Grow. Start with plants purchased from garden centers or through mail-order catalogs.

Heartleaf bergenia needs moisture-retentive soil

Bergenia cordifolia
with Rose 'The Fairy'

that's rich in organic matter. It prefers partial shade but can grow in full sun if the soil is kept moist. It is a great favorite of slugs, which can be controlled with diatomaceous earth or beer traps. Divide the plants in spring or fall when they begin to look sparse.

Uses. Heartleaf bergenia is good for the front of the border, as an edging, or as a groundcover in partial shade. It can be dramatic in mass plantings.

BLACKBERRY LILY. See *Belamcanda chinensis*
BLANKET FLOWER. See *Gaillardia* spp.
BLAZING STAR, PRAIRIE. See *Liatris pycnostachya*
BLEEDING HEART. See *Dicentra* spp.
BLUEBELLS, VIRGINIA. See *Mertensia virginica*

Boltonia asteroides
bowl-TONE-ee-uh as-ter-OY-deez. Boltonia.
Late summer. Zones 3 to 8.
○ ☀ ⚶❧

Characteristics. Height: 3 to 7 feet. Colors: White or pink.

As its species name indicates, boltonia closely resembles its relative, the aster. The tall plants have smooth, narrow, blue-green leaves and burst into bloom in late summer with masses of single, white daisies. (The effect is summed up by the cultivar name 'Snowbank'.) Boltonia blooms for several weeks, providing many flowers for cutting without losing any of the garden display. It has a neat upright habit, is easy to grow, and requires little care in the garden. It spreads quickly enough to give you extra plants every couple of years, but is not invasive.

The species is quite tall and difficult to manage in the perennial border, where it is usually out of proportion to the other plants. Improved cultivars are much better suited for the garden. 'Snowbank' grows only 3 to 4 feet tall and seldom needs staking. 'Pink Beauty' grows to 3 feet and has pretty pink flowers.

How to Grow. To raise your own plants, sow seed of the species directly in a protected area of the garden in midsummer. Move the young plants to their permanent locations in fall or early spring. Cultivars are easy to find as plants at garden centers and through mail-order catalogs.

Boltonias are tolerant of heat, humidity, and drought conditions. They grow well in most soil but prefer moist, rich, well-drained soil in full sun. They tolerate light shade but grow tall and leggy and will not bloom well in too much shade. To encourage bushiness, pinch the plants in spring when they are 6 inches tall. The species requires staking; cultivars need staking only if they are in exposed locations or in too much shade. Divide in spring for propagation. Boltonias are well behaved and are rarely bothered by pests or diseases.

Uses. Boltonia is a perfect plant for the back of the border for late-summer bloom. It can also be used as a background plant or garden accent. The blooms make long-lasting fresh-cut flowers.

Boltonia asteroides
with asters (*foreground*)

Brunnera macrophylla
BRUN-er-uh mak-roh-FILL-uh. Brunnera.
Spring. Zones 3 to 8.
○ ◑ ⚶❧

Characteristics. Height: 15 inches. Colors: Forget-me-not blue.

Brunnera is a fine spring-blooming perennial with exquisite forget-me-not flowers, which bloom for several weeks from April to May. The deep green, heart-shaped foliage is handsome all season. The plants self-sow reliably, providing plenty of

Brunnera macrophylla

seedlings each year to make your colony larger and still have extras to give to your friends and neighbors. 'Variegata' has large leaves that are edged in creamy white. The foliage of this cultivar is beautiful enough that you won't care if the plant blooms. Unfortunately, 'Variegata' does not spread quickly in areas with hot summers, and the foliage has a tendency to burn and turn brown in the sun or in dry conditions.

How to Grow. To raise your own plants, sow seed of the species directly in a protected area of the garden in midsummer. Move the young plants to their permanent locations in fall or early spring. Plants of the species and the cultivar 'Variegata' are not commonly available at garden centers, but you can often find them in mail-order catalogs.

Brunnera thrives in moist, rich soil with good drainage. It is at its best in partial shade but will tolerate sun if the soil is kept moist. The leaves tend to develop brown, crispy edges in hot, dry conditions. Slugs enjoy the large leaves; control these pests with diatomaceous earth or beer traps. Divide crowded clumps in spring or fall. The plants require little care other than moving self-sown seedlings to their new locations in early fall or spring.

Uses. Brunnera makes a fine edging plant or groundcover in partial shade. It thrives in a woodland setting. The tiny flowers can be cut for small bouquets.

BUGBANE. See *Cimicifuga* spp.
BUTTERFLY WEED. See *Asclepias tuberosa*

Campanula glomerata

Campanula spp.
kam-PAN-yew-luh. Bellflower.
Summer. Zones 3 to 8.

Characteristics. Height: 8 inches to 3½ feet. Colors: Blue, violet, and white.

Several species of bellflowers are commonly grown in American gardens. They all have pretty, bell-shaped flowers in shades of blue, purple, or white, produced either singly or in clusters along spikes. Carpathian bellflower (*Campanula carpatica*) is a popular low-growing species that is covered with blue or white blooms from June to July, then sporadically until September. It tends to be short-lived in the garden, especially in areas with hot summers.

Clustered bellflower (*C. glomerata*) bears clusters of small blue flowers on 1- to 3-foot stems from June to July. The flowers are excellent for cutting and have a vase life of up to 2 weeks. The plants are short-lived in the South, lasting only 3 years in the garden.

Peachleaf bellflower (*C. persicifolia*) grows from

1 to 3 feet tall, with elegant spikes of upturned, bell-shaped flowers in white, lavender, or blue. It is ideal for the middle of the border, and naturalizes well in woodlands. The flowers make beautiful, long-lasting cut flowers. Like clustered bellflower, this species tends to be short-lived in the South.

How to Grow. To raise your own plants, sow seed in a protected area of the garden in midsummer. Move the young plants to their permanent locations in fall or early spring. Plants are usually available at garden centers and through mail-order catalogs.

All bellflowers require excellent drainage. Carpathian bellflower and clustered bellflower are more tolerant of dry soil than peachleaf bellflower. The taller types prefer full sun and tolerate light shade; Carpathian bellflower prefers light shade but tolerates full sun if the soil is kept moist. Taller cultivars may require staking. To rejuvenate crowded clumps or to propagate, divide the plants in early spring. Pests and diseases are generally not a problem, though Carpathian bellflower may be bothered by slugs.

Uses. Bellflowers are reliable plants that serve many purposes in the garden. Carpathian bellflowers make attractive groundcovers, edgings, or rock-garden specimen plants. Clustered and peachleaf bellflowers are ideal for flower borders, cutting, or naturalizing in a woodland.

CANDYTUFT. See *Iberis sempervirens*
CARDINAL FLOWER. See *Lobelia* spp.
CATMINT. See *Nepeta* X *faassenii*

*Campanula persicifolia
with poppies and lupines*

Centaurea montana

Centaurea montana
sen-TAR-ee-uh mon-TAN-uh. Mountain bluet.
Early summer. Zones 3 to 8.

Characteristics. Height: 2 feet. Colors: Blue.

This relative of the annual cornflower, or bachelor's buttons, bears spidery flowers that appear for several weeks in May and June. They are a gorgeous shade of deep blue with a hint of a red center. Mountain bluets make good companions for silver-leaved plants, such as artemisias and lamb's ears (*Stachys byzantina*), as well as white- or pink-flowered perennials. The handsome foliage is smooth and narrow, and is attractive even without the flowers. The scaled flower buds look like large versions of those of bachelor's buttons. The plants can have a second bloom period in mid- to late summer if you cut them back after the first flush of bloom in spring.

How to Grow. To raise your own plants, sow seed directly in a protected spot in the garden in midsummer. Move the young plants to their final locations in fall or early spring. Plants are not always available at garden centers, but you can usually find them through mail-order catalogs.

Mountain bluet grows best in poor, well-drained soil in full sun or light shade. The foliage declines rather quickly after the flowers bloom, so cut it back as soon as new growth appears at the base for a second flush of leaves. The plants can spread quickly and have been called invasive, especially in the North. If you want even more plants, divide existing plants in spring or start new ones from seed. Mountain bluets are rarely bothered by pests and diseases, and require little maintenance in the garden other than the yearly haircut.

Uses. Mountain bluet is excellent for the front of the border, where it is valued for the rare, intense blue color of its flowers. The blooms are also good for cutting.

CHRISTMAS ROSE. See *Helleborus* spp.

Chrysanthemum spp.
kris-AN-the-mum. Chrysanthemum, daisy.
Summer. Zones 3 to 9.

○ ✳ ✂❀ ❦ ▼

Characteristics. Height: 1 to 3½ feet. Colors: Pink, red, yellow, purple, orange, and white.

The genus *Chrysanthemum* includes a wide range of annual and perennial daisies for gardens and wildflower meadows. The perennial chrysanthemums most often grown in American gardens are garden mums (*C.* X *morifolium*), Shasta daisies (*C.* X *superbum*), and painted daisies (*C. coccineum*).

Garden mums are to autumn what pansies, crocuses, and daffodils are to spring. Their popularity is due to the great abundance of colorful, attractively shaped blooms, which nearly cover the foliage for

Chrysanthemum X *morifolium*

Chrysanthemum X *superbum* 'Alaska'

many weeks. The glowing flower colors are often a perfect complement to the fiery fall foliage color of deciduous trees. There are always plenty of flowers for cutting, and they last for up to 2 weeks in the vase. Garden mums have a fresh fragrance that is pleasant but not overpowering.

Shasta daisies look like tame versions of the familiar white wildflower daisies. They come in single- and double-flowered forms. 'Starburst Hybrid', developed by Burpee, is the first hybrid Shasta daisy; it features 6-inch-wide, single blooms on 3½-foot-tall plants. 'White Knight Hybrid' is a free-flowering cultivar with 4-inch blooms. The extra-strong stems of this 2-foot-tall cultivar are tolerant of wind and rain, and never need staking.

Painted daisies, also called pyrethrum daisies, have feathery foliage. The flowers are single or double and come in shades of pink, red, lavender, and white. They are one of the prettiest chry-santhe-mums for cutting.

How to Grow. To raise your own plants, sow seed directly in a protected area of the garden in midsummer. Move the young plants to their permanent locations in fall or early spring. Plants are also available at garden centers and through mail-order catalogs. Most mail-order nurseries do not ship garden mums in the fall because many customers expect the plants to be blooming when they arrive. The perennials that *are* shipped out for fall planting are usually dormant, to minimize damage from shipping and transplant shock. When purchasing garden mums in full bloom from nurseries and garden cen-

Chrysanthemum coccineum

ters, make sure you are getting hardy mums, which should survive the winter in Zones 5 to 8. Many cultivars are greenhouse-grown for fall display and may not be hardy.

All chrysanthemums prefer well-drained, moist, rich soil in full sun. Shasta daisies can grow in light shade, and painted daisies can tolerate poor soil. Taller cultivars may need staking. Divide all chrysanthemums every 2 or 3 years in spring or fall.

For a possible second flush of bloom, cut back the stems of Shasta daisies after they bloom. Pinch garden mums two or three times before mid- to late July to encourage bushiness. Make the first pinch when the plants are 6 inches tall.

Uses. There is a place in every sunny garden for chrysanthemums. These plants are terrific for beds, borders, containers, edgings, and cutting gardens. Garden mums are especially useful for fall color. Shasta and painted daisies can be naturalized in a wildflower meadow.

Cimicifuga spp.

sih-miss-ih-FEW-guh. Bugbane.
Summer or fall. Zones 4 to 9.

Characteristics. Height: 4 to 6 feet. Colors: White.

These large, handsome shade-loving perennials offer tall, elegant spires of fluffy white, bottlebrush flowers and coarse, ferny foliage. The two species most commonly grown are branched bugbane (*Cimicifuga racemosa*) and Kamchatka bugbane (*C. simplex*).

Branched bugbane has long, branched flower spikes that look like candelabras. Because they open from the bottom up, from a distance they look as if they taper off into fine smoke. The plants may need staking, especially in exposed locations. They bloom for several weeks in July. An American native, branched bugbane naturalizes well in a woodland setting.

Kamchatka bugbane features 4-foot-tall plants with neat, softly arching flower spikes that appear in October. One of the best cultivars is 'The Pearl'; it is fairly heat-tolerant and has a long blooming period of several weeks. It looks splendid when combined with pink-flowered Japanese anemone (*Anemone* X *hybrida*), which blooms at the same time.

How to Grow. To raise your own plants, sow seed of the species directly in a protected area of the garden in midsummer. You will need to be patient,

Cimicifuga racemosa

because seeds germinate and grow very slowly. Move the young plants to their permanent locations in fall or early spring. Plants of both the species and cultivars are sometimes available at garden centers, but more often through mail-order catalogs.

Both species require rich, moist, well-drained soil and partial or full shade. The plants are rarely bothered by pests and diseases. They seldom need to be divided and require very little maintenance once they are established in the right spot in the garden.

Uses. Both branched and Kamchatka bugbanes make excellent woodland specimen plants or landscape plants, and are welcome additions to the back of the border. The flowers are good for cutting but have a fragrance that not everyone finds appealing.

COLUMBINE. See *Aquilegia* spp.
COLUMBINE MEADOW RUE. See *Thalictrum aquilegifolium*
COMFREY, YELLOW. See *Symphytum grandiflorum*
CONEFLOWER, ORANGE. See *Rudbeckia* spp.
CONEFLOWER, PURPLE. See *Echinacea purpurea*
CORALBELLS. See *Heuchera* spp.

Coreopsis spp.
kor-ee-OP-sis. Coreopsis, tickseed.
Summer. Zones 4 to 9.
○ ◑ ☀ ⚷ ▼

Characteristics. Height: 1 to 2½ feet. Colors: Yellow.

These important perennials are prized for their cheerful, yellow daisylike flowers, which bloom all summer on well-behaved, easy-to-grow plants. Tickseed (*Coreopsis grandiflora*), threadleaf coreopsis (*C. verticillata*), and lanceleaf coreopsis (*C. lanceolata*) are the most popular species, because of their long periods of bloom and their reliable garden performance.

Tickseed is a bushy 1- to 2-foot-tall plant with bright golden yellow single or semidouble flowers and long, narrow leaves. 'Early Sunrise' is an excellent cultivar that won both the All-America Selections and European Fleuroselect awards for its

ability to bloom the first year from seed and for its neat, uniform habit. It blooms continuously from June to August if deadheaded.

Threadleaf coreopsis has very narrow foliage, as wide as its narrow stems. The lightness of the foliage gives the plants an airy texture in the garden. The small single flowers cover the foliage from June through August. 'Moonbeam' is one of the best cultivars; in fact, it is one of the best garden perennials available today. It was selected as the Perennial Plant Association's Perennial Plant of the Year in 1992. The 15-inch plants offer exquisite, creamy primrose-yellow flowers and dark green foliage. The flower color blends well with many other colors, especially blues and purples.

Lanceleaf coreopsis is one of the most forgiving of garden plants. Its lovely, bright yellow, daisylike flowers are 1½ to 2½ inches across. The leaves are lance-shaped, and the plants have a clump-forming habit. It is hardy in Zones 5 to 9.

How to Grow. To raise your own plants, sow

Coreopsis grandiflora 'Early Sunrise'

Coreopsis verticillata 'Moonbeam'

Delphinium elatum hybrids

seed of the species directly in a protected area of the garden in midsummer. Or sow seed indoors in early spring; seed germinates best when the growing medium is kept at about 70°F. Harden off the young plants and move them to their permanent locations in fall or early spring. 'Early Sunrise' will bloom the first year from seed sown indoors about 8 weeks before the last frost date. Plants of other cultivars are available at garden centers and through mail-order catalogs.

All three kinds of coreopsis prefer well-drained soil in full sun. The plants can tolerate partial shade but bloom best in full sun. Tickseed can withstand drought; both threadleaf and lanceleaf coreopsis prefer poorer soil. In fact, too-rich soil can decrease the plants' flowering and make them too sprawling. Regular deadheading can keep tickseed in bloom for months. (If you cut lots of flowers for bouquets, there won't be as many to deadhead.) All three species appreciate a protective winter mulch north of Zone 6. Divide the plants in spring or fall for propagation or to rejuvenate old clumps.

Uses. Coreopsis is valuable for the middle or front of the border and is an ideal addition to dry-soil gardens. This easy-care perennial also performs well in containers. The cut flowers are long-lasting and a welcome addition to fresh arrangements.

DAISY. See *Chrysanthemum* spp.
DAYLILY. See *Hemerocallis* hybrids

Delphinium elatum hybrids
del-FIN-ee-um el-AY-tum. Delphinium.
Summer. Zones 3 to 6.

○ ◑ ❄ ✄❧

Characteristics. Height: 3 to 7 feet. Colors: Blue, purple, pink, and white.

Delphiniums are among the most elegant of all perennials. Their stately flower spires—in regal shades of blue, purple, pink, or white—make us yearn for those perennial borders and cottage gardens we see in picture books of famous British gardens. Unfortunately, however, delphiniums are not as happy in many American gardens as they are in English gardens. Although they thrive in areas of the Pacific Northwest with cool summer nights, they are short-lived in regions with hot summers and should be treated as annuals outside of Zones 3 to 6.

Many fine cultivars are available. 'Pacific Coast' has towering 7-foot spikes of closely packed, single florets in pink, blue, and violet shades; they are magnificent but short-lived. 'Connecticut Yankee' is a 30-inch-tall, semidwarf, well-branched hybrid that is more heat-tolerant than other cultivars. The Blackmore and Langdon Strain tends to be longer-lived and has 4- to 7-foot spikes.

How to Grow. To raise your own plants, sow the seed directly in a protected area of the garden in midsummer. Move the young plants to their permanent locations in fall or early spring. In cool areas, you can allow the plants to go dormant in summer after they flower, then pot them up and overwinter them in a coldframe. Bring them out early the following spring, divide them, then move them to their blooming locations. Plants are also available from garden centers and through mail-order catalogs for fall and spring planting.

Delphiniums require cool, moist, rich soil in full sun or light shade. They need extra watering in dry, hot weather. Taller cultivars must be staked, or the flower spikes will break in stormy weather. Cut back the flower stalks after blooming. Or, if you are growing them as annuals, pull the plants after they bloom.

Uses. Delphiniums are stunning for the back of the border, in cottage gardens, or as accent plants. They also make splendid cut flowers.

Dianthus X allwoodii

Dianthus spp.
dy-AN-thus. Pinks.
Spring or summer. Zones 3 to 9.
○ ☀ ⚶ ❦ ▼

Characteristics. Height: 1 to 2 feet. Colors: Pink, red, salmon, and white.

This large genus of annuals, biennials, and perennials includes many fine species for the garden. All of the species share the fringed, or "pinked," edges of the flower petals; the long, narrow, green-blue or gray foliage; and the color range of pink, red, salmon, and

Dianthus plumarius

white. The perennial species have a decided advantage in that they live longer, coming back for many years if they are happy in their location. They also have evergreen foliage.

Cottage pinks (*Dianthus plumarius*) is named for its early use in cottage gardens—the informal, mixed plantings of flowers, vegetables, and herbs that preceded our modern flower gardens. Cottage pinks feature single red, pink, or white flowers on 18- to 24-inch stems above spreading mats of gray-green, grasslike foliage. The flowers bloom in May and June, and have a spicy fragrance. The plants live for many years but should be divided every 2 or 3 years to maintain their vitality.

The Allwood hybrids (D. X *allwoodii*) were developed by crossing D. *plumarius* with D. *caryophyllus*. They are more compact and vigorous than cottage pinks. Their flowers come in shades of pink, red, and white; most are double, although single forms are available. The plants may be short-lived in areas with hot, humid summers.

How to Grow. To raise your own plants, sow seed directly in a protected area of the garden in midsummer. Move the young plants to their final locations in fall or early spring. Plants are also available at garden centers, and you can find an even wider selection through mail-order catalogs.

All pinks grow well in well-drained soil and full sun. Cottage pinks prefer slightly alkaline soil. Deadheading will encourage more continuous bloom and keep the plants looking neat. Pinks are easy to grow when they are happy and are rarely bothered by pests and diseases.

Uses. Pinks are lovely along the front of the border, as an edging, and in cottage gardens, rock gardens, and containers. They are terrific for cutting, lasting for more than a week in the vase and perfuming the room with their sweet or spicy fragrance.

Dicentra spp.
dy-SEN-truh. Bleeding heart.
Spring. Zones 3 to 7.
◑ ● ❄ ✂

Characteristics. Height: 12 to 30 inches. Colors: Pink or white.

Bleeding hearts are sentimental favorites for their unique heart-shaped flowers with teardrop-shaped, protruding petals, which make them look as though they were bleeding. The spring-blooming flowers are arranged in rows along arching stems over deeply cut foliage.

The old-fashioned common bleeding heart (*Dicentra spectabilis*) has deep pink or white hearts. The plants grow to 2½ feet tall and spread as wide, then die back dramatically in June and disappear until the following spring. They are likely to leave a large gap in your design if you don't plan for their

Dicentra eximia

short season. Fill the space with a late-emerging perennial, such as hardy begonia (*Begonia grandis*), or with medium-sized annuals.

Everything about fringed bleeding heart (*D. eximia*) is smaller or lighter than common bleeding heart. It has lighter pink or white flowers on stems that are not as long and arched as those of the other species. The plants are shorter, growing only 12 inches tall, and have more finely cut foliage, in a lighter shade of green. Unlike common bleeding heart, fringed bleeding heart does not go dormant during the season. It also has one of the longest bloom periods of any garden flower—from April until September.

How to Grow. To raise your own plants, sow seed directly in a protected area of the garden in midsummer. Move the young plants to their permanent locations in fall or early spring. Plants of both species are readily available from garden centers and through mail-order catalogs.

These perennials prefer a woodland environment, with rich, moist, well-drained soil and partial or even full shade. Fringed bleeding heart may

Dicentra spectabilis

need extra watering in hot weather. Common bleeding heart usually goes dormant when hot weather arrives. Deadhead fringed bleeding heart to keep the plants looking neat and for more continuous bloom. When they are happy, both species will self-sow furiously, giving you many seedlings to expand your plantings or to share with friends and neighbors.

Uses. Bleeding hearts are perfect plants for woodland borders and for naturalizing. Fringed bleeding hearts can be used as spring-to-fall groundcovers. The flowers are good for cutting.

Dictamnus albus

dik-TAM-nus ALL-bus. Gas plant.
Early summer. Zones 3 to 7.
○ ❀ ❦

Characteristics. Height: 30 inches. Colors: White or pink.

Gas plant gets its peculiar name from the fact that it releases a flammable gas that can be ignited with a match flame. Don't worry about having the plant around your backyard barbecue or around children; the gas is not highly flammable and is, in fact, remarkably difficult to ignite.

Fortunately, the not-so-pretty common name is offset by the beauty of the flowers. Spikes of white or lavender-pink, star-shaped florets bloom for several weeks in June. The flowers are followed by

Dictamnus albus

interesting seedpods, which can be cut and used in dried flower arrangements. The narrow, deep green foliage is attractive all season.

How to Grow. To raise your own plants, sow seed directly in a protected area of the garden in midsummer. Move the young plants to their final locations in fall or early spring. Plants are not often available at garden centers, but you can sometimes find them in mail-order catalogs.

Gas plants do best in rich, well-drained soil in full sun. They prefer cool summer nights and warm days but are not difficult to grow in Zones 6 and 7. The plants are very long-lived and have a long taproot, which should not be disturbed; propagate by sowing more seed instead of trying to divide them. These perennials are easy to care for and are rarely bothered by pests and diseases.

Uses. Gas plant is a stately, multiseason perennial that is ideal for the middle of the border. The seedpods make interesting additions to dried arrangements. (Be sure to wear gloves when harvesting the seedpods; handling them gives some people a rash.)

Doronicum caucasicum

doh-RON-ih-kum kaw-KASS-ih-kum. Leopard's-bane. Spring. Zones 4 to 7.
○ ❀ ❦

Characteristics. Height: 18 inches. Colors: Yellow.

Unlike most daisies, which bloom in summer and fall, leopard's-bane produces its single, yellow daisy flowers in April and May, in time to accompany spring bulbs and early-spring perennials. The plants grow 18 inches tall, spread 12 inches wide, and have wavy, sharply toothed, heart-shaped foliage. Leopard's-bane goes dormant in the hot summer weather; plant over it with summer annuals or perennials. Sometimes the foliage reemerges in the fall when the weather turns cooler.

How to Grow. To raise your own plants, sow seed directly in a protected area of the garden in midsummer. Move the young plants to their permanent locations in fall or early spring. Plants are not usually available from garden centers, but you can sometimes find them in mail-order catalogs.

Leopard's-bane prefers full sun and rich, moist,

Doronicum caucasicum

cool soil with good drainage. Deadheading helps to prolong the blooming period. The plants die back to the ground in summer and are rarely bothered by pests and diseases. It is important to keep them moist, even when the plants are dormant, or they may not come back the following year. Divide the plants every third year in early spring.

Uses. Leopard's-bane adds a cheerful touch to the front of the border. The flowers combine beautifully with Virginia bluebells (*Mertensia virginica*) or orange, late-blooming tulips. Leopard's-bane blooms are also excellent for cutting.

Echinacea purpurea
ek-in-AY-see-uh per-per-EE-uh. Purple coneflower.
Summer. Zones 3 to 9.

Characteristics. Height: 3 feet. Colors: Pink or white.

Because of its adaptability, long bloom period, and beautiful flowers, this native American wildflower is gaining in popularity. The flowers are large, single daisies with pink or white petals that hang down from the central "cone," which is a wonderful iridescent rust color. The flowers bloom from July into September on sturdy, 3-foot-tall plants with dark green foliage. Even when the plants die back in the fall, the dried seed heads remain to add winter interest.

Echinacea purpurea

How to Grow. To raise your own plants, sow seed directly in a protected area of the garden in midsummer. Move the young plants to their final locations in fall or early spring. Plants are readily available from garden centers and through mail-order catalogs.

Native to the prairies of the Midwest, purple coneflower tolerates heat, drought, and poor soil. It prefers well-drained soil and full sun. For propagation, start new plants from seed, or carefully divide existing plants in spring or fall. Purple coneflowers are a favorite food of Japanese beetles; otherwise, these perennials are rarely bothered by pests and diseases. They normally don't need staking unless the soil is too rich.

Uses. Purple coneflowers are excellent in the middle or back of the border, in a cottage garden, or naturalized in a wildflower meadow. They make a bold statement when massed in a large landscape planting. The blooms are attractive as cut flowers; the "cones" can be used in both fresh and dried arrangements.

Echinops ritro

Epimedium X *youngianum* 'Niveum'

Echinops ritro
EK-in-ops REE-troh. Globe thistle.
Summer. Zones 4 to 9.

Characteristics. Height: 4 to 5 feet. Colors: Steel blue.

Globe thistle has spherical balls of tiny flowers that look like stars shooting out from the center. The icy blue flowers blend well with pink, silver, or white companion flowers. They bloom for 6 to 8 weeks on long, strong, stems and make perfect cut flowers for fresh or dried arrangements. The dramatic plants are rough-textured, with spiny, thistlelike foliage.

How to Grow. To raise your own plants, sow seed directly in a protected area of the garden in midsummer. Move the young plants to their permanent locations in fall or early spring. Plants are not commonly sold at garden centers but are usually available through mail-order catalogs.

Globe thistle prefers rich, well-drained soil in full sun. The plants send down deep roots and can last for many years in the garden. They are difficult to dig up and divide because of the deep roots, but these roots also tend to make the plants drought-resistant. Globe thistle must be staked. To encourage a second flush of bloom on shorter stems, cut the flower stems back to the ground after bloom.

Uses. Globe thistle is useful for the middle or back of the border, or as a background plant. The flowers are good for cutting for fresh or dried bouquets.

Epimedium spp.
ep-ih-MEE-dee-um. Epimedium, barrenwort.
Early spring. Zones 5 to 8.

Characteristics. Height: 12 to 15 inches. Colors: Yellow, pink, red, lavender, orange, and white.

Epimediums deserve to be grown more in American gardens. They have the rare ability to grow well in dry shade, making them an excellent choice for planting under trees. They are grown primarily for their heart-shaped foliage, which often has a reddish edge and is borne on strong, wiry, 12- to 15-inch stems. The foliage is so attractive that many gardeners cut it and use it in fresh flower arrangements. The plants spread and make a fine groundcover. In spring, they produce masses of exquisite, spurred flowers.

Several species are commonly grown. *Epimedium grandiflorum* produces the largest, showiest flowers, which come in shades of pink, lavender, or white and appear in March or April. The plants spread slowly and are deciduous. *E.* X *versicolor* is evergreen in areas with mild winters and produces masses of yellow flowers in April. It spreads more quickly than *E. grandiflorum*. *E.* X *warleyense* produces apricot-orange flowers in April. The plants are deciduous and spread moderately quickly. *E.* X *youngianum* is the smallest hybrid, featuring moderately fast-spreading plants and many lavender or white flowers that appear in April. *E.* X *rubrum* has abundant small, pink flowers, which bloom in April on slowly spreading, semievergreen plants.

How to Grow. Start your epimedium patch with purchased plants. You may not be able to find them at your local garden center, but they're usually available through mail-order catalogs.

Epimediums tolerate dry shade, but they are really at their best in rich, moisture-retentive, well-drained soil in partial to full shade. Cut the remaining leaves to the ground in late winter. Propagate plants from division in fall or spring.

Uses. Epimediums make excellent groundcovers for dry, shady spots. They are ideal for edgings and woodland plantings. These attractive plants are useful for the front of the border, where their foliage provides a nice textural contrast to softer, low-growing perennials or annuals. The foliage is good for cutting as a filler in fresh arrangements.

Eupatorium spp.

yew-puh-TORE-ee-um. Joe-Pye weed.
Summer to early fall. Zones 3 to 8.

Characteristics. Height: 4 to 6 feet. Colors: Pink to lavender.

This genus of hardy native wildflowers is finally coming out of obscurity and taking its rightful and stately place in American gardens. At least two species of Joe-Pye weed are becoming available, *Eupatorium maculatum* and *E. purpureum*. Both form

Eupatorium purpureum
with *Anemone* X *hybrida*

large, tall clumps and have long, lance-shaped leaves arranged in whorls around the stem. Rounded flower clusters at the top of the stems bear handsome, slightly fragrant, pink to purplish lavender blooms.

How to Grow. Joe-Pye weed thrives in full sun to partial shade and moist soil that is rich in organic matter. The plants are extremely low-maintenance and tolerate both heat and drought. They do not have any serious pest or disease problems.

Sow seeds directly in the garden, where you want the plants to grow, in fall or early spring. Or sow them indoors in pots in late winter; leave the pots in the refrigerator for about 3 months, then move them to a warm, bright area. It usually takes 2 years for seed-grown plants to bloom. Divide established clumps every 2 to 3 years to prevent overcrowding. Keep seedlings and transplanted divisions well watered the first season, until they are established. Plants are usually not available at garden centers, but are offered in mail order catalogs.

Uses. Joe-Pye weed is a magnificent plant for the back of the border. It is also ideal for any sunny meadow area.

EVENING PRIMROSE, MISSOURI.
See *Oenothera missouriensis*
FALSE INDIGO. See *Baptisia australis*

Filipendula spp.

fil-ih-PEN-dew-luh. Meadowsweet.
Summer. Zones 3 to 8.

Characteristics. Height: 3 to 8 feet. Colors: Pink, purple, and white.

Meadowsweets are large, shrublike perennials with handsome foliage and clusters of tiny, astilbe-like flowers. Queen-of-the-prairie (*Filipendula rubra*) can reach 6 to 8 feet tall, yet it rarely needs staking. Its fluffy, light pink flowers bloom in June above rough-textured, divided foliage. Japanese meadowsweet (*F. purpurea*) produces large, lobed leaves and fluffy clusters of deep pink flowers that mature to purple in June. It grows to a manageable 4 feet and never needs staking. Queen-of-the-meadow (*F. ulmaria*) grows 3 to 6 feet tall, with divided leaves and fluffy clusters of white flowers that bloom from

Filipendula ulmaria

Gaillardia aristata

Gaillardia spp.
guh-LAR-dee-uh. Perennial blanket flower.
Summer into fall. Zones 2 to 9.

June to July. 'Flore Plena' has double white flowers; 'Variegata' produces variegated leaves. 'Aurea' is a particularly striking cultivar with golden foliage. The golden color is most apparent when the plants are cut back after blooming.

How to Grow. Start with plants purchased from garden centers or through mail-order catalogs.

Meadowsweets prefer well-drained, moist soil in full sun or light shade. They do not tolerate drought well and should be watered in dry weather. Even the tallest plants normally don't need staking. Propagate by division in spring or fall. The plants are rarely bothered by pests and diseases, and are easy to maintain in the garden.

Uses. Meadowsweets are terrific for the back of the border or as accent plants. They naturalize well in moist wildflower meadows. Try cutting the flowers for fresh or dried arrangements. Or, leave the flowers to dry on the plants for winter interest.

FLAG, YELLOW. See *Iris* spp.

Characteristics. Height: 1 to 3½ feet. Colors: Yellow and red.

Perennial blanket flower bears mostly single, daisylike flowers in bright combinations of red and yellow. It has an exceptionally long season of bloom—from June to October. The seed heads that follow the flowers are also attractive and add winter interest to the garden. The "hot"-colored flowers are very bright, so choose companion flowers carefully. The two most popular types of perennial blanket flower grown in American gardens are *Gaillardia aristata*, a native wildflower hardy in Zones 2 to 8, and G. X *grandiflora*, a hybrid species developed by crossing G. *aristata* and annual blanket flower (G. *pulchella*). G. X *grandiflora* is hardy in Zones 3 to 9.

How to Grow. To raise your own plants, sow seed directly in a protected area of the garden in midsummer. Move the young plants to their final locations in fall or early spring. Sometimes they bloom the first year from seed sown early indoors.

You can also start the seed indoors in late winter and set hardened-off transplants outdoors after all danger of frost has passed. Seed should germinate in 5 to 10 days at around 70°F. Gaillardias are usually available at garden centers and from mail-order catalogs.

The plants prefer well-drained, poor soil and full sun. They are tolerant of drought. Deadhead for continuous bloom. Divide the plants every 2 or 3 years in spring or fall.

Uses. Perennial blanket flowers are excellent for the middle of the border, for a cottage garden, and for naturalizing in a wildflower meadow. They are especially valuable for dry-soil areas, and are very striking when planted in large numbers. The blooms make terrific cut flowers.

GAS PLANT. See *Dictamnus albus*
GAYFEATHER. See *Liatris pycnostachya*

Geranium sanguineum

Gaillardia X grandiflora

Geranium spp.

jer-AY-nee-um. Hardy geranium.
Early summer to fall. Zones 4 to 9.

○ ◑

Characteristics. Height: 12 to 24 inches. Colors: Blue, pink, lilac, purple, and white.

These understated perennials bear no resemblance to their namesake, the tender perennial zonal geranium (*Pelargonium* X *hortorum*). Hardy geraniums are low-growing plants with divided, ferny foliage and small, single or double flowers. Several species are becoming popular as gardeners are discovering these wonderful plants.

Geranium endressii features 15- to 18-inch plants with glossy green, finely cut foliage and pretty, light pink, 1-inch-wide flowers that bloom in spring and summer. The best-known cultivar is 'Wargrave Pink', which has notched, salmon-pink flowers. It performs best in cooler areas, where it blooms all summer.

G. himalayense is 12 to 18 inches tall, with blue, 2-inch-wide flowers and deeply lobed foliage. 'Plenum' has double flowers. The most popular cultivar is 'Johnson's Blue', which has a graceful, sprawling habit and more, but smaller flowers than the species.

G. sanguineum has a very long blooming season—from May to September—and is the most

Geranium 'Johnson's Blue'

adaptable species. The mounded, 1-foot-tall plants produce 1- to 2-inch magenta flowers and finely divided, starry foliage.

How to Grow. To raise your own plants, sow seed of the species directly in a protected area of the garden in midsummer. Move the young plants to their permanent locations in fall or early spring. You can find plants at well-stocked garden centers; mail-order catalogs often list a good selection.

Hardy geraniums prefer rich, well-drained, moist soil in full sun or partial shade. They are rarely bothered by pests and diseases, and are easy to care for once they are established. The plants often self-sow where they are happy. If these self-sown seedlings aren't enough, you can also propagate plants by division in spring or fall.

Uses. Hardy geraniums make a lovely, light-textured, deciduous groundcover for partial shade. They are also effective in the front of the border, in a rock garden, as a woodland plant, or as an edging.

Geum quellyon
JEE-um KWEL-ee-on. Geum.
Spring. Zones 4 to 8.
○ ◑ ❄ ✄❦

Characteristics. Height: 1 to 2 feet. Colors: Yellow, orange, and red.

These low-growing perennials make a cheerful display in the spring garden. The mostly semidou-

Geum quellyon 'Mrs. Bradshaw'

ble, yellow, orange, or red flowers bloom in great abundance on 1- to 2-foot stems starting in May. The coarse-textured, hairy foliage has frills at the base of the stem. Even when it is healthy, the foliage can be weedy-looking; in hot, dry conditions, it tends to turn brown and look especially unattractive. The plants are short-lived in the garden, usually lasting only 2 or 3 years. They last longer in areas with cool summer nights and mild winters, such as the Pacific Northwest. The most popular cultivar is 'Mrs. Bradshaw', which has striking scarlet, semidouble flowers.

How to Grow. To raise your own plants, sow seed directly in a protected area of the garden in midsummer. Move the young plants to their final locations in fall or early spring. Plants are also readily available from most garden centers and through mail-order catalogs.

Geum prefers rich, well-drained, moist soil in full sun or partial shade. The plants need extra watering in hot, dry conditions. They are not generally bothered by pests or diseases, and are very easy to care for in the garden. Geums do not usually live long enough to require division.

Uses. Geum is useful for the front of the border or as an edging, especially in combination with late-spring-blooming bulbs, such as late tulips. The flowers are good for cutting.

GLOBE THISTLE. See *Echinops ritro*
GOATSBEARD. See *Aruncus* spp.
GOLDENROD. See *Solidago* spp.

Gypsophila paniculata

jip-SOF-ih-luh pan-ih-kew-LAY-tuh. Perennial baby's breath. Summer. Zones 4 to 8.

Characteristics. Height: 15 to 36 inches. Colors: White or pink.

Perennial baby's breath provides masses of airy, white or pink, mostly double or semidouble flowers for many weeks from June to August. The plants have very handsome, narrow, gray-green foliage. They provide a welcome light texture wherever they grow.

How to Grow. In spring to midsummer, sow seed directly in the garden where you want the plants to bloom. They develop long taproots and do not like to be disturbed once they are established. Plants are sometimes available from garden centers and can usually be purchased through mail-order catalogs.

Gypsophila paniculata

This well-known florist's flower is easy to grow in the right garden conditions: full sun and well-drained soil. The plants do not do well in clay or acid soil; in deep, sandy, alkaline soil, they may live for many years. If your soil is acid, add lime in the fall to raise the pH. The plants have a spreading habit, and taller plants generally need staking; support them with twiggy brush, metal staking hoops, or bamboo stakes and thin green string. They may rebloom if you cut them back immediately after the first flush of bloom.

Uses. Perennial baby's breath is invaluable for fresh or dried arrangements. It is also an attractive plant for borders and rock gardens. For a striking display, allow it to cascade over a wall. The airy plants are particularly useful for covering areas left empty by dormant spring bulbs.

HARDY GERANIUM. See *Geranium* spp.
HEARTLEAF BERGENIA. See *Bergenia cordifolia*

Helenium autumnale

hel-EE-nee-um aw-tum-NAL-ee. Sneezeweed. Late summer. Zones 3 to 9.

Characteristics. Height: 2 to 5 feet. Colors: Yellow, orange, red, and rust.

Helenium autumnale 'Copper Spray'

This native American daisy blooms for several weeks in late summer, adding welcome color just before the perennial garden begins its fall finale. The single flowers have a prominent, almost spherical, central cone surrounded by a row of yellow, orange, or red petals. They bloom on strong, bushy plants that can grow up to 5 feet tall. Despite its common name, sneezeweed does not cause people to sneeze. Like goldenrod, it blooms at the same time as ragweed and is unfairly blamed for causing allergy symptoms.

'Brilliant' is a 4-foot-tall cultivar with fascinating, bronze-rust flowers that blend beautifully with the deep blues of asters. 'Butterpat' offers pretty, creamy yellow flowers on 4- to 5-foot stems. 'Bruno' is a lower-growing, 2- to 3-foot cultivar with mahogany-red flowers.

How to Grow. To grow your own plants, sow seed of the species directly in a protected area of the garden in midsummer. Move the young plants to their permanent locations in fall or early spring. Plants arc also available through mail-order catalogs and sometimes at garden centers.

Sneezeweed requires rich, well-drained, moist soil and full sun. Pinch the shoot tips in June to encourage bushiness and more prolific blooms. Taller cultivars may need staking. Divide the plants every third year in spring, since they decline when they become overcrowded.

Uses. Sneezeweed is ideal for the middle or back of the border for late-summer color. The flowers are excellent for cutting. The plants naturalize well in wildflower meadows.

Helianthus spp.
hee-lee-AN-thus. Perennial sunflower.
Late summer to fall. Zones 4 to 9.

Characteristics. Height: 3 to 10 feet. Colors: Yellow.

The perennial relatives of common annual sunflowers have smaller flowers and bear them in clusters. The plants can be as large as the tall, annual types, although shorter, better-behaved cultivars have been developed for garden use. Perennial sunflowers can be invasive, but the species described here are easy to control.

Helianthus salicifolius

Swamp sunflower (*Helianthus angustifolius*) grows to 10 feet, with handsome narrow foliage and 2-inch flowers that bloom from September to November. When grown in full sun and pinched in spring, the plants can stay a manageable 7 feet. They generally need staking to avoid breaking in windy or rainy weather, although in poor soil they can be self-supporting.

Willowleaf sunflower (*H. salicifolius*) has very narrow, willowlike foliage; golden yellow daisies appear on the 6- to 8-foot stems from September to October. *H. X multiflorus* is a bushy, lower-growing, 3- to 6-foot hybrid that offers masses of sunny yellow daisies from July through September. The double-flowered 'Flore Pleno' is one of the most popular cultivars, producing numerous chrysanthemum-like flowers for months.

How to Grow. To grow your own plants, sow seed directly in a protected area of the garden in midsummer. Move the young plants to their final locations in fall or early spring. Plants are usually available at garden centers and through mail-order catalogs.

Sunflowers perform best in moist soil and require plenty of water during dry spells. As their name suggests, they need to grow in full sun. In shade they grow absurdly tall, tend to fall over and break, and bloom poorly. The plants tend to spread when they are happy; dividing them every 2 or 3 years in fall or spring will help keep them under control. Pinch them in July for shorter plants. They are remarkably free of pests and diseases, and are generally very easy to grow.

Uses. Perennial sunflowers are wonderful for bright color in late summer through autumn. Grow them at the back of the border, as a hedge or screen, as a garden accent, or in a wildflower meadow. The flowers are good for cutting for fresh bouquets.

Helleborus spp.
hel-eh-BORE-us. Hellebore, Christmas rose,
Lenten rose. Early spring. Zones 4 to 9.
◑

Characteristics. Height: 18 to 24 inches. Colors: Pink, green, red, and white.

These understated plants provide long-lasting, hauntingly beautiful, single or double blooms in late winter and early spring. They have divided, rough-textured leaves that look like many-fingered hands. The gray-green or dark green foliage can have

Helleborus orientalis

sharply toothed or smooth edges and a shiny or dull surface.

Christmas rose (*Helleborus niger*) does not bloom as early as Christmas, but it *can* bloom in February or early March. It has white or pink-flushed flowers and dull green foliage. It spreads more slowly than other species and does not tend to perform as well in the garden.

Lenten rose (*H. orientalis*) spreads more quickly and recovers faster from division than Christmas rose. It also blooms later, in March or April. The flowers are white, pink, or garnet red, often with darker speckles. The plants have semievergreen, glossy foliage with toothed edges.

Bear's-foot hellebore (*H. foetidus*) is much more difficult to find, but if you have a friend with a plant, he or she probably has some seedlings to share. This beautiful species self-sows reliably and blooms more quickly from seed than other species. It has thick stems topped with green flowers that look like inverted cups. The flower buds appear in fall, open as early as January, and continue until April or May. This species also has the rare ability to perform well in dry shade.

How to Grow. Hellebores will grow from seed, but they mature slowly and may not bloom for several years. It is easier to start with purchased plants from a garden center or mail-order catalog.

Hellebores prefer moist, rich soil in partial shade. Provide extra watering in hot, dry summer weather; otherwise, the leaves may burn. Cut winter-damaged foliage back before bloom to give the plants a neater appearance and to allow more room for new foliage. Hellebores are easy to care for, and the slow-growing plants seldom need to be divided. They often self-sow and can form a nice colony in time. Or, you can lift seedlings and use them to start new plantings elsewhere in the garden. Double forms may revert to single forms when they self-sow; divide the plants carefully in spring or fall.

Uses. Hellebores are excellent specimen plants for woodland gardens and are valuable for adding winter interest to borders. They also make good edgings and can be attractive landscape accents when planted in groups. Bear's-foot hellebore and Lenten rose both form unusual groundcovers. Hellebores are toxic, so plant them with caution or avoid including them in gardens frequently visited by small children.

Hemerocallis hybrid

Hemerocallis hybrids
hem-er-oh-KAL-iss. Daylily.
Summer. Zones 3 to 8.

○ ◑ ☀ ⚘ ❦ ▼

Characteristics. Height: 1 to 4 feet. Colors: Yellow, pink, lilac, purple, red, orange, white, and bicolors.

Daylilies are nearly perfect perennials. They grow easily in all kinds of soil and weather conditions, and they offer beautiful flowers in a wide range of colors, sizes, and shapes. The narrow, arching leaves are handsome all season, and the plants are rarely bothered by pests and diseases. If you divide them every 3 or 4 years, you'll have a continuous supply of plants for your garden and for your friends and neighbors, too. In short, daylilies are very tough plants that are also very pretty.

The trumpet-shaped flowers of daylilies come in many colors, including creamy white, brassy gold to soft primrose yellow, pumpkin orange to glowing apricot, deep red to pastel pink, and lavender to deep purple. There are also many bicolors and "eyed" types. The single or double flowers can be as large as 6 inches wide or as small as 2 inches across. Each flower lasts only 1 day (the characteristic that gives the plants their common name), but each stem has many buds, so the plants can be in bloom for several weeks. Some are even repeat bloomers. If

you select cultivars carefully, you can enjoy the flowers for up to 4 months.

Daylilies are often confused with true lilies, which belong to the genus *Lilium* and grow from bulbs. It's easy to tell them apart: Daylily flowers bloom on leafless stems; true lilies bloom atop stems that have short, narrow leaves all along them. Many people use the name "tiger lily" for the common roadside daylily (*Hemerocallis fulva*), even though it most correctly refers to a true lily with black-spotted orange petals and swept-back petals.

How to Grow. Unless you want to grow species daylilies, it is best to purchase plants. Many different daylilies are readily available at garden centers; for the widest selection, however, buy plants from specialty mail-order nurseries. To raise plants from seed, sow seed directly in a protected area of the garden in midsummer. Move the young plants to their final locations in fall or early spring.

Daylilies can adapt to poor, clay, or sandy soil but prefer a soil that is rich, with good drainage. The plants do best in full sun; they can tolerate partial shade but do not bloom as prolifically. Repeat bloomers flower more continuously if you remove the spent flowers. For propagation, divide the plants in fall or spring. Daylilies are rarely bothered by pests and diseases, and are among the easiest, lowest-maintenance perennials you can grow. Just plant them and enjoy them!

Uses. Daylilies come in all sizes for the front, middle, and back of the border. They make excellent edgings or landscape features planted in long rows. Grow the smaller cultivars in containers. All types can be cut for fresh flowers, and some cultivars are sweetly fragrant. Daylilies are ideal for a beginning perennial gardener, since they are practically indestructible.

Heuchera spp.
HEW-ker-uh. Heuchera, coralbells.
Summer. Zones 4 to 8.

○ ◑ ⚘

Characteristics. Height: 1 to 2 feet. Colors: Pink, coral, and creamy white.

These low-growing perennials are grown primarily for their attractive, multicolored foliage. They multiply quickly in the right conditions and

Heuchera sanguinea

Heuchera americana 'Dale's Strain'

make a striking woodland groundcover or edging plant. They bloom in summer, but the flowers are often insignificant.

Coralbells (*Heuchera sanguinea*) is the best species for flowers. It blooms continuously all summer when deadheaded, and provides plenty of airy wands of tiny coral or red bells to add to fresh arrangements. *H.* X *brizoides* is a hybrid with similar decorative flowers but better resistance to heat and humidity. 'June Bride' produces abundant clouds of white flowers on vigorous plants. 'Pluie de Feu' features bright cherry-red flower sprays.

H. americana is grown for its handsome, evergreen foliage with multicolored veins. The flowers are creamy white and not particularly attractive. 'Dale's Strain' has silvery green leaves with purple veins. *H. micrantha* var. *diversifolia* 'Palace Purple' has attracted a great deal of attention since it was selected as the Perennial Plant Association's Plant of the Year in 1991. This outstanding selection has broad purple leaves; waving wands of greenish white flowers appear in June and July.

How to Grow. To grow your own plants, sow seed directly in a protected area of the garden in midsummer. Move the young plants to their permanent locations in fall or early spring. Plants are also available from garden centers and through mail-order catalogs.

Heucheras prefer well-drained, rich, moist soil in partial shade or full sun. Divide the plants in spring or fall when the centers of the crowns get woody; discard the woody part and replant the side shoots. The

plants often self-sow when they are happy. Deadhead coralbells for continuous blooming.

Uses. Heucheras are wonderful as a woodland groundcover or specimen plant. They are also attractive in the front of the border or as an edging. The blooms of showy-flowered types are good for cutting.

HOLLYHOCK. See *Alcea rosea*

Hosta hybrids
HOS-tuh. Hosta. Summer. Zones 3 to 8.

Characteristics. Height: 3 to 36 inches (foliage). Colors: Lavender or white flowers; blue, lime green, green, and variegated foliage.

Hostas are the quintessential foliage plants for shade gardens. They send up attractive shoots in spring to accompany spring-blooming bulbs, then unfurl their leaves conveniently to hide the yellowing foliage of the bulbs after they have bloomed. The foliage forms undulating waves when planted in masses, giving a cool look to the garden.

Hosta foliage can be any shade of green, from greenish yellow to medium green, dark green, gray-green, or blue-green. Many cultivars are variegated with yellow, cream, white, or darker or lighter green edges or markings. The leaves can be long and narrow, short and broad, heart-shaped, puckered, or stiffly upright.

Hosta plantaginea

and hosta enthusiasts can rival orchid lovers for their depth of knowledge about their passion.

Because there are so many wonderful hostas, it seems unfair to mention specific ones. Some, however, stand out for their excellence or popularity. For instance, *Hosta sieboldiana* produces large, landscape-sized plants with rounded, blue-green foliage and white or lavender flowers. Cultivars of this species include 'Frances Williams', which has blue-green leaves edged with gold; 'Golden Sunburst', with golden yellow leaves; and 'Elegans', which features steely blue leaves.

H. venusta is a dwarf species that grows 3 to 4 inches tall and 6 to 8 inches across. *H. ventricosa* has wide, dark green leaves; the popular cultivar 'Aureo-marginata' sports yellow-and-green leaves. Plantain lily (*H. plantaginea*) produces large green leaves and pretty, often sweetly fragrant, lilylike flowers; cultivars include 'Honeybells' and 'Royal Standard'.

How to Grow. Start your hosta collection with purchased plants. They are always available at garden centers and through mail-order catalogs. Specialty mail-order nurseries can provide enough interesting selections—both new and old—to keep collectors happy.

Hostas are essentially shade plants, and their broad foliage tends to burn in full sun in warm, dry summer weather. Some cultivars are more tolerant of full sun, but all need extra watering in dry weather to keep the foliage looking fresh. Hostas prefer rich, well-drained, moist soil and can tolerate as much shade as almost any garden plant. They do

Some plants are miniature, growing 6 inches across and 3 to 4 inches tall; others are enormous, up to 5 feet tall. Most are somewhere in between— 1 to 2 feet wide and 1 foot tall, not counting the tall flowers when they are in bloom. The larger cultivars can be very slow-growing and may not bloom for years after they are planted. Even the smaller cultivars can be slow to mature and may take 3 or 4 years to look like their catalog pictures. However, they are well worth the wait.

Hosta flowers appear on spikes for several weeks in midsummer to fall, depending on the cultivar. Some gardeners dislike the flowers and cut them off when they appear. However, many cultivars can be grown primarily for their attractive flowers. The single or double blooms may be lavender or white, in thick, stocky clusters or on tall, graceful spikes. Some are lightly fragrant and most are excellent for cutting. There are so many interesting new cultivars that collecting hostas can become an addiction! Entire books have been written about these plants,

Hosta undulata 'Albo-marginata'

not appreciate the competition for water that shallow-rooted trees such as maples, beeches, or dogwoods provide, but they can grow well under deep-rooted trees such as oaks.

Hostas seem to be the very fruit of life for slugs and snails. Check for these pests regularly (don't forget to look for them *under* the leaves, too), and remove and destroy any within sight. Diatomaceous earth and beer traps can help control their damage. Hostas do not die gracefully in fall, so cut them back when the foliage turns yellow. Division is an easy way to propagate hostas. Some cultivars self-sow.

Uses. Hostas are excellent foliage plants for a deciduous groundcover in shady areas and for the front or middle of a shady border. The larger cultivars make stately landscape specimen plants; lower-growing cultivars are popular as edging plants. Hostas look great in containers in the shade, especially when they are combined with longer-blooming annuals or perennials. The flowers are good for cutting for fresh bouquets, and many have a sweet fragrance. Miniature cultivars are sometimes grown as bonsai companion plants.

Iberis sempervirens
eye-BEER-iss sem-per-VY-renz. Perennial candytuft. Early spring. Zones 4 to 8.
○ ◑ ❋

Characteristics. Height: 16 inches. Colors: White.

In early spring, perennial candytuft bursts into thick clouds of white blooms that almost completely cover the foliage. It blooms for up to 10 weeks, making a charming complement to tulips and other brightly colored spring bulbs. The shrubby plants have handsome, narrow, dark green leaves. Perennial candytuft is evergreen and spreads into mats, making it an ideal low-growing groundcover.

How to Grow. To grow your own plants, sow seed directly in a protected area of the garden in midsummer. Move the young plants to their final locations in fall or early spring. Plants are also available from garden centers and through mail-order catalogs.

Perennial candytuft grows best in well-drained, slightly acid soil in full sun. Cut back the spent flowers to keep the plants looking neat. This perennial does not normally require division. For propa-

Iberis sempervirens

gation, take cuttings from soft tip growth in late summer and overwinter them in a coldframe. The plants are relatively free of pests and diseases, and require little care once they are established.

Uses. Perennial candytuft is a popular spring-blooming perennial for borders, edgings, and rock gardens. It also makes an attractive evergreen groundcover.

INDIGO, FALSE. See *Baptisia australis*

Iris spp.
EYE-riss. Iris. Spring or summer. Zones 3 to 9.
○ ◑ ❋

Characteristics. Height: 6 inches to 4 feet. Colors: Blue, violet, yellow, pink, purple, apricot, deep red, bronze, white, and bicolors.

This important genus includes bulbs and perennials. They all share the familiar iris flower form, with upright or drooping "standards" and drooping "falls." The species differ in flower form and size, foliage, height, color range, bloom time, and soil requirements. With so many plants to choose from, you're sure to find at least one that is perfect for almost any site. The most popular perennial iris species include bearded iris hybrids, Siberian iris (*Iris sibirica*), Japanese iris (*I. ensata*, also known as *I. kaempferi*), yellow flag iris (*I. pseudacorus*), and dwarf crested iris (*I. cristata*).

The bearded iris hybrids are perhaps the best-

Tall bearded iris

known iris group. They grow from fleshy underground stems called rhizomes. They bloom from May to June, and some cultivars repeat their bloom in late summer or early fall. The flowers are characterized by the hairy "beards" on their lower petals, often in a contrasting color from the standards and falls. Bearded iris blooms are often bicolored and may have striking veins in contrasting colors. Many are fragrant. The color range is truly immense and includes every color in the rainbow. One of the prettiest shades is the glowing apricot-peach of 'Beverly Sills'.

Bearded irises vary in height from 8 inches to 3 feet, although most cultivars grow from 2 to 3 feet tall. The taller cultivars tend to have larger flowers but generally need to be staked. Medium-height cultivars are self-supporting. Bloom times vary, too; careful selection can give you a garden of bearded iris that blooms for many weeks. The upright, sword-shaped foliage is handsome, although it has a tendency to burn at the tips in the heat of summer.

Siberian iris is a vigorous perennial with long, narrow, straplike leaves. It has classic iris flowers that look more streamlined than those of bearded iris and do not have the beards. The flowers come in shades of blue, purple, pink, and white, and many have attractive veins. They bloom in May or June for about 2 weeks on 2- to 4-foot stems. The foliage always looks fresh and is more useful in the border than that of bearded iris, since it usually does not burn at the tips and is not as subject to the foliage diseases that attack bearded iris.

Japanese iris has breathtakingly beautiful flowers—perhaps the prettiest of all iris. They are large

and elegant, with gently drooping standards and falls. When they are caught by breezes, they look like graceful birds in flight. Japanese irises come in shades of blue, purple, lavender, and white, and many have beautifully etched veins. They bloom in June or July for a short period—about 2 weeks. Their foliage is like that of Siberian iris, only wider. The plants grow from 2 to 3 feet tall but rarely need staking.

Yellow flag is a water-loving iris that can grow in ponds or along moist stream banks. It has big, bright yellow flowers and blooms just after the Japanese irises have finished. The plants grow over 3 feet tall and have attractive bluish green, straplike foliage.

Dwarf crested iris is a compact wildflower that reaches only 6 to 8 inches tall. This vivid, charming plant bears blue to violet flowers; the petals are highlighted with white and yellow markings. The narrow, sword-shaped leaves grow taller than the

Iris sibirica 'Dewful'
with peony 'Kansas', *Clematis recta*, and *Baptisia australis*

flower stems, so the flowers bloom amid a leafy carpet. This species is hardy in Zones 4 to 9.

How to Grow. Start your iris collection with purchased plants. Plants are available at any nursery and through mail-order catalogs. There are many specialty iris mail-order nurseries.

Irises vary in their soil requirements. Bearded iris prefers rich, well-drained soil and can rot if the drainage is poor. Siberian iris also does best in rich, well-drained soil. Dwarf crested iris will grow fine in average garden soil as long as it gets adequate moisture, but good drainage is critical; waterlogged soil will cause the roots to rot. Japanese iris and yellow flag, on the other hand, can grow in wet soil, and even water. Most types grow best in full sun, but many can tolerate light shade. Dwarf crested iris can take full sun if the soil is evenly moist; otherwise, it prefers partial shade. Plant bearded irises so the rhizomes are level with the soil surface. Deadhead irises after they bloom, to keep the plants looking neat.

Bearded irises are susceptible to iris borer, a wormlike insect that bores holes in the rhizomes, causing them to rot. Divide your bearded irises every 2 or 3 years in early July and check them for borer holes; discard pieces with borers or borer damage. On the rest, cut back the foliage by half and replant the rhizomes. Divide other irises every 3 or 4 years in spring or fall, whenever they become overcrowded. Siberian irises form sturdy clumps that can be difficult to divide without a very sharp spade and a strong back.

Uses. Irises are ideal for the front, middle, or back of the border, depending on the height of the plants. Naturalize them in wildflower meadows, or plant them in masses. Japanese iris and yellow flag can be grown in water gardens and wetland areas; they are also popular in Japanese gardens. Dwarf crested iris makes an excellent seasonal groundcover and is especially good for slopes, since it thrives in well-drained soil. It is also useful as an edging plant and for spring color at the front of borders, in woodland gardens, and in rock gardens. The taller irises produce flowers that are terrific for cutting. Irises are often grouped with daylilies as the perfect perennial plants for beginners.

JOE-PYE WEED. See *Eupatorium* spp.

Kniphofia hybrid

Kniphofia hybrids
nih-FOE-fee-uh. Red-hot poker.
Summer. Zones 5 to 8.

Characteristics. Height: 2 to 5 feet. Colors: Orange, red, yellow, cream, and bicolors.

These fascinating perennials have spikes of two-toned flowers that look as if they were on fire. The two-toned effect is a result of uneven blooming of the tubelike florets along the spike: The bottom flowers turn yellow and start to wither before the top flowers are finished blooming. Some fade to creamy white and have red or coral tops. There are also some striking all-yellow cultivars in shades of light primrose to bright lemon yellow. Red-hot pokers bloom for several weeks in June, July, or August, depending on the cultivar. The grasslike foliage looks fresh and handsome until after the plants bloom, when it tends to look overgrown and tired.

How to Grow. To start your own plants, sow seed directly in a protected area of the garden in midsummer. Move the young plants to their permanent locations in fall or early spring. Plants are also available at some garden centers and through mail-order catalogs.

The plants prefer rich, moist, well-drained soil in full sun. They are fairly drought-tolerant and long-lived where they are happy. They need a protective winter mulch in areas with cold winters. After the plants bloom, cut the foliage back by half for a neater appearance. Divide the plants in spring in areas with cold winters; in warmer regions, divide them after bloom.

Uses. Red-hot pokers are useful for the middle or back of the border. Plant them in masses for an interesting landscape feature. The flowers are fascinating in fresh arrangements.

LADY'S-MANTLE. See *Alchemilla mollis*
LAMB'S EARS. See *Stachys byzantina*
LENTEN ROSE. See *Helleborus* spp.
LEOPARD'S-BANE. See *Doronicum caucasicum*

Liatris pycnostachya

lee-AT-riss pik-no-STAKE-yuh. Gayfeather, prairie blazing star. Midsummer to fall. Zones 3 to 9.

Characteristics. Height: 2 to 5 feet. Colors: Pink to lavender.

The tall, wandlike flowers of gayfeather, a native

Liatris pycnostachya
with *Monarda fistulosa*

wildflower, sway gracefully in the breeze, looking as grand in the garden as they once did among tall prairie grasses across the Midwest. The flowers are unusual in that the blooms at the top of the spike open first, followed by those below. Gayfeather's long stems are covered with grasslike foliage.

How to Grow. To start your own plants, sow seed directly in a protected area of the garden in midsummer. Move the young plants to their permanent locations in fall or early spring. Plants are also available at some garden centers and through mail-order catalogs.

Give gayfeather full sun and well-drained soil that's rich in organic matter. It will not tolerate wet soil. The plants may need staking, especially in exposed, windy sites. They benefit from a good winter mulch, particularly in Zones 3 to 6, to prevent the roots from being pushed out of the ground by alternate freezing and thawing.

Uses. This plant is excellent for adding color, height, and texture to borders and meadows. It also makes a wonderful cut flower. Try planting it next to bee balm (*Monarda didyma*) and asters for a gorgeous display of pinks, reds, and lavenders.

Ligularia spp.

lig-yew-LAIR-ee-uh. Ligularia.
Summer. Zones 4 to 7.

Characteristics. Height: 4 to 6 feet. Colors: Yellow.

Ligularias are large, landscape-sized plants with big, undulating leaves that have sharply toothed edges. The bright yellow flowers bloom for several weeks in July. Ligularias add a rough, bold texture to the garden. When they are well sited, they can be unforgettable. When poorly sited, however, they are sorry reminders that in gardening, as in real estate, location can be everything.

Big-leaf ligularia (*Ligularia dentata*) is grown primarily for its foliage. The purple-green, kidney-shaped leaves have sharply toothed edges and can grow up to 20 inches wide. The brassy yellow daisies are often droopy-looking and have a surprising subtle, sweet fragrance. 'Desdemona' is the most heat-tolerant cultivar. A companion, 'Othello', is a more compact version.

Ligularia stenocephala 'The Rocket'

'The Rocket' ligularia (*L. stenocephala* 'The Rocket') has rounder, heart-shaped leaves; they are light green with purple undersides, and have sharply toothed edges. The lemon yellow flowers grow on dramatic 2-foot-tall spikes and make a highly visible display when the plants are used as accent plantings or in a large border.

How to Grow. To grow your own plants, sow seed of the species directly in a protected area of the garden in midsummer. Move the young plants to their final locations in fall or early spring. Plants are also generally available from garden centers and are commonly listed in mail-order catalogs.

Ligularias need rich, moist soil that does not dry out. In hot, dry conditions, they will wilt dramatically and make you wonder why you ever thought of planting them. Although they usually recover in cooler evening temperatures, it's best to avoid dry sites altogether, since the wilting plants are not an attractive sight. Divide the plants in spring to reju-

venate overgrown clumps or for propagation.

Uses. Ligularias are dramatic at the back of the border or as specimen landscape plants in wet spots. They are also ideal for planting on the edges of ponds and bog gardens where the soil remains moist.

LILYTURF. See *Liriope muscari*
LILY, BLACKBERRY. See *Belamcanda chinensis*

Liriope muscari
leer-EYE-oh-pee mus-KAR-ee. Lilyturf.
Late summer. Zones 6 to 9.

Characteristics. Height: 1 foot. Colors: Purple or white.

This reliable perennial is grown primarily for its handsome, grasslike foliage. The leaves are usually a rich, deep green, although some cultivars have variegated foliage. Spikes of purple or white flowers bloom in late summer and give way to attractive black berries. The flowers resemble grape hyacinths, as reflected in the species name *muscari*. Lilyturf spreads quickly and is easy to divide whenever you want more plants. In fact, some species can become positively invasive, but *Liriope muscari* is fairly well behaved. When you want it to stop, it is easy to weed out.

How to Grow. To start your own plants, sow seed directly in a protected area of the garden in midsummer. Move the young plants to their final locations in fall or early spring. Plants of the species and cultivars are also widely available from garden centers and through mail-order catalogs.

Lilyturf thrives in well-drained, moist soil in partial shade, but it can adapt to a range of soil types in both sun and shade. It will even grow in dry shade, a useful virtue for a perennial. The foliage is usually evergreen but can look ratty after a hard winter; cut the plants back in spring to improve their appearance and to allow room for new growth. You can divide the plants anytime, although the cool weather of fall and spring is probably the easiest on the plants.

Uses. Lilyturf makes an excellent groundcover or edging in sun or shade. It is a good choice to plant around the base of deep-rooted trees or shrubs. The blooms are charming as cut flowers.

Lobelia cardinalis

Lobelia spp.

loh-BEE-lee-uh. Perennial lobelia, cardinal flower.
Summer. Zones 2 to 9.

Characteristics. Height: 2 to 5 feet. Colors: Red or blue.

The two most commonly grown perennial lobelias are cardinal flower (*Lobelia cardinalis*) and blue lobelia (*L. siphilitica*). The upright plants of both species produce tall flower spikes and long, narrow leaves that begin the season as basal rosettes.

Cardinal flower is the more popular of the two species. It features very attractive, dark green to reddish bronze leaves and showy, 3- to 5-foot spikes of brilliant red flowers that bloom from late summer into early fall. This American native naturalizes well in boggy wildflower meadows, along stream banks, and in other areas with wet soil. It spreads when it is happy, forming nice-sized colonies in time.

Blue lobelia grows only 2 to 3 feet tall and has green foliage. The flower spikes are covered with deep blue flowers in mid- to late summer. Blue lobelia blooms for several weeks and is more tolerant of hot, dry conditions than cardinal flower. Its display will never match that of cardinal flower, but it has a cooler, more subtle, look that blends well with other colors. It, too, spreads obligingly to form colonies.

How to Grow. To start your own plants, sow seed directly in a protected area of the garden in midsummer. Move the young plants to their permanent locations in fall or early spring. Cardinal flower is readily available from some garden centers and through mail-order perennial and wildflower sources. Blue lobelia is less widely available but can be obtained from some mail-order nurseries.

Both species prefer moist, rich soil. In dry soil, cardinal flower wilts sadly, and blue lobelia is weak and stunted. These plants prefer full sun but tolerate partial shade. They never need staking. Perennial lobelias tend to be short-lived unless you divide the basal rosettes in spring or fall every 2 or 3 years. They are relatively free of pests and diseases, and thrive with little care once they are established in the right location.

Uses. Perennial lobelias are useful for difficult wet locations in full sun or partial shade. Cardinal flower is attractive in the middle or back of the perennial border. Both species naturalize well in woodlands or along stream banks. They make interesting landscape accents when planted in masses. The flowers are good for cutting.

LOOSESTRIFE. See *Lysimachia* spp.
LUNGWORT. See *Pulmonaria saccharata*

Lupinus Russell hybrids

lew-PIE-nus. Lupine.
Early summer. Zones 3 to 8.

Characteristics. Height: 3 feet. Colors: Blue, pink, purple, yellow, white, and bicolors.

This perennial member of the pea family is unmatched in its gorgeous spikes of pealike flowers,

Lupinus Russell hybrids

which come in cool shades of blue, pink, white, pale yellow, and purple, plus many attractive bicolors. The flowers appear in June on bushy plants with handsome smooth, handlike, blue-green foliage. The Russell hybrids are perennial relatives of the native wildflower Texas bluebonnet (*Lupinus texensis*) and *L. polyphyllus*, which is naturalized from California to British Columbia.

How to Grow. To raise your own plants, sow seed directly in a protected area of the garden in midsummer. Move the young plants to their final locations in fall or early spring. Lupines often bloom the same year from seed if you start them indoors 8 to 10 weeks before the last frost date. Transplant hardened-off seedlings to the garden after danger of a heavy frost has passed. Plants are also available from garden centers and through many mail-order catalogs.

Lupines are cool-season plants that are at their best in areas with cool summer nights. They prefer full sun or light shade and rich, cool, moist, lightly acidic soil with good drainage. Lupines often require staking. If you cut the spent flower stalks back after blooming, the plants may reward you with a second flush of bloom in late summer or fall. Lupines dislike being moved and tend to be short-lived even where they are happy. Because they can bloom the first year from early-sown seed, they are often grown as annuals.

Uses. These spiky plants are dramatic at the back of the border and beautiful for cut flowers. They also naturalize well in wildflower meadows.

Lychnis spp.
LIK-niss. Maltese cross, rose campion.
Early summer. Zones 4 to 8.

Characteristics. Height: 2 to 3 feet. Colors: Scarlet, pink, magenta, and white.

The genus *Lychnis* contains many colorful species. Two of the most popular for perennial gardens are Maltese cross (*L. chalcedonica*) and rose campion (*L. coronaria*).

Maltese cross produces rounded clusters of bright scarlet, white, or pink blooms in June. The plants are 2 to 3 feet tall and have green foliage. Double-flowered forms are available in white, rose, or red.

Lychnis chalcedonica

Lychnis coronaria
with *Begonia grandis*

Rose campion is a shorter-lived species with extraordinarily intense magenta flowers and silvery foliage. No one can see rose campion without asking what it is or commenting on its eye-catching beauty. 'Alba' is a white-flowered cultivar that makes a hauntingly beautiful impression in an all-white garden. It is also a much easier color than magenta to work with in a perennial design. The foliage of rose campion is attractive all season and blends well with blues and other pinks.

How to Grow. To grow your own plants, sow seed directly in a protected area of the garden in midsummer. Move the young plants to their final locations in fall or early spring. Plants are not commonly available for sale, but you may be able to get seedlings from a friend who already has plants.

Both Maltese cross and rose campion prefer rich, well-drained soil in full sun. They tend to rot in poorly drained soil. Deadhead for a possible second flush of bloom, leaving a few seed heads. These plants can be short-lived, but they redeem themselves by self-sowing reliably; move the seedlings in fall or spring to their permanent locations.

Uses. Maltese cross and rose campion are eye-catching additions to the middle of the border in May or June. The blooms make pretty cut flowers.

Lysimachia spp.
ly-sih-MAK-ee-uh. Loosestrife.
Summer. Zones 3 to 8.
○ ◑ ☀ ✿

Characteristics. Height: 3 feet. Colors: White or yellow.

Two species of *Lysimachia* are commonly grown in perennial gardens: yellow loosestrife (*L. punctata*) and gooseneck loostrife (*L. clethroides*). The latter bears fascinating flower clusters that look very much like the neck of a goose, as its common name suggests. The clusters of tiny white flowers bloom for several weeks in July on very vigorous, 3-foot plants. The attractive deep green foliage has a reddish tinge; in autumn, it turns a deep red color, which lasts for many weeks until the plants are killed to the ground by a severe frost. Yellow loosestrife bears its flowers along the stems in early summer.

Lysimachia clethroides

Lysimachia punctata

Macleaya cordata
mak-LAY-uh kor-DAH-tuh. Plume poppy.
Summer. Zones 3 to 8.
○ ◑

Characteristics. Height: 8 to 10 feet. Colors: White.

This towering perennial is guaranteed to attract attention in the garden. It grows 8 to 10 feet tall every season and has big, gray-green, divided leaves that loosely resemble oak leaves. It is topped by tall spikes of creamy white, fluffy-looking flower plumes for several weeks in July.

Plume poppy is not an appropriate perennial for small gardens. Not only would it be out of proportion to its surroundings, but it is also a rampant spreader that would colonize the whole garden quickly. This spreading habit is plume poppy's main defect and must be considered when siting the

Keep in mind that gooseneck loosestrife is an extremely invasive perennial. If you decide to include it in your garden, sink a bottomless bucket in the planting spot, fill it with soil, and plant in that to control the spread. Or simply plant gooseneck loosestrife where the spread isn't a problem. Some bold designers use it as a large landscape feature. Yellow loosestrife is a vigorous plant, but not as invasive as gooseneck loosestrife.

How to Grow. To grow your own plants, you can sow seed directly in a protected area of the garden in midsummer. Move the young plants to their final locations in fall or early spring. Plants are also available from some garden centers and through mail-order catalogs. Or gardeners who already grow the plants may be able to give you a few pieces to start.

Loosestrifes can grow in just about any kind of soil and also tolerate quite a bit of shade. However, moist, well-drained, rich soil in full sun is best. Both species are rarely bothered by pests and diseases. To get more plants or to keep them within bounds, divide them in fall or spring.

Uses. Loosestrifes are striking in the middle of the border, as long as they can be controlled. Because it spreads so quickly, gooseneck loosestrife can also be very effective in mass plantings. Cut the flowers for fresh arrangements.

Macleaya cordata

plants. The roots send out runners that can emerge many feet away from the original plants. You can try to control them by slicing around the plants several times a season with a sharp spade. Under ideal growing conditions, however, this can be a never-ending job. The best site for plume poppy is a wild area where you want some height and are willing to let the plants roam; in such a spot, they are a spectacular sight that can be matched by few other perennials.

How to Grow. To grow your own plants, sow seed directly in a protected area of the garden in midsummer. Move the young plants to their final locations in fall or early spring. Plants are not usually available at garden centers, but you can often find them in mail-order catalogs.

Plume poppy grows well in all soils, but does best in well-drained, rich soil. It prefers full sun or partial shade. Despite their enormous height, the plants are self-supporting and never need staking. The work involved with plume poppy is to prevent if from taking more space that you are willing to give it. If you want even more plants, you can divide them in fall or spring.

Uses. Plume poppy makes an excellent herbaceous hedge, screen, or landscape accent. It can be planted in the back of very wide borders if it will not be way out of proportion, and if you take precautions to contain it. Try plume poppy in very large containers for a truly unusual patio plant.

MALTESE CROSS. See *Lychnis* spp.
MEADOW RUE, COLUMBINE. See *Thalictrum aquilegifolium*
MEADOWSWEET. See *Filipendula* spp.

Mertensia virginica
mer-TEN-see-uh ver-JIN-ih-kuh.
Virginia bluebells. Early spring. Zones 3 to 8.
◐ ⁂

Characteristics. Height: 1 to 2 feet. Colors: Blue.

Virginia bluebells is one of our best native American perennials for woodland naturalizing. It sends up beautiful purple shoots in spring, just as many spring bulbs are emerging. Soon after the

Mertensia virginica

leaves unfurl and take on an olive green tinge, stalks with clusters of small bell-shaped flowers appear. The flowers are purplish pink in bud and open to a rare sky blue; they last for just a couple of weeks and then disappear. Soon afterward, the foliage also disappears. The plants go completely dormant by June until the following spring.

Depending on how you look at it, the ephemeral nature of Virginia bluebells is part of their charm or their greatest drawback. If you think of them as spring bulbs, such as daffodils or tulips, it is not difficult to reconcile yourself to their short garden life. They actually have an advantage over bulbs, since their ripening foliage lasts a very short time and does not present a problem in June, when the foliage of bulbs becomes unsightly and must be hidden with other plants. But Virginia bluebells *do* leave a gap, which you might want to fill with annuals or later-blooming perennials.

How to Grow. To grow your own plants, try sowing fresh seed in a protected area of the garden in midsummer. Move the young plants to their final locations in fall or early spring. Bareroot plants are sometimes available at local garden centers and through mail-order bulb and nursery catalogs for spring or fall planting.

Virginia bluebells prefer moist, rich, well-drained, woodland soil in partial shade. They can tolerate full sun in cooler areas but do best in partial shade in warmer areas. The plants are easy to care for and are rarely bothered by pests and diseases. They do not need to be divided unless they become invasive.

Uses. Virginia bluebells is an excellent perennial to naturalize in a woodland. You can use it in borders if you replace it in summer with annuals or later-blooming perennials. Try it in scattered clumps as landscape accents or as companions for spring bulbs. The blue color combines beautifully with yellow and white daffodils or orange and red tulips. The flowers are good for cutting.

MISSOURI EVENING PRIMROSE. See *Oenothera missouriensis*

Monarda didyma
moh-NAR-duh DID-ih-muh. Bee balm.
Summer. Zones 3 to 9.

Characteristics. Height: 3 feet. Colors: Pink, purple, red, and white.

This American native produces colorful masses of fluffy-looking flowers in early to midsummer. The plants grow vigorously in ideal conditions, forming

Monarda didyma

colonies when they are allowed to spread. They provide many fresh cut flowers for summer arrangements, and attract bees and hummingbirds to the garden. The flowers are followed by attractive seed heads. When it is in bloom, it is difficult to find fault with bee balm.

But bee balm is not without its drawbacks. The plants are often disfigured by powdery mildew (a white, powdery coating on leaves and stems) in the humid weather of late summer. They can also be rampant spreaders. Ideally, you should plant them where they can spread freely without crowding out other plants. If you decide to grow bee balm in a border, plant it in a sunken, bottomless bucket, or thoroughly weed out all unwanted runners each year.

How to Grow. To grow your own plants, sow seed directly in a protected area of the garden in midsummer. Move the young plants to their permanent locations in fall or early spring. They are sometimes available at garden centers and can always be purchased from mail-order nurseries and wildflower specialty nurseries. Neighbors who have colonies of bee balm will always have plants to spare.

Bee balm thrives in rich, moisture-retentive, well-drained soil in full sun. The plants tolerate light shade, and in fact prefer soil that is on the dry side. Bee balm is very susceptible to powdery mildew, although some cultivars have been selected for resistance. Giving plants plenty of room, or at least thinning out the crowded stems, will allow for good air circulation around the leaves and decrease problems with powdery mildew. The stems are strong and normally do not need to be staked. Divide the plants in spring when they begin to crowd each other. Pull out wandering plants that show up where you don't want them.

Uses. Bee balm is useful for the middle or back of the border and wonderful for naturalizing in a wildflower meadow. The cut flowers are attractive in fresh arrangements. This perennial also makes a colorful addition to herb gardens; use the leaves to make a pleasant-tasting tea.

MOSS PINK. See *Phlox* spp.
MOUNTAIN BLUET. See *Centaurea montana*

Nepeta X faassenii

Nepeta X faassenii
NEP-eh-tuh fas-SEN-ee-eye. Catmint.
Summer. Zones 4 to 8.
○ ◑

Characteristics. Height: 18 inches. Colors: Lavender-blue.

Several species of *Nepeta* are commonly called catmint or catnip. The name "catnip" is usually reserved for the herb *N. cataria*, which is not as ornamental as other species. Catmint (*N. X faassenii*) is a cross between *N. mussinii* and *N. nepetella*. This vigorous hybrid has a spreading, sprawling habit, which makes it a good choice for a groundcover. It produces masses of lavender-blue flowers from June to August—sometimes even longer, if you shear the plants back after bloom. The attractive gray-green foliage adds a light texture to borders; it is ornamental even when the plants are not in bloom.

How to Grow. Unlike many other *Nepeta*

species, this catmint does not set seed, so it will not self-sow. Start with plants purchased from garden centers or through mail-order catalogs.

Catmint requires well-drained soil that is not rich. It grows best in full sun but tolerates light shade. For a second flush of bloom, cut the plants back by half after flowering. They are rarely bothered by pests and diseases, and are easy to maintain in the garden. Propagate plants by division in spring or fall.

Uses. Catmint is a fine perennial for the front of the border and for edgings. It also performs well in rock gardens. The mounding plants make an interesting spring-through-fall groundcover. Although *N. X faassenii* is not the plant normally grown for catnip, it still looks at home in an herb garden. Try a few in containers, too!

OBEDIENT PLANT. See *Physostegia virginiana*

Oenothera missouriensis
ee-no-THEE-ruh miz-er-ee-EN-sis. Missouri evening primrose, Ozark sundrops.
Summer. Zones 3 to 8.
○ ✻

Characteristics. Height: 9 to 12 inches. Colors: Bright yellow.

When this plant is flowering, it is like having a burst of sunlight in your garden. There are hardly any other garden plants whose color can match the

Oenothera missouriensis

dazzlingly clear, clean, and lustrous yellow of the flowers. The 3- to 4-inch blooms are borne in summer on short, hairy stems with lance-shaped leaves.

How to Grow. Missouri evening primrose needs full sun and well-drained soil. It prefers dry—even sandy, rocky, or gravelly—soil; wet conditions can lead to root rot.

The plants grow readily from seed sown directly in the garden in fall or early spring. They are also easy to divide in fall or spring. Plants are often available at garden centers and are easy to find in mail-order catalogs.

Uses. The sprawling habit of Missouri evening primrose makes it an excellent plant for raised beds and rock gardens. This cheerful, drought-tolerant perennial is especially suitable for dry-soil areas. For a beautiful combination, try planting Missouri evening primrose with Mexican hat plant (*Ratibida columnifera*), purple coneflower (*Echinacea purpurea*), and lanceleaf coreopsis (*Coreopsis lanceolata*).

ORIENTAL POPPY. See *Papaver orientale*
OZARK SUNDROPS. See *Oenothera missouriensis*

Paeonia lactiflora

pee-OH-nee-uh lak-tih-FLOR-uh. Peony.
Late spring to early summer. Zones 3 to 8.

○ ◑ ✄❀ ❦

Characteristics. Height: 2 to 4 feet. Colors: Pink, coral, yellow, red, white, and bicolors.

Peonies are among the best-loved perennials in northern gardens. They thrive in Zones 3 to 8 but perform poorly in frost-free or nearly frost-free areas. Every year, Burpee customers who have moved from cooler zones to warmer climates say they miss growing peonies more than any other garden plant.

Peonies are popular for their big, softly colored flowers. The blooms of some look like fluffy powder puffs; others resemble cabbage roses. Single, semidouble, and fully double forms are available in a wide range of colors. Many are wonderfully fragrant, and mass plantings of mixed cultivars always yield a delicious scent in the garden.

The beauty of peonies extends beyond their flowers. In spring, their emerging red leaves are as important a part of the garden as the accompanying spring bulbs. Their spherical flower buds have a

Paeonia lactiflora 'Gay Paree' (*background*),
'Krinkled White' (*center*), and
'Mrs. Wilder Bancroft' (*foreground*)

charm of their own, suspended over the foliage in anticipation of the big flowers to come. The divided foliage is handsome all summer and often takes on a glorious red color in late summer to early fall.

Gardeners often ask about the ants that are sometimes present around peony flowers and flower buds. One theory is that they are attendant ants for aphids, tiny pests that like to feed on new growth, including flower buds. But aphids may not be present while the ants are. Another theory suggests that the ants are needed to help the flowers open. But the ants aren't always present, and the blooms open well enough without their assistance. According to yet another theory, the ants are attracted to the sugary nectar that exudes from the buds and is present in the flowers. Some peony experts say they have never noticed ants around peony flowers. Whatever the reason, the ants do not harm the plants and can be easily washed off when the flowers are brought indoors after being cut.

In the proper environment, peonies are exceptionally long-lived perennials, often outliving the gardeners who planted them. They resent being moved as they age, so choose an appropriate permanent location and leave them alone. They will reward you with a lifetime of reliable performance.

How to Grow. Peonies take up to 2 years to germinate from seed, which is clearly inconvenient for even the most adventurous gardener! You're better off starting bareroot plants, which are available through many mail-order catalogs.

Most suppliers will deliver bareroot plants—with 3 to 5 "eyes" (buds)—for planting in spring or fall, although experienced gardeners agree that fall is the best time for planting. The soil should be well drained and rich, in a sunny or lightly shaded location. Prepare the soil as deeply as possible, at least 1 to 2 feet deep. Set the roots so the reddish eyes are 1 to 2 inches below the soil surface. The plants may take their time to bloom—sometimes 2 or 3 years after they are planted. However, once they start blooming, you'll forget their slow start.

Peonies benefit from support, which you can easily provide by using inconspicuous peony "hoops." The plants are heavy feeders, so scratch some bonemeal or superphosphate into the soil in spring or fall. They also need plenty of water, especially during long dry spells. Peonies are subject to botrytis, a fungal disease that kills shoots and flower buds and disfigures foliage. Cutting the plants to the ground in the fall will help prevent this problem, since the pathogen overwinters in the dead foliage.

Uses. Peonies are at their best when planted in masses as landscape features. They make wonderful herbaceous hedges with three seasons of interest. They are also splendid flowers for cutting; try them in dinner-table bouquets. (Don't forget to wash off the ants!) The cut flowers take up an astonishing amount of water, so check the water level in the vase every day.

PAINTED DAISY. See *Chrysanthemum* spp.

Paeonia 'Lotus Queen'

Papaver orientale

Papaver orientale
PAH-puh-ver or-ee-en-TAL-ee. Oriental poppy.
Late spring. Zones 3 to 8.
○ ☀ ✿ ❀

Characteristics Height: 2 to 4 feet. Colors: Pink, orange, red, salmon, and white.

This perennial cousin of the summer-blooming annual poppy is always a focal point when it is included in the late-spring garden. The flowers are much larger than those of their annual relatives and come in very bright, even gaudy colors, with contrasting centers and blotches in black, purple, or white. The flowers may be single, semidouble, or double. They are followed by very interesting seed-pods, which make attractive additions to dried-flower arrangements. The rough-textured, hairy, fernlike foliage is a giant version of the delicate foliage of Shirley or Flanders poppy (*Papaver rhoeas*).

The plants go dormant during the summer, leaving a gap in the border that should be filled with annuals or later-blooming perennials. (Plant the annuals carefully to avoid damaging the poppy roots.) The foliage sometimes reappears in the fall.

How to Grow. To grow your own plants, sow seed directly in a protected area of the garden in midsummer. Move the young plants to their final locations in fall or early spring. To reduce the danger of transplant shock, you can also grow them in peat pots. Plants are available from garden centers.

For the widest range of colors, check out mail-order nurseries. The plants are usually shipped in pots to protect the roots.

Oriental poppies prefer well-drained, rich soil in full sun. They can tolerate summer drought when they are dormant. Like most poppies, they have long, easily damaged taproots and should not be moved once they are established. Also, avoid dividing the plants unless they become very crowded; then divide them carefully in late summer or early fall.

Uses. The brightly colored, late-spring flowers of Oriental poppies are striking in borders. Plan for companions to fill the space left when the plants go dormant. Cut the flowers for fresh bouquets; save the seedpods for interesting additions to dried arrangements.

PEONY. See *Paeonia lactiflora*

Perovskia atriplicifolia
per-OFF-skee-uh ah-trih-plih-sih-FOE-lee-uh.
Russian sage. Summer. Zones 3 to 9.

Perovskia atriplicifolia

Characteristics. Height: 3 feet. Colors: Blue flowers, silver foliage.

Russian sage is gaining in popularity in American gardens for several reasons. The plants make striking landscape accents and look good the same year you plant them. Plus, they are very drought-resistant and are easy to grow and maintain. Russian sage is an excellent choice for hot, dry locations where so many other perennials burn out. Landscapers use it in one of the most difficult areas any perennial will ever have to deal with—parking-lot islands surrounded by a sea of concrete. The only place this plant is not happy is in a wet, poorly drained location, or in the shade. Russian sage is such a valuable perennial the Perennial Plant Association selected it as the Perennial Plant of the Year for 1995.

Russian sage has attractive foliage that persists from spring through fall and into the winter. The silvery color contrasts beautifully with both hot and cool colors in borders. The plants practically glow in the dark and can be haunting when plant-ed near a deck or patio that is used at night. The flowers are not especially showy but add to the plants' interest for several weeks in July and August, when the perennial border often has a decidedly tired look.

How to Grow. Start with plants purchased from garden centers or through mail-order catalogs.

Russian sage prefers poor, well-drained soil in full sun; wet soil means certain death. The stems tend to become woody but will produce fresh new growth if cut back in fall or spring; they can be an interesting winter accent if you leave them until spring. Propagate by division in spring or fall or by stem cuttings in late summer. These durable, easy-to-grow plants are rarely bothered by pests or diseases and are ideal for beginners.

Uses. Russian sage is useful for the back of the border or as a landscape plant. The flowers and fragrant foliage are great for cutting for fresh arrangements. Even though the flowers are blue, Russian sage is an excellent choice for an all-white garden because of its silver foliage.

Phlox paniculata

Phlox spp.

FLOKS. Phlox. Spring or summer. Zones 3 to 8.

○ ◑ ⁂ ❧

Characteristics. Height: 4 inches to 4 feet. Colors: Blue, pink, lilac, purple, red, salmon, and white.

There is a phlox for just about any garden use. Some species are low-growing and mat-forming, and make good groundcovers. Others are tall and narrow, and can be used in the middle or back of the border. There are also medium-sized types, which make good edging plants.

Garden phlox (*Phlox paniculata*) is the species most commonly grown in perennial borders. It grows 3 to 4 feet tall and has an exceptionally long bloom period—from July to August, sometimes even into October. The flowers appear in clusters at the top of the plants. Cultivars are available in shades of pink, red, lavender, salmon, and white,

many with contrasting eyes. The plants have handsome green foliage, although the leaves are often marred by powdery mildew (a fungal disease that produces dusty white deposits). Fortunately, you can choose from several mildew-resistant cultivars, including 'David' (white), 'Eva Callum' (clear pink with a red eye), and 'Franz Schubert' (lavender with darker eyes). 'Starfire' is not particularly mildew-resistant, but it's worth growing for its exquisite, long-lasting, magenta to cherry red blooms.

Creeping phlox (*P. stolonifera*) is a shade-tolerant species that spreads by underground stems (stolons) to make a handsome woodland groundcover. The foliage is evergreen or semievergreen. Masses of light blue, lavender, or white flowers bloom in May well above the foliage on 6-inch stems. Creeping phlox is easy to grow and not susceptible to mildew. All you need to do is keep it from creeping where you don't want it to go. Wild sweet William (*P. divaricata*) is a 12- to 15-inch phlox for the front of the border or for the woodland. It has blue, pink, purple, or white flowers with slightly notched petals. The flowers practically cover the plants in April or May and are very striking when combined with spring-blooming bulbs.

Moss pinks (*P. subulata*) are grown primarily as groundcovers in full sun. They have narrow, almost grasslike, evergreen foliage and form thick mats that completely choke out weeds. They are often used for erosion control on hillsides. Moss pinks are a sight to behold in spring when they are covered with

Phlox subulata

blooms, which come in magenta, coral, scarlet, light pink, white, or blue. This species is also good for rock gardens, as long as it has plenty of room.

How to Grow. Start your phlox collection with plants purchased from garden centers or through mail-order catalogs.

Garden phlox prefers well-drained, rich soil in full sun or very light shade. The plants need good air circulation to help prevent severe powdery mildew problems. They also require staking. Deadheading encourages continuous bloom. Propagate by division in spring or fall, root cuttings in early spring, or stem cuttings in summer.

Creeping phlox and wild sweet William prefer moist, rich, slightly acid woodland soil and partial shade. They are mildew-resistant and require little care in the garden. For propagation, divide the plants in fall or spring, or take cuttings in summer.

Moss pink prefers dry, well-drained, slightly acid soil in full sun. It is resistant to mildew and is rarely troubled by other diseases or pests—just plant it and let it go. Propagate by cuttings in summer.

Uses. Garden phlox is excellent for the middle of the border and for cutting. Creeping phlox makes a good woodland groundcover. Wild sweet William is attractive at the front of the border or as an edging. Moss pink is ideal as a groundcover, for erosion control, and for rock gardens.

Physostegia virginiana
fy-soh-STEE-jee-uh ver-jin-ee-AY-nuh.
Obedient plant. Late summer. Zones 2 to 8.

○ ◑ ⋇✿

Characteristics. Height: 2 to 3 feet. Colors: Pink, purple, and white.

Obedient plants grow 2 to 3 feet tall and have clean, handsome green foliage all season. They burst into bloom in late summer, when flowers are very much appreciated, and continue on as asters and other fall bloomers join the display. The pink, purple, or white flowers are arranged neatly on spikes and resemble little dragons' heads—hence its alternate common name, false dragonhead. A very striking variegated form, 'Variegata', has pink flowers. This cultivar could be grown for its variegated foliage alone.

The name "obedient plant" comes from the ability of the individual flowers on each stalk to maintain whatever position they are bent into. The name is ironic, as these plants are anything but obedient in the garden. They spread rampantly in sandy soil and seem to form colonies twice their size every year. Keep this habit in mind when you decide where to place the plants.

How to Grow. If you have a friend with obedient plants, you can probably get a start of this plant whenever you want them just by asking. Otherwise, start with plants purchased from garden centers or through mail-order catalogs.

Obedient plant prefers rich, well-drained soil in full sun or light shade, although it can adapt to a wide range of conditions. Under ideal growing conditions, it is often invasive; the plants tend to be less invasive in poorly drained, clay soil. They do not grow as tall in well-drained, sandy soil. Obedient plants do not need to be staked and are rarely bothered by pests and diseases. The only garden care they demand is keeping them under control. Divide plants every other year in spring or fall to keep them in bounds; share extra plants with friends.

Uses. Obedient plant is an attractive late bloomer for the middle of the border or for massing as a landscape accent. The blooms make terrific cut flowers, although they attract ants; immerse the blooms in water to soak the ants out before you bring the flowers in the house.

PINK, MOSS. See *Phlox* spp.
PINKS. See *Dianthus* spp.

Physostegia virginiana

Platycodon grandiflorus

Platycodon grandiflorus
plat-ee-KOH-don gran-dih-FLOR-us. Balloon
flower. Summer. Zones 3 to 8.

Characteristics. Height: 10 to 36 inches.
Colors: Blue, pink, and white.

This easy-to-grow perennial is valued for its
unusual buds and pretty flowers, which provide a
rare blue color at a time when almost any flowers are
welcome in the perennial border. They are also
available in an attractive shell pink, as well as
white. The puffy, round flower buds look like little
balloons, which burst open to become elegantly
simple, star-shaped flowers. The plants are late to
emerge in spring; mark plantings with stakes to
avoid digging into them accidently in spring. They
combine well with spring bulbs, which will fill the
space until the balloon flower shoots emerge; these,
in turn, hide the ripening foliage of the bulbs.

'Mariesii' is the most popular cultivar; it grows to a
very manageable height of 1 to 2 feet and bears single blue flowers. 'Albus' is a 2-foot-tall cultivar with
white, yellow-veined flowers. 'Shell Pink' offers
light pink flowers on 20-inch stems.

How to Grow. To grow your own plants, sow
seed directly in a protected area of the garden in
midsummer. Move the young plants to their final
locations in fall or early spring. Plants of all three
colors are available at many garden centers and
through mail-order catalogs.

Balloon flower prefers moderately rich, slightly
acidic, well-drained soil in full sun. The plants can
tolerate partial shade but may grow taller than you
would like in too much shade. If you cut the taller
cultivars back halfway in June, you may not need to
stake them. However, if you want to avoid staking
or cutting the plants back altogether, try the shorter cultivars. Deadheading encourages more continuous bloom. The plants have long roots and are difficult to move unless they are dug very deeply. They
are relatively slow growers and do not need to be
divided often. When they are happy, they will self-
sow and spread by underground runners. Balloon
flowers tend to be long-lived under ideal conditions.

Uses. Grow balloon flower for mid- to late-
summer bloom in the middle of the border. The
flowers are good for cutting for fresh arrangements.

POPPY, ORIENTAL. See *Papaver orientale*
POPPY, PLUME. See *Macleaya cordata*
PRAIRIE BLAZING STAR. See *Liatris
pycnostachya*
PRIMROSE. See *Primula X polyantha*
PRIMROSE, MISSOURI EVENING.
See *Oenothera missouriensis*

Primula X polyantha
PRIM-yew-luh pol-ee-AN-thuh. Primrose.
Spring. Zones 3 to 8.

Characteristics. Height: 10 inches. Colors: All
colors, often with yellow centers.

There are many kinds of primroses, and whole
books have been written about the genus. The most
common garden type is *Primula X polyantha*. These

Primula X *polyantha*

Pulmonaria saccharata

charming plants produce rosettes of long, crinkly-edged leaves. The flower stalks rise above the foliage and are topped with clusters of small, single flowers looking out in all directions. The sweetly fragrant flowers bloom in spring, along with daffodils and tulips, and are available in any flower color you may want. The best and longest-lived cultivars are from the Barnhaven strain. The Pacific Giant strain, which is usually available in pots from florists in early spring, is short-lived in the garden and usually treated as an annual.

How to Grow. To grow your own plants, sow seed directly in a protected area of the garden in midsummer. Move the young plants to their permanent locations in fall or early spring. Plants are also available at garden centers and through mail-order catalogs. Pacific Giants strain primroses are sold in pots at nearly every florist shop in early spring.

Primroses thrive in moist, well-drained soil and light to partial shade. In hot weather, water regularly to keep the soil from drying out. Divide crowded plants in spring. The plants require little care once they are established in the right place.

Uses. Grow primroses at the front of the border, as woodland accents, or along a stream bank. Naturalize them in moist, but well-drained locations. Primroses can also grow in pots; just be sure the soil doesn't dry out. The flowers are good for cutting and are sweetly fragrant, though never overpowering.

Pulmonaria saccharata
pul-mun-ARE-ee-uh sak-uh-RAH-tuh.
Pulmonaria, lungwort. Spring. Zones 3 to 8.

Characteristics. Height: 1 foot. Colors: Blue, pink, and white.

Pulmonarias are low-growing perennials valued for their ornamental foliage and tolerance of shady conditions. The long, hairy leaves are dotted with showy, silvery blotches. In April and May, the leafy clumps produce clusters of small, bell-shaped flowers. 'Mrs. Moon' bears pink flower buds that open and mature to blue flowers. 'Sissinghurst White', named for the famous white garden at Sissinghurst Castle in England, has pure white flowers.

How to Grow. To start your own plants, try sowing fresh seed directly in a protected area of the garden in midsummer. Move the young plants to their final locations in fall or early spring. To grow cultivars that have been selected for particularly attractive foliage or flowers, buy plants at garden centers or through mail-order catalogs.

Pulmonarias need a rich, moist soil in partial shade. If the plants are allowed to dry out, they will wilt dramatically, and constant wilting will seriously weaken them. When they are well sited, they can live for many years and form a very attractive, tightly knit groundcover. For propagation, divide the plants after they bloom or move self-sown seedlings to new locations.

Uses. Pulmonarias are excellent for the front of a shade border, as an edging, or as a spring-through-fall groundcover.

RED-HOT POKER. See *Kniphofia* hybrids
ROSE CAMPION. See *Lychnis* spp.
ROSE, CHRISTMAS. See *Helleborus* spp.
ROSE, LENTEN. See *Helleborus* spp.

Rudbeckia spp.

rude-BEK-ee-uh. Coneflower. Summer. Zones 3 to 9.

Characteristics. Height: 2 to 7 feet. Colors: Yellow-orange.

Coneflowers are among the best-loved perennials for sunny sites. They range in size from 2 to 7 feet, with single daisy or fluffy double flowers in many shades of yellow. Several species and cultivars are popular for garden use.

'Goldsturm' coneflower (*Rudbeckia fulgida* 'Goldsturm') is on most gardeners' list of top-ten perennials. It has a long season of continuous bloom that extends from July into September. The flowers are single, orange-yellow daisies with dark brown centers—perfect replicas of the beloved black-eyed Susans that grow along American roadsides and in

Rudbeckia fulgida

Rudbeckia laciniata

wildflower meadows. The blooms are produced on sturdy stems with handsome, dark green foliage. The plants are a civilized size for the middle of the border: tall enough to be visible, yet short enough that they don't need staking.

Cutleaf coneflower (*R. laciniata*) is so named because of its coarsely divided foliage. It grows to a towering 6 feet, making it a good plant for the back of the border or for a screen to hide an unsightly view. The yellow daisies bloom from July to September.

Shining coneflower (*R. nitida*) ranges from 7 feet down to a manageable 2 or 3 feet. 'Goldquelle' is a 2-foot cultivar with 3-inch, fluffy, double flowers that look like double zinnias. They are a very pretty shade of bright, clear yellow—lighter than gold, but darker than butter.

How to Grow. To grow your own plants, sow seed of the species directly in a protected area of the garden in midsummer. Move the young plants to their final locations in fall or early spring. Plants are also readily available at garden centers and through mail-order catalogs.

Coneflowers tolerate a wide range of soil conditions, from moist to dry, but they grow best in rich, well-drained soil in full sun. When they are happy, the plants will knit together into a vigorous groundcover that will choke out weeds. Divide overcrowded plants in spring, or after flowering in late summer or early fall. The plants are relatively pest- and disease-free.

Uses. Coneflowers provide a long season of bloom for the middle or back of the border. Try shining coneflower in masses for a striking landscape feature. Naturalize tall-growing coneflowers in a wildflower meadow, or use them as a screen or hedge. The flowers of all types are great for fresh arrangements.

SAGE. See *Salvia* spp.
SAGE, RUSSIAN. See *Perovskia atriplicifolia*

Salvia spp.

SAL-vee-uh. Salvia, sage. Summer. Zones 4 to 10.

○ ◑ ✻ ✁❖ ❀

Characteristics. Height: 18 inches to 6 feet. Colors: Blue, pink, purple, and white.

This useful genus includes many fine annual, biennial, and perennial garden plants. The three species described here stand out among the hardy perennial salvias for their reliable garden performance, long period of bloom or garden display, and particularly beautiful flowers or foliage.

Violet sage (*Salvia* X *superba*) is the best-known perennial salvia. It grows 18 to 24 inches tall, with spikes of blue, purple, or pink flowers that form waves of color from June to August. It is most effective when planted in groups of at least six or seven plants. The foliage loosely resembles that of its relative, culinary sage, and stays handsome all season. Violet sage is hardy in Zones 4 to 8. 'East Friesland' is a popular cultivar with regal, violet-purple flower spikes on compact, well-behaved, 18-inch plants. 'Amethyst' is an unforgettable mid-violet shade. 'Rose Queen' is a pink companion for the rich violet 'Blue Queen'.

S. guaranitica is a fairly recent introduction to North American gardens and a superb performer. The strong 4- to 6-foot plants bloom from July right up to the first frost in fall. They are so vigorous that they can be divided every year (or you can give them extra space so they won't have to be divided as often). 'Argentina Skies' produces heavenly flowers in a rare shade of sky blue. It is hardy to Zone 6, and should be protected with a winter mulch in that zone.

Salvia X *superba*

Silver sage (*S. argentea*) looks completely different from other salvias. It is planted for its woolly, silver-gray foliage, which grows in rosettes. The leaves, which measure up to 8 inches long, are covered with fine, silky hairs and have a puckered texture. The plants reach 3 feet tall and produce spikes of yellowish white flowers in summer. The flowers tend to detract from the foliage effect, however, and can weaken the plants; many gardeners cut back the flower stems either before or just after they bloom. Because the plants are not long-lived in the garden, they may never have to be divided. Silver sage is hardy in Zones 5 to 9.

How to Grow. To grow your own plants, sow seed of the species directly in a protected area of the garden in midsummer. Move the young plants to their final locations in fall or early spring. Plants of the species and cultivars are also available at garden centers and through mail-order catalogs.

Salvias generally tolerate drought conditions but appreciate extra water during prolonged dry periods. They grow best in rich, well-drained soil in full sun, although they may take partial shade. Silver sage requires better-drained soil than other salvias and should be grown in full sun. *S. guaranitica* needs staking unless you cut the plants back by half in early to midsummer; provide a protective winter mulch in Zone 6. Divide salvias in fall or spring for propagation or to rejuvenate crowded clumps.

Uses. Salvias are excellent accents for borders; use silver sage near the front and the others in the middle or back. Silver sage also looks stunning in a rock garden or in masses as a landscape feature. The flowers of violet sage and *S. guaranitica* are good for cutting; violet sage is a fine plant for drying.

Sedum spp.

SEE-dum. Sedum, stonecrop. Late summer.
Zones 3 to 9.

○ ☀ ✥ ❀

Characteristics. Height: 2 inches to 2 feet. Colors: Pink, turning copper in fall.

This large genus includes many species. One of the best for perennial gardens is *Sedum* X 'Autumn Joy', which, unlike most plants, provides interest over four seasons. The reddish green leaf buds, which look like clusters of tiny roses, appear in early spring. They grow into 2-foot-tall, upright plants with handsome, light to medium green, succulent foliage that remains attractive all season, in all kinds of weather. In mid- to late August, flattish clusters of tiny pink flowers start blooming and continue for many weeks. They dry on the plant into a rich rust color that does not fade, regardless of whether the flowers are picked and dried, or are allowed to remain on the plant to add interest to the garden in winter. All winter long, the dried flower heads add height and color to the border. Cut them back in spring, and watch as the new growth begins to emerge to start the cycle again.

There are many excellent ground-covering sedums that are available as well, including kamschatka stonecrop (*S. kamtschaticum*) and two-row sedum (*S. spurium*). Both are low-growing plants that form dense mats of foliage. Kamschatka stonecrop bears bright yellow flowers; two-row

Sedum X 'Autumn Joy'

sedum, rosy red ones. 'Dragon's Blood' is a popular cultivar of two-row sedum, with burgundy foliage.

How to Grow. Start with purchased plants. Sedums are easy to find at most garden centers and are readily available through mail-order nurseries.

Like most succulent plants, sedums grow best in dry, poor soil and require full sun. The plants are exceptionally heat- and drought-tolerant; they also tolerate cold and humidity. Propagate plants by division in fall or spring, or take cuttings in summer. Sedums are rarely bothered by pests or diseases and are virtually maintenance-free.

Uses. Plant 'Autumn Joy' sedum in the middle of the border, as an edging, in a rock garden, or in masses as a landscape feature. Cut the flowers for fresh or dried arrangements. Use ground-covering sedums in rock gardens and to cover hot, dry sites, including slopes.

SNEEZEWEED. See *Helenium autumnale*
SNEEZEWORT. See *Achillea* spp.

Solidago X 'Peter Pan'

Solidago spp.
sol-ih-DAY-go. Goldenrod. Late summer.
Zones 4 to 8.
○ ◑ ☀ ✄❀ ❁ ❦

Characteristics. Height: 2 to 6 feet. Colors: Yellow.

The genus *Solidago* includes wildflower species, many of which are native to North America. The fluffy clusters of tiny bright to deep golden yellow flowers, which appear atop stems with narrow, medium to dark green foliage, can dominate the late-summer landscape in open fields. While some of the wildflower species are too invasive for gardens, many fine, well-behaved species and cultivars are suitable for garden use.

Seaside goldenrod (*S. sempervirens*) is an excellent noninvasive species. The graceful, 4- to 6-foot plants produce bright yellow plumes from September to October. They combine beautifully with Tartarian aster (*Aster tataricus*) in the border and in bouquets of fresh-cut flowers. This species is tolerant of salty, sandy, seaside conditions. S. X 'Peter Pan', a hybrid goldenrod, features clusters of long, elegant, canary yellow flower plumes on 2- to 3-foot plants from July to September.

Goldenrod is often blamed for causing hay fever symptoms, but it does not deserve this reputation. The actual cause of the symptoms is ragweed, which blooms at the same time, but is not as noticeable.

How to Grow. Start with purchased plants. You can sometimes find them at garden centers, and they are usually available through mail-order catalogs. Specialty wildflower nurseries often stock the plants, too.

Goldenrods prefer well-drained soil in full sun or light shade. They are generally drought-tolerant. Cut back the taller cultivars by half in midsummer to keep them to a manageable height. Divide the plants in spring for propagation.

Uses. Goldenrods are attractive in the middle or back of the border, or massed as a landscape feature. They are perfect for naturalizing in a wildflower meadow. The flowers are good for cutting and drying; they have a wonderful, subtle fragrance.

SPEEDWELL, SPIKED. See *Veronica* spp.
SPIDERWORT. See *Tradescantia* spp.

Stachys byzantina
STAY-kiss biz-an-TEE-nuh. Lamb's ears.
Summer. Zones 4 to 9.
○ ◑ ☀

Characteristics. Height: 15 inches. Colors: Purple flowers, silver foliage.

Lamb's ears are grown for their fuzzy, silver-gray, oval-shaped foliage, which has the downy texture of a lamb's ear. The silvery foliage contrasts nicely with blues, pinks, and purples, and is hauntingly beautiful when combined with white flowers in an all-white garden. The plants spread obligingly to make a striking groundcover or edging. They provide color and texture in the garden from early spring until they are killed by frost.

From June to July the plants send up flower spikes equally as velvety as the foliage, with purple flowers. Many gardeners think the flowers detract from the foliage effect and cut them back before or after they bloom. Others appreciate the interesting texture the flowers add to the border. Some cultivars, including 'Silver Carpet', have been selected because they produce few or no flowers. 'Helene Von Stein' is an especially attractive, very vigorous

Stachys byzantina

cultivar with broad foliage. It seldom blooms and is less prone to rot.

How to Grow. To start your own plants, sow seed directly in a protected area of the garden in midsummer. Move the young plants to their final locations in fall or early spring. Plants are also readily available at garden centers and through mail-order catalogs.

These drought-tolerant plants prefer poor, well-drained soil in full sun or light shade. Like many silver-foliaged plants, lamb's ears tend to rot in hot, humid weather. Divide the plants every year to keep them vigorous and to prevent overcrowding: Dig them up in fall or spring, break them into rooted pieces 6 inches long, and replant them 6 inches apart. They will knit together quickly. You will have many plants left over; start a new colony, or share the extras with friends and neighbors.

Uses. Lamb's ears work well in the front of the border, as an edging or groundcover, or grouped in front of another perennial as a landscape feature.

STARFLOWER, BLUE. See *Amsonia tabernaemontana*
STONECROP. See *Sedum* spp.
SUNDROPS, OZARK. See *Oenothera missouriensis*
SUNFLOWER. See *Helianthus* spp.
SWEET WILLIAM, WILD. See *Phlox* spp.

Symphytum grandiflorum

sim-FY-tum gran-dih-FLOR-um. Yellow comfrey.
Spring. Zones 3 to 8.
◑ ● ✸

Characteristics. Height: 1 foot. Colors: Whitish yellow or blue.

This low-growing perennial deserves to be planted more in American gardens. It has handsome, dark green foliage that is topped with pretty, nodding, bell-shaped flowers in May. The flowers of the species are whitish yellow; blue cultivars are also available. The vigorous plants spread quickly, forming a thick groundcover that chokes out weeds. They have the rare virtue of performing well in dry shade, and can fill in those difficult areas under trees. 'Blau Glocken' has blue flowers, deep green leaves, and a vigorous spreading habit.

How to Grow. To start your own plants, sow

Symphytum grandiflorum

seed directly in a protected area of the garden in midsummer. Move the young plants to their final locations in fall or early spring. Plants are not readily available for purchase at garden centers, but you can get them through some mail-order catalogs.

Yellow comfrey prefers rich, well-drained soil in partial or full shade. It is drought-tolerant, but the leaf edges may burn in full sun. The plants are well loved by slugs, which can be controlled with diatomaceous earth or beer traps. When the leaves die back in the fall, they have a charred look, as if they had been set on fire. This look persists into spring, until the new foliage emerges. For propagation, divide plants in fall or spring. You will always have many extras to give away to friends.

Uses. Yellow comfrey is an excellent choice for a groundcover in dry shade. It also looks good in the front of a shady border, or as an edging.

Thalictrum aquilegifolium
thal-IK-trum ak-will-lee-jih-FOE-lee-um.
Columbine meadow rue. Late spring. Zones 5 to 9.
○ ◑ ❧

Characteristics. Height: 2 to 4 feet. Colors: Pink, lavender, and white.

The genus *Thalictrum* includes native wildflowers, many of which are too tall to be suitable for garden use. However, several fine species are available,

Thalictrum aquilegifolium 'Purpureum'

the most popular of which is columbine meadow rue (*T. aquilegifolium*). Its flowers are really stamens without petals and look like tiny, fluffy pink, lavender, or white powder puffs. They are clustered into mounded, irregularly shaped plumes that add a misty, cloudlike effect to the garden. The flowers are followed by nodding clusters of seedpods that shimmer in the breeze. The handsome, gray-green, finely divided foliage looks very much like that of columbine—hence the common name. 'Album' is a creamy white-flowered cultivar that grows to 4 feet tall. 'Dwarf Purple' is a 2-foot cultivar with lilac flowers. 'Roseum' has light pink flowers.

How to Grow. To grow your own plants, sow seed directly in a protected area of the garden in midsummer. Move the young plants to their permanent locations in fall or early spring. Plants are often available at garden centers and through mail-order catalogs.

Columbine meadow rue prefers moist, well-drained soil in full sun or partial shade. The plants do not need staking unless they are in too much shade or the soil is too rich. To propagate, sow seed or divide them in spring or fall when they become overcrowded—usually in 4 or 5 years. They are rarely bothered by pests or diseases.

Uses. Columbine meadow rue adds a light texture to the middle or back of the border. It also naturalizes well in a wildflower meadow. The flowers are excellent for cutting. You can also use the foliage for fresh arrangements.

THISTLE, GLOBE. See *Echinops ritro*
TICKSEED. See *Coreopsis* spp.

Tradescantia spp.
trad-es-KAN-tee-uh. Spiderwort.
Summer. Zones 3 to 9.
○ ◑

Characteristics. Height: 1½ to 2 feet. Colors: Purple, blue, white, and pink.

The long, narrow, bent foliage of spiderworts does indeed resemble the legs of a spider. Two types that are commonly grown in American gardens are Virginia spiderwort (*Tradescantia virginiana*) and common spiderwort (*T.* X *andersoniana*).

Virginia spiderwort is a native perennial with a dense, clumping habit. It bears numerous three-petaled purple flowers; although each flower lasts only one day, the plants produce so many buds that they can bloom almost all summer long. This species is hardy in Zones 4 to 9.

Common spiderwort, a hybrid species developed from Virginia spiderwort, comes in a variety of colors. 'Iris Pritchard' has white petals blushed with pale blue. 'Zwanenburg Blue' bears exceptionally large, clear blue flowers. 'Red Cloud' features rosy red flowers. Common spiderwort is hardy in Zones 3 to 9.

How to Grow. Spiderworts need full sun to partial shade. They can grow in somewhat dry, poor soil. For best flowering and shape, however, site them in moist, rich, well-drained soil. After the plants flower, the foliage can look rather bedraggled; for more compact foliage (and to encourage new blooms), cut the plants down to about 6 inches.

Spiderworts grow quickly and easily from seed sown indoors or out in early spring. Divide established plants every 3 or 4 years in spring to prevent overcrowding and to keep them from spreading too quickly. They can be vigorous to the point of being invasive. Plants are often available at garden centers and through mail-order catalogs.

Uses. Plant spiderworts in the front of a border or along a walkway. These plants are ideal in naturalized areas and partly shady sites.

Tradescantia virginiana

Veronica spicata

Veronica spp.

ver-ON-ih-kuh. Veronica, spiked speedwell.
Summer. Zones 4 to 8.

Characteristics. Height: 1½ to 3 feet. Colors: Blue, pink, purple, and white.

Veronica is a large genus that includes rock garden plants, wildflowers, and lawn weeds. Several species of veronicas are ideal for the perennial garden. They have long spikes of blue, pink, purple, or white flowers that create a wonderful haze of color for weeks, or even months, during the summer. These strong plants have handsome, dark green to gray-green foliage that looks attractive all season.

Spiked speedwell (*V. spicata*) is a compact species with strong, upright plants. The flower spikes bloom in shades of blue, white, rose-pink, and purple, and last for 7 or 8 weeks in summer. 'Blue Fox' offers lavender-blue flowers and dark green, narrow foliage on 15- to 20-inch plants. 'Red Fox' is a companion to 'Blue Fox', with masses of deep rose-red flowers. 'Icicle' features icy white spires and glossy green foliage on 2-foot plants.

Longleaf veronica (*V. longifolia*) is 2 to 3 feet tall and has long, narrow leaves. Its long-lasting flower spikes are among the best of the veronicas for cutting. 'Blue Giant' is a strong, 3- to 4-foot plant with pale lavender-blue flower spikes that bloom for many weeks in summer. 'Alba' is a lower-growing, 18-inch, white-flowered cultivar.

V. X 'Sunny Border Blue' was selected as the Perennial Plant Association's Plant of the Year for 1993 for its superb garden performance. It bears thick spikes of dark blue flowers from June to August. The plants are compact and never need staking. If you can have only one veronica, this is the one to choose.

How to Grow. To grow your own plants, sow seed of the species in a protected area of the garden in midsummer. Move the young plants to their final locations in fall or early spring. Plants are also readily available at garden centers and through mail-order catalogs.

Veronicas are easy to grow in rich, well-drained soil and full sun. They are rarely bothered by pests and diseases, and do not require staking. They benefit from occasional deadheading. Divide the plants in spring or fall every 3 or 4 years when they become overcrowded.

Uses. Veronicas are among the best perennials for the front or middle of the border. Tuck them into cottage gardens, or plant them in masses for an eye-catching landscape feature. The spiky blooms make excellent cut flowers.

VIRGINIA BLUEBELLS. See *Mertensia virginica*
WILD SWEET WILLIAM. See *Phlox* spp.
YARROW. See *Achillea* spp.
YELLOW FLAG. See *Iris* spp.

WELCOME SPRING. *Nothing brightens up a garden quite like a showy display of spring bulbs. Here,*
tulips and poppy windflowers (Anemone coronaria) *line a simple gravel walkway.*

CHAPTER FIVE

BULBS

The use of bulbs is at an all-time high. We aren't just growing tulips; we are experimenting with species tulips. We have discovered that onions are not only edible, but often incredibly beautiful, too. From winter-flowering irises to fall-flowering colchicums, the wonderful world of bulbs is being rediscovered by adventurous gardeners across the country.

WHAT ARE BULBS?

Bulbous plants, which may be annual or perennial, include plants that grow from true bulbs, corms, tubers, and rhizomes. Every scholarly work on bulbs takes great pains to explain the specific differences between all of these types of "storage organs." But does it really matter if we talk about the tubers or rhizomes of calla lilies, or if we know for sure whether cyclamen grows from a bulb or a corm? Of course, you don't have to be able to recite the specific traits of true bulbs or tubers to grow gorgeous daffodils or cheerful spring crocuses. But as you gain more gar-

dening experience, it's helpful to be familiar with the different structures. For one thing, the method for propagating each type of bulbous plant varies depending on the type of storage organ it has.

So keep in mind that not all "bulbs" in this chapter grow from true bulbs, as daffodils and tulips do. Crocuses and gladioli, for example, grow from corms. If you really want to know the specifics, check the plant portraits, which indicate what kind of storage organ the plants have.

WHY GROW BULBS?

Why not grow bulbs? They are a part of the gardener's plant palette; they are tools for excitement, creativity, and therapy in the garden. And the netted packages or boxes of red tulips and yellow daffodils are just the tip of the iceberg. Gardeners looking for more than the usual bulbs to grace their gardens will find an incredible array of shapes, colors, and growth habits from which to choose in the pages of mail-order catalogs.

Bulbs are often inexpensive and always interesting. If you take a little time to learn about where they came from, bulbs will allow you to travel the world without ever having to leave your garden. For instance, you can grow tulips from Turkey, irises from the Pyrenees, grape hyacinths from Europe and Asia Minor, calla lilies from South Africa, resurrection lilies from Peru, and zephyr lilies from America.

Bulbous plants blend easily into any garden and can provide beauty in all seasons of the year. Snowdrops and crocuses bring immense pleasure to the winter-weary. Resurrection lilies (*Lycoris* spp.) and fall crocuses (*Crocus speciosus*) glorify the fall garden. Anemones and gladioli combine nicely with roses and daisies in vases of cut flowers. And hyacinths and tuberoses (*Polianthes tuberosa*) fill the air with sweet fragrance.

Some gardeners may be tempted to segregate bulbs from other plants to create a cutting garden and to keep unsightly foliage isolated from the rest of the garden. Admittedly, it is difficult to love the gladiolus plant as much as its flower, and it is definitely a challenge to enjoy the dying leaves of ornamental onions. However, bulbs are all good garden plants and deserve to enjoy the company of the rest of garden society. In fact, they look their best when combined with other plants.

BULB COMPANIONS. *Spring-blooming annuals and perennials make excellent companions for hardy bulbs. Here, tulips are mixed with pansies, forget-me-nots,* Anemone pulsatilla, *and leopard's bane (*Doronicum caucasicum*).*

nitely a challenge to enjoy the dying leaves of ornamental onions. However, bulbs are all good garden plants and deserve to enjoy the company of the rest of garden society. In fact, they look their best when combined with other plants.

To get the most pleasure from your bulbs, pair them with companions that can accent their colorful flowers and then fill in when the bulbs go dormant. Low-growing shrubs, such as spireas (*Spiraea* spp.) and summersweets (*Clethra* spp.), are great for this purpose. Late-emerging perennials, such as balloon flower (*Platycodon grandiflorus*), and vigorous species, such as meadow rues (*Thalictrum* spp.), are excellent for hiding dying bulb foliage and covering the bare stems that are common to many bulbs. Shallow-rooted annuals such as marigolds or impa-

MASS BULBS FOR COLOR. *Most bulbs are at their best when planted in clumps of a dozen or more. This clump of brilliant tulips is a good example. Who could overlook this eye-catching display?*

GROWING TIPS AT A GLANCE

The following plant portraits includes simple symbols to highlight special features you need to know about each bulb. If you're not sure what any of the symbols mean, refer back to this key.

- ○ Full sun (more than 6 hours of sun a day; ideally all day)
- ◐ Partial sun (some direct sun, but less than 6 hours a day)
- ● Shade (no direct sun)
- ✳ Drought-tolerant
- ✄ Good as a cut flower
- ❦ Fragrant
- ▼ Grows well in containers

tiens are also handy for filling in the spots that are left bare when the bulbs disappear.

PLANT PORTRAITS

The bulbous plants described in the following plant portraits are a sampling of some of the best for garden use. Most are relatively easy to find; a few are slightly more elusive but definitely worth the search. If you can't find the bulbs you're looking for at your local garden center, it's time to investigate the many wonderful mail-order catalogs that offer a wide variety of bulbs.

The portraits in this section are alphabetized by their botanical names, which are set in bold type. These names are recognized all over the world, while common names often vary from region to region. If, like many gardeners, you're stumped by the prospect of pronouncing the botanical names, don't despair; pronunciations are provided under the entry names. You'll also find the common name or names of the plant, its main season of interest (generally when it blooms), and its hardiness zones. In addition, there is a description of the plant, including its height and colors, along with growing guidelines and suggested garden uses.

Acidanthera bicolor

as-ih-DAN-ther-uh BY-kul-er.
Abyssinian gladiolus. Summer. Zones 7 to 10.

Characteristics. Height: 30 to 36 inches. Colors: White with purple center.

Abyssinian gladiolus (also known as *Gladiolus callianthus*) is a fascinating summer corm that is not grown nearly as much as it should be in American gardens. The light green, pleated foliage and the sweetly scented white flowers with their deep purple throats are a great addition to any garden. In ideal conditions, each stem can produce 6 to 8 wonderfully fragrant flowers. Native to southern and tropical areas of Africa, the corms are winter-hardy to about Zone 7 (6 with winter protection), but you can grow them in all areas as an annual. The flowers are produced from July to October and are relatively disease- and insect-free. The plants may flower a little too late for northeastern or upper midwestern gardens, where early frosts can nip the buds.

A variety of this species was discovered in Ethiopia in 1896. These stronger-growing, larger-flowered plants are known as *Acidanthera bicolor* var. *murieliae* (or as 'Muralis'). Most of the corms sold today are this variety. When looking for Abyssinian gladioli, search spring bulb catalogs under both

Acidanthera bicolor var. *murielae*

Acidanthera and *Gladiolus*; they may be listed in either spot.

How to Grow. These plants need full sun and well-drained soil; they abhor "wet feet" in the summer. Abyssinian gladiolus looks best when planted in large groups. (Fortunately, the corms are relatively inexpensive.) Set the corms 4 to 6 inches deep and 6 to 10 inches apart after all danger of frost has passed.

In northern areas, lift the corms in the fall, brush off any clinging soil, and store them in dry peat moss in a cool, frost-free area, such as a basement. The corms multiply rapidly and need to be divided every 2 to 3 years. Otherwise, the plants produce too much foliage and too few flowers, and end up looking like tall green weeds.

Uses. *Abyssinian gladioli* are ideal for interplanting in a perennial bed. They make excellent cut flowers, lasting for 5 to 7 days in fresh water.

ACONITE, WINTER. See *Eranthis hyemalis*

Allium spp.

AL-ee-um. Ornamental onion.
Spring. Zones 4 to 8.
○ ◑ ✂ ▼

Characteristics. Height: 4 inches to 5 feet. Colors: Purple, lilac, pink, yellow, and white.

The genus *Allium* is wonderfully diverse. Some of its bulbs are the size of a pea; others are so large that they barely fit in your hand. The flowers may be as small as a quarter, as large as a softball, or somewhere in between. The foliage of some species is handsome, although the leaves of the bulbous species disappear by early summer.

A. aflatunense is one of the best gardening values around. Its large, purple-lilac flowers bloom atop 2- to 3-foot plants in early to mid-spring. The bulbs are inexpensive, so it's easy to plant them by the dozens rather than in ones or twos. (Who wants to see one onion, anyway?) An excellent selection of this fine species is 'Purple Sensation', which has deep violet-purple flowers.

Some of the most attractive foliage is found on *A. karataviense*, which sports 4- to 6-inch-wide,

Allium aflatunense

blue-green leaves mottled with red. The lilac-white flowers are borne on strong 6- to 10-inch-tall stems.

Star of Persia (*A. christophii*) offers perhaps the most impressive flowers of the group. The flower heads are made up of amethyst-purple, star-shaped flowers and can be as large as 12 inches across. They appear in spring to early summer on 12- to 18-inch stems.

As its name suggests, giant onion (*A. giganteum*) is the tallest species, with stems reaching up to 5 feet. It produces large heads of lilac-purple flowers in late spring to early summer. Giant onion is often seen in florist shops as a cut flower.

Allium christophii

One of the longest-lived and easiest species to grow is drumstick allium (*A. sphaerocephalon*), with its dense heads of purple flowers. The plants multiply rapidly and grow 2 to 2½ feet tall. Drumstick allium is also an exceptionally good cut flower.

Other tall choices among the ornamental onions are *A. rosenbachianum*, which grows to 3 feet and bears lilac or white flowers, and *A. atropurpureum*, with smaller purple flowers. There are also some more expensive but magnificent hybrids. These include 'Globemaster', probably the best large purple-flowered allium yet produced, and 'Lucy Ball', which bears deep lilac-purple flowers on 3- to 4-foot-tall stems. To offset these giants, *A. moly* and its offspring 'Jeannine' only stand 6 to 10 inches tall and provide bright yellow flowers; *A. oreophilum* is 4 to 6 inches tall and bears deep pink flowers.

How to Grow. Ornamental onions prefer full sun and well-drained soil. They will tolerate partial shade, particularly in the South, but they may not "perennialize" as well where shade is dense. (All onions are listed as perennials, but some are longer-lived than others.) Southern gardeners treat most ornamental onions as annuals or 2-year plants; none of the species are expected to live more than 3 years. In more northerly climates, including the Northwest, some ornamental onions will multiply well or reseed, providing many years of enjoyment.

Plant these bulbs in the fall, with about 3 to 4 inches of soil above the nose of the bulb. Propagation is usually accomplished by offsets from the mother bulb. For most ornamental onions, though, division is hardly worth the bother; except for the pricey bulbs like *A. giganteum* or some of the hybrids, most are no more expensive than a 6-pack of petunias. Thrips, white rot, and mildew can attack ornamental onions, but should not discourage anyone from including a few of these great plants in the garden.

Uses. Ornamental onions blend very well in any flower garden. Plant them near bushy annuals or perennials that can hide the foliage as it goes dormant by midsummer. The medium and short types grow well in containers. Nearly all the garden-worthy species are also useful as cut flowers. Cut the flowers when about half the flower head is open, plunge the cut stem in clean water, and enjoy them by themselves or combined with other flowers.

Anemone blanda

Anemone spp.

ah-NEM-oh-nee. Anemone, windflower. Spring.
Zones 4 to 8.

Characteristics. Height: 4 to 24 inches. Colors: Pink, red, purple-blue, and white.

Anemone is a large genus consisting of bulbous plants, as well as plants commonly grown as perennials. The bulbous species flower in the spring and provide many bright colors that can be enjoyed both indoors and out. The flowers measure 1 to 3 inches across, depending on the species, and are actually made up of sepals that resemble petals. The foliage is generally fernlike and handsome; in all bulbous forms, it tends to go dormant and disappear in early summer. All of the species prefer temperate summers and are annuals in Zone 7 and south.

One of the most popular species is Grecian windflower (*A. blanda*). It grows 6 to 9 inches tall and produces single daisylike flowers in many colors. Some of the best cultivars are 'Charmer', with deep rose flowers; 'Pink Star', which bears large, deep pink flowers; 'Radar', with reddish, white-centered flowers; and 'White Splendor', one of the hardiest cultivars.

The wonderful poppy windflower (*A. coronaria*), also known as Mediterranean windflower, is also worth mentioning. Hardy only to Zone 6, it has been admired for centuries and grown as a garden and cut flower for almost as long. The plants are not as hardy as Grecian windflowers (only as far north as Zone 7). The parsleylike foliage is attractive, and the cultivars are magnificent. The best known are the DeCaen hybrids, consisting of single flowers of mixed colors. Separate colors are also available, such as the violet-rose 'Sylphide' and the bright scarlet 'Hollandia'. The St. Brigid hybrids offer double flowers; they are usually multicolored, although they also come in solid colors. 'The Admiral', with violet blooms, and 'Mount Everest', a double white form, are just two examples. Treat this species as an annual; it is a poor perennial at best.

Other species to try include wood anemone (*A. nemorosa*) and European anemone (*A. apennina*). Both are only 6 to 9 inches tall and prefer partial shade and woodland conditions. Wood anemone is more at home in the North than the South, while European anemone, which is hardy to Zone 6, performs best in the Northwest.

How to Grow. Plant Grecian, wood, and European anemones in the fall. Set poppy windflowers out in early spring in the North; plant them in autumn in the South. To encourage sprouting, soak the tubers in warm water for about 24 hours before planting. Set them 2 to 3 inches deep in full sun in the North, or in a spot with afternoon shade in the South. Few insects bother anemones, but look out for slugs, as well as squirrels, gophers, voles, and anything else that likes to dig around. Diseases are seldom a problem.

Uses. Plant Grecian, wood, and European windflowers in large groups (at least 25 plants) and allow them to naturalize. They are terrific in rock gardens, borders, and containers. Mediterranean windflowers are wonderful as cut flowers; combine them with spring bulbs and early perennials.

Arisaema spp.

ar-iss-EE-muh. Jack-in-the-pulpit, green dragon.
Spring to summer. Zones 3 to 9.

Characteristics. Height: 1 to 3 feet. Colors: Purple, green, and white.

Compared to other bulbs, some of the plants of

Arisaema triphyllum

Arisaema are quite unusual. The flowers consist of two parts: a spikelike spadix, which bears either male or female flowers, and the spathe, which wraps loosely around the flowers like a large trenchcoat. The foliage of all *Arisaema* species is handsome. In fact, some gardeners find the foliage more appealing than the unusual flowers.

Two of our native species are marvelous. Jack-in-the-pulpit (*A. triphyllum*) is quite variable and may grow from 18 to 36 inches tall. It flowers in early spring through midsummer, and is hardy to Zone 3. Both the stalk of the plant and the spathe can have purple mottling on the outside. Our other common native is green dragon (*A. dracontium*). It sports a long (up to 10-inch), yellow-green spadix, which sticks out from the green spadix—weird but wonderful. Under good conditions, berries may appear on either of these species in autumn. They are bright red on Jack-in-the-pulpit and orange-red on green dragon. Both species love moisture and are often found in moist, shady woodland areas.

Of the many other species, two foreigners are very attractive. *A. candidissimum*, from China, bears a white spathe striped with pink and green. The plants are 9 to 15 inches tall. The Japanese form, *A. sikokianum*, produces a beautiful, pure white spadix surrounded by a stippled, purplish spathe. The plants can grow up to 2 feet tall but generally reach 12 to 18 inches.

How to Grow. Plant the tubers in spring or fall, at least 6 inches deep in a moist, shady location, then stand back and enjoy the show. Propagate the plants by lifting them in early fall and separating the tubers. These woodland plants prefer partial shade, and are among the few plants that tolerate heavy shade. Insects and diseases are rarely a problem.

Uses. Use the various Jack-in-the-pulpit species and green dragons in shade and woodland gardens. Ferns, hostas, and rodgersias (*Rodgersia* spp.) are all good companions.

Arum italicum
AIR-um eye-TAL-ih-kum. Arum lily.
Nearly year-round interest. Zones 5 to 8.
◑ ● ✿ ▼

Characteristics. Height: 9 to 12 inches. Colors: Greenish white.

Arum lilies lack the stately quality of tulips or

Arum italicum

the fragrance of hyacinths, but they are terrific plants for shady areas, where the subtle beauty of the foliage is more important than the color of the flowers. The green, arrow-shaped, leaves first emerge in autumn and provide color and interest through the winter months. In summer, the foliage goes dormant only to appear again in autumn. The leaves look particularly nice in the winter garden, where they glisten in the winter sun. In early spring, the plants bear interesting Jack-in-the-pulpit-like flowers; a greenish white "pulpit," or spathe, surrounds a pencil-like spadix. The flowers aren't particularly showy and can be hard to find among the vigorous foliage, but if you look closely, you can see that the male and female flowers on the spadix are separated by a distinct space. In the fall, the plants produce orange berries before the new leaves emerge. In areas with hot summers, the berries often do not develop, although the plants perform perfectly well.

Arum italicum usually has plain green leaves, but the cultivar 'Pictum' (also called *A. italicum* subsp. *italicum*) offers wonderful 9- to 12-inch-tall foliage mottled with white markings that stand out in shady corners. Another useful offering is 'Marmoratum', which has much more subdued markings on the foliage.

How to Grow. Plant the tubers in spring or fall, 3 to 4 inches deep and about 12 inches apart. They generally prefer shade, although they can grow well in full sun in the North. A spring top-dressing of organic matter, such as garden compost or well-rotted manure, helps the plants grow their best. Propagate arum lilies by lifting and dividing the tubers from the parent root structure; you can also break the tubers and replant them. Pests and diseases do not pose a problem.

Arum lilies aren't commonly offered at garden centers, but are available from some mail-order catalogs. You can get divisions from a gardening friend or sow seed (remove the pulp of the berry) outdoors in a protected location in fall.

Uses. Arum lilies make excellent woodland plants. They are also useful in the front of the border and in containers. Since the foliage goes dormant in the summer, site them where annuals or other perennials will grow over them. The foliage is attractive in arrangements.

ATAMASCO LILY. See *Zephyranthes* spp.

Begonia Tuberhybrida 'Memory Mix'

Begonia tuberhybrida hybrids

be-GO-nee-ah. Tuberous begonia.
Summer to fall. Zone 10.

Characteristics. Height: 12 to 18 inches. Colors: Red, pink, orange, yellow, and white.

The showy tuberous begonias add glorious color to shady parts of the garden. Their thick, fleshy tubers produce juicy stems with hairy, heart-shaped to pointed, green leaves. The upright or trailing stems also bear single or double flowers up to 4 inches across, in a range of colors and shadings. The male flowers tend to be large and showy; they are usually flanked by smaller, single female flowers.

How to Grow. Tuberous begonias need partial shade and moist but well-drained soil. Work plenty of compost into the soil before planting. Start these plants indoors in pots (plant the tubers 1 inch deep) about 4 weeks before the last frost date. Set them out when night temperatures stay above 50°F. Stake upright types. Mulch the plants well, and water during dry spells to keep the soil moist. Pinch off spent flowers to keep the blooms coming. In all but frost-free areas, lift the tubers before or just after the first frost and store indoors in a frost-free spot such as a cool basement or garage over winter.

Uses. Add tuberous begonias to lightly shaded beds and borders or container plantings. Trailing types are well suited for growing in hanging baskets.

CALLA LILY. See *Zantedeschia* spp.

Camassia spp.

kuh-MASS-ee-uh. Camassia, quamash. Summer. Zones 5 to 7.

Characteristics. Height: 2 to 3 feet. Colors: Purple, blue, and white.

When you plant camassias, you are planting a little history in your garden. These plants provided a staple food for the native Americans of the Northwest, who boiled or roasted the bulbs to extract a molasses-like sweetener. Most species of *Camassia* are native to the Pacific Northwest and are useful garden plants, particularly when planted in groups of 5 or more.

C. quamash is the most commonly grown species, and the least expensive, too. It is also probably the most variable species in the genus. The flowers generally range from pale blue to violet-blue. Named cultivars, such as deep blue 'San Juan', are sometimes offered in bulb catalogs.

C. leichtlinii may be the most ornamental of the camassias, bearing whitish to purple-blue flowers on 3-foot-tall stems. Variation is also common in this

Camassia leichtlinii 'Blue Danube'

species. 'Alba' has white blossoms; 'Blue Danube' dependably produces dark blue flowers; and 'Atroviolacea' bears beautiful, deep purple blooms. There are also double-flowered whitish forms, such as 'Semiplena'. Plants with double flowers live longer than single-flowered ones, but are also more expensive.

The last of the common garden species is C. *cusickii*, whose main claim to fame is its very large bulb, which can weigh up to 8 ounces. The flowers are generally pale blue, but cultivars are also available of this species: 'Nimmerdor' and 'Zwanenburg' bear deeper blue flowers.

In truth, there is not a great deal of difference between the three species to the beginning gardener; simply try a few and stick with those you enjoy the most. After all, it is worth a few dollars to have a little Americana in the garden.

How to Grow. Plant the bulbs in the fall, about 5 inches deep and 4 to 6 inches apart. They are at home in most sunny to partly shaded gardens, but prefer moist sites over dry ones. These plants are generally insect- and disease-free.

Uses. Try camassias at the back of the border or around ponds and water gardens. They also work well in meadow gardens with moist soil.

Chionodoxa spp.

ky-on-oh-DOKS-uh. Glory-of-the-snow.
Early spring. Zones 5 to 7.

○ ◐ ✂ ❀ ▼

Characteristics. Height: 4 to 6 inches. Colors: Blue or pink.

These early-flowering bulbs are native to Crete and Turkey. The handsome, starlike flowers are usually some shade of blue and are borne in clusters of 2 to 10 blooms. As indicated by their common name, they stay open even during snow or sleet. These tough little flowers are better suited for northern climates than southern ones, since they prefer cold winters and cool summer soils.

Chionodoxa luciliae is the most commonly sold species. It generally has blue-lavender flowers with white centers on 6-inch stems. Cultivars bearing pink or rose-colored flowers are also available. Other useful species are C. *gigantea*, which produces

Chionodoxa luciliae

1 or 2 large, upward-facing, light blue flowers; and C. *sardensis*, with numerous, clear gentian-blue flowers, each with a small white eye.

How to Grow. Plant these bulbs in the fall in well-drained soil; set them 2 to 3 inches deep and 2 to 4 inches apart. A sunny location is best, although the plants will tolerate some shade. For best performance, glory-of-the-snow requires moist conditions in both winter and spring; avoid planting it near the base of trees, since the tree roots would compete with the bulbs for water. Propagation is simple: Lift a clump of bulbs, remove the offsets, and replant.

Uses. Plant glory-of-the-snow where you can enjoy it up close, such as near a deck or patio. The bulbs naturalize particularly well; for best effect, plant them in masses of 25 or more. Or, try combining them with other early-flowering bulbs, annuals, or perennials in containers.

Colchicum spp.

KOHL-chih-kum. Colchicum, meadow saffron.
Fall. Zones 5 to 7.

○ ◐

Characteristics. Height: 6 to 12 inches. Colors: Lilac-pink, pinkish purple, mauve-pink, or white.

Colchicums are among the most interesting flowers in the fall landscape. Established plants produce their foliage in the spring. The leaves send

Colchicum 'Waterlily'

food down to the corm, then disappear in early summer. The flowers appear from September to November, depending on the location and the species, and range in color from lilac to purplish pink or white. The corms are expensive, but they are worth every penny if they perform to their potential.

Many species and cultivars are available from bulb catalogs. *Colchicum autumnale* bears pink to purplish flowers; there are also cultivars with white flowers, as well as double-flowered forms ('Pleniflorum'). One of the earliest species to flower is C. *byzantinum*, which bears pale pink flowers 4 to 6 inches above the soil. C. *speciosum* produces large red-violet, tuliplike flowers in late September. A few hybrids are also worth trying: 'Lilac Wonder' has lilac flowers with white lines along the sides; 'Violet Queen' bears deep purple flowers; and 'Waterlily' produces pale pink, double flowers.

How to Grow. Since the corms send up their flowers in the fall, you need to buy and plant them by late summer, while they are still dormant. Plant them in a well-drained site with about 4 inches of soil above the top of the corm. Keep the soil moist as long as the foliage remains green. Colchicums generally appreciate morning sun and afternoon shade. They grow well when left undisturbed, although you can divide them just before the foliage dies down for propagation.

Uses. Plant colchicums in beds and borders with low-growing perennials and groundcovers that can support the delicate blooms.

Convallaria majalis

kon-vuh-LAIR-ee-uh muh-JAL-iss.
Lily-of-the-valley. Spring. Zones 2 to 8.

Characteristics. Height: 4 to 8 inches. Colors: White or pink.

Bringing a handful of lily-of-the-valley flowers indoors is like bringing in the fragrance of spring. The flowers and foliage arise from rhizomes, which are generally available from perennial growers and bulb specialists. The small white flowers are held on a many-flowered stalk just above the light green leaves. The plants are much more aggressive in the North than the South; removing unwanted lily-of-the-valley requires a pickax and shovel, and can occupy a small boy's entire weekend. In areas with hot summers, the plants are more docile and are valued more for their fragrance than their ability to cover the ground.

There is only one species, although it can be variable. The flowers are usually creamy white; *Convallaria majalis* var. *rosea* bears pink flowers. 'Fortin's Giant' has white flowers and is bigger and stouter than the species. One interesting cultivar—offered as 'Albistriata', 'Variegata', or simply 'Striata'—has yellow-and-green variegated foliage.

How to Grow. Plant the rhizomes (often referred to as "pips") 2 to 4 inches deep and 6 to 8 inches apart in spring or fall. They are happy in

Convallaria majalis

moist soil and struggle in hot, dry sites. The plants tolerate full sun in the North if moisture is available; partially shaded areas are best in the South. Propagate by digging a clump with your shovel, separating it, then replanting the pieces in a prepared area.

Uses. In northern gardens, lily-of-the-valley is vigorous enough to make a solid groundcover. It is especially attractive growing around rocks, along the sides of paths, or in containers. Snip a few flowers to enjoy indoors.

Crocosmia hybrids
kroh-KAWZ-mee-uh. Crocosmia, montebretia.
Summer. Zones 6 to 8.

Characteristics. Height: 2 to 4 feet. Colors: Red, orange, and yellow.

Crocosmias are excellent plants for sunny locations. Although they have been around since 1880, they are relatively unknown in American gardens. A few years ago, it was difficult to find these wonderful plants, but now they are readily available. The flowers range in color from yellow or gold to orange or red. The soft, pleated foliage resembles flat fans.

Both large- and small-flowered forms are available. A few of the better cultivars with large blooms are 'Citronella', with yellow flowers; 'Emily McKenzie', which produces orange-red blooms; 'Lucifer', with red flowers; and 'Queen Alexandra', which has red-blotched, orange flowers. Small-flowered cultivars include red-flowered 'Fire King', yellow 'George Davidson', and red-and-yellow 'Venus'.

How to Grow. Crocosmias are very easy to grow where they are hardy. They are ideal for soils high in organic matter and will grow in full sun or very light shade. Plant the corms in spring, 1 to 2 inches deep and 8 to 10 inches apart. Propagate crocosmias from offsets. Thrips can be a major problem, causing distortions of the foliage and flowers; spray infested plants with insecticidal soap.

Uses. Enjoy crocosmias as a colorful, mid-border accent. They also make excellent cut flowers.

Crocus spp.
KROH-kus. Crocus. Spring or fall. Zones 3 to 8.

Characteristics. Height: 3 to 6 inches. Colors: Blue, lavender, purple, yellow, and white.

How can anyone not like crocuses? They are available in a dozen colors and hues, will flower in the spring or fall, are inexpensive, and are practically foolproof. There are more than 80 species of crocus, many of which are offered by bulb specialists, as well as many commonly available hybrids.

Crocosmia hybrid

Crocus sp.

The main group of spring-flowering crocuses available to gardeners are the Dutch hybrids, often listed as *Crocus vernus*. They bear the largest flowers and come in an assortment of colors. They are excellent, reliable, and long-lived plants. 'Remembrance' has blue flowers; 'Jeanne d'Arc' bears white blooms; 'Pickwick' produces flowers striped in purple-blue and white. As its name suggests, 'Yellow Mammouth' bears large golden yellow blooms.

While the Dutch hybrids may be the most common, other crocuses are equally as good. Snow crocus (*C. chrysanthus*) flowers earlier than Dutch crocus and is available in many colors. The species bears golden yellow blooms in late winter. Some excellent cultivars include creamy yellow 'Advance', yellow-and-bronze 'E. P. Bowles', and straw-yellow 'Moonlight'. 'Ladykiller' is purple outside and white inside; 'White Triumphator' is white with blue markings. Another fine early-blooming species is *C. tomasinianus*, which bears lilac flowers that are paler on the outside. 'Barr's Purple' is a cultivar with large, deep purple flowers; 'Ruby Giant' has violet flowers. This species is said to be more squirrel-proof than the others.

The fall-flowering species are fabulous, since they bloom at a time when the garden is winding down. One of the best known is saffron crocus (*C. sativus*), which bears lilac flowers with long orange stigmas. The stigmas are harvested for use as a dye and as a spice. (It is estimated that more than 4,000 flowers are required to produce 1 ounce of saffron). *C. speciosus*, sometimes called showy crocus, is easy to establish and bears lavender-blue flowers in early fall. It is available in a number of selections, such as 'Atabir', which offers violet flowers, and 'Cassiope', with blue blooms.

How to Grow. Crocuses require well-drained soil and 3 to 4 hours of sun per day. Plant the corms 3 to 4 inches deep and as close together as possible. Set out the spring-flowering kinds in autumn, and the fall-flowering types as soon as they are available in mid- to late summer. Crocuses are generally problem-free, although squirrels and chipmunks dig and eat them.

Uses. Crocuses are ideal for beds, borders, and containers, as well as for naturalizing. Plant them in groups of at least 12—preferably a couple dozen—to make a good show.

Cyclamen hederifolium

Cyclamen hederifolium
SIKE-luh-men hed-er-ih-FOE-lee-um.
Hardy cyclamen. Fall. Zones 6 to 8.

Characteristics. Height: 4 to 6 inches. Colors: Pink or white.

Unlike the large-flowered florist cyclamen, hardy cyclamen are suitable for outdoor cultivation. Their rounded green leaves are often mottled with silver and are as beautiful as the flowers. The foliage emerges in late summer or fall, soon after the flowers appear, and stays handsome throughout the winter, finally disappearing when the weather gets hot. The lightly scented flowers are always borne singly on stalks just above the foliage. As the flowers finish, the flower stems coil, forcing the seeds to the soil at the base of the plants. A white form of hardy cyclamen, 'Album', is available, though it can be difficult to find. Other species of cyclamen are also available, but *Cyclamen hederifolium* is easier to establish than most of the others.

How to Grow. Plant cyclamen corms in well-drained soil in a shaded area as soon as you receive them in summer. Set them relatively shallowly, with about an inch of soil above the corm. Leave cyclamen undisturbed to form large colonies; self-sown seedlings will increase the size of the planting.

Uses. There is nothing prettier than a sea of pink cyclamen flowers in the fall landscape. They are excellent plants for dry, shady areas, and look good even at the base of shade trees. They are also lovely in large containers on a deck or patio.

DAFFODIL. See *Narcissus* hybrids

Dahlia hybrids
DAL-ee-uh. Dahlia. Summer to fall.
Zones 8 to 10.

Characteristics. Height: 1 to 5 feet. Colors: Red, pink, orange, yellow, purple, and white.

Few flowers say "summer" like the bold blooms of dahlias. These popular plants come in two basic types: compact bedding forms and tall border types. Both have upright stems and divided leaves, and grow from tuberous roots. They come in an amazing range of colors and flower forms, from single, small, daisylike blooms to huge, ruffled flowers up to 8 inches across.

How to Grow. Dahlias need well-drained soil and full sun. Grow bedding types from seed started indoors 6 to 8 weeks before the last frost. Set the plants out about a week after the last frost date. To grow border dahlias, buy the roots in spring. In the North, plant them indoors in pots 2 to 3 weeks before the last frost. Set the plants out about a week after all danger of frost has passed. In milder areas,

Dahlia 'Blazeway'

Dahlia 'Claire de Lune'

plant the roots outside around the last frost date. Dig a deep hole so that the top of the roots will be about 3 inches below the soil surface. Insert a stake at planting time; otherwise, you'll run the risk of stabbing the roots later in the season. Mulch the plants and water during dry spells. Deadhead regularly to keep the plants blooming.

In mild-winter areas, dahlias can stay in the ground all winter (give them a good winter mulch in Zone 8). In other areas, dig them in the fall, before or just after the first frost. Store the roots indoors in a frost-free area. Divide the root clumps into 2 to 4 sections before replanting in the spring. (Make sure each section has a part of the stem.)

Uses. Compact bedding dahlias are ideal for container gardens and for edging beds. Use the border types to add height and color to gardens in late summer to fall. Dahlias also make great cut flowers.

Eranthis hyemalis
er-AN-thiss hy-MAL-iss. Winter aconite.
Winter to early spring. Zones 3 to 7.

Characteristics. Height: 2 to 8 inches. Colors: Yellow.

The botanical name of this plant means "flower of spring," reflecting its tendency to bloom early in the season. Along with snowdrops (*Galanthus* spp.),

Eranthis hyemalis

winter aconites literally bloom through the snow. At the first hint of warmth, the dark green leaves begin to poke through the newly thawed soil. The bright yellow flowers are nestled on top of the leaves, on stems that grow 3 to 6 inches tall. Most bulb catalogs list only *Eranthis hyemalis*, but you may occasionally see others. *E. cilicica* is a little more robust than *E. hyemalis*. *E.* X *tubergenii*, a hybrid between the two species, is taller (up to 8 inches), with sulfur-yellow flowers.

How to Grow. Winter aconites grow best in full sun or in the shade of deciduous trees. They prefer humus-rich soil and do not perform particularly well in acid soil (below pH 5.5). Soak the tubers overnight, then plant them in fall about 1 inch deep and 3 inches apart. These plants do much better in the North than in the South, since a period with cold soil temperatures is necessary for good growth. Once planted, the tubers should not be disturbed. Where they are content, the plants will reseed themselves and form deep yellow carpets within a few years. Squirrels and other digging animals seem to enjoy the tubers; otherwise, these plants are generally pest- and disease-free.

Uses. Winter aconite is very popular not only for its ornamental value but also because it blooms so early. For a colorful spring show, plant the tubers in masses of 25 or more under deciduous shrubs and trees, such as witch hazels (*Hamamelis* spp.). Winter aconites are also useful for containers on a patio or deck.

Galanthus spp.

gah-LAN-thus. Snowdrop.
Late winter to early spring. Zones 3 to 7.

Characteristics. Height: 4 to 10 inches. Colors: White.

Snowdrops are a wonderful group of early-flowering bulbs which, like winter aconites (*Eranthis hyemalis*), can bloom through the melting snow. They are also called milk flowers, due to the milky white color of the blooms. The drooping flowers consist of inner petals and outer sepals; the inner segments are shorter than the outer ones. In some species, there are green markings on the petals.

The most common species are giant snowdrop (*Galanthus elwesii*) and common snowdrop (*G. nivalis*). The former is larger in every way than the latter and tends to bloom a week or two later. There are many selections, including *G. nivalis* var. *viridi-*

Galanthus nivalis

apicis, whose outer segments are tipped in green. 'Flore Pleno', a double form, is a handsome addition to the garden. Another marvelous plant is G. *nivalis* subsp. *reginae-olgae*. It is unusual in that it flowers in the fall, before the foliage has fully emerged.

How to Grow. Plant the bulbs in the fall, 2 to 3 inches deep and 4 to 5 inches apart. Snowdrops are more tolerant of shade than other early-spring-flowering bulbs, although sunny sites are best. They love frigid weather and cold soil, and struggle in warm climates. The flowers produce a good deal of seed, and self-sown plants arise freely in established plantings. To propagate, lift and divide the clumps after they flower, or transplant self-sown seedlings. Gray mold, slugs, and snails can cause significant damage to emerging foliage; otherwise, these plants are rarely bothered by pests or diseases.

Uses. Plant masses of snowdrops for a welcome spring show. Grow them in beds, borders, or containers, or allow them to naturalize in grassy areas.

GLADIOLUS, ABYSSINIAN. See *Acidanthera bicolor*

Gladiolus hybrids
glad-ee-OH-lus. Gladiolus. Summer.
Zones 5 to 8.

Characteristics. Height: 1 to 3 feet. Colors: Red, orange, yellow, greenish, purple, and white.

One of America's all-time favorite flowers, the gladiolus has undergone significant changes over the years. Although over 150 species have been named, nearly all of the plants in cultivation today are hybrids. Hybrid gladioli, commonly called glads, first appeared in 1823, and new cultivars of both small- and large-flowered forms have been selected every year. Numerous divisions of glads occur, ranging from the early-flowering *Gladiolus nanus* hybrids to the summer- and fall-flowering forms of the G. *primulinus* hybrids. The most common garden glads are the large-flowered forms, although recently there has been a resurgence of interest in dwarf and butterfly glads.

All glads, regardless of the type, are easy to grow. Their showy, colorful blooms are very popular

Gladiolus hybrids

as cut flowers. The foliage is sword-shaped and usually light green.

How to Grow. Glads need well-drained soil and full sun. Plant the corms 4 to 6 inches deep and 6 to 10 inches apart in spring after danger of frost has passed. North of Zone 7, you will need to lift the corms in the fall; place them in peat moss in a fine-mesh bag, and hang them from posts in a well-ventilated area where temperatures do not fall below 40°F, such as a slightly heated garage or basement. For propagation, you can separate the cormels (small corms clustered around the corm) when you dig the corms in fall. Or, you can separate them after flowering and plant the cormels to grow on in a prepared area. By the time you lift them in the fall, many will be of flowering size.

Glads are susceptible to all sorts of problems. Botrytis and Fusarium wilt can cause the corms to rot, while aphids, thrips, and corn borers can wreak havoc with the foliage and flowers. But don't be discouraged from trying these magnificent plants; you can help prevent problems by preparing a good planting area and starting with healthy corms from a reputable supplier.

Uses. Because they have historically been used as cut flowers, large-flowered glads are often relegated to a bed of their own or to a "cut flower" bed. However, while not the most ornamental of plants, glads deserve to be combined with other garden-worthy plants—for instance, other perennial species or small shrubs. The shorter cultivars blend well into any garden; annuals and short perennials are useful for hiding the "ankles" of the glads.

GLORY-OF-THE-SNOW. See *Chionodoxa* spp.
GRAPE HYACINTH. See *Muscari* spp.
GREEN DRAGON. See *Arisaema* spp.
HARLEQUIN FLOWER. See *Sparaxis tricolor*

Hyacinthus orientalis
hy-uh-SIN-thus or-ee-en-TAL-iss. Hyacinth.
Spring. Zones 3 to 7.

Characteristics. Height: 12 to 18 inches. Colors: Purple-blue, pink, red, yellow, salmon, and white.

Hyacinths are among the most fragrant flowers in the plant kingdom. While Abyssinian gladiolus (*Acidanthera bicolor*) produces a subtle sweet fragrance and lily-of-the-valley (*Convallaria majalis*) brings a hint of perfume, hyacinths knock us over. For some people, they are simply overwhelming and too intense to bring into the house. Others can't get enough of the aroma.

Hyacinthus orientalis

The tubular, bell-shaped flowers are borne on spikes and emerge above the dark green leaves in early spring. They bloom for a long time, particularly if spring temperatures remain cool. Many cultivars are available, including 'Blue Jacket', 'Blue Giant', and 'Blue Magic', which has purple-blue flowers with white throats. 'Carnegie' and 'L'Innocence' offer white blooms. 'Gypsy Queen' has fabulous salmon-colored flowers. 'Pink Pearl' and 'Marconi' both produce pink blooms. Many others may be found in bulb catalogs. Some companies offer multiflora hyacinths, which produce a number of smaller spikes and can be very pretty.

How to Grow. Hyacinths require a sunny site with well-drained soil. Plant the bulbs in the fall (October in the North, November in the South), with about 4 inches of soil over the top of the bulb. In the South, set the bulbs an extra inch or two deeper to take advantage of the cooler soil temperatures. Space the bulbs about 9 inches apart. Forced pots of hyacinths may be placed in the garden after flowering is complete, but subsequent flowers will not be as large as the original.

In all but the coldest climates, treat hyacinths as 1- or 2-year plants for best results. Although the plants will bloom for 3 to 4 years, the quality of the spikes and the number of flowers per spike decline over time. Compared to the first spring's flowers, subsequent blossoms will be shorter and the flowers farther apart on the spike. Some gardeners dig the bulbs after they flower and store them at 40°F, then replant them in the fall. However, the resulting blooms seldom compare with the first year's flowers.

Hyacinths are not easy to propagate at home. Offsets form slowly, but you can encourage them by lifting the bulbs and making slices with a knife about 1 inch deep on the bottom of each bulb in the shape of a cross. Bulblets will form on the cuts.

Starting with clean, firm bulbs will prevent many of the bacterial and fungal diseases that commonly affect hyacinths. Aphids and thrips can disfigure the flowers, especially if the weather warms up. To control these pests, spray with insecticidal soap.

Uses. Hyacinths add wonderful color and scent to spring beds, borders, and container gardens. Try planting them under windows so you can enjoy the fragrance both indoors and out.

Ipheion uniflorum 'Wisley Blue'

Ipheion uniflorum
IF-ee-on yew-nih-FLOR-um. Spring starflower.
Spring. Zones 5 to 9.

Characteristics. Height: 6 to 12 inches. Colors:
Blue or white.

Although this bulb has been in cultivation
since 1836, it is far from common in gardens today.
Part of the confusion is that it constantly undergoes
name changes; over time, it has been known as
Ipheion, Brodiaea, Milla, or *Triteleia.* By any name,
this is a terrific little plant: It is easy to grow, spreads
well, and is always bright and cheerful in the early-
spring garden. Each plant bears a 6- to 9-inch stem
tipped with a single, star-shaped, creamy white, fragrant flower with a deep blue midrib on the back.
The grasslike foliage smells a little like onion when
crushed. The most popular cultivar is the larger-
flowered 'Wisley Blue', with deep blue blooms.
'Froyle Mill' produces rosy-purple flowers and is also
very attractive.

How to Grow. Spring starflower tolerates full
sun but performs best in partial shade. Plant the
bulbs in the fall, about 2 inches deep and 3 to 5
inches apart. The foliage appears early in the spring,
and the flowers bloom from March to early May.
The bulbs produce bulblets, which, if left undisturbed, quickly fill the planting area. To propagate
spring starflower, dig the plants in late spring or

early summer as the foliage declines, remove the
bulblets, and replant. Seed-propagated bulbs take
about 2 years to reach flowering size.

Uses. While spring starflower cannot compete
with brightly colored tulips or hyacinths, it provides
reliably handsome flowers year after year. This
cheerful flower looks best in borders or containers.

Iris spp.
EYE-riss. Iris. Spring. Zones 5 to 8.

Characteristics. Height: 4 inches to 3 feet.
Colors: Blue, purple, violet, yellow, and white.

Irises are such exceptional plants and the genus
is so diverse, it is not surprising that they are among
the most popular garden flowers. Bearded, Siberian,
Dutch, English, Japanese, and Louisiana irises are
just a few of the groups that have captured the imagination of American gardeners. The majority of garden irises grow from rhizomes and are covered in
Chapter 4, Perennials; only the bulbous forms are
discussed here.

Danford iris (*Iris danfordiae*) seldom grows more
than 4 inches tall. The plants bear showy, bright
yellow flowers in late winter and early spring. In
some areas, they will bloom again the following
year. In most cases, however, the bulbs have a tendency to break up into small bulblets, which do not

Iris danfordiae and *I. reticulata*

flower the next year. For best results, treat Danford irises as annuals.

Unlike Danford iris, reticulated iris (*I. reticulata*) reblooms dependably. The blue to purple flowers are sweetly scented and appear in February to March. The plants are about 4 to 6 inches tall and bear grasslike, blue-green leaves. Once established, these plants continue to bloom for many years. There are many cultivars, including pale blue 'Cantab', dark blue 'Harmony', violet-and-orange 'Jeannine', and sky blue-and-orange 'Joyce'.

Dutch iris hybrids have long been produced as cut flowers in Holland and elsewhere around the world, and are sold by most florists. The bulbs are winter-hardy only to Zone 7 (Zone 6 with winter protection), but they provide spectacular flowers on 2- to 3-foot stems in suitable areas. The foliage arises in the winter, and the 4- to 6-inch-wide flowers appear in March and April. The flowers can become badly damaged if late frosts occur after the buds have swollen.

How to Grow. All bulbous irises require full sun and good drainage. Plant the bulbs in the fall with 2 to 3 inches of soil above them. Thrips and aphids can be a problem if the weather warms up while the plants are in flower; to control these pests, spray with insecticidal soap. To prevent Fusarium wilt and other fungi that can cause the bulbs to rot, choose a well-drained site.

Uses. Irises are ideal for beds, borders, and containers. They also make fine additions to rock gardens. For a good show, plant Danford and reticulated irises in drifts of at least 25. Dutch irises are a little more difficult to find and also more expensive, but they are showy even in groups of 3.

JACK-IN-THE-PULPIT. See *Arisaema* spp.

Leucojum spp.

lew-KOH-jum. Snowflake.
Spring to summer. Zones 4 to 9.

○ ◑ ▼

Characteristics. Height: 12 to 18 inches. Colors: White.

Snowflakes bear charming, white, drooping flowers in early spring to midsummer. Some people

Leucoium aestivum

get snowdrops (*Galanthus* spp.) and snowflakes mixed up, but snowflake flowers are bell-shaped, while snowdrop flowers have an inner cup and three longer outer petals. (The sepals and petals of snowflake flowers are the same length, while the flowers of snowdrops have longer sepals than petals.)

Snowflakes generally bear 1 to 6 bell-shaped flowers on each stem, and the flower tips are often tinged with yellow or green. Spring snowflake (*Leucojum vernum*) and summer snowflake (*L. aestivum*) are the most common species. The former blooms a little earlier and usually bears only 1 or 2 flowers per stalk; the latter flowers later and produces 2 to 8 flowers per stalk. Otherwise, there are few differences between them. *L. aestivum* 'Gravetye Giant' is more robust and free-flowering than the species.

How to Grow. Plant snowflakes in the fall in a sunny to lightly shaded site that is well drained but receives adequate moisture. Set the bulbs 4 to 6 inches apart, with approximately 2 inches of soil over the bulbs. Propagate the plants by lifting the bulbs after the foliage has died and removing the offsets. Snowflakes have few problems with pests or diseases.

Uses. Snowflakes are a welcome addition to any planting of spring bulbs. Add them to beds and borders, or naturalize them under tall dedicuous trees. For best effect plant in clumps of a dozen or more. They also can be used in containers for spring to summer interest.

Lilium 'Enchantment'

Lilium candidum

Lilium spp.

LIL-ee-um. Lily. Late spring to summer.
Zones 3 to 8.

○ ◑ ⊱❀ ❦ ▼

Characteristics. Height: 2 to 8 feet. Colors: White, yellow, orange, red, maroon, and bicolors.

Lilies are the undisputed bulb queens of the summer garden, providing classic beauty for many months. The choice of flower colors, shapes, sizes, and heights is almost endless. There is a plethora of Asiatic and Oriental hybrids, not to mention at least a half-dozen species of these spectacular garden plants.

The terms "Asiatic" and "Oriental" refer to the ancestry of the parents used to create the hybrids. The Asiatics generally have short, dark green leaves and upward-facing, cup-shaped flowers, which are borne near the top of the stem. They often flower earlier than the Oriental hybrids. Orange-red 'Enchantment' and yellow 'Citronella' are two well-known examples.

The Oriental types have longer leaves and larger flowers than the Asiatics. The flowers are usually downward- or outward-facing and are bowl-shaped, flat-faced, or have recurved petals. They bloom in the leaf axils on the top third of the stem, as well as at the end. Reddish, white-edged 'Star Gazer' and

spotted, white 'Everest' are well-known Oriental forms. Numerous cultivars are available, and some specialist catalogs list literally hundreds.

Not to be outdone by the hybrids, a few species are also excellent additions to the garden. These include orange-flowered Henry's lily (*Lilium henryi*); the fragrant, white regal lily (*L. regale*); the white, gold-marked gold band lily (*L. auratum*); and the ubiquitous orange tiger lily (*L. tigrinum*).

How to Grow. Full sun is best, but the plants tolerate a little afternoon shade in the North and enjoy it in the South. No lilies like "wet feet," so good drainage is essential. Plant the bulbs twice as deep as they are long. (For example, a bulb that measures 3 inches from top to bottom should be planted 6 inches deep.) The only exception is Madonna lily (*L. candidum*), which should be planted about 1 inch deep. For an extra boost, apply a little 10-10-10 fertilizer around the outside of the emerging foliage in the spring and again when the flower buds become visible. If the plants become overcrowded, lift them after they bloom and separate the various bulbs and bulblets. Bulbs that are larger than 3 inches in diameter may flower the next year; the smaller ones will take longer. It is important that you do not allow the lifted bulbs to dry out; replant them immediately.

Lilies are a favorite food for aphids, slugs, snails, and thrips, but you can keep these pests at bay by monitoring the plants carefully and simply using a spray of water from your hose to wash them off the plants. Insecticidal soaps are also effective. Some species and hybrids can carry a number of viruses, which can wipe them out in no time and infect other established lilies. Infected plants generally have foliage that is mottled with yellow and/or deformed. Buying healthy bulbs from reputable suppliers is the best way to prevent these problems. Destroy infected plants to prevent the virus from spreading to other lilies.

Uses. Lilies suffer from the same problem as glads; the stems are not particularly attractive when the flowers are not present. (The same is true of tulips and daffodils, but their leaves disappear after flowering.) Growing lilies in groups of 3 or more makes a decent-size stand, which seems to make them look better. You can also site them to grow up through mid-sized shrubs and perennials in beds and borders. Lilies are ideal for fresh arrangements, if you can bear to cut them; many have a delightful fragrance. Try dwarf types in containers.

LILY, ARUM. See *Arum italicum*
LILY, ATAMASCO. See *Zephyranthes* spp.
LILY, CALLA. See *Zantedeschia* spp.
LILY-OF-THE-VALLEY. See *Convallaria majalis*
LILY, RESURRECTION. See *Lycoris* spp.
LILY, ZEPHYR. See *Zephyranthes* spp.

Lycoris spp.
ly-CORE-iss. Resurrection lily.
Late summer to fall. Zones 5 to 8.
○ ◑ ⅌⚗ ▼

Characteristics. Height: 18 to 30 inches. Colors: Mauve or red.

Resurrection lilies are perfect for forgetful gardeners who can't remember where anything is planted, since the flowers seem to magically arise where nothing appeared to be growing. In the winter and spring, the daffodil-like leaves cover the ground, only to disappear by late spring. Meanwhile, other perennials or annuals fill the space. Then, in late summer or early fall, the pink-mauve amaryllis-like flowers of the common resurrection lily (*Lycoris squamigera*) emerge on leafless flower stems. This is

Lycoris squamigera

the hardiest species and performs well as far north as Zone 5.

Gardeners in warmer areas can also enjoy the blood red flowers of *L. radiata*, which emerge in early to late fall. The plants, which are hardy to Zone 7, are much shorter than *L. squamigera*, and the flowers are smaller, but their bright hue makes them stand out immediately. The foliage of *L. radiata* is also smaller and less messy as it dies back than that of the common resurrection lily. Yellow and white species are sometimes available; if you can find them, they are definitely worth a try.

How to Grow. Resurrection lilies prefer well-drained soil and full sun to light shade. Plant the bulbs as soon as they become available, which is usually in late summer or early fall. Set them 3 to 4 inches deep and 6 to 10 inches apart. *L. squamigera* spreads rapidly and requires more space than *L. radiata*. Propagate by lifting the bulbs when they get crowded, preferably when the leaves begin to die down.

Uses. Resurrection lilies are wonderful for adding an unusual accent to beds, borders, and containers at a time when many other garden plants are in decline. The blooms make excellent cut flowers, lasting for many days in fresh water.

MEADOW SAFFRON. See *Colchicum* spp.
MONTEBRETIA. See *Crocosmia* hybrids

Muscari sp.

Muscari spp.
muh-SCARE-ee. Grape hyacinth.
Spring. Zones 3 to 8.

○ ◐

Characteristics. Height: 3 to 12 inches. Colors: Blue-violet or white.

Grape hyacinths are one of the easiest bulbs to grow. There are more than 30 species, but only a few are commonly available. The common grape hyacinths (*Muscari armeniacum* and *M. botryoides*) differ slightly in the number and length of their leaves, but otherwise are very similar. The individual cup-shaped flowers are mildly fragrant and are borne on many-flowered spikes. Numerous cultivars are available at reasonable prices, including 'Cantab', which has pale blue flowers; 'Christmas Pearl', with violet blossoms; 'Fantasy Creation', which produces blue double flowers; and 'Album', with white blooms.

Tassel hyacinth (*M. comosum*) grows 8 to 12 inches tall and bears blue flowers; the flowers of the variety, *M. comosum* var. *plumosum*, look like large feather dusters. One-leaf hyacinth (*M. latifolium*) usually produces only one large leaf; the tall spikes bear light blue flowers at the top and violet flowers at the bottom. This terrific plant is valued for its attractive flowers, neat foliage, and reliability in the garden.

How to Grow. Grape hyacinths grow and mul-

tiply well in a sunny location with well-drained soil. Plant the bulbs 2 to 4 inches deep and 4 to 5 inches apart in fall. To propagate, lift the bulbs as the leaves die down, and separate the offsets. Grape hyacinths are generally trouble-free.

Uses. Common grape hyacinths make useful markers in the garden for other dormant bulbs, such as crocuses. Their leaves, which emerge in the fall, will remind you not to dig there as you search for a spot to plant new bulbs, shrubs, or trees. Planted in large masses, grape hyacinths look like sweeping rivers of blue.

Narcissus hybrids
nar-SIS-us. Daffodil. Spring. Zones 3 to 9.

Characteristics. Height: 6 inches to 2 feet. Colors: Yellow, orange, and white.

Daffodils are universally popular in the United States, both with gardeners and non-gardeners alike. Even people who don't care much about gardening are likely to put a few dozen daffodils in their yard. Daffodils are easy to plant, require minimal maintenance, multiply rapidly, and are inexpensive. Combine these great features with the diversity of height, form, and color found in the genus, and it's

Narcissus bulbocodium

Narcissus 'King Alfred'

easy to understand why even the most ardent gardener considers daffodils indispensable.

There are so many different cultivars that daffodil experts have created 10 different divisions, or groups, to categorize them all. Most of the packaged daffodils found in the retail markets are those with large "cups" and long petals on the flowers; usually, one flower is produced per stem. However, many other forms are available through garden centers and bulb outlets. For example, the petals and the cup may be the same or different colors, and the size of the individual flowers can vary greatly. Some types produce as many as 3 to 5 flowers per stem or bear double flowers. The height of the plants can also vary; some are barely 6 inches tall, while others can grow to 2 feet. The most popular cultivars include 'Unsurpassable', 'Carlton', 'Barrett Browning', 'Cheerfulness', 'Tresamble', 'February Gold', 'Pipit', 'Cragford', 'Actaea', and 'Hawera'.

How to Grow. Full sun is best, but many daffodils also do well in the dappled shade of deciduous trees. Plant the bulbs in the fall, approximately twice as deep as the height of the bulb and 6 to 9 inches apart. Fertilize the bulbs in the spring when the leaves first emerge; use a balanced fertilizer. Allow the foliage to remain until it dies down on its own. When the bulbs become too crowded, they may not flower; lift and divide them after the foliage has begun to yellow. If you start with healthy bulbs,

you should have few problems. Daffodils are rarely bothered by pests or diseases.

Uses. Daffodils are perfect for beginning gardeners: You can start with a bag of daffodils from a local retail outlet, graduate to a few named cultivars from the garden center, then pore over bulb catalogs for different forms or the newest cultivars. These bulbs are also excellent for naturalizing; good bulb retailers usually sell mixtures of cultivars and forms suitable for this purpose. Daffodils make wonderful cut flowers that will last for about a week. (If you put other flowers in the same container, be sure to change the water every day.) The dwarf forms of daffodils are terrific for containers, rock gardens, or other spots where something small, but colorful, is needed in the spring.

ONION, ORNAMENTAL. See *Allium* spp.

Ornithogalum spp.
or-nith-OG-al-um. Star-of-Bethlehem, silver bell. Spring. Zones 5 to 9.

Characteristics. Height: 8 to 18 inches. Colors: White.

Many species of *Ornithogalum* are used as commercial cut flowers. The two most important cut flower species are Arabian star flower (*O. arabicum*)

Ornithogalum umbellatum

and chincherinchee (*O. thyrsoides*), both hardy only to Zone 8. Although they are sold for planting in the garden, they seldom perform well outdoors. The two most common garden species are true star-of-Bethlehem (*O. umbellatum*) and silver bell or drooping star-of-Bethlehem (*O. nutans*).

True star-of-Bethlehem is quite beautiful. It bears up to 20 pure white flowers, with green stripes on the outside of the petals. These flowers have an interesting trait: They open late in the morning—hence, their other common name, 11-o'clock flower. The plants can be very invasive, particularly in rich soils. If you would like some of these bulbs, you will find that many gardeners are more than willing to share a few with you.

Silver bells bear 3 to 12 white flowers with green midribs on 12- to 18-inch stems. They are better behaved than star-of-Bethlehem and not quite as invasive. Often, the flowers are borne more on one side of the stem than the other. These are great, easy-to-grow plants.

How to Grow. Like glads, star-of-Bethlehem species that are not hardy may be dug up and stored indoors over winter. The bulbs prefer well-drained soil and full sun, although they tolerate afternoon shade. Plant them in the fall, about 2 to 3 inches deep and 4 to 6 inches apart. Propagate by lifting and dividing the bulbs after the flowers have finished blooming. Thrips can be a problem; spray affected plants with insecticidal soap.

Uses. Try star-of-Bethlehem in beds, borders, and container plantings. The blooms make nice cut flowers.

Polianthes tuberosa
pah-lee-AN-theez tew-ber-OH-suh. Tuberose. Late summer to fall. Zones 7 to 10.

Characteristics. Height: 30 to 36 inches. Colors: White.

Tuberose was well known for its fragrant flowers as early as the 16th century and has been an important part of the cut flower industry for decades. Up to two dozen flowers bloom in each long, spikelike flower cluster. They may start opening as early as mid-August and continue until the first frost. Well-

grown plants can reach 3 feet tall. 'Mexican Single' and 'The Pearl' bear single and double flowers, respectively. The double flowers stay on the stem longer, and double-flowered forms are probably slightly better garden plants. However, the single-flowered types produce better cut flowers.

How to Grow. Set the bulbs out in spring when the ground has begun to warm up and after the danger of frost has passed. Plant them about 3 inches deep and 8 to 10 inches apart; choose a sunny, well-drained site. In colder areas, treat tuberose like a gladiolus; in milder climates, the bulbs can stay in the ground over winter. Dig and separate the offsets as the bulbs become crowded. Nematodes like to feast on the roots of tuberose, and thrips can disfigure the flowers. Otherwise, these bulbs are not generally bothered by pests or diseases.

Uses. Tuberose looks best when mixed with other garden plants: The flowers are extraordinary, but the plants themselves are rather ordinary-looking. The blooms make terrific cut flowers.

QUAMASH. See *Camassia* spp.

Scilla spp.
SIL-uh. Squill. Spring. Zones 4 to 8.

Characteristics. Height: 3 to 10 inches. Colors: Blue or white.

Although best known for their beautiful bright blue flowers in the spring, squills are a surprisingly large genus that includes spring-, summer-, and fall-flowering species. The spring-flowering are the easiest to find, although some of the others are also well worth trying. All the plants are small; the tallest usually reach no more than 10 inches.

Siberian squill (*Scilla siberica*) is the most common of the spring-flowering group. The brilliant blue, bell-like flowers bloom on 4- to 6-inch-tall plants; usually, 4 to 6 flowers are produced on each stem. Most catalogs offer the cultivar 'Spring Beauty', with bright blue flowers. A white form, 'Alba', is sometimes available.

A very early-spring species with flat, blue flowers is the unpronounceable *S. mischtschenkoana*. The flowers have a dark blue stripe along the center of

Scilla siberica

each flower. Another early-spring bloomer is two-leafed squill (*S. bifolia*). It is easy to grow and provides handsome, starry blue flowers.

More adventuresome gardeners may want to try Peruvian squill (*S. peruviana*), which blooms in summer. The plants are vigorous and provide up to 100 small blue flowers packed on a 10- to 12-inch flower head. They are hardy only to Zone 7, or to Zone 6 if well mulched. Peruvian squills are excellent plants for warm-summer gardens.

How to Grow. All squills do well in filtered sun and tolerate afternoon shade. Plant the spring-flowering species in fall, 3 to 4 inches deep and about 6 inches apart in well-drained soil. Set Peruvian squill just beneath the surface. Squills are slow to propagate, but you can lift clumps and remove the offsets when they become crowded; seed may be a quicker way to increase their numbers. As long as they have good drainage, these plants have few problems.

Uses. Grow squills in beds, borders, containers, and rock gardens. They also look attractive under trees and shrubs.

SILVER BELL. See *Ornithogalum* spp.
SNOWDROP. See *Galanthus* spp.
SNOWFLAKE. See *Leucojum* spp.

Sparaxis tricolor
spuh-RAK-sis TRY-kuh-ler. Harlequin flower, wandflower. Spring to summer. Zones 7 to 9.

Characteristics. Height: 10 to 12 inches. Colors: Red, orange, yellow, and white.

These wonderful plants are native to South Africa, and in a land where brightly colored flowers are the norm, this is one of the brightest. The colors range from pure white to yellow, orange, and red; the flowers are often outlined in black. The plants bloom in early summer on 10- to 12-inch-tall stems above fanlike leaves.

How to Grow. Plant the corms in full sun and well-drained soil in early spring (or fall in warmer areas). Set them about 2 inches deep and 3 to 4 inches apart. Cormels form relatively slowly; separate them from the parent corms for propagation. As with glads, the corms may be stored over winter.

Sparaxis tricolor

The main reason these plants are not more popular is that they suffer if they get too much water during the summer. They prefer to be on the dry side in summer and wet during winter. For this reason, they grow well in drier parts of the West, including Southern California. To prevent problems, be sure the soil is well drained.

Uses. Try harlequin flowers for a real show in the summer garden. For best effect, plant them in groups of at least 25. They also make a dramatic addition to both fresh arrangements and container plantings.

SQUILL. See *Scilla* spp.
STARFLOWER, SPRING. See *Ipheion uniflorum*
STAR-OF-BETHLEHEM. See *Ornithogalum* spp.

Tulipa 'Gudoshnik'

Tigridia pavonia

ty-GRID-ee-uh pav-OWN-nee-uh. Tiger flower.
Summer. Zones 7 to 9.

Characteristics. Height: 20 to 24 inches. Colors: Red, orange, yellow, and white.

Tiger flower is native to Mexico. The 3- to 5-inch-wide flowers range from yellow to white, red, or orange, often with purplish blotches on the inside. Individual flowers may last only one day, but many are formed on each stem.

How to Grow. Purchase the corms in early spring and plant them immediately in full sun and well-drained soil. Set them 3 to 4 inches deep and 6 to 10 inches apart. Where little or no frost occurs, the plants may return each year; in cold climates, you can lift and store the corms with your glads, caladiums, and other tender bulbs. For best results, however, treat tiger flowers as annuals and replace the corms each year. Like harlequin flowers (*Sparaxis tricolor*), tiger flowers need excellent drainage in order to thrive.

Uses. Tiger flowers are eye-catching in summer beds, borders, and containers.

TUBEROSE. See *Polianthes tuberosa*
TUBEROUS BEGONIA. See *Begonia tuberhybrida* hybrids

Tulipa spp. and hybrids

TEW-lih-puh. Tulip. Spring. Zones 2 to 8.

Characteristics. Height: 6 to 36 inches. Colors: Red, orange, yellow, purple, pink, and white.

Tulips are an indispensable part of the garden. The Dutch have taken this native of Turkey and created spectacular palettes for the spring landscape. While *Tulipa* includes many interesting flower forms, it is the simplicity of the classic tulip that makes it such a well-loved flower.

Tulips may flower as early as March or as late as June, depending on the type you have chosen and your climate. If you are just learning about tulips, choose some single-early types, such as 'Apricot Beauty', as well as a few single-late kinds, such as 'Kingsblood'. Then, when you are ready to try something different, plant some Kaufmanniana or Greigii cultivars for early flowering and a few Bouquet types (for example, 'Toronto') for multiple blooms from the same bulb. Kaufmanniana types to try include 'Stresa' and 'Waterlily'; Greiggi cultivars include 'Sweet Lady' and 'Pinocchio'.

Once you have the tulip bug, you will want to try one or two of the dozen or so species tulips offered for sale. Nearly all of these are short (6 to 12 inches), and most are relatively early. Three out-

Tulipa 'Fringed Beauty'

standing species tulips are *T. clusiana*, with red-and-white flowers; *T. batalinii*, which offers yellow-and-apricot blooms; and *T. turkestanica*, a multiflowered, white tulip with an orange center.

How to Grow. Tulips thrive in full sun and well-drained soil rich in organic matter. Plant the bulbs at least 6 inches deep—8 inches is best, especially in the South. Set them close enough together to make a splash in the spring. If you buy your bulbs from a reputable outlet, insects and diseases will be minimal. Chipmunks and other rodents will eat the bulbs, unfortunately.

The tulip is botanically an annual, since the mother bulb is replaced each year by a daughter bulb. The daughter bulb must grow to sufficient size to flower the next spring. If the soil is poor, or if conditions are not to their liking, the daughter bulbs may not get large enough to flower well, or even to flower at all. Bulbs that are too small to flower often produce one large, straplike leaf and nothing else. To encourage tulips to "perennialize,"

especially in areas where they are not commonly long-lived, put some extra effort into preparing a loose, rich planting area. Fertilize in the fall at planting time with an appropriate bulb fertilizer. Then feed again after the bulbs flower and allow the foliage to die back on its own. Some species and cultivars are naturally more perennial than others in a given climate; Darwin Hybrid tulips, Single Late tulips, and many species tulips are among the longest-lived, but be sure to experiment with a variety of them to see which perform best in your garden.

Uses. The key to good-looking tulip plantings is generosity. Don't plant sparse, straight lines of tulip soldiers; paint the landscape with drifts of at least a dozen of each cultivar. Use a broad stroke with the tulip brush, stand back, and enjoy the scenery in the spring.

To help hide the ripening foliage, plant the bulbs to come up through annuals or perennials. Tulips also grow well in containers. Don't forget to plant a few extras for cutting, too.

WANDFLOWER. See *Sparaxis tricolor*
WINDFLOWER. See *Anemone* spp.
WINTER ACONITE. See *Eranthis hyemalis*

Zantedeschia spp.

zan-teh-DESK-ee-uh. Calla lily.
Spring to summer. Zones 7 to 10.

Characteristics. Height: 1 to 3 feet. Colors: White, reddish pink, yellow, and green.

There are few flowers as dramatic as the calla lily. The plants are related to Jack-in-the-pulpits (*Arisaema* spp.) and bear narrow flowers enveloped in a white or colorful coat, called a spathe. Callas can grow 3 feet tall and produce 6 to 12 flowers. The common calla lily (*Zantedeschia aethiopica*) is evergreen, with dark green leaves and a pure white spathe. 'Little Gem' and 'Childsiana' are dwarf selections. 'Crowborough' is supposed to be a little hardier than the species. Many of the newer species and hybrids depicted in catalogs produce deciduous mottled foliage and yellow, pink, or red spathes. One interesting selection is 'Black Magic', which sports a black throat inside the yellow spathe. Other colorful hybrids include salmon-colored 'Cameo', pink-flowered 'Pink Persuasion', and creamy yellow 'Solfatare'.

How to Grow. In its native habitat, the white-flowered common calla lily may be found growing in wet, marshy ground. In the garden, the plants tolerate normal garden soils but flourish in moist, sunny areas. The colored hybrids do not tolerate such wet conditions; site these in well-drained soil.

Plant the rhizomes about 4 inches deep and 12 to 18 inches apart. For best flowering, the plants need sun, but they appreciate afternoon shade. The greatest drawback of calla lilies is their relative lack of cold hardiness, which limits them as perennials to southern zones. In the North, you must dig them in the fall, dry them off, and store them in a cool, dry area over winter. You can also divide the rhizomes in the fall; just be sure to allow the cut ends to dry out well before storing, since soft rot can infect the rhizomes. (This problem tends to occur more in storage than in the garden.) Some leaf-spotting fungi can be a problem on lower leaves; pinch off infected leaves.

Uses. Calla lilies are striking in beds, borders, and containers. They are also excellent as cut flowers.

Zephyranthes spp.

zeh-fir-ANTH-eez. Atamasco lily, zephyr lily.
Spring or fall. Zones 7 to 10.
○

Characteristics. Height: 4 to 12 inches. Colors: White, pink, and rose.

Underused by all but seasoned gardeners, these bulbs produce marvelous crocuslike white, pink, or rose flowers. The largest and earliest flowers are those of our native Atamasco lily (*Zephyranthes atamasco*). The 3-inch-wide, white blooms are tinged with pink and are produced on 9- to 12-inch-long stems in late spring. They are hardy to Zone 7, and sometimes Zone 6 with winter protection.

Zephyranthes atamasco

Atamasco lilies have escaped from gardens in the Southeast and are spectacular weeds by the roadsides in late spring.

Another terrific species is *Z. candida*, probably the hardiest of the zephyr lilies. The 2-inch-long flowers are often flushed with rose, with green toward the base. They bloom on 4- to 8-inch stems in late summer and fall.

Rose zephyr lily (*Z. rosea*) is occasionally offered but is less hardy than the other two species. The rosy pink flowers appear about 6 inches above the narrow leaves and open in late summer.

How to Grow. Plant the bulbs in the spring, 1 to 2 inches deep and 3 to 4 inches apart, in a sunny location. Leave them in the ground in warm climates; lift and store them indoors in a cool, dry place over winter in areas where temperatures regularly stay below 20°F. Propagate by digging and separating the bulbs or by sowing seed. Pests and diseases are seldom a problem.

Uses. Zephyr lilies are attractive in beds and borders or in containers. As winter approaches, bring container-grown plants indoors.

ROSES FOR ALL OCCASIONS. *There is a place for roses in nearly every garden, whether you grow ramblers or hybrid teas, miniatures or shrub roses. This brick-walled scene features two climbing roses—'Climbing Pink Pet' and an old, unnamed orange-flowered polyantha.*

CHAPTER SIX

ROSES

Roses ARE PERHAPS THE MOST BELOVED—AND THE MOST RECOGNIZABLE—OF ALL FLOWERS. For centuries, people have found roses both captivating and mysterious, and have grown them for their stunning flowers as well as for their practical uses. Rose fruits, usually called hips, are an excellent source of vitamin C and are often used to make a delicious tea. The petals of cabbage rose (*Rosa centifolia*) are used to make rose water, which is a common ingredient in both cosmetics and food. True attar of roses (also known as oil of roses) is extracted from the petals of *R. damascena* 'Trigentipetala'. Rose petals are also sometimes candied and eaten as a sweet.

While roses clearly have practical value, it is ultimately their beautiful blooms that make them garden favorites. In this chapter, you'll learn the secrets of planting and caring for your roses to keep them naturally healthy, vigorous, and practically problem-free. You'll also find tips for combining roses with other great garden plants—including shrubs, vines, herbs, perennials, and annuals—for season-long landscape interest.

195

GROWING ROSES

Rose growing should and can be fun and rewarding. The trick is to put your energy into the species and cultivars that are consistently good performers. Roses have received a bad reputation in recent years as temperamental, chemically dependent, high-maintenance plants. Of course, this is true of some roses, but not all of them deserve to be cast aside. For instance, some gardeners are discovering the virtues of the long-neglected old cultivars growing untended in cemeteries and abandoned places. There are even rose groups around the country, like the "rose rustlers" in Texas, who go to places where roses have survived, take cuttings of the plants, and grow them for garden use. Modern rose breeders are also attuned to gardeners' demands for hardy, problem-resistant roses, and are releasing many excellent new selections. These recent introductions, along with the old cultivars, give both ardent and would-be rose growers a great selection of roses to choose from.

SHOPPING FOR ROSES

Always buy roses from a reliable grower. Bargain roses for sale at a local discount store may be inexpensive, but you'll get what you pay for. It's worth paying a few dollars more to a reputable garden center or mail-order source to get a healthy, vigorous plant that's more likely to thrive in your yard.

When you buy your plants, you may have a choice between "grafted" and "own-root" roses. Many roses are sold as grafted plants, since grafting is a fast way to propagate a large quantity of similar plants. Grafted plants usually have a knob or swelling just above the roots. This area, called the graft union, is where the top part of the desired rose was joined to the roots of another. Own-root roses

ROSE TYPES AND TERMS

With so many roses to choose from, it's sometimes hard to know where to start. To make things a little easier, roses have been divided into several groups, based on their origins and growth habits. Understanding the names for these different categories can help you choose roses that are ideal for your needs.

Below you'll find a brief overview of the main rose types. Some of the best of these are highlighted in the plant portraits in this chapter.

Albas: These disease-resistant roses offer clusters of fragrant, midsummer flowers and blue-gray-green leaves on long, arching canes.

Bourbon Roses: These reblooming roses have double flowers. The shrubby plants are susceptible to black spot and powdery mildew.

Cabbage or Provence Roses: Also known as "the rose of 100 petals," these showy flowers are famous for their depiction in paintings by the Dutch masters in the 17th and 18th centuries. The double blooms are usually pink or white blushed with pink.

China Roses: *Rosa chinensis* was the first rose introduced into Europe from China. It was a popular parent for rose-breeding work, due in large part to its everblooming qualities. China roses are less hardy than the European roses and are better suited for growing in warm climates, where they tend to be long-lived.

Damask Roses: Popular for their perfume, Damasks produce semidouble to double flowers on open shrubs, mainly in summer. Autumn Damasks have a prolonged blooming period.

Floribundas: This class resulted from mixing Hybrid Tea roses with Polyanthas. Floribundas are compact and bear many blossoms per stem, usually over a long period.

Gallica Roses: These compact plants produce richly colored, single to double summer flowers, which are used in medicine and to flavor confections. The plants are prone to mildew.

Grandifloras: This class of roses was developed in the 1950s. They are distinguished by large flowers and profuse bloom.

Hybrid Perpetuals: These roses are crosses between Bourbon Roses and a variety of other types of garden roses. Hybrid Perpetuals are the link between the modern and the old roses. They have many of the same characteristics as Hybrid Tea roses, but with less continuous bloom and a better perfume.

Hybrid Teas: Hybrid Teas come in a wide range of beautiful flower colors. The elegant buds and long

are just that—the top and the roots are from the same plant.

If possible, buy roses that are on their own roots. That way, if the top of the plant is killed by the cold, the roots can send up new growth that will be just like the original. When the tops of grafted roses die back, the new shoots that come up from the roots will look completely different, and will probably not be what you want for your garden.

CHOOSING THE SITE

Starting with durable, dependable plants is one part of successful rose growing; the other is choosing the right site. A minimum of 6 hours of direct sunlight per day is essential for good rose growth. If you can only choose from sites that are shaded for part of the day, a spot with morning sun and afternoon shade is preferable; the morning sunlight will dry the leaves off faster and possibly decrease disease problems.

Roses generally prefer soil that's moist but not waterlogged. Tree roots tend to dry out the soil, so avoid planting your roses near trees. You will also need a spot that is big enough for your roses to mature without being crowded. Dense, crowded growth limits air circulation around the plants and can lead to disease problems.

PREPARING THE SOIL

Roses grow best in well-prepared soil. For good root growth, work the soil deeply, loosening the top 2 feet. As you dig, add ample amounts of organic matter, such as compost or manure. (Some gardeners recommend using chicken manure, which is rich in micronutrients.) If possible, dig over an entire bed rather than just a single hole where the rose will go. This will encourage wide-spreading, healthier root growth.

Check the soil pH; it should be between 6.4 and

stems make them popular as cut flowers. However, because these roses tend to require regular spraying to stay healthy, many gardeners are beginning to pass them up in favor of other roses that need less care.

Moss Roses: Moss roses are mutations of cabbage roses that were selected for their "moss"-covered, sticky buds and calyx. Otherwise, they are similar to their parents.

Noisette Roses: The first Noisette rose, 'Champney's Pink Cluster', was bred in Charleston, South Carolina, by John Champney, a rice planter. He sent the rose to nurseryman Phillip Noisette in France, who went on to develop this new class of roses. Noisette roses are known primarily for their climbing habit and showy flower clusters.

Old Roses: This general term refers to the large group of fine roses that have been garden favorites for hundreds of years, including the Albas, Damasks, and Bourbons, as well as Moss, Noisette, Provence, and Tea roses.

Polyanthas: Most Polyantha roses are small plants with abundant flowers. They are ideal for containers or small gardens and tend to have a wide range of hardiness.

Ramblers: Ramblers are known for their vigor-

ous, sprawling habit. They tend to produce masses of blooms all at once.

Rugosa Roses: R. rugosa is a tough, cold-hardy rose known for its salt tolerance, disease resistance, and showy hips. Both the species and its many cultivars and hybrids are excellent garden plants, especially for hedges.

Shrub Roses: This is a catch-all category for many of the new roses that serve as dependable landscape plants and require less pruning.

Species Roses: Species or wild roses are those types that occur naturally. There are approximately 200 such roses in existence. They often have single flowers with 5 petals. Most species roses produce attractive hips in the summer or autumn and can often be grown successfully from seed. Many of the great new shrub roses are species selections or species hybrids.

Tea Roses: It is widely believed that these roses are so named because they first arrived on tea ships from China. The long-blooming plants tend to be disease-resistant, and perform well in Zones 7 to 10.

6.8. If your soil is too acidic, add ground limestone to raise the pH. If it is too alkaline, add sulfur or leaf compost, or both. If the pH is out of balance, nutrient deficiencies will show up later. For example, the leaves may turn yellow, or the plants may not grow as vigorously as they should.

PLANTING

The ideal time to plant roses is when they are dormant—in late fall or early spring. Many mail-order rose nurseries will ship bareroot plants (plants with just packing around the roots) in November, although this can vary by region. If bareroot roses arrive and you cannot plant them immediately, place them in a refrigerator or another cool spot. Before planting, soak the roots in a tub of water. Prune off any injured or broken roots.

Dig a generous planting hole; make it large enough to hold all of the roots in their natural position without bending them. Make a mound of soil in the middle of the hole, set the plant on top, and spread the roots around it.

Before filling in the hole, check the planting depth. The bud or crown (the point where the roots and the stem meet) should be 1 to 2 inches below the soil surface. Adjust the height of the soil mound until the plant is sitting at the right height. Tamp the soil gently, but firmly as you place it back in the hole around the roots. After planting, mound more soil around the base of the plant to give added protection during the first winter; remove the soil mound in spring.

Until the plants are well established, you'll need to water them during dry periods. A good irrigation program—including a morning rinse of the foliage and absolutely no wetting of the foliage at night—can be extremely helpful with roses. Most roses need no pruning during the first year and little or no pruning the second year.

FERTILIZING

Since roses are heavy feeders, many growers recommend a regular fertilization program. For newly planted roses, wait until after the first bloom cycle. For established roses, fertilize every 3 weeks during the blooming season. Some gardeners use a combination of organic and chemical fertilizers. Mix the fertilizer with water and then pour the mixture around the base of the plant, following the direc-

MIXED-UP ROSES. *One excellent way to use roses in a landscape is to mix them into perennial gardens and shrub borders. Here, 'Henne Martin' rose is growing with* Filipendula purpurea.

tions on the label. Good organic fertilizers for this purpose include sea kelp and dried blood. There is also a wide array of good fertilizers on the market specially formulated for roses.

To give your roses an extra boost, apply chicken manure over the area every third winter. As a winter mulch, chicken manure also provides protection against severe frost. In early spring, before new growth begins, fork the manure into the soil.

PRUNING

Rose pruning doesn't have to be a big deal; you just need to keep a few simple rules in mind. Always start by removing all dead, diseased, damaged, or crossing branches. Any further pruning depends on the growth habit of the plant and on your desired objective. Pruning should be a gradual process that includes deadheading on a regular basis and an

HAPPY COMPANIONS. *Herbs and other perennials can make terrific groundcovers when grown under roses. Here, 'Betty Prior' rose is growing with lavender and yellow columbine* (Aquilegia chrysantha).

occasional summer pruning to encourage more blooms.

Do all your pruning with high-quality pruning shears. If you prune a diseased rose, clean the shears off with rubbing alcohol before using them on another rose. Each time you prune, make the cut about ¼ inch above an outward-facing bud, and angle the cut so it slopes away from the bud. You may want to paint the cut cane ends with Elmer's wood glue or nail polish to discourage cane borers (insect pests that attack rose canes).

If possible, prune in late winter or early spring, when the roses are still dormant. Assess the winter damage and remove any dead top growth. (If you can't tell whether it's dead or not, just watch for signs of growth.) Once you've done this basic work, the remainder of your pruning tasks will depend on whether your rose blooms on new wood (the current

year's growth) or old wood (last year's stems). Climbers and ramblers also need special care.

Pruning Roses That Bloom on New Wood: Roses that bloom on the current year's growth include Hybrid Teas, Floribundas, Polyanthas, Grandifloras, Hybrid Perpetuals, Miniatures, China roses, and reblooming shrub roses. These roses generally need hard pruning to produce new flowering growth.

Begin in late winter by cutting out all weak or dead growth, followed by any diseased portions of the plant. Remove any crossing branches or inward-growing stems.

On Floribundas, Polyanthas, Hybrid Teas, Grandifloras, and Hybrid Perpetuals, cut back the strong stems by one-quarter (for Floribundas and Polyanthas) to one-third (for Hybrid Teas, Grandifloras, and Hybrid Perpetuals).

On China roses and repeat-blooming shrub roses, thin out crowded growth, and remove one or two of the oldest canes each year. Prune the longest of the remaining canes back by no more than one-third to shape the plants, and cut all side shoots back to 6 inches. In the fall, cut off the tips of very long canes to keep them from being whipped around by the wind.

On Miniatures, remove a few of the oldest canes at the base, then trim back the remaining stems by one-quarter to one-third to shape the plant.

Pruning Roses That Bloom on Old Wood: Roses that tend to bloom on the previous year's stems include many species roses, Albas, Moss roses, and once-blooming shrub roses.

In late winter, prune out damaged or dead stems, and thin out crowded canes. Remove one or two of the oldest canes each year. Cut the remaining long new canes back by up to one-third. Prune the previous season's side shoots to 6 inches.

Pruning Climbers: Trim repeat-blooming climbers during their dormant period and once-blooming climbers immediately after flowering. The third year after planting, remove any weak, diseased, or dead wood. On repeat bloomers, also shorten the side shoots to 3 to 6 inches; on established climbers, remove one or two of the oldest (dark gray-brown) canes at the base, and train the new canes to the support.

Pruning Ramblers: Ramblers are known for their vigorous sprawling habit. Prune them immedi-

FRAGRANCE CLOSE TO HOME. *What better way to enjoy the blooms of the old garden rose 'Zephirine Drouhin' than to train them on a porch?*

ately after flowering, since the new growth in summer will hold the next year's flower buds. To keep them in bounds, cut out all of the stems that flowered in the current year, and train the remaining unbloomed canes to the support. Or, if you really want your rambler to ramble, simply let it spread, tying it to the support as needed. Remove dead or damaged wood whenever you notice it. For more flowers, you can trim the side shoots to 6 inches in early spring.

Other Pruning Pointers: On reblooming roses, deadheading (cutting off the old, faded flowers) will promote the formation of more flowers. Cut individual flowers or an entire cluster, if appropriate.

On grafted roses, watch for sucker growth (very vigorous shoots that spring up from the roots). Remove the suckers as soon as you spot them. Scrape away the soil from the base of the sucker so you can cut it off as close to the base as possible.

HANDLING PEST AND DISEASE PROBLEMS

Because weather conditions are so variable, the problems you encounter with your roses are apt to change from year to year. For example, there are years when the Japanese beetles come marching in and other years that you do not see one. There are wet years when mildew has a heyday and dry years when the spider mites take over. It is wise to start with the roses that perform best in your area and stick with them as long as they grow well. If you repeatedly have problems with a particular plant, then simply replace it with a more dependable plant that will perform happily without your constant attention.

There are environmentally safe products and techniques that will effectively control most of the problems you may encounter. For instance, insecticidal soap sprays are useful for controlling aphids and thrips. If spider mites attack, causing yellow-stippled leaves, wash them off with a strong spray of cold water. Handpicking is best for Japanese beetles.

Controlling diseases safely is more challenging. It is actually easier to prevent problems than to cure them. Start with roses that are suited to your climate, and give them a site with good drainage, lots of sun, and good air circulation.

If you notice a few spotted or damaged leaves, picking them off and destroying them right away may keep the problem from spreading. If fungal diseases such as black spot and powdery mildew are a problem every year, a program of spraying with lime-sulfur and baking soda can control them well. (Just avoid spraying lime-sulfur when the temperature is above 80°F. Also, be sure to wait at least 14 days after using lime-sulfur before you apply horticultural oil sprays.) Apply lime-sulfur in early spring and again just as the buds are sprouting. Once the plants have a good number of leaves (at least 2 weeks after the last lime-sulfur spray), apply a baking soda spray—1 tablespoon of baking soda mixed with 1 gallon of water—weekly. Use a spreader-sticker or a few drops of lightweight horticultural oil to help the spray stick to the leaves.

(For more detailed information on identifying and controlling pest and disease problems, see Chapter 13, Pests and Diseases.)

PROTECTING ROSES IN WINTER

Gardeners in cold climates accept that their roses must be protected in winter. Even in milder areas, it's a good idea to devote a little time to winter protection, since rapid temperature swings can damage even normally hardy roses.

One of the simplest methods is to tie up the branches, surround the plant with chicken wire, and stuff it with leaves. Just be sure to wait until the roses have been through a hard freeze and are beginning to enter their dormant period before you try this method. Then, in early spring, you should gradually uncover the plants over a period of a few days, before they begin growing inside their cover.

In very cold regions of the United States and Canada, some gardeners protect their roses by digging a trench in front of each plant, carefully lower-

FLOWERING FOUNDATION. *Whether you are looking from the inside out or the outside in, climbing rose 'Blaze' and* Rosa rugosa *make attractive companions.*

ing the branches into the trench, then covering them with a mound of soil or mulch. Be on the lookout for animal pests, such as mice, that might chew on the canes. Uncover the plants in spring.

LANDSCAPING WITH ROSES

There is a perfect rose for every style or type of garden. The broad variation in habit and form makes roses suitable in a formal garden, casual cottage garden, or naturalized meadow-type garden. Some roses perform well in foundation plantings, shrub borders, or hedges; others grow well as groundcovers. Train them up pillars, walls, or fences, or let them trail out of planters and hanging baskets. In the plant portraits in this chapter, you'll find suggestions on how you can use each type of rose; start with these and then experiment to find other uses for them.

Traditionally, roses have been used in formal gardens with large beds consisting primarily of roses. More recently, roses have found a home in informal gardens, where they mingle beautifully with a wide range of other plants, from perennials and grasses to annuals and bulbs. There are literally hundreds of plants that could be combined with roses. Here are just a few suitable rose companions:

Germander (*Teucrium chamaedrys*): an ideal low, green hedge

Lady's-mantle (*Alchemilla mollis*): airy, yellow-green summer flowers; best in a bit of shade in hot climates

Lavandin (*Lavandula X intermedia* 'Grosso'): gray-green leaves and purple flower spikes; excellent as a hedge

Mealy-cup sage (*Salvia farinacea* 'Victoria'): continuously blooming violet-blue flowers on compact, 18-inch plants

Mexican sage (*Salvia leucantha*): 3-foot plants with narrow green leaves and showy spikes of violet-purple flowers

Perennial candytuft (*Iberis sempervirens*): a fine border plant with evergreen leaves and white spring flowers

Rue (*Ruta graveolens* 'Blue Beauty'): lacy, blue-green foliage

Russian sage (*Perovskia atriplicifolia*): gray leaves with long-lasting spikes of blue flowers in late summer to fall

Southernwood (*Artemisia abrotanum*): mounds of aromatic, silvery leaves

Violet (*Viola odorata*): dainty purple spring flowers that thrive in the shady spots under arching rose canes

PLANT PORTRAITS

The following compilation is just a sampling of the many beautiful roses that are suitable as landscape plants. All of these are excellent selections.

CLIMBING AND RAMBLING ROSES

Place ramblers where they can climb up an old tree stump or sprawl over something large. Train climbers on a wall or a pillar. Climbing roses have stiffer growth and a more upright habit than rambling roses. Climbers also tend to be more repeat-flowering and to have larger flowers than ramblers.

When growing climbers and ramblers, be sure the structure they are growing on is strong enough to support their growth. Use raffia to fasten the canes; it is a natural fiber and will give, if necessary. Plastic-coated wire also works well, but you must check the ties regularly to be sure that old wire is not cutting into the expanding canes.

Rosa 'Aloha'
Climbing Hybrid Tea. Spring through fall.
Zones 5 to 8.

Characteristics. Height: 8 to 10 feet.

The flowers of 'Aloha' are large, with pink petals that are deeper pink on the back. They are extremely fragrant and excellent for cutting. The foliage is strong, leathery, dark green, and disease-resistant. 'Aloha' is similar to many of the Hybrid Perpetual, roses, but its bloom is more prolific.

Cultural Notes. Good air circulation will help prevent black spot and powdery mildew. Deadhead as needed, and prune hard to encourage large flowers.

Uses. An excellent pillar rose; also ideal for a trellis.

Rosa 'America'
Climbing rose. Spring through fall.
Zones 6 to 8.

Characteristics. Height: 8 to 12 feet.

The pointed buds of 'America' open to vibrant, coral-pink blooms with a classic Hybrid Tea form. The fragrant flowers are 3 inches across, with good repeat bloom. In 1976, 'America' was the All-America Rose Selection.

Cultural Notes. Good general rose care—including regular fertilization, pruning, and deadheading—will keep 'America' looking its best.

Uses. Train on a wall, trellis, or pillar.

Rosa 'American Pillar'
Rambler. Late spring through early summer.
Zones 6 to 8.

Characteristics. Height: 12 to 20 feet.

This vigorous, disease-free rambler blooms for a long period in late spring and summer, with large flower clusters. The individual flowers are pink with a white center and showy golden stamens. The leathery green foliage is attractive. The flowers are followed by red hips in the fall.

Cultural Notes. In humid areas, 'American Pillar' may be prone to powdery mildew. This rose

Rosa 'American Pillar'

grows in a wide variety of soil types and also is shade-tolerant.

Uses. Great for arbors, trellises, arches, and training up trees.

Rosa banksiae var. *lutea*
Species rose. Early spring. Zones 7 to 9.

Characteristics. Height: 15 to 25 feet.
Commonly known as yellow Lady Banks rose, this elegant climbing species rose bears clusters of small, pale lemon yellow, double blossoms with a mild fragrance. It is almost thornless and has attractive foliage. Many large, old specimens can be seen in gardens in the South. It is vigorous enough to grow through the branches of a tree or will thrive when trained on a sunny wall, especially in a protected site.

The original Chinese species, *R. banksiae*, is extremely vigorous, reaching over 40 feet tall. It has

several different types, or clones, with small (1-inch), slightly fragrant, white or yellow flowers.

Cultural Notes. This is a disease-free rose that tends to be relatively low-maintenance. It must have full sun.

Uses. Ideal trained up against a wall or on a trellis.

Rosa 'Blaze'
Climbing rose. Summer through fall.
Zones 5 to 8.

Characteristics. Height: 7 feet.
'Blaze' bears brilliant scarlet, semidouble flowers in huge clusters. The 3-inch, cup-shaped blooms begin in June and continue through September. The handsome foliage is dark green and leathery. 'Improved Blaze' is an even better form of this already wonderful rose.

Cultural Notes. 'Blaze' is a vigorous rose with good disease resistance. It is not fussy about soil and will tolerate some shade.

Uses. Great along a fence or trained up a trellis or pillar.

Rosa bracteata
Species rose. Summer. Zones 7 to 9.

Characteristics. Height: 10 feet.
Commonly known as Macartney rose, this species has handsome glossy foliage that is evergreen in warm climates. The striking, single white flowers have showy golden stamens and are followed by large, showy orange-red hips. The stems are very prickly.

The cultivar 'Mermaid' is a hybrid between Macartney rose and a double yellow Tea rose. It has creamy yellow, fragrant, single flowers and recurrent bloom. 'Mermaid' is a reliable, disease-free climber that also makes a suitable groundcover in warm climates.

Cultural Notes. Little pruning is necessary on *R. bracteata*. It is naturalized in parts of the southeastern United States.

Uses. Excellent as an espalier or trained against a north wall.

Rosa 'Buff Beauty'
Hybrid Musk. Late spring. Zones 6 to 9.

Characteristics. Height: 8 to 12 feet.

'Buff Beauty' bears clusters of distinctive, fragrant, apricot-colored flowers. The foliage is semiglossy, and the new shoots are an attractive dark red. The plants take a few years to establish before they bloom well.

Cultural Notes. This rose will grow in shade but will not flower unless it has at least 5 hours of direct sunlight. It does not need much pruning.

Uses. Ideal as a pillar rose, 'Buff Beauty' can also be grown as a shrub rose, if it is pruned.

Rosa 'Cécile Brünner'
(climbing form)
Climbing Polyantha. Spring through fall.
Zones 6 to 9.

Characteristics. Height: 14 to 18 feet.

Commonly referred to as sweetheart rose, this charmer is easily recognized by the miniature, Hybrid Tea-like blossoms. The fragrant pink flowers open from pointed buds. The stems have few thorns. The shrub form of 'Cécile Brünner' is a compact, 3- to 4-foot-tall plant.

Cultural Notes. 'Cécile Brünner' is a long-lived, healthy plant that is not fussy about soil conditions; it also tolerates some shade. It requires minimal pruning.

Uses. Grows well against a wall or on an arbor, trellis, or pillar.

Rosa 'Champney's Pink Cluster'
Noisette. Spring through fall. Zones 7 to 9.

Characteristics. Height: 6 to 9 feet.

The forerunner of the Noisette class, this rose produces clusters of beautiful pink buds that bloom throughout the growing season. The flowers have a sweet perfume. The attractive foliage is light green and slightly glossy.

Rosa 'Cécile Brünner', Climbing form

Cultural Notes. 'Champney's Pink Cluster' performs well as a climber in warm areas. It is disease-resistant.

Uses. Grows well up through trees or along fences.

Rosa 'Chevy Chase'
Climbing rose. Late spring through early
summer. Zones 6 to 8.

Characteristics. Height: 12 to 16 feet.

'Chevy Chase' is a spectacular, once-blooming rose. In late spring to early summer, it is covered with small, double, dark crimson flowers in clusters of 10 to 12 blooms. The flowers are moderately fragrant. The light green leaves are soft and wrinkly.

Cultural Notes. This vigorous rose can tolerate poor soil and some shade.

Uses. Grows well up trees or on large structures; good along the edge of a wooded area.

Rosa 'City of York'
Large-flowered climbing rose.
Spring through early summer. Zones 5 to 8.

Characteristics. Height: 15 to 20 feet.

'City of York' is an excellent climbing rose that offers a strong spring or summer display of white-yellow flowers with showy golden stamens. The blooms are fragrant and large—3 to 4 inches across. In 1950, this rose won the American Rose Society National Gold Medal Certificate.

Cultural Notes. 'City of York' is both vigorous and disease-free. It tolerates a wide range of growing conditions.

Uses. Climbs well on trees, arbors, and trellises.

Rosa 'Dortmund'
Kordesii climber. Spring through fall.
Zones 5 to 8.

Characteristics. Height: 10 to 12 feet.

'Dortmund' is a spectacular rose with fragrant, single, medium-red flowers with white centers. It is a vigorous grower that provides recurrent, although not continuous, bloom. Since it is quite thorny, place it where its long branches and thorns will not create a problem.

Cultural Notes. A reliable, disease-free rose, 'Dortmund' is one of the best of all climbing roses to grow. It tolerates poor soil and some shade.

Uses. Ideal for training on pillars, arches, arbors, or walls.

Rosa 'Golden Showers'
Large-flowered climber. Spring through fall.
Zones 6 to 8.

Characteristics. Height: 8 to 12 feet.

'Golden Showers' is one of the most popular climbers. This easy-to-manage, free-flowering rose has lovely, 3- to 4-inch, lemon yellow blooms with a mild lemon fragrance. The shiny, dark green foliage is very attractive.

Cultural Notes. 'Golden Showers' needs good air circulation to prevent black spot. The thorns are fairly substantial, so it is best to keep the plants away from pathways.

Uses. Train to climb a pillar or to cover a wall.

Rosa
'Madame Alfred Carrière'
Noisette. Spring through fall. Zones 7 to 9.

Characteristics. Height: 12 to 15 feet.

Over 100 years old, 'Madame Alfred Carrière' is still one of the best white-flowering climbers. It is known for its disease resistance, its fragrance, and its free-flowering creamy white blossoms. The blossoms are tinged pink and last long into autumn. (It may even bloom in December.)

Cultural Notes. 'Madame Alfred Carrière' is a vigorous climber in warm climates. In colder areas within its hardiness range, place it against a warm wall to protect it against cold damage.

Uses. Great for training along a fence or in a fan shape against a wall.

Rosa 'New Dawn'
Large-flowered climber. Spring through fall.
Zones 5 to 8.

Characteristics. Height: 14 to 18 feet.

'New Dawn' was the world's first patented plant. Its abundant, pale pink flowers are fragrant and reliably disease-resistant. The attractive foliage is a shiny, medium green. 'New Dawn' is considered to be the everblooming form of 'Dr. W. Van Fleet', and the two roses are sometimes confused.

Cultural Notes. 'New Dawn' can take hard pruning, if necessary, and still bloom well. It can grow up through trees, although it will bloom less when grown in shade.

Uses. The perfect rose for a large trellis or arbor.

Rosa 'Rêve d'Or'
Noisette. Spring through fall. Zones 6 to 9.

Characteristics. Height: 12 to 18 feet.

The name 'Rêve d'Or', which means "dream of gold," comes from the buff-yellow, butterscotch blossoms. This rose has a loose habit and few thorns. It blooms all season.

Cultural Notes. It takes 2 to 3 years for this rose to establish itself and provide a beautiful show. Like most Noisettes, it has few problems with insects or diseases.

Uses. Great as a porch pillar, where the branches can arch over to show off the fragrant flowers. Or, train it against a garden shed.

Rosa 'Seven Sisters'
Rambler, Hybrid Multiflora. Summer.
Zones 5 to 8.

Characteristics. Height: 15 to 20 feet.

The flowers of 'Seven Sisters' are much larger than those of its close relative, multiflora rose (R. multiflora). This once-blooming rambler has distinctive, fragrant flowers that change color as they age, from carmine-purple to mauve, fading to pale pink and cream. Its name is derived from the many different colors in each cluster of flowers. The foliage is dark green and coarse, on rather stiff stems.

Cultural Notes. This is not a picky rose; it tolerates poor soil and shade, and needs no special care.

Uses. Site 'Seven Sisters' to cover a large trellis or old tree stump. It also makes a great addition to a cottage garden.

Rosa 'Sombreuil'
Climbing Tea rose. Spring through fall.
Zones 7 to 9.

Characteristics. Height: 8 to 12 feet.

'Sombreuil' is an exquisite rose. Its perfect white blooms have large, full, textured, well-formed petals. The dark, leathery foliage blends well into the garden.

Cultural Notes. This disease-free plant requires no pruning. Deadhead throughout the growing season to encourage continuous blooming.

Uses. Ideal for a cottage garden, since it blends well with antique flowers; train it as a fan on a wall or as a shrub. Grow as a pillar or along a fence.

Rosa 'Veilchenblau'
Rambler, Hybrid Multiflora. Summer.
Zones 6 to 8.

Characteristics. Height: 12 to 16 feet.

This plant is sometimes referred to as "the blue rose" because of the strong blue tones in the flower color. The German name 'Veilchenblau' means "violet-blue." The flowers open violet, turn crimson-mauve streaked with white, then fade to a blue-gray color with showy golden stamens. The small flowers bloom in abundant clusters and smell like green apples. Although 'Veilchenblau' has one primary flush of bloom in midsummer, it sometimes blooms again in autumn.

Cultural Notes. This rose is vigorous and thornless. The long, stiff canes require almost no pruning. A reliable, low-care plant, it tolerates poor soil and some shade.

Uses. Grows well on a large trellis or in combination with other climbing roses. It can be used as a tall background hedge.

Rosa 'White Dawn'

Large-flowered climber. Spring through fall.
Zones 5 to 8.

Characteristics. Height: 15 feet.
'White Dawn' has clusters of medium-size, double white flowers that resemble gardenias. It is a vigorous climber with a strong fragrance. The foliage is shiny and attractive.
Cultural Notes. This rose is similar to 'New Dawn' except that the flowers are white. It is reliably free of insect and disease problems.
Uses. Suited to a large trellis, tree, or arbor.

Rosa 'Gourmet Popcorn'

MINIATURE AND PATIO ROSES

Miniature roses are small versions of larger roses. Most are everblooming and range in height from 8 to 24 inches. Many are susceptible to fungal diseases. They are excellent in containers, as borders, or in rock gardens. More recently, the patio roses have become popular for growing on terraces or balconies. Both miniature and patio roses grow best on their own roots, rather than as grafts.

Rosa 'Baby Betsy McCall'

Miniature. Spring through fall. Zones 6 to 8.

Characteristics. Height: 8 inches.
'Baby Betsy McCall' is a vigorous, compact miniature with pale pink, double flowers that are cupped and fragrant. The foliage is leathery and medium green.
Cultural Notes. This rose needs good air circulation and plenty of light. Prune off old flowers to keep the plants in bloom.
Uses. Suitable as a low border or in a container.

Rosa 'Cupcake'

Miniature. Spring through fall. Zones 6 to 8.

Characteristics. Height: 18 inches.
'Cupcake' has a Hybrid Tea form, with fully double, high-centered flowers that are medium pink. This reliable performer has a bushy habit and attractive, medium green foliage with no prickles.
Cultural Notes. Prune 'Cupcake' hard in the spring. Deadhead regularly for continuous bloom.
Uses. Grow in a flower bed or container, or indoors under lights.

Rosa 'Gourmet Popcorn'

Miniature. Spring through fall. Zones 6 to 8.

Characteristics. Height: 2 feet.
'Gourmet Popcorn' has beautiful buds that open to fragrant white flowers with yellow centers.
Cultural Notes. This rose is generally insect- and disease-free. Be sure to deadhead as needed.
Uses. Works well in a large container or as an accent plant in a border.

Rosa 'Green Ice'

Miniature. Summer through fall. Zones 6 to 8.

Characteristics. Height: 8 to 10 inches.
'Green Ice' is a fascinating miniature with a wonderful bushy growth habit. Its sprawling canes are covered with slightly fragrant, whitish pink blooms that change to light green as they age. The high-centered flowers resemble those of a Hybrid Tea.

Rosa 'Red Cascade'

'Sunblaze' bears clusters of 1½-inch, fully double, orange-red flowers. The blooms are slightly fragrant. The abundant foliage is dark green with a matte finish. This rose has a dense, bushy growth habit.

Cultural Notes. Cut off old flowers to encourage continuous bloom.

Uses. Excellent in containers and borders, or as an edging.

SHRUB ROSES

Shrub roses come from diverse backgrounds, but they share the ability to blend into many different landscapes. These excellent plants are generally easy to care for and problem-free.

Cultural Notes. 'Green Ice' is one of the most reliable miniatures. It tends to be disease-free and winter-hardy. Prune back any dead tips in the spring.

Uses. Ideal when grown in a border, hanging basket, or container.

Rosa 'Red Cascade'
Climbing or Weeping Miniature. Summer through fall. Zones 6 to 8.

Characteristics. Height: 8 to 12 inches.

The well-formed, strong-red, cupped flowers of 'Red Cascade' are showy but have little fragrance. The plant produces long canes that spread up to 3 feet, with dark green, semiglossy foliage.

Cultural Notes. 'Red Cascade' is susceptible to powdery mildew in warm, humid areas.

Uses. Superb in a hanging basket or on a low trellis.

Rosa 'Sunblaze'
Miniature Floribunda, Patio rose.
Spring through fall. Zones 6 to 8.

Characteristics. Height: 12 to 16 inches.

Rosa 'Agnes'
Hybrid Rugosa, Shrub rose.
Spring through summer. Zones 5 to 8.

Characteristics. Height: 5 to 6 feet.

The flowers of 'Agnes' are pale amber-yellow, which is very unusual for a Rugosa. The double blooms have a deep center and are extremely fragrant. The leaves are a dull light green and coarse in texture.

Cultural Notes. 'Agnes' is a tough, disease-resistant rose. It is extremely thorny and relatively vigorous. Once it establishes itself, it will bloom repeatedly throughout the season.

Uses. Great as a hedge or in the back of a border.

Rosa 'Blanc Double de Coubert'
Hybrid Rugosa, Shrub rose. Spring through fall.
Zones 4 to 8.

Characteristics. Height: 4 to 6 feet.

'Blanc Double de Coubert' is a distinguished shrub rose recognized for its superior double, white, strongly perfumed flowers. The leathery leaves have excellent fall color, and the hips are attractive in the fall and winter garden.

Cultural Notes. Like so many white flowers, the blooms of 'Blanc Double de Coubert' do not age gracefully. Clip off the browning flowers until midsummer, then remove only the faded petals so the showy hips can form.

Uses. Attractive in a shrub or flower border, or as a hedge or foundation plant.

Rosa 'Bonica'
Shrub rose. Spring through fall. Zones 5 to 8.

Characteristics. Height: 4 to 5 feet.

'Bonica' is one of the finest of the Meidiland group of new shrub roses. It blooms profusely, bearing large clusters of soft pink, fully double flowers.

Other fine Meidiland roses include 'Scarlet Meidiland' and 'Alba Meidiland'. 'Scarlet Meidiland' has vivid scarlet flowers and attractive dark green foliage. It grows as a mounding groundcover (3 to 4 feet tall) and can tolerate some shade. 'Alba Meidiland' has pure white flowers and a low growing habit, making it ideal for covering a slope.

Cultural Notes. Little pruning is necessary other than a light tip pruning in early spring. Plants will bloom most freely in moist soil.

Uses. Makes an attractive landscape shrub in borders, mass plantings, or hedges.

Rosa 'Carefree Beauty'

Rosa 'Carefree Beauty'
Shrub rose. Spring through fall. Zones 4 to 8.

Characteristics. Height: 3 feet.

'Carefree Beauty' has large, semidouble, medium pink flowers. It is worthy of its name, requiring little maintenance while blooming endlessly. A newer, improved form of 'Carefree Beauty', known as 'Carefree Wonder', blooms even more freely and is more resistant to black spot.

Cultural Notes. Cut the shoot tips back lightly in spring; otherwise, this is a reliably carefree plant.

Uses. Blends well in a border and in mass plantings.

Rosa 'Frau Dagmar Hartopp'
Hybrid Rugosa, Shrub rose. Spring through fall. Zones 4 to 8.

Characteristics. Height: 2 to 3 feet.

'Frau Dagmar Hartopp', also sometimes listed as 'Frau Dagmar Hastrup', is a distinctive thorny shrub that perfumes the garden with its clove-scented blooms. The silvery pink flowers are followed by showy hips. The leaves are green and crinkled.

Cultural Notes. Remove suckers regularly to keep the plants in bounds. Deadhead early in the season, but stop in summer so the hips can form.

Uses. Excellent as a low hedge or as an accent in the garden.

Rosa 'Heritage'
Shrub rose. Spring through fall. Zones 5 to 8.

Characteristics. Height: 4 feet.

'Heritage' is the best of the David Austin roses, which are also referred to as English Roses. It has a compact habit and is covered with exquisite, shell pink, fully cupped flowers that appear throughout the growing season. The fragrance is similar to that of an old rose, with strong lemon overtones. This sensational plant has few thorns.

There are many other new David Austin roses

Rosa 'Heritage'

on the market. They tend to be large plants (to about 6 feet tall) and vary in their disease resistance. They possess many of the delightful characteristics of the old garden roses, such as intense fragrance and cupped and quartered flowers.

Cultural Notes. Give 'Heritage' full sun, good air circulation, and rich soil. Remove the spent flowers regularly.

Uses. Blends well into flower borders and cottage gardens. Also looks great as a specimen plant.

Rosa 'Roseraie de l'Häy'
Hybrid Rugosa, Shrub rose. Spring through fall.
Zones 3 to 8.

Characteristics. Height: 6 to 8 feet.
'Roseraie de l'Häy' is an early bloomer with large flowers that offer a strong fragrance and intense color: crimson-red changing to rosy magen-

ta. The leaves are large, dark green, and wrinkled. The canes are quite thorny.

Cultural Notes. Like most Rugosas, 'Roseraie de l'Häy' produces suckers; remove them if they spread out of bounds. Deadheading can prolong the bloom season.

Uses. A tall rose to use as a hedge or at the back of a border.

Rosa 'Stanwell Perpetual'
Hybrid Spinosissima. Spring through fall.
Zones 3 to 8.

Characteristics. Height: 4 feet.
'Stanwell Perpetual' is characterized by abundant white, fragrant flowers that cover small gray-green leaves on arching, free-flowing branches. It has a soft look, even though it is prickly, and it is completely hardy, tough, and everblooming.

Cultural Notes. In spring, after the first major flush of blooms, it is quite a task to deadhead the hundreds of small, faded flowers. However, it is worth the effort to encourage the continuing bloom of this delightful, mounding rose. 'Stanwell Perpetual' adapts to many conditions, including sandy soil, although it may drop some leaves when summer temperatures are extreme. It does not produce suckers.

Uses. Suitable as a corner planting, in a container, or along a sloped border.

POLYANTHAS AND FLORIBUNDAS

Polyanthas are noted for their continuous bloom and many-flowered clusters. They have a bushy habit and tend to be quite hardy. Floribundas are the result of crossing the carefree Polyanthas with the larger-flowered Hybrid Tea roses. They have a more open habit than the Polyanthas and tend to be healthier and a little smaller than the Hybrid Teas. Floribundas are also sometimes called Cluster-Flowered Roses.

Rosa 'Betty Prior'
Floribunda. Spring through fall. Zones 4 to 8.

Characteristics. Height: 4 feet.

When 'Betty Prior' is covered with flowers, it's hard to see any of the foliage. Some have said it looks like an American dogwood in bloom. The individual flowers are single, with carmine-pink petals that have a beautiful overlapping pattern. They are held in abundant clusters and have a spicy scent. The plant has a full habit, making it useful in the landscape.

Cultural Notes. 'Betty Prior' is hardy and easy to grow. Its flowers are darker in cooler weather.

Uses. A great plant for mass plantings or use it in a shrub or perennial border.

Rosa 'Country Dancer'
Shrub rose. Spring through fall. Zones 4 to 8.

Characteristics. Height: 3 to 4 feet.

Rosa 'Country Dancer'

The large flowers of 'Country Dancer' are rose-red, double, and fragrant. The foliage is large, dark green, and leathery. This bushy plant has a compact, upright habit and it is an also an excellent repeat bloomer.

Cultural Notes. 'Country Dancer' is a tough, hardy, low-maintenance rose. Trim the shoot tips back a little in spring, and it should bloom profusely most of the growing season. Deadhead as needed.

Uses. Attractive when used in a cottage garden or flower bedor border, where it can be planted alone or in a mass.

Rosa 'Gruss an Aachen'
Floribunda. Spring through fall. Zones 5 to 8.

Characteristics. Height: 3 to 4 feet.

'Gruss an Aachen' has sumptuous, pearly pink, 3-inch-wide blossoms that emerge from salmon-yellow buds with a hint of fragrance. It is free-blooming throughout the season, with rich green foliage and a compact habit.

Cultural Notes. 'Gruss an Aachen' is one of the few roses that will bloom well in some shade. It is a reliable performer and will grow well with minimal care.

Uses. A good rose for the front of a border.

Rosa 'Marie Pavié'
Polyantha. Spring through fall. Zones 5 to 8.

Characteristics. Height: 3 feet.

'Marie Pavié' is one of the most beautiful roses for a small space. Its sweetly fragrant pink buds open to white, double, 2-inch-wide blooms. The nearly thornless stems have attractive, dark green leaves.

Cultural Notes. Little pruning is necessary, other than a light trim in spring. Deadhead as needed to keep the plants blooming.

Uses. An outstanding landscape plant. Use near patios, as a low hedge, or in borders or cottage gardens.

Rosa 'The Fairy'
Polyantha. Spring through fall. Zones 4 to 8.

Characteristics. Height: 3 feet.

'The Fairy' is easy to recognize by its characteristic clusters of dainty pink buds, which are borne in charming bouquets. 'The Fairy' also makes a wonderful "standard" or "tree" rose. Left untrained, it has a rounded, free-flowing, mounded shape that allows it to blend well in gardens. The flowers are very double and have little or no fragrance. The small green leaves are shiny and attractive.

Cultural Notes. 'The Fairy' is a hardy and disease-resistant rose. In hot summers, it may stop flowering for a period; otherwise, it is a generous bloomer.

Uses. A fine small border accent, specimen, or container plant.

OLD GARDEN ROSES

"Old garden" refers to any rose that was grown before the development of the first Hybrid Tea in 1867 or that belongs to one of the categories of roses that is considered "old" (such as the Albas, Damasks, and Gallicas). Most old roses from Europe bloom for several weeks in spring and are known for their distinctive rose fragrance, unique flower forms, and many petals. Old roses from China are very different; they bloom continuously throughout the growing season and tend to be less fragrant and less hardy. They are some of the best shrubs for warm regions because they do not require a dormant period in order to bloom.

Rosa 'Celsiana'
Damask. Spring through fall. Zones 5 to 9.

Characteristics. Height: 5 feet.

'Celsiana' offers enchanting flowers with silky pink petals that have a translucent glow about them. They have the distinct Damask citrus-and-spice fragrance. The downy foliage is light gray-green and has many prickles.

Cultural Notes. 'Celsiana' is usually disease-free, especially in cooler climates.

Uses. Ideal for the back of a flower border.

Rosa chinensis 'Mutabilis'
China. Spring through fall. Zones 6 to 9.

Characteristics. Height: 4 to 8 feet.

Often called "the butterfly rose," 'Mutabilis' has exquisite, silky flowers that flutter above the foliage. The flowers are single and cup-shaped and have

Rosa 'The Fairy'

Rosa chinensis 'Mutabilis'

Rosa damascena 'Semperflorens'

petals that range from yellow or orange to red or crimson. The blooms are set off by the strikingly beautiful, reddish leaves on maroon stems. The foliage and flowers, which appear from summer into fall, change color as they mature—an outstanding feature of this rose. 'Mutabilis' has also been sold as 'Tipo Ideale'.

Cultural Notes. 'Mutabilis' is generally healthy and trouble-free. For best results, look for plants that have been grown on their own roots, rather than from grafts.

Uses. An extraordinary shrub for the border; it can also be trained up a pillar in warmer climates.

Rosa damascena 'Semperflorens'
Autumn Damask. Summer through fall. Zones 5 to 8.

Characteristics. Height: 6 to 8 feet.
Commonly called "the four seasons rose," this plant is important in the long history of roses. Unlike most other Damask roses, it flowers again after its primary flush of bloom in late spring. Its blooms are medium pink, very double, and intensely fragrant. The foliage is rather gray, downy, and soft.

Cultural Notes. This rose is occasionally sus-

ceptible to disease problems but is generally a strong grower. Deadhead to keep the plant blooming in summer and fall. Although it does repeat bloom, it produces only scattered flowers after its big show in spring.

Uses. A tall shrub that is suitable for training up a trellis or fence, or use it as a specimen in an herb garden.

Rosa 'Souvenir de la Malmaison'
Bourbon. Spring through fall. Zones 6 to 9.

Characteristics. Height: 4 feet
'Souvenir de la Malmaison' is a well known rose that is often referred to as the "queen of beauty and fragrance." The large, double, quartered flowers are a blend of cream, flesh, and rose tones and have an intense, spicy fragrance. The leaves are large and dark green in color. The plants tend to rebloom more than other Bourbon roses.

At its best, 'Souvenir de la Malmaison' is considered the finest of all the Bourbon roses. At its worst, it is dreadful—the flowers often turn into a soggy brown mess after a rain.

Cultural Notes. Keep the plants deadheaded, especially after a rain.

Uses. Suited to a small garden or container.

Rosa 'Zéphirine Drouhin'
Climbing Bourbon. Spring and fall.
Zones 6 to 9.

Characteristics. Height: 10 feet.

'Zéphirine Drouhin' is popular for its strong cerise flower color, fragrance, long blooming period, bronzy red young shoots, and lack of thorns. The plants occasionally repeat bloom in autumn.

Cultural Notes. To grow 'Zéphirine Drouhin' as a shrub, prune it hard in spring. As a climber, it just needs a light spring pruning to thin the canes and remove the dead wood.

Uses. Superb for a pillar or post. A good choice for porches and near walkways, since it is thornless.

SPECIES ROSES

There are many fine species roses to choose from. These plants are suitable for a natural garden or as large mounded shrubs.

Rosa carolina
Species rose. Summer. Zones 4 to 9.

Characteristics. Height: 3 to 5 feet.

Commonly called pasture rose, *R. carolina* bears fragrant, single, dark pink flowers up to 2 inches across in July or August, followed by small red hips. The slender stems have narrow prickles and dark green, slightly glossy foliage. The variety *alba* bears white flowers; the variety *grandiflora* has larger leaves than the species. 'Plena' produces double flowers and is a repeat bloomer when grown under ideal conditions.

Cultural Notes. Pasture rose can grow in some shade. It produces many suckers.

Uses. Excellent for a native plant collection, habitat planting, or any natural area.

Rosa eglanteria
Species rose. Spring. Zones 5 to 8.

Characteristics. Height: 12 feet.

You know you are near the eglantine when the air smells of sweet apples. Also known as sweetbrier, this garden giant was a favorite of Shakespeare, who described it in *Midsummer Night's Dream*. The arching branches have hooked prickles and fragrant, dark green leaflets. The single, pink June flowers are followed by large red hips in autumn.

Cultural Notes. Like many species roses, *R. eglanteria* does not require the rich soil that most roses prefer. However, they all appreciate an application of chicken manure every third or fourth winter. The foliage is disease resistant.

Uses. Traditionally used in cottage gardens. Also suitable for "wild" gardens when you have plenty of space, or trained along a fence.

Rosa glauca
Species rose. Spring. Zones 5 to 8.

Characteristics. Height: 8 feet.

This exceptional rose, which is also listed as *R. rubrifolia*, has grayish purple foliage and a graceful habit. The branches are lovely in flower arrangements. Single pink flowers are produced in spring, followed by small red hips.

Cultural Notes. *R. glauca* needs little care.

Uses. Suitable for cottage gardens, shrub or perennial borders, foundation plantings, or "wild" gardens.

Rosa X harisonii
Hybrid Foetida. Spring. Zones 5 to 8.

Characteristics. Height: 8 feet.

This once-blooming rose, which is commonly called "Harison's Yellow," has bright lemon yellow flowers and is valued for its ability to survive with no care. It is said to have been discovered on a farm in Manhattan in the 1830s and, because it was so popular, it travelled west with the settlers—the origin of the "yellow rose of Texas."

Cultural Notes. This rose needs no special care. It will grow well in poor soil.

Uses. Great for neglected areas such as roadsides, or as an informal hedge.

Rosa X harisonii

Rosa moschata

Species rose. Summer through fall. Zones 6 to 9.

Characteristics. Height: 4 to 6 feet.

Musk rose is a late-blooming, shrubby species that bears small, white, single or double flowers with golden stamens in the center.

Cultural Notes. Musk rose is easy to grow and has few, if any, disease or insect problems.

Uses. Works well as a hedge, in a natural garden, or combined with perennials.

Rosa setigera

Species rose. Summer. Zones 4 to 8.

Characteristics. Height: 6 to 12 feet.

Commonly called prairie rose, *R. setigera* is one of the most beautiful North American rose species. It is late-blooming (July or August) and bears single, dark pink, 6-inch-wide flowers, followed by orange-red-brown, rounded hips. It has climbing stems with long, curved prickles and bright green leaves.

Cultural Notes. Prairie rose is easy to grow and requires no special care.

Uses. Great in a native plant garden or a naturalized setting. Use with caution because it spreads.

Rosa virginiana

Species rose. Summer. Zones 5 to 8.

Characteristics. Height: 3 to 4 feet.

This very attractive species rose has outstanding autumn color. Its leaves turn brilliant shades of orange, red, purple, and green, somewhat like those of sugar maples. In summer, it produces single, pink flowers, followed by 1/2-inch hips that last through the winter.

There is tremendous variation among the strains of *R. virginiana*, since most are seed-grown. The varieties include *alba*, with white flowers; *grandiflora*, which bears larger, dark pink flowers; and *plena*, with double pink flowers.

Cultural Notes. This vigorous plant produces

Rosa 'Apricot Nectar'

Rosa 'Dainty Bess'

suckers; remove them as needed to keep the plants in bounds.

Uses. Excellent for a natural-style garden, wildlife habitat planting, native plant garden, or woodland edge.

HYBRID TEAS

For many people, Hybrid Tea roses symbolize the classic rose. The flowers are exquisite, but the plants themselves are usually less appealing. For best bloom, Hybrid Tea roses need hard pruning, since they flower on new wood. They require regular fertilizing, pruning, deadheading, spraying for insects and diseases, and winter protection.

Rosa 'Apricot Nectar'
Hybrid Tea. Spring through fall. Zones 5 to 8.

Characteristics. Height: 6 feet.
The flowers of 'Apricot Nectar' are apricot-colored and as large as 5 inches across, with slightly ruffled petals that have a tea rose fragrance. This constantly blooming, bushy, sturdy plant has large, dark green foliage. 'Apricot Nectar' was an All-America Rose Selections in 1966.

Cultural Notes. Like other Hybrid Tea roses, 'Apricot Nectar' needs regular care to stay healthy and vigorous.

Uses. Attractive in a rose garden or a border.

Rosa 'Dainty Bess'
Hybrid Tea. Spring through fall. Zones 6 to 8.

Characteristics. Height: 3 feet.
'Dainty Bess' produces lightly fragrant, single flowers that measure up to 4 or 5 inches across; they are a unique silvery rose-pink-lavender with distinctive wine-colored stamens. The plant blooms continuously over attractive, disease-resistant foliage.

Cultural Notes. 'Dainty Bess' is a vigorous and very popular Hybrid Tea.

Uses. Blends well in perennial borders.

Rosa 'Mister Lincoln'
Hybrid Tea. Spring through fall. Zones 6 to 8.

Characteristics. Height: 6 feet.
'Mister Lincoln' is considered the best red rose in its class. Its rich, deep red buds open to velvety petals and classic Hybrid Tea flowers that do not fade in intensity. The incredibly fragrant flowers bloom atop long stems. The large leaves are a glossy dark green.

Cultural Notes. 'Mister Lincoln' is one of the

most reliable Hybrid Tea roses. It needs well-prepared, rich soil and benefits from regular fertilization and pruning.

Uses. Great in a rose garden or as an accent plant.

Rosa 'Peace'
Hybrid Tea. Spring through fall. Zones 6 to 8.

Characteristics. Height: 6 feet.

Often referred to as "the rose of the century," 'Peace' was given its name the day Berlin fell at the end of World War II. It has won all the major rose awards. The flower possesses the classic Hybrid Tea form, with yellow petals edged in pink and a slight fragrance. The long, sturdy stems make this a great rose for cutting.

Cultural Notes. 'Peace' needs regular care to thrive. It is particularly susceptible to fungal problems such as blackspot.

Uses. Wonderful in a rose garden or as an accent plant.

GRANDIFLORAS

These roses are known for producing large, clustered flowers on long stems. They were created as bedding plants, although they can grow to 6 feet tall. Their flowers open more quickly than those of Hybrid Teas and are exceptionally colorful. Like the Hybrid Teas, they need severe pruning to produce large blossoms. Most Grandiflora roses are susceptible to a broad range of pests.

Rosa 'Love'
Grandiflora. Spring through fall. Zones 6 to 8.

Characteristics. Height: 3 feet.

'Love' is a unique, shapely flower with scarlet-red petals that are silvery white on the back. This upright plant is known as a good exhibition rose.

Cultural Notes. 'Love' tends to be one of the tougher Grandifloras. Give it good general rose care. If you want few, but larger flowers, pinch off the smaller side buds to leave one main flower bud per stem.

Uses. Attractive in a rose or flower garden.

Rosa 'Love'

Rosa 'Queen Elizabeth'
Grandiflora. Spring through fall. Zones 6 to 8.

Characteristics. Height: 5 feet.

This outstanding rose has received a great deal of attention, and with good reason. It has clusters of long, high-centered buds that open to clear pink flowers. The plant is vigorous and upright, with large, dark green leaves.

Cultural Notes. This rose needs a little pampering to perform well; fertilize, prune, and mulch regularly.

Uses. Suitable for a rose or flower garden.

Rosa 'Sonia'
Grandiflora. Spring through fall. Zones 6 to 8.

Characteristics. Height: 3 feet.

The long buds of 'Sonia', which is also sometimes listed as 'Sweet Promise', open to large, superbly shaped flowers that are silky pink tinged with coral-yellow. Frequently used as a cut flower, this rose is free-blooming and has a fruity fragrance. The foliage is dark green, glossy, and leathery.

Cultural Notes. 'Sonia' needs good regular maintenance to look its best.

Uses. Good for bedding or in a rose or flower garden.

HOME-GROWN RICHES. *From tender, sweet lettuce and spinach in early spring to late-season pumpkins for tasty pies and scary jack-o'-laterns, there's no end to the bounty of a home vegetable garden.*

218

CHAPTER SEVEN

VEGETABLES

FEW THINGS CAN COMPARE WITH THE SATISFAC-TION OF PICKING AND EATING GARDEN-FRESH PRO-DUCE. The rich taste of a sun-warmed, vine-ripened tomato or the crisp snap of a just-picked snow pea are just two examples of the many joys awaiting the home vegetable gardener.

In this chapter, you'll learn the secrets to growing vegetable crops successfully, from seed starting to harvest. And if you can resist the temptation to enjoy your vegetables before you even get them to the kitchen, you'll find some great suggestions on ways to prepare them for unforgettable meals.

WHY GROW VEGETABLES?

Vegetable gardeners are often asked, "Why do you grow vegeta-bles at home when they are so easy to buy at the store?" This question assumes that gardening is basically work, that we only grow vegetables because we have to eat, and that the fruits of our labor are no more valuable than the fruits of anyone else's labor.

219

ALL MIXED UP. *Who says you have to grow vegetables, herbs, and flowers separately? To grow a garden that provides vegetables and herbs for the table—and cut flowers to decorate it—plan to grow all your favorites together.*

Once you've raised your own vegetables, you know that you just can't put a price on the feeling you get from growing your own food. The process of planting and nurturing crops is as spiritually gratifying as the knowledge that you're doing something productive and worthwhile. But beyond the emotional value of the gardening experience, there are also very practical reasons for choosing to grow produce at home: flavor and freshness. Homegrown vegetables are simply superior to purchased produce on both counts.

When commercial growers choose their crops, they look for cultivars that adapt well to large-scale production. They want cultivars that ripen all at once and that are easy to harvest mechanically. They want uniformity so that the crop is easy to package. And they want cultivars that hold up well when they are shipped long distances.

As a home gardener, you don't need to worry about mechanical harvesting or shipping. And you may even consider uniform ripening a drawback, since it will give you a big yield all at one time, rather than extending your harvest over a longer season. Freedom from these constraints allows you to judge cultivars by their taste, not their durability and uniformity. You can try new cultivars each year for a new taste sensation, or stick with dependable favorites—it's up to you.

As for freshness, it's impossible for anyone else to grow vegetables as fresh as those you pick yourself, minutes before preparing them or seconds before eating them right there in the garden. And any cook knows that the best-tasting meals are made from the freshest ingredients.

Most gardeners and cooks also care about the amount of pesticides used on the food they eat, and with good reason. Unless you know the grower, you cannot be sure how the vegetables you eat were grown. More and more organically grown vegetables are becoming available, but they are not always the most flavorful cultivars, and they are still not as fresh as homegrown produce. In your own garden, you can use a variety of safe, effective pest control techniques to ensure that your food will be both fresh and chemical-free.

VEGETABLE-GROWING BASICS

No matter where you live, you can grow at least a few vegetable crops. Cold-climate gardeners succeed easily with cool-weather vegetables such as peas, broccoli, and cabbage; southern gardeners grow heat-loving melons, okra, and sweet potatoes to perfection. With a little extra planning, such as late-season plantings for cool-weather crops in the South and indoor seed-starting for long-season crops in the North, gardeners in nearly all areas can have luck with a wide range of vegetables.

You don't have to have a lot of room to grow vegetables, either. Even some of the most space-hungry crops, such as squash and cucumbers, are now available in compact bush forms. If you don't have room for a separate vegetable garden, try planting vegetables in flower borders. Or, grow them in containers on a deck or balcony, or in a sunny window.

The real key to successful vegetable gardening is giving your crops plenty of light. A site that gets full sun is ideal; at least 6 hours a day is okay. Some crops, such as beets, can get by on as little as 4 hours of sun, but most will grow poorly in too much shade.

When choosing a site, you should also consider convenience. If you have a choice of spots, site the garden fairly near the house, to make harvesting and maintenance easier. It's also handy to have a water source nearby, so you don't have to lug water buckets or haul hoses a long distance during dry spells.

Loose, rich soil is also important for good crop growth. When you prepare the soil, dig or till the top 8 inches or so (at least 1 foot for carrots and other root crops), and work in plenty of compost or other organic matter.

Other than that, your vegetable crops need the same basic care as all other garden plants. (For guidelines on planting and maintaining your vegetable garden, see Chapter 11). For details on growing specific crops, see the plant portraits in this chapter.

PLANT PORTRAITS

The following plant portraits include those vegetables that are most commonly grown in home gardens, along with a few others that deserve to be more widely grown. Unlike most of the other entries in this book, these plants are listed by their common name rather than their botanical name. Most, if not all, seed companies list vegetables by their common name, and few gardeners ever have occasion to use the botanical names.

Under the common name for each entry, you'll find the crop's family affiliation. (For instance, cabbage, broccoli, and cauliflower all belong to the cabbage family, while tomatoes, eggplants, and potatoes are all members of the tomato family.) While it's not necessary to know the botanical names of your crops, it *is* important to know what botanical family they belong to. That's because crops in the same family often share the same pests and diseases. When you plan your garden each year, try to shuffle your crops around so plants in the same family don't grow in the same spot two years in a row. This simple precaution can prevent the buildup of soil-borne pests and diseases, and minimize plant problems.

The plant portraits also tell you whether a vegetable is an annual, biennial, or perennial. Most annual and biennial crops are grown for just one year—planted in spring or late summer each year and harvested at the end of the growing season. Perennial vegetables, such as rhubarb and asparagus, are treated slightly differently, since they can stay in the same place for many years. Give them a separate area of the vegetable garden, so they won't get in

GROWING TIPS AT A GLANCE

The following plant portraits includes simple symbols to highlight special features you need to know about each vegetable. If you're not sure what any of the symbols mean, refer back to this key.

○ Full sun (more than 6 hours of sun a day; ideally all day)

◑ Partial sun (some direct sun, but less than 6 hours a day)

❄ Cool-weather crop

✳ Warm-weather crop

▼ Grows well in containers

Globe artichoke

the way when you prepare the soil for other crops each year.

The height of each crop is indicated to give you a general idea of how big it will get. Different cultivars can vary widely in spread, so it is best to check the seed packet or plant tag for specific spacing recommendations.

Finally, guidelines are provided on planting, growing, harvesting, and using each crop. The ideas for the vegetable's use are intended to help beginners, as well as to inspire more experienced gardeners to try something new.

Artichoke, Globe
Aster family. Perennial.
 ○ ❄ ▼

Characteristics. Height: 5 feet.

Globe artichokes are grown for their thistlelike flower buds, which consist of layers of tender bud scales that are peeled off at the table as they are eaten. The tender hearts, found at the center of the buds, are delicious in salads or stuffed with meat, fish, or vegetables and served cold.

These plants are limited in their growing range, preferring damp weather, cool summer temperatures, and mild winters. They are grown commercially in coastal areas of northern California.

Globe artichokes are perennials and can survive for 5 or 6 years in mild-winter areas. Adventurous

northern gardeners can grow them as annuals by starting the seed early indoors and harvesting in the fall, or raising the plants in large tubs and moving them to a protected area for the winter. 'Green Globe' is the most popular cultivar for the home garden.

How to Grow. If you are growing globe artichokes as perennials, keep them separate from annual vegetables so they won't be in the way as you turn the soil for spring or fall planting. The large plants are heavy feeders and love moist, well-drained soil enriched with plenty of manure or other organic matter.

Grow globe artichokes from seed or roots. Sow seed early indoors, 6 to 8 weeks before the last frost in spring. Transplant hardened-off seedlings outside after the danger of heavy frost has passed. Or set roots in the garden in early spring, after the danger of heavy frost has passed, with the buds just above the soil line. Allow at least 4 to 6 feet between the plants.

While artichokes cannot survive cold winters, a thick layer of loose winter mulch may be enough to protect the plants in areas with moderate winters. The bud scales tend to become tough in hot weather; gardeners in warmer regions can improve their chances of success by providing plenty of water when temperatures rise.

The plants are sometimes attacked by aphids or slugs. Spray with insecticidal soap to control aphids; handpick slugs or lure them away with beer traps. Cut the stems to the ground in the fall to discourage overwintering pests. In areas with moderately cool winters, leave 10 to 15 inches of the stalks above ground for the winter, and mulch the roots heavily in the fall.

How to Harvest. Pick the flower buds when they are about the size of an orange. Cut them off with 1 to 2 inches of the stem attached.

Uses. Serve cooked bud scales and hearts hot or cold, with a sauce for dipping. The plants themselves are dramatic-looking and can serve as landscape features. If you lose track of time or go away on vacation when the buds are ready to harvest, they will bloom into 6-inch, blue, thistlelike flowers that are good for drying.

Arugula
Cabbage family. Annual.
○ ◑ ❊ ▼

Characteristics. Height: 6 to 24 inches.

Also known as roquette, rugola, and rocket, this member of the cabbage family has a strong—some might even say fanatic—following among those who have tasted it. The leaves have a unique, pungent flavor that is almost peppery. The flowers are edible, too, and can be added to salads or used as garnishes. The plants are easy to grow and quick to mature, so you can plant them for both spring and fall crops. They are also ideal for container growing.

How to Grow. Arugula grows best in cool, moist, well-drained soil and full sun or light shade (especially during warm spells). It performs best in cool weather and tends to become bitter in high temperatures.

Sow seed directly in the garden in early spring, after danger of heavy frost has passed. For a longer harvest, keep sowing at 2-week intervals until the weather becomes hot. Sow again in mid- to late summer for a fall crop. Cover the seeds with ¼ inch of fine soil and keep the seedbed evenly moist until they germinate.

Arugula plants appreciate plenty of water during dry periods. They grow fast and are ready to pick about 35 days after sowing. This crop is sometimes bothered by flea beetles; cover the developing plants with floating row cover to keep these insects out. Otherwise, arugula is relatively free of pests and diseases.

How to Harvest. Pick the tender young leaves when they are about 4 to 6 inches tall. They stay fresh for 4 to 5 days in plastic bags in the refrigerator. When the plants flower and begin to set seed, pull them up, cut the usable leaves off at the base, and compost the rest.

Uses. Pick the tender young leaves and flowers for salads, or serve them by themselves with a vinaigrette. Cook the mature leaves as greens.

Asparagus
Lily family. Perennial.
○ ◑

Characteristics. Height: 4 to 6 feet.

Asparagus is probably the longest-lived vegetable in the garden. A well-sited, well-maintained asparagus patch can be productive for 20 years or more. This crop is grown for its tender shoots, or spears, which emerge in the warm temperatures of late spring and early summer. If they are not harvested, they develop into bushy plants with ferny foliage. In fall, they take on an attractive golden color.

Asparagus produces male and female plants. Mature female plants are pollinated by male plants when they bloom, and produce beautiful red berries in the fall. The fruit contains seed, which self-sows to produce many seedlings. This is a disadvantage, since the seedlings can crowd out older plants, and seed production weakens the female plants. Research has been underway for many years to develop asparagus strains that produce predominantly male plants. 'Jersey Giant' is one of the more popular cultivars that produce mostly male plants.

Asparagus

Because the plants need a dormant period triggered by the first frost in fall, they do not perform well in frost-free areas. Cultivars are being bred that are more tolerant of mild winters, including 'UC 157', a predominantly male cultivar that is resistant to Fusarium wilt disease.

How to Grow. Asparagus prefers rich, well-drained, slightly acid soil in full sun or light shade. Choose a location apart from your annual vegetables so the soil won't be disturbed every year. The more care you give to soil preparation before you plant asparagus, the better it will produce and the longer it will live.

You can grow asparagus from seed or from 1- or 2-year-old roots. Your choice will depend on how long you're willing to wait for your first crop. (The roots should be 3 years old before you start harvesting.) First-year spears are about as thick as the lead in a pencil, second-year spears are as thick as a pencil, and third-year and older spears are as thick as a finger.

To plant asparagus, dig a trench 12 inches wide and 15 inches deep for each row, and space the rows 4 feet apart. Mound up 8 to 9 inches of soil at the bottom of the trench.

If you're starting with roots, soak them overnight before planting, so they can take up water more easily. Set the crowns 18 inches apart on the mounds, and spread the roots out as evenly as possible. Then cover them with only 2 inches of soil.

If you're starting with seed, scatter it on top of the mounds. Cover it with ½ inch of soil, and keep the soil moist until the seed germinates.

As the stalks grow up, carefully mound the soil around them throughout the summer, so that by fall the soil level is even. (Be very gentle with the seedlings.) The patch needs plenty of water the first year, especially if you are planting roots. Since the roots will be as many as 6 inches below the soil surface by the end of the summer, the water must penetrate at least 8 inches deep each time you irrigate. Once the plants are established, they are more tolerant of dry conditions. Allow the foliage to die back in the fall before cutting it to the ground. That way, the plants can store plenty of energy for next year's crop.

Weeding is especially important in an asparagus bed, since you won't be cultivating the soil each year; a summer mulch can help keep weeds to a minimum. Plants are susceptible to rust and asparagus beetles; sometimes Fusarium wilt can also be a problem. Look for disease-resistant cultivars, and handpick pests as you spot them.

How to Harvest. To enable your plants to get a vigorous start, wait to begin harvesting from seed-grown plants until the third spring after sowing; wait until the second spring after planting 1-year roots, and the first spring after planting 2-year roots. During the first harvest season, pick for only 2 weeks. The second harvest season, pick for 3 weeks; the third season, pick for 4 weeks. Fully mature plants can be harvested for 4 to 6 weeks, until the stalks become progressively thinner. Harvest only spears that are thicker than a pencil. Cut them just above the soil level when they are 6 to 8 inches tall.

White asparagus is considered even more of a delicacy than green asparagus, and it's fairly easy to produce: Simply pile another 8 to 10 inches of soil over the bed. When the spears push through, remove the soil and harvest them at ground level, just as you would with green asparagus. The soil protects the stalks from the sun, preventing them from developing their green color. Do not try to grow white asparagus until your patch is at least 4 years old.

Uses. Asparagus does not retain its freshness for more than a day or two, so enjoy your harvest as soon as possible. This vegetable is delicious boiled or steamed, served with a sauce or by itself. The ferny plants add a light texture to the garden. The foliage with berries can be picked for fresh flower arrangements.

ASPARAGUS BEAN. See *Bean*

Bean
Bean family. Annual.
○ ✳ ▼

Characteristics. Height: 20 inches for bush beans; 5 to 8 feet for pole beans.

There is probably more diversity among beans than any other garden vegetable. Whole cookbooks—and whole gardens—have been devoted exclusively to beans. Some beans are grown for the pods and seeds; others are grown for the seeds only. They come in shades of green, yellow, purple, and red, and some have spots, stripes, speckles, or black "eyes." The pods can be short or long, round or flat, broad or narrow, on bushy or vining plants. In short, there's a bean for everyone and every sunny garden.

Snap beans, also known as string beans, are the familiar crisp green beans that snap when you bend them. They are eaten whole, with their ends snipped off. The bushy or vining plants can have yellow, purple, or green pods. (The yellow-podded types are also called wax beans.) 'Romano' is a popular, flat-podded pole bean. 'Roma II' is a bush version of 'Romano'. Snap beans are great raw (served with dips or in salads), steamed, or boiled. Most types freeze well after they are blanched. Bush types are usually ready for harvesting 45 to 60 days after sowing, while pole cultivars take from 60 to 80 days.

Filet beans, also called haricots verts, are long, narrow, and crunchy, and usually grow on bush-type plants. They are produced in great numbers starting about 45 to 55 days after sowing and should be harvested every day for continuous production. Pick them when they are about 4 to 6 inches long and about 1/8 inch wide, before the pods begin to swell. 'Triomphe de Farcy' is a popular heirloom cultivar that has green pods with faint purple stripes.

Lima beans, also called butter beans, are considered shell beans because the seeds are removed from the shell, which is then discarded. There are both bush and pole cultivars. The pods and beans vary in size: Baby lima pods are 2½ to 3 inches long, with 3 or 4 small beans in each, while the large "potato"-type limas are 3 to 6 inches long, with 3 to 5 large beans inside. 'Florida Speckled' has buff-colored beans splashed with maroon. Lima beans generally require warmer temperatures than snap beans. The bush types mature in 70 to 80 days, the pole types in 75 to 90 days. Lima beans are usually cooked and can be combined with corn to make succotash.

Other shell beans include soybeans, kidney beans, pinto beans, and French horticultural beans. Some can also be grown as dried beans. The horticultural beans produce colorful pods, which may be striped or speckled with red.

Mung beans are grown primarily for their seeds, which make the crunchy sprouts used in salads and stir-fried dishes. They have a long period of maturity—from 90 to 100 days—and are mostly grown in the South. Mung beans grow on bush-type plants and should be harvested as dried beans. To sprout for eating, put them in containers with holes for

Snap bush bean 'Topper'

drainage, and keep them constantly moist in a warm, dark area. They are ready to use in 5 to 10 days.

Fava beans are also called broad beans, Windsor beans, or horse beans. They grow on bush-type plants and are harvested as green shell or dried beans. The pods contain 5 or 6 oblong beans and mature in about 85 days. Since fava beans are more tolerant of cool temperatures, they are sometimes used as a substitute for lima beans in areas with short, cool summers. Some people are allergic to fava beans and their pollen.

Garbanzo beans, or chickpeas, have a chestnutty flavor. They can be boiled or roasted and are popular additions to salads and soups. Garbanzo beans grow on bush-type plants and are harvested as dried beans. They take a long time to mature—about 100 days.

Cowpeas are also known as black-eyed peas, Southern peas, or crowder peas. They are popular in the South but mature quickly enough (75 to 85 days) to be grown in the North as well. These beans perform best in areas with hot summer days and warm summer nights. They grow on vines but do not have tendrils, so they must be tied to their supports. Most gardeners prefer to harvest and eat cowpeas at the shell stage, but this crop can also be used as dried beans. 'California Blackeye' is a disease-resistant cultivar that produces cream-colored beans with black eyes. 'Purple Hull' is also disease-resistant, and has purple pods and light green to white beans with purple eyes.

Asparagus beans grow on vines and produce prolific crops of beans that can grow over 2 feet long (although they are best when harvested at less than 18 inches long). The fresh beans have a nutty flavor and can be stir-fried or sautéed as snap beans. You can also let them mature fully on the vine for dried beans.

How to Grow. Beans require full sun and well-drained, rich soil. These warm-season crops cannot tolerate any frost and grow slowly in cool temperatures. Like other members of the pea family, beans act as a host for beneficial bacteria that live on their roots. These bacteria take nitrogen from the air and convert it to a form that the plants can use. If you are planting beans in a new spot, you may need to add an inoculant (readily available from seed companies) to the seed to make sure the right bacteria are present. Once you have grown beans in that spot, the bacteria can survive in the soil for several years until the next planting.

Sow seed directly in the garden in late spring or early summer, after all danger of frost has passed and the soil is warm. Plant seed of bush cultivars 2 to 3 inches apart, cover it with 1 inch of soil, and keep it moist until seedlings appear. Thin the seedlings to about 6 inches apart when they are large enough to handle.

Vining types need some kind of support, such as poles (spaced 2 or 3 feet apart) or a fence or trellis. Sow the seed 2 to 3 inches apart around each pole or along the fence or trellis. Cover the seed with 1 inch of soil and keep the soil moist until seedlings appear. When the seedlings are large enough to handle, thin them to 5 or 6 plants per pole or 6 to 10 inches apart along the fence or trellis.

The plants may stop producing pods temporarily in hot summer weather, since temperatures over 80°F can kill the pollen before the flowers are pollinated. When temperatures become cooler, the plants should resume production.

Beans are susceptible to a variety of problems, including root rot diseases, anthracnose, bacterial diseases, and bean beetles. Check with your local Cooperative Extension office to find out which problems are most common in your area, and look for cultivars that are resistant to those problems. Planting beans in a different part of the garden each year can help prevent soil-borne root rot diseases. Avoid working around bean plants when they are wet to prevent the spread of diseases.

How to Harvest. Pick snap beans when the pods are firm and crisp, and the seeds are still small or undeveloped. Hold the stem with one hand and pull off the pod with the other to avoid breaking the branch of the plant. Harvest constantly, or the pods will become tough and stringy. Regular harvesting also keeps the plants more productive.

Harvest shell beans when the pods are firm, plump, and fully mature, after they change color but before the beans dry out completely. Harvest dry beans after the pods dry on the plants. You can pull up the whole plant and hang it upside down to dry the pods more fully. When the pods split open, shell the beans and store them in tight-lidded jars in a cool, dry location.

Uses. There are as many uses for beans as there are types of beans. Enjoy snap beans raw in dips and salads, or serve them cooked. Limas and other shell beans are shelled and cooked. Shell and dried beans can be baked. Mung beans are grown for sprouts, which are tasty in salads and stir-fried dishes.

Beans are excellent crops for children to raise, because the seed is easy to handle and the plants grow quickly. You can even train vining types on poles to make tepees for children to play in.

Beet
Goosefoot family. Biennial grown as an annual.
○ ❋ ▼

Characteristics. Height: 8 inches.

Beets are a cool-season crop grown for their fleshy, round, oblong, or cylindrical roots and their leafy tops. Both plant parts are highly nutritious; together, they are rich in carotene, potassium, calcium, iron, and vitamins A, B_1, B_2, and C. 'Detroit Dark Red, Medium Top' is a popular cultivar with perfectly round, dark red roots that grow to 3 inches across. 'Little Ball' is a gourmet baby beet that can be served whole.

The red roots of traditional beets are well known for their habit of "bleeding" all over kitchen counters and sinks, as well as other ingredients. Golden and white cultivars, such as 'Burpee's Golden', do not have this problem.

How to Grow. Beets appreciate loose, friable, deeply worked soil that's been enriched with organic matter. They cannot tolerate very acidic soil, so add lime to your growing beds the fall before planting.

This vegetable prefers cool temperatures and can be planted as both spring and fall crops. (In areas with frost-free winters, you can also plant beets as winter crops.) Sow the seed directly in the garden in early spring, as soon as you can work the soil. Sow again in midsummer for a fall crop. Or plant successive crops every 3 weeks for a continuous harvest. The seed you plant is actually a dried fruit—a cluster of 3 or 4 seeds—so try not to plant too thickly. Plant the seed in rows spaced 8 inches apart. Thin the plants to 2 to 3 inches apart when they are 2 to 3 inches tall.

Beets tolerate both cold and hot temperatures but may produce seed stalks in prolonged tempera-

Beet

tures below 50°F. If your beet roots have bitter black spots on them, there may be a boron deficiency in the soil. You can have your soil tested to verify this. If it is a problem, amend the soil as recommended on the test results.

How to Harvest. Pick beet greens when they are 4 to 6 inches long. The roots are usually best when they are less than 2 inches in diameter. Fall-harvested beets can be stored at 33° to 35°F and in 95 percent humidity. (Do not allow them to freeze in storage.) You can also can or pickle the roots.

Uses. Cook beet greens as you would spinach. The roots are delicious baked, grilled, or boiled. Add them to salads, make them into borscht, or serve them as a side dish.

BELGIAN ENDIVE. See *Chicory*
BLACK-EYED PEA. See *Bean*

Broccoli
Cabbage family. Annual.
○ ❋ ▼

Characteristics. Height: 2 to 3 feet.

Broccoli is one of the most nutritious garden vegetables you can grow. It is high in vitamins A and C, and is an excellent source of fiber. While some people have been known to publicly denounce broccoli, many more prize it for its exceptional flavor, whether cooked or eaten raw. This crop is gaining in popularity, and more than

Broccoli 'Love Me Tender'

half of all vegetable home gardeners in this country now grow it.

Broccoli is grown for its edible flower buds and foliage. Cultivars are available with different maturity dates, so if you choose carefully, you can enjoy broccoli fresh from the garden for months. 'Green Comet' is an early-maturing All-America Selections winner with big central heads up to 7 inches across, followed by many side shoots. It matures in 55 days after transplanting. Purple-headed cultivars are also available and are sometimes offered as a purple cauliflower. 'Romanesco' is an old-fashioned Italian type with chartreuse-colored central heads that appear to spiral out from the center. It has a long maturity period of 75 days.

How to Grow. Broccoli is a slow-growing, cool-season crop that grows best in a rich, well-drained soil in full sun. Start seed indoors 4 weeks before the last frost in spring. The seedlings need a great deal of light and can grow tall and leggy if they don't receive enough. To be on the safe side, have plant

lights available as a backup if you plan to grow the seedlings in a sunny window; just a day or two of cloudy weather after they sprout can cause them to skyrocket on spindly stems. If you don't have the time or space to start the seed early, you can purchase bedding plants, which are often available at garden centers.

Transplant hardened-off seedlings to the garden after the last hard frost. Plant them slightly deeper than they were growing previously, with the soil almost up to the lowest leaves. Set the seedlings 1 to 2 feet apart in rows spaced 2 feet apart.

For a fall crop, sow the seed directly in the garden in midsummer, 3 months before the first fall frost. Plant the seeds 1 inch apart in the rows and thin to 1 to 2 feet apart when the seedlings are large enough to handle. The plants can tolerate a light frost in the fall.

Broccoli plants need lots of water for vigorous, steady growth. Water regularly and mulch the plants to keep the soil moist.

This crop is susceptible to flea beetles, aphids, cabbageworms, and cabbage loopers. To keep pests out, protect the developing plants with floating row cover. To prevent problems with diseases such as black rot, black leg, and wilt, avoid planting broccoli or its relatives in the same spot each year.

How to Harvest. Pick broccoli when the heads have tight, firm buds. Cut off the central head with 6 inches of stem attached. After the central head has been cut, most cultivars will produce many smaller side heads, which can also be harvested. Enjoy broccoli heads fresh, store them in the refrigerator for a week or so, or freeze them.

If you don't harvest the heads at the right time, they will become looser and the yellow petals will begin to show. If you see yellow, the heads may be past their peak; pull the plants out for the compost pile, or let them bloom to have the flowers, which are edible.

Uses. This versatile vegetable can be eaten raw or cooked. Try it in salads, as a side dish, or in soups, casseroles, stir-fries, or stews. Broccoli makes a tasty stuffing for baked potatoes, too. You can also eat the foliage, either raw or cooked as greens. For a special taste treat, try peeling the thick stems and chopping and adding them to salads. They have a sweet, nutty taste. Even the yellow flowers, if allowed to bloom, can be used in salads or as a garnish.

Brussels sprouts 'Jade Cross'

Brussels sprouts
Cabbage family. Biennial grown as an annual.
○ ❄

Characteristics. Height: 3 feet.

Brussels sprouts have one of the most fascinating plant habits of all the vegetables. Their blue-green foliage is similar to that of other cabbage family members, but they grow much taller and produce sprouts, which look like miniature cabbage heads, all along the central stems. They are planted in spring for fall harvesting, and take 90 to 100 days to mature from transplanted seedlings.

Unfortunately, brussels sprouts are not popular in American gardens, possibly because they take up space in the garden for such a long time, or because many people simply do not like the taste. Brussels sprouts can taste bitter if they are harvested before frost has a chance to sweeten them. For this reason, most gardeners wait to harvest them until after the first frost in fall. You can eat the sprouts right off the plant in the garden while you are doing your fall cleanup, or enjoy them cooked.

How to Grow. Brussels sprouts prefer full sun and well-drained soil enriched with plenty of organic matter. They take a long time to mature from seed, so start them indoors 4 weeks before the last frost in spring. The seedlings need a great deal of light; if you grow yours on a windowsill, you may need to have plant lights as a backup during cloudy weather. Transplant hardened-off seedlings to the garden after all danger of frost has passed. Set them 2 feet apart in rows spaced 3 feet apart. The plants need 1 to 1½ inches of water per week for steady growth.

Brussels sprouts are susceptible to the same pests and diseases as other cabbage family members, so avoid planting any of their relatives—such as cabbage, broccoli, or cauliflower—in the same spot 2 years in a row. 'Jade Cross' and 'Long Island Improved' are resistant to Fusarium wilt and yellows.

How to Harvest. If possible, wait until after a light frost to begin harvesting. Start from the bottom of the stalk and work your way up. Harvest sprouts that are 1 to 1½ inches in diameter. Remove the row of leaves under the row of sprouts you are harvesting, but leave the top leaves on the plant until you work your way up. Twist the sprouts off the stems. Harvest as many sprouts as you need at each picking and leave the rest; they can remain on the plant through part of the winter, if necessary. Extra sprouts can also be blanched and frozen after they are harvested. They can be stored in the refrigerator for up to 3 weeks.

Uses. Eat the sprouts raw, or steam or boil them and serve as a snack or side dish with melted butter or a sauce. Try them au gratin, cooked with chestnuts.

Cabbage
Cabbage family. Biennial grown as an annual.
○ ◑ ❄

Characteristics. Height: 18 to 20 inches.

Cabbage is one of the most popular and versatile vegetables grown in home gardens. It is rich in vitamins A, C, and K, as well as essential minerals. And homegrown cabbage has a sweet flavor that store-bought cabbage just doesn't seem to have.

Cabbage 'Fast Ball'

Cultivars are red or green, with smooth or savoyed (wrinkled) edges and flat, round, or pointed heads. Early-, mid-, and late-season cultivars are available, so cabbage devotees can harvest cabbage throughout much of the summer into fall.

'Early Jersey Wakefield' is a popular, yellows-resistant heirloom cultivar with compact, pointed heads that are ready to harvest 63 to 65 days after transplanting. 'Danish Roundhead' is another heirloom, valued for its large heads, which mature in 105 days after transplanting. It should be planted as a fall crop.

Chinese cabbage has a mild, sweet flavor and crinkled leaves on elongated heads. It is usually grown as a fall crop, although 'Two Seasons Hybrid' has been developed for both spring and fall crops. Pak choi is a related crop grown for its leafstalks, which are tasty raw or cooked in Oriental dishes.

How to Grow. Cabbage prefers full sun or light shade and well-drained soil enriched with organic matter. It is a cool-season crop and does not tolerate hot temperatures. Start spring crops early to give the plants a chance to mature before hot weather. Sow seed indoors 5 to 6 weeks before the last frost in spring. Transplant hardened-off seedlings outside after danger of heavy frost has passed. Or plant seedlings purchased from a local garden center after danger of heavy frost. Direct-sow fall crops in midsummer. Set plants 12 to 18 inches apart in rows spaced 2 feet apart.

Cabbage plants benefit from rapid, uninterrupted growth, which is aided by 1 to 1½ inches of water every week, plus liberal applications of compost or 10-10-10 fertilizer. They are susceptible to the same diseases and pests as their relatives, so avoid planting any cabbage family crops in the same spot 2 years in a row. Floating row covers can protect the developing plants from many pests.

How to Harvest. Gather cabbage heads when they are firm. Cut the stem at soil level and remove the outer leaves, or leave several inches of stem and leaves in the garden. After the central head is harvested, smaller heads may develop near the base of the leaves. Harvest Chinese cabbage when the leaves are loose and 10 inches tall, or wait until they form heads. Fall-harvested cabbage heads can last for several months if you store them at 40°F and in high humidity.

Uses. Serve cabbage cooked or raw, in combination with other vegetables or with meat dishes; it can be stir-fried, steamed, boiled, sautéed, or baked. Or shred it for cole slaw or sauerkraut.

CANTALOUPE. See *Melon*

Carrot

Carrot family. Biennial grown as an annual.

Characteristics. Height: 12 inches.

Carrots are grown for their sweet-tasting, bright orange roots, which are high in vitamin A. While the large cultivars require loose, deep, sandy soil for good root development, gardeners with heavy clay soil can have success with shorter cultivars, some of which grow no deeper than 2 or 3 inches. These short-rooted types also grow well in containers.

Carrot roots develop inner and outer cores as they mature. The outer core tastes sweeter and contains more vitamins and minerals, while the inner core tends to be tougher in texture. The best-quality carrots have small inner cores and large outer cores.

The roots vary in length from 1½ to 9 inches. They can be long and narrow or short and rounded; they can taper toward the tip or be cylindrical. 'Thumbelina' is an All-America Selections winner with round, golf ball-size roots that can be eaten whole. 'Little Finger' is a delicious gourmet type that grows 3½ inches long and ⅝ inch wide, with a small inner core. 'Imperator' grows 8 to 9 inches long; the slender roots are only 1½ inches wide.

How to Grow. Carrots require a sunny location with well-drained soil that is free of stones and has been worked at least as deep as the length of the cultivar's roots. (If the roots reach a hard-packed layer or stones, they will either stop growing or split apart.) This cool-season crop tolerates light frost. Sow seed directly in the garden in early spring, after danger of heavy frost has passed. Sow again at 2-week intervals for a continuous supply, or just make one large repeat sowing in midsummer for a fall crop. Space the rows 6 inches apart. Water regularly to keep the soil moist while the seeds are sprouting, which can take up to 2 weeks. Thin the seedlings to 3 inches apart when they are large enough to handle.

The tops of the roots will turn green if they are exposed to sunlight. To prevent green "shoulders," feed and water the plants regularly; this will promote rapid growth of the foliage, which can shade the tops from the sun. You can also heap soil around the roots about 40 days after sowing.

Carrots are bothered by few pests and diseases, with the exception of root nematodes, which are microscopic worms that can severely disfigure the roots. If the roots are stunted and hairy-looking, you may want to have your soil tested for nematodes. You can prevent the buildup of these pests by planting your carrots in different parts of the garden each year.

Shallow watering can also damage the roots. Remember that each time you irrigate, the water must soak in slightly deeper than the length of the roots.

How to Harvest. You can begin to harvest carrots at thinning time. The harvested thinnings make great snacks right in the garden. Leave the rest of the carrots in the ground until you are ready to use them. They are easier to harvest if you soak the bed with water before you begin pulling. Gently grab the tops and twist them as you pull the roots up. If there are still some carrots left in the fall, you can leave them in the ground after the first frost, but in cold climates you'll need to pull them up before the ground freezes. Store them in a root cellar or other cool, humid area until you are ready to use them. In mild areas, you can leave carrots in the ground and harvest them all winter long.

Uses. Raw carrots, especially the smaller cultivars, make great in-the-garden snacks. They are important ingredients for salads, either shredded or sliced, and can be used for dipping. You can also cook them in various ways, including steaming, boiling, baking, glazing, or sautéing in olive oil. Carrots are ideal in soups and stews, and as garnishes for meat dishes. They make a terrific curry soup, which can be served hot or cold. The young tops can be used to flavor soups. If you allow carrots to overwinter, they produce pretty flowers that look like Queen-Anne's-lace.

Carrot 'Short 'n Sweet'

Cauliflower
Cabbage family. Annual.
○ ❄

Characteristics. Height: 2½ feet.

Cauliflower is the most challenging member of the cabbage family to grow. When gardeners are successful, the plants produce delicious heads of creamy white flower parts called "curds." When they are not successful, the heads can turn yellow, or the curds can fall apart or become "ricey." The secret to success is to maintain continuous, rapid growth in cool temperatures.

Cauliflower 'Early White'

avoid planting cabbage family relatives in the same spot 2 years in a row. Floating row covers can protect developing plants from pests.

Cauliflower must be shielded from the sun to maintain its white color. Some cultivars have long leaves that grow close to the heads, offering "self-blanching" protection. If your cultivar is not self-blanching, you'll have to do it yourself, by tying the foliage over the heads: When the heads are 2 to 3 inches across, tie the foliage over them with rubber bands, or hold them with one or two clothespins. (Clothespins are easier to move as the heads grow larger.)

How to Harvest. This crop is ready to harvest when the heads are the appropriate size for the cultivar, and the curds are held tightly together. Cut the heads off the main stem, leaving 1 to 2 inches of stem on each head. Use the heads as soon as possible after harvesting, or freeze them for future use.

Uses. Cauliflower can be served raw or cooked. Raw curds are great for snacks or dipping, or in salads. Cauliflower is also good stir-fried, sautéed, steamed, boiled, or baked, alone or combined with meats or other vegetables. It is especially delicious in a cauliflower curry dish with Indian spices and yogurt.

The cultivars differ in their maturity dates, resistance to diseases, and ability to maintain their quality when frozen. 'Early White Hybrid' is an excellent 52-day cultivar with 9-inch heads that do not tend to become loose and "ricey."

How to Grow. Cauliflower needs full sun and rich, well-drained soil. Start seed indoors 4 weeks before the last frost, and give the seedlings plenty of light to keep them compact. Transplant hardened-off seedlings to the garden after danger of a heavy frost. Sow fall crops directly in the garden in midsummer. Set transplants or thin seedlings to stand 2 feet apart in rows spaced 30 inches apart.

Too much heat will prevent cauliflower heads from forming, and too much cold will slow them down. It is important to water and fertilize regularly to encourage continuous growth, as any interruption will delay the production of heads. Cauliflower is susceptible to the same pests and diseases as other cabbage family crops, including black rot and cabbageworms. To prevent the buildup of diseases,

Celery

Carrot family. Biennial grown as an annual.

○ ❄

Characteristics. Height: 15 to 18 inches.

Celery has a reputation for being one of the most challenging vegetables for home gardeners to grow. It has a very long season, maturing 90 to 120 days after transplanting. Celery is also fussy about temperatures. It is basically a cool-season crop that cannot tolerate heat, but when temperatures drop below 55°F for a prolonged period, it will produce flower stalks and go to seed. It can be grown during the winter in areas with mild winters, as an early-spring crop in the South, or as a fall crop in the North.

Gardeners grow celery for the crunchy, elongated leafstalks, which make a tasty, low-calorie snack. Despite its daunting, technical-sounding name, 'Tall Utah 52-70 R Improved' is a great cultivar for the home garden. It produces long, dark green stalks with great flavor, and the plants are resistant to Western celery mosaic disease.

How to Grow. Celery requires full sun and cool, moist, deep soil that has good drainage and is rich in organic matter. Start seed indoors 10 to 16 weeks before the last hard frost in spring. The seed takes a long time to germinate; to aid germination, soak it overnight before sowing. Sow the seed in trays of seed-starting medium and cover it with a sprinkling of the medium. When the seedlings are 2 inches tall, move them to individual pots. If you don't have the time or space to start the seed indoors, you can buy transplants, which are often available at garden centers in early spring.

Transplant hardened-off seedlings outside after all danger of frost has passed. Set them 6 to 10 inches apart in rows spaced 2 feet apart. If you know that nighttime temperatures will drop below 50°F, cut the bottoms out of plastic milk jugs and set the jugs over the transplants at night. Water and fertilize regularly throughout the season to promote steady growth. When the plants are 12 inches tall, heap soil around their bases to keep them upright. Be careful not to get soil into the center of the plants, or they may rot in the middle. If you want your celery to be light-colored and the cultivar you've chosen isn't self-blanching, wrap brown paper around the stems.

Celery plants are susceptible to aphids and earwigs, as well as virus diseases and nematodes. Look for disease-resistant cultivars, and use floating row covers to keep pests off the plants.

How to Harvest. Start harvesting the outer stalks when the plants are 6 to 8 inches tall. Cut the taproot below the soil surface if you want to harvest the whole plant. Celery can tolerate light frost, but be sure to finish harvesting before a heavy frost; plants that are harvested too late can become pithy and stringy.

Uses. The stalks are good for dipping and party trays or in vegetable salads. They also add flavor and crunch to potato, egg, chicken, and seafood salads. Celery is a useful ingredient in soups, stews, and casseroles. Braised celery makes an unusual side dish. Use the foliage as a basting brush when grilling on the barbecue.

CHICKPEA. See *Bean*

Chicory
Aster family. Perennial.
 ○ ❄ ▼

Characteristics. Height: 16 to 18 inches.

Chicory is considered a real delicacy. It is grown for its leaves, which can have a sharp, tangy flavor that many people enjoy.

When chicory is grown for the small heads of fresh leaves, it is called radicchio. The foliage varies from dark red to deep burgundy. Radicchio matures relatively slowly—85 to 110 days from seed sown in early spring to harvest. Belgian, or French, endive is grown for its roots. Gardeners then dig the roots in the fall, bring them indoors, and force them to produce "chicons" for use in salads. The pale gold sprouts, which look like small corn husks, are not as bitter as radicchio. Forcing them is not particularly easy but can be tremendously rewarding when it works.

How to Grow. Both kinds of chicory prefer full sun and deep, rich soil. In most areas, sow seed for radicchio in spring, after danger of a heavy frost. In frost-free areas, sow in the fall for a spring harvest. Plant the seed ¼ inch deep in rows spaced 18 inches apart. Thin the seedlings to 8 inches apart when they are large enough to handle. On some radicchio cultivars, you'll need to cut the foliage back in the fall for the heads to form. Tie the leaves loosely together at the top when they are about 10 inches long. After 2 to 3 weeks, the inner leaves will be smooth and mild-tasting, with a pale gold color. Radicchio can stand a light frost, and the flavor can even be improved by it.

Belgian endive requires deeply dug soil for its long taproots to form properly. Sow seed in the garden after all danger of frost, when the weather stays warm. Sow it ½ inch deep in rows spaced 12 to 18 inches apart. Thin the seedlings to stand 4 to 5 inches apart.

Dig the long taproots after the first light frost in fall, about 110 days after sowing. Remove all the leaves except the small ones coming out of the crown on top of the roots. Store the roots at 35° to 40°F in damp peat moss or sand until you are ready to force them.

When you are ready to force some roots, take as many as you need, and cut off the tips so they are 8 to 10 inches long. Large roots tend to produce clustered heads; medium-size roots that are 1 to 2 inches in diameter produce the best heads. Stand them with the small leaves on top in boxes or barrels, and bury them in moist peat moss or sand. Water them thoroughly. Keep them at 60°F in darkness and high humidity. (You may want to cover them with black plastic with some holes punched in it for air circulation.) If you maintain the right conditions, the same roots can produce 2 or 3 harvests.

How to Harvest. Gather radicchio heads after a light frost by cutting them just below the soil surface. Harvest Belgian endive chicons when they are 4 to 6 inches tall; cut them just above the crown.

Uses. Enjoy radicchio as a tangy lettuce substitute in salads, stuffed with caviar, used with dips, or as a colorful garnish. The leaves can also be steamed or sautéed. The red-foliaged plants are very decorative in the garden and in containers, even window boxes. Belgian endive roots can be forced to produce gourmet sprouts, which are tasty in salads or stuffed with caviar for hors d'oeuvres.

Collards
Cabbage family. Biennial grown as an annual.

Characteristics. Height: 2 to 4 feet.

A close relative of cabbage and kale, collards form rosettes of handsome blue-green leaves rather than heads. They are very rich in vitamins and minerals, and have a delicious, mild, cabbagelike flavor. Collards are easier to grow than cabbage, as they tolerate a wider range of temperatures and growing conditions. They can withstand temperatures as low as 10°F but also grow well in hot summer weather. They are grown as a spring and fall crop in the North and all year in the South.

How to Grow. Collards prefer rich, well-drained soil in full sun. For a spring crop, sow seed directly in the garden ¼ to ½ inch deep after danger of heavy frost. Space the rows 30 inches apart. Thin the seedlings to 6 to 8 inches apart. You can also start seed indoors 4 to 6 weeks before the last frost date; transplant the hardened-off seedlings 6 to 8 inches apart after the danger of heavy frost has passed. For a fall crop, sow in midsummer. Collards can be grown year-round in the South.

The plants need 1 to 1½ inches of water every week. They benefit from a scattering of nitrogen fertilizer 1 month after planting. Collards are susceptible to the same pests and diseases as other members of the cabbage family; cabbageworms, aphids, downy mildew, and black leg are the most common problems. To prevent the buildup of diseases, plant cabbage family crops in a different spot each year. Cover the developing plants with floating row covers to protect them from pests.

How to Harvest. You can harvest whole collard plants when they are 6 to 8 inches tall. Or, pick the bottom leaves as you need them, and the inner buds will keep producing more foliage. Wait until after a light frost to harvest fall crops, as frost sweetens the flavor.

Uses. Enjoy collard greens steamed, sautéed, or boiled. They can be used to flavor soups or stews, or cooked and served with ham and pork.

Corn
Grass family. Annual.

Characteristics. Height: 4 to 9 feet.

Eating fresh sweet corn is one of the greatest delights of summer. Nothing can match the flavor of the luscious, succulent, sweet kernels of corn on the cob, fresh-picked from the garden. Although the plants take up a great deal of room and yield as little as an average of 2 ears per plant, anyone who has ever tasted fresh sweet corn from his or her own garden knows that growing this wonderful crop is well worth it.

Most corn plants look like giant blades of grass and grow from 4 to 9 feet tall. Sweet corn cultivars can be yellow, white, or bicolored (with both yellow and white kernels). Sweet corn has been the subject of much hybridizing in the seed industry, and recent breakthroughs in breeding programs have led to the sugary-enhancer hybrids and the super-sweet hybrids.

The super-sweet cultivars can be up to 4 times as sweet as other types of sweet corn. They do not even have to be cooked or amended in any way to taste as delicious as standard cultivars smothered in butter and salt.

The sugary-enhancer hybrids can stay sweet much longer than earlier cultivars. Most corn has a

Sweet corn 'Breeder's Bicolor', 'Silver Choice', and 'Breeder's Choice'

small window of ripeness—usually just 2 or 3 days—before the sugar turns to starch and the corn tastes stale. The sugary-enhancer hybrids stay sweet up to 2 weeks after picking. This means you do not have to harvest your entire crop as soon as it ripens in order to avoid starchy, overripe corn.

The part of corn that we eat is the kernel, or seed. The immature seeds swell when the female flowers, or silks, are fertilized by pollen carried by the wind from the male flowers, or tassels. The silks must be pollinated by the same corn cultivar, or the kernels will be uneven in size and quality. For good pollination, plant your corn in blocks at least 4 rows wide. If you want to plant more than one cultivar, separate them by at least 400 yards to prevent cross-pollination, or choose cultivars that mature at least a month apart. (One advantage of choosing the sugary-enhancer hybrids is that they do not need to be isolated from other sweet corn cultivars.)

Popcorn is a type of corn that produces hard, starchy kernels, which explode when they are heated. The plants look like those of sweet corn but are often shorter. The husked cobs are shorter—only about 4 inches long—and are filled with the familiar hard kernels that are somewhat pointed, unlike the broader, flatter kernels of most sweet corn.

Ornamental corn is grown for its colorful kernels, which can be combinations of blue, red, maroon, yellow, and orange—even on the same cob. The husks may also be decorative, sometimes with red and purple markings. The cobs vary in size from

2 inches to the size of sweet corn cobs. They generally have a longer maturity period (over 100 days) and mature in the fall, in time for harvest-season decorations. 'Strawberry' is a popular cultivar with strawberry-colored ears measuring only 2 inches long and 1½ inches wide.

Some gardeners are becoming interested in older cultivars of sweet corn, which are open-pollinated rather than hybrids. These types tend to be less sweet than the hybrids but reportedly have more "corn" flavor. Some seed companies now offer traditional cultivars, such as 'Black Aztec', with blue-black kernels, or 'Mandan Red Nueta', a pre-Columbian cultivar that produces up to 6 small ears of reddish brown to orange kernels per plant.

Burpee customers often ask about the gourmet "mini-corn" found at salad bars and in Oriental dishes. Cultivars that have been bred to produce very small ears are not widely available in this country. If you want to grow your own "mini-corn," harvest the ears of sweet corn a few days after they produce silks, then pickle them.

How to Grow. If you have the space, corn is relatively easy to grow. This crop prefers rich, well-drained soil and requires full sun. Sow the seed after all danger of frost in spring and after the soil has warmed up.

Corn seed looks like very dry corn kernels (which is, in fact, what they are). The seed of supersweet and sugary-enhancer hybrid types is more shriveled than that of standard sweet corn. The more shriveled the seed is, the longer it will take to soak up water when it germinates. For this reason, many gardeners soak corn seed overnight before sowing. When the seed is planted in cool soil, it takes longer to germinate, and if it has not been presoaked, it may rot.

Sow the seed 5 to 6 inches apart in rows spaced 2 to 3 feet apart, and cover with 1 inch of soil. When the seedlings are large enough to handle, thin them to 12 inches apart. Corn is a heavy feeder and appreciates a side-dressing of 5-10-5 fertilizer when the plants have produced 6 to 8 leaves. The plants need 1 to 2 inches of water every week. Suckers tend to form at the base of the plants; they help support the stalks and make food for the plant. The stalks may have to be staked in windy areas, but in general they are self-supporting.

Dry conditions can stunt corn growth. Under severe stress, the plants may tassel when the stalks are only 2 to 3 feet tall, before the silks are produced. If the pollen dies before the silks appear, the corn will not have a chance to be pollinated. To prevent this problem, mulch the plants and water regularly.

Pests and diseases generally aren't too serious in corn patches. If you see ugly gray, swollen masses that open to release what looks like black soot, your corn has corn smut, a fungal disease. Smut can appear on the foliage, the silks, and the kernels. When it gets in the kernels, it can make them swell to immense irregular shapes. Smut is not toxic and is even harvested as a delicacy in some cultures, but affected plant parts should be removed before the spores are released. Corn earworms can also be a problem. They enter the ears through the silks and feed on the upper kernels. Once they are in the ears they cannot be controlled, but they do not usually cause severe damage; break off and discard the damaged tips after harvest.

How to Harvest. The ears are ready to harvest about 17 or 18 days after the silks appear. The kernels of sweet corn should be milky when you pierce them with your fingernail. If they are thick and creamy, they are overripe; if they are watery, they are not ready yet. There are obvious drawbacks to this method of determining ripeness, and it should only be used when you are learning what a ripe ear feels like. If you open the husk before the ear is ripe, put a paper bag over it to protect it from birds and insects. Harvest by snapping the ear off the stalk with a quick, twisting motion. Store standard cultivars in the refrigerator for up to 3 days; you can refrigerate the super-sweet and sugary-enhancer hybrids for up to 2 weeks. Harvest popcorn and ornamental corn when the husks and plants are dry.

Uses. It's hard to resist snacking on fresh-picked sweet corn right in the garden. If you manage to get some to the kitchen, boil the husked ears lightly and eat the kernels right off the cob. Or cut the kernels off the ears, steam them, and enjoy them alone or added to other vegetable dishes. Corn can be combined with lima beans to make succotash. It can also be used in stuffings, and makes great fritters, breads, and puddings. Pop popcorn for a nutritious snack. Use ornamental corn for autumn decorations.

COWPEA. See *Bean*

Cucumber 'Bush Champion'

Cucumber
Squash family. Annual.

Characteristics. Height: 2 to 4 feet for bush types; up to 9 feet for vining types.

Cucumbers are vine or crops grown for their green fruits, which have a refreshing, mild, cool flavor. Standard cucumbers have straight, narrow fruits with spiny, waxy skins that range from medium to dark green. Most cultivars grow on vines, which should be supported with trellises. Bush cultivars are also available; they take only one-third as much space as vining types and can even be grown in containers. 'Bush Champion' produces prolific crops of straight, slender, bright green fruits up to 11 inches long on bush-type plants. Pickling cultivars—both vining and bush-type—produce shorter, plumper fruits with lighter skins for fresh eating or for pickles.

Many other types of cucumbers make interesting additions to the vegetable garden. For instance, Oriental cucumbers are long and curved, with a rough texture. They are good for slicing and adding to salads or for making into pickles. Armenian cucumbers, also called snake or serpent cucumbers, grow 3 feet long. They have thin skins and a sweet flavor that is never bitter. "Burpless" cucumbers lack the gene that makes some cucumbers bitter and difficult for many people to digest. They taste sweet and do not need to be peeled before you eat them. Lemon cucumbers are bright yellow and look like their namesake. They do not taste like lemons, however, but are sweet and crisp.

Cucumbers produce male and female flowers on the same plant. The male flowers pollinate the female flowers, which in turn produce the fruit. Many newer cultivars produce only female flowers and are called "gynoecious." They bear considerably more fruit per plant than other cucumbers. However, they still need some male flowers to produce the pollen, so seeds of a standard cultivar are included in packets of gynoecious cucumber seeds. The seeds are not always marked, so if you don't want to plant all the seeds in the packet, you'll need to distinguish the pollinator from the other seeds. The pollinator seeds tend to be a little larger and plumper than the gynoecious seeds. (Under stress, the female plants may also produce male flowers.)

How to Grow. This warm-season crop prefers rich, warm, well-drained soil in full sun. In areas with short summers, you can start the seed indoors about 4 weeks before the last frost date and transplant the hardened-off seedlings to the garden after all danger of frost. In areas with long summers, sow seed in the garden after all danger of frost has passed. Sow the seed of vining types 1 inch deep in rows spaced 3 to 4 feet apart, and thin the seedlings to 12 inches apart when they are large enough to handle. Or plant the seed in "hills"—groups of 3 plants with 2 to 3 feet between groups. Plant bush types in containers, or 12 inches apart in rows spaced 2 to 3 feet apart.

Provide a trellis for vining types to climb; otherwise, they will produce curved fruits. Cucumbers tend to be shallow-rooted and need extra water in dry weather. They can stop growing if they become too dry but will usually start growing again when conditions improve. Mulching the soil can help keep the roots evenly moist.

Cucumber flowers are pollinated by bees, which must visit the blooms many times before enough pollen is transferred to produce full-size, straight fruits. If the flowers are not properly pollinated, the fruits can be distorted, or the plants may produce no fruit at all. Bees tend to be less active in cloudy weather and in gardens where pesticides are used. If your bees aren't doing their job, you can pollinate the flowers yourself: On a cloudy day or early in the morning, simply remove the male flower and rub it on the female flower. (The female flowers have a tiny fruit behind them, which will eventually swell into a cucumber.) Contrary to popular opinion, cucumbers do not cross-pollinate with melons, and bitter cucumbers are not produced by other vine crops growing in the vicinity.

Cucumbers are susceptible to a number of pests and diseases common to squash family members, including anthracnose, powdery or downy mildew, cucumber mosaic virus, aphids, cucumber beetles (which spread bacterial wilt disease), and vine borers. Many cultivars have been selected for resistance to these problems. Check with your local Cooperative Extension Service office for recommended cultivars for your area. Avoid planting squash family crops in the same spot 2 years in a row.

How to Harvest. Pick cucumbers at any stage of growth, but before they become larger than the cultivar should grow. The more you harvest, the more the plants will produce; pick the fruits daily, or at least every other day, when the plants are at peak production.

Uses. Slice standard types for salads, chop or grate them to add a cool taste to dips, or combine them with yogurt and Indian spices to make raita. They can also be sautéed, stir-fried, added to casseroles, or made into a terrific soup that can be served hot or cold. Pickling types are good for pickling or eating fresh.

Eggplant
Tomato family. Annual.

Characteristics. Height: 2 to 3 feet.

Eggplant is a close relative of tomatoes and peppers. It produces beautiful fruit with a luscious, succulent texture and mild flavor. The fruit can be egg-shaped or long and cylindrical, with glossy purple, lavender, pink, yellow, or white skin. The deep purple-fruited heirloom 'Black Beauty' was introduced by Burpee in 1902 and is still popular.

Eggplant 'Purple Blush'

water in prolonged dry weather. They do not normally require support.

Eggplants are susceptible to the same pests and diseases that attack tomatoes. Common pests include flea beetles, aphids, Colorado potato beetles, and Japanese beetles; use floating row covers to protect the plants. To prevent diseases, grow resistant cultivars and plant in a different site each year.

How to Harvest. You can harvest the fruits at any stage of maturity, from gourmet baby eggplants to full-size fruits. For regular-size fruits, pick them when they are 4 to 5 inches long, while the skin is still glossy. When the skin turns dull, the fruit is probably overripe. Use a sharp knife or pruning shears to cut the fruits, leaving 1 inch of stem attached. Eggplants do not keep well, so eat them as soon as possible after harvesting.

Uses. Eggplant can serve as a vegetable substitute for meat in many cooked dishes, soups, and stews. Try it stir-fried, deep-fried, sautéed, baked, or stuffed. It is an important ingredient in many Middle Eastern dishes, such as baba ganoush. For a taste treat, prepare eggplant curry with Indian spices and yogurt. The miniature cultivars are great stuffed and served whole as hors d'oeuvres.

Endive

Aster family. Biennial grown as an annual.

Characteristics. Height: 16 to 18 inches.

This close relative of chicory is grown for its pungent, slightly bitter foliage, which livens up salads. When it has frilled foliage, it is called endive; when it has flat leaves, it is called escarole. One type, called Belgian or French endive, can be forced indoors in midwinter to produce small sprouts ("chicons") from roots grown in the garden during the summer.

How to Grow. Endive is a cool-season crop that prefers rich, well-drained soil and full sun. It is planted all winter in areas with mild winters and as a spring and fall crop in the North. In too-warm temperatures, the plants will produce a seed stalk, and the leaves will taste bitter. Long-season cultivars are best grown as a fall crop. The plants can tolerate a light frost, which can sweeten their flavor.

Eggplants vary in size from miniature, thumb-size fruits to large, oval-shaped fruits. Italian types are long and slender, growing to 10 inches long and 2½ inches wide. Japanese types are narrower and can reach 12 inches long and 2 inches wide. Most eggplants form bushy plants that grow 2 to 3 feet tall, although miniature cultivars are available; they grow just 12 inches tall and are perfect for patio containers.

How to Grow. Eggplant thrives in warm, rich, well-drained soil in full sun. This warm-season crop cannot tolerate any frost. It takes a long time to mature, so start the seed indoors 10 to 12 weeks before the last frost in spring. Transfer the seedlings to individual containers when they are 2 inches tall. Transplant hardened-off seedlings to the garden after all danger of frost. Set the plants 12 inches apart in rows spaced 30 inches apart.

The plants are fairly tolerant of dry conditions once they are established, but they appreciate extra

For a spring crop, sow seed directly in the garden after danger of a heavy frost; sow in midsummer for a fall crop. For a head start, you can start the seed indoors 6 to 8 weeks before the last heavy frost and transplant the hardened-off seedlings to the garden after danger of a heavy frost. Set the plants 8 to 10 inches apart in rows spaced 18 to 30 inches apart.

Endive and escarole plants are relatively free of pests and diseases, although they can be attacked by slugs; handpick these pests, or surround the plants with diatomaceous earth. The plants may require extra water during dry periods. When the leaves are 10 inches long, tie them together to blanch the center leaves. Blanching takes 2 to 3 weeks.

How to Harvest. Cut the entire plant off at the base 2 to 3 weeks after tying the leaves together for blanching. The tough outer leaves are usually discarded at harvest.

Uses. Enjoy endive and escarole as a lively lettuce substitute in salads. They can also be braised and served as a side dish.

ESCAROLE. See *Endive*
FAVA BEAN. See *Bean*
FILET BEAN. See *Bean*
GARBANZO BEAN. See *Bean*

Garlic
Onion family. Perennial.
○ ▼

Characteristics. Height: 1 to 2 feet.

Garlic is grown for its large bulbs, which are made up of sections, or "cloves," and have a unique, tangy flavor. This onion family member is nutritious as well as delicious, and is believed to help lower blood pressure.

Garlic is grown not from seed but rather from the cloves. The larger the clove, the larger the bulb it will produce. Elephant garlic produces extra-large cloves in enormous bulbs measuring 2 to 3 inches long and 4 inches wide. Its flavor is milder than that of standard garlic.

How to Grow. Garlic plants require deep, friable, well-drained soil in full sun. Dig plenty of organic matter into the soil before planting. In the South, plant garlic cloves in the fall for a spring

Garlic

crop. In the North, plant in early spring for a fall crop. Elephant garlic is usually planted in the fall in both the North (with winter protection) and the South. Plant the cloves with the pointed side up. Set them 1 inch deep and 4 inches apart in rows spaced 1 to 2 feet apart.

Give the plants extra water during dry periods; otherwise, the bulbs may be stunted. They have the same pest and disease problems as onions, including thrips and root maggots. Rotate planting sites each year to prevent the buildup of soil-borne problems.

How to Harvest. Gather garlic when the foliage dies back. Carefully dig the bulbs with a pitchfork, and allow them to cure in a warm, dry place for a week. Store the cured bulbs in a cool, dry place. You can leave the stalks on the plants and braid them.

Uses. Garlic is useful as a seasoning. Roasted cloves have less bite than raw cloves and may be eaten as a snack or side dish. Garlic foliage has a milder flavor than the bulbs. Harvest and chop leaves and add them to salads, dips, or garlic bread. Don't harvest too many leaaves from a single plant, though, because it will reduce bulb size. The blooms make attractive cut flowers.

GLOBE ARTICHOKE. See *Artichoke, Globe*
HARICOTS VERTS. See *Bean*
HONEYDEW. See *Melon*

Horseradish
Cabbage family. Perennial.
○ ◑ ✳

Characteristics. Height: 15 to 20 inches.

This cool-season perennial is grown for its fleshy roots, which are grated and used as a condiment or in sauces. Fresh, homegrown horseradish has a special pungency that cannot be found in store-bought horseradish. The plants produce enormous, coarse-textured leaves that emerge in the spring and die back in the fall. After the foliage dies back, you can dig up the roots and prepare them for use during the winter.

Horseradish thrives in regions with cold winters and does not perform well in the South. It is a vigorous grower and can become a troublesome weed in moist areas in the North. Growing horseradish as an annual—by digging up all the roots every fall and saving just a few for spring replanting—can help prevent the roots from spreading into areas where they do not belong.

How to Grow. Choose a location apart from annual vegetables, where the soil will not be disturbed every year. This crop prefers moist, deep, rich soil in full sun or partial shade. Plant in early spring, as soon as you can work the ground. Horseradish does not produce seed and can only be grown from root cuttings or crown divisions. Root cuttings are generally pencil-size side shoots taken from the main root; plant them on a slant, with the top 3 inches below the soil surface. (The end that was attached to the main root is considered the top.) Set them 18 inches apart in rows spaced 30 inches apart.

The plants prefer moist locations and need extra water during dry periods. They grow fastest in cool temperatures in spring and fall. When the largest leaves are 10 inches long, dig up the main root and gently remove the side roots on the top, but not on the bottom. Remove all but the best leaves on the crown of the plant, then replant the crown. Do this again after 6 weeks. This "lifting" will encourage production of the best-sized main roots.

Horseradish is generally trouble-free, although it may be attacked by flea beetles. Floating row covers can keep pests off the plants.

How to Harvest. Gather the roots when the foliage is killed by frost in the fall. Dig them up with a spade and store them in the refrigerator in an airtight plastic bag. To prepare horseradish, cut the roots into cubes. Put the cubes in a blender with a small amount of cold water and crushed ice; add 2 to 3 tablespoons of white vinegar and ½ teaspoon of salt. Blend the ingredients together, pour the mix in a jar with a tight lid, and store in the refrigerator.

Uses. Use the grated root as a condiment on sandwiches, or add it to dips or meat sauces.

HOT PEPPER. See *Pepper*

Jerusalem artichoke
Aster family. Perennial.
○

Characteristics. Height: 6 to 8 feet.

Jerusalem artichokes bear no resemblance to globe artichokes and have nothing to do with Jerusalem. They are tall, perennial, sunflower-like plants that produce edible tubers similar to potatoes. The tubers have a multitude of culinary uses, and can be used as a substitute for potatoes. The flowers are very pretty and look nice in fresh arrangements. The plants can become terrible weeds unless you grow them in a confined area; keep them away from regular garden beds where they could become a problem.

How to Grow. Jerusalem artichokes tolerate poor, dry soil, but they perform best in full sun and well-drained soil enriched with plenty of organic matter. Choose a location apart from annual vegetables, where the tall plants will not shade other sun-loving plants. Jerusalem artichokes are available as tubers rather than seed. Plant the tubers in early spring, as soon as you can work the soil. Set them 3 inches deep and 2 feet apart in rows spaced 3 feet apart. These plants are rarely bothered by pests and diseases, and are very easy to care for in the garden.

How to Harvest. The tubers are ready to harvest when the tops are killed by frost in the fall. In areas where the ground does not freeze hard, you can harvest the tubers all winter. Remove the tops and dig the tubers with a fork. Try to harvest all the tubers to prevent a serious weed problem the next year. The tubers do not store very well, so don't dig them up until you need them. If there are still some tubers in the soil when the ground begins to freeze, harvest them and keep them in moist peat in a root cellar or in plastic bags in the refrigerator.

Uses. Eat Jerusalem artichokes raw as a snack or in salads. They can be boiled, sautéed, stir-fried, creamed, or pickled. Try roasting them and serving them with hazelnut butter and maple syrup. The plants make attractive garden accents, and the flowers are good for cutting.

Kale
Cabbage family. Biennial grown as an annual.
○ ❄ ▼

Characteristics. Height: 12 to 16 inches.

Kale is a close relative of collards and cabbage. It tolerates frost and is usually grown as a fall crop; the first frost can sweeten the flavor of the slightly bitter leaves. The foliage is a handsome blue-green and has frilled or wavy edges, adding color and texture to the fall and winter garden. Kale is rich in vitamins A and C, and is a good source of fiber.

How to Grow. Kale prefers rich, well-drained soil in full sun. In most areas, sow seed in early summer for a fall crop. In areas with mild winters, sow in late summer for a winter crop. Space rows 18 to 24 inches apart. Thin the seedlings to 8 to 14 inch-

Kale 'Dwarf Blue'

es apart when they are large enough to handle. The thinnings make tasty additions to salads.

The plants may need extra water during dry periods. Kale is prone to the same pests and diseases as other cabbage family members. To prevent the buildup of diseases, avoid planting any of these crops in the same place 2 years in a row.

How to Harvest. If possible, wait until after the first frost to begin harvesting, since it can sweeten the flavor. Pick the outer leaves as needed, starting when they are about 6 to 8 inches long. Be sure to leave the central bud, which will keep producing new leaves. The plants may survive the winter in some areas.

Uses. Use kale as a substitute for lettuce in salads. It also makes a good substitute for cooked cabbage or collards. Kale is attractive in the fall and winter garden, adding color in containers or as an edging.

Kohlrabi
Cabbage family. Biennial grown as an annual.
○ ❄ ▼

Characteristics. Height: 8 to 12 inches.

This relative of kale and cabbage has a flavor similar to that of turnips. It is grown for its enlarged, bulblike stem, which grows above the ground. The leaves that grow out of the bulbous stem can be harvested when they are young and used as a substitute for spinach. The bulb may be light green with creamy white flesh or deep purple with greenish white flesh. The purple cultivars are pretty enough to leave in the garden in fall. 'White Vienna' is a popular white cultivar with tender, mild flesh and exceptional flavor. 'Purple Vienna' has purple skin and greenish white flesh.

How to Grow. Kohlrabi plants prefer rich, well-drained soil in full sun. You can plant this cool-season crop for a spring or fall harvest in the North, or for a winter harvest in the South. For a spring crop, sow the seed outside after danger of a hard frost; sow in midsummer for a fall crop, or in fall for a winter crop. Space the rows 12 to 18 inches apart. Thin the seedlings to 4 inches apart when they are large enough to handle. You can also grow kohlrabi in containers.

Kohlrabi 'Grand Duke'

The plants need at least 1 inch of water every week. They perform best when their growth is not interrupted by drought or very hot weather. In areas with hot summers, many gardeners grow kohlrabi as a fall crop. This relative of cabbage should be planted in a different spot every year to avoid the buildup of pest and disease problems.

How to Harvest. Kohlrabi is best when the bulbs are about 2 to 3 inches in diameter. If they are allowed to grow much larger, they can become tough and woody. Harvest the foliage when it is young and tender.

Uses. Try eating the stems fresh, like an apple. They can also be shredded as salad greens, sautéed, stir-fried, boiled, or steamed and served with a sauce as a side dish. The tops are edible; use them as salad greens or cook them as a substitute for spinach.

Leeks

Onion family. Biennial grown as an annual.

○ ❋

Characteristics. Height: 12 to 15 inches.

Leeks are closely related to onions but have a sweeter, creamier, more delicate flavor. They are prized by cooks as a flavoring for dishes of all types. They are also used to make a tasty soup, and are served cooked or raw as a side dish. Unlike onions, leeks do not form bulbs. Instead, they resemble giant-sized scallions. Because they take a long time to mature, they are usually harvested as a fall crop. They tolerate frost and can be left in the ground all winter, even in areas with cold winters. Leeks are easier to grow than garlic or onions and are gaining in popularity in American gardens. 'Broad London' is a mild-flavored leek that stores well; 'Titan' has extra-long stalks and sweet mellow flavor.

How to Grow. Leeks prefer deep, rich soil in full sun. Start the seed indoors 10 to 12 weeks before the last frost in spring. Transplant hardened-off seedlings to the garden after danger of a heavy frost has passed. Set the plants 4 to 6 inches apart in rows spaced 12 to 18 inches apart. In the South, you can sow seed directly in the garden in the fall for a spring harvest. Seedlings are sometimes available from garden centers in spring.

Leeks are heavy feeders and benefit from a sprinkling of 10-10-10 fertilizer 6 weeks after transplanting. When the plants are about the size of a pencil, wrap the base of the stalks with paper to blanch them. (Many gardeners heap soil around the base of the plants, but this can cause the stems to rot.) Thrips may be a problem during prolonged periods of drought; water as needed so the soil is evenly moist and the plants stay vigorous. To avoid common pest and disease problems, avoid planting leeks and other onion family members in the same place 2 years in a row.

How to Harvest. Leeks are ready to harvest when the base of the stalks is ³⁄₄ inch to 2 inches in diameter. Use a trowel or spade to sever the roots under the stalks. Gently twist the stalks back and forth to loosen them and ease them out of the ground. Cut off the remaining roots and all but 2 inches of the leaves. Take only what you need each time, and leave the rest for winter harvest. Mulch leeks heavily in areas with cold winters, and harvest them during the winter when the ground is not frozen. If any are left in spring, harvest them as soon as the ground thaws, or let them bloom.

Uses. Use leeks to make a hot or cold soup, as a flavoring for meat and vegetable dishes, or pureed and served as a side dish or as a stuffing for tomatoes. They can be braised, or served cold with a vinaigrette dressing. The flowers are good for cutting and are also edible.

*Lettuce types: 'Great Lakes' Iceberg, 'Burpee Bibb',
'Paris Island' Cos or Romaine, and Leaf Lettuce*

Lettuce
Aster family. Annual.
○ ◑ ❄ ▼

Characteristics. Height: 9 to 15 inches.

Lettuce is one of the easiest vegetables to grow. It thrives in full sun or partial shade, in the garden or in containers. It also grows quickly, and pests and diseases are usually not a problem. Lettuce foliage can be sweet or slightly bitter; it may be bright red, yellowish white, or light to deep green, with smooth, curled, frilled, or deeply lobed edges. Lettuce is an important source of fiber and is high in vitamins A and C, as well as calcium. Some cultivars are also high in iron.

There are four major types of garden lettuce. Iceberg, or crisphead, lettuce is the closest to the round heads of pale green salad lettuce found in supermarkets. The foliage is thin and crisp, and the heads are firm and round. The leaves blanch to a creamy white in the middle. Their maturity season is relatively long—80 to 90 days from seed. Burpee introduced one of the most popular cultivars, 'Iceberg', in 1894.

Butterhead, or bibb, lettuce forms looser, softer heads than crisphead types, and the foliage has a more delicate flavor. Butterhead types are also more heat-tolerant, and their foliage is more easily bruised. The inner leaves are a creamy yellow, and the outer leaves are medium to dark green. Butterhead lettuce matures in 45 to 75 days. It is higher in iron than other types of lettuce. 'Buttercrunch' is an All-America Selections winner that has a luscious, buttery texture and tolerates high temperatures.

Cos, or romaine, lettuce has an upright habit and long, loose leaves. The outer leaves are green and the inner leaves are creamy white. Romaine lettuce matures in 65 to 70 days. It is the most nutritious type of lettuce, as well as the most shade-tolerant. 'Parris Island Cos' is a classic cultivar with thick, crisp leaves that tolerate high temperatures.

Leaf, or loosehead lettuce, does not form heads. Its leaves can be curly, deeply lobed, serrated, or savoyed (wrinkled). Some cultivars are bright red and look attractive in containers or window boxes. 'Oak Leaf' has deeply cut foliage that resembles the leaves of a white oak tree. 'Black-Seeded Simpson' was introduced by Burpee in 1879 and is still popular today. It has light green, frilly leaves. 'Red Salad Bowl' has deeply cut burgundy leaves and is heat-resistant. Looseleaf types mature in 45 to 50 days and are more tolerant of high temperatures than other types.

How to Grow. Lettuce prefers rich, well-drained soil in full sun or light shade. It is a cool-season vegetable that "bolts," or forms flowers and seeds, in high temperatures. The leaf edges also burn in hot weather. Once lettuce bolts, the leaves turn bitter.

Sow seed directly in the garden in early spring, after danger of a heavy frost. For a fall crop in the North, sow in late summer, after the worst of the summer heat is over. (Lettuce will not germinate in high temperatures.) You can start the seeds indoors if conditions there are cooler; transplant the seedlings when outside temperatures cool down. For a winter crop in the South, sow in the fall. Space the rows 12 to 18 inches apart. Thin the plants or set the transplants to stand 4 to 6 inches apart for leaf types, 6 to 8 inches apart for romaine and butterhead types, and 10 to 12 inches apart for crisphead types.

Keep plants well watered during dry periods to promote rapid, uninterrupted growth. Lettuce does not have many pest and disease problems, although slugs and cabbageworms may be troublesome; hand-pick these pests. Lettuce is shallow-rooted, so avoid disturbing the soil around the plants when weeding.

How to Harvest. Pick crisphead types when the heads are firm. Harvest loosehead types anytime the leaves are large enough to use. Harvest romaine and butterhead types when they have formed heads and the leaves are a good size. Cut the heads below the crown. On leaf types, you can just pick a few leaves at a time, if you like.

Uses. Lettuce is the classic ingredient in salads. It adds crispness to sandwiches and can be used as a garnish, braised, or added to soups. Many of the loosehead cultivars are decorative in the garden.

LIMA BEAN. See *Bean*

Melon
Squash family. Annual.

○ ✳

Characteristics. Height: 1 to 2 feet; vines spread to 9 feet or more.

Melons—including cantaloupes, winter melons, and watermelons—are popular garden crops that grow on vining plants, which can spread out over the garden or be trained up a trellis or other support.

Honeydew melon 'Venus Hybrid'

Cantaloupes are a delight both to taste and to smell. The fragrance of ripe cantaloupe is second only to quince in sheer ambrosial quality. In fact, cantaloupes are also called muskmelons (for their delicious, musky fragrance), and one of the most popular cultivars is 'Ambrosia'. The flavor of the extra-sweet, juicy flesh is never a disappointment, and the skin has a special beauty of its own: finely textured, intricately netted, and the color of dried grass with a hint of green, with evenly spaced ridges that look like the latitude lines on a world globe. The plants are vining, although bush types, such as 'Sweet Bush Hybrid' and 'Honeybush', are also available.

Winter melons are so called because they have a longer season of maturity. They generally have smooth skin and lack the aroma of cantaloupe. Honeydews have pale green flesh; crenshaws have salmon-pink flesh. Exotic melons, such as 'Early Silver Line', can have bright yellow skin and crisp white flesh. 'Sunrise' has canary yellow skin and sweet white flesh.

Watermelons are practically symbolic of summertime. Their refreshing, vivid red flesh is a common sight at summer barbecues, especially on the Fourth of July and Labor Day. The fruits are large—from 12-pound "ice box" types to giant, 200-pound monsters. Some cultivars have beautiful lemon yellow flesh and a slightly milder flavor. The large black seeds are considered by some to be the one drawback of watermelons, since they are difficult to dispose of discreetly. "Seedless" cultivars have been developed, including 'Redball Seedless', which may have a few small, edible white seeds. Watermelons generally take a long time to mature, although faster-maturing cultivars are available for northern gardens. Bush types are also available, including 'Bush Sugar Baby'.

How to Grow. All melons are warm-season crops that prefer rich, warm soil in full sun. In long-season areas, sow the seed directly in the garden after all danger of frost. In areas with shorter seasons, sow the seed indoors 3 to 4 weeks before the last frost date; transplant hardened-off seedlings to the garden after the danger of frost has passed. Sow the seeds 1 to 1½ inches deep, and thin the seedlings or set the transplants to stand 1 foot apart. Grow melons in rows spaced 3 to 4 feet apart or in "hills," with groups of 2 plants every 3 feet or 3 plants every 4 feet. You can also train melons on a fence or trellis, as long as it is strong enough to support the weight of the fruit.

Melons have the same cultural requirements as cucumbers. They appreciate ample water during dry periods and a side-dressing of 5-10-5 fertilizer after they begin to vine. They are normally pollinated by bees, but you can also hand-pollinate the flowers as you would for cucumbers, if fruits aren't forming. Long spells of cloudy weather occasionally cause the fruit to taste bitter. Melons are subject to the same pests and diseases as cucumbers, so avoid planting these and other squash family members in the same place 2 years in a row.

How to Harvest. All melons should be allowed to ripen on the vine. Cantaloupes have a delicious aroma when they are mature. The fruit color changes from green to yellow or tan, and the fruit generally breaks away (or "slips") easily from the vine with only slight pressure. (Some cultivars do not exhibit this "full slip" quality; cut them off the vine when they have the right aroma and the blossom end is soft.) Winter melons are ready when they turn the appropriate color and the blossom end is soft. The undersides of watermelons turn from white to yellow when they are ready to harvest, and the tendrils closest to the fruit turn brown and dry up. The skin becomes dull and hard, and the fruit should make a dull "thudding" sound when tapped.

Uses. Melons make delicious, refreshing snacks in hot summer weather. Serve them as breakfast foods, as a side dish for lunch, or as a dessert for dinner. Cut them into cubes or scoop them with a melon baller for fruit salads. Watermelon rinds can be pickled.

MUNG BEAN. See *Bean*

Mustard
Cabbage family. Annual.
○ ❄

Characteristics. Height: 15 to 18 inches.

This fast-maturing relative of collards and cabbage is grown for its foliage, which has a pungent, tangy flavor. (The mustard seed used to make the condiment added to Middle Eastern and Indian dishes is a different species, and is not commonly grown in home gardens.) Use the immature greens raw as a substitute for lettuce or spinach in a salad, or allow them to mature and cook them as you would cabbage or collard greens. Mustard is an excellent source of fiber and is rich in calcium, iron, and potassium.

How to Grow. Mustard appreciates rich, well-drained soil in full sun. This cool-season vegetable can be planted as a spring or fall crop in the North and as a winter crop in the South. For a spring crop, sow the seed directly in the garden after danger of a heavy frost; sow in August for a fall crop. Space the rows 15 to 24 inches apart, and thin the seedlings to 12 inches apart when they are large enough to handle. For a continuous supply, sow small amounts at 2-week intervals until the weather turns warm.

Water well in dry weather. Prolonged periods of warm temperatures will cause the plants to produce a seed stalk; pull out these plants. To prevent the buildup of diseases, avoid planting mustard and other cabbage family crops in the same place for 2 years in a row. Mustard is sometimes bothered by aphids and cabbageworms; use floating row covers to protect the plants from these pests.

How to Harvest. Begin to harvest the young foliage for salad greens when it is 6 to 8 inches long. Pick the lower leaves as needed, or harvest the whole plant at once. Pick the foliage before it becomes tough.

Uses. Use young mustard greens in salads, or wait until they mature and use them as cooked greens. The foliage can be boiled, sautéed, or added as a flavoring to broths.

Okra
Mallow family. Tender perennial
grown as an annual.
○ ❋

Characteristics. Height: 2 to 7 feet.

Okra is one of the prettiest vegetables you can grow. It is related to hollyhock and has gorgeous, single, hibiscus-like flowers that look more at home in the flower garden than in the vegetable garden. The plants are tender perennials that are usually grown as annuals. They produce long, narrow seedpods that may be round or ridged, with or without spines, in green, red, burgundy, or purple. They are rich in vitamin A. The leaves are also edible and are high in vitamins A and C, protein, calcium, and iron. 'Clemson Spineless' is an All-America Selections winner that produces dark green, spineless pods on 4-foot plants. 'Annie Oakley Hybrid' is the first hybrid okra cultivar that produces spineless pods on 5-foot plants 52 days after sowing.

How to Grow. Okra is a warm-season crop that prefers rich, well-drained soil in full sun. Sow seed directly in the garden after all danger of frost, when the temperatures remain warm. Space the rows 3 to 5 feet apart (depending on the cultivar), and thin the seedlings to 1 to 2 feet apart when they are large enough to handle. Plant taller cultivars at the northern edge of the garden so they won't shade other crops. The plants need 1 to 1½ inches of water every week. Grow okra in a different area every year to avoid the buildup of pest and disease problems.

How to Harvest. Pick the pods when they are young and 2 to 3 inches long. Keep harvesting the pods every other day to encourage continuous production. Cut them from the stem just above the cap with a sharp knife. You can store the pods for several days in the refrigerator in a plastic bag.

Uses. Use the pods to thicken soups, stews, ketchup sauces, and relishes, or to make gumbo. Okra can also be stewed or sautéed and served as a side dish.

Onion
Onion family. Biennial grown as an annual.
○ ❄

Characteristics. Height: 10 inches.

No kitchen would be complete without onions for flavoring a wide variety of cooked or raw dishes, including salads, stuffings, soups, stews, and omelettes. Use them on sandwiches, for onion rings, add them to casseroles, or cooked as a side dish. Indeed, it is difficult to think of a meal in which onions would be out of place.

Onions vary in size from large, 4-inch-wide, globe-shaped bulbs to small "pearl" types measuring less than 1 inch in diameter. They can be white, yellow, or red, and globe-shaped, oval, flattened, or shaped like a lemon. Green onions, or scallions, can

Onion sets for 'Red Hamburger', 'White Bermuda', and 'Yellow Globe'

be either harvested as immature onions or grown from cultivars that do not produce bulbs. 'Walla Walla Sweet' produces 4-inch, flattened globe-shaped bulbs with sweet, yellow flesh. 'Granex', the popular Vidalia onion from southern Georgia, produces large, flat bulbs with yellow skin and mild white flesh. 'Crystal Wax Pickling PRR', a pearl-type onion, produces creamy white, round, ½- to ¾-inch onions that are perfect for pickling.

The formation of onion bulbs is triggered by day length. Long-day cultivars form bulbs when the day length is more than 13 hours; they are best suited for northern gardens. Short-day cultivars form bulbs when the day is less than 13 hours long; they are suitable for growing in the South.

How to Grow. Because onions are grown for their underground bulbs, they require deep, well-drained soil free of stones and enriched with organic matter. They also need full sun. You can grow onions from seed, plants, or sets.

Seeds take from 100 to 300 days to mature. Start them indoors 8 to 10 weeks before the last frost in spring. Make sure the seedlings receive plenty of sunlight, and supplement a sunny windowsill with plant lights to offset cloudy weather. Transplant hardened-off seedlings outside after the danger of heavy frost has passed. Set the plants 2 to 3 inches apart in rows spaced 12 to 16 inches apart.

Onion plants are available for spring or fall planting. In the North, set them out in early spring as soon as you can work the soil; in the South, plant them in the fall for a spring harvest. Set them 1 to 1½ inches deep and 3 inches apart.

Onion sets are small, dry onions that have already begun to form bulbs. They produce full-size onions in about 85 days. In the North, plant them as soon as you can work the soil; in the South, plant them in the fall.

Onions are heavy feeders and appreciate a scattering of 10-10-10 fertilizer twice during the season. They do not compete well with weeds for water and nutrients in the soil, so weed regularly. These vegetables can be grown successfully in containers. To prevent the buildup of diseases and pests, avoid planting onions and other onion family members in the same place 2 years in a row.

How to Harvest. Pick green onions when the plants are 6 to 8 inches tall. For bulbous onions, gently bend the tops over when about one-quarter of the tops have already fallen over and turned yellow naturally. Avoid nicking or breaking the bulbs, or diseases and insects may enter the wounds. After a few days, pull the bulbs and cover them with the foliage to prevent sunburn. Allow them to dry in the garden for up to a week, then cure them indoors in a warm, dry place with good air circulation for 2 to 3 weeks. After curing them cut off the foliage, leaving 1 inch above the top of the bulb. Place the bulbs in mesh onion bags or old panty hose and store them in a cool, dry location.

Uses. Onions can be sliced into rings or chopped into small pieces and used as a garnish, condiment, or salad ingredient. Raw or sautéed onions make a tasty topping for sandwiches or hamburgers. The larger cultivars can be used to make deep-fried onion rings, and the smaller pearl types may be creamed and served as a side dish. You can also pickle onions. Add scallions to salads, soups, or stir-fried dishes. Onion foliage is also edible, as are the flowers (before they become dry).

ORNAMENTAL CORN. See *Corn*

Parsnip
Carrot family. Biennial grown as an annual.

Characteristics. Height: 10 to 15 inches.

Parsnips deserve to be planted more in American gardens. Devotees who know of their unmatched sweet, chestnutty flavor can hardly get enough of them when they are available in fall and winter. These tasty vegetables can be prepared in many ways and can improve any dish to which they are added. Like carrots, parsnips are grown for their long, tapering roots, which are a creamy tan color and have a fine-grained, snowy white interior. They grow best in cool temperatures and are usually harvested in the fall, after frost sweetens their flavor. 'Hollow Crown' is one of the more popular cultivars. It produces 12-inch-long roots that are 2¾ inches thick at the shoulders and have no side roots. The flesh is fine-grained and has a sweet, nutty flavor.

How to Grow. This crop requires deep, rich, stone-free soil and full sun. If your soil is heavy or rocky, you can grow parsnips in deep containers. In the North, sow seed in the spring after danger of heavy frost, when the weather is somewhat settled. In the South, sow in the fall and harvest before the hot weather of midsummer. The seed should not be more than 1 year old, as it loses its viability quickly. Sow in rows spaced 18 inches apart, and thin the seedlings to 3 inches apart when they are large enough to handle.

As long as you give parsnips good soil, they are fairly easy to care for and are rarely bothered by pests and diseases.

How to Harvest. Frost sweetens the flavor of parsnips, so if possible, wait until after a light frost to begin harvesting. (They can, however, become tough and woody if left too long in the ground.) Parsnips will stop growing after frost and can be harvested all winter long when the ground is not frozen. In areas with severe winters, mulch the area in early winter to keep the ground from freezing as long as possible. If there are still some parsnips left in the ground in spring, harvest them as soon as possible before they begin to grow again.

Uses. Raw parsnips can be shredded and added to salads, or sliced and served with dips. Parsnips are most often prepared as cooked vegetables, however. Try them shredded, sliced, chopped, or diced, then sautéed in olive oil with carrots or by themselves. Or boil, steam, grill, or roast them—you can even bake them to make terrific potato pancakes, or fry or mash them. Parsnips are also used to add flavor to blander-tasting potatoes. They are especially tasty when pureed and combined with roasted garlic and chestnuts, or when mixed with carrots and apple cider. Try them as a side dish, mixed with different herbs and spices.

Snap Peas

Pea
Bean family. Annual.
○ ❊ ▼

Characteristics. Height: 18 inches to 8 feet or more for vining types.

Only home gardeners and their lucky friends really know how delicious homegrown garden peas can be. Peas lose their freshness soon after harvest, so store-bought peas are never as fresh and sweet as homegrown ones. Peas are produced on either bushy plants or vines. They can adapt well to life in containers. Three types that are commonly grown in American gardens are garden peas, edible-podded peas, and snap peas.

Garden, or English, peas are harvested after the seeds mature and are shelled from their inedible pods. The pods range from 3 to 4½ inches long and contain 7 to 12 peas. The seeds can be small

and tender, as in the French 'Petit Provencal', or large, like those of 'Burpeeana Early'.

Edible-podded peas—generally known as snow, sugar, or China peas—are grown for their crunchy, succulent, flat pods, which contain immature peas. If you don't harvest them early enough, you can shell them and prepare them as you would garden peas. They may be stir-fried, steamed, or eaten fresh, and are frequently included in Oriental dishes.

Snap peas are a fairly recent development in pea breeding. They are harvested when the seeds are mature and when the pods are thick and fleshy. The peas are sweet and crunchy and can be eaten raw or cooked. The pods are also edible. Snap peas freeze well but are not recommended for canning. 'Sugar Snap' is one of the most popular cultivars and has the distinction of being a Number-One All-Time All-America Selections vegetable winner.

How to Grow. These cool-season vegetables prefer rich, well-drained soil in full sun. In the North, you can plant them as early as St. Patrick's Day, if the weather is fairly warm. (If the soil is too cold, the seeds will take a long time to germinate and can rot in the soil.) In the South, grow peas as a winter crop. Bush cultivars are self-supporting; vining cultivars climb by tendrils, so put a trellis in place before planting. To encourage earlier germination, soak the seed overnight before planting. Sow the seeds 2 inches deep in rows spaced 18 inches apart. Thin the seedlings to 8 to 10 inches apart when they are large enough to handle.

Peas may need extra water under dry conditions, but they often mature before dry weather sets in. They do not perform well in overly wet conditions, and the seeds can rot in wet soil before they germinate. The plants do not normally require fertilizer. However, as with beans and other legumes, certain bacteria must be present in the soil for the peas to grow vigorously, so coat untreated seed with an inoculant (readily available from seed companies). After you have grown peas once, the bacteria can survive in the soil.

This crop is susceptible to various diseases and pests, but disease-resistant cultivars are available. Check with your local Cooperative Extension Service office to find out which problems are common in your area and which cultivars perform best.

How to Harvest. Pick garden peas when the pods are well filled but not dry or faded in color. For the freshest peas, pick as close to mealtime as possible. Pull the pods from the plants with care to avoid damaging the plants. The peas do not all ripen at the same time and may require several harvests. Freeze extras before the end of the harvest season.

Edible-podded peas are ready to harvest when the pods are 3 to 5 inches long (depending on the cultivar) and before the peas inside mature. They are usually ready about a week after the flowers bloom. Edible-podded peas must be picked frequently, or they will become overripe. If they swell too much, harvest and shell them as you would garden peas.

Pick snap peas when they are plump and the full size for the cultivar.

Uses. Shell garden peas, then steam or boil them; enjoy them alone, or combine them with other vegetables as a side dish. Many cultivars are good for freezing. Edible-podded peas can be stir-fried, steamed, boiled, sautéed, or eaten raw. Steam snap peas, or use them for dips or stir-fries.

Peanut
Bean family. Annual.
○ ☀

Characteristics. Height: 3 to 4 feet.

Peanuts, which are related to peas and beans, form hard seeds in shells underground. They require 4 months of reliably warm temperatures to mature and are normally grown only in the South. The plants produce yellow flowers, which send "pegs" down into the soil after they are pollinated. The pegs mature into the hard-shelled fruits and seeds we know as "peanuts." Virginia peanuts have 1 or 2 seeds in each pod; Spanish types produce 2 or 3 seeds per pod.

How to Grow. Peanuts need full sun and rich, deep, well-drained soil that is free of stones. Sufficient calcium is important to prevent empty shells, so add lime or gypsum if a soil test indicates a deficiency. This warm-season crop cannot tolerate cold temperatures. Sow seed 1 to 2 inches deep when all danger of frost has passed and the weather is warm. Space rows of Spanish types 2 feet apart, and thin plants to 6 inches apart in the rows. Thin Virginia types to 8 inches apart in rows spaced 3 feet apart.

The plants may need extra water when they are flowering and sending down pegs. However, too much water near harvesttime can cause the "nuts," or seeds, to sprout underground. Peanuts are susceptible to corn earworms, cutworms, and various caterpillars. The stems, roots, and pods are all susceptible to stem rot diseases. Plant peanuts in a different spot each year to help prevent disease problems. Floating row covers can keep pests off the plants.

How to Harvest. Harvest the plants when their leaves begin to turn yellow, before freezing weather. Dig up the entire plants and allow them to cure in a warm, dry area for 2 weeks, then shell the pods.

Uses. Roast shelled peanuts for a snack. Cooked or raw, they add crunch and flavor to hot or cold dishes with meats or vegetables. Peanut soup is delicious, and peanut butter is a classic for sandwiches or crackers.

Pepper
Tomato family. Annual.
○ ☀ ▼

Characteristics. Height: 2 to 2½ feet.

Whole seed companies, cookbooks, and gardens are devoted to peppers, and pepper fanciers can be among the most fanatical of vegetable gardeners.

Hot peppers, mixed types

There is a wide range of types to choose from, including sweet and hot peppers in red, green, yellow, purple, lilac, and orange. These popular vegetables also come in many shapes, sizes, flavors, and maturity dates. Many are pretty enough to grow in the flower garden, and the fruits make attractive table decorations before they are eaten. All peppers are rich in vitamin C and carotene, and are a good source of fiber.

Sweet bell peppers are blocky in shape, with thick walls that make them good for stuffing. They can be elongated or nearly cube-shaped. They may be huge (up to 6 inches long and 5 inches across) or tiny (just 2 inches long and 1¼ inches across). Green peppers are actually red, yellow, or purple peppers that are harvested before they turn their characteristic color.

Hot peppers can be bell-shaped, round like cherry tomatoes, or long and slender. They may be red or green and have varying degrees of heat. 'Habanero' is a blocky, extra-super-hot type. Cayenne types are long, slim, and slightly curved; they grow from 2 to 12 inches long. Chili types are long and slim and grow about 3 inches long. All-America Selections winner 'Mexi Bell Hybrid' is the first hot bell-shaped pepper.

How to Grow. Peppers prefer rich, well-drained soil in full sun. Start seed indoors 8 to 10 weeks before the last frost in spring. Set the plants outside in the garden after all danger of frost has passed and the weather is warm. Space the plants 18 inches apart in rows spaced 2 feet apart. They are also easy to grow in containers.

Peppers need 1½ inches of water every week. They appreciate watering in dry periods and an extra feeding with 5-10-5 fertilizer as the fruits begin to form. Peppers are subject to the same pests and diseases as tomatoes and eggplants. To prevent the buildup of diseases, avoid planting peppers and other tomato family crops in the same place 2 years in a row. To prevent the spread of tobacco mosaic virus, smokers should avoid handling the plants.

How to Harvest. Pick the fruits when they are the proper size and color for the cultivar. Break or cut off the fruit with a bit of stem attached. Hot peppers can be dried and strung together for handy kitchen use.

Uses. Enjoy raw sweet peppers in salads, for dipping, as a crunchy hors d'oeuvre, or sliced and added to sandwiches. They can also be grilled, sautéed, stir-fried, roasted, stuffed and baked, or added to soups, stews, and sauces. Use hot types carefully to spice up many dishes. Hot peppers can also be pickled. Always use rubber gloves when preparing hot peppers, as they can burn cuts on your hands. Be especially careful not to touch your face when handling hot peppers; the hottest types will cause severe burning in your eyes and nose.

POPCORN. See *Corn*

Pepper 'Yellow Cayenne'

Potato
Tomato family. Annual.
○ ❀ ▼

Characteristics. Height: 18 to 24 inches.

The potato is one of the most important staple foods in our diet. It is rich in vitamins B and C, potassium, protein, complex carbohydrates, and fiber. Potatoes can be prepared so many ways that you can eat them every day for a year and not grow tired of them. They have a delicious flavor of their own, yet they also blend well with herbs, spices, sauces, and stronger-flavored vegetables and meats. When you grow potatoes at home, you get the

Potatoes 'Kennebec' and 'Red Pontiac'

added treat of harvesting fresh new potatoes in mid-summer.

Many kinds of potatoes are available, including standard white-fleshed baking types and heirloom types with blue, yellow, pink, or white flesh. Potatoes can be round, elongated, oval-shaped, or narrow "fingerling" types that can be 2 to 5 inches in length. They can have red or tan skins. 'Yukon Gold' has a light yellow skin and golden yellow flesh that tastes as though it has been smothered in butter. 'Kennebec' is a popular all-purpose, white-fleshed potato that is resistant to late blight. 'Red Pontiac' is a red-skinned cultivar that performs well in heavy soil.

How to Grow. Potatoes are thickened underground stems called tubers. For good tuber development, potatoes require deep, loose, well-drained soil that is free of stones. They also need full sun for the tops of the plants to grow well. Seed companies and garden centers sell "seed potatoes"—tubers with buds (called "eyes")—for planting in spring. Always purchase certified disease-free tubers to avoid disease problems. (Don't buy grocery-store potatoes for planting; they are chemically treated to prevent sprouting.) Plant the tubers as soon as you receive them, after danger of heavy frost in spring in the North, and in fall through February in the South. Either plant the tubers whole, or cut them into pieces with 2 or 3 "eyes" each and spread them out in a well-ventilated place to dry for 24 hours before planting. Plant them with the eyes up, 2 to 3 inches deep and 10 to 12 inches apart in rows spaced 2 feet apart.

The tops of the developing tubers should not be exposed to sunlight, or they will turn green. (Green patches on potato tubers are poisonous and should be discarded.) When the plants are about 5 to 6 inches tall, begin to heap soil around the base of the stems, or surround the plants with a thick layer of mulch. Potatoes need regular watering throughout the season. If their growth slows due to dry weather and then starts again in wet weather, the tubers can form knobs. The tubers can also develop cavities inside when the plants don't have a consistent supply of water.

Potatoes are subject to various pests and diseases. Plant only certified disease-free stock to prevent serious potato diseases. To avoid the buildup of soil-borne diseases, avoid planting potatoes and other tomato family members in the same spot 2 years in a row. One of the worst pests of potatoes is the Colorado potato beetle, a small orange-and-white-striped insect. Many gardeners plant their potatoes as early as possible so that the plants are a fairly good size before the beetles are a problem. (Vigorous plants are better able to survive an attack.) Covering plants with floating row covers can also protect them from pests.

How to Harvest. For "new" potatoes, harvest about 10 weeks after planting. When potato blossoms appear, it is a sign that the frist new potatoes are ready for harvest, simply feel around in the soil with your fingers for the small tubers. Try not to damage the roots of the plant or you may reduce the main harvest.

Harvest mature potatoes after the tops die back and before the first frost. Dig carefully to avoid damaging the tubers. After harvesting mature potatoes, store them in a dark, dry place for a week at 65° to 70°F. Then store them at 35° to 40°F at fairly high humidity. Some cultivars store better than others; if you know you will be storing your potatoes, choose suitable cultivars. Potatoes do not freeze well.

Uses. The culinary uses of potatoes are limited only by your imagination. They can be boiled, baked, roasted, deep-fried, grilled, sautéed, stir-fried, braised, glazed, mashed, creamed, or scalloped. Enjoy them as a soup or side dish; stuff them, make them into a soufflé, or combine them with other vegetables or meats in soups, stews, breads, or casseroles. They can also be made into potato chips, potato pancakes, or hash browns.

Pumpkin 'Prize Winner'

Pumpkin
Squash family. Annual.
○ ✳

Characteristics. Height: 1 to 2 feet; vines spread to 10 feet or more.

A front doorstep decorated with pumpkins—combined with chrysanthemums and ornamental corn—is as symbolic of the fall season as holiday greens are of the Christmas season. But pumpkins are also prized for their delicious, coarse-grained flesh, which can be used to make pies, breads, muffins, and soups. The seeds make great snacks when they are roasted. One cultivar, 'Triple Treat', is named for the three main uses of pumpkins: carving, pies, and seed.

Pumpkins are actually winter squashes and are produced on spreading vines. The fruits vary in size from miniature 'Jack Be Little' pumpkins, which grow 3 inches across and 2 inches high, to 'Atlantic Giant', which can weigh over 700 pounds but usually ranges from 300 to 400 pounds. Pumpkins can be round or oblong, with black or tan stems. The outer skin is traditionally orange, but the cultivar 'Lumina' has white skin.

When choosing a cultivar to grow, think of what you want to do with your pumpkins. If you want to carve jack- o'-lanterns, choose a round cultivar about 10 to 12 inches across, such as 'Jack o'Lantern'. If you want to cook pies, choose a sweet cultivar, such as 'Small Sugar'. Choose 'Prizewinner Hybrid' if you want to win a prize for growing the largest pumpkin. If you do not have a huge garden, choose 'Bushkin', which produces 10-pound fruits on 6-foot vines.

How to Grow. This warm-season crop needs space, plenty of sun, and well-drained, fertile soil. If the fruit will not be very heavy, you can train the vines on a trellis to save space. Large-fruited cultivars need lots of room to ramble. In long-season areas, plant the seed directly in the garden after all danger of frost, when the weather is warm. In short-summer areas, choose a fast-maturing cultivar and plant the seed outdoors, or start plants indoors 3 to 4 weeks before the last frost date and transplant the seedlings to the garden after all danger of frost. Sow the seed 2 inches deep. Thin the seedlings or space the transplants so that you have groups of 3 plants every 5 to 10 feet. Bush types can grow closer together, with 1 plant every 3 feet.

Pumpkins need plenty of water and fertilizer through their long growing season. Like their close relatives, cucumbers and melons, they produce male and female flowers on the same plant. You can hand-pollinate the flowers as you would for cucumbers if the bees aren't doing their job. If you are trying to grow extra-large pumpkins, allow only one fruit per plant to mature. To prevent the buildup of diseases, avoid planting pumpkins and other squash family crops in the same spot 2 years in a row.

How to Harvest. Pumpkins are ready to harvest when the rinds are hard and the proper shade of orange or white for the cultivar. Sometimes the vines are killed by light frost before the pumpkins are harvested; cut the fruits from the vines—with 3 to 4 inches of stem attached—before they are damaged by heavy frost. Pumpkins can be stored for weeks or months in a warm, dry place at 50° to 60°F.

Uses. Use the flesh for baked pies, soups, casseroles, muffins, or bread. Or cook pumpkin as you would winter squash, and serve as a side dish. Roast the seeds for a tasty snack. The flowers are also edible and can be dipped in batter and deep-fried, stir-fried, or sautéed. Pumpkins are important autumn decorations: Leave them unadorned, paint them, or carve them for jack-o'-lanterns.

RADICCHIO. See *Chicory*

*Radish 'French Breakfast', 'Cherry Belle',
and 'White Icicle'*

Radish
Cabbage family. Biennial grown as an annual.

○ ◐ ❋ ▼

Characteristics. Height: 4 to 6 inches.

Radishes are one of the easiest and fastest vegetables you can grow, making them a good crop for children and other beginning gardeners. They require little care, are rarely bothered by pests and diseases, and even perform well in containers or window boxes. They are one of the first vegetables you plant in spring, and one of the first to be harvested. Besides providing a quick, tasty crop, radishes are also useful for marking vegetables that are slower to germinate, such as carrots. (To use radishes to mark a crop, just mix seeds of the two crops together and sow them together.) As a trap crop, radishes can entice insects away from other vegetables in the garden.

Radishes come in many sizes, shapes, colors, and flavors. Most have a pungent, tangy flavor, although milder cultivars, such as 'French Breakfast', are available. They can be long and narrow, such as 'White Icicle'; short, round, and bright red, such as 'Cherry Belle'; or flat and white, such as 'Burpee White'. Some oval kinds, such as 'Easter Egg', come in shades of purple, lavender, pink, scarlet, and white. Oriental, or daikon, types produce long, narrow roots that can weigh up to 50 pounds.

How to Grow. This cool-season crop needs full sun to light shade and deep, well-drained soil that is free of stones. In the North, grow radishes as spring and fall crops; in the South, grow them as a winter crop. Spring radishes grow quickly; you can plant them in early spring after danger of a heavy frost and harvest them about a month later. Plant winter radishes in midsummer or fall for a fall or winter crop. (The winter types are slower to mature and generally have a stronger, more pungent flavor.) Oriental, or daikon, types are usually grown as a fall crop.

Sow radish seed ½ inch deep in rows spaced 12 inches apart. Thin the seedlings of standard types to stand 1 to 3 inches apart, depending on the cultivar. Thin the seedlings of large-rooted types to stand 4 to 6 inches apart, depending on the cultivar.

Too-fertile soil or too much fertilization can cause excess foliage to grow at the expense of root development. In warm temperatures, radishes grow slowly and may produce seed stalks. If you can provide good soil, cool temperatures, and even, continuous watering, you should have high-quality radishes with few problems.

How to Harvest. Pull spring radishes when they are the proper size for the cultivar. Finish the harvest before warm weather sets in, and before the roots become woody and pithy. Store them in plastic bags in the refrigerator for up to 3 weeks with their tops cut off. Harvest winter or fall radishes as needed in the fall. Dig all remaining roots before the ground freezes, and store them as you would carrots or beets until needed during the winter.

Uses. Radishes are tasty served raw and dipped in salt. They make beautiful garnishes when they are carved to look like roses. Stuff them for hors d'oeuvres, or cut them up and add them to salads. Most radishes, especially the Oriental (daikon) types, can be used as a substitute for turnips. They also make a great snack-while-you-garden crop.

Rhubarb

Rhubarb
Buckwheat family. Perennial.
○ ◑ ❀

Characteristics. Height: 18 to 36 inches.

Rhubarb is a perennial vegetable grown for its juicy leafstalks, which have a tart, tangy flavor. The leafstalks grow up to 22 inches long and can be green or red; the red cultivars are the sweetest and the most prized by gardeners and cooks. The plants look dramatic in the garden, with their large, coarse-textured leaves and colorful leafstalks.

This hardy, cool-season perennial grows without a great deal of care in areas where the ground freezes in winter. It does not perform as well in the South. The plants can be productive for more than 10 years in favorable conditions. Rhubarb foliage is highly toxic; be sure to discard it when you harvest the stalks.

How to Grow. Rhubarb prefers deep, rich, well-drained soil in full sun or light shade. As a perennial, it should be kept apart from annual vegetables; otherwise, it is easy to damage the plants by mistake when you dig or till the garden in spring. It is grown from roots rather than seed. Plant the roots in early spring, with their tops 2 inches below the soil surface. Space the plants 3 feet apart.

The plants are heavy feeders and appreciate a scattering of 10-10-10 fertilizer or an organic mulch in spring. They need adequate water in dry weather

during the growing season. If they produce a seed stalk, cut it off at the base, as seed production weakens the plants. Some gardeners surround the developing plants with cardboard boxes to encourage the leafstalks to stretch and become longer.

How to Harvest. Do not harvest from your plants the year you set them out. The second year, you can harvest for 2 weeks; the third year, harvest for 6 weeks. After that, you can harvest until the stalks become thinner. Always leave at least one-third of the leafstalks on each plant to avoid weakening the plants too much. After you pick the stalks, remove the leaves and discard them. Do not harvest from frozen plants; the oxalic acid that makes the leaves toxic can move into the stems when they freeze.

Uses. The tart leafstalks can be eaten raw by the brave but are usually sweetened with brown sugar or maple syrup. Try them cooked in a pie with strawberries, as an ingredient in baked dishes with ginger or cinnamon, or poached with sugar, butter, and ginger.

ROCKET. See *Arugula*
ROQUETTE. See *Arugula*
RUGOLA. See *Arugula*
RUTABAGA. See *Turnip*
SCALLION. See *Onion*

Shallot
Onion family. Biennial grown as an annual.
○ ❀

Characteristics. Height: 12 inches.

Shallots are related to garlic and onions. Like garlic, they produce clusters of bulbs, but they have a milder, onionlike flavor. They cook more quickly than onions and have a more tender texture. Shallots are prized by cooks for their delicate flavor, which adds a subtle touch to cooked meat and vegetable dishes, soups, stews, and sauces.

How to Grow. Shallots are a cool-season crop that thrives in full sun and deep, rich, stone-free soil with good drainage. They grow from bulbs rather than from seed or plants. Plant the bulbs in the garden after danger of a heavy frost in spring. Set them with their pointed tops up, 2 inches deep and 4 inches apart in rows spaced 12 inches apart.

Water during dry spells to keep the soil evenly moist, and apply a scattering of 10-10-10 fertilizer in midsummer. The plants are subject to the same pests and diseases as onions, so avoid planting shallots and their relatives in the same spot 2 years in a row.

How to Harvest. Gather shallots when the foliage dies back. They are hardy, so you can leave them in the ground over winter, but it's best to harvest as many as possible before the ground freezes. Cure them in a warm, dry location with good air circulation for a week before storing them in a cool, dry place for use during the winter. You can keep the tops on and braid them for storage or decoration.

Uses. You can use shallots the same way you use onions and garlic. They add a subtle, mild taste to cooked dishes, especially soups, stews, sauces, and casseroles. For a superb meat sauce, sauté them in olive oil with mushrooms. You can also harvest the foliage as a flavoring, but be sure to leave some of the leaves if the bulbs are not ready to harvest.

SNAP BEAN. See *Bean*
SNAP PEA. See *Pea*
SNOW PEA. See *Pea*

Spinach
Goosefoot family. Annual.
○ ◑ ❄ ▼

Characteristics. Height: 10 to 12 inches.

Almost anyone can learn to enjoy this cool-season green—even people jaded by childhood experiences when they were forced to consume overcooked, unadorned, boiled spinach. You can sneak spinach into quiches, pancakes, crepes, and omelettes. It is valued by cooks for its distinctive, slightly bitter flavor, which blends well with both stronger and weaker flavors in cooked and raw dishes. It is also rich in vitamin A and iron. Gardeners like spinach because it is quick and easy to grow for a spring or fall crop.

Spinach has thick, succulent, glossy green leaves that may be savoyed (wrinkled) or semi-savoyed. 'Avon Hybrid' is prized for its heat tolerance and its large, succulent, semi-savoyed leaves. 'Bloomsdale Long-Standing' produces heavy crops of very savoyed, dark green leaves on upright, heat-resistant plants. 'Melody Hybrid' is an All-America

Spinach 'Melody'

Selections winner that is resistant to downy mildew and mosaic virus.

New Zealand spinach is often grown as a warm-weather substitute for spinach. Although it is not really a spinach, it produces succulent, brittle green leaves that can be used raw as a salad green, or as a cooked green.

How to Grow. This crop prefers a rich, well-drained soil in full sun or light shade. For a spring crop, sow seed in spring, after danger of heavy frost; for a fall crop, sow in midsummer. In the South, plant in fall for a winter crop. Space the rows 12 inches apart. Thin the plants to 4 inches apart when they are large enough to handle.

Spinach is shallow-rooted and requires 1 to 1½ inches of rain each week for continuous, rapid growth. It does not have many serious pest and disease problems, although cabbageworms, aphids, and leafminers are common. Choose disease-resistant cultivars to prevent problems with specific diseases in your area. Protect the plants with floating row covers to keep pests off the plants.

How to Harvest. Cut the entire spinach plant to the ground when it has 3 to 5 leaves, or just harvest the outer leaves as needed when they are 3 inches long. When the weather turns warm and a seed stalk begins to develop, harvest the whole plant right away.

Uses. Spinach makes a delicious raw green salad and an attractive garnish. It can also be boiled, steamed, sautéed, stir-fried, or creamed. Add it to tomatoes in a tomato and cheese loaf, or combine it with mushrooms and cheese in pancakes. Spinach is commonly used in omelettes, quiches, and soufflés.

Squash

Squash family. Annual.

Characteristics. Height: 2½ feet; vines spread to 10 feet or more.

Squash is a warm-season crop related to cucumbers, melons, and pumpkins. It is grown for its fruit, which forms on vining, semivining, or bush-type plants. There are two basic types of squash: summer squash and winter squash.

Summer squash is grown for its immature fruit, which is harvested at any stage of growth in summer, before frost kills the vines. The kinds of summer squash range from long, slender zucchini and butterstick types to flat pattypan types with scalloped edges. The fruits

Squash 'Butterboy'

can be yellow or various shades of green; some have silver stripes. Crookneck summer squash has a bulbous, elongated shape with a hooked, gooseneck end. Summer squash grows on bush or vining plants.

Winter squash is grown for its hard-shelled fruit, which matures in the fall, often after frost kills the vines. The fruits vary from acorn-shaped to butternut types (with a distinctive elongated shape that widens at the base) to pumpkin-shaped, in various colors. The warty or smooth skins may be metallic blue, green and yellow, orange, tan, or white; many are striped or spotted. Vegetable spaghetti squash has an oblong shape with a yellow rind. It is grown for the stringy fibers inside, which can be used as a substitute for spaghetti. Winter squash usually grows on vining plants.

Gourds are similar to winter squash but are grown for ornamental purposes. They also vary widely in their shapes and colors. Loofas are grown for their fibrous flesh, which is dried and used to make bath sponges.

How to Grow. All squash prefer full sun and well-drained soil that is rich in organic matter. Sow seed outdoors after all danger of frost has passed and the weather is warm. Sow seed 2 inches deep, in groups of 4 seeds. For vining types, space the groups 5 feet apart in rows spaced 8 feet apart; thin the seedlings to leave 2 or 3 in each group. For semivining types, space the groups 4 feet apart in rows spaced 6 feet apart. Thin bush types to stand 30 inches apart in rows spaced 3 feet apart.

Squash plants appreciate extra water in dry weather. You can use a trellis to support vining types, as long as it is sturdy enough to hold the weight of the fruit. The plants are susceptible to the same pests and diseases as cucumbers and pumpkins. Choose disease-resistant cultivars, and avoid planting squash family crops in the same spot 2 years in a row, to prevent the buildup of diseases.

How to Harvest. Pick summer squash fruits when they are immature and still tender, at whatever size you wish. To get the fruit at peak quality, harvest daily or every other day by cutting it from the plants with a sharp knife. The plants are extremely prolific, and you will have plenty of squash to share with friends, neighbors, relatives, and passersby! Use the fruits as soon as possible after harvest.

Harvest winter squash after the shells harden. Cut the fruits from the vines with 1 or 2 inches of stem attached, then cure them for a week in a warm,

Summer squash, mixed types

dry location with good air circulation. Store them in a cool, dry place at 50° to 55°F for use throughout the winter.

Uses. Harvest summer squash as a gourmet mini-vegetable, then stuff it and serve it as hors d'oeuvres. Larger summer squash can be sliced and sautéed, steamed, boiled, grilled, stuffed, or baked in casseroles. You can also use it to make soup, zucchini bread, fritters, or corn bread. Use winter squash to make pumpkin pie, or bake it and serve it as a delicious side dish. It can also be made into soup or added to casseroles, as well as baked meat and vegetable dishes. Try marinating the cubed or sliced flesh in soy sauce and ginger before grilling, steaming, or stir-frying. The flowers of all squash types are edible and can be stir-fried, breaded and deep-fried, or stuffed with cheese.

STRING BEAN. See *Bean*
SUGAR PEA. See *Pea*
SWEET BELL PEPPER. See *Pepper*
SWEET CORN. See *Corn*

Sweet potato
Morning glory family.
Perennial grown as an annual.

Characteristics. Height: 18 inches.

Sweet potatoes are more closely related to morning glories than to potatoes. They are native to tropical America and are grown for their delicious enlarged roots, which are popular at holiday dinners in fall and winter. They have orange, yellow, or white flesh that can be dry or moist, depending on the cultivar. Sweet potatoes are high in vitamin A and are a good source of fiber. The plants are usually vining, but bush types have been developed that are more suitable for smaller gardens. They are not related to yams (which are native to Africa), although the two crops are similar in culture and taste.

How to Grow. These warm-season plants grow best in full sun and well-drained soil. They need a long season to mature and cannot tolerate any frost. Sweet potatoes are available as rooted cuttings called "slips," or as transplants. If you use slips, start them in pots 8 weeks before the last frost in spring. Set them so the bottom 3 inches of stem are buried in the soil. Keep them moist but not wet. Grow them until the last frost date, then transplant them to the garden after all danger of frost. If you start with transplants, you can set them directly in the garden after all danger of frost, when the weather is warm. Sweet potatoes are generally planted in ridges 8 to 15 inches high, spaced 3 to 4 feet apart. Space the plants 12 to 16 inches apart in the ridged rows.

The plants need ¾ inch of water every week when they are young, and more as they mature. Too much water after a dry period may cause the roots to split, but they generally heal with little loss in quality. Do not water during the 2 weeks before harvest. Cultivate around the plants to prevent weeds and to keep side roots from developing. Sweet potatoes are rarely bothered by pests and diseases. Use certified disease-free slips or plants to prevent serious disease problems.

How to Harvest. Gather small roots anytime, or wait for the full-size roots in the fall. Before frost, dig the roots with care, and cure them in a warm, humid location for 10 days. Store them at 55°F at high humidity.

Uses. Enjoy sweet potatoes baked, mashed, candied, caramelized, deep-fried, stuffed, or boiled; try them as a substitute for white potatoes. Their sweet flavor combines well with many fruits and nuts, including pineapples, oranges, lemons, apples, raisins, and pecans. Their taste is enhanced by ginger, brown sugar, maple syrup, and nutmeg.

Swiss chard
Goosefoot family. Biennial grown as an annual.
○ ☀ ▼

Characteristics. Height: 10 to 12 inches.

Swiss chard is a close relative of beets. It is often grown as a summer substitute for spinach because of its tolerance for warm temperatures. It also withstands cool temperatures and can be grown from early spring right up to frost. The plants are very attractive, resembling small rhubarb plants. They have thick, succulent leaves and long leafstalks that can be either green or red. The leaves may be savoyed (wrinkled) or smooth. Swiss chard is high in vitamins A and C, potassium, and iron. 'Fordhook Giant' is a popular cultivar with dark green, savoyed leaves and green stalks. 'Burpee's Rhubarb Chard' has beautiful red stems and deep green leaves with red midribs. The plants are pretty enough for the flower border!

How to Grow. Swiss chard plants prefer rich,

Swiss chard

well-drained soil in full sun or light shade. In the North, sow from early spring to midsummer for a fall crop; in the South, sow in fall to spring. Sow the seed ½ inch deep in rows spaced 18 inches apart. The seeds are clustered, so try to space them evenly. Thin the seedlings to 12 inches apart when they are large enough to handle.

The plants benefit from an application of a high-nitrogen fertilizer 4 weeks after sowing. They are rarely bothered by pests and diseases, and are very easy to grow.

How to Harvest. Use the thinnings as salad greens. Harvest the outer leaves as needed, when they are more than 6 inches long. Cut the leaves off about 1 inch from the ground. Harvest continually to keep the plants productive. Before a hard freeze in fall, dig up the plants with the roots still attached, and with some soil covering the roots. If you keep the plants cool and moist, you can keep harvesting from them during the winter.

Uses. Use Swiss chard as a green, either cooked or raw. Use the leafstalks with the leaves, or cook the stalks separately like asparagus. The leaves are good as wrappers for stuffings.

Tomato
Tomato family. Annual.
○ ☀ ▼

Characteristics. Height: 12 inches to 4 feet or more.

The tomato is America's favorite garden vegetable. There are many reasons for tomatoes' popularity, but probably the most important is flavor. Anyone who has ever tasted a homegrown tomato and compared it with one purchased at the supermarket knows there's a real difference. While this is true of many vegetables, it is especially the case with tomatoes.

Tomatoes are among the most important and versatile foods we eat. They are used to make many products and dishes we consume on a regular basis, from soups and sauces to condiments and salads. Cultivars have been developed especially for the commercial market to improve their yields, uniformity, shippability, and shelf life. Because of the longer period between harvest and consumption for

Tomatoes, mixed types

commercially grown tomatoes, they are generally harvested green and then ripened artificially by exposure to ethylene gas. The flavor of these tomatoes just can't compare with those grown in the home garden and vine-ripened in the sun.

The tomato cultivars available to home gardeners are rarely available in supermarkets. There is a tomato for every gardener and for every garden. Tomato plants range from large, sprawling vines to dwarf bush plants that grow only 12 inches tall. Cultivars have been developed for hanging baskets, window boxes, and patio containers. Tomato fruits range from small, cherry types to big, juicy beefsteak types that can weigh over 7 pounds! Plum tomatoes are pear-shaped and are often used to make paste, sauces, and ketchup. Tomato fruits can be red, pink, orange, or yellow, and some cultivars have stripes.

Some tomatoes have been bred for resistance to various diseases and pests. The letters "V", "F", "N", and "T" refer to Verticillium, Fusarium, nematodes, and tobacco mosaic virus, respectively. Cultivars that have these letters in their names or descriptions are resistant to these diseases or pests.

Tomato cultivars have been bred to produce from as early as 54 days after transplanting to as late as 90 days, allowing you to harvest tomatoes from early summer to the first frost in autumn. Some cultivars bear fruit continuously; others produce their crops all at once. Some cultivars are hybrids, while others are open-pollinated. Many heirloom culti-

vars with unusual shapes, colors, or flavors are becoming available.

Tomatoes are classified as determinate or indeterminate. Determinate plants grow to a specific height and produce a crop all at once. They are the best type for gardeners who need large numbers of tomatoes at one time to can or process into soups or sauces. Indeterminate types keep producing smaller numbers of tomatoes continually throughout the season until frost kills the vines. These are a good choice for gardeners who want to be able to run into the garden now and then to pick a tomato or two for salads or sandwiches.

How to Grow. Tomatoes need full sun and warm, rich, well-drained soil. These warm-season plants cannot tolerate any frost. They take a fairly long time to mature, so start the seed indoors 6 to 8 weeks before the last frost in spring. Transfer the seedlings to individual containers when they are 2 inches tall.

Set supports up before you move the plants to the garden. You can train tomatoes on stakes, over A-frame supports, on a trellis or fence, or in circular tomato cages. Transplant hardened-off seedlings to the garden after all danger of frost. Set the plants 18 inches apart in rows spaced 3 feet apart.

The plants need 1 inch of water every week. Water container plants when they are partially dry, but not wilted; they may need watering every day. All tomatoes appreciate a scattering of 5-10-5 fertilizer in midsummer. If you are training the plants to trellises or stakes, prune the developing plants to keep one or two strong stems. Every week, remove the side shoots that develop from where each leaf meets the main stem.

In general, tomatoes will stop producing fruit when temperatures drop below 50°F or rise above 90°F, although some cultivars are more tolerant of these temperature extremes than others. In hot, dry weather, plants may drop their flowers or fruit, but when conditions improve, they generally recover fully. When the weather is very dry and then very wet, tomatoes are liable to produce cracked fruit, because the fruit grows too quickly when the wet weather arrives; some cultivars are more resistant to cracking than others. Tomatoes can also develop "green shoulders," which occur when they ripen unevenly; cultivars differ in their resistance to this problem.

Tomato 'Winter Red'

Sometimes the blossom end of the tomato develops a tough, black leathery patch—a sign of blossom end rot. This common problem is caused by a calcium deficiency in the soil, or by uneven watering. If your soil is deficient in calcium, add lime in the fall for next year's crop. Try to keep the watering schedule as consistent as possible.

Tomatoes may be scalded by the sun in too-hot temperatures, when the fruit is not shaded from the direct sun. The fruit needs warmth—not light—to ripen, so you can cover the developing tomatoes with the leaves to shield them. Do not plant tomatoes near black walnut trees; the plants are susceptible to a toxin exuded by the roots of the tree, which causes "walnut wilt." The plants may grow well for many weeks, but one day they will wilt dramatically and never recover.

The most common tomato pests and diseases are Verticillium and Fusarium wilt, nematodes, and tobacco mosaic virus. There are no cures for any of these, so choose resistant cultivars. To prevent the buildup of soil-borne diseases, avoid planting toma-

to family crops in the same spot 2 years in a row.

How to Harvest. Pick tomatoes when they are as ripe as possible—they should be fully colored and firm. When you know there will be a frost, pick all the almost-ripe tomatoes you can, and ripen them in brown bags or spread on newspapers at room temperature. Many cultivars will store for months. ('Long-Keeper' stores for at least 5 or 6 months. Every year, customers write to Burpee to report that they managed to keep 'Long-Keeper' fruits from one crop to the next!) Store only sound fruit, at 50° to 60°F.

Uses. The foliage of tomatoes is toxic and should not be eaten. The fruit, however, is another matter! Tomatoes are enjoyed in many cooked dishes as a flavoring. Use them to make soups, sauces, stews, ketchup, paste, juice, quiche, and pies. Add them to curries, casseroles, and chutney. They can be stuffed, stewed, pickled, preserved, canned, or made into relish. Slice them raw for sandwiches and salads. Cherry tomatoes make great in-the-garden snacks.

Turnip
Cabbage family. Annual.
○ ❄ ▼

Characteristics. Height: 10 to 12 inches.

Turnips are closely related to rutabagas. Both are cool-season crops grown primarily for their flavorful roots.

Turnip roots can be eaten raw or cooked. They are globe-shaped to flattened, with white flesh and white or purple skin. They mature fairly quickly, in 35 to 70 days from sowing. Their young tops are high in vitamin A, calcium, potassium, and iron, and can also be harvested; try them as cooked greens.

Rutabagas are sometimes called swedes, or Canadian or yellow turnips. They originated in the Middle Ages as a cross between cabbage and turnip. Their roots are sweeter, larger, and starchier than those of turnips. They take longer to mature and also store longer. Their flesh is generally yellow, turning bright orange when cooked. Rutabagas are usually grown as a fall crop in the North and are normally prepared as a cooked vegetable.

How to Grow. Turnips and rutabagas grow best in full sun and deep, rich, well-drained soil that is free of stones. For a spring crop of turnips, sow as soon as you can work the soil in spring. For a fall crop of turnips or rutabagas, sow as late as possible in summer for the roots to mature before a heavy fall frost. In the South, sow either vegetable in fall for a winter crop. Sow seeds ½ inch deep in rows spaced 12 to 18 inches apart. When the turnip seedlings are large enough to handle, thin them to stand 2 to 3 inches apart; thin rutabagas to 6 inches apart.

Cabbage root maggots can be a problem. To prevent the buildup of soil-borne pests and diseases, avoid planting turnips, rutabagas, and other cabbage family members in the same spot 2 years in a row.

How to Harvest. Pick turnip greens 4 weeks after sowing. Harvest turnip roots when they are 2 to 3 inches in diameter, before the weather turns hot, if you are growing them as a spring crop. If the roots grow too large or mature in too-hot weather, they tend to be woody and pithy. Harvest fall crops after frost, which can sweeten their flavor. Dig up rutabagas when they are 3 inches in diameter. Both crops can be harvested as long as the ground is not frozen. To extend the harvest season, mulch the area heavily in the fall to keep the ground soft.

Uses. Eat turnips raw or cooked. Serve them with game or as a side dish, or add them to soups and stews. They can be boiled, mashed, steamed, browned, glazed, scalloped, or stuffed. Steam young turnip greens and serve them as a side dish, or use them as a wrapper for a stuffing with ham or bacon. Rutabagas can be steamed and then mashed with a little sugar. Try them boiled, baked, or deep-fried. They are also excellent mashed with potatoes and served with pork or beef.

WATERMELON. See *Melon*
WAX BEAN. See *Bean*
ZUCCHINI. See *Squash*

TASTY AND ORNAMENTAL, TOO. *Chives are a popular herb that make attractive additions to both flower and herb gardens. Grow a single clump, or plant a row as an edging.*

CHAPTER EIGHT

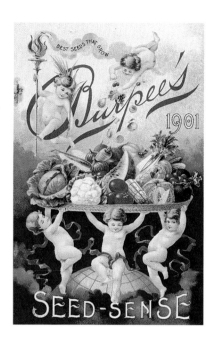

HERBS

WHEN YOU THINK OF HERBS, WHAT COMES TO MIND? Probably traditional culinary standbys like parsley, thyme, and oregano. But what about charming pink-flowered calamint, tangy-leaved lemon grass, or aromatic, silvery southernwood? There's a whole world of exciting and versatile herbs out there just waiting for you to try. Whether you grow herbs for cooking, healing, crafts, or just enjoying in the garden, they are sure to bring you lots of satisfaction.

WHAT ARE HERBS?

Loosely defined, herbs are plants that are of use to humans. (This does not include vegetables, or plants that we just grow for ornament.) These plants may be valued for their flavor, fragrance, medicinal qualities, or insecticidal properties. Some herbs have economic or industrial use (for example, as a source of fiber, rubber, or oil); other herbs provide coloring material for dyes. Spices are plants that are used like herbs but are from tropical or subtropical regions.

263

WHY GROW HERBS?

Vegetables give us a useful yield. Flowers beautify our yards. Herbs give us the best of both worlds: Not only can they be used in a multitude of ways, but many also have attractive leaves or flowers and are good garden plants in their own right.

HERBS FOR COOKING

It has long been known that herbs improve and enhance the flavor of food. The trick, however, is having a handy supply of fresh herbs at your disposal. With a home herb garden, you can dash outside and snip a few chives or mint leaves to add just the right touch to any dish. And if the luxury of having a steady supply of fresh herbs isn't enough, you can grow extra and preserve their flavors any number of ways, including drying, freezing, or making vinegars, sauces, and jams. Growing a wide variety of herbs will encourage you to experiment with different flavors and uses, making boring meals a thing of the past.

HERBS FOR HEALING

Herbs have been valued for their medicinal properties for thousands of years. Today, they are still used to alleviate various physical ailments. For example, a cup of mint tea can be a soothing way to settle an upset stomach; a cup of chamomile tea can be just the thing to help you unwind after a stressful day at work. New discoveries are emerging that validate the immense value of herbs in medicine. To be on the safe side, it's best to use herbs under a doctor's supervision; some can be extremely toxic if ingested accidentally or in large doses. You also need to be careful if you're pregnant, nursing, or taking medications for other ailments.

HERBS FOR FRAGRANCE

Often, just the scent of herbs is enough to refresh even the most harried gardener. In fact, the natural essences of many herbs are used for healing and relaxation in a technique known as aromatherapy.

FRAGRANT PAVEMENT. *Several herbs will thrive when planted between stepping-stones or in rock crevices. Creeping thyme will provide a fragrant cover-up when planted in pavement cracks, as shown here.*

GROW HANDY HERBS. *One of the best places to grow herbs is wherever they are most handy. This garden puts herbs within a few steps of the kitchen door.*

You can enjoy the scents from your own plants simply by brushing the leaves to release their aroma. Grow them where they are within easy reach—for instance, in a planter on a deck, in a raised bed by a door, or along a path to the driveway. Many of these aromatic herbs keep their fragrance when dried, so you can preserve their scent for winter enjoyment in potpourris, wreaths, arrangements, and a variety other crafts.

HERBS FOR BEDS AND BORDERS

While herbs are traditionally grown together in a separate herb garden, many of these great plants are showy enough for the flower garden. The leafy green rosettes of parsley, for instance, make an attractive—and edible—edging. The flowers of lavender, calamint, and anise hyssop look lovely with other perennials and annuals. Rose geranium makes an elegant container specimen. And low-growing

KNOT GARDEN DESIGN. *Traditional herb gardens feature square or rectangular beds with low, clipped hedges used either as edging for the beds or to form an ornamental pattern, or "knot." The individual beds can be filled with formal, mirror image plantings or a somewhat more casual mixture of useful herbs, as shown here.*

herbs, such as creeping thyme and sweet woodruff, are marvelous as groundcovers. Mixing herbs with flowers in beds and planters is a great way to save space if your garden area is limited.

HERB-GROWING BASICS

Herbs can grow successfully just about anywhere in the United States. If you want to grow the widest possible range of herbs, you'll need to take into account the special needs of the particular plants. In

the North, for instance, you may need to grow tender herbs in pots and bring them indoors in winter, or give them special protection outdoors. In the hot, dry West, moisture-loving herbs will need supplemental watering to survive a drought. If easy maintenance is more your style, you can choose herbs that are naturally suited to your climate's conditions so you won't have to worry about watering or winter protection.

Good soil conditions are essential for growing herbs successfully. In general, the soil should be

SUMMERING TENDER HERBS. *Many herbs make ideal container plants. In fact, growing tender herbs such as sweet bay, shown here, and rosemary makes it easy to move the plants indoors over winter.*

loose and light, with some organic matter and moderate fertility. A too-rich soil will produce weak herbs that are prone to disease problems. The pH should be approximately 6.5, although most herbs will grow in soil that is slightly acidic or slightly alkaline.

To grow healthy, productive herbs, you must also provide them with adequate light. Most herbs thrive in full sun (at least 6 hours of sun a day; more is generally better). In too much shade, sun lovers tend to be spindly and unproductive. Your choice of herbs is somewhat more limited for shady areas, but there are some—parsley, peppermint, and sweet cicely, for example—that grow well in light shade.

Water is most important while new plants are getting established. Once the plants have taken hold, watering is usually only necessary in times of extreme drought. To avoid disease problems, water in the morning. Unless you are trying to encourage growth, there is no need to add fertilizer. If you do choose to fertilize, try an organic fertilizer such as kelp or fish emulsion.

For best results, prune your herbs throughout the growing season; regular pruning will produce fuller, more compact plants. Cut back woody perennials—such as thymes, lavender, and savory—in spring and then as needed through the summer. Annuals benefit from pinching, which encourages branching and produces fuller plants. Just pinch out the stem tips with your fingers, or snip them with scissors to shape the plants. Use the pinched tips for cooking or as cuttings for starting more plants.

Herbs tend to be fairly pest-resistant, but aphids, whiteflies, mites, and other common pests may occasionally attack the plants. If you can, remove the pests by handpicking them (if they're large) or by pinching off infested plant parts. If you're not planning to harvest within a week or so, you can also use soap sprays. However, avoid spraying anything on herbs you plan to eat.

HARVESTING HERBS

For best flavor, harvest your herbs just as they are about to bloom; very young or end-of-the-season herbs tend to have less flavor. Cut your herbs in the morning, after the dew has dried and before the sun is too bright. If you plan to harvest a large quantity, select a cloudy day; otherwise, the herbs may wilt or lose some of their flavor as you cut and prepare them.

If you like to use fresh herbs, simply pick a few leaves or sprigs here and there as needed throughout the season. If you want to harvest a lot at one time for drying, leave some of the foliage so the plant can continue to grow. On most annuals, take no more than 60 percent of the foliage at any one harvest. (When harvesting short-lived annuals, such as dill and coriander, you can cut the whole plant at once and then replant for a new crop.) On perennials, leave about half of the foliage. If you're harvesting biennial herbs, you can pick the leaves as needed the first year, but you may want to wait until seeds set the second year to increase your supply of plants.

Use sharp scissors or garden shears to snip off the parts you want to harvest. On bushy herbs, you can take the tips; on clumping herbs, such as parsley, just cut off the outer leaves. As you harvest, place the herbs in a water-filled container to keep them from wilting.

Use the herbs right away, or store them in the refrigerator. To keep them from drying out, leave them in a container of water or wrapped in moistened paper towels in a plastic bag.

PRESERVING HERBS FOR STORAGE

If you want to store your herbs for more than a few days, you can either freeze them or dry them. Air drying is the traditional method, although oven drying and freezing are quicker, and microwave drying is handy for small batches. Remove all damaged, discolored, or diseased leaves, then try one of the methods described below.

FREEZING HERBS

Freezing is a quick and easy way to preserve many herbs. It's especially good for herbs that tend to lose their flavor when dried, including basil, chives, French tarragon, lovage, and parsley. Once they are thawed, however, frozen herbs are limp and not especially attractive, so they're best used for cooking.

To prepare leaves for freezing, chop them and place them in plastic containers or bags. Or, put the herbs in a blender with water or olive oil, then pour the puree into ice cube trays for easy-to-use chunks. (Store the frozen cubes in plastic containers or bags.) Label all frozen herbs with the date of storage, and use them within 6 months.

AIR DRYING HERBS

Air drying is a time-honored technique for preserving many kinds of herbs. Leafy herbs are usually hung upside down to dry. Gather the fresh herbs in small bunches—approximately 3 to 5 stems each of large, leafy herbs (such as sage) or 6 to 8 stems of smaller herbs (such as thyme). Secure the stem end of each bundle with a rubber band. You can also spread leaves and flowers out on screens to dry. To dry seeds, hang the seed heads on their stalks upside down in a paper bag, so the seeds will fall into the bag as they dry.

Keep the drying herbs away from direct sunlight, as exposure to the sun will cause deterioration in color and flavor; a room that is dark, dry, and well ventilated is ideal. Hang the bundles from a line or on drying racks; space them evenly for thorough drying. To dry herbs on screens, support the screens between two chair backs or on unused tomato cages so air can circulate evenly around the herbs. Depending on the humidity, herbs can take a few days to a few weeks to dry thoroughly.

The best way to judge whether your dried herbs are ready for storage is to touch them: If they crumble to powder, they are probably too dry. On the other hand, if they feel at all moist, they are not ready; simply continue the drying process until they are completely dry.

OVEN DRYING HERBS

The quicker herbs dry, the more colorful and flavorful they will be. For this reason, oven drying generally gives better results than air drying, especially for delicate flower petals and thick leaves, such as those of scented geraniums.

The temperature for herb drying should be between 90° and 110°F. A gas oven with a pilot light is ideal; just allow the flame to dry the herbs slowly. If you have a gas oven without a pilot light, try setting it at the lowest temperature. Electric ovens— even at the lowest temperature—will cook the herbs rather than dry them.

Spread the herbs out evenly on cookie sheets,

then set them in the oven. Leave the oven door open a little so the moisture can escape. Most herbs will dry to the touch in 1 to 4 days, depending on the amount of humidity in the air.

MICROWAVE DRYING HERBS

Herbs—especially flowers and flower petals—maintain extremely good color, form, and in some cases, flavor when dried in the microwave. One disadvantage of microwave drying is that certain herbs seem to cook and get too crispy and flavorless. Experiment to see which herbs dry best in your microwave.

To prepare your herbs for microwave drying, wash them, pat them dry, then spread them out evenly between two paper towels on a microwave-safe dish. The first time you dry an herb, follow the timing suggestions in "Microwave Drying Tips" below. Keep a close eye on the drying herbs, and stop the oven if you see any signs of smoke or charring. If this happens, try a new batch for a shorter period of time. When you find the right timing, jot it down for future reference.

PLANT PORTRAITS

The following plant portraits are a sampling of some of the best annual, biennial, and perennial herbs you can grow. Some are popular for cooking; others

GROWING TIPS AT A GLANCE

Each of the following plant portraits includes simple symbols to highlight special features you need to know about each herb. If you're not sure what any of the symbols mean, refer back to this key.

○ Full sun (more than 6 hours of sun a day; ideally all day)
◐ Partial sun (some direct sun, but less than 6 hours a day)
● Shade (no direct sun)
✻ Prefers cool temperatures
✁ Good as a cut flower
❀ Good as a dried flower or foliage
▼ Grows well in containers

MICROWAVE DRYING TIPS

Experimentation is the key to getting the best drying results from your particular oven. To get you started, here are some guidelines:

Herb	Drying Time	Shrinkage	Flavor Reduction	Notes
Basil	7 min.	50%	70%	Remove leaves from stem; lay them flat and do not overlap.
Bay	12 min.	5%	None	Stays green. Do not use weak topgrowth. Remove leaves from stem.
Chives	4 min.	50%	90%	Keeps nice green color but loses most flavor.
Parsley	6 min.	50%	85%	Remove leaves from stem; lay them flat and do not overlap.
Rosemary	4 min.	30%	None	Dries well on or off the stem.
Sage	7 min.	20%	None	Dries well on or off the stem; may want to remove leaf stems. Needs turning to dry evenly.
Tarragon, French	4 min.	70%	40%	Easy to dry on stem; holds color well.
Thyme	5 min.	50%	None	Dry leaves on the stem.

are great for crafts. All of these herbs are attractive and productive. Most are easy to grow from seed or are commonly found at local garden centers. A few are a little less common but are worth the search; check out specialty herb nurseries or catalogs.

The herbs in this section are listed by their common name, in large bold type. Under the common name, you'll find the botanical name, along with its pronunciation. You'll also find the herb's bloom time, along with its hardiness range, if it is a perennial. (Remember that annual herbs don't live over winter, so you can grow them in virtually any climate.) A general description, growing guidelines, and suggested uses complete the entries to ensure your herb gardening success!

Angelica
Angelica archangelica. an-JEL-ih-kuh
ark-an-JEL-ih-kuh. Summer. Zones 4 to 8.

Characteristics. Height: 4 to 5 feet. Spread: 2 feet.

Angelica features big, bold foliage, which gives

Angelica

gives the plants a kind of tropical appearance. This herb has a large, deep taproot and is usually grown as a biennial; if you remove the flowers, it may act like a short-lived perennial. The flower heads give off a distinctive fragrance that attracts beneficial insects to the garden.

How to Grow. Angelica thrives in cool, rich, moist soil and full sun or light shade. It is at home by a pond or stream, or in an herb or vegetable garden. During hot summers, the plants may stop growing, but they will perk up again when cool weather returns. Start with purchased plants. To propagate, sow the fresh seeds immediately or mix them with moist vermiculite and store them in the refrigerator for spring sowing.

Uses. All parts of angelica are aromatic. You can eat the leaves fresh in fruit salads or crystallize the stems for dessert decorations. The root is used as a fixative in potpourri. The plant's bold, statuesque form makes an eye-catching accent in the garden.

Anise hyssop
Agastache foeniculum. ag-ah-STAH-chee
fee-NIK-yew-lum. Summer. Zones 5 to 9.

Characteristics. Height: 3 feet. Spread: 1½ to 2 feet.

This large, showy herb has prolific purple flower

Anise hyssop

spikes and looks equally at home in flower, herb, and vegetable gardens. Both the leaves and flowers have a pungent licorice scent. There is a white-flowered form known as 'Alba'. Korean anise hyssop (*Agastache rugosa*) is a related species with pinkish flowers and slightly scalloped leaves.

How to Grow. Anise hyssop prefers rich, moist soil in a sunny location. Start with purchased plants, or grow it from seed sown indoors or out in spring. This herb tends to be a short-lived perennial, but it will reseed in locations where it is happy.

Uses. Use the anise-flavored leaves and flowers as a seasoning or to make a pleasant-tasting tea. The flowers attract many interesting insects, including honeybees. They also look wonderful in fresh or dried arrangements.

Basil
Ocimum basilicum. OH-sih-mum bah-SIL-ih-kum. Summer. Tender annual.

○

Characteristics. Height: 2 feet. Spread: 1 foot.
Basil lovers have a marvelous variety of flavors to choose from. One of the best loved is sweet basil (*Ocimum basilicum*), a bushy, upright plant with broad, smooth, shiny green leaves. The cultivar 'Napoletano' has large wrinkled leaves. Lemon basil (*O. basilicum* 'Citriodorum') is a sturdy grower with delightful lemony basil flavor. 'Cinnamon' is also used in cooking or for its fragrance. 'Purple Ruffles', a Burpee introduction, is an All-America Selections

winner; the beautiful, crinkly, rich purple leaves make it a terrific bedding plant. 'Dark Opal' has smooth, dark purple leaves that are especially striking when combined with gray foliage. 'Minimum' has a compact habit and forms a delightful little rounded shape. It is ideal for a container or as a low hedge.

How to Grow. Basil needs full sun and evenly moist—but not wet—soil. Sow seed indoors 6 to 8 weeks before the last frost date. Set hardened-off seedlings into the garden after all danger of frost has passed. To promote branching, pinch the shoot tips when the plants are 4 to 6 inches tall. To encourage the production of more leaves, pinch off the flower heads as they form.

Uses. Basil is considered the premiere culinary herb. Use the fresh leaves to make pesto or as a seasoning for fresh or cooked tomatoes. Basil is also a great flavoring for oils and vinegars. The bushy plants, especially the purple-leaved types, look great in the flower garden.

BAY, SWEET. See *Sweet bay*

Borage
Borago officinalis. bore-AY-goh oh-fish-in-AL-iss. Summer. Tender annual.

○

Characteristics. Height: 2 feet. Spread: 1 foot.
Borage is a hairy annual herb with lovely sky blue, star-shaped flowers. The large, rounded, coarse

Basil

Borage

leaves form a rosette at the base of the flower stems. 'Alba' has attractive white, star-shaped flowers.

How to Grow. Borage grows best in a sunny spot with light, well-drained to dry soil. Sow the large seeds directly in the garden in early spring. This herb will self-sow where it is happy.

Uses. Both the flowers and the young leaves are edible. Add the flowers to wine, use them to decorate cakes, or try crystallizing them. Borage is an attractive flowering annual in cottage gardens or borders, or planted with herbs and vegetables.

BURNET, SALAD. See *Salad burnet*

Calamint
Calamintha spp. kal-uh-MIN-thuh. Summer. Zones 5 to 10.
○

Characteristics. Height: 15 inches. Spread: 15 inches.

Calamints are attractive, bushy, perennial herbs with creeping roots. Lesser calamint (*Calamintha nepeta*) features rounded, slightly hairy leaves and small lavender flowers on long stalks. It is known for its strong odor and pungent taste. In Italy, the leaves are used for flavoring mushrooms. The flowers of C. *grandiflora* are larger (up to 2 inches long) and pink. The variegated form known as 'Bert's Beauty' has green leaves spattered with cream.

How to Grow. Calamints must have full sun and good drainage. They will grow in average to poor soil. Start with purchased plants. Calamints tend to be short-lived perennials, but they will reseed readily.

Uses. Enjoy the leaves in teas or as a flavoring. Calamints make excellent plants for flower borders.

CALENDULA. See *Pot marigold*

Caraway
Carum carvi. KARE-um KAR-vee.
Summer. Zones 3 to 8.
○

Characteristics. Height: 2 feet. Spread: 1 foot.

This biennial herb produces ferny green leaves during its first growing season. The second year, it bears flat clusters of white flowers that resemble those of Queen-Anne's-lace. Once the flowers set seed, the plants die.

How to Grow. Caraway thrives in full sun and rich, moist soil. It resents transplanting, so start plants from seed sown directly in the garden in fall or spring. It normally reseeds readily; thin out the seedlings as needed.

Uses. Caraway seeds are most often used to flavor bread, cakes, and cheeses. The seeds are also eaten to aid digestion. Enjoy the fresh leaves with vegetables; cook the root as a vegetable. Grow car-

Calamint

Caraway

away in an herb garden, with vegetables, or in a border.

CATMINT. See *Catnip*

Catnip
Nepeta spp. NEP-eh-tuh. Early summer.
Zones 3 to 9.

Characteristics. Height: 2 to 3 feet. Spread: 2 feet.

Several species of *Nepeta* are grown in herb and flower gardens. Catnip (*N. cataria*) is not especially ornamental, but it is the species used primarily for catnip tea and to excite cats. This tall, coarse herb has gray-green leaves and small white flowers. Lemon-scented catnip (*N. cataria* 'Citriodora') combines the flavor of catnip with that of lemon. The more ornamental members of the genus are generally known as catmints. This group includes *N. X faassenii* 'Blue Wonder', which is shorter than catnip (18 inches tall) and produces large, deep blue flowers. *N. mussinii* 'Dropmore' grows to 1 foot tall and bears prolific, deep blue-lavender flowers that last well over a month. It has a loose, sprawling habit and will self-seed in the garden.

How to Grow. Place both catnip and catmint in a sunny to lightly shaded location with good drainage. Start with purchased plants, or sow seed of catnip indoors or out in spring. (Cultivars of catmint are best grown from purchased plants.) In areas with high humidity, the plants are susceptible to fungal problems. To improve air circulation around the plants, cut them back by about one-half after the first flush of bloom. Cutting them back will also encourage another flush of bloom in late summer. Divide the plants every 2 or 3 years to keep them vigorous and to prevent them from spreading too much.

Uses. Grow catnip for your feline friends, or use it yourself for a soothing tea. Catmints are marvelous as edgings for perennial beds and borders, as groundcovers under roses, or cascading over the edge of containers.

Chamomile
Chamaemelum nobilis, Matricaria recutita.
kam-ee-MEL-um no-BILL-iss, mah-trih-KARE-ee-ah reh-cue-TEE-tah. Spring. Zones 4 to 8.

Characteristics. Height: Roman chamomile, 4 to 12 inches; German chamomile, 2 to 3 feet. Spread: 1 foot.

Roman chamomile (*Chamaemelum nobilis*) is a creeping perennial herb with lacy leaves. Its delicious applelike scent is most noticeable in the flowering tips and young leaves. The flowers are small white daisies.

The plant commonly known as German chamomile is actually an annual, *Matricaria recutita*. Also known as sweet false chamomile, German chamomile looks similar to Roman chamomile, but is more upright and has a pineapple-like flavor and fragrance. It comes up in early spring, then sets seed and dies in late spring.

How to Grow. Both types of chamomile prefer full sun and dry soil. Start with purchased plants, or sow seed indoors or out in the fall. To encourage the plants of Roman chamomile to spread outward, mow off the flowers. For propagation, divide Roman chamomile; German chamomile tends to reseed readily.

Uses. The flowers of both types of chamomile make a soothing tea. Roman chamomile grows well in cracks and crevices, between stones in a walkway, or in a wall. Grow German chamomile in any open, sunny site in the herb garden.

Roman chamomile

Chervil

Anthriscus cerefolium. an-THRISS-kus seer-eh-FOE-lee-um. Late spring to summer. Hardy annual.

Characteristics. Height: 18 to 24 inches. Spread: 15 inches.

Chervil has a short life cycle: It comes up, flowers, sets seed, and dies within a period of 6 to 8 weeks. Its ferny foliage adds a fine texture to the garden, and its clusters of white flowers are lacy and delicate.

How to Grow. Chervil prefers cool soil enriched with generous amounts of compost. In areas where summers are hot, the plants require some shade. Chervil will produce more abundant foliage in the cool seasons. Sow seed directly in the garden in early spring or late summer.

Uses. Fresh chervil leaves are highly prized for their anise flavor and are traditionally a common ingredient of fine herb mixtures. Add the young leaves to fish, poultry, salads, omelettes, and sauces. Chervil has a delicate appearance; plant it in an herb, vegetable, or naturalized garden.

Chives

Allium schoenoprasm. AL-ee-um skee-noh-PRAZ-um. Mid-spring. Zones 3 to 10.

Characteristics. Height: 12 inches. Spread: 10 inches.

Chives

Chives produce clumps of upright, hollow leaves and showy pink-lavender flowers. They are distinguished by their onion flavor. When interplanted with other garden plants, chives can repel insect pests; they are excellent companions for roses. This herb is also a good choice for growing in containers indoors or out.

How to Grow. Chives grow best in full sun and rich, moist, well-drained soil. Sow seed indoors or out in spring. Cut the clumps to the ground after blooming to encourage the production of new leaves. Divide the clumps every 3 to 4 years to keep them vigorous.

Uses. Harvest the leaves by clipping them back to 1 inch above the ground; new leaves will emerge. Add fresh leaves to salads, soups, cream cheese, butter, or sandwiches. Sprinkle the florets on salads. The leaves and flowers make a flavorful vinegar. Try adding the pink-lavender blooms to a white vinegar—they will give it a light onion flavor and a beautiful pink color.

Chives, Garlic

Allium tuberosum. AL-ee-um tew-ber-OH-sum. Late summer. Zones 5 to 10.

Characteristics. Height: 15 inches. Spread: 10 inches.

Garlic chives

Starry, white, sweet-scented flowers make garlic chives a beautiful plant. Its mild onion-garlic flavor makes it tasty, too.

How to Grow. Give this easy-care herb in full sun and well-drained soil. Sow the seed outdoors in early spring. Divide the plants every 3 or 4 years to keep the clumps vigorous. To prevent rampant self-sowing, pinch off spent flowers.

Uses. Harvest the flat leaves by cutting them to 1 inch above the ground. Use them fresh in soups, salads, sauces, and sandwiches. Sprinkle the white florets on salads. After the plants flower, the attractive seed heads can be harvested and used in herbal wreaths and arrangements. Include garlic chives in perennial borders, herb gardens, vegetable gardens, and containers.

CICELY, SWEET. See *Sweet cicely*
CILANTRO. See *Coriander*

Coriander
Coriandrum sativum. kore-ee-AN-drum sat-EE-vum. Late spring. Tender annual.

Characteristics. Height: 2 feet. Spread: 1 foot.

Coriander is a short-lived annual. The green, parsleylike leaves are known as cilantro and are used in Mexican and Asian cuisine. The flowering stem is topped with a flat cluster of white to pink flowers. 'Long Standing' is slow to go to flower, so it produces more leaves from a single sowing than the species.

How to Grow. Coriander likes good garden loam in full sun. Grow from seed sown directly in the garden once the danger of heavy frost has passed. Sow seed every 3 weeks during the growing season to ensure a steady supply.

Uses. Harvest the leaves before the flower stem has developed. Harvest the seeds once they start turning from green to gray-brown. The leaves do not dry well, so use them fresh; the taste is better than the smell. The ripe seeds are an important ingredient in curry. They are also used as a pickling spice or sugar-coated and eaten as a candy. Grow coriander with herbs and vegetables in the garden or in a container.

CORSICAN MINT. See *Mint*
CREEPING THYME. See *Thyme, creeping*

Dill
Anethum graveolens. an-EE-thum grav-ee-OH-lenz. Spring to summer. Tender annual.

Characteristics. Height: 3 feet. Spread: 2 feet.

Dill has handsome, feathery, blue-green foliage topped with clusters of delicate golden flowers. The plants prefer cool weather and quickly go to seed during the heat of summer. Once they begin going to flower, they stop producing foliage. 'Bouquet' is considered one of the best dill cultivars for flavor. 'Dukat' is a tall (4-foot) cultivar that was selected for its high yields of foliage and seeds. 'Fernleaf' is perhaps the best cultivar. This Burpee selection, which won the All-America Selections Award, has many fine qualities. Compared to the species, it is slower-growing and less apt to bolt quickly, and it has a more compact growth habit (to 18 inches). 'Fernleaf' is a great dill for growing in containers. Dill will reseed in spots where it is happy.

How to Grow. Choose a site with full sun and moist, fertile soil. Sow seed directly in the garden in early spring. Make successive sowings every few weeks as space permits until the weather heats up.

Dill

Removing the flowers as they appear can help prolong leaf production for a short time. Pinching off spent flowers can also prevent prolific self-sowing. At the end of the season, let some plants go to seed to provide a crop next year.

Uses. The fresh, young leaves are a popular flavoring for fish, poultry, seafood, eggs, soups, salads, sauces, and new potatoes. Use the seeds for pickling; enjoy the blooms as cut flowers. Grow dill in herb or vegetable gardens.

Elecampane

Inula helenium. IN-yew-luh hel-EN-ee-um.
Late summer. Zones 3 to 9.
○

Characteristics. Height: 6 feet. Spread: 3 feet. Elecampane is used primarily as a medicinal herb. Extremely coarse in texture, the plant has a basal rosette of large green leaves and smaller leaves that appear along the towering flower stem. The stem is topped with bright yellow flowers similar to small sunflowers. If you plan to harvest elecampane for its roots, wait until late fall of the plant's second year.

How to Grow. This perennial herb grows in a wide variety of conditions but prefers sun and moist, fertile soil. Start with purchased plants. Propagate by separating rooted offshoots from the parent plant.

Uses. The root of elecampane is used to make a tea to aid digestion and to relieve minor respiratory problems. This giant plant makes a showy addition to the back of the flower border or herb garden.

Fennel

Foeniculum vulgare. fee-NIK-yew-lum vul-GAR-ee.
Summer. Zones 4 to 10.
○

Characteristics. Height: 5 feet. Spread: 2 to 3 feet.

Fennel—with its feathery foliage, wonderful flavor, and many uses—is a favorite among herb gardeners. Sweet fennel (*Foeniculum vulgare*) is a short-lived, lacy-leaved perennial; the yellow flower clusters can be used in fresh cut arrangements. Bronze fennel (*F. vulgare* 'Rubrum') has gorgeous purple-bronze leaves and combines beautifully with bulbs, such as Madonna lily (*Lilium candidum*). It is a welcome addition to both perennial borders and herb gardens.

The vegetable fennel, commonly known as finocchio or Florence fennel (*F. vulgare* var. *dulce*), is grown as an annual. In autumn, it produces a delicious bulbous base that is eaten raw or cooked.

How to Grow. Fennels prefer well-drained loam in full sun. Sow seed outdoors after the last frost date. As a perennial, sweet fennel is short-lived, but it will reseed abundantly.

Uses. Enjoy the young leaves as a garnish and flavoring for soups, salads, and fish. Use the tasty seeds crushed or whole in sausage and other meats, as well as to make a refreshing tea with a warm, sweet, anise flavor. Fennel's lacy texture makes it a valuable garden plant.

Elecampane

Feverfew

Germander

Feverfew

Chrysanthemum parthenium. kris-AN-thuh-mum
parth-EN-ee-um. Spring to summer. Zones 4 to 10.

Characteristics. Height: 1 to 2 feet. Spread: 1
foot.

The aromatic, finely cut leaves of feverfew form
an attractive mound. The flowers appear in loose
clusters and consist of a yellow center edged with
white petals. The double-flowered form bears white
buttonlike flowers and is an especially decorative
plant. 'Aureum' has beautiful golden foliage that
looks elegant in beds and borders.

How to Grow. Feverfew likes full sun and soil
that is relatively dry and well drained. Sow seed
indoors or out in spring. The plants will reseed profusely if you do not remove the spent flowers.

Uses. Feverfew leaves are used for a medicinal
tea to ease the pain of migraine headaches. The
flowers are attractive in fresh arrangements. They
also dry well (especially the double form) and are
used in wreaths or in potpourri to repel insects.
Grow this herb with roses and in flower borders.

FRENCH TARRAGON. See *Tarragon, French*
GARLIC CHIVES. See *Chives, garlic*
GERANIUMS, SCENTED. See *Scented
geraniums*
GERMAN CHAMOMILE. See *Chamomile*

Germander

Teucrium spp. TEW-kree-um. Summer.
Zones 5 to 10.

Characteristics. Height: 24 inches. Spread: 20
inches.

Germanders are bushy herbs that are often evergreen where winters are not too harsh. Common
germander (*Teucrium chamaedrys*) is grown more for
its attractive, dark green foliage and tidy, upright
growth habit than for its pleasant, pale lavender
flowers. There is a variegated form that is sometimes
called 'Wellsweep'; it has cream-and-green leaves
that sometimes revert to green. *T. marum* has an
unusual pungent fragrance, a compact habit, and
small gray leaves. *T. scorodonia* 'Crispum' has beautiful crisped leaves and tiny yellow flowers. Tree germander (*T. fruticans*) is a tender plant with showy
blue flowers and beautiful leaves; it makes a great
topiary plant trained as a standard.

How to Grow. Germanders are not particular
about conditions but prefer full sun to light shade
and light, moderately moist and fertile, well-drained
soil with a slightly acid pH. Start with purchased
plants. Prune the plants back as often or as little as
you like. If the top dies or is damaged, cut back the
top growth, and new shoots will grow from the
roots. Divide the plants as needed for propagation,
or take tip cuttings in summer.

Uses. These herbs are grown primarily for their attractive leaves. They can be clipped into a charming low hedge.

Hyssop
Hyssopus officinalis. hih-SOP-us oh-fish-in-AL-iss.
Summer. Zones 4 to 9.
○ ◑

Characteristics. Height: 18 inches. Spread: 18 inches.

Hyssop is an upright, semiwoody herb with medium green leaves and blue, white, or pink flowers. The leaves have an interesting odor. The cultivar 'Aristatus', commonly known as rock hyssop, is more compact, with dark blue flowers and narrow, fragrant leaves.

How to Grow. Hyssop grows best in dry, light, well-drained soil and full sun to partial shade. Sow seed indoors or out in spring, or start with purchased plants. Regular clipping will help keep the plants compact. To propagate, divide the plants in spring or early fall, or take tip cuttings in summer.

Uses. Hyssop is occasionally used as a culinary herb in small amounts—it has a pungent camphor-mint flavor. It is also used to make a medicinal tea to relieve coughing and lung problems. This herb makes a great hedge, low border, or knot garden plant.

HYSSOP, ANISE. See *Anise hyssop*

Hyssop

Lavender 'Hidcote'

Lavender
Lavandula spp. luh-VAN-dew-luh. Late spring.
Zones 5 to 9.
○

Characteristics. Height: 12 to 24 inches. Spread: 12 to 30 inches.

The handsome gray foliage of lavenders gives them year-round interest. The flower colors range from dark blue to light lavender and even white. Many new cultivars of English lavender (*Lavandula angustifolia*) have been introduced recently. 'Lady' is an exciting new Burpee introduction that can be grown from seed and will bloom the same year. It is compact, reaching only 10 inches high and 12 inches wide, and bears blue flowers. 'Munstead' is distinguished by green leaves and dark violet buds that open into dark violet-blue flowers; it grows 15 to 30 inches tall. 'Hidcote', perhaps the most frequently grown cultivar, is known for its dark purple flowers, small silver leaves, and compact, slow-growing habit.

Most promising of the new lavender groups are the *L. X intermedia* cultivars. These plants, commonly called lavandins, are the result of crosses between *L. angustifolia* and *L. latifolia*. Their advantages include superior fragrance, wider gray or gray-green leaves, and longer flowering spikes. Lavandins bloom in mid-season and are hardy to 0°F. 'Grosso' is perhaps the most stunning of all, with large flowers on spikes over 2 feet high. It makes an outstanding addition to perennial borders, rose gardens, and containers.

How to Grow. Lavenders need full sun and average to dry, well-drained soil. Start with purchased plants, or sow seed outdoors in the fall or indoors in the spring. Trim the plants in early spring to keep them compact. To encourage repeat flowering, cut back the flowers after they bloom. To propagate, dig up rooted stems, or take cuttings in summer.

Uses. Lavender leaves and flowers are valued for their fragrance. Use them fresh or dried to make a soothing tea; add the dried parts to potpourris. Lavenders are excellent plants for a border, container, or rock garden; they also make a great low hedge.

Lavender cotton
Santolina spp. san-toe-LEE-nuh. Late spring.
Zones 5 to 8.

Characteristics. Height: 2 feet. Spread: 2 feet.

Lavender cotton (*Santolina chamaecyparissus*) has aromatic, silvery, almost furry-looking leaves. The plants form a rounded mound. In summer, yellow puffy-button flowers decorate the top of the plant. 'Pretty Carroll' is a dwarf form. Green lavender cotton (*S. virens*) has a similar habit but produces green leaves.

How to Grow. Give lavender cotton excellent drainage, good air circulation, moderately rich soil, and full sun. Start with purchased plants. Some gar-

Lavender cotton

deners prefer to cut off the flowers before they bloom; this will not hurt the plant and may in fact encourage bushier growth. To propagate, divide the plants, dig up rooted stems, or take cuttings in summer.

Uses. The dried flowers can be used for potpourri, and the dried leafy stems are excellent for herb wreaths. Lavender cotton is grown primarily as an ornamental for knot gardens and edgings.

Lemon balm
Melissa officinalis. mel-ISS-uh oh-fish-in-AL-iss.
Summer. Zones 5 to 9.

Characteristics. Height: 1 to 2 feet. Spread: 2 feet.

Lemon balm resembles many mints, to which it is closely related. The plants produce clumps of coarse, lemon-scented leaves. Golden-leaved cultivars, such as 'All Gold', are very attractive, especially when interplanted with blue flowers; just be sure to give them some shade to avoid leaf burn.

How to Grow. This herb will grow in a wide variety of conditions, although it prefers sun to partial shade and rich, moderately moist soil. Sow seed indoors or out in spring, or start with purchased plants. Cut the plants back by up to two-thirds after they bloom to encourage new growth. Lemon balm is mildly invasive, so divide the plants every year or two in spring or early fall to keep them in bounds.

Uses. Lemon balm is one of the easiest lemon-scented herbs you can grow. Use the fresh leaves to add flavor to foods and teas, or toss them into your bathwater. Include the dried leaves in potpourri. Lemon balm is suitable for flower borders, herb gardens, containers, or vegetable gardens.

Lemon grass
Cymbopogon citratus. sim-boh-POH-gon
sit-RAH-tus. Summer. Zones 10 to 11.

Characteristics. Height: 5 feet. Spread: 3 feet.

Lemon grass is a robust grass that forms dense clumps of long, thin, pointed leaves. It rarely flowers. It is also sometimes called fevergrass and West Indians lemon.

How to Grow. This herb will grow in a variety of soil types, but is most vigorous with plenty of moisture and full sun. In Zones 9 and north, keep lemon grass in a pot so you can bring it indoors over winter. In summer, set the ppots out in a protected location. Or plant lemon grass directly in the garden after the last frost and just pot up a small piece in the fall to overwinter indoors. To harvest the leaves, snip them and use them fresh anytime during the summer. Leaves can also be harvested and dried for winter use; for best flavor, dry them quickly.

Uses. The leaves of lemon grass make a delicious herbal tea. The tender inner portion on the base is used in Thai food to make lemon grass soup and to season chicken. This herb has a relaxing effect when added to bathwater. The lovely grassy texture adds interest to the garden and to container plantings.

Lemon verbena
Aloysia triphylla. al-OY-see-uh try-FILL-uh.
Summer. Zones 10 to 11.

Characteristics. Height: 6 feet. Spread: 3 feet.

Lemon verbena is a somewhat deciduous shrub that produces narrow, green leaves with a wonderful lemon scent; just rubbing them will make your mouth water. Clusters of lavender-white flowers appear in summer but rarely set seed. The plants will not survive a hard frost.

How to Grow. This herb prefers full sun and light, well-drained soil that is slightly alkaline. Start with purchased plants. In Zones 9 and north, grow lemon verbena in a container so you can bring it indoors over winter. Cut plants back in fall and keep them in a cool, sunny spot. Spider mites can be a problem on indoor plants; keep the temperature cool and spray with insecticidal soap, if necessary.

Uses. Lemon verbena leaves have the best lemon scent and flavor of all the herbs you can grow. Snip the leaves and shoot tips as needed throughout the summer to use fresh or dried. Add them to foods or use them in tea, herbal baths, or (when dried) potpourri.

Lovage
Levisticum officinale. leh-VISS-tih-kum
oh-fish-in-AL-ee. Late spring. Zones 4 to 8.

Characteristics. Height: 6 feet. Spread: 3 feet.

Lovage is a large herb with towering yellow flower heads that appear over succulent, green, divided leaves. (Do not confuse lovage with some of its similar-looking poisonous relatives, such as *Conium maculatum*, the deadly, white-flowered poison hemlock.) The large green leaves at lovage's base are ideal for harvesting and can be used fresh or frozen.

How to Grow. Lovage thrives in sun to light shade and cool, rich, moist soil. In hot summers, it gets a bit ragged but will often revive when cool nights return. Sow seed outdoors in fall or early spring, or start with young purchased plants. To encourage healthy leaf production, cut the flowers back after they bloom. Lovage has large taproots that go down deep into the soil, so they prefer not to be dug up for division. It's generally easiest to start new plants from seed.

Uses. The entire plant has a celery flavor, which goes nicely in soups, sauces, or chicken. Use the stems as celery-flavored straws for tomato juice or Bloody Marys. In the garden, lovage blends well with vegetables; it also looks good toward the back of a perennial border.

Marjoram, Sweet
Origanum majorana. oh-rig-AH-num
mah-jer-AH-nuh. Summer. Zones 9 to 10.

Characteristics. Height: 1 foot. Spread: 1 foot.

Sweet marjoram has pungent, gray leaves that are satiny in texture. The bloom clusters consist of handsome, green petal-like bracts with small white flowers. The plants grow as perennials in the warmest climates; in Zones 9 and north, grow them as annuals.

Several other marjoram relatives are also popular herbs. *Origanum* X *majoricum*, commonly known as hardy marjoram or Italian oregano, is a sterile hybrid, probably between *O. vulgare* subsp. *virens*

Sweet Marjoram

and *O. majorana.* It possesses the flavor of marjoram and some of the hardiness of oregano. 'Compact Greek' has a smaller habit and exceptionally beautiful, velvety gray leaves.

How to Grow. A sunny spot with good drainage and slightly acid soil is ideal for sweet marjoram. Sow seed indoors about 6 weeks before the last frost date; set hardened-off plants into the garden after the danger of frost has passed. Pinch or harvest from the plants frequently throughout the season to encourage bushy, upright growth. Propagate from seed.

Uses. The warm, sweet flavor of marjoram makes it one of the best culinary herbs. Try it in vinegars, salads, and sauces; add it to dishes with meat, fish, pasta, or mushrooms. Marjoram is attractive in the garden and makes a good edging or rock garden plant.

Mint

Mentha spp. MEN-thuh. Late spring to summer. Zones 4 to 9.

Characteristics. Height: 15 inches to 2 feet. Spread: 2 feet or more.

A variety of mints make excellent additions to herb gardens. Peppermint (*Mentha* X *piperita*) is noted for its dark, purplish stems and the strong minty fragrance of all of its above-ground parts. There are many cultivars, including 'Todd Mitcham', with an especially intense peppermint flavor, and 'Chocolate Mint', which supposedly has a slight chocolate taste.

Spearmint (M. *spicata*) is perhaps the best loved of all the mints. This herb bears lavender flowers in late spring; the leaves are dark green and sharply pointed. Curly mint (M. *spicata* 'Crispata') is an especially decorative selection with distinctive, crinkled, rounded, bright green leaves. Red mint (M. X *gracilis*) is a close relative, with red-tinged leaves and a mild spearmint flavor. It is considered the best culinary mint for use with rice, salads, or fruit desserts.

English pennyroyal (M. *pulegium*) low-growing mint that looks superb as a groundcover in the spaces between stepping-stones or planted in a hanging basket. Hardy to Zone 7 (6 with protection), it is a valuable companion plant for repelling insects. As a dry herb, it is used to make herbal flea collars and insect-repellent sachets.

Corsican mint (M. *requienii*) is another low-growing species with tiny leaves that smell like crème de menthe. It makes a fine shade-loving groundcover.

Both apple mint (M. *suaveolens*) and white-leaved pineapple mint (M. *suaveolens* var. *variegata*) bear leaves with a fruity fragrance.

How to Grow. Most mints thrive in full sun or partial shade with evenly moist, rich soil; Corsican mint prefers a shady site. Start with purchased plants; pinch a leaf before buying a plant to make sure you get one with good fragrance. In the right spot, mints can spread rapidly. To control the spread of these enthusiastic colonizers, grow them in a pot, contain them with metal edging, or plant them in a bottomless container sunk into the soil. Another option is to plant mints in an out-of-the-way spot where their spreading isn't a problem. To encourage a flush of new growth, cut the stems back to the ground after the plants flower. To propagate, divide the plants in spring or fall.

Uses. Fresh or dried, spearmint, peppermint, and apple mint leaves make a healthful and delicious tea. Add the fresh leaves and flowers to salads and desserts. Pennyroyal and Corsican mint are usually grown as ornamental plants. Include mints in herb gardens, container plantings, and children's gardens.

Oregano

Origanum spp. oh-rig-AH-num.
Summer. Zones 5 to 9.

○ ❀ ▼

Characteristics. Height: 18 inches. Spread: 24 inches.

The most commonly grown of this group of herbs is Greek mountain oregano (*Origanum vulgare* subsp. *hirtum*, formerly known as *O. heracleoticum*). It has dark green leaves, hairy stems, and white to lavender flowers. Wild oregano (*O. vulgare* subsp. *vulgare*) is an invasive plant with attractive purple flowers that are great for drying. Unlike its culinary relative, wild oregano produces leaves that are flavorless and have no value in cooking. 'Compactum Nanum' is a very dwarf form of this oregano and is often used as a low border plant. Another cultivar, 'Aureum' has golden leaves and is very decorative. *O. onites* is considered an oregano, despite its common name, pot marjoram. It has an upright habit and leaves that are a paler green than other oreganos; its flavor has a real bite. Pot marjoram makes an attractive container plant.

How to Grow. All oreganos need full sun and average, well-drained soil. Seeds tend to produce plants with varying flavor, so it's generally best to start with purchased plants. (Pinch a leaf before you buy a plant, to make sure it has a good aroma.) Pinch or harvest from the plants frequently to keep them bushy. Once you find an oregano with a flavor you really like, propagate it by division in spring or cuttings in summer.

Uses. Greek mountain oregano is one of the best hardy oreganos for cooking, and it has one of the strongest flavors, too. Grow it in a children's garden, a "pizza" garden (with tomatoes, onions, and peppers), or in a container.

Parsley

Petroselinum crispum. peh-troh-seh-LY-num
KRIS-pum. Summer. Zones 4 to 9.

○ ◐ ▼

Characteristics. Height: 15 to 24 inches. Spread: 18 inches.

Parsley

Parsley has many fine ornamental qualities. The dark green leaves have a beautiful, ferny appearance, and they grow in mounded clumps that look especially attractive along a border. Although this herb is actually a biennial, it is normally grown as an annual. Once parsley flowers, the flavor of the leaves deteriorates, and the plants die after they set seed.

There are many kinds of parsley to choose from. They vary in the curl of the leaves and in the shade of green. The curly types are classified as *Petroselinum crispum* var. *crispum*. The most commonly grown flat-leaf type is Italian parsley (*P. crispum* var. *neapolitanum*).

How to Grow. Give parsley full sun to light shade and rich, deeply dug soil that has ample moisture. Sow seed outdoors in spring (it can take several weeks to germinate), or start with young purchased plants. To increase leaf production, fertilize several times during the growing season, and remove any flowering stalks that appear. If you let one or two plants go to seed, parsley will often self-sow.

Uses. Parsley leaves are rich in vitamins and minerals. Harvest the outer leaves by cutting them at the base of the leafstalk. They are delicious in salads and make an excellent accent for vegetables and potatoes. Chewing on a fresh leaf can freshen your breath. Parsley is superb as a border plant or as an underplanting for roses. Try it in a container, or grow it in the vegetable garden.

PENNYROYAL, ENGLISH. See *Mint*
PEPPERMINT. See *Mint*

Pot marigold
Calendula officinalis. kuh-LEND-yew-luh
oh-fish-in-AL-iss. Spring or fall. Hardy annual.
○ ◑ ❀ ▼

Characteristics. Height: 1 foot. Spread: 1 foot.

Pot marigolds, also called calendulas, are decorative, hardy annuals that bring a burst of color to the spring and autumn garden. The plants produce light to medium green leaves and leafless flower stems. The sticky flower buds open into orange to lemon yellow, daisylike blooms.

How to Grow. Pot marigolds will grow in most good garden soil; they bloom abundantly in full sun. In warmer regions, some shade is helpful to keep the plants cool, but they still need adequate light to flower well. Sow seed of this cool-season annual directly in the garden in early spring or late summer. Pinch off the old flowers to keep new blooms coming.

Uses. Use the flower petals in salads and to give flavor and coloring to other foods. They are also valued for their soothing and antiseptic qualities; add them to herbal baths. You can grow pot marigolds in borders, flower beds, containers, cottage gardens, and vegetable gardens.

ROMAN CHAMOMILE. See *Chamomile*

Rosemary
Rosmarinus officinalis. rose-mah-RINE-us
oh-fish-in-AL-iss. Late winter to early spring.
Zones 7 to 10.
○ ▼

Characteristics. Height: 2 to 6 feet. Spread: 2 to 6 feet.

Rosemary is a classic culinary herb with short, needlelike leaves that have a pungent aroma and taste. The plants can grow to be large shrubs in warm climates; elsewhere, you'll need to bring them indoors over winter. Small blue flowers bloom along the stems in late winter to spring. 'Arp' is a hardier cultivar that can survive outdoors in Zone 6 with a loose winter mulch. 'Prostrata' is a creeping form of rosemary.

Rosemary

Pot Marigold

How to Grow. Rosemary thrives in average, well-drained soil and full sun. Sow seed of the species indoors in spring. (Fresh seed works best; old seed may germinate poorly.) Plants of the species and cultivars are commonly available for purchase from garden centers in spring. Propagate by cuttings in summer. In cold-winter areas, grow rosemary in pots so you can bring it indoors for the winter.

Uses. The fresh, frozen, or dried leaves are great for seasoning poultry, beef, fish, lamb, and pork; chop them before adding them to food. Sprinkle the fresh flowers over salads. Shrubby rosemary plants look great in the garden and in container plantings.

Rue
Ruta graveolens. ROOT-uh grav-ee-OH-lenz.
Summer. Zones 4 to 8.

Characteristics. Height: 2 feet. Spread: 1 foot.
Rue is a valuable foliage plant because of its unique blue-green-gray leaf color. The yellow summer flowers are followed by attractive four- or five-lobed capsules. The whole plant has an unusual smell and bitter taste. There are some improved ornamental selections of rue, including 'Jackman's Blue' and 'Blue Mound'.

How to Grow. Rue likes full sun and well-drained clay loam with a pH of around 7. Sow seed

indoors about 8 weeks before the last frost date. Set out hardened-off seedlings after the danger of frost has passed. In hot, humid summers, rue is prone to soil fungal diseases; if the plants suffer, remove them and try new plants in a different location. Prune the stems back by one-half to two-thirds to keep the plants bushy. Propagate by cuttings in summer.

Uses. Many people have an allergic skin reaction to rue, similar to that caused by poison ivy. It's best to use rue strictly as an ornamental herb; plant it with roses, in knot gardens, or in perennial beds and borders.

Sage
Salvia spp. SAL-vee-uh. Late spring. Zones 5 to 8.

Characteristics. Height: 2 feet. Spread: 3 feet.
Sage is a shrubby herb with a distinctive rounded shape and a striking leaf texture. It has long been a symbol of wisdom, as well as a valuable addition to herb gardens. Ornamental forms of culinary sage (*Salvia officinalis*) bring great color to the garden. 'Icterina' has gold-and-green variegated leaves. 'Purpurea' (also known as 'Purpurascens') bears purple foliage. 'Tricolor' is variegated with cream, purple, gray, and white. Pineapple sage (*S. elegans*) is a tender plant with a pineapple flavor; the leaves and flowers add a refreshing touch to desserts. The

Rue

Sage

bright red fall flowers are also ornamental, and they attract hummingbirds. Clary sage (*S. sclarea*) behaves like a biennial. It forms a rosette of large serrated leaves, which are topped with billowing clusters of lilac flowers.

How to Grow. These herbs must have full sun and well-drained soil. Sow seeds of the species indoors or out in spring; start with plants of the cultivars. Prune established plants back by one-half to two-thirds in early spring if they are getting too large or leggy. In humid areas, sage is susceptible to fungal diseases. If the leaves or branches start to die, remove them, and the plant may recover. If removing the leaves or branches does not solve the problem, start with a new plant in a different site. If mites are a problem, treat the plants with a soap spray. In frost-prone areas, bring pineapple sage inside for the winter. Clary sage often reseeds; propagate others by cuttings in summer.

Uses. Sage leaf tea is useful in treating colds and for aiding digestion. Try the leaves as a flavoring in breads and stuffing or with meats or vegetables. The large size, attractive mounding habit, and textural leaves of the plants make them highly ornamental in the garden. Use them as a corner accent, or mix them with perennials, annuals, and other herbs in a cottage garden.

Salad burnet

Salad burnet
Sanguisorba minor. san-gwih-SOR-buh MY-ner.
Summer. Zones 4 to 8.
○ ◐ ❄

Characteristics. Height: 15 inches. Spread: 15 inches.

Salad burnet is a short-lived perennial with a mounding habit and gracefully arching leaves that are almost evergreen in many climates. The plants love cool weather and can produce a usable harvest well into winter if grown in a coldframe.

How to Grow. This herb grows best in full sun to light shade and rich, moist, well-drained soil. Sow seed directly in the garden in spring. The flowers are not showy; to encourage more leaf production, trim them back after blooming. To propagate, divide the plants in spring. They will also self-sow if you allow a few flowers to mature.

Uses. Salad burnet leaves have a refreshing

cucumber flavor and are used in salads, vinegars, and beverages. This herb is a beautiful plant in the landscape, especially after a rain, when the delicate leaves are accented with sparkling water drops. Try salad burnet in a formal or informal border, or in an herb garden.

Savory
Satureja spp. sat-yew-REE-yuh.
Summer. Zones 5 to 8.
○

Characteristics. Height: 18 inches. Spread: 20 inches.

Winter savory (*Satureja montana*) is a perennial herb with lance-shaped leaves on thin, woody stems. 'Nana', the dwarf form, makes a superb knot garden plant because of its neat, compact habit. Summer savory (*S. hortensis*) is the annual form of savory. It has a much looser, more open habit and grows to 2 feet tall. Its pungent peppery flavor makes it a valuable culinary herb.

How to Grow. Both winter and summer savory like sun and loose, well-drained soil. Sow winter savory seed indoors in spring, or start with purchased plants. Summer savory grows easily from seed sown indoors or directly in the garden in spring. Pinch or harvest from the plants frequently to promote bushy growth. Cut back winter savory after flowering. Propagate winter savory from divi-

Savory

heart-shaped leaves and a beautiful habit. There are many fine scented geraniums to choose from, with a range of fragrances, textures, sizes, and colors. A few of the most popular include rose geranium (*Pelargonium graveolens*), a large plant with deeply cut leaves, and 'Prince Rupert' lemon geranium (*P. crispum* 'Prince Rupert'), a small plant with stiff, serrated, variegated leaves. Apple geranium (*P. odoratissimum*) is a dense, bushy plant with soft, apple-scented leaves. Peppermint geranium (*P. tomentosum*) offers magnificent, large, velvety leaves that smell like peppermint.

How to Grow. Scented geraniums generally grow best in full sun and average to dry, well-drained soil. Seed is sometimes available, but it's usually easiest to start with purchased plants. In Zones 9 and north, grow scented geraniums in pots and bring them indoors for the winter, or take cuttings from garden plants in summer.

Uses. Use the leaves of rose geranium to add a rose taste to jellies, teas, and cakes. Rose geranium grows into a large plant that makes a fine summer hedge. Grow other types in containers, along paths, or in raised beds, where you can easily rub the leaves to release their refreshing fragrance.

sion or summer cuttings; propagate summer savory from seed.

Uses. Medicinally, summer savory has been used as an antiseptic and as a tonic. It has also been called the "bean herb," for its ability to relieve flatulence. Its strong-flavored leaves may be crushed and used as a salt substitute. You can use both types of savory as a seasoning for a variety of meat and vegetable dishes. Winter savory has great ornamental value and is often evergreen; the leaves can turn a rich purple color in winter.

Scented geranium
Pelargonium spp. pel-ar-GOH-nee-um.
Summer. Zones 10 to 11.
○

Characteristics. Height: 2 feet. Spread: 2 feet. This excellent tender perennial features large,

Sorrel
Rumex spp. REW-meks. Late summer.
Zones 4 to 8.
○

Characteristics. Height: 30 inches. Spread: 24 inches.

Garden sorrel (*Rumex acetosa*) forms upright clumps of pointed, arrow-shaped leaves with a light green midrib. The brownish flowers are followed by flat brown seeds. Sorrel has a refreshing, tangy, acid flavor, due to its high oxalic acid content; enjoy a few leaves now and then, but avoid eating large quantities. Buckler-leaf French sorrel (*R. scutatus*) has a milder, more lemony flavor and is the preferred form in France. The names of both garden sorrel and French sorrel have been confusingly interchanged.

How to Grow. Sorrels can grow in full sun or light shade. They must have rich, moist soil to grow well and produce harvestable leaves from late spring through autumn. Sow seed directly in the garden in early spring. To promote better leaf production, cut off the flower heads. Divide the clumps every 3 or 4 years to keep the plants healthy.

Uses. The fresh leaves are used to make sorrel soup, which is served hot or cold. They also make a wonderful spicy addition to salads, green sauces, and omelettes. Or, cook them and eat them as you would spinach. Sorrel fits well into herb and kitchen gardens.

Southernwood
Artemisia abrotanum. ar-teh-MEEZ-ee-uh ab-ro-TAN-um. Summer. Zones 3 to 9.

Characteristics. Height: 2 feet. Spread: 2 feet.
Southernwood is a hardy, shrubby herb with fragrant, finely textured, gray foliage that forms a beautiful round shape. You can allow it to grow tall, or prune it in early spring to keep it smaller. The tiny yellowish white flowers bloom in loose panicles; they are not noticeable.

Wormwood (*Artemisia absinthium*) is a bitter herb that was once used to make the alcoholic beverage known as absinthe. It has silvery white foliage coated with silky hairs. 'Lambrook Silver' is a superior selection with a broader growing habit; it blends especially well with roses. A. 'Powis Castle' is

thought to be a hybrid between A. *absinthium* and A. *arborescens*. It gets very large—up to 3 feet by 4 feet—and is popular in perennial gardens for its silvery foliage and mounding habit.

How to Grow. Artemisias need full sun and light to medium-textured, well-drained soil. Start with purchased plants. Prune the plants in spring to promote neater, bushier growth.

Uses. Southernwood is grown primarily as an ornamental, although its aromatic leaves add a nice touch to herbal baths. Use the dried leaves to repel insects, such as clothes moths. Artemisias look marvelous in cottage gardens, perennial borders, herb gardens, and rose plantings.

SPEARMINT. See *Mint*
SWEET BASIL. see *Basil*

Sweet bay
Laurus nobilis. LORE-us no-BILL-iss.
Early spring. Zones 9 to 11.

Characteristics. Height: 15 feet. Spread: 4 feet.
Sweet bay is an aromatic evergreen tree with sturdy, flavorful green leaves and an elegant shape. It is a slow grower and can last many years in a container. Golden bay (*Laurus nobilis* 'Aurea') has golden leaves and requires some shade to prevent the

Southernwood

Sweet bay

leaves from burning. Willow-leaf bay (*L. nobilis* 'Angustifolia') has narrower leaves than the species.

How to Grow. Plant sweet bay in full sun to light shade and rich, moist, well-drained soil. Choose a site protected from winds. In Zones 8 and north, grow the plants in containers; bring them indoors over winter and put them outside during the warmer months. Sweet bay is frost-tolerant and has been known to die back to the roots and still come back. Start with purchased plants. Bay trees are susceptible to scale insects, which can be treated with horticultural oil. For smaller, pot-grown specimens, use a Q-tip dipped in alcohol to control scale insects. Sweet bay can be difficult to propagate; try taking cuttings from soft, new growth.

Uses. Use the dry leaves to flavor soups and stews and sauces. (Remove them before serving.) You can also use the leaves to make herbal wreaths or add them to bathwater to relieve aching limbs. Bay makes an excellent topiary or is an especially attractive container plant.

Sweet cicely

Myrrhis odorata. MER-iss oh-door-AH-tuh. Early summer. Zones 4 to 9.

◑

Characteristics. Height: 3 feet. Spread: 2 feet.

The finely cut, textured leaves of sweet cicely give it a fernlike appearance. The dark seeds, which have a nutty flavor, are ornamental when standing upright above the foliage. The whole plant has a pleasant scent.

Sweet cicely

How to Grow. Sweet cicely grows best in light shade, as the leaves will burn in the hot summer sun. The soil should be rich and moist. Sow fresh seed directly in the garden in late summer to fall, or start with purchased plants. Established plants will often reseed profusely.

Uses. All parts of sweet cicely have a sweet, licorice flavor. Use the young leaves to season soups and stews; add the seeds to salads. The root is eaten as a cooked vegetable with oil and vinegar. Sweet cicely is well suited to a woodland or naturalized garden. It also looks good in front of shrubs or tall perennials.

SWEET MARJORAM. See *Marjoram, sweet*

Tarragon, French

Artemisia dracunculus. ar-teh-MEEZ-ee-uh druh-KUNK-yew-lus. Summer. Zones 6 to 8.

 ○ ◑

Characteristics. Height: 2 feet. Spread: 1 foot.

French tarragon is prized as a culinary herb for its delicate anise flavor. True French tarragon can only be grown from root or stem cuttings or from division. (Although the plants sometimes bloom, they almost never set seed.) Russian tarragon, which is sometimes sold as tarragon or French tarragon, is weedy and has no value in cooking. It is seed-grown. When you buy plants, always pinch a leaf to make sure the ones you are buying have the anise flavor of true French tarragon.

How to Grow. French tarragon prefers full sun to light shade and well-drained soil enriched with organic matter. Start with purchased plants. Pinch the shoots when they are 4 to 6 inches tall to encourage branching. For best growth, remove the flowers as they appear. Divide the plants every 3 years in spring or fall. You can grow French tarragon indoors in winter, just pot young divisions or plants in late summer and cut the foliage back to just above the soil.

Uses. Use the fresh leaves to enhance fish and chicken dishes, sauces, and salads. French tarragon also makes a superb vinegar. The plant has no special ornamental qualities other than its bright green foliage.

Thyme, Common

Thymus vulgaris. TY-mus vul-GAIR-iss.
Summer. Zones 5 to 9.
○

Characteristics. Height: 1 foot. Spread: 1 foot.
Common thyme is a small herb with an upright
growth habit and gray-green leaves that are highly
aromatic. There are many variations of thyme to
choose from. They have been confused in the trade
because of their ability to cross with one another. Be
careful when shopping for thymes—pinch the
leaves to make sure you get the fragrance you want.
'French' is distinguished by its superior flavor and
narrow gray leaves; 'English' has flatter, greener
leaves. Both are upright in habit. 'Orange Balsam'
features a wonderful orange-spice fragrance and
attractive, dark green leaves; the plant thrives in
rock gardens.

Lemon thyme (*Thymus* X *citriodorus*) has a number of marvelous cultivars. 'Aureus', commonly
known as golden thyme, doubles as a culinary herb
and an outstanding ornamental with attractive gold-
en foliage. 'Silver Posie' has silver-edged leaves. It is
similar to silver thyme (*T. vulgaris* 'Argenteus'),
which is highly ornamental and a bit less hardy (to
Zone 6).

How to Grow. Thymes need full sun and well-
drained soil. Sow seed of common thyme indoors or
out in the spring; start with purchased plants of cultivars. The life span of thyme plants averages about
5 to 6 years. If you notice that the plants are beginning to deteriorate, you can take cuttings and start
new ones, or prune the existing plants back hard to
rejuvenate them.

Uses. This classic herb is traditionally added to
many meat and vegetable dishes. It makes a great
low, evergreen hedge or rock garden or border plant.

Thyme, Creeping

Thymus praecox subsp. *arcticus.* TY-mus
PRAY-koks ARK-tih-kus. Summer. Zones 4 to 9.
○

Characteristics. Height: 1 to 2 inches. Spread:
12 to 18 inches.
Creeping thyme makes a superb evergreen, low-

Creeping thyme

growing groundcover well suited for sunny spots.
'Alba' has white flowers; 'Coccineus' has pinkish red
flowers. 'Lanuginosus', commonly called woolly
thyme, has woolly, silvery leaves. (It needs perfect
drainage to keep from rotting.) 'Minus' has the
smallest leaf of any thyme and requires the same sort
of conditions as woolly thyme. One of the toughest
and most versatile creeping thymes is caraway
thyme (*Thymus herba-barona*), which has a caraway
fragrance to its leaves.

How to Grow. Give creeping thymes a warm
site with full sun and loose, infertile soil. In the right
spot, these plants generally need little care. Cut
them back after blooming and in early spring, if necessary, to keep them neat. If you plant many different kinds of creeping thymes, keep them separated;
otherwise, they will grow together in a thick, entan-
gled mass.

Uses. Creeping thymes are most frequently used
as groundcovers in the cracks between rocks or
pavers in a walkway, in rock gardens or crevices
such as walls, and in hanging baskets. The plants are
attractive to bees.

WORMWOOD. See *Southernwood*

EASY-CARE COVER. *Groundcovers are low-maintenance solutions to many garden problems. They can control weeds, reduce erosion, and cover tough sites like dry shade with lush, leafy cover. This planting of hostas 'Blue Umbrellas' and 'True Blue' accomplishes all that and more—it also creates an appealing shade garden.*

CHAPTER NINE

GROUNDCOVERS

THERE'S SOMETHING ABOUT A LUSH, FINELY CLIPPED LAWN—AN OPEN, FRIENDLY SPACE THAT INVITES YOU TO PLAY, STROLL, OR JUST LOUNGE AROUND. The downside of lawns is all the maintenance they need—regular mowing, plus edging, watering, fertilizing, and pest control. And sometimes, no matter how hard you try, there are areas where grass just won't thrive—under trees, in wet spots, or on dry slopes, for instance—and you are left with ugly bare patches. Fortunately, there is an easy and attractive solution to all of these problems: groundcovers!

In this chapter, you'll learn about the wide variety of groundcovers that can reduce lawn maintenance significantly and add multi-season interest in the process. You'll find lots of ideas for incorporating these tough, adaptable plants into your landscape, along with information on selecting and growing more than 20 great groundcovers. In addition to the groundcovers listed in this chapter, many perennials make excellent groundcovers. For a list of some of the best, see "Perennial Groundcovers" on page 292.

COVER WITH PERENNIALS. *Groundcovers generally have stems or underground roots that spread at a rather rapid rate, but perennials that don't spread that rapidly, such as these astilbes, can be used as groundcovers, too. Just place the plants close together from the start to create a groundcovering blanket of flowers and foliage.*

PERENNIAL GROUNDCOVERS

The perennials listed below also make ideal groundcovers. For more information on any of these plants, read about them in Chapter 4.

Alchemilla mollis (lady's-mantle)
Astilbe chinensis 'Pumila' (dwarf astilbe)
Bergenia cordifolia (heartleaf bergenia)
Epimedium spp. (epimediums, barrenworts)
Helleborus orientalis (Lenten rose)
Heuchera spp. (heuchera, coralbells)
Hosta hybrids (hostas)
Iberis sempervirens (candytuft)
Pulmonaria saccharata (pulmonaria, lungwort)
Stachys byzantina (lamb's ears)

WHAT ARE GROUNDCOVERS?

Groundcovers are plants that spread out to form a living carpet over the soil. The term is usually used for low-growing, creeping plants that are no more than 1 or 2 feet tall. Lawn grasses can technically be considered groundcovers, since they are short and they spread to cover the soil. In most cases, though, "groundcovers" refers to creeping nonlawn plants, including perennials, herbs, sprawling vines, and even low shrubs. In low-maintenance areas, low-growing weeds such as ground ivy and English daisies can serve as groundcovers. Even moss can make a marvelous groundcover in shady areas.

WHY GROW GROUNDCOVERS?

Flowers are pretty; vegetables are productive; groundcovers are practical. By shielding the soil from the sun and wind, groundcovers can help keep it moist and cool, providing ideal rooting conditions for plants. They discourage weed seeds from sprouting and, if they are vigorous enough, can even crowd out weeds that do get started. English ivy (*Hedera helix*), common periwinkle (*Vinca minor*), and several other popular groundcovers are adaptable enough to tolerate sites where few other plants

MIXED-UP GROUNDCOVERS. *One of the most effective ways to use groundcovers is to mix them together. This bed combines hostas, astilbes,* Heuchera 'Palace Purple', *Lenten roses* (Helleborus orientalis), *and ferns to create a planting filled with lush color and texture.*

will grow, such as dry, shady spots under trees.

Groundcovers can also prevent soil erosion and help solve water runoff problems. Once you get plants established and growing on a slope, the tangle of roots and stems will slow the water running down the slope and keep it from carrying off valuable topsoil.

Groundcovers reduce your overall workload, too. By replacing part or all of your lawn with these easy-care plants, you can cut down on (or eliminate) mowing and lawn-maintenance time. Growing groundcovers also eliminates the need for tedious hand-trimming under trees and shrubs and in other spots the mower usually misses.

As if all these practical benefits weren't enough, groundcovers have a lot to offer to the beauty of your yard. The wide variety of leaf textures, colors, and shapes add interest while creating an aesthetically pleasing tapestry effect. Groundcovers are ideal for layering and can be used to create varying heights in beds and borders, along walkways, and even in containers.

GARDENING WITH GROUNDCOVERS

Which groundcovers you choose will depend on what you want them to do and what conditions you have to offer. Some, such as ajuga (*Ajuga* spp.) and Japanese spurge (*Pachysandra terminalis*), spread dependably outward to form broad carpets. They adapt to different growing conditions and climates, making them suitable for a wide range of sites. These kinds of spreaders are ideal for covering large areas, such as beds under shrub groupings or along driveways.

In smaller areas, you can experiment with slightly less vigorous spreaders, such as hens and chicks (*Sempervivum* spp.), Bethlehem sage

(*Pulmonaria saccharata*), European ginger (*Asarum europaeum*), and hostas. These tend to look best in small patches, tucked under shrubs in foundation plantings, along garden steps, or mixed with other plants in beds and borders.

Like all other garden plants, groundcovers grow best when you match their needs to the conditions you have to offer. For a hot, sunny site, stick with drought-tolerant species, such as creeping juniper (*Juniperus horizontalis*) or beach wormwood (*Artemisia stellerana*). For more sheltered spots, plant shade lovers such as epimediums (*Epimedium* spp.) and dead nettle (*Lamium maculatum*). By matching the plants to the site, you'll end up with a planting that is naturally healthy and vigorous without a lot of fussing on your part.

Keep in mind that some groundcovers are evergreen, while others are deciduous (that is, they die back to the ground each winter). Lady's-mantle (*Alchemilla mollis*), lamb's ears (*Stachys byzantina*), and other deciduous groundcovers tend to be very showy during the growing season, and they can work fine for discouraging weeds. During the winter, however, you'll be left with bare soil, which doesn't look especially attractive. For spots where you really need year-round interest, stick with English ivy, Japanese pachysandra, and other evergreen plants. You can add seasonal interest to patches of evergreen groundcovers by planting them with short spring- or fall-blooming bulbs, such as crocuses, snowdrops (*Galanthus* spp.), colchicums (*Colchicum* spp.), and small daffodils.

PLANT PORTRAITS

The following portraits highlight some of the best groundcovers for home gardens. Some are evergreen; others are deciduous. They may have showy flowers, attractive leaves, or both. You can buy all of these groundcovers from retail sources—either mail-order catalogs or local nurseries and garden centers.

The plants are listed by their botanical name, in large, bold type. Under the botanical name, you'll find its pronunciation, along with the common name, bloom season, and hardiness zones. Each entry also provides a description of the plant, including its average height and spread, as well as growing guidelines and suggested garden uses. With

GROWING TIPS AT A GLANCE

Each of the following plant portraits includes simple symbols to highlight special features you need to know about each groundcover. If you're not sure what any of the symbols mean, refer back to this key.

- ○ Full sun (more than 6 hours of sun a day; ideally all day)
- ◑ Partial sun (some direct sun, but less than 6 hours a day)
- ● Shade (no direct sun)
- ✳ Drought-tolerant
- ❧ Fragrant

this information at hand, you'll be able to find the perfect groundcover for nearly any spot in your yard.

AARON'S-BEARD. See *Hypericum calycinum*

Ajuga spp.
ah-JEW-guh. Ajuga, bugleweed.
Spring. Zones 3 to 9.
○ ◑

Characteristics. Height: 6 inches. Spread: 18 inches.

Ajuga, also commonly known as bugleweed, is a fast-spreading, semi-evergreen or evergreen groundcover. It forms dense carpets of flat or crinkled leaves that are accented by spikes of blue, pink, or white flowers in spring. The most common species

Ajuga reptans

is *Ajuga reptans*, which comes in a variety of attractive leaf forms. There are several cultivars with bronze-colored leaves, most notably 'Bronze Beauty'. The leaves of 'Burgundy Glow' are pink edged with cream; new growth is burgundy-colored. 'Multi-color' (also known as 'Rainbow') has shiny leaves with a mixture of colors, including pink, cream, and bronze. 'Silver Beauty' produces lovely grayish leaves with white around the edges. 'Catlin's Giant' has taller flower spikes (to 8 inches) and large, bronze-green foliage. *A. pyramidalis* spreads less and is a little taller than *A. reptans*. It has attractive foliage and prefers a damp location.

How to Grow. In warm southern climates, ajugas grow best in some shade. In cool climates, they prefer sun. They are happiest in a rich, moist soil, although most will tolerate dry shade. Crown rot, a fungal disease that causes the plants to wilt and die, is often a problem in areas with high humidity; look for a spot with well-drained soil and good air circulation. Ajugas are quite vigorous and can quickly creep into adjacent lawn areas; keep them separate with an edging strip, or be prepared to trim the edge 2 or 3 times a year. Propagate by division in spring.

Uses. Ajugas are ideal for covering large areas quickly. They are especially useful under trees and shrubs.

ALLEGHENY PACHYSANDRA.
See *Pachysandra* spp.

Arctostaphylos uva-ursi

ark-toe-STAFF-ill-ose EW-vuh ER-see. Bearberry.
Late spring. Zones 2 to 7.

○ ✳

Characteristics. Height: 6 inches. Spread: 2 feet.

Bearberry is an attractive, slow-growing, mat-forming groundcover with shiny, evergreen leaves. The small, pendulous, white to pink flowers are followed by lovely red fruit. In winter, the leaves turn a beautiful bronze color.

How to Grow. Bearberry prefers full sun and poor, acid, sandy soil. It can tolerate salt spray but does not grow well in areas with high heat and humidity. Do not fertilize. Bearberry can be tricky

Arctostaphylos uva-ursi

to propagate; try cuttings in summer.

Uses. This tough groundcover is excellent for seaside gardens and for acid-soil areas, especially on slopes.

Artemisia stellerana

ar-teh-MEEZ-ee-uh stel-er-AH-nuh.
Beach wormwood. Late spring. Zones 3 to 8.

○ ✳

Characteristics. Height: 1 foot. Spread: 2 feet. Beach wormwood forms low-growing clumps of

Artemisia stellerana 'Silver Brocade'

grayish white foliage. The leaves have a beautiful lobed shape and a soft, feltlike appearance. Small yellow flowers appear in late spring.

How to Grow. Beach wormwood tolerates a wide variety of conditions but prefers full sun and good drainage. Cut back faded flowers to keep the plants neat. To propagate, divide the plants in spring or take cuttings in summer.

Uses. This plant makes a superb groundcover for seaside, perennial, or cottage gardens. Try it as an edging for a border or path. It blends well with annuals and bulbs.

Asarum spp.

uh-SAR-um. Wild ginger. Spring. Zones 3 to 9.

◖ ●

Characteristics. Height: 10 inches. Spread: 15 inches.

Wild gingers produce carpets of heart-shaped foliage and interesting, brown-speckled, spring flowers that hide beneath the leaves. The root has a spicy, gingerlike aroma. Canada wild ginger (*Asarum canadense*) is a deciduous species with broad, medium to dark green leaves; it is quite hardy. European wild ginger (*A. europaeum*) has shiny, dark green, evergreen leaves; it is slightly less hardy (Zones 4 to 8). Mottled wild ginger (*A. shut-*

tleworthii) produces beautiful evergreen leaves that are spotted with silver. This species is more heat-tolerant and less hardy (Zones 7 to 9) than European wild ginger.

How to Grow. Wild gingers prefer shade and humus-rich, slightly acid soil that is moist but well drained. To propagate, divide the plants in spring.

Uses. Wild gingers are ideal groundcovers for shady rock gardens and terrace gardens, as well as woodland and naturalized gardens.

BEACH WORMWOOD. See *Artemisia stellerana*
BEARBERRY. See *Arctostaphylos uva-ursi*
BIGROOT GERANIUM. See *Geranium macrorrhizum*
BUGLEWEED. See *Ajuga* spp.

Ceratostigma plumbaginoides

ser-at-oh-STIG-muh plum-badge-in-oh-EYE-deez. Leadwort. Summer to fall. Zones 5 to 9.

○ ◖

Characteristics. Height: 10 inches. Spread: 18 inches.

Leadwort is a vigorous, mat-forming groundcover. It is evergreen in warm climates but dies back to the ground each winter in cold climates. The flow-

Asarum canadense

Ceratostigma plumbaginoides

ers, which bloom from summer to fall, are a spectacular electric blue, and the shiny, dark green leaves turn rich red colors in autumn.

How to Grow. Give leadwort a site with full sun or partial shade and well-drained soil enriched with generous amounts of organic matter. In areas where the foliage is evergreen, shear the plants back by hand or with a lawn mower on a high setting to encourage fresh, new growth.

Uses. Leadwort is excellent for a shady rock garden, in the front of a border, or combined with bulbs in a mass planting.

Chrysogonum virginianum

kris-OG-oh-num ver-jin-ee-AY-num. Golden star, green-and-gold. Spring through summer. Zones 5 to 9.

○ ◑

Characteristics. Height: 6 to 8 inches. Spread: 12 inches.

Golden star, also known as green-and-gold, is a delightful, small, mat-forming plant with small, hairy leaves. Bright yellow daisylike flowers bloom over a long season. This fast spreader is sometimes evergreen in warm climates.

How to Grow. This groundcover grows in sun or partial shade and rich, moist soil that is slightly acid. To propagate, divide the plants in spring.

Uses. Golden star is not always reliable for creating solid mats over large areas. However, it blends beautifully with other plants in a naturalized or wildflower garden.

Convallaria majalis

kon-vuh-LAIR-ee-uh muh-JAL-iss.
Lily-of-the-valley. Spring. Zones 2 to 8.

◑ ●

Characteristics. Height: 10 inches. Spread: 12 inches.

The sweet, fragrant, nodding white flowers of lily-of-the-valley are a symbol of spring. In addition to the flowers, the deciduous plants offer attractive, broad leaves and a vigorous, spreading habit that makes them great groundcovers. The variegated form 'Aureovariegata' has leaves with striking yellow stripes. 'Fortin's Giant' features larger flowers. 'Prolificans' is a double-flowered form. 'Rosea' bears pink flowers.

How to Grow. Plant lily-of-the-valley in a partially to fully shaded site with moist to dry soil that has been amended with organic matter. Mulch with compost each autumn to keep the soil rich. In cool climates and moist soil, lily-of-the-valley can become a weed because it is such a strong grower. To keep it under control, or to expand your plantings,

Chrysogonum virginianum

Convllaria majalis

divide the plants in fall or spring after flowering.

Uses. Lily-of-the-valley is ideal for a shade garden. Choose a spot where its spreading won't be a problem.

CREEPING JENNY. See *Lysimachia nummularia*
CREEPING JUNIPER. See *Juniperus horizontalis*
DEAD NETTLE. See *Lamium maculatum*
ENGLISH IVY. See *Hedera helix*

Galax urceolata

GAY-laks er-see-oh-LAH-tuh. Wandflower.
Late spring to early summer. Zones 3 to 8.

Characteristics. Height: 15 inches. Spread: 15 inches.

This reliable, striking groundcover has rounded, shiny, evergreen leaves that turn bronze in fall and winter. Spikes of delicate white flowers appear in late spring to early summer.

How to Grow. Wandflower needs shade and moist, humusy, loam soil that is slightly acidic. To propagate, divide the plants in spring or fall.

Uses. Wandflower is an ideal groundcover for spots under trees and shrubs.

Galium odoratum

GAL-ee-um oh-dor-AH-tum. Sweet woodruff.
Spring. Zones 4 to 8.

Characteristics. Height: 6 inches. Spread: 12 inches.

Sweet woodruff offers bright to dark green, whorled leaves on square stems. Its beautiful, starry, white flowers appear in spring. The deciduous plants die back to the ground each winter.

How to Grow. This groundcover grows best in soil that is constantly moist. It prefers shade (especially in hot climates), but will grow in full sun in cool areas. Divide the plants in spring or fall for propagation.

Uses. Sweet woodruff is perfect for a wild gar-

Galium odoratum

den, in the dappled shade of large trees, or in damp nooks and crannies. It can be invasive, so plant it where the spread isn't a problem. The dry leaves and stems smell like new-mown hay and are wonderful in sachets.

Gaultheria procumbens

gall-THEER-ee-uh proh-KUM-benz. Wintergreen.
Summer. Zones 3 to 8.

Characteristics. Height: 4 inches. Spread: 12 inches.

Gaultheria procumbens

This attractive, creeping, evergreen groundcover is a native woodland wildflower. It has leathery, rounded leaves that turn reddish in autumn. The leaves and fruit smell like wintergreen when crushed. The small white to pink, pendulous summer flowers are followed by large red berries.

How to Grow. Wintergreen must have partial to full shade and moist, acid soil that is high in organic matter. It is slow-growing and doesn't transplant well; leave established plants to form handsome clumps.

Uses. Wintergreen is great for woodland and shade gardens.

Geranium macrorrhizum

jer-AY-nee-um mak-roh-RY-zum.
Bigroot geranium. Spring. Zones 3 to 9.

Characteristics. Height: 18 inches. Spread: 18 inches.

This vigorous hardy geranium tolerates a wide range of growing conditions, making it a super groundcover. The large, aromatic, semievergreen leaves are 6 to 8 inches wide, with divided segments; they grow from large, fleshy, spreading roots. Because of its fragrance, this plant is sometimes confused with scented geraniums (*Pelargonium* spp.). The purplish pink flowers of bigroot geranium bloom in small clusters in spring and are borne above the leaves. 'Bevan's Variety' has magenta flowers with deep red sepals. The cultivar 'Alba' bears white flowers. 'Ingwersen's Variety' has light pink flowers.

How to Grow. The plants will tolerate a range of conditions but prefer full sun in cool climates and some shade in hot climates. Although they thrive in soil that is constantly moist, they can withstand dry conditions well. Divide the plants in spring or fall for propagation.

Uses. Bigroot geranium is useful as a groundcover in hot, dry areas or in light shade under trees.

GINGER, WILD. See *Asarum* spp.
GOLDEN STAR. See *Chrysogonum virginianum*
GREEN-AND-GOLD. See *Chrysogonum virginianum*

Hedera helix

Hedera helix

HED-er-uh HE-liks. English ivy. Evergreen.
Zones 5 to 10.

Characteristics. Height: 6 to 8 inches. Spread: 3 feet.

English ivy creates a lovely evergreen groundcover under trees and in shady spots where few other plants will grow. Although it is a vigorous plant, it is not terribly invasive. 'Thorndale', also known as Baltic ivy, features large, attractive leaves. It is very hardy and is useful for stabilizing slopes and preventing other erosion problems. 'Gold Heart', one of the most beautiful ivies, is popular for its heart-shaped, gold-striped leaves and its reliable growth habit.

How to Grow. English ivy tolerates a wide range of conditions, including full sun, deep shade, and poor soil. However, it prefers humus-rich, moist soil in partial shade. Cut the plants back as needed to keep them from spreading out of bounds. To propagate, dig up and transplant rooted stems or take cuttings in summer.

Uses. This groundcover is excellent for dry shade under trees or on slopes. Add extra interest by interplanting it with small bulbs, such as crocuses and dwarf daffodils.

HENS AND CHICKS. See *Sempervivum* spp.

Hypericum calycinum

hy-PEAR-ih-kum kal-ih-SIGH-num.
Aaron's-beard. Summer. Zones 5 to 8.

○ ◑

Characteristics. Height: 18 inches. Spread: 24 inches.

This fast-growing, evergreen or semievergreen groundcover produces blue-green leaves and brilliant yellow blossoms with showy stamens on low, arching branches. It blooms on new wood and flowers over a long season.

How to Grow. Aaron's-beard grows well in full sun or partial shade and lean, well-drained soil. It performs best in the cooler parts of its range. If the plants lose their leaves over winter, shear them back by one-half to two-thirds to promote fresh, new growth. To propagate, divide the plants in fall or spring.

Uses. Use Aaron's-beard to cover hillsides, slopes, or berms.

Hypericum calycinum

IVY, ENGLISH. See *Hedera helix*
JAPANESE SPURGE. See *Pachysandra* spp.

Juniperus horizontalis

jew-NIP-er-us hore-ih-zon-TAL-iss.
Creeping juniper. Evergreen. Zones 3 to 9.

○

Characteristics. Height: 6 inches. Spread: 6 feet.

Creeping junipers are widely grown as groundcovers for hot, dry sites. Many cultivars with different foliage colors are available. One of the most popular is blue rug juniper (*Juniperus horizontalis* 'Wiltonii' or 'Blue Rug'). It offers intense steel blue foliage that hugs the ground on fast-growing, trailing branches. In winter, the foliage takes on a purplish cast.

How to Grow. The plants demand full sun and good drainage. They are very tolerant of heat and dry, sandy sites. Slightly acid soil (pH 5.0 to 6.0) is ideal. Creeping junipers aren't especially easy to propagate at home; buy new plants to expand your plantings, or try cuttings in fall.

Uses. Creeping junipers are ideally suited for covering hot, sunny slopes.

Juniperus horizontalis 'Wiltonii'

Lamium maculatum 'White Nancy'

Lamium maculatum
LAY-mee-um mak-yew-LAY-tum. Dead nettle.
Spring. Zones 3 to 8.
◐

Characteristics. Height: 10 inches. Spread: 18 inches.

Dead nettle has green leaves with silver centers, making it valuable for brightening up dark areas. The species is very vigorous and can be invasive; cultivars may be slightly less aggressive. 'White Nancy' has very silvery leaves, along with white flowers that appear in spring. 'Beacon Silver' is similar to 'White Nancy' but bears pink flowers. 'Aureum' has yellow leaves with a white mid-vein area; it requires some shade.

How to Grow. Dead nettle needs evenly moist soil in partial shade. After the spring bloom, shear the plants lightly to promote fresh, new growth. To propagate, divide the plants in spring.

Uses. Plant dead nettle in or along a border, under trees or shrubs, or with roses.

LEADWORT. See *Ceratostigma plumbaginoides*
LILY-OF-THE-VALLEY. See *Convallaria majalis*
LILYTURF. See *Liriope* spp.

Liriope spp.
ler-EYE-oh-pee. Lilyturf. Summer. Zones 5 to 10.

Characteristics. Height: 10 to 24 inches. Spread: 18 inches

Creeping lilyturf (*Liriope spicata*) forms thick mats of arching, narrow leaves. As a groundcover, it has a wonderful grassy texture. Spikes of pale lavender flowers appear in summer. Blue lilyturf (*L. muscari*) has slightly wider leaves and grows taller (up to 2 feet); it is less vigorous and has a somewhat coarser look. Mondo grasses (*Ophiopogon* spp.) closely resemble lilyturf but are less hardy.

How to Grow. Lilyturfs are adaptable and easy to grow. They will grow in sun or shade; they appreciate some moisture but can take well-drained to droughty soil. The plants tolerate heat well and adapt to seaside conditions. If the leaves turn brown

Liriope spicata

after a harsh winter, shear them back in early spring. To propagate, divide the plants in spring or fall. The round, black seeds that follow the flowers will often self-sow, and you can lift and move seedlings when they appear.

Uses. Lilyturf is well suited to growing on slopes or banks, and under trees or shrubs. It also makes a nice edging.

Lysimachia nummularia

ly-sih-MAK-ee-uh num-yew-LAH-ree-uh.
Creeping Jenny. Early summer. Zones 3 to 8.

Characteristics. Height: 2 to 4 inches. Spread: 2 to 3 feet.

This ground-hugger has small, rounded, green leaves and 1-inch-wide, bright yellow, fragrant flowers, which appear in early summer. It is a good, dense groundcover, although it can become invasive. The golden form, 'Aurea', is especially beautiful and is less vigorous.

How to Grow. Creeping Jenny thrives in moist soil and partial to full shade. To propagate, divide the plants in spring.

Uses. Grow creeping Jenny along streams or pools, where it can spread freely.

Lysimachia nummularia

Microbiota decussata

Microbiota decussata

my-kroh-by-OH-tuh deh-koo-SAY-tuh.
Siberian carpet cypress. Evergreen. Zones 2 to 8.

Characteristics. Height: 2 feet. Spread: 10 feet.

Siberian carpet cypress is an exquisite, dwarf, evergreen shrub with graceful, shiny green, scalelike leaves that turn a bronzy color in winter. The plants are extremely hardy and easy to grow.

How to Grow. Siberian carpet cypress grows equally well in sun or partial shade, as long as it has well-drained soil. It can tolerate drought. The easiest way to expand your plantings is to purchase more plants; you can also try taking cuttings in autumn.

Uses. Use Siberian carpet cypress in rock gardens, borders, or foundation plantings.

Pachysandra spp.

pak-ih-SAN-druh. Pachysandra.
Late spring. Zones 4 to 9.

Characteristics. Height: 8 to 12 inches. Spread: 18 inches.

Japanese spurge (*Pachysandra terminalis*) is one of the most popular groundcovers. Its shiny, whorled, evergreen leaves are a lovely bright green

Pachysandra terminalis

Sarcococca hookerana var. *humilis*

color when young, aging to a rich dark green. The leaves are topped with creamy white flowers in late spring. 'Green Carpet' is a lower-growing cultivar with darker green leaves. 'Silver Edge' has leaves with thin silver-white margins. Allegheny pachysandra (*P. procumbens*) is a native species that is more clump-forming. Its light green summer leaves turn darker and develop silvery mottling during the winter. Brushy white flowers emerge from the center of the clumps in spring.

How to Grow. Pachysandra prefers a shady location with a rich, moist, slightly acid (pH 5.5 to 6.5) soil. Cut off old leaves as needed to promote new growth. To propagate, divide the plants in spring.

Uses. Pachysandras are perfect for growing under trees and in heavy shade.

PERIWINKLE. See *Vinca* spp.

Sarcococca hookerana var. humilis

sar-koh-KOH-kuh hook-er-AH-nuh HEW-mil-iss.
Sweet box. Early spring. Zones 5 to 8.
◑ ●

Characteristics. Height: 2 feet. Spread: 2 feet. Sweetly fragrant, late-winter flowers and attrac-

tive, glossy, evergreen foliage make this a wonderful shrubby groundcover. Sweet box bears small black fruits and spreads slowly.

How to Grow. Sweet box grows well in shady sites. It prefers some moisture but can adapt to drier conditions. To propagate, try summer cuttings.

Uses. Grow sweet box as a groundcover under trees and shrubs or in a shady border.

Sempervivum spp.

sem-per-VY-vum. Hens and chicks.
Summer. Zones 3 to 8.
○ ◑

Characteristics. Height: 8 to 10 inches. Spread: 16 inches.

Hens and chicks are loved for their charming, evergreen rosettes, which consist of fleshy leaves with pointed tips. The thick, upright, flower stalks are topped with starry, purplish red flowers in summer. New plants are produced around the base of mature rosettes—hence the name "hens and chicks." The "hens" often die after flowering, but the "chicks" quickly fill in the space.

How to Grow. Hens and chicks tolerate a wide range of growing conditions, including hot, dry, and rocky places. They can take sun or light shade and grow best in well-drained, neutral soil.

Sempervivum spp.

Vinca minor

Uses. Try a patch of hens and chicks along or in a wall or walkway. They also make superb additions to rock gardens.

SIBERIAN CARPET CYPRESS. See *Microbiota decussata*
SWEET BOX. See *Sarcococca hookerana* var. *humilis*
SWEET WOODRUFF. See *Galium odoratum*

Vinca spp.

VING-kuh. Periwinkle. Spring. Zones 4 to 9.

Characteristics. Height: 4 to 6 inches. Spread: 24 inches.

Periwinkles are widely used groundcovers with glossy, evergreen leaves and rich blue flowers that appear in spring. The nonflowering trailing stems take root as they creep across the ground. Common periwinkle (*Vinca minor*) has small leaves. The cultivar 'Alba' has white flowers. Greater periwinkle (*V. major*) produces large leaves and is less hardy (generally Zones 7 to 10). 'Variegata' has cream-and-green leaves and is a popular addition to hanging baskets and window boxes.

How to Grow. These plants prefer loose, humus-rich soil with plenty of moisture. They can grow in full sun or shade but generally do best in partial shade. Weed carefully the first few years, until the plants get established. To propagate, divide the plants in spring or fall.

Uses. Periwinkles are ideal for controlling erosion on shady slopes and for covering the soil under trees and shrubs.

WANDFLOWER. See *Galax urceolata*
WILD GINGER. See *Asarum* spp.
WINTERGREEN. See *Gaultheria procumbens*
WOODRUFF, SWEET. See *Galium odoratum*
WORMWOOD, BEACH. See *Artemisia stellerana*

CLIMBING COMPANIONS. *Vines make ideal decorative coverings for walls, fences, and trellises. Both of these climbers—Boston ivy (*Parthenocissus tricuspidata*) and variegated Persian ivy (*Hedera colchica 'Dentata Variegata'*)—cling to supports with holdfasts.*

CHAPTER TEN

VINES

V INES HAVE MUCH TO OFFER THE ADVENTUROUS
GARDENER. Trained up trellises or allowed to spread gracefully over the ground, vines grow quickly to provide cover, shade,
or privacy. They make a beautiful backdrop for borders and foundation plantings, and they can provide vertical accents for flower
beds. Vines can also add seasonal interest—for example, when
allowed to twine through trees and shrubs.

   In this chapter, you'll learn more about these and other ways
that vines can add excitement to your landscape. Plus, you'll find
a gallery of plant portraits covering more than 15 popular vines,
along with descriptions and growing guidelines. So read on to
enter the wonderful world of vines!

WHAT ARE VINES?

Vines are plants that need support to hold themselves upright.
Some can grab onto a support by themselves; others will need
some help from you to hang on. You'll know what kind of assis-

FLOWER-FILLED SHADE. *This pergola spanning a walkway is decked with* Clematis armandii. *It provides a lightly shaded spot from which to enjoy the rest of the garden.*

tance your vines need by seeing how they grow. There are three basic ways vines can climb.

CLINGING VINES

The first group includes climbers that are self-clinging. Some, such as English ivy (*Hedera helix*), have aerial roots; others, including Virginia creeper (*Parthenocissus quinquefolia*), have adhering tendril tips. These vines need little training and are able to climb walls, trellises, and tree trunks without additional support.

TWINING VINES

The second group consists of twining vines, which climb by wrapping themselves around a support. Some, including clematis, have twining petioles (leaf stems) or tendrils that need wire, string, or netting for support. Other twining vines, such as trumpet honeysuckle (*Lonicera sempervirens*) and wiste-

rias (*Wisteria* spp.), wrap their whole stems around a support; they also need wires, poles, fences, or trellises to climb. If you want them to go up a trellis or thick post, you'll need to train the young vines in the right direction by securing the base of the plant to the support with strings or wire.

When training a twining vine to cover a solid structure, such as a fence or wall, leave at least 1 inch of space between the wires or trellis and the structure. This will allow for good air circulation around the plant and greatly reduce possible disease problems. Also, attach the trellis to the wall or fence with hooks at the top and hinges at the base. That way, you can easily uncover the structure when you need to paint or do other maintenance.

CLIMBING ROSES

The third group includes long-caned roses that adapt well to vertical training. These plants don't actually climb, but they can hang onto rough supports (such as tree trunks) with their hooked thorns. Climbing roses need a sturdy support—along with pruning, training, and tying—to look their best. (To learn more about choosing and growing climbing roses, see Chapter 6 Roses.)

WHY GROW VINES?

Clematis twining up an old tree trunk, honeysuckle covering a garden shed, wisteria climbing over a large arbor with its dangling, jewel-like flowers—all of these are glorious additions to the garden. Vines growing on and over things can create depth and dimension in outdoor spaces. Their twining stems and cascading flowers provide a sense of motion in the garden. Vines can weave together plants of different heights and textures, giving a unified look to a design. They can also add a vertical element, raising the eye above ground level to accentuate or obscure particular features. Some vines even make attractive groundcovers if you allow them to spread rather than climb.

GARDENING WITH VINES

Versatile vines deserve a place in every part of the yard. Training them to grow up trellises, walls, arbors, and fences is both a traditional and an attractive way to display many vines. Leafy vines, such as crimson glory vine (*Vitis coignetiae*) and wisteria, are ideal for providing cool summer shade for porches, patios, and decks. These plants also make a perfect screen to add a sense of privacy or block an unpleasant view without the permanence or expense of a solid fence.

But don't forget that vines have much more to offer than just leaves. Flowering vines, such as morning glories (*Ipomoea* spp.) and clematis, are ideal for adding height and color to beds and borders. Train them to climb posts in the middle or back of the border, or create a tepee of bamboo poles for the vines to cover as a garden centerpiece.

For even more excitement, combine vines with each other and with other plants. Climbing roses, for instance, look simply stunning blended with clematis and honeysuckle. Delicate clematis also looks great growing up through spring-blooming shrubs, such as lilacs (*Syringa* spp.), sweet mock orange (*Philadelphus coronarius*), and viburnums (*Viburnum* spp.); the shrub blooms early in the season, and the clematis flowers add welcome summer-to-fall color. If you have a dead tree trunk that needs covering, choose a more vigorous vine, such as silver lace vine (*Polygonum aubertii*).

TRAINING AND PRUNING VINES

Most vines will grow just fine without a lot of fuss. If they need some help holding onto their support, you can tie them with soft string. (Check the ties every few months to make sure they aren't cutting into the vine stems.) Woody vines benefit from some pruning and shaping to control their growth; regular pruning of very vigorous vines, such as wisteria, is especially important to keep them in bounds. For details on how and when to prune specific vines, see the individual plant portraits that follow.

PLANT PORTRAITS

The following plant portraits cover some of the best evergreen and deciduous vines for your garden. Most are relatively easy to find at nurseries and garden centers. Mail-order catalogs offer a wide selection of cultivars, along with species of unusual vines, so be sure to check them out.

The plants are listed by their botanical names, in bold print. Below the botanical name, you'll find

GROWING TIPS AT A GLANCE

Each of the following plant portraits includes simple symbols to highlight special features you need to know about each vine. If you're not sure what any of the symbols mean, refer back to this key.

○ Full sun (more than 6 hours of sun a day; ideally all day)

◐ Partial sun (some direct sun, but less than 6 hours a day)

● Shade (no direct sun)

❦ Fragrant

its pronunciation, along with the common name, the bloom time or main season of interest, and the hardiness zones. Each entry also includes a description of the plant, including its height and color, plus growing guidelines and suggested garden uses.

Actinidia kolomikta

ak-tih-NID-ee-uh koh-loh-MIK-tuh. Hardy kiwi.
Spring. Zones 4 to 8.
○ ◑

Characteristics. Height: 15 to 20 feet.

Hardy kiwi produces male and female flowers on separate plants. The male vine is distinguished by its attractive, tricolored variegation, with young leaves that are richly colored in pink, white, and green in early summer. The female vine bears small, fragrant flowers, followed by small, greenish yellow, edible fruits.

How to Grow. This deciduous, twining vine grows in full sun or partial shade and tolerates a wide range of soil conditions. Male plants may take several years to produce their colorful leaves. A sunny location on a south- or west-facing wall and alkaline soil can enhance the variegation. To get fruit from the vines, generally you must grow both male and female plants, although 'Issai' is a self-pollinating cultivar. Hardy kiwi needs little pruning; simply trim and thin as needed in late winter or early spring.

Uses. Train hardy kiwi to climb a large wall or fence.

Akebia quinata

uh-KEE-bee-uh kwin-AH-tuh. Fiveleaf akebia.
Spring. Zones 4 to 9.
○ ◑ ●

Characteristics. Height: Over 30 feet.

Fiveleaf akebia is a twining, semievergreen vine with beautiful bluish green leaves that have five leaflets. The small, purplish, fragrant flowers appear in spring and may be followed by long, sausage-shaped, dark purple fruits with white flesh.

How to Grow. This vigorous vine grows well in most conditions, from sun to shade, in moist or dry soil. To tidy and shape the young plants, trim them

Actinidia kolomikta

Akebia quinata

in summer. If the mature plants get out of control, cut them to the ground in late winter or early spring; train the new shoots to reclimb the support.

Uses. Train this fast-growing vine to climb up trees or cover large structures.

Ampelopsis brevipedunculata

am-pel-OP-sis brev-ih-peh-dunk-yew-LAH-tuh. Porcelain ampelopsis. Spring. Zones 5 to 10.

○ ◑

Characteristics. Height: Up to 25 feet.

Porcelain ampelopsis is a vigorous vine that climbs by means of curling tendrils. The deciduous, three-lobed, green leaves are 2 to 3 inches across. Inconspicuous summer flowers are followed by clusters of rounded fruits that turn an exceptional color of porcelain blue in autumn. 'Elegans' is a less vigorous form with white-and-pink mottled leaves.

How to Grow. This vine grows in most soil types, in sun or partial shade. It needs a long, sunny summer for the fruits to turn blue. The plants may reseed in the garden; pull out unwanted seedlings while they're small. In late winter to early spring, cut the previous season's growth back to 2 or 3 buds.

Uses. Allow porcelain ampelopsis to cover a large structure or rock pile.

Aristolochia durior

Aristolochia durior

uh-riss-toe-LOW-kee-uh DER-ee-or. Dutchman's-pipe. Late spring. Zones 4 to 8.

○ ◑

Characteristics. Height: Up to 30 feet.

This twining, deciduous vine has heart-shaped leaves and unusual, 3-inch-long, brownish yellow flowers.

How to Grow. Dutchman's-pipe grows well in full sun to partial shade. Although it prefers moist, rich, well-drained soil, it will tolerate less ideal conditions. After flowering, trim the vines as needed for shape. To rejuvenate old or overgrown vines, cut the plants to the ground in late winter.

Uses. Train Dutchman's-pipe up a tree, fence, or stump. It is often used as a fast-growing screen on a porch or arbor.

Ampelopsis brevipedunculata

Bignonia capreolata

big-NO-nee-uh kap-ree-oh-LAH-tuh. Cross vine. Spring. Zones 7 to 9.

○ ◑

Characteristics. Height: 50 feet.

Cross vine is a fast-growing, semievergreen climber with twining leaf tendrils. It has large leaflets, dense foliage, and showy, orange-red, tubu-

Bignonia capreolata

Clematis X jackmanii

lar flowers. It can be rampant in warm, moist places.

How to Grow. This vine will grow in sunny or partially shady locations. It prefers moist soil. Trim as needed in late winter or early spring.

Uses. Cross vine looks best growing up a wall or tree.

BOSTON IVY. See *Parthenocissus* spp.
CAPE HONEYSUCKLE. See *Tecomaria capensis*
CHINESE WISTERIA. See *Wisteria* spp.

Clematis X jackmanii

KLEM-uh-tiss jak-MAN-ee-eye. Jackman clematis.
Summer to fall. Zones 4 to 8.
○

Characteristics. Height: 6 to 14 feet.
The original large-flowered clematis, Jackman clematis is a thin-stemmed, deciduous vine. It climbs by wrapping its leafstalks around its support. It is known for its profusion of rich violet-purple flowers, which are 4 to 7 inches across. The flowers bloom on the current season's growth, over bright green leaves.

There are many fine cultivars to choose from. 'Comtesse de Bouchaud' bears large mauve-pink flowers in summer and is known to be very free-flowering. It is especially lovely growing up a tree trunk. 'Duchess of Edinburgh' has medium double, white flowers and is well suited for growing over shrubs or on walls. 'Ernest Markham' has large, magenta-red flowers with light brown anthers; it is one of the best red-flowered clematis. 'Superba' is the most popular clematis because of its large, dark purple flowers and free-flowering habit. 'Nelly Moser' bears distinctive mauve-lilac flowers with a deep pink bar and red anthers.

How to Grow. This vine prefers moderately moist soil with good drainage; dig in plenty of compost or aged manure before planting. Clematis grow best with their tops in the sun and their roots in the shade. To satisfy these seemingly incompatible conditions, choose a sunny spot where the base of the plant will be shaded by a shrub or a planting of perennials. Or, mulch the plants to keep the roots cool. Avoid planting Jackman clematis in extremely hot, exposed areas. If the individual stems or entire plants wilt suddenly, remove and destroy the affected parts; there is no cure for clematis wilt. Since plants bloom on the current season's growth, prune in February or March, leaving a strong pair or two of buds at the base of each stem.

Uses. Train Jackman clematis on fences or walls, or up through shrubs. It also makes an interesting groundcover when allowed to sprawl.

Clematis montana
KLEM-uh-tiss mon-TAN-uh. Anemone clematis.
Late spring. Zones 5 to 9.
○

Characteristics. Height: 20 to 30 feet.

Anemone clematis is a fast-growing woody vine that climbs with twining leaf stems. The green leaves are roughly toothed and made up of three leaflets. New growth is tinged with purple. The white to pink, 2-inch-wide flowers are borne singly

Clematis montana

or in clusters; most have a vanilla scent. The feathery seed heads that follow are ornamental. The variety *Clematis montana* var. *rubens* is variable but usually has deep mauve-pink flowers with creamy stamens.

Other early-flowering clematis include *C. alpina*, which climbs to 6 feet and bears bell-shaped, violet-blue, nodding flowers; and Armand clematis (*C. armandii*), a fast-growing, evergreen species suitable for warm climates (Zones 8 and south). Armand clematis has large, glossy leaves with prominent veins and fragrant white flowers that appear in early spring. The feathery seed heads are decorative. *C. macropetala* grows to 10 feet tall and offers bright blue, 4-inch-wide flowers in early spring, followed by silvery seeds in fall.

How to Grow. Plant anemone clematis and other early-flowering species in full sun, but keep the roots covered with mulch or a groundcover. The soil should be fertile, well drained, and evenly moist. Provide wire or string supports to prevent the brittle stems from breaking. Prune the current season's shoots back to 2 or 3 buds after flowering. These plants are subject to clematis wilt; remove and destroy infected parts.

Uses. Both anemone and Armand clematis can climb high into trees and cover large trellises. Train smaller early-blooming species on fences or posts.

Clematis viticella
KLEM-uh-tiss vih-tih-SELL-uh. Italian clematis.
Summer. Zones 4 to 8.
○

Characteristics. Height: To 12 feet.

An excellent climber, Italian clematis is a semiwoody vine with 1- to 2-inch-long leaves that are divided into three leaflets. It blooms prolifically on the current season's growth for 2 to 3 months. The nodding, saucer-shaped flowers are 1½ to 2½ inches across and deep purple with green stamens.

How to Grow. Italian clematis is vigorous and easy to grow. Prune the stems back to 6 to 12 inches above the ground every several years in late winter or early spring. Unlike many of the large-flowered clematis, this species is not susceptible to clematis wilt.

Uses. Allow Italian clematis to climb over shrubs up trees or on trellises..

CLIMBING HYDRANGEA. See *Hydrangea anomala* subsp. *petiolaris*
CRIMSON GLORY VINE. See *Vitis coignetiae*
CROSS VINE. See *Bignonia capreolata*
CYPRESS VINE. See *Ipomoea* spp.
DUTCHMAN'S-PIPE. See *Aristolochia durior*
FIVELEAF AKEBIA. See *Akebia quinata*
HONEYSUCKLE, CAPE. See *Tecomaria capensis*
HONEYSUCKLE, TRUMPET. See *Lonicera sempervirens*

Hydrangea anomala subsp. petiolaris

hy-DRAN-jee-uh uh-NOM-uh-luh
pet-ee-oh-LAIR-iss. Climbing hydrangea.
Summer. Zones 5 to 8.

Characteristics. Height: Up to 75 feet.
This self-clinging vine attaches to structures with aerial rootlets. It has large, circular leaves and showy flower clusters. Each cluster is made up of many small, fragrant, white flowers surrounded

Hydrangea anomala subsp. *petiolaris*

by larger petal-like bracts.
How to Grow. Plant climbing hydrangea in full sun or partial shade and fertile, moist, well-drained soil. It can be slow to establish itself, but it's worth the wait. Prune lightly in early spring to remove damaged growth or to shape the plants.
Uses. Climbing hydrangea is excellent for growing on a wall, arbor, porch, or tree.

Ipomoea spp.

ih-poh-MEE-uh. Morning glory, cypress vine.
Summer. Zone 10.
○

Characteristics. Height: Up to 20 feet.
These plants are fast-growing, soft-stemmed, twining vines. They are hardy in frost-free areas; elsewhere, they are grown as annuals. Common morning glory (*Ipomoea purpurea*) is popular for its broad, heart-shaped leaves and showy purple or reddish, white-throated, funnel-shaped flowers. 'Heavenly Blue' bears gorgeous true-blue flowers. Cypress vine (*I. quamoclit*) offers dainty, fernlike foliage and striking, brilliant red, star-shaped flowers that attract hummingbirds. Cardinal climber (*I. X multifida*) produces small scarlet trumpets.
How to Grow. Morning glories and cypress vines thrive in full sun and average, well-drained soil. Soak the seeds overnight, then sow them outdoors after the last spring frost, when the soil is warm.
Uses. Train morning glories, cypress vines, and cardinal climbers on strings or wires to cover walls, fences, trellises, or arbors.

JAPANESE WISTERIA. See *Wisteria* spp.
KIWI, HARDY. See *Actinidia kolomikta*

Lonicera sempervirens

lon-ISS-er-uh sem-per-VY-renz. Trumpet honey-suckle. Summer. Zones 3 to 8.
○ ◐

Characteristics. Height: 12 to 20 feet.
Trumpet honeysuckle is a twining vine that is

Lonicera sempervirens with yarrow (foreground)

Parthenocissus tricuspidata

evergreen in the South and semievergreen or decid-uous in the North. It has 3-inch-long leaves and scentless, scarlet-and-yellow, tubular flowers that are 2 inches long and bloom in summer. The flow-ers are followed in autumn by bright red berries, which are popular with birds. 'Magnifica' blooms later and features red flowers. 'Sulphurea' has true yellow blooms that continue flowering well into fall.

How to Grow. Trumpet honeysuckle prefers rich, moist soil but will grow in any good garden soil. It thrives in full sun or partial shade and toler-ates urban conditions. Prune as needed after flower-ing to keep the plants in bounds.

Uses. Allow trumpet honeysuckle to climb up a trellis or arbor, or let it scale a support on the side of a building. It also grows well with climbing roses.

MORNING GLORY. See *Ipomoea* spp.

Parthenocissus spp.

par-then-oh-SIS-us. Boston ivy, Virginia creeper.
Summer. Zones 4 to 8.

○ ◑ ●

Characteristics. Height: 30 to 50 feet.
These vigorous, deciduous vines have adhesive-tipped tendrils that cement themselves to walls;

they need no support to climb. Boston ivy (*Parthenocissus tricuspidata*) has shiny, 3-lobed leaves that are 8 inches wide. Clusters of small, greenish, summer flowers are followed by dark blue-black berries. 'Purpurea' produces leaves that remain pur-ple throughout the growing season. 'Veitchii' has smaller leaves that are purplish when young. Virginia creeper (*P. quinquefolia*) is a similar species with 5-leaflet leaves. Also commonly called wood-bine, or simply American ivy, it produces small flowers in summer, followed by clusters of blue-black berries. Both species turn brilliant scarlet or crimson in fall.

How to Grow. These vines grow in any good garden soil, in sun or shade. They tolerate city con-ditions. Trim as needed during the summer to remove damaged growth or to shape the plants.

Uses. Both Boston ivy and Virginia creeper are excellent for covering walls, fences, and tree trunks. The berries are attractive to birds.

Polygonum aubertii

Polygonum aubertii
poh-LIG-oh-num aw-BER-tee-eye.
Silver lace vine. Summer. Zones 4 to 8.

Characteristics. Height: 25 feet or more.
Silver lace vine, also called fleece vine, is a fast-growing, twining climber. Its creamy white, fragrant flowers bloom in long fluffy or airy-looking clusters through the summer and into fall. They cover the top of the vine, giving it a lovely, lacy appearance.

How to Grow. Silver lace vine grows in sun or partial shade; it tolerates dry soil and urban conditions. Another common name for this vigerous vine gives a clue to its only drawback—it is also called mile-a-minute vine. Plants can grow between 20 and 30 feet per year in ideal conditions. Prune severely in late winter or early spring to keep it under control, especially in small spaces.

Uses. Allow silver lace vine to climb up sturdy supports on large structures and on trees. This handsome climber can also be used to disguise a chain-link fence; space plants at 25-foot intervals, and they will cover it completely.

PORCELAIN AMPELOPSIS. See *Ampelopsis brevipedunculata*
SILVER LACE VINE. See *Polygonum aubertii*

Tecomaria capensis

Tecomaria capensis
tek-oh-MARE-ee-uh kuh-PEN-sis. Cape honeysuckle. Summer to late fall. Zones 9 to 10.

Characteristics. Height: 6 to 20 feet.
This evergreen vine is suitable for mild climates. Its beautiful, dark green foliage makes a great backdrop for the orange-red or scarlet, 2-inch-long flowers.

How to Grow. Cape honeysuckle needs full sun. It grows well in sandy soil and tolerates salt and drought. Prune in spring to thin out crowded stems.

Uses. Train cape honeysuckle over a bank or low wall. It also makes a good espalier trained against a wall or fence.

TRUMPET HONEYSUCKLE. See *Lonicera sempervirens*
VIRGINIA CREEPER. See *Parthenocissus* spp.

Vitis coignetiae
VY-tiss coin-YAY-tee-ee. Crimson glory vine.
Summer. Zones 5 to 8.

Characteristics. Height: 50 feet or more.
Crimson glory vine is an ornamental, fast-grow-

Vitis coignetiae

Wisteria floribunda

ing vine that climbs by wrapping its tendrils around a support. It has dense, heavy, rounded leaves that are up to 12 inches long. Its most notable feature is the brilliant red autumn color. The insignificant summer flowers are followed by clusters of black berries.

How to Grow. Crimson glory vine prefers full sun to partial shade and moist, well-drained soil. Prune the plants as needed in late winter or early spring to keep them in bounds.

Uses. Train crimson glory vine on large pergolas, or use it as a groundcover to cover slopes.

Wisteria spp.

wis-TEER-ee-uh. Wisteria. Spring. Zones 4 to 9.

○

Characteristics. Height: 30 feet or more.

Wisterias are large, vigorous, twining vines that require a strong (preferably metal) structure to support their weight. Japanese wisteria (*Wisteria flori-*

bunda) is the most widely planted species. It produces a spectacular spring show of lightly fragrant, lavender-blue flowers in long, cascading clusters. 'Macro-botrys' bears very fragrant flowers in clusters up to 3 feet long. Chinese wisteria (*W. sinensis*) offers blue-violet, less-fragrant flowers; the clusters are 6 to 12 inches long.

How to Grow. Wisterias thrive in full sun and fertile, moist, well-drained soil. When purchasing a wisteria, try to buy a named cultivar, because seedlings will vary in their flowering habits. Every year, prune the plants back severely after flowering. Pruning will encourage them to bloom more abundantly and keep them in bounds; if left unchecked, the vines can take over structures and cause severe damage.

Uses. Train wisterias to climb large, strong structures such as freestanding arbors or pergolas. They can also be trained on sturdy wires affixed to concrete or brick walls. They are powerful twining vines, and with time will pull apart all but the sturdiest structures. They will also pull down downspouts and gutters if left to ramble at will.

PART III

THE PRACTICAL GARDENER

ONCE YOU HAVE DEVELOPED A DESIGN THAT APPEALS TO YOU AND HAVE SELECTED THE PLANTS YOU WOULD LIKE TO GROW, IT'S TIME TO GET YOUR HANDS DIRTY. Sure, planting and caring for a garden takes work, but it's work that's enjoyable and relaxing. It's very good exercise, too.

In the chapters that follow, you'll learn all the basic techniques you need to know to have a healthy garden. Chapter 11 covers everything from preparing the soil, making compost, mulching, and fertilizing, to growing plants from seed, planting, and propagating. You will also find chapters on handy tools, pest and disease control, and answers to some of the questions Burpee customers ask most often. As you read these pages and work in your garden, keep in mind that you'll learn much of what you need to know just by going out and experimenting with different plants and techniques, to see which work best for you. That's because gardening conditions vary so much from one area to another. So use the basic guidelines that follow, but don't be afraid to experiment. Above all, have fun!

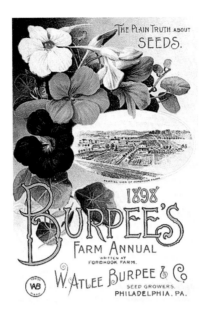

CHAPTER ELEVEN

PLANTING AND CARING FOR YOUR GARDEN

ONCE YOU'VE FINALIZED YOUR PLANTING PLAN, IT'S TIME TO GET OUT AND GET STARTED. Spend some time preparing the soil thoroughly so your carefully chosen plants will grow and thrive. Get the plants you need, either by growing them from seed or by purchasing healthy transplants. Plant them at the right depth and spacing, then stand back to watch them produce masses of beautiful blooms, tasty vegetables, or pungent leaves.

During the growing season, keep your plants vigorous and productive with good care, including mulching, fertilizing, watering, staking, pinching, and deadheading. If the urge to increase your perennial gardens strikes, propagate your existing plants with easy techniques such as division and cuttings. At the end of the season, prepare your garden for winter with a good fall cleanup. Pretty soon, the new seed and plant catalogs will start arriving, and it will be time to start the fun all over again!

PREPARING THE SOIL

The hardest work, and by far the most important for successful gardening, is preparing a site for planting. It's especially challenging when you're starting a site that's never been planted before. But if you do it right the first time, you'll see your plants growing strong and healthy, and you'll know it was worth the effort.

The goal in soil preparation is to develop a fertile, loose, crumbly soil. This kind of soil provides seeds and plants with

321

what they need to grow: essential nutrients; aeration for strong and healthy root development; and good drainage so that roots get as much moisture as they need but aren't waterlogged. If you are starting with a clay or sandy soil, don't expect to have the fluffy kind of soil that's ideal for gardening the first season. It takes several years of steady work to transform poor or mediocre soil into great garden soil. But no matter what kind of soil you're starting with, you can improve it every time you dig.

DIG IN!

You can dig your garden beds virtually any time of year, as long as the soil is ready. Obviously, you can't dig when the ground is frozen. Soil that is either too wet or too dry isn't in prime condition for cultivation, either. Working the soil when it's too wet can destroy its good, crumbly structure and leave it tight and compacted—less-than-ideal conditions for good root growth. (This is especially a problem if your soil is on the clayey side.) If the soil is too dry, it will be harder for you to dig, and you may be left with a powdery soil that's prone to compaction and crusting.

So how do you know when the ground is ready to dig? Pick up a clump of soil in your hand, squeeze it, and roll it into a ball. Then tap the ball with your fingers: If it falls apart into smaller pieces, the soil is ready to be worked. If the ball does not come apart, your soil needs at least a few days to dry out. If the soil is dry and will not even form a ball, then water it well, wait a day, and perform the test again. If your soil is so clayey that the soil ball

HEALTHY SOIL MEANS HEALTHY PLANTS. For a garden that thrives with minimal care, feed the soil with regular applications of organic matter. Testing the soil periodically, and adjusting the pH if necessary, is another good way to ensure healthy plants.

won't fall apart even after the ground has dried out some, try digging a few shovelfuls. If the soil feels very sticky and clings to your tools and boots, wait another few days (and remember to work in lots of organic matter to loosen the soil when you finally do dig!).

When both you and your soil are ready, begin by removing any weeds or other unwanted vegetation. Rake it away and place it in your compost pile. If you don't have a compost pile, this is a great time to start one!

You can loosen the soil by hand-digging or by using a rotary tiller. For most flowers, bulbs, and vegetables, it is sufficient to work the soil to a depth of at least 10 to 12 inches. However, the deeper the soil is loosened, the better, especially for large or deep-rooted plants. Once you've dug your beds deeply, you don't need to do it again every year. In vegetable gardens and annual flower beds, just

scatter some organic matter over the surface and dig it into the top few inches with a garden fork.

Using a Rotary Tiller: A rotary tiller can make soil preparation much easier on your back and takes much less time than it does to do the job by hand. If you don't want to spend the money to purchase a tiller, keep in mind that many home rental centers have tillers for rent.

By tilling in several passes and setting the blades deeper at each pass, you can usually loosen the soil to a depth of 6 to 8 inches. While this is a help, it's not the last step in soil preparation. For best results, you should still hand-dig the area to break up the soil at least 2 to 4 inches below that.

Digging by Hand: If you choose to dig by hand, use a shovel to turn over the top 10 to 12 inches of soil. "Turning over the soil" means just that—taking each shovelful of soil and turning it over. Break up soil clods by hitting and separating them with a garden fork. Then dig over the area again with a garden fork to loosen the lower level where the shovel didn't reach. Remove any large to medium-sized rocks from the area; you can leave a few smaller rocks, since they help the soil drain.

There is another method of garden bed cultivation called double-digging. Double-digging involves loosening the soil to a depth of as much as 24 inches. To do this, you make a series of trenches and refill one trench with soil from another, along with generous amounts of organic matter.

Double-digging is hard work, and there is still some debate about whether all the extra effort is really worth it. It probably *is* worth the effort if you have heavy, poorly drained clay soil that needs intensive improvement. Double-digging also provides ideal conditions for root crops, such as carrots and potatoes. If you want to try this method, follow these steps:

1. After removing the existing vegetation, spread a 1- to 3-inch layer of organic matter over the planting area.

2. Take a sharp, flat-bladed spade and dig a trench about 2 feet wide, 1 foot deep, and as long as you want the new garden bed to be. Put the soil from this trench in a garden cart, or lay a sheet of plastic near the trench and place the soil on the sheet. Remove any large stones or other debris as you dig.

3. Add an inch or two of organic matter to the bottom of the trench. Also apply lime or any other soil amendments your

DOUBLE-DIG FOR DEEP ROOTS. *Double-digging a bed improves soil drainage and makes plants more drought resistant, by encouragnig them to send roots deep into the soil.*

First, work organic matter into the bottom of the first trench.

Next, fill the first trench with soil from the second one.

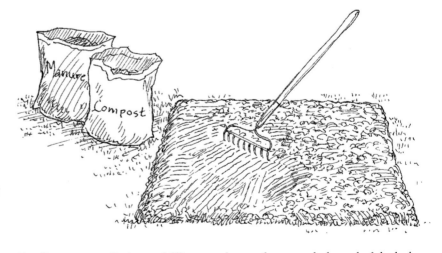

Finally, continue digging and filling trenches until you reach the end of the bed, then rake the entire bed smooth.

GETTING RID OF GRASS

Removing turf grass and weeds from new garden sites can be a big job. There are a few ways to approach this task, depending on how much time and energy you have.

If you can wait several months to plant, try smothering the grass with mulch: Mow the grass as short as possible, then cover it with a dense mulch, such as newspapers or old wool or cotton carpeting. Top that with a layer of more attractive mulch. After a few months, the grass should be dead, and you can dig or till the site to prepare it for planting.

If you want to plant soon, you need to take more direct action. For a relatively small area, you can remove the sod by hand. Slide a sharp spade between the grass and the soil to sever the grass roots. Pull up the sod pieces, shake off the loose soil, and toss the pieces upside-down onto your compost pile. As you expose the soil, carefully pick out any remaining weeds or weed roots. Don't be tempted to simply till live turf into the soil; tilling will only chop up the weed and grass roots and spread them all over the area, leaving you with serious weed problems in your new beds.

soil may need (as indicated by the soil test you took back when you were investigating your garden site).

4. Using a garden fork, dig the organic matter and amendments into the soil at the bottom of the trench.

5. Dig another 2-foot-wide trench next to the first trench. Place the topsoil and organic matter into the first trench.

6. Repeat steps 2 through 5 until the entire bed has been worked. Fill the last trench with soil from the first trench.

7. Rake the bed, breaking up any surface clods to make a smooth, level surface.

While digging the trenches, never stand on the soil that you've already loosened. Your weight will compact the soil, which defeats the purpose of double-digging.

IMPROVE YOUR SOIL WITH ORGANIC MATTER

Soil improvement is an ongoing process; it doesn't stop after the first digging session. To achieve any kind of success in gardening, you must put as much time and care into growing rich, healthy soil as you do in designing your garden and selecting your plants.

All kinds of soil benefit from regular and generous additions of organic matter. What exactly is organic matter? Organic matter is just dead plant or animal tissue, material such as rotting vegetables, leaves, stems, and roots. As it breaks down, it releases nutrients and humus. Humus promotes good soil structure by helping soil particles stick together. Soil organisms are a critical part of this process, since they help to break down the organic matter.

While you can add just about any kind of organic matter to the soil, the most common types used in gardening are peat moss, animal manures, and compost. Every time you prepare a new or existing garden bed for planting, don't forget to include some form of organic matter to keep the soil in prime condition.

Peat Moss: Peat moss is often recommended as a soil amendment, especially for loosening clay soil. It does not, however, have any significant nutrient value, so you still need to mix in manure or compost.

Animal Manures: Manures from cows, horses, chickens, and rabbits are excellent sources of organic matter for any garden. Manure adds nutrients, especially nitrogen, and it also improves soil structure.

Fresh manure can "burn" tender plant roots, so wait several months to plant after applying it, or use manure that has been aged until it's dry and odorless. Animal manures, even if aged, often carry weed seeds, so don't be surprised to see some new weeds cropping up in your garden not long after you have spread manure.

Compost: A compost pile, made from all your yard and fruit and vegetable scraps, is your best source of organic matter for your garden. There is nothing difficult or expensive about making compost—you simply mix together different kinds of organic matter and allow it to decompose. The organic matter is right at your fingertips, since it is constantly being produced in your yard and kitchen. Compostable items include leaves (shredded, if possi-

MAKING COMPOST

You can begin composting any time of the year. Select a spot in your yard that is level, well drained, and near a water source, if possible. Make a free-standing pile, or buy or build a compost bin. Bins are a more attractive way of composting, especially for small yards where there may not be room to hide the compost pile. You can make bins from readily available and inexpensive materials, such as chicken wire, wooden pallets, snow fencing, or two-by-fours. Garden supply catalogs and garden centers sell different styles and sizes of wooden and plastic bins. For good decomposition, your bin or pile should be at least 3 feet high and wide; it can be as long as you like.

Start building the compost pile by alternating layers of high-carbon and high-nitrogen materials. High-carbon materials tend to be dry and brown, like leaves or straw. High-nitrogen materials are usually green and moist or sloppy; these include grass clippings, weeds, vegetable and fruit scraps, animal manures, and spent garden plants. To speed up the composting process, add a few shovelfuls of garden soil, manure, or finished compost. These materials are rich in microorganisms, which help decompose organic matter.

Keep the pile moist at all times, but never waterlogged. Do not allow the pile to dry out completely, or decomposition will slow down. It's a good idea to cover the pile with a black plastic tarp, especially during very rainy, snowy, or cold periods. The cover will hold in the heat and prevent the pile from getting waterlogged. A tarp will also help to conserve moisture during hot, dry spells.

Turning the pile every month or so will help speed up the decomposition process, although it's not absolutely necessary. Your pile should produce usable compost in about 4 to 12 months. The compost is ready to use when it has broken down into small, crumbly pieces that have a dark brownish black color. Work in a 1- to 2-inch layer each year before planting annuals or vegetables; for perennials, use it to improve the soil before planting and as a mulch after planting.

SIMPLE COMPOSTING.
Compost bins can be made from a variety of materials you may have on hand. This one is made from hardware cloth attached to wood frames on three sides; boards fit in tracks in front so the finished compost is easily accessible.

THREE-BIN COMPOSTER. *This more elaborate setup makes it easy to turn compost from one bin to the next. The third bin can be used to collect new compost ingredients or to store finished compost.*

ble), vegetable and fruit scraps from the kitchen, shredded woody stems, spent annual and perennial plants, dead flowers, wood ashes, eggshells, coffee grounds, grass clippings, and manure from cows, horses, chickens, and rabbits.

The heat that builds up in a compost pile accelerates the natural decomposition of organic matter and kills weed seeds, pests, and many diseases. If properly tended, a backyard compost pile will not be a source of unpleasant odor or a hangout for rodents. To prevent animal pest problems, avoid adding meat, fat, bones, or dairy products to your pile. Other materials to keep out of your pile include diseased plants, diseased fruits and vegetables, weeds that have gone to seed, corncobs (unless shredded first), citrus fruit, coal or charcoal ashes, and manure from dogs, cats, or humans.

GETTING YOUR PLANTS

Now that you've prepared an ideal site, you're ready to get your plants. You can start them yourself from seed, or buy them from a local or mail-order source. Your choice will depend on what kinds of plants you need, how much time you have, and what kind of budget you're working with.

PURCHASE GROWING PLANTS

Shopping at a local outlet or through a mail-order catalog is obviously the most direct and fastest way to get the plants you need. As long as you know what to look for in plants, you can buy them from any source.

Buying by Mail-Order: Buying plants through catalogs can be a little intimidating, since you can't see what you're buying until it arrives at your doorstep. But when you order from an established, reputable company, you can be fairly sure that you'll get good-quality plants at fair prices. Keep in mind that if a particular nursery has unbelievably low prices, the quality of the plants may be unbelievably poor. If you're nervous about buying by mail-order, try placing a small order the first year to see if you like what you get.

Most mail-order nurseries will ship your plants at the right

planting time for your area. When the plants arrive, they will probably appear a little bedraggled; bareroot plants may even look like they are dead. Read the packing slip that comes with the plants to find out how to handle them. If you can't set out your plants right away, pot them up in a mix of potting soil and compost so they can keep growing.

Buying at a Nursery or Garden Center: Shopping for your plants at a retail outlet is fun and easy. The choice is usually more limited than what you can buy through mail-order, but you'll see exactly what you're getting for your money. It can be hard to resist impulse buying when confronted with rows of great-looking plants, but be strong and stick to the lists you made back in the planning stages. Otherwise, you may end up bringing home plants that you don't have the right location or any room for.

As you find the plants on your list, inspect them carefully. If possible, purchase younger plants that haven't yet flowered. A plant can be permanently stunted if grown for too long in a container that's too small. If it hasn't set flowers yet, you'll know it is still young and hasn't matured too quickly.

Gently lift each plant out of its container and inspect the roots. You should see some healthy-looking, white roots on the outside of the rootball. If you don't see any roots, the plant may be unhealthy; put it back. Also, avoid buying plants that are pot-bound. If the roots are thickly matted and circling around each other, the plant has outgrown its container. If the plant is too large to take out of the container,

check to see if roots are starting to grow out of the bottom of the pot—another sign that the plant is pot-bound.

Look at the overall appearance of the plant. Don't buy plants that appear wilted—they may not fully recover even when well watered. Also, avoid plants that have any symptoms of insect or disease infestations, such as sticky leaf surfaces, leaves that look as though they've been chewed, and yellowed, discolored, or blackened foliage. If container plants are full of weeds, you'll know the nursery has been sloppy in its maintenance, and plants may not have been fed and watered properly. The weeds are also a sign that the plants are probably old and pot-bound. Don't waste your money; shop elsewhere.

START YOUR OWN PLANTS FROM SEED

Growing your own garden plants from seed takes more time and planning than buying them, but it's a tremendously rewarding experience. There's a special feeling of satisfaction when you see the plants you've nurtured from tiny seeds finally burst forth with beautiful blooms or bountiful produce. Growing plants from seed also lets you grow new or unusual plants that haven't yet made it to your local nursery. Best of all, buying seed is much cheaper than buying plants, so you can fill your garden for a fraction of the cost of using store-bought plants.

Some plants—such as melons, pumpkins, squashes, and many wildflowers—are so tough that you can sow them directly in the garden where you want them to grow. And some grow so

lift up the seedlings to be transplanted. Carefully separate the tiny plants, disturbing the roots as little as possible. Lift each seedling gently by the leaves— *never* by the stem—and set it in its planting hole. If the seedlings are leggy, plant them a bit deeper than they were in the germination container. Pat the soil medium back into the hole around the roots; it is important that the roots have proper contact with the soil. Label each new container with a waterproof marker.

Water the transplants as necessary to keep the soil evenly moist. Apply a liquid fertilizer about once a week at half the recommended strength. Keep the young plants in bright sunlight or under fluorescent lighting.

Hardening Off Seedlings: Transplants need to be hardened off before being planted directly outdoors. Hardening off plants is the process of gradually acclimating indoor-grown plants to tougher outdoor conditions. It takes anywhere from one to two weeks, depending on the plant and your climate.

Start the process around the last frost date. (Check the seed packet or the plant portraits in Part Two of this book for the best timing for specific plants.) The plants should have developed at least six true leaves by this time. Place them outdoors during the daytime, in a sheltered area that is out of the wind and direct sunlight. For the first two or three days, keep the plants outdoors for about 3 hours, then bring them back in. After this period, keep them outside for about 5 hours each day for the next several days. Make sure they are well

COLDFRAMES FOR WARM SEEDLINGS

A coldframe is an outdoor, unheated, bottomless, boxlike structure with a glass or plastic lid. The temperature inside a coldframe can be anywhere from 10° to 25°F warmer than the outdoor temperature. The sides and top protect plants from wind, heavy rain, snow, and hail, making coldframes great places to shelter seedlings during the hardening-off process. Coldframes are also handy for rooting cuttings and forcing winter bulbs. Since they are usually set on bare ground, you can sow cool-weather vegetables—such as lettuce, radishes, and spinach—right in the frame, even when the weather is too cold for regular outdoor planting.

You can buy ready-made coldframes or build your own from lumber. Old glass windows or clear plastic sheets stretched over wooden frames make great lids. The lid needs a hinge at the back so you can prop it open. The coldframe should be in full sun and facing south to southeast, with the lid tilted at least 45 degrees to catch the most spring sunlight.

During sunny days, prop the lid open to provide proper ventilation for the plants and to prevent them from overheating. (Some coldframes have a device that automatically opens and closes the frame to maintain the right temperature.) Close the lid at night to hold in the heat. If it is going to be particularly cold at night, you can provide extra insulation by throwing an old blanket over the lid, banking the sides with straw bales, and covering the plants inside with a layer of straw.

CONTAINER GARDENING BASICS

No matter what size garden you have, container-grown plants can add beauty and bounty to your yard. You can grow many kinds of plants in containers—flowers, vegetables, herbs, vines, and even shrubs and small trees! (For specific ideas, see the list of "Flowers for Containers" on page 402.) Pots, planters, window boxes, and hanging baskets of all kinds add a special welcoming touch to doorways, decks, and patios.

Suitable containers range from wooden barrels to ornate terra-cotta and porcelain containers. If possible, choose containers that have drainage holes at the bottom. Without holes, it's sometimes hard to tell if a plant's roots are sitting in water. Even if the top of the soil is dry, the bottom area may still be quite wet. The container should be large enough to hold the mature plant comfortably, so the roots don't become too pot-bound as the plant grows.

Fill the container about halfway with potting soil. Set in and arrange the plants as you would in the garden. Remember to loosen the rootballs if the roots are circling, and leave room around each plant to allow for growth. When you have finished planting, fill in around the roots with more potting soil until the surface is about 1 inch below the top of the container. Water thoroughly.

After planting, fertilize with a slow-release fertilizer (which should last all growing season), or every 10 days with a liquid fertilizer. Check the containers every day, especially during warm weather, to see if they need watering. The soil in containers tends to dry out very quickly, particularly in full-sun locations. Water when the top inch or so of the soil is dry or if the plants are wilting.

EASY COOL-WEATHER PRO-TECTION. Plastic milk jugs—with the bottoms removed—make excellent cloches for protecting newly transplanted seedlings from cold weather. Poke a hole in the handle and stick a thin stake through it to hold the jug in place.

watered and protected from any animal pests.

If the plants seem to be doing well at this point, leave them out all day and night. (Move them to a sunny spot if they are full-sun plants.) If frost threatens while you are hardening off your plants, bring them indoors overnight. After the last frost date, move the hardened-off plants to the garden.

PLANTING YOUR GARDEN

Now that you have a good collection of healthy plants, you're ready to get them in the ground. If you can, choose an overcast day for planting so the plants are less stressed while they're adjusting to their new growing conditions. If the soil is very dry, water the area a day or two before planting. Also, water container plants thoroughly before planting.

Set the plants out at the proper spacing, arranged according to how you had them on your garden plan. Avoid the temptation to overplant to get an instant, more mature, garden effect. If the plants have good growing conditions, they will quickly fill in their allotted space, and you will have a better-looking and healthier garden in the long run.

For easiest planting, start at the back of the garden and work toward the front. Set boards over the area to walk and kneel on so you don't compact the soil.

Setting Out Container-Grown Plants: To remove a plant from a container, set one hand over the top of the pot, with the plant's stems between your fingers. Turn the pot over so it is resting on your first hand, then use your other hand to pull off the container. If the plant's roots are circling around the outside of the container, use your fingers to gently untangle and loosen them.

If you are setting out plants in peat pots or peat pellets, you can plant the entire pot directly into the ground. With peat pots, however, it's best to peel off the upper rim and use a sharp knife to cut a few slits in the sides to help roots grow out.

Use a trowel or shovel to dig a hole about half again as wide as the root area and a little deeper. The hole should accommodate the root system of the plant with-

SIMPLE SHADE. *Since hot sun can wilt newly transplanted seedlings, it's best to transplant on an overcast day. A board propped up on stakes (left) can provide much-needed shade until plants become established. Floating row covers on simple wire hoops (right) help to protect plants from drying winds and insects.*

out bending the roots. The plant should sit as deep in the ground as it did in the container before planting. (If the plant is a bit leggy, you can set it slightly deeper for better support.) Fill around the roots with the soil you removed from the hole. Firm the soil lightly, then water thoroughly.

If the soil needs a fertility boost, scatter some compost or a balanced fertilizer near the base of each plant after planting. Always follow the package directions for the exact amount needed. Never add fertilizer—especially chemical fertilizers—directly into the planting hole, since it

can burn the roots. After you've planted the whole area, add a layer of mulch to the bed.

Planting Bareroot Perennials: Plant out bareroot perennials by digging a hole large enough to hold all the roots without bending them. Build a little cone or pyramid of soil inside the planting hole so that the top of the mound is just even with the soil surface. Set the crown of the plant (the point where the roots meet the stem) on top of this mound, and spread the roots evenly over the sides. Fill around the roots with soil, making sure you get good contact between the soil and the roots. After planting, water thoroughly and mulch.

MULCHING

Mulch is an essential part of successful gardening. It can be any material that you spread over a garden area to help retain soil moisture, moderate soil temperatures, prevent soil erosion, and

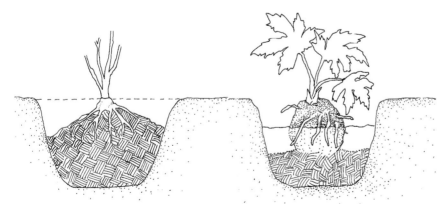

PLANTING TRANSPLANTS. *When planting bareroot plants, spread the roots over a cone of soil in the bottom of the hole (left), making sure the crown of the plant is level with the soil surface. For container-grown plants, take the plant out of the container, loosen the roots on the side of the rootball with a knife or screwdriver, then set the plant in the hole at the same depth it was growing in the pot (right). Water both types of transplants thoroughly after planting, then every other day until growth resumes.*

keep weeds down. Mulch materials are usually divided into two groups: inorganic and organic. Inorganic mulches include black and clear plastic sheeting and polyester landscape fabrics. Organic mulches include materials such as compost, grass clippings, straw, and bark. The kind you choose will depend on what you want it to do and where you want to use it.

Inorganic mulches are very effective for keeping the soil moist and weeds smothered, but they are not very attractive. Plastic mulches can also be harmful around permanent plantings. Recent research indicates that the roots of many plants, such as trees and shrubs, do not grow as deep or as well under plastic mulches as they do under landscape fabric or an organic mulch. This can lead to shallow-rooted trees that are more likely to blow over in high winds. And shallow-rooted plants in general are less drought-tolerant, since roots near the surface will dry out and die faster than roots extending deeper into the soil. Over time, plastic mulches can also encourage fungal disease problems and reduce soil oxygen levels.

Plastic and fabric mulches *can* be handy if you use them properly. For example, you can use black plastic for the vegetable garden to provide nice, warm growing beds for heat-loving crops such as sweet potatoes, peppers, eggplants, and squash. Use landscape fabric around trees and shrubs, and cover it with an attractive organic mulch, such as shredded bark or pine needles. But if you decide to use landscape fabric, keep in mind that it is difficult or impossible to remove

around trees and shrubs because plant roots grow up into the fabric. Removing it damages roots.

In most parts of the garden, organic mulches are your best choice. Not only do they look very natural, they also add nutrients and organic matter to the soil as they break down. Pine needles will help to keep the soil acidic, so they are an ideal mulch for acid-loving plants such as rhododendrons, azaleas, and camellias. Straw is great for vegetable gardens, but it's too coarse for ornamental plantings. Shredded bark, wood chips, and compost mulches blend in well in many garden settings.

For more information on the characteristics of different mulches, see "Mulch Materials" on the next page.

Applying Mulch: Before mulching, prepare the area by removing any existing weeds. Water thoroughly if the soil is dry.

Spread organic mulches about 2 to 3 inches deep around annuals, perennials, and vegetables, and 3 to 4 inches deep around trees and shrubs. Leave a few inches between plant stems and the mulch. Some settling will occur after you first apply the mulch; replenish the mulch as needed throughout the year to maintain the proper depth. For wintertime protection in northern zones, you can apply a deeper layer of mulch in late fall. Just be sure to remove the extra winter layer in early spring as the weather warms up.

If you are using black plastic in your vegetable garden, spread it over the prepared area several weeks before planting. (To make later watering easier, install a drip irrigation system before applying

the plastic. For information on drip irrigation, see "Watering" on page 341. When you are ready to plant, make slits—in the form of a cross—where you want to set transplants in the ground. Plant the transplants in the center of each cross, and water well.

When using a landscape fabric, lay it in strips around plantings of trees, shrubs, and roses. Leave a few inches of unmulched space around the base of each plant for good root growth. Mulch piled around plant stems can also cause disease problems. Top the fabric with a layer of organic mulch to help it last longer and to make it look more natural.

Avoiding Mulch Problems: While mulching is beneficial for most plants, sometimes it can be more damaging than helpful. To use mulch most effectively, keep these points in mind:

• Do not mulch freshly seeded beds or very young seedlings— a cover of mulch is often too heavy for them. However, if your seedbed is on a slope or if it's exposed to heavy rains, it's okay to add a very light layer of straw over the area for protection.

• Do not mulch clay soil in early spring, or it may stay too wet. Wait until late spring or early summer, when the soil has dried out somewhat.

• Do not mulch cool-weather crops, such as lettuce, spinach, and peas, in early spring. If you do, the soil may remain too cool and wet even for these crops.

• Wait until the soil has warmed in early or mid-summer to apply mulch around heat-loving crops, such as peppers and eggplants.

• Avoid piling mulch against

MULCH MATERIALS

Not sure which mulch is best for you? Read the following descriptions to find out about a variety of popular organic and inorganic mulches:

Bark: Both shredded bark and bark chips make a very long-lasting and attractive mulch for trees, shrubs, and ornamental beds. Shredded bark is better for an informal or more natural garden design.

Black Plastic: Black plastic keeps the soil warm, making it ideal for heat-loving vegetable crops. It is also excellent for suppressing weeds. Plastic does not degrade and can be a litter problem. Avoid using it in ornamental plantings.

Buckwheat Hulls: If you have access to buckwheat hulls, use them as a lightweight and attractive mulch, especially for ornamental beds. In windy areas, you may need to top the hulls with a layer of heavier mulch to keep them from blowing away. They also break down quickly, so you'll need to replenish them more often than you would other kinds of mulch.

Clear Plastic: Like black plastic, clear plastic will heat up the soil quickly. It is ideal for warming cold vegetable garden soil in early spring. It is not as good as black plastic at suppressing weeds, however. Cover clear plastic with an organic mulch in summer to discourage weed seeds from sprouting and to keep the soil from getting too hot.

Cocoa Bean Hulls: Cocoa bean hulls make a very attractive mulch. Plus, your garden will smell like chocolate for the first few weeks after you apply fresh hulls! They add nitrogen to the soil and can be dug or tilled into the garden bed at the end of the season to improve soil structure.

Compost: Finished compost is a pleasing dark color and is effective for warming up the soil. It quickly adds nutrients and improves soil structure. Compost usually needs to be replenished during the growing season.

Grass Clippings: Clippings are readily available, but they decompose quickly and need to be replenished frequently. Don't mulch with clippings from a lawn that's been treated with herbicide unless they've been composted first. Grass clippings are best for informal areas and vegetable gardens.

Landscape Fabrics: Landscape fabric works the same way as black plastic, but is more durable and allows water and air to reach the soil. Fabrics are useful in foundation plantings, under walkways, and in areas around trees, shrubs, and roses. Cover them with a layer of attractive organic mulch. Pull out any weeds that poke through.

Leaves: Composted or shredded leaves make a good mulch for any type of garden. Till or dig them into the soil at the end of the season to add organic matter. For larger quantities, see if your municipality offers free leaf compost.

Newspaper: Newspaper is excellent for suppressing weeds between vegetable rows and on pathways. Apply a layer of heavier mulch over it to keep it from blowing away. Don't use colored ink or magazine print, since they may contain toxic inks or lead.

Nut Shells: Crushed or uncrushed nut shells form long-lasting, attractive mulches. Their sharp edges repel slugs.

Pine Boughs: Branches from pines and other evergreens are great for protecting perennials over the winter. Lay them over planted areas after the ground has frozen in winter; remove them in early spring. Christmas trees are a good source of pine boughs for mulching.

Pine Needles: Pine needles form a lovely natural mulch that's slow to decompose. They are especially good for mulching acid-loving plants. Do not use them if your area is subject to wildfires, as they are very flammable when dry.

Rice Hulls: Rice hulls make a lightweight and long-lasting mulch. They absorb a lot of water, though, so don't use them on soils that are naturally on the wet side.

Salt Hay: Salt hay is cut from wild seaside grasses. It decomposes more slowly than regular hay and has fewer weed seeds, but is more expensive. Save it for the vegetable garden.

Seaweed: Seaweed makes a durable mulch that's rich in trace elements. It's especially good for vegetable gardens. Wash seaweed by spraying it with a hose before using it as a mulch, to wash off the salt.

Stone: Crushed pebbles, marble chips, and other stone mulches are durable and long-lasting. They are particularly good for pathways. Marble chips may be too alkaline for acid-loving plants.

Straw or Hay: These materials form a nice, loose mulch for vegetable gardens. Hay adds nutrients to the soil as it breaks down but may also contain weed seeds. Both hay and straw are flammable when dry.

White Plastic: White plastic keeps the soil cool, since the white color reflects light. It's used mostly in very warm areas to moderate soil temperatures in summer.

Wood Shavings and Sawdust: Finely ground wood-based mulches are useful for pathways and vegetable gardens. They can draw some nitrogen from the soil as they decompose, so apply a layer of compost beneath them or add a little extra nitrogen fertilizer to the soil. Shavings and sawdust can acidify the soil. They are also flammable.

plant stems. Mulch around the base of some plants can cause rotting and disease problems, especially if the weather is cool and damp.

• Mulch can attract pests, such as slugs, rodents, and insects. Remove the mulch around plants suffering from a pest problems. It's easier to water a bit more and pull weeds than to deal with these loathsome pests.

FERTILIZING

If you have been amending your soil regularly with compost and other organic matter, it is on its way to becoming naturally fertile. However, even with naturally fertile soil, there are times when plants need a boost of fertilizer for proper growth and development. For example, if you grow corn in the same place for several years, the area may be low in nitrogen, since corn is a heavy nitrogen user. To fertilize effectively, you need to know what kinds of nutrients to apply, the best time to apply them, and how much to use.

Deciding If You Need to Fertilize: Too much fertilizer can be as bad as too little, so don't be tempted to apply it just on general principles. It is difficult to determine exactly which nutrients your soil may be deficient in unless you have it professionally tested in a lab. Ideally, you should do a soil test when you are planning the garden and preparing the soil for planting. But if you didn't do it then, or if it's been a few years since you tested the soil and the plants look like they may need some help, take samples for testing now. Contact your county Cooperative Extension Service office for directions on how and where to send soil samples for testing. The results will indicate any nutrient imbalances and give recommendations on how to correct them.

Even if you have fertile soil, there may be times when your plants could use a nutrient boost, depending on the weather and on the particular kinds of plants. Container plants often need frequent fertilizing, since the space available for their roots is limited. If you notice any plants with yellowish or bronzy leaves, fewer-than-normal flowers, or particularly slow growth, try giving them a dose of liquid fertilizer to see if they perk up.

In general, trees and shrubs don't need extra fertilizer unless the soil is poor. Annual flowering plants and vegetables need more fertilizer than perennials. Lawn and ornamental grasses usually benefit from some additional nitrogen each year. Herbs, native plants, and wildflowers need very little, if any, fertilizer, especially if they are growing in fair to good soil.

Understanding Your Fertilizer Options: Fertilizers come in many different forms. They may be derived from organic materials or synthetic; they can be solid or liquid. Each kind has advantages and disadvantages. Organic gardeners *only* use fertilizers that are derived from organic materials.

Pound for pound, manures, compost, and other bulky organic materials supply less nitrogen, phosphorus, and potassium than chemical fertilizers. They also release their nutrients much more slowly. However, organic fertilizers provide a good balance of many different kinds of nutrients.

They also add organic matter, which naturally promotes good soil structure and drainage. Yearly additions of these materials to already-fertile soils usually provide enough nutrients to grow most garden plants.

For a slightly more concentrated nutrient source, you can apply processed organic fertilizers. These materials include blood meal, bonemeal, fish meal, cottonseed meal, and hoof-and-horn meal. While processed organic fertilizers break down fairly slowly

APPLYING ORGANIC FERTILIZERS

Chemical fertilizers are generally sold in tidy, labeled boxes or bags, so it's easy to find out how much to apply. But if you're dealing with organic fertilizers, it's not so easy to tell. Here are some guidelines to help you:

Alfalfa Meal: 40 to 50 pounds per 1,000 square feet

Animal Manure: 30 pounds per 1,000 square feet

Blood Meal: 10 to 30 pounds per 1,000 square feet

Compost: 1- to 3-inch layer

Cottonseed Meal: 20 to 30 pounds per 1,000 square feet

Earthworm Castings: 8 pounds per 1,000 square feet

Fish Emulsion: 2 ounces per gallon of water to cover 1,000 square feet (repeat 2 or 3 times during the season)

Fish Meal: 20 pounds per 1,000 square feet

Granite Dust: 10 pounds per 1,000 square feet

Seaweed Extract: 1 ounce per gallon of water to cover 1,000 square feet

in the soil, they release their nutrients faster than non-processed organic fertilizers.

Synthetic (chemical) fertilizers release their nutrients in a matter of hours or days, instead of weeks or months for some organic fertilizers. A scattering of balanced chemical fertilizer applied several times during the growing season will provide fast-growing vegetables, annual flowers, and container plants with nutrients immediately. You can also buy slow-release chemical fertilizers, which break down gradually over the season to provide a steady supply of nutrients.

If your plants need a fast-acting nutrient boost, a dose of liquid fertilizer may be in order. Use a liquid-form organic fertilizer, such as fish emulsion or seaweed extract, or a chemical fertilizer that is made to dissolve quickly in water. Mix the materials according to package direc-tions and spray them on the leaves of your plants. The plants will absorb the nutrients through their leaves and put them to use right away. In most cases, you'll notice improved growth within days. Liquid fertilizers are good for a quick fix or midsummer boost, but don't rely on them completely for fertilizing your plants. Concentrate on improving the natural fertility of the soil so your plants won't need this special treatment repeatedly.

Buying Fertilizers: Any fertilizer on the market must provide information about its N-P-K ratio, that is, the percentage of nitrogen (N), phosphorus (P), and potassium (K) it contains. When the three numbers are the same, such as 5-5-5 or 10-10-10, the fertilizer is said to be "balanced." If one number is higher than the others, as in 20-10-10, then you know that the fertilizer contains a higher concentration of that particular nutrient (in this case, nitrogen). This kind of fertilizer is useful if you know your soil is low in a certain nutrient. Organic fertilizers have a lower nutrient analysis than chemical fertilizers and will be marked as "certified organic" or "organic."

SOIL NUTRIENTS AND SOURCES

Here are some materials you can apply to correct nutrient deficiencies in your soil:

MAJOR NUTRIENTS

Nitrogen: Ammonium sulfate, ammonium nitrate, compost, manure, green cover crops, cottonseed meal, fish meal, blood meal.

Phosphorus: Bonemeal, colloidal phosphate, rock phosphate, greensand.

Potassium: Granite meal, greensand, kelp meal, wood ashes, potash rock, potassium sulfate, potassium nitrate.

MINOR NUTRIENTS

Boron: Green cover crops, granite dust.

Calcium: Limestone, gypsum, ground-up eggshells, kelp meal, wood ashes.

Copper: Compost, grass clippings, manure, sawdust.

Iron: Compost, manure, blood meal, greensand.

Magnesium: Green cover crops, dolomitic limestone, manure, greensand.

Manganese: Alfalfa meal, oak leaves, leaf mold.

Sulfur: Alfalfa, clover, pea, or soybean cover crops; gypsum.

Zinc: Manure, compost.

GROW YOUR OWN FERTILIZER

Before the invention of concentrated organic and chemical fertilizers, gardeners and farmers relied on animals and plants to provide material for soil improvement. Nowadays, keeping a herd of cows to supply fertilizer isn't a viable option for most of us. However, you can still use plants to improve and enrich your garden soil. This technique is called cover-cropping.

Cover crop seeds are planted in the garden, allowed to grow, and then dug or tilled into the soil in early spring. Like animal manures or compost, the turned-under crops release nutrients—especially nitrogen—back into the soil. At the same time, they add lots of organic matter, which helps to improve the soil structure. Cover crops are also an excellent way to prevent soil erosion during the winter due to wind and rain.

Try planting clover, alfalfa, rye, winter rye, peas, or winter wheat in the fall and turning it under in the spring. Or, you can plant soybeans, peas, or buckwheat in the spring and turn it under in the fall. During the growing season, mow or hand-cut your cover crop before it goes to flower so it won't reseed. When you're ready to dig it under, mow it again to chop up some of the top growth.

Besides indicating the balance of nutrients, the N-P-K ratio also tells you how many pounds of nutrients the material contains. For example, if you have a 100-pound bag of fertilizer that is marked 20-10-10, this means there are 20 pounds of nitrogen, 10 pounds of phosphorus, and 10 pounds of potassium. The rest of the ingredients are "filler" materials.

Deciding When to Fertilize: Fertilize your garden beds naturally each fall by incorporating compost, shredded leaves, grass clippings, or manure (or a combination of these) into the soil. These materials will break down over the winter and release nutrients for spring planting.

Spring is a good time to apply more fertilizer if your soil needs extra nutrients. (Have a soil test done if you're not sure.) When preparing beds for planting, work in organic or chemical fertilizers as needed. Feed established perennials and roses with a balanced, slow-release fertilizer when they first begin to grow in early spring. At the same time, fertilize rhododendrons, azaleas, and other acid-loving plants with an acidic fertilizer, such as cottonseed meal.

After setting out annual, perennial, and vegetable transplants, give them a dose of a liquid fertilizer high in phosphorus to help them develop a good root system quickly. Vegetables and annual flowers benefit from an additional application of fertilizer during the growing season. Scatter a balanced granular fertilizer around the plants and scratch it into the top ½ inch of soil. Do not put fertilizer directly on the leaves or stems, as it can "burn" the plants.

During the growing season, give container plantings and other fast-growing plants a dose of liquid fertilizer if they need a nutrient boost. Stop fertilizing all plants by late summer. Otherwise, you may encourage them to produce tender new growth that won't have time to harden off before cold weather arrives.

Applying Fertilizers: When applying packaged fertilizer, always follow the label directions for exact application amounts. It's better to apply fast-acting chemical fertilizers in several small doses than in one large dose. Use a measuring cup to scatter the right amount of chemical fertilizer around each plant. If you're fertilizing with compost or other bulky organic materials, the amounts don't have to be as exact; just apply a 1- to 3-inch

WATERWISE GARDENING

"Waterwise gardening" means planning and maintaining any garden to conserve water by means of careful plant selection, efficient irrigation methods, and good general care. These practices are essential in arid or drought-stricken areas. In fact, there are regions in California, particularly those with restricted water use, where water-efficient landscapes are mandated. But even if your water use isn't limited, it's still smart to practice waterwise gardening, since it can save water, money, and time. Here are some gardening tips for conserving water:

Choose and Site Plants Carefully. Group plants according to their water needs to make efficient watering easier. Keep moisture-loving plants near the house, where you can reach them easily; choose drought-tolerant species for hot, south-facing sites and outlying areas that are hard to reach with the hose. Reduce the overall lawn area by paving part of the front or back lawn with a decorative paving like sandstone, brick, or gravel. Or replace part of the lawn with drought-tolerant groundcovers or wildflowers. (You'll find a list of suggested drought-tolerant plants on page 397.)

Use Water Efficiently. Update your irrigation system: Use a drip system or pop-up sprinklers targeted at areas in greatest need of water. Maintain sprinklers and faucets by cleaning clogged heads and fixing leaks. If you have installed an automatic watering system, remember to adjust the watering schedule to reflect changing weather conditions. Place buckets under outdoor faucets, especially leaky ones, to collect water; use that water to irrigate nearby plants.

Try Smart Planting and Maintenance Techniques. Before planting, add organic matter or compost to sandy soils that drain too quickly. Set out new plants in fall or early spring, when the weather is cool and damp, so they will need less water. If you must plant in warm weather, install shade cloth over young seedlings and new plants. Build berms or basins around new plants to direct water to the roots. Apply mulch to retain moisture in the soil. Pull weeds around the plants to limit water competition. Hold off on fertilizing during dry spells to avoid encouraging lush new growth.

layer over the area, and dig or till it into the soil.

When working with dry fertilizers, wear gloves to protect your hands and a mask to avoid breathing the dust. Apply liquid fertilizers with a hand mister or pump sprayer to thoroughly cover the leaves.

WATERING

Improper watering is the number-one cause of garden plant deaths. Plants use water for all of their vital functions. The roots need water so they can absorb dissolved nutrients. Plant stems and foliage need water to remain upright and transport food within the plant. Plants also use water to keep themselves cool in summer.

Water requirements can vary widely, depending largely on the soil, the plant, and the weather. Clay or loam soils retain more water than sandy soil, so they don't require as much watering. Mulched soil of any kind will stay moist much longer than bare soil.

Most plants thrive when the soil is evenly moist, but some can tolerate either extreme. For example, rose moss (*Portulaca grandiflora*) and coneflowers (*Echinacea* and *Rudbeckia* spp.) thrive under the hot, dry conditions that would cause a meltdown for plants like impatiens, ferns, and roses. You took these different needs into consideration when you were choosing plants for your garden. But during periods of high heat mixed with little rainfall, even drought-tolerant plants may need a little extra watering.

When to Water: Plants respond much better if given one good deep watering when the soil

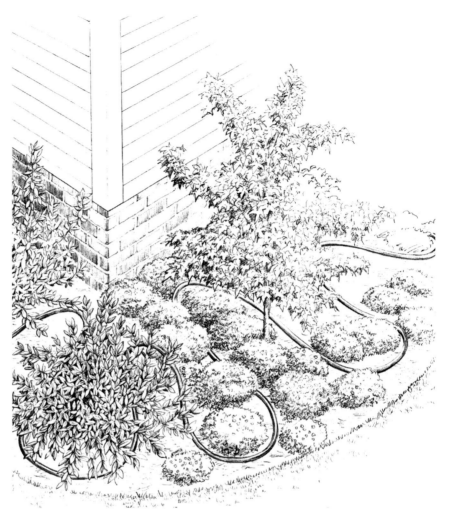

SIMPLE, EFFICIENT WATERING. *Soaker hoses make it easy to deliver water directly to plant roots, which reduces water waste and helps control diseases by keeping leaves dry. Snake soaker hoses through a bed at the beginning of the season and leave them in place. To water, connect them to a regular hose and turn the faucet on about one-quarter turn to let moisture seep into the ground.*

surface becomes dry, rather than frequent, light waterings. The only exception is seeds, whether started indoors or out—they do require frequent watering so that the soil surface doesn't dry out. Young transplants also need more frequent watering than established plants for the first several weeks after planting.

Most garden plants do fine with about 1 inch of water per week, either from rainfall or irrigation. If there is not enough natural rainfall, a sprinkler or irrigation system left on for about 1 hour should be enough each week. To check how long it takes for your sprinkler to emit 1 inch of water, set a coffee can in the garden. To check a drip irrigation system or soaker hose, set a can into the ground below part of the hose. Turn on the water at the tap and let it run until there is 1 inch of water in the can. If plants are spaced very close together, as in an intensively planted vegetable bed, allow the water to run an extra 20 minutes or so. If you notice puddles building up, stop watering in that area until the extra water drains off.

Throughout the growing season, you may need to water your garden plants about once a week if rain is lacking. During very hot weather, water whenever the top 1 inch of soil is dry. Drought-tolerant plants can get by with less water; experiment to find out exactly how much they need to survive.

The best time of day to water is either early morning or late evening. If you water in the late morning or afternoon, you will lose a lot of water to evaporation. Watering in the middle of a hot, sunny day can also scald and discolor foliage. Plants susceptible to fungal problems, like roses and delphiniums, should be watered in the morning so the foliage doesn't remain damp throughout the night. However, if you notice any plants wilting due to lack of moisture, *water them immediately!* If you must water plants in the middle of the day, water at soil level to reduce leaf scald.

How to Water: The home gardener can choose from among many different kinds of irrigation equipment. For example, a sprinkling can or hose-attached mist nozzle is fine for watering seedbeds, container plantings, and hanging baskets, and for emergency spot watering.

Overhead sprinklers are best suited for lawns. They are not recommended for ornamental or vegetable gardens, because they lose a lot of water to evaporation. They also get the foliage wet, which can lead to plant disease problems.

A soaker hose or drip irrigation system, or a combination of the two, is the best choice for giving garden plants a regular deep watering at soil level. Drip irrigation involves using a main hose with emitters or special valves that connect to a network of attached tubes. These tubes emit water directly into the root area of plants. Soaker hoses are simply garden hoses that are porous throughout their entire length. Soakers are especially efficient for watering vegetable and flower gardens, and are usually spaced about 2 feet apart. Both drip systems and soaker hoses can be buried under mulch. (For more information on watering equipment, see Chapter 12, Tools and Equipment.)

STAKING

Tall or floppy plants like tomatoes, peonies, dahlias, sunflowers, and hollyhocks need support as they grow. Staking will extend

SINGLE STAKING. *To stake plants with tall, heavy blooms, such as delphiniums, tie them loosely to individual stakes with soft yarn.*

the life of these plants by preventing the stems from breaking due to wind or rain. Staking plants will also give your garden a more well-groomed and tidy appearance. There are two kinds of staking: peripheral and single.

Peripheral staking involves setting a circle of supports around a clump or group of plants. These are usually plants that grow fairly tall but have thin or sprawling stems, such as peonies, snapdragons, and tomatoes. Metal cages, which come in a range of sizes, are probably the easiest and most effective way to stake a wide variety of flowering plants and vegetables. The cages are hidden by leaves as the plants grow.

If you don't have cages, you can make your own out of stakes and twine. While the plants are still young, space four or five stakes evenly around the clump, and hammer them into the

STAKING CLUMPS. *Perennials that grow in clumps, such as peonies, are easiest to stake with wire hoops. Or use wooden stakes around the clump and support the stems with string wrapped around the stakes and through the middle of the clump.*

ground. Attach strong twine to one of the stakes, near the base, and string it around the other stakes to enclose the clump. As the plants grow, continue adding twine further up the stakes and around the plant clump. You can also place twine diagonally within the staked area for further support. As the plants mature, they will eventually cover the twine and stakes.

Single staking is best for supporting very tall plants, as well as plants with very large flowers, such as sunflowers, delphiniums, dahlias, and hollyhocks. Set a

tall, sturdy stake next to the plant just as it begins to grow. Hammer the stake about 6 inches into the ground and roughly 3 inches away from the center of the plant. As the plant grows, tie the stem to the stake every foot or so with twine or plant ties. Be careful not to crush the stem as you tie it.

Staking should be as inconspicuous as possible. Dark-colored metal, wooden, or bamboo stakes are excellent for any style of staking. Twiggy branches stuck in the ground around clumps of plants also work well for support and

give a lovely, English-cottage look to the garden.

PINCHING AND DEADHEADING

Pinching controls the shape of your plants, especially those that have leafy stems and a somewhat bushy habit, such as coleus, petunias, phlox, basil, and mint. To make these plants look fuller, pinch off the shoot tips several times during the season. To prevent your chrysanthemums from flowering too early, keep pinching off the flower buds until midsummer.

Deadheading, which involves removing spent flowers and developing seedpods, is another important technique for keeping plants looking their best. Take a box or bucket and a pair of garden shears with you every time you walk through your garden, and pinch or cut off dead flowers and new seedpods. (When you've collected a few, toss them into the compost pile.) This will encourage your plants to produce more blooms and will keep the garden looking fresh. And by

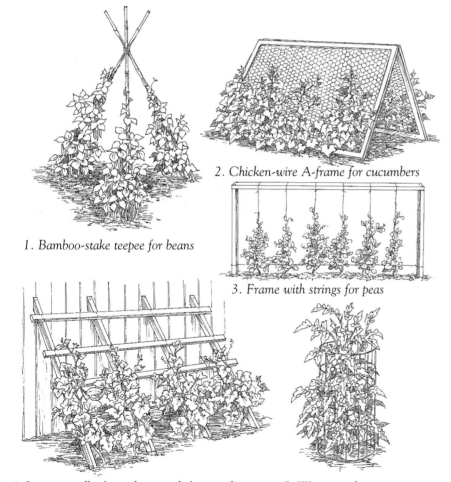

1. Bamboo-stake teepee for beans

2. Chicken-wire A-frame for cucumbers

3. Frame with strings for peas

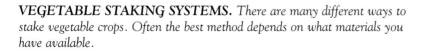

4. Leaning trellis for melons, with fruit in slings   *5. Wire cage for tomatoes*

VEGETABLE STAKING SYSTEMS. *There are many different ways to stake vegetable crops. Often the best method depends on what materials you have available.*

PINCHING. *Pinching out the top leaves on a plant encourages branching. To promote bushy growth, pinch the side branches as well.*

deadheading herbs, you can encourage them to produce more of their desirable leaves. Deadheading can also help cut down on disease problems in the garden. Do not deadhead if you want to save seed, or if you want flowers such as cleome, foxgloves, and hollyhocks to self-sow for next year.

PROPAGATING PERENNIALS

Once you've been bitten by the gardening bug, you'll probably want to grow more and more plants. But while your desire for more plants may be unlimited, your budget probably isn't. The solution? Grow your own plants!

You may already be raising your own annual and vegetable transplants from seed. The same techniques will work for growing a wide range of wonderful perennials. (For a review, see "Start Your Own Plants from Seed" beginning on page 326.) You can also propagate perennials using other methods, including division, cuttings, and layering. The advantage of these three options is that they will give you plants that are identical to the original plants. Seedlings often look similar, but can vary somewhat in height and color

Dividing: One of the easiest ways to propagate perennial plants is to simply dig them up and divide them. Besides giving you more plants, division will keep your garden from getting crowded and overgrown. Most ornamental perennials—including bulbs, ornamental grasses, and groundcovers—need to be (or at least benefit from being) divided every three to four years.

The best time of year to divide is in early spring, just after

DIG AND DIVIDE. *It's easy to propagate many perennials, by digging the entire clump and gently separating it into individual plants. Replant the divisions in the garden, or pot them up to plant later or to share with friends.*

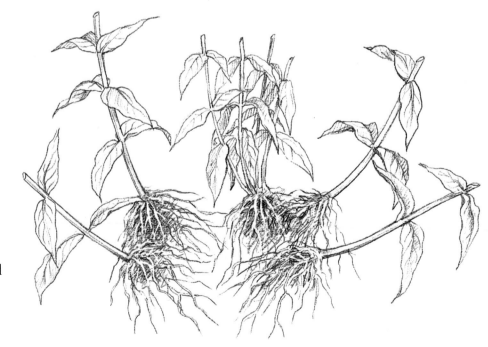

the plants have begun to grow again, or in the fall. To reduce plant stress, try to divide on overcast days. Water the area around the plants you want to divide. Take a shovel or spading fork and dig around each plant. As you dig, try not to disturb the root system of the plant too much.

Lift up the entire rootball area of the plant and shake off as much soil as possible. Usually, the rootball will naturally divide itself as you begin to gently pull it apart with your hands or cut it in half with a sharp knife. An easy way to separate larger rootballs is to stick two pitchforks into the middle of the rootball area so they are both pointing outward in opposite directions. Then gently pull the handles in opposite directions—the rootball should come right apart. Repeat as needed. For really tough rootballs, such as those of big ornamental grasses, you may need to use an ax to chop the pieces apart.

Depending on how large the rootball is, you should get two to four good-sized divisions—maybe more, if the plant hasn't been divided for many years. Make sure each section has some roots and some buds or top growth. Replant divisions as soon as possible, according to their recommended spacing. If the plant has top growth, cut it back by about a third. Mix a little phosphorus into the planting holes, set one clump in each hole, and water thoroughly. If you're dividing in the spring, top-dress with a balanced fertilizer.

If you don't have the time to replant your extra divisions, pot them up and keep them watered until you can plant them. If you don't need them, pot them up and give them away to your gardening friends and neighbors. Many church, school, or horticultural organizations would welcome your extra plants for their spring plant sales!

Hardy bulbs such as tulips, daffodils, hyacinths, snowdrops, and crocuses can be divided after flowering, when the foliage is turning yellow and the bulbs are going dormant. If you cut into or scrape the bulbs as you dig them up, throw them away; they'll probably rot anyway. Gently pull apart the bulbs and the roots. Replant them at the proper depth and spacing.

Tender bulbs, corms, and tubers should also be divided as they go dormant in the fall. But instead of replanting them right away, allow them to dry, then place them in containers or paper bags filled with peat moss or sand. Label all of the containers with the bulb name and color. Store them in a cool, dry, frost-free area until it's time to replant in spring.

Taking Cuttings: When you want to propagate a plant but don't want to dig it up or disturb its root system, you can take cuttings from the shoot tip or the stems. Tip cuttings include the top growing point of the plant. Stem cuttings take part of the stem without the top growing point.

Take cuttings of perennial plants starting in early to late spring. Tip and stem cuttings should be 4 to 6 inches long, depending on the size of the plant (short cuttings from shorter plants, and long ones from taller plants). Make the cuts at a 45-degree angle using a clean, sharp knife or razor blade. (Wipe the blade with rubbing alcohol to sterilize it before cutting.) Strip the leaves from the lower half of each cutting, leaving two to four sets of leaves. Also, remove flowers and seedpods from tip cut-

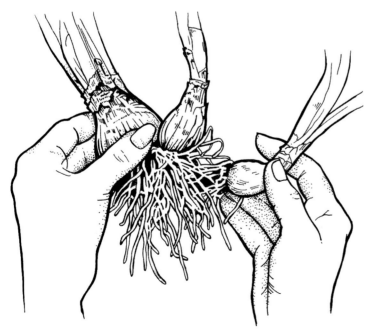

DIVIDING BULBS. *Propagate bulbs like daffodils by digging the clumps in spring, after the leaves have turned yellow. Pull the individual bulbs apart and replant them as soon as possible.*

TAKING CUTTINGS. *To propagate perennials and groundcovers from cuttings, take 4- to 6-inch-long shoots, remove the lower leaves, then stick the stems in moist vermiculite or perlite. Cover the cuttings with plastic to maintain high humidity.*

tings. Work quickly, before the cuttings wilt. To keep the cuttings from wilting, you can mist them frequently as you're preparing them.

Some propagators like to dip the base of cuttings into a rooting hormone powder before sticking them into the rooting medium. Plants will root without the hormone, but it can stimulate the development of a vigorous root system. Rooting hormone powders are readily available from most garden centers.

Stick prepared cuttings into a container filled with moistened vermiculite or perlite, or a 50/50 combination of the two. Use a pencil to make a hole in the medium for each cutting. Set the bottom third to half of the stem in the hole, and gently firm the medium around it. Space the cuttings far enough apart so they aren't touching. After you've set all the cuttings in the medium, water and mist them. Then cover the container with a tent of clear plastic to keep the humidity level high. If necessary, support the plastic with stakes or wire hoops so it doesn't rest on the cuttings. Place the covered container in a

warm and partially shaded area; avoid exposing the cuttings to direct sunlight.

Depending on the plant, the cuttings should begin to form roots in two to three weeks. You can check on their progress by tugging on them lightly—the more resistance there is, the greater the root development. Once the cuttings have begun to develop a strong, vigorous root system with roots over 2 inches long, you can transplant them into the garden or into a container with a soilless potting mixture. To get them off to a good start, feed them with a dilute dose of liquid fertilizer.

Growing Root Cuttings: Some perennials—including Oriental poppy (*Papaver orientale*), plume poppy (*Macleaya cordata*), hardy geraniums (*Geranium* spp.), and garden phlox (*Phlox paniculata*)—can even grow new plants from root pieces. For most plants that can be propagated this way, it's best to take cuttings in early spring, when the plants are eager to start growing again. (Propagate Oriental poppy in summer, while it is dormant.) Unpot or dig up the plant that

you'll be propagating. You don't need to sacrifice the mother plant for root cuttings, as long as you leave about half of the roots and cut back about a third to half of its top growth (if it has any). Be sure to use a clean, sharp knife to do the cuttings.

For plants with very fine, hairlike roots, cut the root pieces into 2- to 4-inch sections and scatter them directly onto a well-prepared soil bed outdoors, or into a tray filled with a soilless potting mixture. Lightly cover the pieces with about ½ inch of the soil or potting medium, and gently water with a fine-mist nozzle. Keep the area well moistened until the roots begin to form plantlets.

For larger and fleshier roots, such as those from Oriental poppies and plume poppies, dig up the plants and cut the roots with a sharp, clean knife into sections about 3 inches long. Stick them into a rooting medium of equal parts perlite and soilless potting mixture. Stick the roots into the mixture vertically, with the root end that was closest to the center of the plant sticking about ¼ inch out of the medium. Keep the cut-

LAYERING. *Herbs, groundcovers, and many vines and perennials are easy to propagate by layering. Just bend a stem to the ground, hold it in place with a length of wire bent in half, and cover with a mound of soil. Cut off the new plant when roots have formed, which can take several months.*

tings well moistened and misted. Once the roots have formed leafy growth, plant them where they are to grow, or hold them over in a coldframe during the winter and plant them out the following spring.

Layering: Whether you know it or not, you may already be propagating plants in your garden by layering. Many plants— including roses, sedums, azaleas, rhododendrons, and clematis— propagate themselves naturally through layering.

Layering occurs when one of a plant's branches touches the soil and eventually forms roots. You can mimic this natural process quite easily with plants that have sprawling or vining stems. Gently bend a stem until part of it behind the tip touches the ground. (Don't bend the branch sharply, or you may break it or cut off nutrients and water to the growing area.)

Take a knife or razor blade and slightly nick the bottom section of the branch where it touches the soil. Cover the nicked section with 2 to 3 inches of soil. If necessary, place a rock over the soil to hold the branch

down. It usually takes at least several months for enough roots to form so you can cut the branch away from the mother plant. At that point, you can dig up the new plant to transplant it, or just leave it where it is to add to the existing planting.

CONTROLLING WEEDS

Weeds are to gardeners what mosquitoes are to campers— pesky intruders that make an otherwise pleasant pursuit an unpleasant experience indeed. In the war against weeds, you need to be vigilant, or else they will quickly claim victory in your garden.

The best way to get the upper hand with weeds is to stop them early in the season. Take some time to weed thoroughly in early spring, when weeds begin to come up. Follow by adding or replenishing mulch to a depth of about 2 to 3 inches around established and new plants. If weeds are a particular problem in a garden bed or pathway, lay landscape fabric over the area and cover that with a few inches of organic mulch.

To keep ahead of weeds

before they become large and numerous, make it a practice to weed all garden areas at least once a week. The easiest time to weed is when the ground has dried out slightly after a rain or after the area has been irrigated. Take a sharp, long-handled hoe and rake it firmly across the soil surface over weeds; smaller weeds should come right out of the ground. Hoe harder under larger weeds, or hand-pull them. If it is a sunny day, you can leave pulled weeds where they are—the sun and heat will dry out the roots. Or, if you want to be tidy, gather the weeds and add them to the compost pile.

Some weeds have deep roots that allow them to survive a simple hoeing; when you hoe off the top, the root will just send up another batch of leaves and flowers. For weeds with long taproots, such as dandelions and thistles, use a trowel or taproot weeder. A taproot weeder has a long, metal probe that is perfect for digging down under the base of the plant and pulling up the entire root.

Chemical weed killers, known as herbicides, can be used to eliminate large weedy areas or individual weeds. Herbicides do save considerable labor and time. However, they can also harm microorganisms in the soil, con-taminate groundwater, and injure fish and other wildlife if they end up in rivers, streams, and ponds. Avoid using herbicides unless you have a very severe weed problem that you can't control any other way. Organic gardeners stay away from nearly all commercial herbicides with the exception of soap sprays.

There are two types of herbicides: selective and nonselective. Selective herbicides are used mostly by large-scale farmers and kill only certain types of weeds or grasses. Nonselectives, in various concentrations, will kill any plant. They are popular for controlling weeds in patios and pathways where you don't want weeds to grow.

You can apply herbicides directly onto plant foliage or onto the soil. Preemergent herbicides are applied to the soil to kill weed seeds before they sprout. They are usually applied in the spring or early summer, after the garden has been planted and mulched.

Always read the label to make sure the herbicide will control the kinds of weeds you want it to. When applying herbicides, follow the exact directions on the label and wear protective clothing, such as a long-sleeved shirt, long pants, rubber gloves, rubber boots, and goggles. Never apply herbicides on a windy day, as they can drift off and damage nearby plants. If you've treated

an area with herbicides and have composted the weeds, do not use this compost for at least one to two months, to allow the herbicide time to break down. Most important, make sure herbicides are clearly labeled as poisonous, and keep them out of children's reach.

CONTROLLING PEST AND DISEASE PROBLEMS

Careful garden planning, proper plant selection, and good general maintenance are the secrets to keeping your plants free of pest and disease problems. This is one area where you can really see how a little care can go a long way!

When plants are growing vigorously, they are less prone to attack by insects, fungi, and bacteria. But occasionally, even the best-planned and best-maintained gardens may have a few problems. As you walk through your yard, make a habit of looking for signs of damage, such as chewed leaves, discolored flowers or foliage, or rotted stems. As soon as you spot a problem, turn to Chapter 13, Pests and Diseases, to find out how to control it quickly and effectively.

WINTERIZING THE GARDEN

The process of getting your garden ready for winter starts while you are still enjoying the late-summer sun. At this time, stop fertilizing and decrease watering so plants will grow more slowly and stop producing new growth. Also, in all areas but Zones 9 to 11, stop pinching back plants;

otherwise, new growth may be damaged by an early frost.

In fall, weed the garden beds one last time. Dig up and compost frost-nipped annuals. (Be sure to discard any diseased plants.) Cut perennial leaves and stems to the ground, and rake all of the old plant parts out of the bed to help prevent disease and insect problems next year. Lift tender bulbs, such as dahlias and glads, for indoor storage. To build up the soil for spring planting next year, add compost or other organic matter to the vegetable garden and annual flower beds.

Right after the ground freezes, apply or replenish a winter layer of mulch over perennials and bulbs to keep the cycles of freezing and thawing from pushing the plants out of the ground. Evergreen boughs are excellent for this purpose, and they are easy to clear away in the spring before plants begin to grow and flower.

Winterizing your garden doesn't have to mean an end to your garden enjoyment. You may decide to leave some plants in the garden all winter so you can enjoy their attractive seed heads or berries. If you leave tall ornamental grasses standing until early spring, you can admire their lovely straw color against the snow and listen to the sound of the wind swirling through them. While you're appreciating the garden from the warmth and comfort of indoors, grab your notebook and seed catalogs, and start thinking about your great new plans for next year!

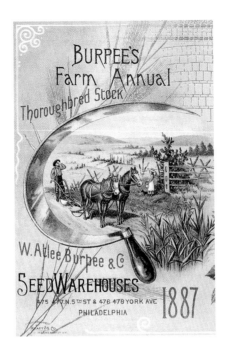

TOOLS AND EQUIPMENT

THERE'S NO WAY AROUND IT: GREAT GARDENS TAKE HARD WORK. Fortunately, you can make that work as painless as possible by using high-quality tools and equipment made for the job at hand.

BUYING THE RIGHT TOOLS

How can you tell the difference between a good-quality tool and an average or poor one? For starters, check the price. A very low-priced tool is probably low in quality, too. If you see three shovels at varying prices from the same place, you're usually better off buying one of the higher-priced models. Chances are, it will last longer and therefore be less expensive in the long run.

The second thing you should check is the weight of the tool. A heavier tool is often better than a lighter one, because higher grades of metal are heavier. If you aren't especially strong, however, you may prefer lightweight tools. To be sure you get a good tool, regardless of its weight, check the label: It should say that the tool is made from "tempered," "heat-treated," or "forged" metal. Buy stainless steel metal tools if you can afford them. Although they are the most expensive, they won't rust and are an excellent investment if you plan to use them for many years.

The third step is to see how the metal tool is attached to the handle. The best-quality tools have a "solid shank," "solid socket," or "solid strap" handle construction, which means that the whole metal part of the tool is one piece. Also, make sure the metal part of the tool is secured to the handle with rivets. If it isn't, the tool head may pop off the handle when you're doing heavy work.

Next, take a good look at the handle. The best tools usually

SHOP FOR QUALITY. *High-quality tools are worth every penny. Not only are they comfortable to use, but they also do the job they are intended for easily and efficiently.*

TIP-TOP TOOLS. *A well-made tool will last a lifetime with proper care. Regular sharpening will ensure that tools like spades and shovels will slice through soil when you dig and will separate clumps of perennials cleanly when you divide.*

have all-wooden handles. Ash and hickory are the preferred types of wood; avoid buying tools with handles made of Douglas fir, which is a poor-quality wood. Also, make sure there are no knots, cracks, or flaws in the wood.

Finally, "try on" the tool before you buy it. Try out the weight of the tool, as well as the feel of the handle. Look for handles that fit your hand well and are comfortable. If you're looking at trowels or other ground-level tools, check that the grip area of the handle is long enough so you won't scrape your hand against the ground when you use the tool. For longer-handled tools like hoes, shovels, and rakes, buy the handle size that matches your height best.

KEEPING TOOLS IN TOP SHAPE

Once you find the right tools, you'll want to make them last. Carefully collect and clean off all garden tools after you are finished for the day, then place them in a dry, well-organized garden storage shed or garage. Before storing the tools, be sure to wipe off all metal parts with an oiled cloth to keep them rust-free. Keep a sharpening stone or hand file in the storage area for regular tool and blade sharpenings, or have the tools professionally sharpened once or twice a year.

No matter how careful you are, it's almost inevitable that you'll misplace tools at one time or another. One way to prevent this from happening is to paint all the tool handles a bright color. They'll be easier to spot lying around your yard, and they'll also be easier to identify if you loan them out to neighbors or friends.

STARTING YOUR TOOL COLLECTION

What are the basic tools every gardener needs? And how do you know which tools are best for which jobs? In gardening, there are four primary kinds of tools: digging, weeding, raking, and pruning. It's also handy to have a wheelbarrow or garden cart, watering equipment, and a few other miscellaneous items. As you gain more experience, you may need or want to acquire more specialized garden tools. However, the following tools should suffice for most gardening tasks.

DIGGING TOOLS

The essential digging tools all gardeners should have include a trowel, spade, shovel, and short-handled spading fork.

Trowel: A good trowel is indispensable for planting, transplanting, and smaller plant-dividing jobs. The sturdiest trowels are of one-piece construction and have a stainless steel blade. Trowels come in regular and narrow sizes. Narrow trowels are useful for digging between closely spaced plants and for planting bulbs. Some trowels have inches marked along the blade to help you gauge how deep to plant various bulbs.

Spade: A spade has straight sides and a rectangular shape with a sharp, flat edge. For some jobs—such as digging, planting, and transplanting perennials,

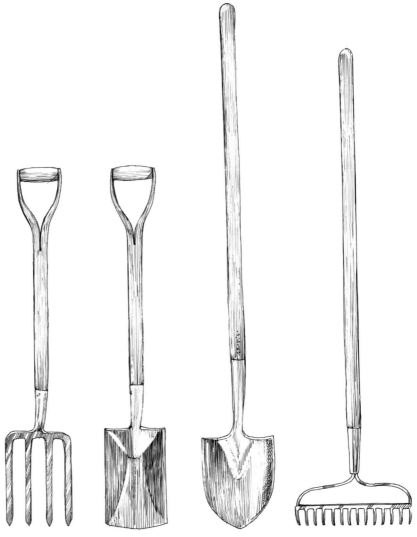

A GARDENER'S ARSENAL. *Every gardener needs an assortment of basic tools for preparing the soil, including (left to right) a spading fork, a spade, a shovel, and a rake.*

trees, and shrubs—spades and shovels can be used interchangeably. But a spade is the tool of choice for jobs where a sharp, clean cut is important, such as when you need to lift sod, edge beds, or work in closely planted areas to divide or transplant larger plants. A spade is also the best tool for digging into compacted soil or into beds with large roots from nearby trees or shrubs. If you can't afford to buy both a spade and a shovel, purchase the spade, which is more versatile.

Look for a spade with a "Y-D" handle. This type of handle, which divides at the top and is linked by a horizontal grip at the end, gives you a better grip than "T" handles. The spade should be solidly constructed, with a stainless steel or carbon-steel blade. Stainless steel can be expensive but is the best. The carbon-steel blade is just about as good and should also last a lifetime. Keep the blade sharp so it will be easier to use.

Shovel: Shovels are useful for

larger digging and lifting jobs, such as digging up large beds, removing soil from an area, filling in soil around newly planted trees or shrubs, working compost into a bed, or moving sand, cement, or other material from one area to another.

Shovels come in long- and short-handled types. The long-handled ones are used for most garden tasks, since they give greater leverage and require less stooping than short-handled shovels. The highest-quality shovels are made from high-car-

bon, heat-treated steel with a forged construction.

The most useful type is probably the round-point shovel. Scoop shovels are larger, yet more lightweight and are used primarily for scooping up lighter-weight materials, such as sawdust, dry

POWER TOOLS FOR EASIER GARDENING

If you have a small or medium-size garden, you'll probably do just fine with a good assortment of standard garden tools. But if you have a large property to take care of, or if your energy is limited, you may want to consider investing in some power garden tools to make your life a little easier. The three most popular pieces of power equipment are lawn mowers, rotary tillers, and chipper/shredders.

LAWN MOWERS

If your lawn is very small, you may choose to stick with a push or reel mower. These tools are blessedly quiet and almost never need repair, except for sharpening the blades. For most of us, though, a power mower is a faster way to get through the weekly mowing. When purchasing a lawn mower, go for the best quality you can afford. A quality mower will have various attachments and should have good safety features. It is best to buy a model that allows you to adjust the blade height easily—a feature not all mowers share. Only buy from established, reputable dealers who can also service your machine. Test-drive several models before buying.

There are self-propelled power mowers and nonpropelled or walking mowers. The self-propelled mowers are good for hilly yards or

yards with a lot of curving borders or walkways to mow around. However, they are heavier, more expensive, and subject to more repair problems than regular walking mowers. Walking mowers are less expensive but require more stamina to operate. For lawns larger than ¾ of an acre, a riding lawn mower is generally recommended. Some have attachments, such as snow blowers and front plows, that allow you to use the machine year-round.

Power mowers may be powered by gas or electric engines. Electric machines have long extension cords or run on batteries. Most battery-powered machines can work for about 45 minutes before they need recharging.

A mulching mower is your best buy because it finely shreds grass clippings, thus eliminating the job of raking up the clippings. Plus, leaving the clippings on the lawn is an excellent way to improve soil fertility and structure naturally. However, if you cut your grass infrequently, it's better to use a mower with a grass bag to collect the trimmings; otherwise, you'll be left with big clumps and mats of clippings on the lawn, which can cause discoloration and possible disease problems.

Keep all mower blades sharp; sharp blades cut more efficiently and cleanly, minimizing the damage

to your grass. There are now nylon string mowers on the market that, like string trimmers, cut grass with a high-speed nylon cord. These types of mowers may prove safer than traditional whirling metal blades, which can propel stones and other debris into the air. There are also "floating string mowers," which are self-propelled and literally float over the ground on a cushion of air. They are excellent for rough, rocky lawns where it is difficult or dangerous to use a traditional mower.

ROTARY TILLERS

Rotary tillers are used to mechanically cultivate the soil and to work organic matter into the top 4 to 8 inches of soil. While having a rotary tiller is not an absolute necessity, it can seem that way if you have large garden beds to prepare each year. These machines can save you much back-breaking work and are effective in producing loose, fluffy soil. You can use them in spring to prepare planting areas, and in spring and fall to incorporate cover crops, and organic matter such as compost into the soil.

Rotary tillers come in two basic models: front-tine or rear-tine. Use the heavier, rear-tined types for heavier and more difficult jobs—especially for areas that have never been cultivated before, or for heavy compost, manure, and leaves.

Short-Handled Spading Fork: This tool is indispensable for turning over already-loosened garden beds and for breaking up heavy soil and soil clods when you are preparing a site for planting. You can also use a spading fork for lifting and dividing bulbs and perennials, for lifting and moving dry materials such as hay and straw, and for digging up underground crops such as potatoes, peanuts, and beets.

A short-handled spading fork has four flat tines and is usually about 42 inches long. The best-quality ones are made from high-carbon tempered steel. Make sure the fork's tines have a bit of "spring" to them. This flexibility helps the tines absorb pressure so they won't get bent when you're digging into heavy or rocky soil.

clay and rocky soil. Front-tined tillers are fine for soil that has been previously cultivated and for loamy or sandy soil that is easy to cultivate. Rear-tined tillers cost more than front-tined models, but they are the tool of choice if you have difficult soil or a large area to handle.

The width and depth a rotary tiller will cultivate on one pass varies. Choose a model that suits your garden size and soil type. The highest-quality tillers have high carbon-steel tines that can be adjusted for width. Make sure any rear-tined tiller you are considering has a safety cover. Test several models and select one that is easy to start up and operate. Electric-powered models are generally less noisy than gas-powered types.

Many rental centers rent rotary tillers for daily or weekly use. If you have a small garden or only need a rotary tiller to prepare a bed in the spring, renting may make more sense than purchasing.

CHIPPER/SHREDDERS

These machines grind leaves, weeds, plant debris, twigs, and small branches into finely shredded material, quickly reducing piles of garden debris into useful mulch. The ground-up organic matter will also make finished compost much faster than nonshredded materials. Chipper/shredders are excellent for chopping up leaves to produce leaf mold mulch for garden beds.

Chipper/shredders come in different sizes and vary in the size of woody branches they can handle; look for one that meets your needs. If you have an average-size garden, you may just want to rent a machine once or twice a year to shred leaves and trimmings for mulch and compost. Always use protective eyewear, and be careful when feeding woody twigs and small branches through these machines.

WORK-SAVING ROTARY TILLERS. *Tillers are handy for working organic matter like compost into the soil. When using them for weed control, avoid tilling in perennial weeds like thistles, because every cut piece of root will resprout.*

A garden pitchfork is a slightly different type of fork that has slightly rounded and thinner tines. It is very useful for lifting lightweight, bulky materials such as hay, straw, and leaf mold.

WEEDING TOOLS

For many of us, weeding is the least enjoyable garden task. Fortunately, there are many tools you can use to make the job a little easier. Some of the most common "weed weapons" include a hoe, hand fork, and asparagus weeder.

Hoe: This ancient device is one of the most effective weeding tools and a good all-around garden tool. Use it to scrape weed seedlings from the soil and to hack out annual weeds and other fairly shallow-rooted weedy plants. You can also use a hoe to break up soil clods, cultivate already-loosened soil, make furrows to plant seeds, or hill up soil around seedlings and plants. A scuffle hoe is a special type of weeding hoe with a double-edged blade that cuts on both the push and pull strokes.

Garden hoes come in long- and short-handled types. For most people, the long-handled kind is easier to use, because it requires less bending over.

Hand Fork: This tool is handy for both eliminating weeds and cultivating the soil when you are sitting or kneeling in the garden. It is also useful for pulling rocks, leaves, and other debris away from the base of plants.

Asparagus Weeder: This tool has a long, narrow metal shaft with a V-shaped blade at the bottom. It is very handy for getting rid of dandelions, dock, and other taprooted weeds in lawns and borders without disturbing the grass or other ornamental plantings. Insert the blade into the soil an inch or so from the weed, and push it down into the soil to pop out the weed. Be sure to get the entire root; otherwise, the remaining piece may sprout a new plant.

RAKING TOOLS

A variety of gardening tasks involve raking, including preparing beds for planting, cleaning debris out of garden beds, and, of course, cleaning up dropped leaves in fall. These tasks require two different kinds of rakes: a bow rake and a lawn rake.

Bow Rake: Once the soil in a planting area has been cultivated and broken up with other

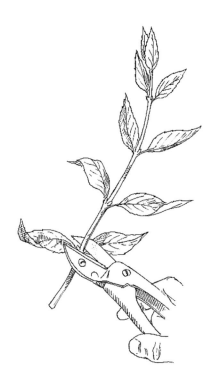

HANDY PRUNERS. Pruners are useful for a variety of tasks, from taking cuttings or pruning shrubs to deadheading flowers or cutting back perennials at the end of the season.

tools, a metal-toothed bow rake is the best tool for smoothing over the site and removing small sticks and stones from the surface. It is also useful for evenly scratching fertilizer, lime, or other soil amendments into the soil. Never use a bow rake on a lawn, as it can easily tear up the grass.

Before purchasing a rake, test it out to be sure the handle length and weight are comfortable for you.

Lawn Rake: A lawn rake ranks up there with a trowel and hoe as an essential garden tool. This fan- or broom-shaped rake is lighter than a bow rake and is useful for collecting leaves, grass clippings, twigs, and other lightweight lawn and garden debris.

Rubber-tipped lawn rakes are handy for removing debris in flower beds without harming the plants. Avoid purchasing plastic rakes, because they tend to break in cold weather. Bamboo lawn rakes are a better choice, since they are sturdy, inexpensive, and lightweight. They also have a natural "springy" feel to them.

PRUNING TOOLS

Pruning tools range from small handheld shears for cutting fresh flowers to large loppers and saws for pruning off tree and shrub limbs. High-quality tools will help make your cutting chores much easier and safer than cheap tools. Essential pruning tools for most home gardens include hand pruners, long-handled loppers, hedge shears, and short-handled grass shears. If you prune trees and shrubs regularly, you should also have a pruning saw.

Hand Pruners: It's a good idea to carry pruning shears with you whenever you're out in the garden. You'll use them for innumerable tasks, from snipping off spent blooms and harvesting fresh flowers and herbs to trimming small twigs, cutting back perennials and roses, and snipping pieces of twine.

There are two types of hand pruners: bypass and anvil. The bypass type has two curved blades that cut like a pair of scissors. Anvil-type pruners have only one cutting blade, which cuts against a straight, flattened edge. Bypass types tend to make cleaner cuts, while anvil types give you better stability for cutting woody plant parts. Choose the kind that feels best to you.

Long-Handled Loppers: This tool gives you additional leverage and cutting strength for pruning small- to medium-size shrub and tree branches that are too large for hand pruners. The long handles extend your reach so that you don't have to step into a wide garden bed or use a ladder. Like hand pruners, long-handled loppers come in anvil and bypass types.

Hedge Shears: These are mostly used to prune and shape shrubs and to cut back or deadhead perennials. While hand pruners can be useful for cutting back one or two plants at a time, hedge shears are easier and faster to use for cutting back larger perennial plantings. This tool is also suitable for cutting back taller grasses or weeds where a lawn mower can't reach.

Short-Handled Grass Shears: These shears are a smaller, one-hand version of hedge shears. They are used for cutting back grass along edgings, walkways, and borders, and around places where a lawn mower can't

reach. If you have to do a lot of this kind of trimming in your garden, you may want to invest in electric- or battery-powered shears or string trimmers. (String trimmers are especially effective and easy to use; just use caution when working around the base of trees or shrubs, as the fast-spinning plastic line can nick and damage the bark of woody plants.)

Pruning Saws: When loppers aren't big enough for a pruning job, you need a pruning saw or bow saw. These handheld tools will quickly cut through woody branches if you keep them sharp. They are both equally effective, although the pruning saw can sometimes be easier to maneuver when you're working around crowded stems.

WHEELBARROWS AND GARDEN CARTS

Wheelbarrows and carts are invaluable for moving heavy loads of soil mix, mulch, peat moss, compost, garden debris, gravel, and cement.

The single front wheel of a wheelbarrow makes it easier to

maneuver than a garden cart, which has two wheels. There are generally two kinds of wheelbarrows available: those for professional construction jobs, and those for garden use. The construction types are heavier and sturdier and can support more weight than the lighter garden models. Unless you are unable to lift a heavier wheelbarrow, the professional kind is better, since it is more durable. No matter which kind of wheelbarrow you choose, make sure it has good bracing on the legs. Keep the wheel well oiled, and don't allow water to sit in metal wheelbarrows, or they may rust. Store wheelbarrows and carts in a dry location.

When using a wheelbarrow, be careful to keep the load balanced; otherwise, it may tip over. If the load shifts and the wheelbarrow becomes difficult to control, just let it tip over; if you try to keep it upright, you may end up straining your back or other muscles. Also, to avoid back injury, never lift more than you can easily manage.

A garden cart allows you to

ESSENTIAL CARRYALLS. *Wheelbarrows are handy for carrying mulch, fertilizer, or other heavy loads. Although they don't carry as much as garden carts, they are easier to maneuver on narrow garden paths.*

carry heavy loads with more relative ease than a wheelbarrow, since the weight is distributed over two wheels instead of just one. Carts can usually hold more material than wheelbarrows, although they are more difficult to unload. Be careful when using them on inclines; a heavily loaded cart can easily push or pull you downhill!

WATERING TOOLS

The right kind of watering equipment will help ensure that your plants get the right amount of moisture and will help you conserve water. Equipment can range from a basic watering can to fancy, electrically timed drip irrigation systems. For the average home garden, you can get by with a watering can, a regular hose, and a soaker hose, plus a hose reel and hose guides, several hose nozzles, and possibly a sprinkler.

Watering Can: A galvanized steel watering can is both attractive and functional. Make sure the nozzle is fairly large so it doesn't clog up too much and so it can be cleaned out easily.

For many gardeners, a 2-gallon type is the easiest to lift when full. A smaller can with a misting nozzle is handy for watering freshly planted seeds and seedlings.

Watering cans are especially useful for watering container plantings in areas you can't reach easily with a hose.

Hoses: Garden hoses are made of many different materials, including rubber, nylon, vinyl, canvas, and polyester fabric. When buying hoses, keep in mind that the rubber types with good-quality fittings are the most durable. Avoid plastic hoses, which can crack or break in cold weather.

Soaker hoses look like regular garden hoses, except that they have small holes along their entire length. They are used to slowly deliver a steady flow of water at ground level or just under the soil surface. These hoses are easier to use than drip emitter systems, since they don't clog up as much as emitters do. Soaker hoses come in lengths of 25 to 500 feet. Place them in the garden permanently, or move them as necessary to water the entire garden. It is important to adjust the water pressure, since the hose may burst open if the pressure is too high. Start with a low water flow, then raise the pressure gradually until water is oozing out slowly over the whole length of the hose.

Hose Reels and Guides: While hoses are necessary for getting water to different parts of the garden, they can cause problems when they kink, knock over

LOW-TECH WATERING. *The ideal way to deliver a gentle spray of water to newly sown flats of seedlings is to use a watering can. This tool is also handy for watering seedbeds out in the garden.*

plants, or twist into knots. You can make your hoses much easier to manage with a hose reel and hose guides.

A hose reel keeps your hose neatly coiled in a roll, preventing it from getting knotted up and making it a much simpler task to wind up the hose when you're finished with it. Hose guides are metal or wooden stakes that are placed in strategic spots in the yard to guide hoses around plants and borders. As you drag the hoses around, the guides keep them from damaging your plants.

Nozzles: There are many kinds of hose nozzles to choose from. The best are those that allow you to adjust the flow of water at the free end of the hose. With fan-type nozzles, you can use a gentle spray for seedbeds and seedlings, and a stronger flow for irrigating more established plants. A watering wand can also

make watering much easier. This long wand has a nozzle at one end and attaches to the hose at the other end. It is great for watering outdoor hanging baskets and for spot-watering hard-to-reach plants in wide borders. The wand also allows you to deliver water at soil level without getting the plants' foliage wet.

Sprinklers: Sprinklers are most useful for watering large lawns and gardens that need frequent irrigation. They are not as efficient as soaker hoses or drip irrigation systems for ornamental and vegetable gardens.

Oscillating sprinklers are handy for distributing water evenly over a wide swath of garden or lawn. Most of these sprinklers can cover about a 55-by-65-foot area. Avoid buying cheap models, since they tend to pause at the extremes of their arc and cause puddling at those spots.

Revolving sprinklers whirl water around a circular area. At high water-pressure levels, most revolving types can cover a 50-foot circular area. They can water a smaller area if you reduce the water pressure.

Impulse sprinklers shoot water straight up through a nozzle. As it shoots up, it is deflected by a little metal arm that goes back and forth, scattering the stream of water into smaller droplets over a given area. These sprinklers are most often used to water large lawns. At higher water pressures, they can cover a diameter of lawn up to 100 feet. When used to water ornamental beds, they are usually placed atop 4- to 6-foot stands.

In general, the highest-quality sprinklers are made of stainless steel or brass. Choose one that is easy to clean (debris can clog the emitter holes) and that is appropriate for the size of your lawn.

When you use the sprinkler, adjust the water pressure as necessary so the water can be absorbed by the soil. If water is coming out faster than it can soak into the soil, it will run off and be wasted. If you notice runoff, turn the sprinkler off for an hour or two to let the water soak in.

MISCELLANEOUS EQUIPMENT

Open up any gardening supply catalog, and you'll see dozens of products designed to make gardening easier and more successful. Having these items readily available, in a well-organized storage space, will save you from having to hunt them down each time you are ready to go out and work in the garden.

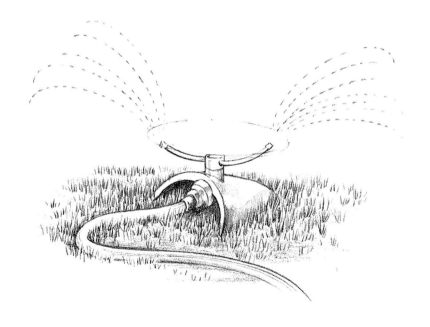

SPRINKLERS. *Although not as efficient as soaker hoses, sprinklers come in handy for spot-watering lawns and other areas of the garden.*

Sprayers: Fertilizers, pesticides, and herbicides are often applied in a spray form. If you need to spray small seedlings, houseplants, or just a small area of your garden, you can buy a simple plant mister or simply recycle a used window cleaner-type plastic bottle. For most jobs, though, a simple compressed-air sprayer is the best choice.

A home garden compression sprayer varies in capacity size but usually holds 1 to 5 gallons. Of course, if you have a large garden, you may want to go with a large sprayer. However, remember that 1 gallon of water weighs about 8 pounds, so don't get a larger sprayer if you can't comfortably tote around the extra weight.

The compression sprayer is very simple to operate: Simply pump the handle up and down several times to compress the air inside the pump. Push in the attached trigger to release the spray solution through the wand and spray nozzle. (For safety's sake, don't let a compressed sprayer sit in the hot sun too long before using it; the heat could cause the sprayer to explode.) Plastic compression sprayers are fine for most home gardens, although metal sprayers are, of course, more durable. Try to find a sprayer with a good mist nozzle; a fine mist is the best way to deliver most fertilizers and other chemicals to plants.

Instead of a compression sprayer, you can purchase a hose-end sprayer that is attached to the end of a hose nozzle. The sprayer either comes prepackaged with a concentrated solution or gives directions on how to prepare your own concentrated fertilizer or pesticide solution. The sprayer attachment releases the solution it contains into the stream of water coming from the hose. This kind of attachment is very efficient for frequent fertilizing jobs. It is also a handy device if you have trouble carrying around the heavier compressed-air sprayer.

If possible, buy one sprayer for fertilizing and another for pesticides and herbicides. Never use fertilizers in sprayers with any amount of residue from pesticides or herbicides. In fact, the safest practice is to have a sprayer marked for each specific pesticide or herbicide you use. If you can't afford to buy more than one sprayer, thoroughly clean and rinse the sprayer and all nozzle parts after each application. No matter what chemical spray you are using, mix only the amount you will need for the immediate job. Do not store and try to reuse any of the unused chemical solution.

Mechanical Spreader: A mechanical spreader is a very useful device for evenly distributing dry fertilizer or lime over a large lawn or vegetable garden. Most home-garden types of spreaders are pushed by hand. An oscillating shuttle device at the bottom of the spreader disperses the particles evenly, which is virtually impossible to do if you scatter material by hand.

Tool Sharpeners: Nothing is as frustrating for a gardener and damaging to a plant as dull garden tools. Buy a hand file or other sharpening tool, and use it according to the package directions. Or have your tools professionally sharpened once or twice a year.

Gloves: For general garden work, lightweight cotton gloves are the most comfortable on hot days and for easier tasks like pulling annual weeds. Keep a good pair of leather gloves for tough garden jobs, such as pruning roses or other prickly shrubs. If you are working around poison ivy, wear rubber gloves, a long-sleeved shirt, long pants, and rubber boots. Thoroughly wash all of these items in warm water and detergent before putting them back on again.

Boots: If you are using a shovel, spade, pitchfork, or other sharp digging implement, wear sturdy footwear, such as leather work boots. Wear rubber boots when spraying pesticides and herbicides in the garden.

Knee Pads: Sometimes gardening seems like a rough contact sport! Knee pads can go a long way toward making many weeding and planting tasks much more comfortable. They will also extend the life of your favorite gardening pants and keep all your jeans from getting grass stains at the knees!

Kneeling Bench: This item is excellent for lending support as you get up and down while weeding or planting an area. It is a padded device that also acts as a little bench when turned upside down.

CHAPTER THIRTEEN

PESTS AND DISEASES

PART OF THE JOY OF CAR-
ING FOR A GARDEN IS
WATCHING IT CHANGE
THROUGH THE SEASONS
AND THE YEARS. Perennials
grow into large, showy clumps;
groundcovers fill in to form
attractive carpets; vegetables
mature into plump roots, succulent leaves, or juicy fruits. But
there are some changes that are
not for the better: those caused
by pests and diseases attacking
your plants. Fortunately, there are
simple techniques you can use to
keep these unwelcome visitors to
a minimum. In this chapter,
you'll learn how to prevent problems from starting, how to identify pests and diseases that do

appear, and how to deal with
them before they damage your
garden.

WHAT ARE PESTS?

The most common garden pests
are insects. All insects have three
pairs of legs, a pair of antennae,
and three body sections. Many
have a hard, protective outer
skeleton and a set of wings.
These features can make control
difficult, since the hard coat can
be impervious to insecticides, and
the wings enable the pests to
escape quickly when you start
spraying.

Some insects, including beetles and weevils, attack plants by

chewing on the plant parts.
Others, such as aphids and whiteflies, suck the juices from plant
parts, causing a stippling effect or
an uneven loss of color. Besides
directly damaging tissues as they
feed, pest insects can also spread
diseases from plant to plant.

While insect pests cause
plenty of damage on their own,
they're not the only creatures
that feed on your plants. Slugs
and snails, for instance, are actually mollusks—soft-bodied creatures related to shellfish. They
eat plant foliage and can devastate young crops and seedlings.
Their feeding can also severely
disfigure foliage plants, such as
hostas.

359

Mites are another kind of noninsect pest that's common in the garden. These eight-legged creatures are related to spiders. However, unlike spiders, which feed on insect pests, mites actually feed on your plants. They are almost microscopic in size but are extremely prolific, so they can spread quickly before you even notice them.

Larger pests in the garden include rabbits, squirrels, and deer. Animals can be the most difficult type of garden pest to manage, and they are often the most destructive.

WHAT ARE DISEASES?

Plant diseases are microscopic organisms that can weaken, disfigure, or kill a plant. Some attack only specific plants or plants in the same botanical family; others can affect almost any plant.

For a disease to damage a plant, three factors must be present: the host plant, the disease pathogen, and the environment in which the disease is active (such as warm, moist weather or hot, dry conditions). If any of these factors is missing, the disease will not affect the plant.

Diseases are caused by three major types of pathogens: fungi, bacteria, and viruses. Fungi are the cause of 70 percent of plant diseases. Fortunately, they are also the easiest pathogens to control. Fungi are threadlike organisms that infect plant tissues with microscopic strands of even tinier cells. They can kill plant tissue by producing toxins and enzymes that destroy the plant cells. Fungi grow on living plant tissues and decomposing organic matter.

Some fungi are edible; others are extremely toxic to both plants and humans.

Most fungi reproduce by spores, which can be spread by water or wind, or (inadvertently) by gardeners. The spores act as seeds and germinate when they land in a favorable location, under favorable environmental conditions. Fungicides prevent spores from germinating, thus preventing them from infecting the plant. However, fungicides generally cannot kill spores that have already germinated.

Bacterial diseases are caused by single-celled organisms that have rigid cell walls. They are considerably smaller than most fungal spores. Bacteria multiply very quickly in favorable conditions and produce toxins and enzymes that can kill plant cells. They usually enter a plant through wounds or openings in the tissue, just as they enter human wounds to cause infections. Plants or plant parts infected with bacterial diseases cannot be cured and are usually discarded if the infection spreads. (When bacteria infect large, valuable trees or shrubs, the plants may be treated with antibiotics.) Gardeners can only try to prevent bacteria in the garden, by controlling insect vectors that carry them, and by removing infected plants before the disease spreads.

Viruses are even smaller than bacteria. They are smaller than a cell and are composed of nucleic acid and protein. The nucleic acid in viruses, which is usually ribonucleic acid (RNA), causes enzymes in plant cells to manufacture more of the viral RNA and proteins, thereby creating

more of the virus. As viruses are being reproduced, energy is taken away from the normal growth of the plant. This causes symptoms such as green flowers (on plants that normally have colored blooms), abnormal growth, or mottling of the foliage (the "mosaic" symptom).

Like bacterial diseases, viruses cannot be cured; all you can do is control the insects that spread the diseases and remove infected plants. To prevent the spread of tobacco mosaic virus, smokers should not handle susceptible plants (for example, tomatoes, eggplants, peppers, or petunias) until they have washed their hands after smoking. The disease can be present in the tobacco leaf that was used to make the cigarette and is so strong that it can affect related crops in the garden even after it is smoked.

Other disease pathogens are less common than fungi, bacteria, and viruses, but they can still cause serious problems. These include mycoplasmas, parasitic plants, and nematodes.

Mycoplasmas are single-celled organisms that do not have rigid cell walls. For many years, diseases caused by mycoplasmas were thought to be caused by viruses. Yellows is the most troublesome mycoplasma-caused disease in the garden. It produces abnormal growth and can make the whole plant look jaundiced. It is transmitted by leafhoppers, and controlling these pests is the only way to prevent yellows from spreading to susceptible plants.

Parasitic plants are often classified as pathogens, since they live off the nutrients and water of the host plant. They may or may

SIMPLE PEST AND DISEASE CONTROL. *Following good basic gardening practices is an extremely effective way to prevent pest and disease problems. Plants that are growing in healthy soil and that are kept mulched, watered, and fed are much less likely to have serious problems than plants that are struggling to survive.*

not kill the plant, but they inhibit its growth and weaken it as they take the water and nutrients the plant needs for its own growth. Examples of parasitic plants include mistletoe and dodder.

Nematodes are also classified as disease pathogens, although they could also be considered pests. They are microscopic worms that live in the soil. Most are not harmful to plants, but some feed off of plant roots, restricting plant growth and severely disfiguring root crops such as carrots and radishes. They feed by means of a needlelike structure, which they insert into roots, stems, or leaves and use to suck the juices out of the plant. They reproduce by laying eggs, which hatch into the next nematode generation. Pest nematodes are difficult to control, although you can try treating the soil with beneficial nematodes that eat the pest species.

PREVENTING PESTS AND DISEASES

Before pests and diseases can become a problem in your garden, three things must be present: the pest or disease organism, a susceptible plant, and the right environmental conditions. If you take steps to control any of these three factors, you can keep pests and diseases to a minimum.

KEEP PESTS AND DISEASES AWAY

Let's face it—there's no way you can eliminate pests and pathogens altogether. Insects have short life spans, but they compensate by reproducing in astronomical numbers. Disease organisms can also produce millions of spores in a single plant. Even if you could get rid of all the bad bugs and diseases in your garden, new ones would immediately fly, creep, or blow in from

all sides. Fortunately, though, there are steps you can take to keep these troublesome creatures and organisms in a reasonable balance.

One important step is to use good gardening practices, such as providing the right growing conditions for each plant and fertilizing, watering, and mulching properly to keep the plants vigorous. Keeping the garden clean will also help minimize pest and disease outbreaks. Always remove and destroy damaged plant parts and severely affected plants as soon as you see them; they can contain fungal spores, bacteria, viruses, or insect eggs. Getting rid of them will prevent diseases and pests from spreading onto other plants. Pests and pathogens can live through the winter on plant debris, so clean up the garden in the fall to prevent problems from returning in spring.

You can also spread disease organisms and pests through your

ROTATE FOR HEALTHY CROPS. *Crop rotation will help control many insect pests, as well as soilborne diseases. For best results, move crops in the same plant family—such as cabbage, broccoli, and brussels sprouts—to a new location in the garden each year. You can plant again in the original spot after three years for most crops. This illustration shows a sample rotation for one garden bed.*

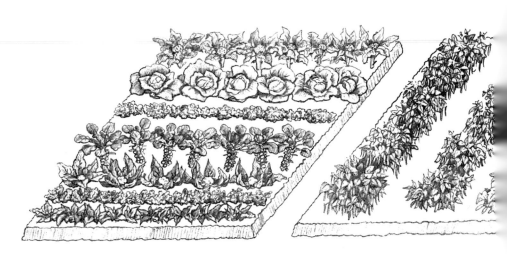

garden without knowing it. Always inspect new plants before you buy them, so you won't bring new problems into your garden. Clean clinging soil off your tools and shoes to prevent problems from spreading from place to place. If you know you've been working around plants that have fungal or bacterial diseases, wipe your tools with rubbing alcohol before using them again. Dipping your tools and hands in milk is also thought to prevent the spread of viral diseases, although no one seems to know why.

If you're growing vegetables or annuals, you can minimize problems by rotating your crops every year. Basically, this means avoiding planting the same or related crops in the same spot each year. (For example, if you planted beans, tomatoes, and onions last year, switch the planting sites this year so each is planted where one of the other crops grew before.) Crop rotation can prevent soil-borne disease pathogens from overwintering in the soil and attacking the same or related crops every year. This method works better for diseases than for pests, because most diseases attack only a few kinds of plants.

If you have limited space and grow many related crops (such as squash, cucumber, and pumpkins, or tomatoes, peppers, and eggplants), you may have difficulty finding a new location for everything you want to grow. In this case, you could try growing some of your plants in containers. Most reasonably sized vegetables and annual flowers can grow in containers, as long as the containers are large enough to accommodate the roots. At the end of every season, remove the growing mix and wash the pots thoroughly. Fill the containers with fresh growing mix in spring, and you can grow your vegetables in the same spot every year without worrying about soil-borne diseases.

ELIMINATE SUSCEPTIBLE PLANTS

If a susceptible plant isn't present, it doesn't matter how many pest insects or disease organisms are around—you simply won't have a problem. While nearly every plant is susceptible to something, you can look for those that are naturally less prone to problems than others: These are said to be "resistant." The popular perennial flower called bee balm (*Monarda didyma*), for instance, is prone to powdery mildew, but the cultivar 'Marshall's Delight' is resistant to the disease. When you are buying new plants for your garden, look for species and cultivars that are resistant to common problems, and you'll save yourself a lot of trouble later on. (If you aren't sure which problems are most prevalent in your area, check with your local Cooperative Extension Service office.)

Providing good care will keep *all* of your plants vigorous and naturally more resistant to problems. Start by giving your plants the growing conditions they prefer. For instance, keep sun-loving plants in bright, sunny spots and shade-loving plants away from

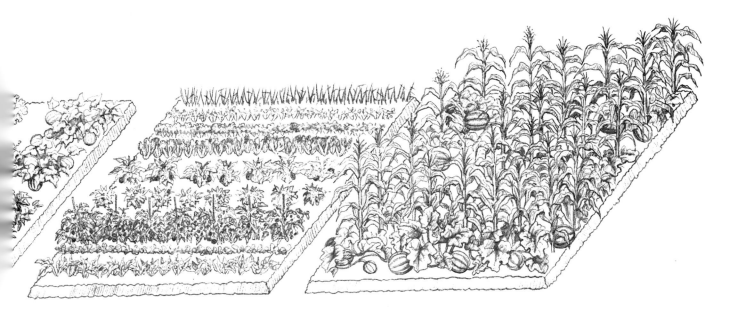

strong, direct sun. (This seems to be common sense, but it is surprising how often people forget.) Through the season, keep your plants weeded, mulched, fertilized, and watered according to their needs.

MAKE THE ENVIRONMENT UNFAVORABLE

The third key to preventing garden problems is to make the environment unfavorable for the pest or pathogen. This can be challenging, since the ideal environment for the pest or disease is generally similar to the ideal environment for the plant. There are, however, some tricks you can use to make pests or diseases less comfortable without adversely affecting your plants.

Avoid Wetting Plant Leaves: Many fungal diseases require water to spread. When you use a sprinkler to water your garden, you end up wetting the plant leaves, which in turn provides ideal conditions for the fungi. If you must use a sprinkler, use it in the morning so the wet leaves can dry quickly. (Also, avoid working around wet foliage, to minimize spreading disease spores from plant to plant.) If possible, use a drip irrigation system, which delivers water right to the soil without wetting the leaves.

Space Plants Properly: Fungi also thrive on high humidity and poor air circulation. Leave ample space between plants to allow air to circulate freely around the leaves and to reduce the humidity around the foliage. Thin vegetable and flower seedlings to prevent overcrowding, and follow the recommended spacing for transplants, perennials, trees, and shrubs.

Protect Plants with Row Covers: Lightweight fabrics called floating row covers can be a real blessing in the vegetable garden. Lay these light covers loosely over seedbeds or transplants, and weight the edges down with soil or boards. As the plants grow, they will push up the covers. Water and light can get through the fabric, but pests are sealed out. You can keep the covers on leafy plants, such as cabbage, until they are ready to pick. If you are growing plants that need to be insect-pollinated, such as cucumbers and squash, remove the covers when the flowers appear; by that time, the plants should be vigorous and able to resist many problems.

ONE-STEP PEST CONTROL.
Floating row covers like Reemay are one of the easiest and best pest controls available. To prevent cucumber beetles, leafhoppers, and other pests from reaching your crops, loosely cover them at planting time. Tuck the edges in along the row with soil, as shown here. Be sure to tuck in the ends as well.

IDENTIFYING PROBLEMS THAT OCCUR

Sometimes, despite your best efforts, pests and diseases can sneak past your defenses. When this happens, you need to be able to identify the problem correctly before you can decide how to deal with it.

KNOW WHAT TO EXPECT

You'll have a head start if you know what pests and diseases your plants are susceptible to, and which problems are most common in your area. If you are new to an area, talk to your gardening neighbors and local garden center staff. Also, get to know your local Cooperative Extension Service agent. The Cooperative Extension Service is sponsored by the state agricultural university in each state. In Pennsylvania, for example, the sponsoring state university is The Pennsylvania State University; in New York, it is Cornell University; and in New Jersey, it is Rutgers University. You can find your local agent by looking in the state offices section of your local telephone directory. Experienced agents can tell you what problems you are likely to encounter, and they can offer suggestions on how to cope with them.

KNOW WHAT IS NORMAL

When you find what looks like a sick plant in your garden, the first question you should ask is: What should the plant look like at this time of the year? At certain times of the year, some plants look better than others. Some trees, for instance, naturally lose their leaves earlier than others and

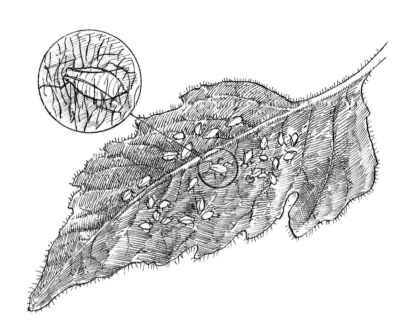

KEEP AN EYE OUT FOR PROBLEMS. *Take time every other day or so to stroll through your garden looking for signs of pests or other problems. Be sure to look under leaves to search for pests like aphids, shown here. If you catch infestations early, they'll be easier to control.*

may not exhibit much fall color. Some annuals cannot tolerate high temperatures and naturally die back or languish in midsummer. Some perennials naturally die back in the summer and reemerge in the fall.

If the plant in question has yellow or mottled leaves, check the name on the tag or in your records: If it says something like "aurea" or "variegata," the leaves are supposed to be an unusual color. When you are familiar with your plants, you will know what looks normal and what does not.

SEARCH FOR A CAUSE

When you know that your plant is damaged, you need to consider all possible causes. Keep in mind that not all problems are caused by pests or diseases. Damage from lawn mowers, for instance, can cause branch dieback on shrubs

and trees. Careless weeding can damage shallow-rooted plants, such as azaleas and blueberries. Unusual weather conditions can cause all kinds of problems, from frost injury and wind damage to sunburn and drought stress. Nutrient imbalances can also cause diseaselike symptoms, such as discolored leaves.

In general, damage caused by environmental factors tends to be more uniform in appearance than damage caused by pests or pathogens. For example, wind damage and sunburn occur on the side of the plant facing the wind or sun. These environmental factors also tend to affect more than one plant in a given area; look at other plants nearby to see if they exhibit the same symptoms. If you can pinpoint what's causing the problem, you can usually take steps to prevent the same damage from occurring in the future. (In the case of wind or sun damage, for example, you may choose to put in a windbreak or sun screen.)

Nutrient deficiencies have characteristic patterns. For example, a nitrogen deficiency causes the lower leaves of a plant to turn yellow. The newer leaves of a plant with an iron deficiency will turn yellowish. A calcium deficiency can cause the leaf tips to curl. A boron deficiency can cause dead patches to form in plant tissues or hollow areas to form in fruits. To determine if your soil is deficient in nutrients, have it tested by the Cooperative Extension Service.

Some plant symptoms are difficult to interpret. Brown leaf edges are a classic sign of drought stress, but they could also come from a salt buildup in the soil, overfertilization, or root damage. Wilting is a sign of drought stress but may also be caused by a wilt disease, such as Fusarium. If you aren't sure that a problem is caused by environmental factors, it's time to investigate possible pests and pathogens.

SIGNS OF DAMAGE FROM PESTS

Start your search by checking the plant for pests. Look closely at the stems, leaves (especially the undersides!), shoot tips, flower buds, flowers, and fruit. Many pests feed only at night, so if you don't see any pests during the day, check out your plants at night with a flashlight. If you can't find any pests, you may have to rely on their damage to identify the culprits.

Holes in Leaves and Flowers: Chewing pests leave

KNOW YOUR PESTS. *It pays to know what pest you are dealing with before you try to control it. Otherwise, you may spend valuable time and money on controls that aren't effective. Caterpillars such as tomato hornworms, shown here, are easy to control with a spray of BT or BTK while they are still small.*

holes in foliage and flowers. Slugs and snails leave huge, gaping holes in leaves or completely devour seedling plants. They also leave a telltale trail of slime, and tend to feed close to the ground. Slugs and snails usually feed at night, but you may find them under plant leaves during the day. Weevils also feed at night and hide in the soil during the day, so unless you look for them at night with a flashlight, you may only see their damage: comma-shaped notches in the edges of rhododendron leaves. Japanese beetles are usually out during the day, feeding on tender leaf tissues and leaving behind a lacy network of leaf veins. Caterpillars can devour entire leaves quickly, leaving only the midvein, if anything.

Mottled or Discolored Leaves: Sucking insects cause spotting or stippling on the foliage and twisted, misshapen young leaves. Aphids are easy to find on the soft, new growth of many plants; they are often evident in large numbers. They produce a sticky substance called honeydew, which attracts ants. Another common sucking insect is the whitefly, which can cause pale or yellowed leaves. If tiny white insects fly up when you shake or brush by a plant, whiteflies are in the area.

Scales or mealybugs are usually visible on stems and in the crotches of branches. Their feeding weakens the plant and causes the leaves to turn yellow. Mites cause stippling when they suck the juices from foliage. If you suspect your plant has mites, hold a piece of white paper under the leaves and shake the plant; if you see tiny red spots moving on the paper, the plant has red spider mites. Mites also spin webs, like their spider relatives. (Unfortunately, when you see the webs, the damage is often too advanced to be controlled.) Other sucking insects cause galls, or swellings, on leaves or stems, although galls can also be caused by diseases.

Other Symptoms of Pest Damage: If a leaf looks rolled and tied together with silklike threads, it could be caused by leaf rollers. If there are irregular squiggly lines marking the leaf surface, it could be from leafminers. And holes at the base of cucumber vines or other vine crops, with sawdust next to the holes, may indicate that borers are present.

SIGNS OF DAMAGE FROM DISEASES

If you can't pin down a pest cause for plant damage, the problem may be a disease instead. Diagnosing diseases can be tricky, since the same pathogen can cause somewhat different symptoms on different plants. But if you have some idea of what diseases might attack a particular plant, you'll have a better idea of what to look for.

Fungal Diseases: Fungi can be the easiest pathogens to identify, since they often have characteristic spores or fruiting bodies. Rust fungal diseases, for instance, form dark orange spots that look very much like metal rust. Smut diseases leave gray or black, sooty-looking spores on leaf blades, stems, flowers, and seeds. Fungi may also cause leaf spots, which usually look like a series of concentric brownish to greenish rings. When a plant wilts and you know that the soil is neither too wet nor too dry, you may be dealing with a fungal wilt disease. If you make a lengthwise slice along

the stem of the plant and see a red substance in the veins, Fusarium wilt is at work; if there is a tan substance, it is probably Verticillium wilt.

Some fungal diseases can look as though they are damaging your plants when, in fact, they are feeding on something else. Sooty mold, for instance, grows on the sticky honeydew left behind by aphids. The fungus produces a black coating on the leaves, but it does not infect the plant. The green algaelike substance and the white mold that form on the soil of containers or seedling flats are usually surface molds that grow on the soil, not on the plants growing in it. It's important to be aware of these fungi, since they can tell you that your plant is affected by sucking insects (in the case of sooty mold) or that the soil is too wet (in the case of soil molds).

Bacterial Diseases: Bacterial diseases may cause leaf spots, a water-soaked appearance on foliage, or a slimy, bad-smelling rot. The leaf spots tend to be irregular or angular, rather than concentric rings. They also tend to be all one color, not shading to brown in the center, like the leaf spots caused by fungi. When the spots dry, they may become translucent or papery thin. Infected wounds typically exude a sticky, bacteria-laden substance that can spread the pathogen to other branches or other plants.

Viral Diseases: Viral diseases cause plant cells to manufacture more of the virus, which inhibits the cells' ability to function normally. Sometimes viruses interfere with the production of chlorophyll, the substance that makes plants green. The lack of

chlorophyll can reveal other pigments in the plant tissues, resulting in discolored foliage or flowers, mottling, or unusual colors—for example, the color "breaks" of the Rembrant tulip.

Other symptoms of viral diseases include mosaic or ring patterns in contrasting colors on the foliage. Sometimes the foliage looks uniformly yellow, although this symptom may also be from yellows disease. The leaf veins may appear translucent or have bands of lighter green or yellow shades. The plant itself may be stunted or exhibit abnormal growths, such as "witches'-brooms," which are densely branched clusters of twigs. Sometimes viruses cause dead tissue or lesions to form, but this is less common than the other symptoms and is difficult to distinguish from bacterial symptoms.

Viruses do not tend to kill plants, since they depend on the plants for reproduction. They can, however, severely reduce your harvest from crops such as tomatoes, cucumbers, and peppers, which depend on healthy, rapid plant growth for fruit production. If you want to be sure you're dealing with a virus, you can send a sample of infected plant tissue to your local Cooperative Extension Service office or to a research university, for analysis. In most cases, though, it's easiest to simply remove and destroy infected plants.

Nematodes: Nematodes feed on roots or shoots. Shoot nematodes cause yellowing or dead tissue to form near the base of leaves. Root nematodes inhibit the plant's ability to take up water and nutrients through its roots, which in turn causes nutrient deficiencies and wilting. The roots may form knots where the nematodes feed, or they may be stunted or misshapen. Because nematodes are microscopic, the best way to find out if they are in your soil is to send a sample for analysis to your local Cooperative Extension Service office or to a major agricultural university.

DEALING WITH PESTS AND DISEASES

Once you have determined that your plant has a pest or disease problem and you have identified the specific culprit, then what? Sometimes, as with viral diseases, your only option is to remove and destroy the infected plant. You can't control damage caused by weather conditions, either; sometimes you can just hope that your plant outgrows the problem. Bacterial diseases and nematodes are also very difficult to handle. But fortunately, you do have a variety of options for controlling the two most common kinds of plant problems: pests and fungal diseases.

PLAN A CONTROL STRATEGY

Before you reach for the sprayer, stop a minute and consider whether you really need to do anything. If your plant just has one or two spotted leaves, simply pinching off the damaged parts may be enough to stop the problem before it spreads. Handpicking large, slow-moving pests such as caterpillars (wear gloves, or use tongs if you're really squeamish), or knocking off tiny, soft-bodied creatures such as aphids and

CONTROLLING ANIMAL PESTS

Many animals—both wild and domestic—can be garden pests. Dogs and cats can dig in the soil or knock over plants as they romp through the yard. The most difficult animal pests to control, however, are wild ones, including squirrels, rabbits, groundhogs, mice, moles, and deer. These creatures feed on garden vegetables, flowers, trees, and shrubs, frustrating and angering even normally calm gardeners.

But before you do anything drastic, try a barrier or repellent to keep the critters away. If squirrels or mice are attacking seedling trays outside or in the greenhouse, cover the trays with chicken wire. If you want to keep pests out of your yard altogether, install some kind of fence. The height and construction will depend on what kind of animals are common in your area. If deer are a problem, you'll need a fence about 8 feet high so they can't jump over. If rabbits are your main problem, the fence doesn't need to be very high (maybe 2 or 3 feet), but you should bury the bottom 6 inches or so to keep bunnies from burrowing underneath. Netting can keep birds from decimating your fruit crops.

If you don't want to bother with barriers, you could try using repellents or scare tactics to keep animals at bay. Purchase commercial repellents to spray on or scatter around plants. An essence of fox scent is available to scare off small mammals that are prey to foxes. Some gardeners deter deer by wrapping human hair in sections of panty hose and hanging the small bundles on trees and shrubs. Fake owls and snakes are available to fool birds and mice.

Finding the perfect control for your garden is usually a matter of trial and error. Talk to other gardeners in your area to find out what works for them. Also, check with the staff at your local Cooperative Extension Service office; they can advise you on different control techniques and fence styles.

HANDPICK PESKY PESTS. *Many pest insects, including Colorado potato beetles, shown here, can be controlled by handpicking. Either squash them or drop them into a bucket of soapy water. Wear gloves if you are squeamish!*

mites with a spray of water from the hose, may prevent further damage.

Trying these mild methods first can give your plants a chance to recover without further help from you. Beneficial insects, for instance, may arrive to feed on remaining pests. Or the plants may begin growing more vigorously and resist further infection. If your plants don't improve, however, you may have to choose a more active strategy. Start with biological controls, then try traps if you need additional help. Organic sprays and dusts are the next option. If no other control measures work, you may choose to try chemical sprays as a last resort.

TRY BIOLOGICAL CONTROLS

"Biological control" basically means using one organism to control another. This simple system can work on either diseases or insects.

Releasing Beneficial Insects: Although your garden naturally contains many different beneficial insects, there may not be enough or the right kinds to deal with your particular pest problem. Many garden supply companies offer the eggs, larvae, and adult forms of insects that feed on plant-damaging species. Ladybugs are perhaps the best-known "good" garden bugs; they feed on aphids, scales, mealybugs, spider mites, and Colorado potato beetle eggs. Green lacewing larvae feed on aphids, mealybugs, whiteflies, thrips, spider mites, and many other pests. Trichogramma wasps are tiny, nonstinging wasps that feed on cabbageworms, cutworms, corn earworms, corn bor-

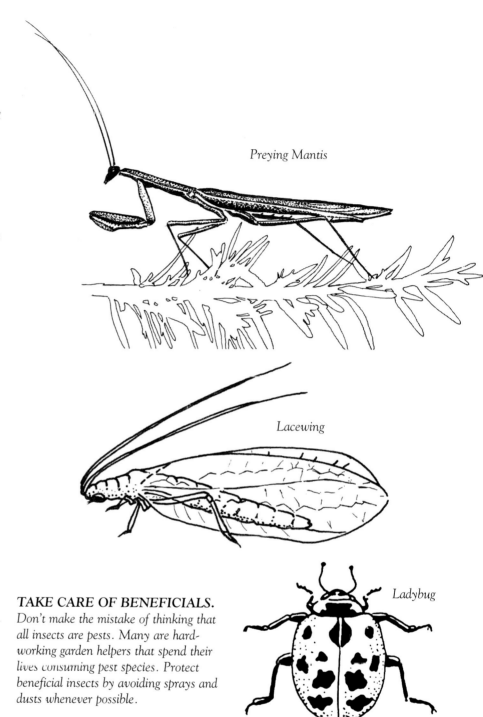

Preying Mantis

Lacewing

Ladybug

TAKE CARE OF BENEFICIALS. *Don't make the mistake of thinking that all insects are pests. Many are hardworking garden helpers that spend their lives consuming pest species. Protect beneficial insects by avoiding sprays and dusts whenever possible.*

ers, codling moths, tomato hornworms, and many other moth and butterfly larvae. Praying mantids will feed on just about any insect, including their own young.

There are some drawbacks to introducing beneficial insects to

your garden. Sometimes they do not want to stay. This has been a problem with ladybugs, which have a tendency to fly away and seek their original home. The best way to keep them in your garden is to have them hatch from eggs there, because their home will then be your garden. Ladybugs are now available that are "preconditioned" to lay eggs when they are released to your garden.

One disadvantage of releasing praying mantids in your garden is that they will eat good as well as bad insects. They are also territorial and chase each other away from areas under a specific size. Most of the praying mantids that hatch from the egg cases you purchase will not remain to control pests in your garden.

Once you release beneficial insects, give them a chance to do the job you bought them for. Don't expect the pest insects to be gone in a day or two; it can take a week or more for beneficials to get settled and start doing their job. Also, remember that spraying any kind of insecticide is incompatible with using beneficial insects, since pesticides kill the good guys, too. If you really feel you must spray, carefully spot-treat affected plants; don't spray a whole bed or garden area at once.

Using Beneficial Microorganisms: Besides releasing predator insects in your garden, you can also introduce diseases to attack pests. These diseases will only attack insects; they will not harm your plants. The best-known biological disease control is the bacterium *Bacillus thuringiensis*, commonly called BT. A particular strain known as BTK is used to control the larvae of moths and butterflies. Strains of BT are also available for fungus gnats (BTI) and Colorado potato beetle larvae (BTSD). When target pests eat leaves that have been sprayed or dusted with BT,

their digestive tracts become paralyzed, and they starve to death. The bacterium is usually only effective for up to four days after application, although there is now a form that lasts four times as long.

You can also fight pests with nematodes. Beneficial, or parasitic, nematodes attack a wide range of soil-dwelling pests, including Japanese beetle and June beetle grubs, borers, cutworms, weevils, cabbage root maggots, fungus gnats, and wireworms. You can also buy parasitic nematodes that feed on destructive nematodes.

Using microorganisms against plant diseases is mostly in the experimental stage at this point. The control organisms work either by attacking the pathogens directly or by competing with the pathogens. Bacterial crown gall disease, for instance, can be prevented by dipping roots into a solution of the bacterium *Agrobacterium tumefaciens* before planting. Researchers are still working on finding parasitic fungi to attack various bacterial and fungal diseases.

USE TRAPS TO CATCH PESTS

If you want to put a dent in pest populations, you can also try trapping them. Commercially available yellow or white sticky boards work like old-fashioned fly paper: Aphids, whiteflies, flea beetles, and fungus gnats are attracted to the traps and get stuck when they touch the glue. To keep caterpillars from climbing up trees, you can wrap sticky tapes around the tree trunks.

Some traps use scent lures to attract pests such as gypsy moths

or Japanese beetles, which then either get stuck or fall into the trap. While these traps can be useful in large areas, such as orchards, they aren't ideal for home gardens. The lures can attract pests from surrounding areas into your yard, and not all of the pests will be trapped, so you may actually end up with more pests than you started with. If you want to try these traps, place them away from the plants the pests normally attack, and empty them frequently.

CONSIDER ORGANIC SPRAYS AND DUSTS

Organic sprays and dusts include materials that are derived from natural sources (for example, plants or minerals). Just because a pesticide comes from an organic source does not mean that it cannot be highly toxic to humans. But organic controls are generally preferable to chemical sprays, because they tend to break down more quickly into safe by-products.

Insecticidal soaps are probably the most popular organic pesticides used by home gardeners. Made from fatty acids and potassium salts, soap sprays kill insects (usually pests and beneficials alike) on contact. Beneficial insects that are not hit by the spray can come back right after it dries.

Many organic pesticides are derived from plants. Rotenone, for instance, is extracted from the roots of tropical plants. It kills aphids, flea beetles, Colorado potato beetles, borers, and leaf miners. Ryania is made from the roots of a shrub and is effective against caterpillars. Sabadilla is made from the seed of a tropical plant in the lily family. It controls adult beetles, worms, caterpillars, squash bugs, stink bugs, and others. Pyrethrin is extracted from pyrethrum daisies (*Chrysanthemum coccineum*) and is used as an all-purpose pesticide to kill aphids, beetles, thrips, caterpillars, weevils, and other pests. Neem products are made from the seeds of the neem tree, which is native to India. They are effective in controlling gypsy moths, whiteflies, aphids, mealybugs, weevils, and leaf miners, among others. Sprays made from garlic or hot peppers can also be effective against a range of garden pests.

Other organic sprays and dusts are prepared from mined materials. Diatomaceous earth, for instance, is made of fossilized diatoms (single-celled aquatic organisms). This material is abrasive to slugs and other soft-bodied creatures, so you can dust it on and around plants to keep these pests at bay. Sulfur- and copper-based sprays and dusts are used to control powdery mildew, botrytis, and other fungal plant diseases.

Horticultural oil sprays, which work by smothering pests, are also becoming popular organic pest-control options. "Dormant" oils are okay to use on leafless, dormant plants, such as fruit trees in late winter. You can use "superior" oils anytime, on plants that have their leaves. Horticultural oil sprays can be very helpful for controlling tough pests, such as scales and mealybugs.

USE CHEMICAL CONTROLS AS A LAST RESORT

If all other methods fail and you really want to save a particular plant, you may decide to try a chemical control. Select the control that is most effective for the pest or disease you are targeting. The chemical should also be safe for the plant you are treating. Read the label before you buy or use any product; it will tell you how much to use, how to prepare and apply it, and what precautions you should take. It will also tell you how to store the chemical, how to dispose of the bottle when you are finished with it, and what to do if anyone accidentally ingests the contents. There should be an EPA registration number, indicating that the product has been registered and approved by the EPA. Always follow the directions, as using a pesticide in a manner inconsistent with what is listed on the label is a violation of federal law.

APPLYING CONTROLS SAFELY

When using either organic or chemical controls, keep in mind these five "right" principles: right time, right material, right amount, right equipment, and right method of application.

APPLY THE CONTROL AT THE RIGHT TIME

"Right time" refers to the proper time for the particular pest or disease. Pesticides are designed to target insects at specific stages of development, and if you apply them at the wrong time, they may be ineffective. Fungicides, for example, must be applied before disease spores germinate. If you apply them too soon, however-

er, they will no longer be effective when the spores land on the plant. Read the label to find out when you should spray the particular product. If the label is not clear, check with your local garden center or Cooperative Extension Service office.

"Right time" also refers to the weather conditions. The best time to spray is in the morning, on a cloudy day when rain is not expected. Obviously, you don't want to spray while it is raining, or within a day of rain; otherwise, the rain will just wash the spray off the leaves. Also, wait for a calm day, since wind can cause the spray to drift onto people and other plants. Do not spray when the temperature is over 90°F, as sprays can burn foliage in hot weather.

CHOOSE THE RIGHT MATERIAL

Make sure the pest you want to spray is listed on the label. The plant you want to spray should also be listed. Although the specific plant may not be listed, the general plant type should be. If you want to spray your bush beans, for instance, look for a product that lists either "beans" or just "vegetables." If you need to spray a plant and cannot find it listed on any label, check with your local Cooperative Extension Service office for advice.

The label may also indicate which plants not to use the spray on. Some plants are more prone to damage from sprays than from the problem itself. Nasturtiums, for example, may show signs of stress when they are sprayed for aphids, even if you only use insecticidal soap. Young plants of any kind may not be able to tolerate a full dose of a particular spray; check the label to see if it recommends a diluted dose for younger plants. Also, check to see if the manufacturer recommends adding a spreader-sticker, a material that will help the spray cling to foliage better. Never mix chemicals that are not specifically recommended to be mixed, since unpredictable chemical reactions can occur.

USE THE RIGHT AMOUNT

Applying the right amount of a spray or dust is extremely important. Using too much of a chemical can not only kill plants—it can kill people, too. Dry powders or granules are relatively easy to measure and don't require mixing. Other materials are sold as wettable powders or as liquids. Wettable powders are mixed with water and sprayed; liquids are either used as is or mixed with water and then sprayed.

When you are mixing a concentrated liquid or wettable powder always follow the label directions carefully. Keep a special set of measuring spoons and liquid measuring cups with your pest controls. (Always keep them separate from your kitchen set!) If you have trouble remembering liquid measuring units, such as pints, quarts, and gallons, refer to a weights-and-measures chart, or get a knowledgeable friend to help you. If you use too much of a pesticide because of improper mixing, it can burn the foliage; if you use too little, it will not be effective. Mix only what you need, because you don't want to leave any in the sprayer when you are finished. It's better to have to make a second batch than to have some left over.

USE THE RIGHT EQUIPMENT

"Right equipment" refers to the equipment you use to apply the pesticide, as well as protective clothing, which you should always wear when applying any kind of pesticide—organic or chemical. A quality sprayer is a good investment if you'll be doing any kind of spraying. The key to a good sprayer is the nozzle; look for one you can adjust from a fine mist to a strong stream. Also, choose a sprayer that is appropriate for the size of your garden and the amount of spraying you will be doing. Small handheld sprayers are convenient but don't hold much material and need to be refilled constantly if you are spraying a large area. On the other hand, a 10-gallon sprayer is too large for a small garden; many gardeners prefer 2-gallon, backpack-type sprayers.

Always clean your sprayer after using it: After you have emptied the tank, fill it with water and spray the whole tank through the hose to clean the hose and nozzle. It's a good idea to run water through the sprayer twice.

You should also run water through the sprayer before using it each year, to make sure everything is in working order and nothing is leaking. When the nozzle gets clogged and does not spray evenly, it's time to either clean it or replace it.

A good sprayer is one part of safe pesticide application; protective clothing is another. Pesticides are dangerous and must be used with caution. Many of the negative effects of pesticides on your health are long-term and do not exhibit symptoms for many years. Some gardeners will tell you that they never take precautions and that they have been spraying for years. But it is simply foolish to believe that if damage to your health is not immediately apparent, then you have nothing to worry about. Not wearing protective clothing because it is inconvenient is no excuse. The fact is, pesticides are dangerous.

Pesticides can enter your system through your mouth and nose, and they can be absorbed through your skin. The skin on your hands and feet absorb the chemicals more quickly than the skin on other parts of your body. Even if you do not want to wear a complete spraying suit when you spray, you should always wear rubber gloves and rubber boots or shoes. You should also wear long sleeves, long pants, and a hat to protect your skin. Always wash your spraying clothes separately from other clothes, and wash them after every use.

It is also a good idea to wear goggles or glasses to protect your eyes. If you are spraying a great deal or for a long time, or if you are using something particularly toxic, you should also wear a respirator with filter cartridges. Make sure that the cartridges on your respirator are clean; many are good for only 8 hours, and after that, you are breathing the same air you would breathe without the respirator. (If you smell the pesticide, the respirator is not working.) Keep the cartridges fresh by storing them in airtight containers when you aren't using them.

APPLY THE MATERIAL THE RIGHT WAY

The right method of application—how you go about spraying

and what you do afterward—is also important. Again, read the label first and follow the directions. When you apply the chemical, make sure you spray the underside as well as the top of the foliage. Direct the spray under the leaves and use the pressure from the sprayer to cover the surface, rather than lifting the leaves by hand. Be careful to spray only the plants you want to treat. Try not to direct the spray above your head, or it will come down over you; use a ladder, if necessary, or position yourself to avoid the drift. Large trees should be sprayed by professionals who have the proper equipment to reach the taller branches.

When you have finished spraying and have cleaned all of your equipment, lock up all your chemicals, measuring spoons, and liquid measures. Make a note of how much you sprayed, as well as where and when you sprayed. Keeping records will help you keep track of treatments and give you the information you'll need to make effective decisions about spraying in the future.

PEST PORTRAITS

APHIDS

Characteristics: Aphids are tiny, soft-bodied, pear-shaped insects that suck the juices from leaves, stems, flowers, and fruit. They come in a variety of colors, including green, yellow, red, brown, black, gray, and white. (They are often the color of the plant on which they are feeding.) Most species have wings, but they do not generally fly away when they are discovered. Aphids are

Aphids

parthenogenetic, which means that the females can reproduce even if no males are present. They can also give birth to female aphids that are already pregnant. It's no wonder aphids are so prolific!

Aphids prefer succulent new growth. You'll usually find them on leaf and flower buds, or on the undersides of new leaves. They are most damaging on young plants, since they can severely disfigure young foliage; they are not as troublesome on mature plants. However, some species transmit viral diseases, which can be much more serious than the damage caused by the aphids.

Aphids secrete a sticky substance called honeydew, which attracts ants. The honeydew can be troublesome when it falls from trees onto cars, plants, or garden furniture. Also, a black sooty mold can grow on the honeydew. While this fungus does not harm leaves directly, it is unsightly and can keep light from reaching the foliage, thereby preventing photosynthesis.

Symptoms: Look for yellowish leaves, leaves with curled edges, sticky leaves and stems, black mold, or ants. The aphids themselves are easy to spot when you look closely; they cluster on succulent new growth and on the undersides of leaves.

Host plants: Aphids are practically everywhere and can attack any kind of plant.

Controls: If you are not squeamish, you can try squashing the aphids right on the plant with your fingers. You can also wash them off with a strong spray of water. Aphids have many natural predators, including ladybugs, green lacewings, praying mantids, and parasitic wasps. You can also trap aphids on yellow sticky boards. If your plants are seriously infested, you can spray or dust with insecticidal soap, pyrethrin, or rotenone. When applying pesticides, don't forget to spray the undersides of the leaves; just treating the tops may not help at all.

APPLE MAGGOTS

Characteristics: Apple maggots are the larvae of dark brown flies that are about ¼ inch long.

The flies lay their eggs on the skins of apples, and the maggots hatch and eat into the fruit. The maggots are small white or yellowish worms that measure about ¼ inch long. They are one of the most serious orchard pests in the Northeast and Canada.

Symptoms: Apples have slight depressions where the maggots enter the fruit. Unfortunately, it's often difficult to detect damage until you cut or bite into the apple.

Host plants: Apple maggots attack apples, apricots, cherries, peaches, pears, and plums. Blueberries are attacked by a similar pest, the blueberry maggot.

Controls: The trick is to control the female flies before they lay eggs on the fruit. To do this, hang round, red sticky traps around susceptible plants before the flowers open.

BEETLES

Characteristics: Approximately 40 percent of all insects are beetles. They have hard shells and two pairs of wings, and come in many sizes, shapes, and colors. Their larvae, sometimes called grubs, can be damaging to plant roots. Beetles feed on organic matter, other insects, and plants. Some, including ladybugs and ground beetles, are beneficial to the garden. Most garden pest beetles either devour plants completely or chew holes in foliage, flowers, stems, and buds. Some beetles are damaging in the garden not because they eat plants, but because they carry diseases. For example, bark beetles are vectors of chestnut blight and Dutch elm disease fungi, which have nearly eliminated the American chestnut and American elm trees from the landscape.

There are many garden beetle pests. Asparagus beetles are either blue-black with 4 white spots and reddish edges, or red or brown with 12 black spots. Mexican bean beetles are yellow with black spots; they feed on beans, peas, and squash. Colorado potato beetles are yellow with black stripes and orange heads. They lay bright yellow eggs on the undersides of leaves. Their feeding can completely devastate potatoes and related crops, including tomatoes and eggplants. Cucumber beetles are yellow with black stripes or spots. They feed on many plants, including asparagus, beans, corn, tomatoes, potatoes, eggplants, and vine crops such as squash and cucumbers.

Flea beetles are small and black with yellow or white markings. They get their name from their tendency to jump like fleas when disturbed. They chew holes in foliage and transmit serious viral and bacterial diseases. Japanese beetles are the scourge of rose gardens in the East. The adults are metallic green with copper-colored wings and black heads. They feed on roses, zinnias, and beans, as well as a wide range of other plants. Their comma-shaped, dark-headed, white grubs feed on turfgrass roots.

Symptoms: You may see holes in leaves, buds, or flowers, or whole plants may be defoliated. Japanese beetles tend to leave lacy-looking foliage. Beetles are easy to detect, since they feed on the plants both day and night.

Host plants: Some species, such as asparagus beetles, only bother specific plants. Others will eat whatever they can find. All beetles have their favorites. Most plants can be bothered by some kind of beetle.

Controls: Cover vegetable crops with floating row covers to keep beetles from reaching the plants. Handpick beetles from other plants in the morning, before the pests are warm enough to fly away, and drop them in a bucket of soapy water. Biological controls, such as milky disease spores and BTSD, are valuable for controlling some beetles, including Japanese beetles, Colorado potato beetles, cucumber beetles, and flea beetles; check garden supply catalogs or garden centers to see what is available. To control serious infestations, you can spray or dust with neem, pyrethrin, sabadilla, ryania, or rotenone. Check the label to make sure the product you buy will be effective against the pest you need to control. Some pesticides and biological controls are targeted for grubs and must be applied at the proper time, or they will be ineffective.

BORERS

Characteristics: Borers are the wormlike larvae of beetles and moths. They bore holes into the stems or roots of trees, shrubs, or perennials, and feed on the plant tissue. There are many species, some of which are named after the plants they feed on. The species commonly found in gardens are rose borers, raspberry root borers, raspberry caneborers, iris borers, peachtree borers, European corn borers, dogwood borers, lilac borers, bronze birch borers, and squash vine borers. They can be very serious pests, because they are almost impossible to control once they are inside the plant. They cause vine crop plants like melons to wilt and can kill trees by girdling the trunk under the bark. They often enter woody stems through a cut or bruise. Trees with thin, easily damaged bark, such as dogwood and birch, are particularly susceptible to borers.

Symptoms: Borers leave a hole with frass, or sawdust, where they enter the plant. They cause vine crops such as squash and melons to wilt suddenly. If you cut the stem of affected vine crops or cane plants lengthwise, you can find the borers in their tunnels.

Host plants: Specific borers attack certain plants. All vine crops—including cucumbers, melons, pumpkins, and squash—are susceptible to squash vine borers. Bearded irises are susceptible to iris borers. Other plants that can be damaged by borers include apricots, blackberries, cherries, corn, peaches, plums, raspberries, birches, dogwoods, and roses.

Controls: There are no good controls for borers once they are in the plants. Sometimes you can insert a wire into the tunnel and kill the borer in the plant. Injecting BT into the hole may also control borers. To prevent damage, clean up garden debris in the fall, and avoid wounding trees with lawn mowers, string trimmers, and other equipment.

CABBAGE LOOPERS

Characteristics: Cabbage loopers are the larvae of night-flying brown moths with a silver spot on each forewing. These green caterpillars have yellow stripes on their backs; as they move, their back curves into a loop. They chew large holes in the foliage and heads of many vegetable crops, especially members of the cabbage family. They can eat whole seedlings to the ground.

Symptoms: Large, jagged holes appear in the foliage of infested plants, or seedlings are eaten. Green, looping worms are evident on the foliage.

Host plants: Many plants are prone to damage, including beans, broccoli, brussels sprouts, cabbage, cauliflower, collards, kale, kohlrabi, lettuce, parsley, radishes, rutabagas, and turnips.

Controls: Rotate crops and don't grow them in the same bed for 5 years. Use floating row covers to keep pests off the plants. Or dust uncovered plants with diatomaceous earth, and handpick pests that appear. Beneficial insects—including lacewings, Trichogramma wasps, and ladybugs—attack cabbage loopers. Organic pesticides, including rotenone and pyrethrin, are effective as a last resort.

CABBAGE MAGGOTS

Characteristics: Cabbage maggots are the larvae of insects that resemble houseflies. The flies lay their eggs at the base of the stem of the plant. The small, white, blunt-headed maggots hatch and tunnel into the roots, interrupting the plant's ability to take up food and water from the soil. Cabbage maggots can kill young plants or severely disfigure radish and turnip roots. They are most active in cool weather.

Symptoms: The lower leaves turn yellow, and young plants stop growing, wilt, and die for no apparent reason. Brown, slimy tunnels are evident in plant roots, especially in radishes and turnips.

Host plants: Susceptible crops include beets, broccoli, brussels sprouts, cabbage, cauliflower, celery, collards, kale, kohlrabi, peas, radishes, rutabagas, and turnips.

Controls: Grow radishes to lure adult flies away from other cabbage-family plants. Crops planted in midsummer for fall harvest are less prone to damage. Parasitic nematodes can attack cabbage maggots.

CABBAGEWORM, IMPORTED

Characteristics: The imported cabbageworm, also called imported cabbage butterfly, causes the same kind of damage as the cabbage looper. The adult is a butterfly with white or yellow wings marked with black spots. The damage is caused by the larvae, which are green caterpillars with a narrow orange stripe down their backs. They feed on the foliage and heads of members of the cabbage family.

Symptoms: You'll see large, ragged holes in foliage and heads, along with green caterpillars.

Host plants: Imported cabbageworms attack broccoli, cabbage, kale, lettuce, mustard, and nasturtiums.

Controls: Cover vegetable crops with floating row covers to prevent damage. Handpick pests from uncovered plants, or spray them with BTK. Imported cab-

CORN EARWORM

Characteristics: The corn earworm is the larval stage of a brown moth. The worm is a 1½-inch, white, green, or red caterpillar with short spines. Early in the season, corn earworms feed on leaves and buds. Later generations enter the corn ears through the silks and feed on the kernels at the tips of the ears. This pest also feeds on many other crops. On tomatoes, it is called tomato fruitworm; on cotton, it is called bollworm.

Symptoms: Corn plants may be stunted and have damaged ears. Tomato fruits are damaged at the stem end.

Host plants: Corn earworms feed on beans, corn, lettuce, okra, peanuts, peppers, squash, and tomatoes.

Controls: Corn cultivars with tight husks are considered generally resistant to this pest. Green lacewings, parasitic wasps, and beneficial nematodes are effective controls. Do not weed out smartweed if you have it, since it works as a trap crop. Spraying with BTK before the worms crawl too far into the ears may help.

CUTWORMS

Characteristics: Cutworms are among the most frustrating of all garden pests, because they come out at night and literally cut seedlings down to the ground. These 1- to 2-inch-long, soft-bodied, gray or brown caterpillars curl up when they are touched. They live in the soil during the day and come out at night to feed. They also eat the roots of seedlings, causing the young plants to wilt and die. Cutworms mature into brown, night-flying moths.

Symptoms: Seedlings are cut to the ground, or they wilt and die.

Host plants: Virtually all kinds of vegetable and flower seedlings are susceptible, including beans, cabbage-family crops, eggplants, lettuce, peppers, potatoes, and tomatoes.

Adult cutworm

Cutworm

Controls: Once cutworms strike, there is nothing you can do but replant. To prevent damage, place stiff paper collars around the base of the plants. (Push the collar into the soil a bit to keep the pests from crawling underneath.) A ring of diatomaceous earth sprinkled around the plants creates an abrasive barrier. Handpick the worms at night. Beneficial nematodes and Trichogramma wasps attack cutworms. Check garden supply catalogs and garden centers for a BTK bait that controls cutworms.

GYPSY MOTH

Characteristics: Gypsy moth caterpillars grow up to 2½ inches long and are covered with tufts of hair. They are dark, with red-and-blue markings and a yellow head. They mature into moths with a 1½-inch wingspan. The male moth is brown and the female is white. They are prevalent in the eastern United States and have also been found in British Columbia and the Pacific Northwest.

Gypsy moths were introduced from Europe to New England in 1869 as a potential replacement for the silkworm. They have no natural enemies in North America and have devastated forest trees and residential landscapes. They can defoliate whole stands of trees in a couple of weeks. The foliage of many hardwoods can grow back, but repeated attacks can kill the trees. Evergreens may die if they are defoliated in one season. Fortunately, gypsy moths produce only one generation in a year.

Symptoms: The caterpillars eat foliage and are evident on trees and shrubs.

Host plants: Gypsy moths feed on hardwood forest trees, hemlocks, spruces, white pines, fruit trees, and many shrubs.

Controls: Sticky tape around the base of trees prevents the larvae from climbing the trunks. Handpicking works when the infestation is not severe and the pests are within reach. Trichogramma wasps and beneficial nematodes can be effective. Spraying with BTK can help, too.

HARLEQUIN BUG

Characteristics: Harlequin bugs are small, shiny, black, beetlelike insects that are triangular in shape and have red markings on their backs. When they are squashed, they give off a bad odor. They suck the juices from foliage, sometimes causing plants to wilt and die. Harlequin bugs lay rows of distinctive, keg-shaped, black-and-white-striped eggs on the undersides of leaves.

Symptoms: Leaves have yellowish, blackish, or whitish spots; young plants wilt. You'll see the adult bugs, as well as their eggs, on the undersides of the leaves.

Host plants: Susceptible crops include broccoli, brussels sprouts, cabbage, collards, eggplants, kale, kohlrabi, radishes, and turnips.

Controls: Plant turnips, mustard, or radishes as trap crops to lure pests away from other crops. Protect susceptible vegetable crops with floating row covers. On uncovered plants, you can control infestations with insecticidal soap, pyrethrin, sabadilla, or rotenone.

LEAFHOPPERS

Characteristics: Leafhoppers are small, wedge-shaped insects that jump like fleas when they are disturbed. They are green, brown, or yellow and sometimes have red or yellow markings. These pests suck the juices from plants and spread diseases as they feed. They leave behind a sticky honeydew, similar to that left by aphids.

Symptoms: Leafhoppers generally feed on the undersides of leaves and hop when disturbed. Damaged foliage has a mottled appearance and is glazed by the honeydew, which attracts a black sooty mold. The plants may show signs of yellows or a viral disease.

Host plants: These pests feed on many plants, including beans, beets, carrots, potatoes, spinach, squash, tomatoes, fruit trees, raspberries, asters, and marigolds.

Controls: Clean up garden debris. Use floating row covers to keep leafhoppers off vegetables. Green lacewings and Trichogramma wasps attack leafhoppers. If infestations occur, try using organic controls, such as insecticidal soap, pyrethrin, sabadilla, or rotenone.

LEAFMINERS

Characteristics: Leafminers are the larvae of small black flies. These larvae tunnel under the surface of leaves and form blotches or squiggly lines on the leaves. Besides disfiguring foliage, leafminers carry fungal diseases, such as black leg and soft rot. Like borers, they are difficult to control once they have entered the plant tissues, because contact pesticides cannot reach them.

Symptoms: Blotches or lines appear on the foliage of susceptible plants.

Host plants: Many plants are susceptible to leafminers, including beans, cabbage, lettuce, peppers, radishes, spinach, turnips, arborvitae, birches, columbines, and hollies.

Controls: Clean up garden debris each fall. In vegetable gardens, till the soil thoroughly to expose overwintering larvae, and protect the crops with floating row covers. On uncovered plants, leafminers are difficult to control except when they are in the adult fly stage, which occurs in early spring. Handpick the eggs on the undersides of the foliage; they are white, the size of a pinhead, and laid in lines of 3 to 5 eggs. Pick off and destroy foliage that shows signs of damage.

MEALYBUGS

Characteristics: Mealybugs are sucking insects that feed on the stems and leaves of plants. They are small and oval-shaped, and look as if they are covered with a powdery white wax. They release honeydew, which attracts ants and supports the growth of black sooty mold. Some species carry viral diseases.

Symptoms: Plants are weakened and have yellowish leaves. The insects are plainly visible on stems and leaves (especially in the crotches of branches).

Host plants: Many houseplants and greenhouse plants are attacked by mealybugs. Outside, fruit trees, grapes, persimmons, azaleas, and wisterias are particularly susceptible.

Controls: After mealybugs begin to feed, they cover them-

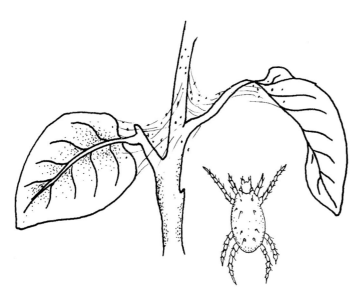

Spider mite

selves with a waxy coating that is difficult to penetrate with insecticides. These pests are easiest to control in the crawler stage, after the eggs hatch but before they begin feeding. Green lacewings are useful predators. Insecticidal soaps, neem, and light horticultural oils can be effective against serious infestations.

MITES

Characteristics: Mites are tiny spider relatives that suck the juices from plant foliage. They are most active in hot, dry weather and multiply quickly when conditions are favorable. The strength of mites is in their numbers, and they are unbelievably prolific: They can produce a new generation in 2 weeks, and up to 8 generations in a single season. If allowed to go unchecked for several weeks, they can quickly infest and kill a plant.

Symptoms: Mites cause distorted growth, especially on stem tips, and stippling on foliage; damaged leaves eventually turn yellow and drop. Mites may also make tiny webs that are visible between the leaves. If you suspect that a plant has mites, hold a piece of white paper under a leaf and shake the plant; the red, black, or brown mites should fall on the paper and move around. If you see more than 5 of these insects, you should take action immediately.

Host plants: Many house-, greenhouse, and garden plants are susceptible to mites. Some that are particularly prone to infestation include dwarf Alberta spruce, roses (especially miniature types), strawberries, and many fruit trees.

Controls: Green lacewings, ladybugs, and predatory mites are natural predators. A strong blast of water on the undersides of leaves can knock mites off a plant. Insecticidal soap sprays are also effective.

SCALE

Characteristics: Scales are sucking insects similar to mealybugs. They find a feeding site on a stem or leaf base, attach themselves to the site with their mouthparts, and begin feeding. They secrete a hard, shell-like covering, or a waxy, cottony coating. The shell-like species are called armored scales. This group includes oystershell scale and euonymus scale. The cottony types include cottony-cushion scale and tortoise-shell scale. Serious scale infestations can kill branches and even entire trees. Scales excrete sticky honeydew, which favors the growth of black sooty mold.

Symptoms: The leaves of infested plants turn yellow; the branches weaken and die. Scale insects are visible on plant stems and foliage. Their honeydew is sticky and often has black sooty mold growing on it.

Host plants: Scales can attack a wide range of both indoor and outdoor plants. In the landscape, particularly susceptible plants include fruit trees, ashes, beeches, birches, bittersweets, camellias, dogwoods, euonymus, hollies, lilacs, maples, and pachysandra.

Controls: Scale is difficult to control once it has attached itself to its feeding place. Green lacewings are natural predators. In the crawling stage, scales can be controlled with insecticidal soap. Oil sprays can also help control scales.

SLUGS AND SNAILS

Characteristics: These ground-dwelling mollusks can be devastating to many kinds of plants. They commonly grow 2 to 4 inches long, although they can reach up to 8 inches long on the West Coast. Slugs can be brown,

Slug

Snail

orange, tan, black, purplish, or yellow, with stripes or spots. Snails are very similar to slugs but have hard shells. Both slugs and snails prefer moist, cool locations. They are hermaphrodites, which means that each slug or snail has both male and female parts. They can live for several years and produce one generation each year. They feed mostly at night, starting about 2 hours after sunset.

Symptoms: Slugs and snails chew ragged holes in plant foliage and can devour young seedlings. They leave a characteristic trail of slime. Sometimes you can find them during the day under boards or stones.

Host plants: Slugs and snails feed on most garden plants, especially those in cool, shady areas and those with foliage close to the ground. They love cabbage, coleus, geraniums, hollyhocks,

hostas, marigolds, primroses, and snapdragons, just to name a few.

Controls: Sprinkling a ring of diatomaceous earth, crushed eggshells, or wood ashes around plants can be an effective way to keep these pests off your plants. Traps can also work. Buy special traps, or make your own by sinking shallow dishes into the soil, so the rim is flush with the soil surface; fill the traps with beer. Some gardeners leave wooden boards in the general area where slugs and snails feed; the pests will collect under the boards during the day, so you can easily remove and destroy them. You can also go out at night with a flashlight and handpick the pests from plants. Sprinkling salt on slugs is not a good idea, because the salt can also harm your plants.

TARNISHED PLANT BUG

Characteristics: Tarnished plant bugs are brown, flat, ¼-inch, oval-shaped bugs with irregular markings in white, yellow, red, and black. They have a characteristic yellow triangle with a black dot on the lower third of each side. These pests suck the juices from plant parts and inject a toxin that deforms foliage and flower buds. They also carry fire blight disease, which can be devastating to fruit trees and shrubs.

Symptoms: Roots, shoots, and flowers may be deformed, and the pests themselves are usually present. Black spots and pitting may be evident on stem tips, flower buds, and fruit. These pests can stop fruit production altogether, especially on dwarf fruit trees and strawberries.

Host plants: Tarnished plant bugs attack a wide range of plants, including strawberries, fruit trees, and vegetables. They also feed on China asters, chrysanthemums, dahlias, marigolds, poppies, salvias, sunflowers, zinnias, and other flowers.

Controls: Clean up the garden in autumn, since the insects overwinter in plant debris. Protect vegetable crops and strawberries with floating row covers. Hang sticky traps near fruit trees to catch these pests. For serious infestations, you can spray or dust with pyrethrin, sabadilla, or rotenone.

THRIPS

Characteristics: Thrips are very small, barely visible, slender insects with feathery wings. They feed by sucking the juices from leaves, stems, flower buds, and fruit. They can also spread disease pathogens as they feed.

Symptoms: Thrip feeding causes streaking on foliage and scarring on fruits; the leaves may eventually wither and die. White- and light-colored flowers may be discolored; severely infested flowers are deformed or destroyed.

Host plants: Many plants are affected, including beans, corn, onions, squash, blueberries, fruit trees, chrysanthemums, and gladioli.

Controls: Green lacewings, ladybugs, and predatory mites are natural enemies of thrips. Use diatomaceous earth or garlic sprays to keep the pests off your plants. Insecticidal soaps, pyrethrin, or rotenone can be effective against infestations.

TOMATO HORNWORM

Characteristics: These big green, white-striped caterpillars are the larvae of a large gray or brown moth with 5 orange spots on each side of its body and a wingspan of up to 4 or 5 inches. The moths can hover like hummingbirds as they sip the nectar of funnel-shaped flowers, such as those of petunias and flowering tobacco. Plants are damaged by the caterpillars, which are 3 to 5 inches long and have a black horn at the end of their bodies. They feed voraciously on tomatoes, tobacco, and other members of the tomato family.

Symptoms: Tomato hornworms chew large holes in leaves and fruit. Brown droppings are visible on foliage and stems. You may also see the pests near the damage.

Host plants: These pests feed on dill, eggplants, peppers, potatoes, tomatillos, and tomatoes.

Controls: Tomato hornworms can be controlled by handpicking; keep an eye out for them so you catch them before they cause too much damage. (If you see a tomato hornworm with white cocoons along its back, it has already been parasitized by Trichogramma wasps and its days are numbered; leave it on the plant so the parasites can hatch and attack other hornworms.) Plant dill as a trap crop to lure the pests away from your crops. Pyrethrin and rotenone are effective against serious infestations.

WEEVILS

Characteristics: Weevils are beetles with hard shells and characteristic long snouts. There are many species, and they feed on a wide range of plants. They generally feed at night and live in the soil during the day, so you may never see them unless you look for them at night with a flashlight. The adults chew on foliage and fruits; their larvae feed on leaves, roots, stems, and fruits. Bean weevils feed on seeds. Weevils are parthenogenetic and do not need males to reproduce.

Symptoms: Look for foliage with notched edges or large holes (with only the midvein remaining). Other symptoms include chewed fruit or zigzag patterns where larvae entered the roots, stems, or fruits. The weevils are evident at night.

Host plants: Many plants are host to weevils, including beans, carrots, peas, rhubarb, blueberries, fruit trees, strawberries, cyclamen, dogwoods, magnolias, rhododendrons, roses, spruce trees, tulip poplars, and yews.

Controls: Clean up garden debris in the fall to remove overwintering sites for the pests. Rotate vegetable crops to prevent overwintering weevils from attacking susceptible plants. Sprinkle diatomaceous earth around plants to form a barrier. Beneficial nematodes can help to control the pests. Weevils are difficult to control with contact sprays unless you catch them at night; pyrethrin or rotenone may be effective.

WHITEFLIES

Characteristics: Whiteflies are small, white flying insects that feed on the undersides of plant foliage. They suck the juices from leaves, stems, and flower buds, and leave behind a honeydew on which black sooty mold grows. They also carry diseases. Whiteflies are one of the worst insect pests in greenhouses.

Symptoms: Whiteflies tend to fly away in a cloud when you

Whiteflies

shake an infested plant. They cause stippling on foliage, which eventually turns yellow and dies. The leaves may be covered with sticky honeydew and black sooty mold. Whiteflies also distort flower buds and weaken plants.

Host plants: Many plants are susceptible, especially tomatoes, flowering tobacco, geraniums, heliotrope, petunias, and verbenas. Certain species feed on citrus plants, grapes, mulberries, strawberries, azaleas, ferns, and irises.

Controls: Use a forceful spray of water to chase whiteflies off foliage temporarily. Green lacewings, ladybugs, and Trichogramma wasps are natural predators; *Encarsia formosa* is recommended as a predator for greenhouse whiteflies. Indoors or out, you can trap these pests with yellow sticky boards. Insecticidal soap works when it hits the flies. (Try not to disturb them before spraying, or they will simply fly away and return later.) Neem, pyrethrin, and ryania sprays can also be effective.

WIREWORMS

Characteristics: Wireworms, the larvae of click beetles, are stiff, hard-shelled, dark brown or yellow worms. They resemble millipedes that have lost all but 3 pairs of legs. They feed on underground plant parts, including roots, stems, tubers, and seeds. These pests are particularly destructive to root crops but are also damaging to other vegetables and flowers. Wireworms are often found in areas that have recently been turned from grass into garden beds.

Symptoms: Plants wilt and may die. When you dig up an infested plant, you may see the worms in the roots or tubers.

Host plants: Wireworms feed on many crops, including beans, beets, carrots, corn, onions, peas, potatoes, radishes, asters, dahlias, gladioli, and phlox.

Controls: Clean up garden debris in the fall, and rotate root crops. Before planting new beds made from lawn areas, skewer pieces of raw potato on the end of sticks and bury them in the soil; after a week or two, lift out and destroy the infested pieces. Beneficial nematodes can be effective against wireworms.

DISEASE PORTRAITS

ALTERNARIA LEAF SPOT

Characteristics: Alternaria leaf spots are caused by fungi that attack many flowers, as well as fruit and vegetable crops. The fungi, which grow on both living and dead tissue, disfigure foliage and fruits. (They can also damage fruit in storage.) The spores are spread by wind and water, and overwinter on plant debris. The disease can spread in a wide range of temperatures—from 40° to 90°F—and prefers moist conditions. Infection is usually worse toward the end of the season as the disease builds up.

Symptoms: Dark brown, circular lesions form on main stems, leaf stems, leaves, and fruits. Leaves may drop prematurely. The spots may have concentric rings or may be long and narrow. Older leaves are normally affected more severely.

Host plants: Many plants are susceptible to Alternaria, including beans, carrots, cabbage-family crops, cucumbers, potatoes, pumpkins, radishes, sweet potatoes, carnations, and zinnias.

Controls: Plant resistant cultivars, and rotate susceptible crops. Space plants properly to allow for good air circulation. Avoid wetting the foliage. If you see damage, remove infected plants and plant parts to prevent the disease from spreading. (Burn, bury, or dispose of infected plants in your trash; do not compost them.)

ANTHRACNOSE

Characteristics: Anthracnose is a fungus that causes sunken lesions to form on stems, leaves, and fruit. It needs warm weather to germinate and is most active when temperatures range from 78° to 86°F. The pathogen overwinters in the soil and on plant debris. It is spread by wind, water, and gardening tools.

Symptoms: Spots with sunken centers appear on leaves, stems, and fruit. Pink spores may be visible in the spots. The foliage may die.

Host plants: Anthracnose infects many plants, including beans, cucumbers and other vine crops, rhubarb, tomatoes, blackberries, raspberries, hollyhocks, lupines, pansies, snapdragons, and sycamore trees.

Controls: Look for resistant cultivars. Rotate the planting sites of susceptible crops. Provide adequate air circulation, and avoid watering the foliage. If anthracnose has been a problem in past years, apply a preventive spray of sulfur- or copper-based fungicide on susceptible plants to keep the spores from germinating. Remove infected plants and plant parts to prevent the disease from spreading. (Burn, bury, or dispose of infected plants in your trash; do not compost them.)

APPLE SCAB

Characteristics: Apple scab is a serious disease that can cause entire apple and pear crops to fail in bad years. This fungal disease attacks leaves, fruit, and stems, causing small, poor-quality fruit and early leaf drop. It is worst in wet, cool weather, when the fungus can spread the fastest.

Symptoms: Yellow or light green spots form on young leaves and flower buds, and eventually turn darker. The leaves may be disfigured or destroyed; they become velvety looking as the spores develop. The spots can spread to form large areas of dead tissue. Fruit and foliage drop prematurely.

Host plants: Apple scab affects both apples and pears.

Controls: Prevent problems by planting resistant cultivars. Remove infected foliage and fruit immediately to help keep the disease from spreading. (Burn, bury, or dispose of infected plants in your trash; do not compost them.) If you choose to spray, check with your local Cooperative Extension Service office for recommendations on suitable materials and when to apply them.

BACTERIAL SPOTS AND BLIGHTS

Characteristics: Spots and blights are caused by a number of different bacteria. They are most prevalent in high humidity and either warm or cool temperatures, depending on the disease. Bacterial spots and blights infect plants through wounded tissue or small holes in plant leaves. The pathogens overwinter in plant debris.

Symptoms: Irregular spots with a water-soaked appearance (and sometimes a foul smell) form on leaves, stems, flowers, and fruit. Foliage, stems, and flowers may be killed quickly.

Host plants: Many plants are susceptible, including beans, peas, peppers, tomatoes, fruits, zonal geraniums, nasturtiums, and tuberous begonias.

Controls: Clean up the garden in autumn. Rotate the planting sites of susceptible crops. Provide adequate air circulation, and avoid watering the foliage or wounding the plants. Keep garden tools clean, and disinfect them after using them on a plant you think might be infected. Bacterial diseases cannot be cured, so remove infected plants and plant parts as soon as possible to prevent the infection from spreading. (Burn, bury, or dispose of infected plants in your trash; do not compost them.)

BACTERIAL WILT

Characteristics: Bacterial wilt diseases clog the water-conducting tissues of infected plants, causing them to wilt and die. The bacteria enter plant tissue through wounds or natural openings in stems. They are spread by flea beetles, cucumber beetles, infected seeds, wind, or water. The bacteria are most active in warm, wet weather, when temperatures are above 75°F. The pathogen overwinters in plant debris and in the soil around infected plants.

Symptoms: Plants wilt even when they are not dry. Streaks may appear on the foliage. Sticky material may ooze from cut stems.

Host plants: Bacterial wilt diseases infect many plants, including beans, corn, cucumbers and other vine crops, tomatoes, astilbes, bleeding hearts, cosmos, dahlias, dianthus, nasturtiums, and sweet alyssum.

Controls: Clean up plant debris in the fall. Rotate the planting sites of susceptible crops, and plant resistant cultivars. Avoid wetting the leaves. Control flea beetles and cucumber beetles, which can carry the disease. Remove infected plants and plant parts to prevent the disease from spreading. (Burn, bury, or dispose of infected plants in your trash; do not compost them.)

BLACK LEG

Characteristics: Black leg is a fungal disease that produces a dry rot. It causes sunken lesions to form on plant stems near the base; the spots may run together and girdle the stem. This disease is spread by infected seeds, rain, and garden tools, and is particularly damaging in warm, wet, or humid weather. The spores overwinter in plant debris in the soil.

Symptoms: Sunken lesions form around the base of the stem. Gray or black spots can appear on stems and leaves, and leaf margins may turn blue or red. Plants can wilt, fall over, and die.

Host plants: Black leg most commonly affects potatoes and cabbage-family plants, including cabbage, broccoli, cauliflower, and kale.

Controls: Purchase seeds

from a reputable seed company. Rotate the planting sites of susceptible crops, and grow resistant cultivars. Avoid wetting the leaves. If the disease was serious in past years, try a preventive copper spray. Remove infected plants and plant parts to prevent the disease from spreading. (Burn, bury, or dispose of infected plants in your trash; do not compost them.)

BLACK SPOT

Characteristics: Black spot is familiar to those who grow roses in the humid environments of midwestern, northeastern, and southeastern states. This fungal disease causes black spots to form on leaves; the spots spread and eventually cause the foliage to drop. The infections are worst in wet, humid weather in spring and fall, but can be a problem all summer in areas with high humidity. Black spot is spread by water and affects the leaves closest to the ground first.

Symptoms: Black spots form on the foliage, which turns yellow and drops. Whole plants can be defoliated by July in severely affected areas.

Host plants: Black spot infects roses.

Controls: Select resistant cultivars. Choose a site with good air circulation, and allow ample space between plants. Avoid wetting the foliage. Remove infected plant parts to keep the disease from spreading. To prevent black spot, some rose growers use a regular spray schedule of fungicidal soaps, sulfur-based fungicides, or chemical fungicides.

BOTRYTIS

Characteristics: Botrytis is a fungal disease that affects fruits, flowers, leaves, and stems. It is also called gray mold, because one of the later symptoms of the disease is a fluffy, gray mold. The fluffy part releases the spores, which are spread by water. Botrytis is most prevalent in wet weather, especially in the cooler temperatures of spring.

Symptoms: Flower petals develop blighted tissue and become soft and watery; eventually, a gray mold develops. The leaves have spots that turn dry and white or brown. Fruits that form from infected flowers develop spots from the blossom end; these spots enlarge and eventually develop a gray mold. Botrytis on peonies causes the plant tissue to rot and emerging foliage to fall over or blacken at the tips. It can also prevent flower buds from opening.

Host plants: A wide range of plants are susceptible, including beets, lettuce, onions, peppers, tomatoes, blackberries, raspberries, strawberries, African violets, azaleas, begonias, dahlias, geraniums, peonies, petunias, snapdragons, and many bulbs.

Controls: Look for resistant cultivars. Rotate the planting sites of susceptible crops. Provide a site with good air circulation, and avoid wetting the foliage. Remove infected plant parts to prevent the disease from spreading.

CLUB ROOT

Characteristics: Club root is a fungal disease that affects plant roots and causes wilting and stunted plant growth. It gets its name from the abnormal swellings it causes on roots. Club root is spread by water and wind, and can survive in the soil for 7 years without a host.

Symptoms: The only above-ground symptom is stunted growth. When you dig up affected plants, you'll see club-shaped swellings on the roots.

Host plants: Club root attacks cabbage, broccoli, kale, and other members of the cabbage family.

Controls: The pathogen that causes club root prefers acid conditions, so try adding lime to the soil to raise the pH. Look for resistant cultivars, and rotate the planting sites of susceptible crops. Remove infected plants and plant parts to prevent the disease from spreading. Avoid planting susceptible crops in that area for at least 7 years.

DAMPING-OFF

Characteristics: Damping-off diseases can attack many types of plants of all ages, but they are most commonly a problem on seedlings. Several fungi can cause this condition. Some damping-off pathogens attack seeds before they sprout, preventing them from germinating; others attack seedlings after they emerge. The pathogen is present in the soil and can be spread by garden tools. It is most troublesome in moist conditions with poor air circulation.

Symptoms: Seeds do not germinate, or seedlings suddenly fall over and die. A brown, crimped area may be visible on the stem at the soil line.

Host plants: Seedlings of all types are susceptible.

Controls: Use sterilized mixes when starting seedlings indoors. Take care not to overwater flats and pots of seedlings. Once the seeds have germinated, remove any covers and allow the soil to dry out a little between waterings. Thin the seedlings as soon as possible to prevent overcrowding, which encourages damping-off.

FIRE BLIGHT

Characteristics: Fire blight is a bacterial disease that attacks the stems of pear and apple trees, causing the limbs to look burned. It is spread by bees, tarnished plant bugs, aphids, and other insects, as well as by rain, dew, tools, and the wind. Infected tissue oozes a sticky substance that drips onto lower limbs, further encouraging the infection to spread. Fire blight can be devastating to some trees, especially fruiting and ornamental pears. The disease is worst in wet spring weather; it sometimes seems to stop magically in June.

Symptoms: Reddish, water-soaked lesions develop on branches, and branch tips wilt and curl. Limbs turn black, as if they have been burned. A sticky substance oozes from the infected branches. Flowers wither and die.

Host plants: Fire blight attacks apples, pears, and ornamental members of the rose family.

Controls: Plant resistant cultivars. The disease prefers succulent growth, so be careful not to overfertilize. Many gardeners prune affected limbs at least 12 inches from the last affected tissue, although some pathologists recommend breaking, not pruning, the limb closer to the infected part. If you do prune, disinfect your pruners before using them on something else. Cut or break limbs during the winter, when the pathogen is dormant. An antibiotic streptomycin spray is now available to home gardeners for controlling the spread of the disease.

FUSARIUM WILT

Characteristics: Fusarium wilt disease is caused by a fungus that clogs the water-conducting tissues of plants, causing them to wilt and die. It thrives in warm, reasonably dry weather and is only active when soil temperatures are between 60° and 90°F. Fusarium is spread by water and cucumber beetles. It can live in the soil for 20 years without a host plant.

Symptoms: Plants may be one-sided, stunted, or wilted. Leaves turn yellow and drop off. The roots rot, and the plants eventually fall over and die. When the stem is sliced lengthwise, a red substance is visible in the tissue.

Host plants: Fusarium attacks many different plants, including asparagus, cabbage, celery, corn, melons, peas, potatoes, radishes, spinach, and tomatoes.

Controls: Clean up garden debris in the fall. Plant resistant vegetable cultivars. (The "F" after the name of a tomato cultivar indicates a resistance to Fusarium.) Rotate planting sites, or grow susceptible crops in containers. Remove and destroy infected plants.

MILDEWS

Characteristics: Mildews are caused by fungi. Powdery mildew creates a powdery look on the top of plant leaves that does not wipe or wash off. Downy mildew causes similar symptoms but appears on the undersides of foliage. Powdery and downy mildews are very host-specific, which means that the powdery mildew you see on your lilacs will not spread to your phlox. This fact can be a relief to gardeners who plant a variety of plants, although similar conditions encourage powdery mildew in all susceptible plants. The diseases are most troublesome in late summer, in high humidity with poor air circulation. They prevent photosynthesis, thus weakening plants; the damage is more serious on some plants than on others. The later in the season the disease occurs, the less damage it tends to cause.

Symptoms: The foliage of infected plants develops a whitish tinge that looks like powder; it appears on the top or bottom of the leaves, depending on the disease. On some plants, such as roses, flower buds can be severely deformed.

Host plants: Mildews can attack many different plants. Those most susceptible to powdery mildew include cucumbers, melons, squash, blueberries, fruit trees, raspberries, strawberries, sage, tarragon, ageratums, asters, bee balm, begonias, black-eyed Susans, China asters, coralbells, cosmos, dahlias, delphiniums, lilacs, phlox, roses, salvias, sunflowers, yarrows, and zinnias. Plants particularly prone to downy mildew include beans, broccoli, lettuce, onions, radishes, spinach, turnips, vine crops such as cucumbers and squash, tarragon, asters, China asters, cornflowers (bachelor's buttons), forget-me-nots, poppies, salvias, and sweet alyssum.

Controls: Clean up garden debris in autumn. Rotate the planting sites of closely related crops. Choose a site with good air circulation, and avoid overcrowding. Plant resistant cultivars. Train vining crops to grow up trellises to keep them off the ground. Remove infected plants and plant parts to prevent the disease from spreading.

MOSAIC VIRUSES

Characteristics: Mosaic viruses do not generally kill plants but may cause stunted or abnormal growth. "Mosaic" refers to the various color pigments that are exhibited in the leaves when the disease causes the plant to stop making chlorophyll. (Chlorophyll is what makes a plant green and enables it to make food for itself.) Tobacco mosaic, which attacks members of the tomato family, is one of the most common forms.

Symptoms: Mottling and unusual colors on plant foliage are common symptoms of mosaic viruses. You may also see stunted or abnormal growth, low vegetable yields, and discolored flowers and fruit.

Host plants: Mosaic viruses can infect many plants, including cucumbers, lettuce, melons, peppers, potatoes, summer squash, tobacco, tomatoes, raspberries, orchids, and petunias.

Controls: Control insect vectors, including leafhoppers and

aphids. Do not smoke in the garden or greenhouse. If you are a smoker, do not handle virus-susceptible plants until you have washed your hands. Plant resistant cultivars. (The "T" after the name of tomato cultivars indicates a resistance to tobacco mosaic virus.) Remove and destroy infected plants.

NEMATODES

Characteristics: Nematodes are microscopic wormlike organisms that live in the soil. Some feed on decomposing plant matter, some feed on plants, and some feed on other nematodes and garden pests. The ones that feed on plants may damage roots, shoots, flowers, or leaves. They cause wilting and stunted growth as they interrupt the ability of plants to take up moisture and nutrients from the soil. These nematodes can severely deform the roots of root crops, such as carrots and potatoes. They tend to be scattered in the soil and may not damage crops that are within several feet of affected plants. If you suspect that nematodes are a problem in your garden, you can send a soil sample to your local Cooperative Extension Service office to have it checked.

Symptoms: Above ground, nematode symptoms include stunted growth and deformed leaves, flowers, and fruit. Root knot nematodes cause knotlike galls to form on roots; aboveground growth may be yellowed or stunted.

Host plants: Many plants are susceptible, including beans, carrots, okra, potatoes, sweet potatoes, tomatoes, and strawberries.

Controls: Rotate planting sites of susceptible crops, and grow resistant cultivars. (The "N" after the name of tomato cultivars indicates a resistance to nematodes.) Apply beneficial nematodes to the soil to prey on the pest species. If you know nematodes are a problem, another option is to plant susceptible crops in containers.

RUSTS

Characteristics: Rust diseases are caused by various fungi. They produce rust-colored spores, usually on the undersides of foliage. (Don't confuse the brown or rust-colored spots scattered on the back of fern foliage with rust; the spots on the fronds are the fruiting bodies of the fern.) Rusts tend to have fairly specific hosts. Some, such as cedar-apple rust, need two hosts to complete their life cycle. Rust spores are commonly spread by the wind.

Symptoms: Rust-colored spores are evident on foliage, flowers, and fruit. Leaves may turn yellow and drop.

Host plants: Many plants are susceptible to rust diseases, including asparagus, beans, apples, blackberries, pears, raspberries, ageratums, asters, black-eyed Susans, cannas, cedar trees, chrysanthemums, coreopsis, cornflowers (bachelor's buttons), cosmos, dianthus, four o'clocks, hollyhocks, irises, lilies, salvias, snapdragons, sweet alyssum, and yarrows.

Controls: Grow resistant cultivars, and rotate the planting sites of susceptible crops. Choose sites with good air circulation. Avoid wetting the leaves. Remove infected plants and plant parts to prevent the disease from spreading.

SMUTS

Characteristics: Smuts are fungal diseases that are spread by wind. Different smuts have specific hosts; corn smut, for instance, will not infect turfgrass. Smuts can cause spots to appear on any plant part. These spots swell and form masses covered with gray membranes, which burst to release millions of black spores. The spores can live in the soil for many years until a susceptible crop is planted in the same spot. Corn smut, the kind you're most likely to encounter, actually looks much worse than it is. You can remove the infected part with little effect on the rest of the plant.

Symptoms: Swollen, gray masses form on leaves, stems, flowers, fruit, or seeds. The masses open to release sooty black spores. Corn smut is sure to attract attention and is easy to diagnose. On turfgrasses, smuts form gray lines that open to release black spores.

Host plants: Smuts mainly attack grasses, including turfgrass and corn. Dahlias and pansies may also be affected by smuts.

Controls: Rotate the planting sites of susceptible crops.

Provide adequate air circulation, and avoid wetting the foliage. Remove infected plants and plant parts as soon as you see them (try to catch them before the spores are released) to prevent the disease from spreading.

VERTICILLIUM WILT

Characteristics: Like Fusarium, Verticillium is a fungus that clogs the water-conducting tissues of plants, causing them to wilt and die. It thrives in cool, humid conditions. Verticillium can be spread by water and by gardeners when they cultivate the soil.

Symptoms: Look for stunted, one-sided, or wilted plants. Leaves turn yellow and drop off. The roots can be rotted, and plants may simply fall over and die. When the stem is sliced lengthwise, a tan substance is visible in the tissue.

Host plants: Verticillium wilt can damage many plants, including eggplants, peppers, potatoes, rhubarb, tomatoes, mint, sage, blackberries, fruit trees, raspberries, and strawberries.

Controls: Plant resistant vegetable cultivars. (The "V" after the name of tomato cultivars indicates a resistance to Verticillium.) Rotate crops to different parts of the garden, or try growing them in containers.

Clean up garden debris in the fall. Remove and destroy infected plants.

YELLOWS

Characteristics: Yellows is caused by mycoplasmas, single-celled organisms spread by insect vectors, including leafhoppers. Like viruses, yellows diseases do not tend to kill plants, but they do stunt plant's growth and prevent normal flower development. They may also cause discolored and distorted growth.

Symptoms: Plants are stunted and may appear stiffer, more branched, and more upright than is characteristic of the plants. The plants and flowers have a yellowish look. Flowers may be deformed or may not develop at all.

Host plants: Many plants are susceptible to yellows, including baby's breath, cannas, China asters, chrysanthemums, coreopsis, cornflowers (bachelor's buttons), delphiniums, marigolds, nasturtiums, pansies, petunias, salvias, strawflowers, and sweet alyssum.

Controls: Clean up garden debris. Control leafhoppers, which spread the disease. Remove infected plants and plant parts to prevent the disease from spreading.

CHAPTER FOURTEEN

New Dahlias.
INTRODUCED IN 1901
PAINTED FROM NATURE
W. Atlee Burpee & Co.
PHILADELPHIA.

GARDENERS' MOST-ASKED QUESTIONS

DESIGNING YOUR GARDEN

Q: **I am overwhelmed by trying to design my garden. Where do I start?**

A: Start by investigating your site so you know what you have to begin with. It's helpful to sketch a map of your yard so you can take notes about existing features or problem sites easily. Mark which areas are sunny, and which are shady. Have your soil tested to find out its fertility and pH. Be sure to note which areas are exposed to winds, and which are more sheltered.

Next, think about how you would like to use the space you have available in your yard. Do you want a vegetable garden, a formally landscaped area, or a landscaped patio area for entertaining? Do you want very fragrant plants around the patio and entryways? Do you need hedges for privacy or to camouflage an eyesore? Do you want a lovely view from your kitchen or living room window? Make a list of the features you really want in your landscape.

Now it's time to start matching what you want with what you can have. If sunny areas are limited but you really want a vegetable garden, put the vegetables in the sunniest spot. If your property tends to slope, save the flattest spots for play or outdoor dining areas. Add hedges or shrub borders where you want to screen off a view or add privacy. Lay out flower beds where they look pleasing to you. Don't forget to plan for views you'll see from inside the house, so you can enjoy the garden even when you're indoors.

Try to fit in as many of your "wants" as you can. If you can't fit in everything, try to combine two features. If you don't have room for both an herb garden and a flower garden, for instance, why not mix herbs and flowers together in one bed? As you plan, ask knowledgeable friends for advice, and check garden design books and magazines for ideas and how-to information. If possible, consult with a professional landscape designer for ideas and help with developing a master plan. Don't expect to do everything in one year—your master plan can be implemented and adjusted over several years as time and money permit.

Q: I can only spend about an hour and a half in my garden every day or every other day. Given my schedule, about how much garden space can I realistically maintain?

A: Many home lots are at least ¼ acre, which includes the home itself, walkways, and driveways. If at least 50 percent of the remaining area is lawn and the rest is ornamental or edible gardens, your schedule should allow you enough time to properly maintain it.

Keep in mind that in the spring, you'll need to spend twice as much time as usual in the garden, to prepare the soil, sow seed, plant, mulch, fertilize, and get the garden cleaned up and in shape.

Q: What can I do to hide eye sores such as my neighbor's dog-house, garbage cans, and compost pile?

A: Erect temporary or permanent fencing and plant it with fast-growing vines, such as grapes (*Vitis* spp.), Virginia creeper (*Parthenocissus quinquefolia*), honeysuckles (*Lonicera* spp.), silver lace vine (*Polygonum aubertii*), or trumpet vine (*Campsis radicans*). Tall-growing ornamental grasses can also provide fast screening. For more long-term solutions, plan your landscape design to include evergreen trees and dense shrubs that can hide the unsightly areas. Select fast-growing conifers such as white pine (*Pinus strobus*), or hedges such as privets (*Ligustrum* spp.) or arborvitae (*Thuja* spp.).

Q: I just bought a new house, and the garden is very overgrown and weedy. What should I do first?

A: Get the soil tested for pH and nutrients. While you are waiting for the results, start removing anything that you know is a weed. If you're not sure if it's a weed or not, look around your property; if that plant is growing in a lot of other areas, it is probably a weed and should be removed. Start a compost pile with the weeds and grass clippings.

As these overgrown beds begin to thin out, keep weeding at least once a week. Add lots of organic matter and compost as you remove plants and prepare the soil. Apply a mulch to bare spaces to keep the weeds from resprouting.

Have an arborist come to prune back any overgrown trees or shrubs that are blocking walkways or hanging over your house. Remove any dead or diseased-looking branches or plants.

After the area is cleaned and opened up, start working on a master garden plan so you can develop the garden bit by bit over the next several years. Take the results of your soil test and begin amending your soil as necessary.

Q: My backyard is long and narrow. How can I design it so it doesn't seem like a bowling alley?

A: Break up the space with garden beds that curve out into the yard at intervals down the length of the yard. Do not build straight pathways or straight plantings down the center of the space; plan curving, meandering pathways instead. Use small to medium-size trees or shrubs to break up the area.

You could construct two or more garden "rooms," by fencing off one area for a patio garden and another for a children's play garden or a vegetable garden. The rooms could be separated by raised beds, hedges, or screening vines over a fence.

Q: My backyard is the size of a postage stamp. What's the best plan or style for a tiny space?

A: Stick to a simple design that repeats a cool color pattern. Cool colors—for example, blue, white, and green—will make a space seem more expansive; hot colors, such as red and bright pink, jump out at you and make a space look smaller.

Pick one special feature—such as a beautiful Japanese maple (*Acer palmatum*) or a small water garden—and design the rest of your landscape around it. You could also take out most of the lawn and install a path to a patio area, with several small trees, shrubs, and flower borders in the rest of the area. If you'd like to grow vegetables but don't have room for a separate garden, mix them into flower gardens or grow them in containers.

Q: How can I design my garden so it's also interesting in the winter?

A: Add a variety of evergreens and berry-producing plants to carry interest through winter. Use evergreens with unusual shapes and colors, like tall columnar cypresses and junipers. Include plants with colorful or showy bark, such as paperbark maple (*Acer griseum*), river birch (*Betula nigra*), red-twig dogwood (*Cornus sericea*), and crape myrtle (*Lagerstroemia indica*). Trees with weeping forms, such as weeping willow (*Salix babylonica*), are especially beautiful in winter.

Also, grow perennials that have interesting winter seed heads, such as 'Autumn Joy' sedum and various *Clematis*

species. The swaying leaves and dramatic seed plumes of ornamental grasses can be wonderful accents in the winter garden, too.

Make sure you site these plants where you can see them from inside, especially from the rooms where you spend the most time during the winter.

UNDERSTANDING YOUR SOIL

Q: How do I know what type of soil I have?

A: Pick up a handful of moist garden soil and squeeze it. If it sticks together like cookie dough, it's probably clay. If it doesn't hold together in a ball and feels gritty, it is probably a sandy soil. If it holds together in a ball but crumbles if tapped lightly, it is a loamy soil.

Color is also a clue to soil texture. Light-colored soils are usually sandy. Some clay soils are light, too, although they are more of a yellow-gray to light brown color. A rich, dark brown color often indicates a loamy soil.

Q: What does "soil pH" mean?

A: The pH of a soil indicates if it is acidic, neutral, or alkaline. The pH scale runs from 1 to 14, with 7 being neutral. Numbers below 7 indicate an acidic soil; those above 7 indicate an alkaline soil. The scale is logarithmic, which means, for example, that a pH value of 6.0 is 10 times more acidic than a value of 7.0.

Q: How do I know what my soil pH is?

A: You must have your soil tested. You can buy a soil-testing kit and do it yourself, or, for a more thorough and accurate reading, you can send soil samples to your state soil-testing laboratory. It is important to take soil samples from different areas in your yard, since the pH can differ somewhat throughout your yard. Follow the directions carefully on the soil-testing kit, or call your local Cooperative Extension Service office for details on how to submit soil samples.

Q: What's the best soil pH value for most garden plants?

A: The ideal pH for most plants is anywhere between 6.0 to 7.0. Most garden plants prefer a slightly acidic soil.

Q: How much ground limestone do I need to add to my soil to raise the pH?

A: It depends on your soil type and on the starting pH of your soil. Sandy soil does not need as much limestone as loam or clay to raise the pH by the same amount. As a general rule, if you want to raise your soil pH by 1 point (from 5.0 to 6.0, for instance), you should add 6 to 8 pounds of ground limestone per 100 square feet for loam or clay soil, and 2 to 4 pounds per 100 square feet for sandy soil.

Q: **When is the best time to apply lime?**

A: You can apply lime to the soil in the fall or early spring. If you add it in the spring, apply it as early as possible before planting crops.

Q: **What can I add to my alkaline soil to lower the pH?**

A: Ground sulfur or aluminum sulfate will lower soil pH the fastest. To lower the pH 1 point (7.0 to 6.0, for example), add 2 pounds of sulfur or 5 pounds of aluminum sulfate per 100 square feet of garden area. The best time to add the materials is in the fall. If you can't add it in autumn, work it into the soil as soon as possible in early spring, well before planting time.

STARTING SEEDS

Q: **When should I start seeds indoors in the spring?**

A: It depends on two factors: the type of plant, and the average frost-free date in your area. Ask other gardeners or your local Cooperative Extension Service office about the average last frost date for your area. Then check the seed package to see how many weeks before that date you should start the seed. Most garden plants can be started indoors 6 to 8 weeks before the frost-free date.

Q: **Can I use leftover flower and vegetable seed from one or two years ago?**

A: Most garden seeds will retain good germination rates for 1 to 2 years if they are stored in a cool, dry location. Keep leftover seed packets in a glass jar with a screw-top lid. Wrap about 4 tablespoons of powdered milk in a paper towel or tissue, and place it in the bottom of the glass jar to absorb extra moisture. Store the jar in the refrigerator until you are ready to plant the seeds.

Q: **Can I use regular garden soil to germinate seed indoors?**

A: No, because garden soil may contain bacteria, fungi, or microorganisms that can attack and kill seedlings. Garden soil in containers also tends to pack down with repeated watering, smothering plant roots. Use a homemade or commercial soilless growing mix specially formulated for germinating seeds.

Q: **How can I make a homemade soilless mixture for germinating seeds?**

A: One reliable formula is Cornell Peat Lite, developed by Cornell University:

   1 bushel of shredded sphagnum peat moss
   1 bushel of horticultural vermiculite
   4 level tablespoons of ammonium nitrate

   2 level tablespoons of powdered 20-percent superphosphate
   10 level tablespoons of finely ground dolomitic limestone

Stir all the ingredients together thoroughly, then moisten them before filling containers with the mixture.

Q: **How deep should I plant seeds?**

A: A general rule of thumb is to cover seed about twice as deep as its diameter. (If a seed is ¼ inch across, for instance, plant it ½ inch deep.) For lettuce, begonias, and other fine seeds, just press them into the soil surface.

Q: **Aren't there some seeds that need light to sprout?**

A: Yes, some seeds need light to germinate and shouldn't be covered with any soil. Among vegetables, these include mustard, lettuce, celery, and garden cress. Flower seeds that need light include ageratum, begonias, browallia, coleus, columbines, foxgloves, impatiens, lobelias, petunias, poppies, primroses, rose moss, Shasta daisies, snapdragons, and strawflowers.

Q: **What temperature is best for germinating most seeds?**

A: It depends on the plant, but most seeds will germinate successfully if you keep the germination medium around 70° to 75°F. Warm-weather crops, such as peppers and eggplants, like warmer soil temperatures of about 80°F.

Q: Why didn't my seeds sprout?

A: A number of factors could be at work. Damping-off fungi are a common culprit. To prevent this problem, rinse seedling trays and pots in a 10-percent bleach solution (1 part bleach to 9 parts water) before filling them with sterile, soilless germinating mix. Avoid overwatering seedlings, and thin them out before they get crowded. Old or improperly stored seeds may germinate poorly; try planting fresh seed. Drying out can be fatal to tender seedlings; make sure you keep the mix evenly moist (but not wet). Other causes of poor germination include covering seeds that need light to sprout, keeping the soil too warm or too cold, or planting the seed too deep.

Q: When should I transplant seedlings to larger containers?

A: Transplant as soon as the seedlings have developed 2 to 4 true leaves. ("True" leaves are those that form after the first 1 or 2 "seed" leaves.) When transplanting, be careful to handle only the leaves to avoid bruising the fragile stems.

Q: How high should I hang fluorescent lights above seed trays?

A: Keep the lights about 3 to 4 inches above seed trays for the first 3 to 4 weeks after germination. After that, move the lights up to keep them 3 to 4 inches above the tops of the seedlings.

PREPARING THE SOIL

Q: When can I start working the soil in the spring?

A: Test the soil's readiness by squeezing a handful of soil into a ball. If it breaks apart when you tap it lightly, it's ready to work. Do not dig if the soil ball is sticky and wet, or so dry that it won't form a ball. If the soil is dry, moisten it so water penetrates to at least 4 inches deep; let excess water drain before cultivating.

Q: Should I turn my vegetable garden under in the fall or in the spring?

A: Turn it under in the fall so organic matter can break down over the winter and release nutrients into the soil for the next growing season. After digging or tilling, cover the area with mulch or a cover crop, such as winter rye. Dig or till in the mulch or cover crop in early spring.

Q: How deep must I cultivate the soil?

A: The deeper the better, but a depth of about 12 inches is good for most flowers and vegetables. Most rotary tillers only cultivate 4 to 8 inches deep, so you'll need to loosen the soil below the top layer with a garden spade or fork.

Q: Why does my soil form large clumps after I've cultivated it? How do I get rid of them?

A: You probably have a heavy clay soil without enough organic matter to loosen it up. Or you may have worked the soil when it was too wet. Use a rotary tiller to go over the clumps, or use a pitchfork to break them up. Add more compost to the soil, and add a layer of organic mulch to the area after it has been planted.

Q: How can I improve the drainage in my flower and vegetable garden?

A: You can do a number of things, including digging beds deeply, adding lots of organic matter to the soil each year, building raised beds, and installing drainage pipes. If the problem is severe, you may need to install a more extensive underground drainage system or have the area regraded.

PLANTING YOUR GARDEN

Q: How far should I space plants from each other?

A: It depends on the plants. Most seed packages will tell you exactly how far apart they should be planted and thinned. Keep in mind that plants generally like to have enough space around them so they are not competing with other plants and weeds for light, water, and nutrients. Give each plant enough space around it so its leaves are only slightly overlapping those of neighboring plants.

Q: When is the best time of year to plant perennials?

A: Early spring or fall is the ideal time to plant most perennials. When planting in the fall, water the bed thoroughly before the ground freezes, and mulch the soil after it freezes, to prevent rapid thawing and refreezing during warm spells.

MULCHING

Q: When should I begin to clear away winter mulch from my plants in spring?

A: Start clearing it away when you see new shoots coming up from the soil. If there is going to be a late frost, cover the shoots until the danger of frost has passed.

Q: How much mulch should I put around my plants?

A: It depends on the material. Most organic mulches—including wood chips, shredded pine bark, and leaf mold—can be applied 3 to 4 inches thick. Loose mulches such as straw can be as deep as 6 inches. Be sure you don't pile mulch directly against plant stems.

FERTILIZING

Q: What is the difference between a balanced fertilizer and a complete fertilizer?

A: A complete fertilizer is any fertilizer that contains nitrogen, phosphorus, and potassium. If the amounts of those nutrients are roughly equal (as in 10-10-10 or 10-5-5), the material is said to be balanced. If there is much more of one or two of the nutrients (as in 10-45-15), the material is complete but not balanced. A material lacking one or more nutrients (as in 0-10-0) is neither complete nor balanced.

Q: What is the best overall fertilizer for most garden plants?

A: A 10-10-10 or a 5-10-5 is recommended for most ornamental and vegetable plants.

Q: What is the difference between a chemical fertilizer and an organic fertilizer? Which is better to use?

A: Organic fertilizers are materials derived from plants, animals, or minerals that contain essential elements for plant growth. These include substances such as blood meal, manure, or compost.

Organic fertilizers may be physically processed in some way, but they are not chemically altered or combined with synthetic materials. Chemical fertilizers are manufactured from mineral or synthetic substances, or both.

Plants don't care where they get their nutrients from as long as they get them when they need them. Organic fertilizers release nutrients as they break down over a period of weeks or months. Chemical fertilizers release their nutrients much more quickly. You may find chemical fertilizers useful to tide plants over while you build up the soil's natural fertility with organic matter. If your soil is naturally fertile and you are regularly adding lots of compost and other organic matter each year, you probably don't need much, if any, extra chemical fertilizer.

Q: If I use a chemical fertilizer, do I still have to add compost to my garden?

A: Yes, you should always be building up the natural fertility and structure of your soil by regularly adding organic materials, such as compost, aged manure, and chopped leaves.

Q: Can I add lime when I add chemical fertilizer?

A: No, never mix the two together. Wait a few months before adding the other material.

Q: When should I add fertilizer to my flower and vegetable gardens?

A: Incorporate organic fertilizer into the soil when you prepare the bed for planting, or spread it over the area in late fall. If you are using chemical fertilizer, add a slow-release material around the base of transplanted vegetable seedlings, and sprinkle a slow-release fertilizer in flower beds in the spring when plants begin to start growing. You can also add a scattering of fertilizer to vegetables and flowers in mid-season if they look like they could use additional nutrients.

MAKING COMPOST

Q: What materials are best for a compost pile?

A: The best and most readily available materials to use are grass clippings (except from herbicide-treated lawns), pulled weeds (without seeds), farm animal manures, leaves (preferably shredded), kitchen scraps (fruits, vegetables, coffee grounds, and eggshells), wood ashes, and garden trimmings (such as dead flowers and annuals that have finished blooming).

Q: What shouldn't I add to my compost pile?

A: Do not add diseased or insect-infested plants, meat or dairy scraps, citrus fruit rinds (they decompose too slowly), colored newspaper or magazines, grass or weeds treated with resid-

ual herbicides, weeds that have gone to seed, or manure from dogs, cats, or humans.

Q: It's been several months since I started a compost pile, but it isn't breaking down at all. What can I do to speed it up?

A: There could be different reasons why it isn't breaking down. You may have too much high-carbon material, such as leaves, hay, straw, and dried plant stalks. Add more high-nitrogen substances (for example, grass clippings, hoof and horn meal, blood meal, and vegetable scraps), and mix them into the pile.

Also, make sure the pile is getting enough air. Poke holes in it, or better yet, turn it over a few times with a pitchfork. If the pile is waterlogged, add more dry organic materials and cover it with a plastic tarp; allow it to dry out a bit, then turn it over. If the pile feels dry, add water to keep it evenly damp. Small piles may not have enough material to break down properly; make your pile at least 3 feet on each side.

Q: How fast can I expect to have usable compost?

A: If you have followed all of the above tips, you should have usable compost in about 2 to 4 months. If you are just allowing the pile to break down on its own, it will take about a year. For really fast compost, try using a 50/50 mix of high-carbon and high-nitrogen materials.

Q: Sometimes my compost pile smells bad. What can I do?

A: Give the pile more air, and add a thin layer of soil and lime. If the pile is wet, mix in some dry material, and cover it with a tarp to keep out rainwater. Try mixing in some chemical or organic nitrogen fertilizer. Make sure you are not adding any meat scraps, dairy products, or fish scraps.

Q: Can I add woody twigs and branches to my compost pile?

A: A general rule of thumb is not to add woody twigs bigger than the diameter of a pencil to the compost pile. Larger woody twigs and branches should be run through a chipper/shredder machine before you add them to the pile.

Q: Can I add rotted or moldy fruit and vegetables to the compost pile?

A: Yes, as long as they are not diseased or infested with insects.

WATERING

Q: How often should I water my garden?

A: Most gardens need a total of about 1 inch of water per week during the growing season. This water can come from rainfall or irrigation, or a combination of the two. As a rule, a sprinkler or other irrigation system left on for about 1 hour should provide enough water for 1 week (or less during extremely hot, dry periods). Bury a can or cup to soil level and turn on your irrigation system for 1 hour; measure the amount of water in the can, and adjust the time as necessary to deliver 1 inch of water. Remember, it is always better to give plants one long soak than frequent, superficial waterings.

Q: When is the best time to water plants?

A: Early morning is the best time to water, because there is less loss of moisture to evaporation at that time of the day. Plus, leaves will dry more quickly, so the chance of fungal problems is reduced. If you can't water in the morning, the next best time is early evening. If your schedule permits only evening watering, try to use a drip irrigation system so plant leaves won't get wet.

Q: How can I use less water in the garden?

A: Mulch around all of your plants, including trees and shrubs. Instead of sprinklers, use drip irrigation systems, which lose very little water to evaporation. Check and repair any leaks in irrigation systems and hoses. Grow drought-tolerant plants, and group plants in the garden according to their water needs. Use rain barrels to collect rainwater from downspouts for later use in the garden.

GROOMING AND STAKING

Q: What is meant by "pinching back"?

A: "Pinching back" means using your fingers to remove the tips of growing shoots to encourage branching. On some plants, you may also pinch off some of the flower buds to get fewer but larger flowers; this technique is commonly used for dahlias.

Q: When is the best time to stake tall plants?

A: Always stake plants when they are young, so they will grow upright and look natural. Once unstaked plants reach full size, they may already be sprawling; it's tough to tie them up and have them still look attractive.

PROPAGATING PLANTS

Q: When is the best time to take stem cuttings from herbaceous plants?

A: Usually, the best time is spring or early summer, when the plants are actively growing. Take 3- to 4-inch stem pieces, remove the leaves from the bottom half, and stick the leafless stems in a moist rooting medium, such as vermiculite or perlite. Keep the cuttings moist, and set them in a bright place out of direct sunlight. Soil temperatures of about 75°F are ideal.

Q: Do I really need to apply a rooting hormone to my cuttings?

A: Given the proper conditions, most herbaceous stem cuttings will root fairly readily. Rooting hormones simply promote faster rooting and a more profuse root system.

Hardwood cuttings do benefit from a rooting powder. Apply it to the base of the cutting before sticking it into the rooting medium.

Q: When should I divide my perennials?

A: In general, it's best to divide early-blooming perennials in the fall and summer- and fall-blooming perennials in early spring. Divide bearded irises in summer, after they bloom.

CONTROLLING PESTS AND DISEASES

Q: What are the best ways to keep my garden free of disease and insect problems?

A: The best defense against attacks from pests and diseases is to give plants good care; strong plants are better able to fight off problems than weak plants. Start by building up your soil so it is well drained and naturally rich in organic matter. Add lots of compost each year when you prepare planting beds. Give your plants the nutrients and water they need so they aren't stressed. Use mulch to keep moisture in the soil and reduce water stress. Plant disease-resistant cultivars whenever possible. Keep the garden free of old plant debris. Do not add diseased or infested plants to the compost pile. Rotate the planting sites of your crops so you don't grow related crops in the same place each year. Water in early morning, or use a drip irrigation system to keep plant leaves dry. Make sure the plants have good air circulation around them, especially if the climate is humid.

Q: **What's the best way to control Japanese beetles?**

A: Handpick them off foliage and drop them into a container of soapy water. Plant trap crops such as borage, white roses, African marigolds, and white or light-colored zinnias; the beetles will tend to congregate on these plants, so they'll be easier to collect. Apply milky disease spores to your lawn to kill the beetle grubs. Don't place Japanese beetle traps in your garden; they will only attract more beetles to the area. If you want to use traps, place them as far from the garden as you can.

Q: **Are there some simple, non-toxic pest sprays I can make at home?**

A: To make a spray that is effective against many kinds of immature insects, mix 1 cup of cooking oil with 1 tablespoon of liquid dish soap. Add 2½ teaspoons of this mixture to 1 cup of water, and spray it on the surface and undersides of leaves. Repeat

the application a few days later if insects are still a problem.

If you have a problem with aphids, mites, or whiteflies, try this soap solution: Mix 2 teaspoons of liquid dish soap (do not use detergent soap) with 1 gallon of warm water. Spray the soap-and-water mixture onto the surface and undersides of leaves. Repeat the treatment every 2 or 3 days for about 2 weeks.

Q: **How can I protect my garden from deer?**

A: For an effective, long-term solution, your only option is to install 8- to 10-foot-tall fencing or an electric fence. Home remedies include hanging bars of deodorant soap around the garden; scattering dried blood meal around plants; spraying a solution of Tabasco sauce on the foliage (3 tablespoons per gallon of water); and constructing chicken wire cages around important plantings. However, these solutions are not very convenient, and they're not particularly dependable, either.

There are some commercial products on the market that are supposed to repel deer, but they must be reapplied after a rain. While hungry deer will eat just about anything, you may be able to discourage them by planting strong-flavored herbs, spiny plants, and low-growing groundcovers.

WEEDING

Q: **How can I keep weeding to a minimum?**

A: If you take the time to weed carefully in the spring, you'll greatly reduce summer weed problems. In early spring, pull up or hoe weeds as they emerge. Before planting, water the area or wait until after a rain, then give weeds a week or two to sprout. Weed thoroughly, then plant and apply a 3- to 4-inch layer of mulch as soon as possible to the garden. Plan to weed your garden a day or two after a rain or after irrigating it; weeds come out much easier when the soil surface is moist. Use a weed-digging tool to remove taproots from dandelions; if you just pull up the foliage without getting the entire root, the plant will quickly grow back.

Q: **How can I get rid of poison ivy in my garden?**

A: Very carefully! First, apply a systemic herbicide to the plants. Wait until the plants begin to wither, then remove them by hand; be sure to wear long-sleeved clothing, long pants, waterproof boots, and rubber gloves. If you see more new growth coming up, apply more herbicide and repeat the process until the poison ivy is eradicated. Do not burn poison ivy or add it to your compost pile; bury it or dispose of it with the household trash.

PROTECTING PLANTS OVER WINTER

Q: **In the spring, I notice that some of my plants are uprooted** and have died. What can I do to prevent this from happening next year?

A: When the soil freezes and thaws repeatedly, plants can be pushed out of the ground—a process called frost heaving. Give the plants a thick cover of mulch in the fall, after the ground freezes solid, and remove it in the spring. The mulch will help to keep the temperature more constant and to prevent rapid freeze-thaw cycles.

Q: How can I protect my plants from cold damage?

A: Water your plants thoroughly and give them a thick covering of mulch in late fall. Wrap burlap around tender plants so they don't dry out from winter winds. There are also commercial sprays available—called anti-dessicants—that you can apply to evergreen foliage to protect the plants from drying winds. Don't brush snow off your plants; snow acts as an insulator to protect them.

Q: How can I keep voles and rabbits from damaging my woody plants over the winter?

A: In late fall, wrap tree trunks with a thick plastic wrap or hardware-cloth cage to prevent animal pest damage. Also, avoid spreading mulch right up to the base of your plants, as voles and other pests like to nest in it.

PLANTS FOR EVERY PURPOSE

THE LISTS THAT FOLLOW WILL HELP YOU GET THE MOST OUT OF YOUR GARDEN. Use them to help you find the perfect plant for a problem site, fill your yard with flowers for cutting, or welcome butterflies and bees.

PLANTS FOR HOT, DRY, AND SUNNY SITES

Have a hot, dry site where nothing seems to thrive? Tired of mowing that sunny slope all summer? Try creating a garden with any of the tough, drought-tolerant plants listed below for an attractive solution to these problem areas.

ANNUALS

Amaranthus tricolor (summer poinsettia)
Catharanthus roseus (vinca)
Centaurea cyanus (bachelor's button)

Chrysanthemum ptarmiciflorum (dusty miller)
Cosmos spp. (cosmos)
Dyssodia tenuiloba (Dahlberg daisy)
Eschscholzia californica (California poppy)
Gaillardia pulchella (annual blanket flower)
Gazania ringens (gazania)
Gomphrena globosa (globe amaranth)
Helianthus annuus (sunflower)
Helichrysum bracteatum (strawflower)
Limonium sinuatum (annual statice)
Melampodium cinereum (melampodium)
Mirabilis jalapa (four o'clock)
Oxypetalum caeruleum (oxypetalum)
Portulaca grandiflora (rose moss)
Sanvitalia procumbens (sanvitalia)
Tagetes spp. (marigolds)
Tithonia rotundifolia (Mexican sunflower)
Zinnia elegans (common zinnia)

PERENNIALS

Achillea spp. (yarrows)
Artemisia spp. (artemisias)
Asclepias tuberosa (butterfly weed)
Centaurea montana (mountain bluet)
Coreopsis spp. (coreopsis)
Echinacea purpurea (purple coneflower)
Echinops ritro (globe thistle)
Gaillardia X *grandiflora* (blanket flower)
Helianthus spp. (perennial sunflowers)
Hemerocallis hybrids (daylilies)
Iberis sempervirens (perennial candytuft)
Liatris spp. (gayfeathers)
Oenothera spp. (evening primroses)
Perovskia atriplicifolia (Russian sage)
Phlox subulata (moss pinks)
Rudbeckia spp. (orange coneflowers)
Sedum X 'Autumn Joy' ('Autumn Joy' sedum)
Solidago spp. (goldenrods)

Stachys byzantina (lamb's ears)

BULBS

Sparaxis tricolor (harlequin flower)
Tigridia pavonia (tiger flower)

HERBS

Calamints (*Calamintha* spp.)
Feverfew (*Chrysanthemum parthenium*)
Hyssop (*Hyssopus officinalis*)
Lavender (*Lavandula* spp.)
Lavender cotton (*Santolina* spp.)
Oregano (*Origanum* spp.)
Sage (*Salvia* spp.)
Savory (*Satureja* spp.)
Southernwood (*Artemisia abrotanum*)
Thyme, common (*Thymus vulgaris*)
Thyme, creeping (*Thymus praecox* subsp. *arcticus*)

GROUNDCOVERS

Arctostaphylos uva-ursi (bearberry)
Artemisia stellerana (beach wormwood)
Juniperus horizontalis (creeping juniper)
Sempervivum spp. (hens and chicks)

PERENNIALS FOR MOIST TO WET SITES

Soggy spots can be a real challenge in the garden. In wet soil, plant roots can't get the air they need to thrive, so the aboveground parts grow poorly and are prone to diseases. If you have a moist to wet spot in your yard, try creating a bed or border with a mix of these moisture-tolerant perennials.

Aruncus spp. (goatsbeards)
Astilbe spp. (astilbes)
Brunnera macrophylla (brunnera)
Cimicifuga spp. (bugbanes)
Filipendula spp. (meadowsweets)

Iris ensata (Japanese iris)
Iris pseudacorus (yellow flag iris)
Ligularia spp. (ligularias)
Lobelia spp. (perennial lobelias)
Lysimachia clethroides (gooseneck loosestrife)
Physostegia virginiana (obedient plant)
Tradescantia virginiana (Virginia spiderwort)

PLANTS FOR SHADY SITES

While few plants tolerate deep, dark shade, many can grow well in a spot with just a few hours of sun. A site that gets bright light but no direct sun can also provide good growing conditions for a wide variety of attractive annuals, perennials, bulbs, and herbs.

ANNUALS AND BIENNIALS

Ageratum houstonianum (ageratum)
Begonia semperflorens (wax begonia)
Browallia speciosa (browallia)
Catharanthus roseus (vinca)
Cleome hasslerana (spider flower)
Coleus blumei (coleus)
Digitalis purpurea (foxglove)
Impatiens spp. (impatiens)
Lobularia maritima (sweet alyssum)
Lunaria annua (honesty)
Myosotis sylvatica (forget-me-not)
Nicotiana spp. (flowering tobaccos)
Torenia fournieri (torenia)
Viola X *wittrockiana* (pansy)

PERENNIALS

Alchemilla mollis (lady's-mantle)
Anemone X *hybrida* (Japanese anemone)
Aquilegia spp. (columbines)
Aruncus spp. (goatsbeards)
Astilbe spp. (astilbes)
Baptisia australis (false indigo)

Begonia grandis (hardy begonia)
Bergenia cordifolia (heartleaf bergenia)
Brunnera macrophylla (brunnera)
Campanula spp. (bellflowers)
Cimicifuga spp. (bugbanes)
Dicentra spp. (bleeding hearts)
Epimedium spp. (epimediums)
Filipendula spp. (meadowsweets)
Helleborus spp. (hellebores)
Hemerocallis hybrids (daylilies)
Heuchera spp. (heucheras)
Hosta hybrids (hostas)
Iris ensata (Japanese iris)
Liriope muscari (lilyturf)
Lobelia spp. (perennial lobelias)
Lysimachia clethroides (gooseneck loosestrife)
Macleaya cordata (plume poppy)
Mertensia virginica (Virginia bluebell)
Phlox divaricata (wild sweet William)
Phlox stolonifera (creeping phlox)
Primula X *polyantha* (primrose)
Pulmonaria saccharata (pulmonaria)
Symphytum grandiflorum (yellow comfrey)
Thalictrum aquilegifolium (columbine meadow rue)
Tradescantia virginiana (Virginia spiderwort)

BULBS

Allium moly (lily leek)
Anemone spp. (anemones)
Arisaema spp. (arisaemas)
Arum italicum (arum lily)
Camassia spp. (camassias)
Chionodoxa spp. (glory-of-the-snow)
Colchicum spp. (colchicums)
Convallaria majalis (lily-of-the-valley)
Crocus spp. and hybrids (crocus)
Cyclamen hederifolium (hardy cyclamen)
Galanthus spp. (snowdrops)

Ipheion uniflorum (spring starflower)
Leucojum spp. (snowflakes)
Lilium spp. (lilies)
Lycoris spp. (resurrection lilies)
Muscari spp. (grape hyacinths)
Narcissus hybrids (daffodils)
Ornithogalum spp. (star-of-Bethlehem)
Scilla spp. (squills)
Zantedeschia spp. (calla lilies)

HERBS

Angelica (*Angelica archangelica*)
Chervil (*Anthriscus cerefolium*)
Lemon balm (*Melissa officinalis*)
Lovage (*Levisticum officinale*)
Parsley (*Petroselinum crispum*)
Peppermint (*Mentha* X *piperita*)
Salad burnet (*Sanguisorba minor*)
Sorrel (*Rumex acetosa*)
Spearmint (*Mentha spicata*)
Sweet cicely (*Myrrhis odorata*)
Sweet woodruff (*Galium odoratum*)

GROUNDCOVERS

Ajuga spp. (ajugas)
Alchemilla mollis (lady's-mantle)
Asarum spp. (wild gingers)
Bergenia spp. (bergenias)
Ceratostigma plumbaginoides (leadwort)
Chrysogonum virginianum (golden star)
Convallaria majalis (lily-of-the-valley)
Epimedium spp. (epimediums)
Galax urceolata (wand flower)
Galium odoratum (sweet woodruff)
Gaultheria procumbens (wintergreen)
Geranium macrorrhizum (bigroot geranium)
Hedera helix (English ivy)
Hosta spp. (hostas)
Lamium maculatum (dead nettle)
Liriope spp. (lilyturfs)

Lysimachia nummularia (creeping Jenny)
Pachysandra spp. (pachysandra)
Pulmonaria saccharata (Bethlehem sage)
Sarcococca hookerana var. *humilis* (sweet box)
Vinca spp. (periwinkles)

PLANTS FOR CUT FLOWERS

Few things seem more indulgent than surrounding yourself with beautiful bouquets of cut flowers. Whether you set aside a separate cutting garden or just snip blooms from your beds and borders, you can always have a supply of great cut flowers—just try any or all of the flowers suggested below.

ANNUALS

Ageratum houstonianum (ageratum)
Amaranthus spp. (love-lies-bleeding)
Antirrhinum majus (snapdragon)
Calendula officinalis (pot marigold)
Callistephus chinensis (China aster)
Celosia spp. (celosias)
Centaurea cyanus (bachelor's button)
Clarkia amoena (godetia)
Cleome hasslerana (spider flower)
Consolida ambigua (rocket larkspur)
Cosmos sulphureus (cosmos)
Dianthus spp. (pinks)
Digitalis purpurea (foxglove)
Eustoma grandiflorum (lisianthus)
Gaillardia pulchella (annual blanket flower)
Gomphrena globosa (globe amaranth)
Gypsophila elegans (annual baby's breath)
Helianthus annuus (sunflower)

Helichrysum bracteatum (strawflower)
Lathyrus odoratus (sweet pea)
Lavatera trimestris (mallow)
Limonium sinuatum (annual statice)
Lunaria annua (honesty)
Matthiola incana (stock)
Melampodium cinereum (melampodium)
Moluccella laevis (bells-of-Ireland)
Myosotis sylvatica (forget-me-not)
Nigella damascena (love-in-a-mist)
Oxypetalum caeruleum (oxypetalum)
Papaver spp. (poppies)
Phlox drummondii (annual phlox)
Salpiglossis sinuata (salpiglossis)
Salvia spp. (salvias)
Scabiosa atropurpureum (pincushion flower)
Schizanthus pinnatus (schizanthus)
Tagetes spp. (marigolds)
Tithonia rotundifolia (Mexican sunflower)
Trachymene caerulea (blue lace flower)
Tropaeolum majus (nasturtium)
Xeranthemum annuum (immortelle)
Zinnia elegans (zinnia)

PERENNIALS

Achillea spp. (yarrows)
Alchemilla mollis (lady's-mantle)
Amsonia tabernaemontana (blue starflower)
Anchusa azurea (Italian alkanet)
Anemone X *hybrida* (Japanese anemone)
Aquilegia spp. (columbines)
Artemisia spp. (artemisias)
Aruncus spp. (goatsbeards)
Asclepias tuberosa (butterfly weed)
Aster spp. (asters)
Astilbe spp. (astilbes)
Baptisia australis (false indigo)
Boltonia asteroides (boltonia)

Brunnera macrophylla (brunnera)
Campanula spp. (bellflowers)
Centaurea montana (mountain bluet)
Chrysanthemum spp. (chrysanthemums)
Cimicifuga spp. (bugbanes)
Coreopsis spp. (coreopsis)
Delphinium elatum hybrids (delphiniums)
Dianthus spp. (pinks)
Dicentra spp. (bleeding hearts)
Doronicum caucasicum (leopard's-bane)
Echinacea purpurea (purple coneflower)
Echinops ritro (globe thistle)
Filipendula spp. (meadowsweets)
Gaillardia X *grandiflora* (perennial blanket flower)
Geum quellyon (geum)
Gypsophila paniculata (perennial baby's breath)
Helenium autumnale (sneezeweed)
Helianthus spp. (perennial sunflowers)
Hemerocallis hybrids (daylilies)
Heuchera spp. (coral bells)
Hosta hybrids (hostas)
Iris spp. (irises)
Kniphofia hybrids (red-hot poker)
Liatris spp. (gayfeathers)
Ligularia spp. (ligularias)
Liriope muscari (lilyturf)
Lobelia spp. (perennial lobelias)
Lupinus Russell Hybrids (lupine)
Lychnis spp. (campions)
Lysimachia clethroides (gooseneck loosestrife)
Mertensia virginica (Virginia bluebells)
Monarda didyma (bee balm)
Paeonia lactiflora (peony)
Papaver orientale (oriental poppy)
Perovskia atriplicifolia (Russian sage)
Phlox spp. (phlox)
Physostegia virginiana (obedient plant)
Platycodon grandiflorus (balloon flower)

Rudbeckia spp. (orange coneflowers)
Salvia spp. (salvias)
Sedum X 'Autumn Joy' ('Autumn Joy' sedum)
Solidago spp. (goldenrods)
Thalictrum aquilegifolium (columbine meadow rue)
Veronica spp. (veronicas)

BULBS

Acidanthera bicolor (Abyssinian gladiolus)
Allium spp. (ornamental onions)
Anemone coronaria (Mediterranean windflower)
Arum italicum (arum lily)
Convallaria majalis (lily-of-the-valley)
Crocosmia hybrids (crocosmias)
Dahlia hybrids (dahlias)
Gladiolus hybrids (glads)
Iris spp. (irises)
Lilium spp. (lilies)
Lycoris spp. (resurrection lilies)
Narcissus hybrids (daffodils)
Ornithogalum spp. (star-of-Bethlehem)
Polianthes tuberosa (tuberose)
Sparaxis tricolor (harlequin flower)
Tulipa spp. and hybrids (tulips)
Zantedeschia spp. (calla lilies)

HERBS

Anise hyssop (*Agastache foeniculum*)
Dill (*Anethum graveolens*)
Fennel (*Foeniculum vulgare*)
Feverfew (*Chrysanthemum parthenium*)
Lavender (*Lavandula* spp.)

PLANTS FOR DRIED FLOWERS

The first fall frost doesn't have to signal the end of your flowers! During the summer, collect and dry a variety of flowers and seedpods to enjoy indoors in fall, for arrangements, wreaths, potpourris, and other crafts. Here's a list of some of the best plants for drying.

Ageratum houstonianum (ageratum)
Amaranthus spp. (love-lies-bleeding)
Celosia spp. (celosias)
Centaurea cyanus (bachelor's button)
Consolida ambigua (rocket larkspur)
Gomphrena globosa (globe amaranth)
Gypsophila elegans (annual baby's-breath)
Helichrysum bracteatum (strawflower)
Limonium sinuatum (annual statice)
Lunaria annua (honesty)
Moluccella laevis (bells-of-Ireland)
Nigella damascena (love-in-a-mist)
Oxypetalum caeruleum (oxypetalum)
Salvia farinacea (mealy-cup sage)
Scabiosa stellata (starflower)
Xeranthemum annuum (immortelle)

PERENNIALS

Achillea spp. (yarrow)
Artemisia ludoviciana 'Silver King' ('Silver King' artemisia)
Aruncus spp. (goatsbeards)
Asclepias tuberosa (butterfly weed)
Astilbe spp. (astilbes)
Baptisia australis (false indigo)
Dictamnus albus (gas plant)
Echinacea purpurea (purple coneflower)
Echinops ritro (globe thistle)
Filipendula spp. (meadowsweets)
Gypsophila paniculata (perennial baby's-breath)
Papaver orientale (oriental poppy)
Salvia spp. (salvias)
Sedum X 'Autumn Joy' ('Autumn Joy' sedum)

Solidago spp. (goldenrods)

HERBS

Anise hyssop (*Agastache foeniculum*)

Chives, garlic (*Allium tuberosum*)

Feverfew (*Chrysanthemum parthenium*)

Lavender (*Lavandula* spp.)

Lavender cotton (*Lavandula* spp.)

Southernwood (*Artemisia abrotanum*)

PLANTS FOR FRAGRANCE

Fragrance is a fairly personal thing: What smells heavenly to one person may be unpleasant to another. The plants listed below, however, are proven favorites for pleasing scents. Not all cultivars of these plants are fragrant, so try to sniff before you buy. On some plants, it's the flower that's scented; on others, it's the leaves. The list tells you what to check on each plant.

ANNUALS

Antirrhinum majus (snapdragon): flowers

Brachycome iberidifolia (Swan River daisy): flowers

Dianthus spp. (pinks): flowers

Heliotropium arborescens (heliotrope): flowers

Lathyrus odoratus (sweet pea): flowers

Lobularia maritima (sweet alyssum): flowers

Matthiola incana (stock): flowers

Mirabilis jalapa (four o'clock): flowers

Nicotiana alata (flowering tobacco): flowers

Petunia X *hybrida* (petunias): flowers

Phlox drummondii (annual phlox): flowers

Tagetes spp. (marigolds): flowers and foliage

Trachymene caerulea (blue lace flower): flowers

Tropaeolum majus (nasturtium): flowers

PERENNIALS

Achillea spp. (yarrow): foliage

Artemisia spp. (artemisia): foliage

Chrysanthemum X *morifolium* (garden mums): flowers and foliage

Dianthus spp. (pinks): flowers

Hemerocallis hybrids (daylilies): flowers

Hosta plantaginea (plantain lily): flowers

Monarda didyma (bee balm): foliage

Paeonia lactiflora (peony): flowers

Perovskia atriplicifolia (Russian sage): foliage

Phlox spp. (phlox): flowers

Primula X *polyantha* (primrose): flowers

Solidago spp. (goldenrods)

BULBS

Acidanthera bicolor (Abyssinian gladiolus): flowers

Convallaria majalis (lily-of-the-valley): flowers

Cyclamen hederifolium (hardy cyclamen): flowers

Hyacinthus orientalis (hyacinth): flowers

Lilium spp. (lilies): flowers

Muscari spp. (grape hyacinths): flowers

Polianthes tuberosa (tuberose): flowers

HERBS

Anise hyssop (*Agastache foeniculum*): flowers and foliage

Basil (*Ocimum basilicum*): foliage

Calamints (*Calamintha* spp.): foliage

Caraway (*Carum carvi*): foliage

Catnips (*Nepeta* spp.): foliage

Chamomile (*Chamaemelum nobile*): flowers and foliage

Dill (*Anethum graveolens*): foliage

Fennel (*Foeniculum vulgare*): foliage

Feverfew (*Chrysanthemum parthenium*): foliage

Lavender (*Lavandula* spp.): foliage and flowers

Lavender cotton (*Santolina* spp.): foliage

Lemon balm (*Melissa officinalis*): foliage

Lemon grass (*Cymbopogon citratum*): foliage

Lemon verbena (*Aloysia triphylla*): foliage

Marjoram, sweet (*Origanum majorana*): foliage

Oregano (*Origanum* spp.): foliage

Peppermint (*Mentha* X *piperita*): foliage

Sages (*Salvia* spp.): foliage

Savory (*Satureja* spp.): foliage

Scented geraniums (*Pelargonium* spp.): foliage

Southernwood (*Artemisia abrotanum*): foliage

Spearmint (*Mentha spicata*): foliage

Sweet bay (*Laurus nobilis*): foliage

Sweet cicely (*Myrrhis odorata*): flowers and foliage

PLANTS THAT ATTRACT BEES AND BUTTERFLIES

Make your yard a haven for butterflies, bees, and other beautiful and beneficial insects. Below are some plants that are favorite food or shelter sources for these fascinating creatures.

ANNUALS

Ageratum houstonianum (ageratum)

Calendula officinalis (pot marigold)

Centaurea cyanus (bachelor's button)
Cosmos spp. (cosmos)
Gaillardia pulchella (annual blanket flower)
Helianthus annuus (sunflower)
Heliotropium arborescens (heliotrope)
Lobularia maritima (sweet alyssum)
Matthiola incana (stock)
Tropaeolum majus (nasturtium)
Verbena spp. (verbenas)
Zinnia spp. (zinnias)

PERENNIALS

Achillea spp. (yarrows)
Alcea rosea (hollyhock)
Aruncus spp. (goatsbeards)
Asclepias tuberosa (butterfly weed)
Aster spp. (asters)
Chrysanthemum spp. (chrysanthemums)
Cimicifuga spp. (bugbanes)
Coreopsis spp. (coreopsis)
Dictamnus albus (gas plant)
Echinacea purpurea (purple coneflower)
Echinops ritro (globe thistle)
Eupatorium purpureum (Joe-Pye weed)
Gaillardia X *grandiflora* (perennial blanket flower)
Helenium autumnale (sneezeweed)
Helianthus spp. (perennial sunflowers)
Hemerocallis hybrids (daylilies)
Iberis sempervirens (perennial candytuft)
Liatris spp. (gayfeathers)
Lobelia cardinalis (cardinal flower)
Lupinus Russell Hybrids (lupine)
Monarda didyma (bee balm)
Nepeta X *faassenii* (catmint)
Phlox paniculata (garden phlox)
Rudbeckia spp. (orange coneflowers)
Salvia spp. (salvias)
Sedum X 'Autumn Joy' ('Autumn Joy' sedum)

Solidago spp. (goldenrods)

HERBS

Catnips (*Nepeta* spp.)
Chives (*Allium schoenoprasum*)
Dill (*Anethum graveolens*)
Fennel (*Foeniculum vulgare*)
Lavender (*Lavandula* spp.)
Mint (*Mentha* spp.)
Parsley (*Petroselinum crispum*)
Rosemary (*Rosmarinus officinalis*)
Rue (*Ruta graveolens*)
Sage (*Salvia officinalis*)

FLOWERS FOR CONTAINERS

Many plants can survive in pots, but some adapt better than others to life in a container. Here are some of the best choices for container gardens.

ANNUALS

Ageratum houstonianum (ageratum)
Antirrhinum majus (snapdragon)
Begonia X *semperflorens* (wax begonia)
Brachycome iberidifolia (Swan River daisy)
Brassica oleracea (flowering cabbage)
Browallia speciosa (browallia)
Calendula officinalis (pot marigold)
Callistephus chinensis (China aster)
Catharanthus roseus (vinca)
Centaurea cyanus (bachelor's button)
Chrysanthemum ptarmiciflorum (dusty miller)
Clarkia amoena (godetia)
Coleus blumei (coleus)
Cosmos spp. (cosmos)
Cynoglossum amabile (Chinese forget-me-not)
Dianthus spp. (pinks)
Dyssodia tenuiloba (Dahlberg daisy)

Eschscholzia californica (California poppy)
Eustoma grandiflorum (lisianthus)
Gaillardia pulchella (annual blanket flower)
Gazania ringens (gazania)
Gomphrena globosum (globe amaranth)
Helichrysum bracteatum (strawflower)
Heliotropium arborescens (heliotrope)
Impatiens spp. (impatiens)
Lavatera trimestris (mallow)
Limonium sinuatum (annual statice)
Lobelia erinus (annual lobelia)
Lobularia maritima (sweet alyssum)
Matthiola incana (stock)
Melampodium cinereum (melampodium)
Mirabilis jalapa (four o'clock)
Myosotis sylvatica (forget-me-not)
Nicotiana spp. (flowering tobaccos)
Nierembergia hippomanica (nierembergia)
Nigella damascena (love-in-a-mist)
Pelargonium spp. (geraniums)
Petunia X *hybrida* (petunia)
Phlox drummondii (annual phlox)
Portulaca grandiflora (rose moss)
Salpiglossis sinuata (salpiglossis)
Salvia spp. (salvias)
Sanvitalia procumbens (sanvitalia)
Tagetes spp. (marigolds)
Torenia fournieri (torenia)
Tropaeolum majus (nasturtium)
Verbena spp. (verbenas)
Viola X *wittrockiana* (pansy)
Xeranthemum annuum (immortelle)
Zinnia spp. (zinnias)

PERENNIALS

Achillea spp. (yarrows)
Aquilegia spp. (columbines)

Aster spp. (asters)
Chrysanthemum spp. (chrysanthemums)
Coreopsis spp. (coreopsis)
Dianthus spp. (pinks)
Hemerocallis hybrids (daylilies)
Nepeta X *faassenii* (catmints)
Primula X *polyantha* (primrose)

BULBS

Allium spp. (ornamental onions)
Anemone spp. (anemones)
Arum italicum (arum lily)
Chionodoxa spp. (glory-of-the-snow)
Convallaria majalis (lily-of-the-valley)
Crocus spp. and hybrids (crocus)
Cyclamen hederifolium (hardy cyclamen)
Eranthis hyemalis (winter aconite)
Galanthus spp. (snowdrops)
Hyacinthus orientalis (hyacinth)
Iphieon uniflorum (spring starflower)
Iris spp. (irises)
Leucojum spp. (snowflakes)
Lilium spp. (lilies)
Lycoris spp. (resurrection lilies)
Narcissus hybrids (daffodils)
Ornithogalum spp. (star-of-Bethlehem)
Scilla spp. (squills)
Sparaxis tricolor (harlequin flower)
Tigridia pavonia (tiger flower)
Tulipa spp. and hybrids (tulips)
Zantedeschia spp. (calla lilies)

HERBS

Basil (*Ocimum basilicum*)
Catnips (*Nepeta* spp.)
Chives (*Allium schoenoprasum*)
Chives, garlic (*Allium tuberosum*)
Coriander (*Coriandrum sativum*)
Dill (*Anethum graveolens*)
Lavender (*Lavandula* spp.)

Lemon balm (*Melissa officinalis*)
Lemon grass (*Cymbopogon citratum*)
Lemon verbena (*Aloysia triphylla*)
Oregano (*Origanum* spp.)
Peppermint (*Mentha* X *piperita*)
Pot marigold (*Calendula officinalis*)
Scented geraniums (*Pelargonium* spp.)
Spearmint (*Mentha spicata*)
Sweet bay (*Laurus nobilis*)
Sweet woodruff (*Galium odoratum*)

BULBS FOR ALL SEASONS

With a little planning, you can enjoy beautiful bulbs nearly year-round. Use the lists below to help plan your plantings for extended blooms. Some genera are listed under more than one season because they contain species that flower at different times.

WINTER OR EARLY SPRING

Arum italicum (arum lily)
Crocus, some species and hybrids (crocus)
Cyclamen hederifolium (hardy cyclamen)
Eranthis hyemalis (winter aconite)
Galanthus spp. (snowdrops)
Ipheion uniflorum (spring starflower)
Iris spp. (irises)
Leucojum spp. (snowflakes)
Muscari, most species (grape hyacinths)
Narcissus, early species (daffodils)
Tulipa, early species (tulips)

SPRING

Anemone blanda (Grecian wind-flower)

Anemone coronaria (Mediterranean windflower)
Arisaema, most species (Jack-in-the-pulpits)
Allium, some species (ornamental onions)
Chionodoxa spp. (glory-of-the-snow)
Crocus, many species and hybrids (crocus)
Hyacinthus orientalis (hyacinth)
Muscari, some species (grape hyacinths)
Narcissus hybrids (daffodils)
Ornithogalum spp. (star-of-Bethlehem)
Scilla spp. (squills)
Tulipa, mid-season types (tulips)
Zantedeschia spp. (calla lilies)
Zephyranthes spp. (zephyr lilies)

SUMMER

Acidanthera bicolor (Abyssinian gladiolus)
Allium spp. (ornamental onions)
Arisaema, some species (Jack-in-the-pulpits)
Begonia Tuberhybrida hybrids (tuberous begonias)
Camassia spp. (camassias)
Crocosmia hybrids (crocosmias)
Dahlia hybrids (dahlias)
Gladiolus hybrids (glads)
Lilium spp. and hybrids (lilies)
Sparaxis tricolor (harlequin flower)
Tigridia pavonia (tiger flower)
Zantedeschia spp. (calla lilies)
Zephyranthes spp. (zephyr lilies)

FALL

Colchicum spp. (colchicums)
Crocus, some species (crocus)
Cyclamen hederifolium (hardy cyclamen)
Lycoris spp. (resurrection lilies)
Polianthes tuberosa (tuberose)
Zephyranthes spp. (zephyr lilies)

SEASON-BY-SEASON GUIDE TO GARDEN MAINTENANCE

GARDEN PLANTING AND MAINTENANCE TIMES VARY FROM ZONE TO ZONE AND WITHIN ZONES FROM YEAR TO YEAR. There is too much variation in climates in this country for one calendar to suit all growing regions of the country. However, the following month-by-month guide is a good general guide for you to begin planning your own maintenance calendar.

EARLY SPRING

- Shop for the garden tools and equipment you will need for the coming season
- Remove winter mulch from perennials as the weather begins to warm up
- Weed early, and weed often!
- Turn or loosen the soil in annual flower beds and vegetable gardens
- Use a spading fork to carefully cultivate soil around plants in perennial beds
- Work manure, compost, and other organic matter into garden beds before planting
- Apply acidic fertilizers to azaleas and rhododendrons
- Rake and aerate your lawn; sow new grass seed as necessary
- Cut ornamental grasses to just above the ground if you didn't cut them down in fall
- Cut back all dead perennial parts that you left standing for the winter
- Start flower and vegetable seed for planting outdoors after the last frost
- Sow seed of lettuce, peas, and other fast-growing, cool-weather crops directly in the garden

MID-SPRING

- Plant perennials, roses, ground-covers, trees, and shrubs; mulch and water them thoroughly
- Weed garden beds and borders
- Divide and replant summer- and fall-blooming perennials
- Snip off spent flowers and developing seedpods from tulips, daffodils, and other bulbs
- Replenish mulch around established roses, and begin fertilizing them
- Prune any shrubs that have finished early-spring flowering
- Mow and fertilize lawns as needed
- Plant out seedlings of broccoli, cabbage, cauliflower, and other cool-season crops

LATE SPRING

- Start mowing your lawn regularly
- Begin harvesting your first crop of lettuce, spinach, and other early greens
- Continue planting perennials
- Set out hardened-off transplants of annual flowers, vegetables, and herbs; mulch beds

as you finish setting out your plants
- Direct-sow annual flower seed
- Lay out irrigation lines in garden beds
- Water during dry spells to make sure your garden gets approximately 1 inch of water per week
- Remove spent flowers from rhododendrons and azaleas and other spring-flowering plants
- Set out stakes or hoops to support lilies, delphiniums, peonies, hollyhocks, foxgloves, and other tall plants
- Continue getting rid of annual and perennial weeds

EARLY SUMMER

- Keep watering and weeding as needed
- Continue planting out annual bedding plants and vegetables
- Scout for insect problems; take control measures as necessary
- Deadhead or cut back spent annual and perennial flowers
- Prune shrubs that have finished flowering
- Continue to fertilize your roses as necessary, and keep an eye out for pests and diseases
- Prune early-blooming clematis after flowering
- Harvest lettuce, peas, and other early vegetables
- If you plan to be away during the summer, make arrangements to have someone water your garden

MIDSUMMER

- Continue watering, weeding, and mulching
- Treat plants that aren't growing vigorously to a dose of fish emulsion or other liquid fertilizer
- Scout for pest and disease prob-

lems; control as necessary
- Continue fertilizing and spraying roses
- Remove faded flowers from annuals and perennials to prolong bloom time
- Stake tall-growing plants as needed
- Divide bearded irises after flowering if they are getting too crowded
- Prune wisteria after flowering
- Pinch off the shoot tips of chrysanthemums and asters to promote more branching and more blooms in fall
- Sow seeds of foxgloves, sweet William, and other biennial flowers in pots or an unused garden bed

LATE SUMMER

- Continue weeding, watering, and deadheading
- Dig up and discard dead or diseased plants
- Stop fertilizing all plants
- Continue treating pest and disease problems
- Prune hydrangeas after they finish flowering
- Trim summer-blooming clematis after flowering
- Sow seeds of spinach, lettuce, and other fall vegetable crops
- Transplant seedlings of biennial flowers to where you want them to bloom next year
- Freeze or can your garden's surplus vegetables

EARLY FALL

- Weed and water as necessary
- Start a compost pile if you don't have one already! Toss in unused produce, weeds (if they haven't gone to seed), spent flowers and plants, leaves, grass clippings, and

other trimmings as you remove them from the garden
- Test your soil for pH and nutrient levels; add amendments as indicated in your results to balance the soil for next year
- Seed new lawn areas or lay new turf, making sure you keep the area well watered during spells of warm, dry weather
- Aerate established lawns
- In colder regions, begin planting crocuses, daffodils, tulips, and other spring bulbs; in warm climates, set out pansies, sweet alyssum, and other hardy annuals for winter bloom
- Plant perennials, roses, groundcovers, trees, and shrubs
- In cold-winter areas, pot up rosemary, chives, and other culinary herbs to enjoy inside for the winter
- Divide spring- and early-summer-blooming perennials
- Harvest late-season vegetables

MID-FALL

- Rake leaves. Add them to the compost pile, or shred them for use as a winter mulch
- Do one final weeding of the garden
- Apply slow-release fertilizer and lime to lawns as needed
- Remove spent annual flowers and vegetable plants from the garden, and toss them into the compost pile
- Unless you live in a frost-free area, dig up dahlias, cannas, glads, tuberous begonias, and other tender bulbs; let them dry for a few days, then store in slightly moist sand or peat moss in a cool, dry place
- Cut back frost-nipped perenni-

als to within several inches of the ground
- Plant new hardy perennials
- Divide any perennials you didn't get to in early fall
- Incorporate compost and other organic matter into empty garden beds
- Plant hardy perennials, spring-flowering bulbs, bareroot roses, trees, and shrubs
- Direct-sow winter rye or other cover crops to protect the soil in empty garden beds for the winter

LATE FALL TO EARLY WINTER

- Add protective mulch to carrots, turnips, parsnips, beets, and other root vegetables you haven't finished harvesting
- Cut chrysanthemums and asters to the ground after flowering
- Continue incorporating compost and organic matter in garden beds
- Continue planting spring bulbs
- Continue raking and composting leaves
- In cold-winter areas, wait until the ground freezes to apply a thick layer of mulch to perennials, trees, and shrubs
- Place wire mesh around the base of woody plants to protect them from animal damage over winter
- Empty hoses of water and store them
- Order new seed and plant catalogs

MID- TO LATE WINTER

- Replenish winter mulch as needed
- Trim trees and shrubs (except spring-flowering kinds) as needed
- Make new plans for garden beds
- Send in seed and plant orders
- Begin sowing seeds indoors (usually late February)
- Look for any perennials that have been heaved out of the ground by freezing and thawing; push them back into the soil
- Gather all tools for cleaning, repair, sharpening, and oiling; store them in a dry, protected area

USDA PLANT HARDINESS ZONE MAP

To get a full-color, 4-foot-square copy of the map on page 407, send a check for $6.50 to: Superintendent of Documents, Government Printing Office, Washington, D.C. 20402. Ask for Item #1417.

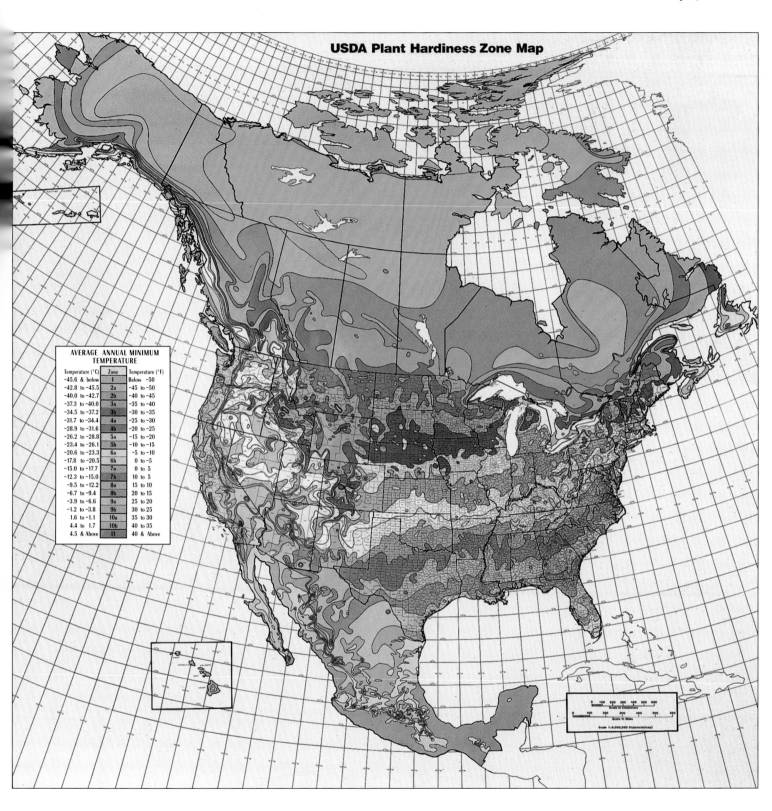

USDA Plant Hardiness Zone Map

AVERAGE ANNUAL MINIMUM TEMPERATURE

Temperature (°C)	Zone	Temperature (°F)
-45.6 & below	1	Below -50
-42.8 to -45.5	2a	-45 to -50
-40.0 to -42.7	2b	-40 to -45
-37.3 to -40.0	3a	-35 to -40
-34.5 to -37.2	3b	-30 to -35
-31.7 to -34.4	4a	-25 to -30
-28.9 to -31.6	4b	-20 to -25
-26.2 to -28.8	5a	-15 to -20
-23.4 to -26.1	5b	-10 to -15
-20.6 to -23.3	6a	-5 to -10
-17.8 to -20.5	6b	0 to -5
-15.0 to -17.7	7a	0 to 5
-12.3 to -15.0	7b	10 to 5
-9.5 to -12.2	8a	15 to 10
-6.7 to -9.4	8b	20 to 15
-3.9 to -6.6	9a	25 to 20
-1.2 to -3.8	9b	30 to 25
1.6 to -1.1	10a	35 to 30
4.4 to 1.7	10b	40 to 35
4.5 & Above	11	40 & Above

INDEX